North Carolina's
Outer Banks

INSIDERS' GUIDE® TO

NORTH CAROLINA'S OUTER BANKS

THIRTY-FIRST EDITION

JULIAN KINGSLEY

INSIDERS' GUIDE

GUILFORD, CONNECTICUT
AN IMPRINT OF GLOBE PEQUOT PRESS

All the information in this guidebook is subject to change. We recommend that you call ahead to obtain current information before traveling.

To buy books in quantity for corporate use or incentives, call **(800) 962-0973** or e-mail **premiums@GlobePequot.com.**

INSIDERS' GUIDE ®

Project Editor: Lynn Zelem
Layout: Joanna Beyer
Text Design: Sheryl Kober
Maps: XNR Productions, Inc. © Morris Book Publishing, LLC

ISSN 1082-9458
ISBN 978-0-7627-6473-0

Printed in the United States of America
10 9 8 7 6 5 4 3 2 1

CONTENTS

Directory of Maps

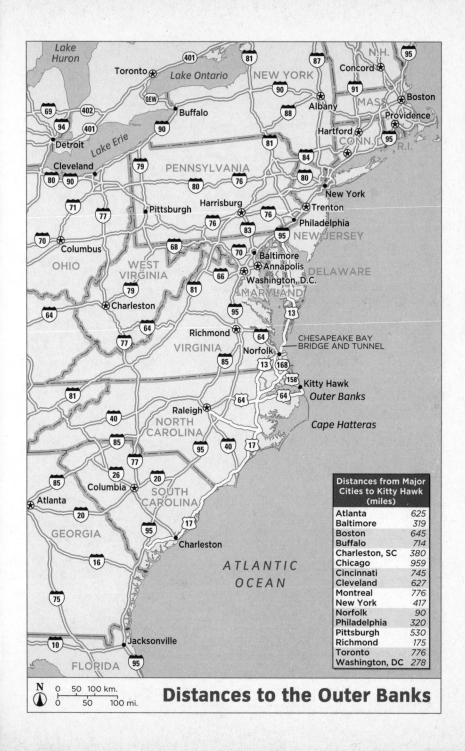

Distances to the Outer Banks

Distances from Major Cities to Kitty Hawk (miles)	
Atlanta	625
Baltimore	319
Boston	645
Buffalo	714
Charleston, SC	380
Chicago	959
Cincinnati	745
Cleveland	627
Montreal	776
New York	417
Norfolk	90
Philadelphia	320
Pittsburgh	530
Richmond	175
Toronto	776
Washington, DC	278

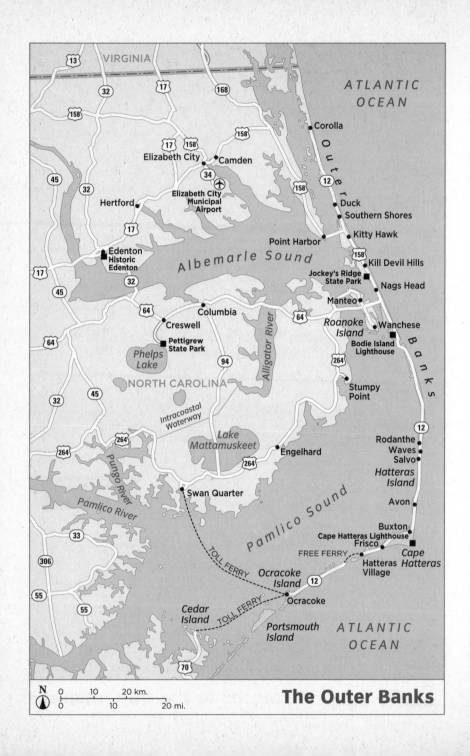

The Outer Banks

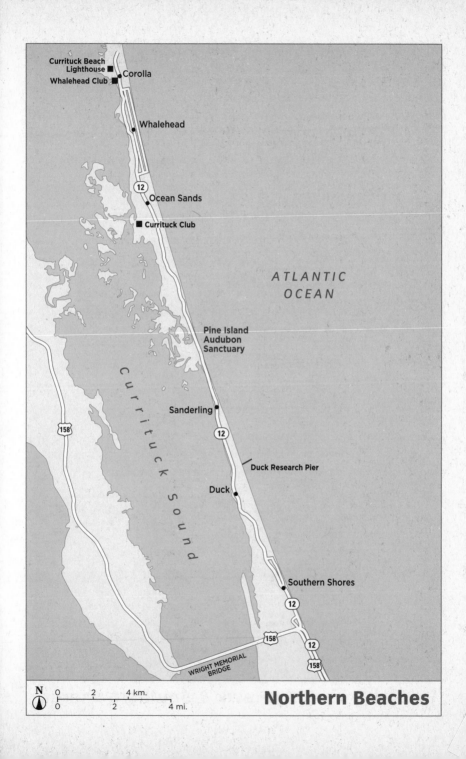

Currituck Beach Lighthouse

Corolla

Whalehead Club

Whalehead

12

Ocean Sands

■ Currituck Club

ATLANTIC OCEAN

Pine Island Audubon Sanctuary

C u r r i t u c k   S o u n d

Sanderling

12

Duck Research Pier

Duck

158

Southern Shores

12

158

12

158

WRIGHT MEMORIAL BRIDGE

N

0   2   4 km.

0   2   4 mi.

Northern Beaches

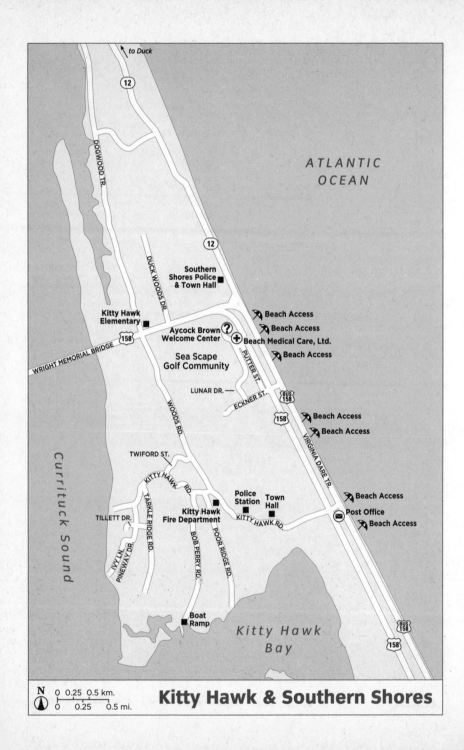

to Duck

12

DOGWOOD TR.

ATLANTIC
OCEAN

12

DUCK WOODS DR.

Southern
Shores Police
& Town Hall

Kitty Hawk
Elementary

158

WRIGHT MEMORIAL BRIDGE

Aycock Brown
Welcome Center ?

Beach Access
Beach Access
Beach Medical Care, Ltd.
Beach Access

Sea Scape
Golf Community

PUTTER ST.

LUNAR DR. —

ECKNER ST.

BUS
158

158

Beach Access
Beach Access

WOODS RD.

VIRGINIA DARE TR.

TWIFORD ST.

KITTY HAWK RD.

TARKLE RIDGE RD.

TILLETT DR.

Kitty Hawk
Fire Department

Police
Station

Town
Hall

Beach Access

Post Office
Beach Access

KITTY HAWK RD.

IVY LN.
PINEWAY DR.

BOB PERRY RD.

POOR RIDGE RD.

Currituck Sound

Boat
Ramp

Kitty Hawk
Bay

BUS
158

158

N

0   0.25 0.5 km.
0   0.25   0.5 mi.

Kitty Hawk & Southern Shores

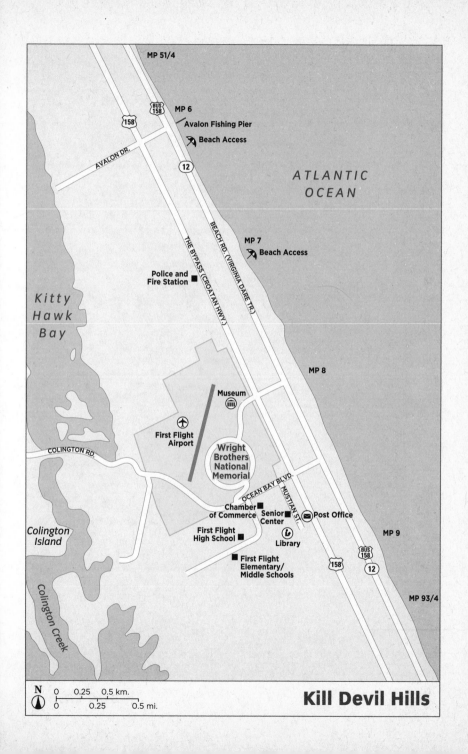

MP 51/4

BUS 158

158

MP 6

Avalon Fishing Pier

Beach Access

AVALON DR.

12

ATLANTIC
OCEAN

BEACH RD. (VIRGINIA DARE TR.)

THE BYPASS (CROATAN HWY.)

MP 7

Beach Access

Police and
Fire Station

Kitty
Hawk
Bay

MP 8

Museum

First Flight
Airport

Wright
Brothers
National
Memorial

COLINGTON RD.

OCEAN BAY BLVD.

MUSTIAN ST.

Chamber
of Commerce

Senior
Center

Post Office

MP 9

Colington
Island

First Flight
High School

Library

BUS 158

12

First Flight
Elementary/
Middle Schools

158

Colington
Creek

MP 93/4

N

0   0.25   0.5 km.

0   0.25   0.5 mi.

Kill Devil Hills

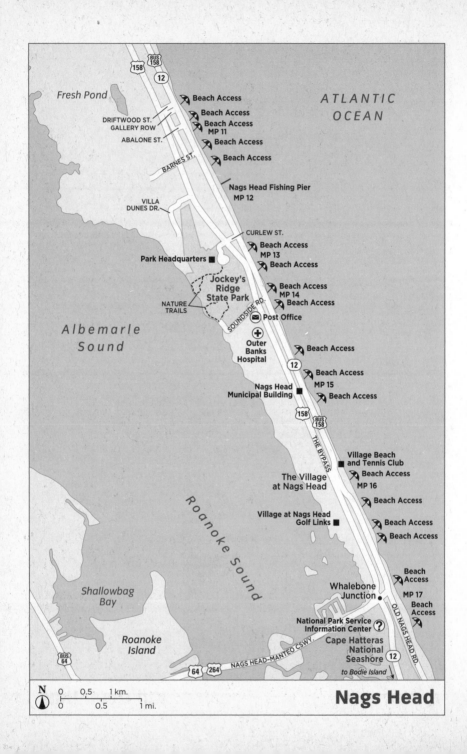

Fresh Pond

BUS 158

12

DRIFTWOOD ST.
GALLERY ROW

ABALONE ST.

BARNES ST.

Beach Access

Beach Access

Beach Access
MP 11

Beach Access

Beach Access

ATLANTIC
OCEAN

Nags Head Fishing Pier
MP 12

VILLA
DUNES DR.

CURLEW ST.

Beach Access
MP 13

Beach Access

Park Headquarters ■

Jockey's
Ridge
State Park

NATURE
TRAILS

Beach Access
MP 14

Beach Access

Post Office

Albemarle
Sound

Outer
Banks
Hospital

Beach Access

12

Beach Access
MP 15

Nags Head
Municipal Building ■

Beach Access

158

BUS 158

THE BYPASS

Village Beach
and Tennis Club ■

Beach Access
MP 16

The Village
at Nags Head

Beach Access

Village at Nags Head
Golf Links ■

Beach Access

Beach Access

Roanoke Sound

Beach
Access

MP 17

Whalebone
Junction

Beach
Access

OLD NAGS HEAD RD.

Shallowbag
Bay

National Park Service
Information Center ?

Roanoke
Island

Cape Hatteras
National
Seashore

12

BUS 64

64   264

NAGS HEAD–MANTEO CSWY.

to Bodie Island

N

0   0.5   1 km.

0   0.5   1 mi.

Nags Head

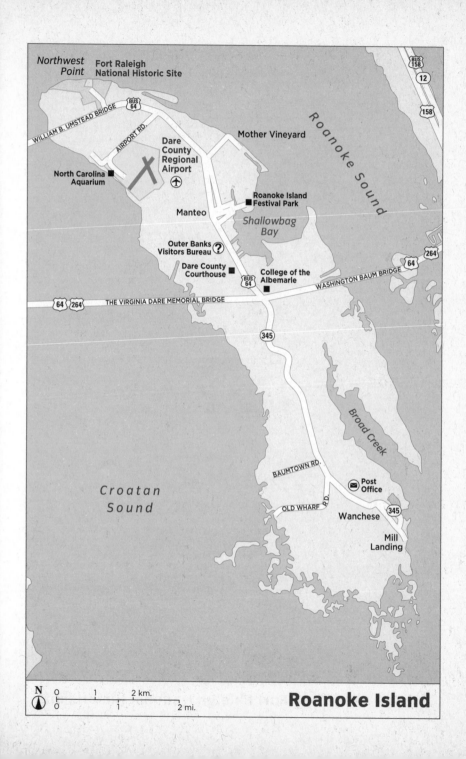

Northwest Point

Fort Raleigh National Historic Site

Mother Vineyard

Roanoke Sound

WILLIAM B. UMSTEAD BRIDGE

AIRPORT RD.

BUS 64

Dare County Regional Airport ✈

North Carolina Aquarium ■

Roanoke Island Festival Park ■

Shallowbag Bay

Manteo

Outer Banks Visitors Bureau ❓

Dare County Courthouse ■

BUS 64

College of the Albemarle ■

WASHINGTON BAUM BRIDGE

64 264

THE VIRGINIA DARE MEMORIAL BRIDGE

64 264

345

BUS 158

12

158

Croatan Sound

Broad Creek

BAUMTOWN RD.

OLD WHARF RD.

✉ Post Office

Wanchese

Mill Landing

345

N

| 0 | 1 | 2 km. |
| 0 | 1 | 2 mi. |

Roanoke Island

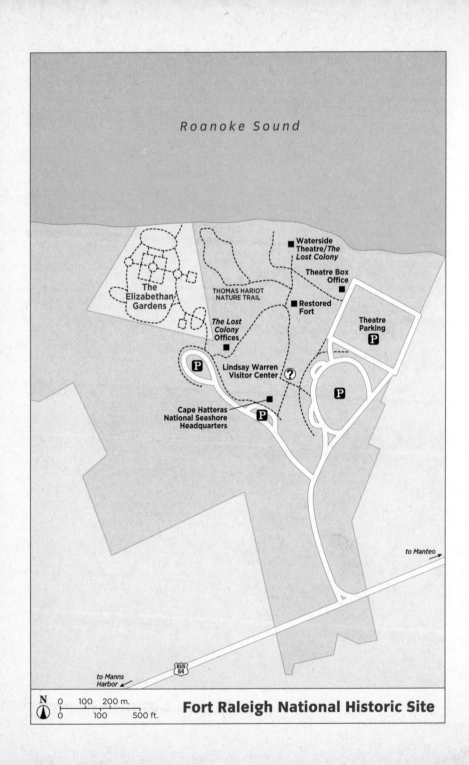

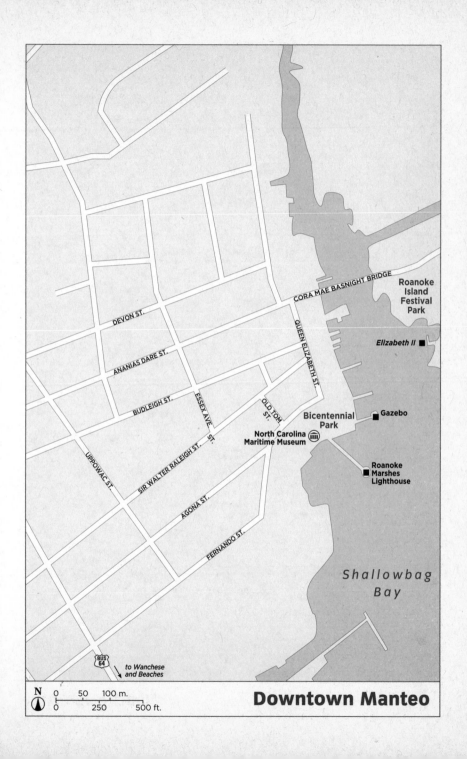

DEVON ST.

ANANIAS DARE ST.

BUDLEIGH ST.

ESSEX AVE.

SIR WALTER RALEIGH ST.

OLD TOM ST.

QUEEN ELIZABETH ST.

CORA MAE BASNIGHT BRIDGE

UPPOWAC ST.

AGONA ST.

FERNANDO ST.

Roanoke
Island
Festival
Park

Elizabeth II ■

Gazebo ■

Bicentennial
Park

North Carolina
Maritime Museum 🏛

■ Roanoke
Marshes
Lighthouse

*Shallowbag
Bay*

BUS 64

to Wanchese
and Beaches

N

0   50   100 m.
0   250   500 ft.

Downtown Manteo

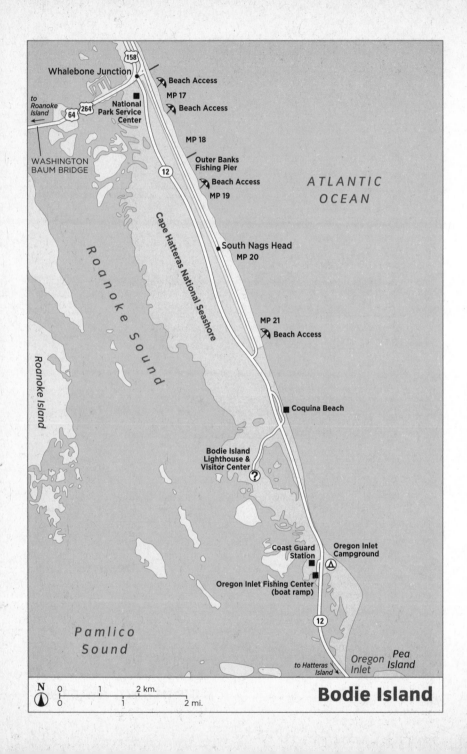

Whalebone Junction

to Roanoke Island

National Park Service Center

WASHINGTON BAUM BRIDGE

Beach Access
MP 17

Beach Access

MP 18

Outer Banks Fishing Pier

Beach Access
MP 19

ATLANTIC OCEAN

South Nags Head
MP 20

Roanoke Sound

Cape Hatteras National Seashore

Roanoke Island

MP 21
Beach Access

Coquina Beach

Bodie Island Lighthouse & Visitor Center

Coast Guard Station

Oregon Inlet Campground

Oregon Inlet Fishing Center (boat ramp)

Pamlico Sound

to Hatteras Island

Oregon Inlet

Pea Island

N

0   1   2 km.
0   1   2 mi.

Bodie Island

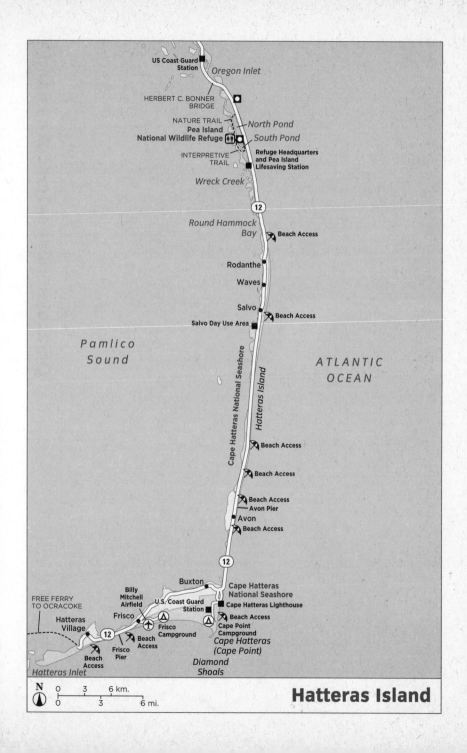

US Coast Guard Station

Oregon Inlet

HERBERT C. BONNER BRIDGE

NATURE TRAIL

North Pond

Pea Island National Wildlife Refuge

South Pond

INTERPRETIVE TRAIL

Refuge Headquarters and Pea Island Lifesaving Station

Wreck Creek

12

Round Hammock Bay

Beach Access

Rodanthe

Waves

Salvo

Beach Access

Salvo Day Use Area

Pamlico Sound

ATLANTIC OCEAN

Cape Hatteras National Seashore

Hatteras Island

Beach Access

Beach Access

Beach Access
Avon Pier
Avon
Beach Access

12

Buxton

Cape Hatteras National Seashore

Billy Mitchell Airfield

U.S. Coast Guard Station

Cape Hatteras Lighthouse

Beach Access

FREE FERRY TO OCRACOKE

Frisco

Frisco Campground

Cape Point Campground

Cape Hatteras (Cape Point)

Hatteras Village

12

Beach Access

Frisco Pier

Diamond Shoals

Beach Access

Hatteras Inlet

N

0   3   6 km.
0   3   6 mi.

Hatteras Island

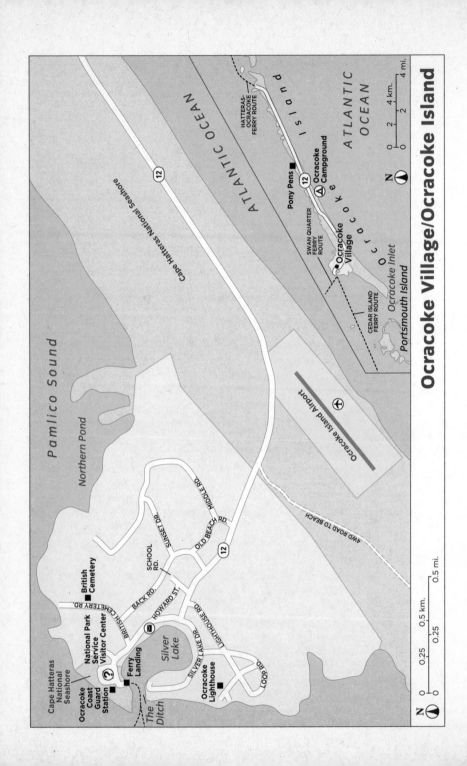

Ocracoke Village/Ocracoke Island

INTRODUCTION

Part of the Outer Banks' charm is the remoteness of the area. Since it's accessible only by ferry or by driving over one of the bridges that connects it to the mainland, once you're here you feel far removed from the rest of the world. It's really not that far. And in recent years, with an ever-growing tourism industry, goods and services have come to us. It's fascinating to hear locals tell of long drives to stores on the mainland to buy groceries or to receive medical care back in the old days. The "old days," however, were barely 25 years ago. Those of us who live here year-round still make excursions to nearby cities for specific services, shopping, and cultural events, but we wouldn't trade island life for anything. Living here is a trade-off that is heavily weighted toward the good life; we're blessed, and we know it.

Welcome to the land of beginnings! Feast your senses on wide beaches, whispering sea oats, and undulating dunes—a land where the pace of life is geared to the unceasing sand-sharpened breezes and wild winds. From the gifts and punishment of the glorious and untamed waters of these indomitable islands have sprung heroes, pioneers, pirates, and inventors. Tales of courage and creativity, bloody battles and savage shipwrecks, resourcefulness and compassion: All are part of the mystique of the Outer Banks. Here the first English colonists set up camp. Blackbeard and his band of buccaneers anchored sloops along the shallow sounds. Wilbur and Orville Wright flew the world's first airplane, buoyed by stiff winds and brazen determination, and Billy Mitchell proved airpower to the world. From remote national wildlife refuges, sheltered seashores, and protected maritime forests to upscale resort communities, these strips of shifting sand offer both peaceful retreat and awesome adventure. Kitesurf or Jet Ski. Surf fish or stroll the endless beaches. Charter a deep-sea fishing boat to fight an ocean giant. Grab the binoculars and watch birds. Soar from the East Coast's highest sand dune in a hang glider. Catch some waves and surf some of the best swells on the Atlantic Seaboard as breakers barrel toward the beach. It's all here for the choosing, and boredom is not an option.

Despite its rise as a favorite resort destination, the Outer Banks continues to be a casual place. Shorts and sandals are accepted garb in even the finest establishments. Shrimp, crab, and dozens of species of fresh-caught fish (often hauled in that very day by Outer Banks fishermen) are available at nearly every one of the slew of restaurants that serves tourists and locals alike.

While you're trekking the dunes, frolicking in the pristine waters, or enjoying the Carolina blue skies and soothing sunsets, don't forget that these overgrown sandbars have provided the setting for some of the most dramatic moments in American history. Remember that you are walking the sands of some of the most dynamic barrier islands on earth. Some things have stayed the same since Sir Walter Raleigh's party first laid eyes on Roanoke Island more than 400 years ago. These barrier beaches still startle visitors as well as natives with their rugged beauty and capricious topography. The fragile landscape remains at the mercy of the sea, furious with storm one day, calm the next.

Summer isn't the only time to enjoy the Outer Banks, although the season from Memorial Day through Labor Day is by far the most packed with people and things to do. Fall offers fabulous fishing and windsurfing, spring brings bird watching and bicycling, and winter is deliciously devoid of almost everyone. Spend time here and you'll understand why many of us came back to stay—or never left.

HOW TO USE THIS BOOK

Celebrating the 31st edition of the *Insiders' Guide to North Carolina's Outer Banks*, we've updated, changed, and revised our extensive collection of favorite restaurants, shops, attractions, events, getaways, activities, and much more.

Most information in our guide is arranged geographically from north to south. Besides introducing you to the area's fascinating history and hidden treasures, we provide practical information on camping, real estate, vacation rentals, ferry schedules, fishing sites, and other areas of interest. Also discover valuable tips—look for the **i**—that you could get only from an insider. We've designed the *Insiders' Guide to North Carolina's Outer Banks* as a handy reference for all aspects of life here. Keep it in hand, and let us accompany and guide you along every step of your Outer Banks journey.

We begin with colorful overviews of each area along the barrier islands, from the sand-tail villages of Carova (at the Virginia–North Carolina border) to the windswept shores of Ocracoke Island; after that you'll find a chapter on the various ways to get to and around on the Outer Banks and sections on our history. Comprehensive chapters tailored to meet your personal needs follow: Accommodations, Kidstuff, Arts & Culture, Annual Events, Recreation, Real Estate, and more. If you're looking for a cozy dinner spot, browse through the Restaurants chapter. If you want to spend the afternoon in search of a special souvenir, turn to Shopping. If you've always wanted to try scuba diving, parasailing, or surfing, all the information you'll need is in Water Sports.

We've arranged this book so you can read it bit by bit, opening to those particular pages that pique your interest while breezing by those that don't. But please go back and thumb through any parts you may have skipped at first. We bet you'll learn something interesting and maybe even discover some new favorite sports or pastimes along the way. To guide you along your adventure, a passel of excellent maps is tucked in at the book's beginning as well.

Scattered throughout the various chapters are special Insiders' tips (as noted above they're indicated by an **i**) for quick insights. The tips are our way of sharing our insider information. You will also find lengthy Close-ups profiling truly unique aspects of the area's lifestyle and culture.

You'll also find listings accompanied by the ✳ symbol—these are our top picks for attractions, restaurants, accommodations, and everything in between that you shouldn't miss while you're in the area. You want the best this region has to offer? Go with our **Insiders' Choice.**

Finally, if you're moving to the Outer Banks or already live here, be sure to check out the blue-tabbed pages at the back of the book. There you will find the **Living Here** appendix that offers sections on relocation, retirement, education, and child care.

AREA OVERVIEW

The Outer Banks is a world unto itself, made of islands linked to the rest of civilization only by a few bridges and ferries. This fact lends a separatist character to the Outer Banks, with residents who are proud to have escaped the trappings of the mainland and vacationers who come here to put aside the city life. Days go by in the indescribable realm of "island time," becoming more surreal the farther south you go.

Cultural traditions and norms seem to fall by the wayside once one has crossed over onto one of the islands. Suddenly it's perfectly acceptable to go barefoot all day, to wear your bathing suit to the grocery store, to get buried up to your neck in sand, to spend hours on the porch staring at the water, to stop to watch the sun set.

The area is a chain of several islands—Roanoke, Colington, Bodie, Hatteras, and Ocracoke—stretching more than 100 miles along eastern North Carolina. Bodie Island, the largest landmass of the Outer Banks, encompassing the land from the north side of Oregon Inlet through Carova, is technically no longer an island. Physically it's connected to Virginia and is therefore a peninsula. However, since the state border is closed to land crossings, Bodie is, in many minds, an island.

OVERVIEW

Some people also consider the islands south of Ocracoke Island, from Cape Lookout and through Bogue Banks, part of the Outer Banks. But for the purposes of this book, the Outer Banks extends from the Virginia line through Ocracoke. If you'd like information on the beaches south of Ocracoke, the best spots in the area are revealed in *Insiders' Guide to North Carolina's Central Coast and New Bern* and *Insiders' Guide to North Carolina's Southern Coast and Wilmington.*

Bodie, Hatteras, and Ocracoke Islands are barrier islands, separated from the mainland by a system of wide, shallow sounds. The barrier islands are reefs of sand protecting the mainland from the ravages of the Atlantic Ocean. What keeps the barrier islands from washing away in the face of all that power is their ability to shift and move, to go with the flow of nature. On the other hand, vegetation plays a huge part in the stabilization of the islands, making them fit for human occupation.

The Albemarle-Pamlico Sounds system that separates the Outer Banks from the mainland is the second largest estuary in the United States, second only to the Chesapeake Bay. These sounds have 3,000 square miles of surface water and 30,000 square miles of watershed. The system consists of seven sounds—Albemarle, Pamlico, Currituck, Croatan, Roanoke, Bogue, and Core.

These individual sounds are fed by inlets, cuts of water that slice through the skinny islands from the ocean, and by five major rivers. The Albemarle-Pamlico system is one of the most biologically productive estuaries in the United States, supporting a huge variety of wildlife, fish, shellfish, and plants.

Three North Carolina counties lay claim to these barrier islands—Currituck, Dare, and Hyde. Dare is the largest county, with 391 square miles of land, 509 square miles of water, and around 34,000 residents. Dare County stretches from north of Duck to the tip of Hatteras Island, including Roanoke Island and a mass of mainland. Currituck County encompasses 255 square miles of land, most of it on the mainland and a small portion of barrier island from north of Duck to the Virginia border. Geographically divided Currituck County has a population of more than 24,000; around 500 reside on Currituck's northern beaches year-round. Hyde County's Outer Banks portion is Ocracoke Island, a 9-square-mile island with around 900 residents.

The 35,000 or so year-round residents of the Outer Banks host more than 7 million visitors a year. Due to bridges and air travel, the Outer Banks islands are now more easily accessible than ever. This has led to rapid development, along with a dramatic increase in the availability of goods and services. Residents have all the accoutrements needed for a comfortable way of life, including a thriving economy with low unemployment, affordable housing, retail stores offering almost everything, and an abundance of restaurants, arts and entertainment, medical care, and recreational opportunities. With all this, however, no one will deny that the pulse of life on these barrier islands is still set by wind and water. The weather and the

natural world play intimate and demanding roles in the lives of barrier island residents.

Much of what keeps the Outer Banks so special is the Cape Hatteras National Seashore, which encompasses more than 75 miles of rugged, undeveloped beaches, dunes, marshes, and flatlands. With commercial and residential development continually increasing on the barrier islands, the Cape Hatteras National Seashore—the first national seashore in the nation—is treasured and appreciated more than ever. Three national wildlife refuges further protect portions of the Outer Banks from development.

Whether it's the sunrise, the sunset, or what goes on between, the Outer Banks offers the most extraordinary of what island life has to offer. "The sunsets here are the prettiest I have ever seen," Orville Wright wrote to his sister in 1900. "The clouds light up with all colors, in the background, with deep clouds of various shapes fringed with gold before. The moon rises in much the same style, and lights up the pile of sand almost like day." We have more than just good looks and personality, though: We have history. We have drama. We have lots of good stories to tell.

In this chapter we offer overviews of the areas that make up the Outer Banks, taking you on a north-to-south tour of Corolla and Currituck beaches, Duck, Southern Shores, Kitty Hawk, Kill Devil Hills, Colington Island, Nags Head, Roanoke Island, Hatteras Island, and Ocracoke Island.

COROLLA & CURRITUCK BEACHES

Not so long ago Currituck County's Outer Banks beaches were the barrier islands' outback. Seeming to stretch infinitely from north of Duck to the Virginia border, wide wind-swept expanses of sandy terrain lay virtually untouched except by winds, blue herons, and wild horses (see the Close-up in the Attractions chapter). For many years the area was blocked to vehicles on both ends—by the state of Virginia on the north end and by a private developer on the south end. In 1984 the state opened Highway 12 into the tiny village of Corolla, and it wasn't long before developers and vacationers started setting their sights on the Currituck Outer Banks.

From these barren dunes harboring a few fishing shacks and a handful of private homes, thousands of upscale houses, including 7,000-square-foot mansions, have sprung up on miles of recently paved subdivision roads. A family-owned convenience store that once supplied the only local goods for fewer than 100 permanent residents has been overshadowed by a modern chain grocery store. A lighthouse completed in 1875 has become more important as a landmark for tourists than as a guide for sailors. Dozens of eateries offer a variety of cuisines, and three quality resort shopping plazas are available to serve the hundreds of thousands of visitors who flock to the northernmost Outer Banks each summer.

The tiny community where everyone knew everyone else has undergone enormous change with its transformation into a favorite travel destination, but development has been tasteful and aesthetically pleasing. (And everyone still knows almost everyone else.)

People now often refer to the whole of the Currituck Outer Banks as "Corolla." Technically, Corolla is only the tiny, old village that sits on the west side of the island near the lighthouse. The Currituck Outer Banks has no incorporated towns and consists of several planned developments. From north to south, these are Ocean Hill, Corolla Light, Monteray Shores, Whalehead Beach, Buck Island, Crown Point, Ocean Sands, Ocean Sands South, and Pine Island.

Currituck National Wildlife Refuge

A few miles north of the Currituck Beach Lighthouse, the multistory mansions become sparser and the paved two-lane highway dead-ends at a sand hill. Here a wildlife sanctuary provides a safe haven for endangered piping plover, wild boar, and other wildlife. A 4-foot-tall fence stretching a mile from sound to sea marks the southern barrier of this 1,800-acre sanctuary, where most of Corolla's wild horses still range (see the Close-up in the Attractions chapter). People can walk through the fence, however, and four-wheel-drive vehicles can cross over a cattle grate.

Once Corolla's most popular tourist attraction, the wild horses no longer roam freely in the populated village. The Corolla Wild Horse Fund is headquartered at the Corolla Wild Horse Museum, located in the heart of Corolla Village.

Isolated Outposts

There is no paved route from Corolla to the Virginia border. Still, a few hundred homes line this expanse of sand. On summer afternoons more than a thousand four-wheel-drive vehicles create their own paths on the beach as they drive into and around a community called Carova—where North Carolina meets Virginia. Note that Carova's name is a melding of both states.

There is an ordinance requiring permits to drive all-terrain vehicles (ATVs) to Carova. Drivers must prove ownership of property in Currituck to gain a free permit. For more specific information call the county satellite office at (252) 453-8555.

Several hundred homes are located along these remote beaches, and the area seems to increase in popularity each year. Residents negotiate tides and the beach not only in off-road and four-wheel-drive vehicles but also in regular cars with big deflated tires. Bicyclists sometimes manage at dead low tide to scoot around the fence into Sandbridge, Virginia, as natives in pre-fence days did routinely.

Although relatively protected from civilization, the area is patrolled by county, state, and federal officers. A system of dirt roads behind the dune line allows residents access to their homes. Most residents and visitors to Swan Beach, Carova, North Swan Beach, and the Seagull subdivisions drive on the beach above the waterline or on well-tread tracks at the base of the dune line.

Without a four-wheel-drive vehicle, you should not drive on the beach. Local guides gladly show visitors around in off-road vehicles. Guided tours of the area are available (see the Recreation chapter). Watch out for tree stumps, though. An ancient forest that historians say grew along the sound more than 800 years ago still thrusts its sea-withered trunks through the waves at an area known as Wash Woods.

Whether you're staying in one of Currituck Beach's exclusive rental homes or camping somewhere on the southern Outer Banks, Corolla and the four-wheel-drive area are well worth exploring.

DUCK

What makes Duck unique is its villagelike atmosphere and the incredible water views that run along the main street of town. In this upscale resort community, you'll find wonderful waterfront boutiques, art galleries, and a variety of fine restaurants and casual eateries within easy strolling distance of one another and within walking or biking distance of many of Duck's neighborhoods. In the busy season Duck teems with visitors, and traffic crawls along the two-lane highway that runs north to Corolla. But even if you're staying elsewhere, it's worth a special trip.

Tourism was slow to find Duck. It began to catch hold in the early 1980s, but once it did the town grew rapidly (too rapidly, according to many locals). Two decades ago, T-shirts that read "Stuck in Duck" seemed to speak for a lot of the young people who craved more excitement than could be found in this sleepy town. Today it is affluent, busy, and thriving, and around 450 residents call Duck their year-round home. In the quaint shops nestled throughout this village, you can find some real treasures, authentic and one-of-a-kind items to bring home as souvenirs. Plan to enjoy at least one meal here: Duck boasts many outstanding restaurants, and some offer outdoor tables. Two bed-and-breakfast inns accommodate nightly guests, but don't expect to find strings of motels. Almost every visitor to Duck rents a vacation home.

Duck makes an excellent jumping-off point for the full range of water sports. You'll find places to rent kayaks, canoes, windsurfing equipment, sailboats, Jet Skis, and WaveRunners, and you can launch very close to restaurants and shops. For extra exhilaration try a few hours of kayaking followed by lunch or dinner at a soundside table.

The town grew up on one of the most slender strips of sand on the Outer Banks.

The ocean and the sound are close enough here so that many cottages offer extraordinary views of both, and, when the weather turns nasty, NC 12 floods quickly in many sections around town. The neighborhoods in and around Duck are a pleasing mixture of graceful older cottages and luxurious new homes. The gently rolling terrain contrasts with the flatter areas of the Outer Banks. This is the place if you crave a shady, tree-lined escape or a hilltop retreat where you can watch the sun rise and set from two sides of the same home.

i The US Army Corps of Engineers research pier north of Duck is the only oceanographic research pier of its kind in the world. See the Attractions chapter for information on touring this facility.

Getting to Duck

If you're heading to Duck from the northern Outer Banks, turn left onto NC 12 at its junction with US 158 in Kitty Hawk, 1.5 miles after crossing the Wright Memorial Bridge. Travel past the homes of Southern Shores, and wind around the dunes on the two-lane highway. On good days Duck is a 10-minute drive from Kitty Hawk. In heavy summer traffic, bottlenecks form in the village, causing backups that stretch for miles and that sometimes last more than 30 minutes.

NC 12 curves through the center of Duck. All the commercial development is along this road, confined to the highway by zoning ordinances, landscaped with lovely local foliage. Drive slowly—even locals are astounded by the fetching sights around every bend.

The sea is quite close to Duck, as is the sound; many rental homes provide the rare opportunity for viewing both bodies of water from upstairs open-air decks. Wild beans, peas, and cattails cover the marshy yards, most of which are at least partially wooded, with the houses tucked among the trees.

True to its name, Duck is both home and passageway for a variety of nesting and migrating shorebirds and waterfowl. Streets are named after these feathered creatures, which often come to call. Loons, cormorants, gannet, and flocks of terns and gulls soak up the sun's warmth near the water's edge. You can sometimes see swans and mallards swimming in the sound at sunrise as well as otters playing in the sound.

On the northern edge of Duck, a US Army Corps of Engineers research facility occupies the site of a former navy bombing range. Military weapons recovery crews have dug up thousands of unexploded shells around here, and an 1,800-footlong pier now provides scientists with an important opportunity to track subsurface currents, study the effects of jetties and beach nourishment projects, and chart the movements of the slender strips of sand (see the Attractions chapter for more information).

Beyond the pier, heading north toward Corolla, you'll find the Duck Volunteer Fire Department, the Dare County Sheriff's Office northern beach station, and the Duck Recycling Center.

About 5 miles north of Duck, through an open wilderness area, Sanderling is the northernmost community on Dare County's beaches—an isolated, exclusive enclave with 300 acres stretching from sound to sea.

The community itself was started in 1978, setting a precedent for excellence among vacation destinations. These neighborhoods, barely visible from the road, approach land planning sensitively, preserving as much natural vegetation as possible and always aiming for architectural excellence. They are well worth searching out.

In 1985 the Sanderling Inn and Restaurant (now known as Sanderling Inn Resort) opened in the restored Caffey's Inlet Lifesaving Station, built in 1874. With cedar-shake siding, natural wood interiors, and English country antiques, it has the appearance of turn-of-the-20th-century Nags Head resorts and the ambience of a European escape. It's large and airy, with wide porches offering plenty of room for conversation, drinks, and soaking in the sunrise while rocking in wooden chairs (see the Accommodations and Restaurants chapters for details).

North of Sanderling, Palmer's Island is a 35-acre development with 15 oceanfront 1-acre lots, 8 of which have estates ranging from 6,000 to 10,000 square feet each. The homes are engineered to withstand 120 mph winds. Signature architectural embellishments are scaled to match the grandeur of the natural environment.

SOUTHERN SHORES

Stretching from sound to sea, Southern Shores is heralded as one of the most beautiful, well-thought-out developments on the Outer Banks. Interwoven with canals, maritime hardwood forests, dunes, and private beaches, its scenic beauty is hard to match. Real estate agents call Southern Shores property one of the best Outer Banks values for long-term investment.

Southern Shores is south of Duck and north of Kitty Hawk. You can enter this community from the south via NC 12; by South Dogwood Trail, which runs alongside Kitty

Hawk School; or by Juniper Trail, which runs perpendicular to the Marketplace shopping center.

A Haven of Solitude

Comprising mostly single-family homes, Southern Shores is predominantly a residential town uncluttered by the commercial aspects of other Outer Banks areas, making it the perfect place to seek solitude. Residents enjoy canoeing or kayaking in the canal system designed by David Stick, a local historian and published author. Though not the painter his father was, David's artistic talent was in full swing when he created these panoramic lagoons that connect interior properties to Jean Guite Bay and Currituck Sound.

The community includes two private marinas, soundside picnic and bathing areas, and ocean beach accesses situated every 600 feet. The accesses are available only to residents and vacationers staying in the area (make sure you display the proper permit), affording every beachgoer enough elbow room to comfortably spread a blanket or throw a Frisbee. A soundside wading beach on North Dogwood Trail is a favorite spot for families because the shallow sound water is a safer place for children to swim than the ocean. In the summer the picnic area has toilet facilities. Paved and unpaved bike trails meander through the town. Anyone can use the facilities, but to park you must belong to the civic association or get a town sticker. In either case, you have to be a property owner or guest to park in Southern Shores.

The golf course at Duck Woods Country Club winds its way through a residential neighborhood of Southern Shores, offering outstanding play in a pristine setting among tall pines, dogwoods, and other foliage. The 18-hole course is the oldest on the Outer

Banks and accepts public play year-round (see the Golf chapter).

The 40 original families who inhabited Southern Shores formed the town's first civic association. The Southern Shores Civic Association acts like a parks and recreation department. It owns, operates, and maintains the marinas, playgrounds, beach accesses, and crossovers for residents, property owners, and guests. Membership dues cover costs, but most of the physical upkeep is done by volunteers in the community.

Today the population has expanded to more than 2,600 year-round residents, swelling to 10,000 in the summer months. Until recently most residents were retirees, but now Southern Shores has an equal number of young families living within its boundaries. The town hall sits on a small hill off US 158 on Skyline Road.

It's been more than half a century since Stick first purchased Southern Shores, but the slow pace of development means there still is real estate available. Raw land on the oceanfront or soundfront is hard to come by these days, but those wanting to purchase property can obtain homes or land in the beach zone, dunes, or woods. Due to careful planning, Southern Shores has land reserved for a future civic center and several plots to be developed for other town needs.

One of the town's three retail establishments, the Marketplace, includes Food Lion and a multitude of smaller shops (see the Shopping chapter). This complex sits at the edge of Southern Shores, just east of the base of the Wright Memorial Bridge. Southern Shores Crossing, situated behind Southern Shores Realty, offers more small shops, a specialty market, a day spa, and an upscale restaurant. The new Sandy Ridge Mall offers a home lifestyle store, a restaurant, and a tanning salon.

Southern Shores was incorporated in 1979 and growth has occurred in the development since Frank Stick's purchase, but the developers' spirit of conservation is felt with every bike ride, every sunset, and every tour of the waterways that weave together flora, fauna, and humankind. The town continues to be environmentally conscious and is the first Outer Banks community to offer curbside recycling.

KITTY HAWK

If you access the Outer Banks from North Carolina's Currituck County mainland, the first town you'll reach is Kitty Hawk. This beach municipality begins at the eastern end of the Wright Memorial Bridge over the Currituck Sound and stretches sound to sea for about 4 miles. Within its town limits are a maritime forest, a fishing pier, a golf course, condominiums, and a historic, secluded village where Wilbur and Orville Wright stayed while conducting experiments with their famed flying machines.

Southern Shores forms the northern boundary of Kitty Hawk, and Kill Devil Hills is to the south. Milepost (MP) markers offer the best means of finding your destination. Most rental cottages, shops, restaurants, attractions, and resorts in this area can be located by green milepost markers along US 158 (insiders call this the Bypass) and NC 12 (insiders call this the Beach Road). The first milepost marker (MP 1) is in Kitty Hawk where the highway splits near the Aycock Brown Welcome Center.

With its name bonded to aviation history and its positioning as one of the gateways to the wide, undeveloped beaches of the Outer

Banks, Kitty Hawk might not be what you expect—at least at first glance. Much of its 4 miles of beachfront is narrower and appears more developed than any other place on the barrier islands. Even though Wilbur and Orville Wright certainly disembarked and stayed with the locals in the village of Kitty Hawk, they didn't fly here. Their experiments and successful flights were accomplished a few miles down the road in Kill Devil Hills.

Now that we've got that straight, enjoy Kitty Hawk for what it is: a vacation getaway offering lots of family-oriented activities, a fishing pier, some great eateries, convenient shopping, and all the fun you could want on a clean beach. Tucked away within the borders of Kitty Hawk's 12 square miles are some of the loveliest and most exclusive communities in the central beach area.

Keep in mind that when you just feel like taking a ride, the Beach Road through Kitty Hawk is one of the few stretches on the entire Outer Banks where you can see the ocean from your vehicle. Cruising south along the beach, you'll notice some weather-beaten houses perched on the shoreline. At high tide and in stormy weather, waves crash under the house pilings and wash out truck-loads of sand. The ocean plays chicken every year with these tired beach cottages, and just about every year a cottage cries uncle and collapses into the pounding surf. After every "big blow," local gossip (we love to talk weather here) inevitably comes around to an update on the Kitty Hawk cottages. You've likely gotten a good view of one of them on the Weather Channel, which, to the tourist bureau's chagrin, seems to delight in showing the wreckage of a Kitty Hawk beach house clinging pitifully to the sands during a storm. Once they're gone, they're gone, as federal coastal management law now

forbids building closer than 60 feet from a coastline's first line of vegetation.

By one popular version, Kitty Hawk owes its colorful name to a derivation of local Indians' references to goose hunting season as "killy honker" or "killy honk." Eighteenth-century documents record this beach community as "Chickahauk," a name adopted by the prestigious southeastern section of Southern Shores. Other theories say the name evolved from "skeeter hawk," mosquito hawks that were prolific in the area, or from ospreys or similar raptors preying on the area's kitty wren.

The Transition to Vacation Destination

Unlike Nags Head, which has been a thriving summer resort since before the Civil War, Kitty Hawk didn't become a vacation destination until about 75 years ago. A group of Elizabeth City businessmen bought 7 miles of beach north of Kitty Hawk Village in the late 1920s and formed the Wright Memorial Bridge Company. By 1930 they had built a 3-mile wooden span across the Currituck Sound from Point Harbor to the Outer Banks. Travelers could finally arrive at island beaches by car from the mainland. Kitty Hawk land became popular—and a lot more pricey. Summer visitors streamed across the new bridge, paying $1 per car for the privilege.

With the sudden boom in tourism, development shifted from the protected soundside hammocks to the open, wind-swept beaches. Small wooden cottages sprung from behind dunes on the ocean-front. As the beach eroded over the years, wind and water had their way with many of the beachfront homes. Houses were swept away during hurricanes and nor'easters, providing newfound ocean frontage for the neighbor cottage across the street. In 2003 Hurricane Isabel took an additional seven homes.

Even the original Kitty Hawk Lifesaving Station had to be jacked up and moved to a more protected site on the west side of the Beach Road to prevent tides from carrying it to a watery grave. The station is now a private residence, but travelers can still recognize the original Outer Banks gabled architecture of this historic structure.

In the western reaches of this community, the maritime forest of Kitty Hawk Woods winds for miles over tall ridges and blackwater swamps. Primarily year-round residents make their homes here on private plots and in new subdivisions. Some lots are much larger than in other central beach communities. The twisting vines, dripping Spanish moss, and abundant tall trees offer seclusion and shelter from the storms not found in the expansive, open oceanfront areas. On summer days locals often ride horses around the shady lanes of old Kitty Hawk Village, reminiscent of the days before bridges.

Although you'll find some businesses tucked back in the trees of Kitty Hawk Village at the western end of Kitty Hawk Road near the sound, most of this town's commercial outposts are along the Bypass and the Beach Road. The Outer Banks' only Wal-Mart is in Shoreside Center near the end of the Wright Memorial Bridge. Regional Medical Center at MP 1½ offers a full range of urgent care and outpatient services.

If you're headed for the beach, you'll find a public bathhouse at MP 4½. The public is also welcome to use the Dare County boat launch at the end of Bob Perry Road, where locals and visitors can set sail during a hot summer day and watch the dolphins frolic in Kitty Hawk Bay.

From waterskiing to fishing, Kitty Hawk presents exceptional recreational possibilities. With all the water fun rounded out with a fine selection of dining establishments, convenient shopping, and medical services, along with history and natural beauty, it's obvious why Kitty Hawk is a favorite beach retreat for families, retirees, and college students.

i When visiting Jockey's Ridge with kids, take along an old boogie board and let them try out the latest pastime—sand surfing.

KILL DEVIL HILLS

Even among all the other romantic and striking names of Outer Banks communities, Kill Devil Hills swirls a little longer in the imagination. One legend has it that Kill Devil Hill, the sand dune where the Wright brothers revolutionized transportation, was named after the wretched-tasting kill-devil rum that may have washed up in barrels from shipwrecks in early colonial days. According to another tale these hills were named after a rogue called Devil Ike, who blamed the theft of shipwrecked cargo on the devil, whom he claimed to have chased to the hills and killed. Other local lore tells of an Outer Banker who, atop one of the dunes, tried to kill the devil he had traded his soul to for a bag of gold.

The Outer Banks' first incorporated and most populous town, Kill Devil Hills is bookended by Kitty Hawk and Nags Head. Spanning the barrier island from sound to sea, this beach community is the geographic center of Dare County, with more than 7,000 permanent residents. Hundreds of thousands of tourists visit this bustling beach town each summer. Indeed, the intersection of Ocean

Bay Boulevard and Colington Road—where the Wright Memorial, a beach bathhouse, the post office, the town municipal center, the county chamber of commerce, the library, a school complex, and the entrance to the only road to Colington Island are grouped—is the busiest junction in the county and possibly the busiest secondary road in North Carolina. Bottlenecks are common in the morning and mid-afternoon hours.

Despite the trend toward bigger and more exclusive resort homes and amenities elsewhere on the Outer Banks, Kill Devil Hills remains a family-oriented beach for visitors and a centrally located town of moderately priced housing for the permanent population. Kite flying, surfing, sea kayaking, windsurfing, sunbathing, air flight tours, shopping, restaurants, motels, churches, and schools combine to make this town a top choice for many, as it has been for more than a half century.

Condominiums and franchise hotels dot the 5 miles of once-barren dunes. More than 41 miles of paved roads have replaced sandy pathways. Fast-food restaurants have sprung up along the five-lane US 158, forming the Outer Banks' commercial hub, known locally as French Fry Alley.

COLINGTON ISLAND

In 1633 Colington Island became the first land in Carolina to be deeded to an individual. Today this 2-milelong, 2.5-mile-wide island, although developing rapidly, is one of the last of the Outer Banks communities to experience growth. Around 3,500 people make Colington their year-round home.

The east end of Colington Island lies a mile west of the Wright Brothers National Memorial, linked by a bridge over Colington Creek, which separates the island from Kill Devil Hills and Dare County beaches. Colington's other borders are surrounded by open water. Kitty Hawk Bay is to the north and Buzzard Bay is to the south. The mouths of four sounds (Currituck, Albemarle, Croatan, and Roanoke) converge on the west side of this family community.

Colington, named after its first proprietor, Sir John Colleton, was originally tilled to grow grapes for a winery shortly after settlers in 1664 founded the first Outer Banks community. The grapes, along with crops of tobacco, fruits, and vegetables, failed after three successive hurricanes. But by the early 1800s, a thriving fishing community had grown on two halves of the island: Great Colenton and Little Colenton, cleaved in 1769 by the Dividing Creek. Fishing, crabbing, and hunting sustained islanders generation after generation. Eventually, years after the rest of the barrier islands, Colington natives got paved roads, telephones, and electric service.

Now they have tourism as well. Just like the four- or five-generation families that live here, Colington Island has its own unique Outer Banks identity. High, uneven dunes meet dank, brackish swamplands. Thick groves of pine, dogwood, live oak, beech, and holly drip Spanish moss over expanses of sandy shoreline. Thin creeks widen to unexpected harbors and bays. In summer months soft-shell crab holding pens illuminate strips of scrubby yard along the sounds at night, the naked light bulbs glaring out of the darkness like a Reno casino. Advertisements for waterfront property in pricey new subdivisions are posted not far from where trailers and campgrounds line the twisting road. Mansions are barely evident, perched on their sandy shelves overlooking Colington Road, the most heavily traveled secondary road in Dare County.

Colington Harbour, the island's first subdivision, was built in 1965. Since then numerous other subdivisions have been constructed along canals, marshlands, and soundfronts and in woodlands throughout Colington Island. After a year of weighing benefits and risks, newcomers and natives hammered out a reasonable zoning plan. Several restaurants, a storage garage, and a go-kart track mingling with crab shedders and fish houses along the road illustrate the conflict and challenges this sheltered community faced over dramatic change. With new development approved every year, residents have accepted the inevitability of growth. The future face of Colington will be determined by the strength of the zoning plan and the people who molded it.

NAGS HEAD

Home of the Outer Banks' first resort, the community of Nags Head is south of Kill Devil Hills and north of Oregon Inlet. It stretches from the Atlantic Ocean to the Roanoke Sound and has remained a popular vacation destination for more than 150 years. Many first-time vacationers mistakenly refer to the whole middle-Banks area as "Nags Head," lumping the town together with neighboring Kill Devil Hills and Kitty Hawk. Most likely this is historically based, due to the fact that at one time Nags Head was the only true destination on the middle Banks.

The booming summer scene was once anchored by cottages towering over the shallow sound, elaborate hotels facing the mainland, and calm-water canoeing, crabbing, and conversation. This relaxed style

of soundside vacationing has long since been altered by shifting sands and changing values.

The Story Behind the Name

The primary resort destination on these barrier islands for more than a century, Nags Head has been the official name of the area since at least 1738, when it first appeared on maps. Historians say the beach town got its name from the horses that once roamed throughout the islands. The much more colorful legend we insiders prefer is that Nags Head was derived from a custom locals used to lure ships to the shores. Securing a lantern from a Banker pony's neck, residents would drive the horse up and down the beach, the light swinging with the same motion as a sailboat. The unsuspecting offshore vessel would steer toward the light and proceed to get grounded on the shoals. The locals would then promptly ransack the hapless ship.

Nags Head Today

Today Nags Head is home to over 3,000 residents. Hotels, restaurants, piers, rambling residences, and luxurious vacation cottages line Nags Head's oceanfront, which remains predominantly vacation oriented. Local residents live in the middle and on the west side of the island, away from the harsh elements of the sea. The sound shores are filled with private cottages, except one portion of lower Nags Head that features water-sports outfitters, go-kart tracks, and minigolf galore. South Nags Head, stretching from MP 17 to MP 21, is an exclusively residential area with no commercial development.

Jockey's Ridge State Park is Nags Head's most popular attraction aside from the beach. The best kite flying, hang gliding, and sunset views are found atop this natural phenomenon, which is the largest sand dune on the East Coast. Every summer day the sprawling dune is dotted with hundreds of people who climb to the top for recreation and for the expansive views of sea and sound.

Another Nags Head natural attraction is the Nags Head Woods Ecological Preserve, actually in both Nags Head and Kill Devil Hills. Hikers, birders, and nature lovers delight in this wooded anomaly, where diverse flora and fauna can be enjoyed in stunning silence (see the Natural Wonders chapter).

Nags Head is well known for its recreational opportunities. A paved bike path stretches almost the entire length of the town. A Scottish links–style golf course, Nags Head Golf Links, is one of the area's most beautiful and challenging courses. It stretches along the Roanoke Sound, offering sound views and the opportunity to see a variety of waterbirds and wildlife. Dolphin tours, airboat rides, boat rentals, Jet Ski rentals, kiteboarding lessons, windsurfing, and sailing are all offered on the sound in lower Nags Head, around MP 16 and on the Nags Head–Manteo Causeway. Miniature golf and go-kart tracks also cluster in this area. Nags Head has the YMCA complex and the area's only bowling alley.

Shoppers flock to Nags Head's name-brand outlet stores and to its several strip malls and grocery stores. Nags Head is home to many art galleries, including an artists' enclave known as Gallery Row (see the Arts & Culture chapter). Restaurants and nightspots lure diners and revelers to Nags Head. Owens' Restaurant has been a Nags Head institution for more than 50 years; Kelly's Tavern is the most well-known nightspot on the Outer Banks.

Since it's centrally located on the Outer Banks, Nags Head is a favorite destination of people who want to take day trips to Hatteras Island and Corolla. If you don't want to get back in the car once you've arrived at your vacation destination, you can get everything you want within walking distance of most Nags Head hotels and cottages.

Whether you're looking to escape the bustle of the beach by taking a quiet hike through the Nature Conservancy's Nags Head Woods Ecological Preserve or dance the night away at a beachside tavern, this Outer Banks town remains one of the area's most popular resorts.

ROANOKE ISLAND

Nestled between the Outer Banks and the North Carolina mainland, Roanoke Island is one of the most historic places in America. People sometimes confuse our island's history with that of Jamestown, Virginia, where the first permanent English colony thrived in the early 17th century. The confusion between the two revolves around the word "permanent." Roanoke Island is the site of England's earliest attempts to plant a permanent colony in the New World. Beginning in 1584, Sir Walter Raleigh dispatched a series of voyages carrying courageous souls to settle in the New World. These journeys culminated in a colony of 117 men, women, and children, sent here in 1587, only to disappear mysteriously; hence the lack of "permanence." The Lost Colony of Roanoke Island remains a puzzle. Theories concerning the colonists' fate abound, but until archaeologists dig up some real proof, we'll continue to wonder what really happened to these early settlers.

For those who appreciate concrete links to the past, relics have been retrieved from the waters surrounding Roanoke Island—artifacts that may provide clues to centuries-old puzzles. Numerous locals and archaeologists alike have combed the island for treasures from the Native American culture, earliest English settlements, and Civil War times. Old English coins, a powder horn, a vial of quicksilver, weapons, bottles, iron fragments, pottery, and arrowheads have been discovered here.

In the winter of 1998–99, a strong nor'easter blew so much water out of the sound that some creek beds and sound bottoms were exposed for the first time in many decades. Locals harvested numerous arrowheads from the exposed muddy tracts. Some remnants can be seen at Fort Raleigh National Historic Site on the north end of the island (see the Attractions chapter), while others found their way into personal collections. Roanoke Island native Hubby Bliven opened the Roanoke Heritage Gallery and Museum on the island mostly with artifacts he's been collecting since his youth.

Roanoke Island tends to bring out the nature lover in all of us. In the spring, summer, and fall, early mornings and late afternoons find marsh rabbits nibbling roadside grasses. Red-winged blackbirds, looking much like holiday ornaments, adorn the bushes alongside the road. They really stand out in winter, when the leaves have left trees barren. Scan the creeks in the warm months, just before entering Roanoke Island from the west, and you can see turtles lined like soldiers on half-sunken logs and along the banks. Crossing the Washington Baum Bridge from the east, we regularly spot osprey flying overhead, clutching dangling snakes or fish in their claws. (Don't take your eyes off the road too long, and definitely do not stop on the bridge!) Of course, a wide variety of fish, such as spot, croaker, pigfish, sea mullet, sheepshead, and stripers, inhabit the surrounding waters. Boats and recreational water vehicles of all sorts share the sounds and bays in fair weather.

By land you can walk back into time at Roanoke Island Festival Park, formerly the Elizabeth II State Historic Site in Manteo. You can also examine history at Fort Raleigh. Make sure to explore the park's nature path, the Thomas Hariot Trail. Hariot, a 16th-century author, wrote the first book about the New World in Elizabethan English. His book is a study of the Native Americans and a survey of the area's natural resources. Only six copies of his literary treatise are said to exist.

Getting Here

Roanoke Island is west of Nags Head and due east of Williamston, North Carolina. It certainly is easier and quicker to get here now than it was centuries or even decades ago due to the construction of several bridges and new highways. While you won't have to forge a path through reeds, as our ancestors did, you still can reach the island by water. If a car is your mode of transportation, you can choose from at least four routes; all are scenic. Some wend through more remote regions than others. One two-lane road, US 64/264, has always carried all the local traffic plus vacationer traffic right down the spine of Roanoke Island, creating backups and bottlenecks. In 2002 the 5-mile Virginia Dare Memorial Bridge came into service. This bridge, the longest in the state, steers vacationer traffic and much of the local traffic away from the island. One end of the bridge is in Manns Harbor and the other is at the Manteo–Wanchese junction, which leads right to the beaches of the Outer Banks. If you wish to travel by air, the Dare County Regional Airport is on the north end of Roanoke Island. Private pilots fly into this airport daily, and charter services are available. It's not unusual to see visitors riding in on bicycles. The Outer Banks' flat terrain makes for excellent bicycle touring. For specific routes and directions see the Getting Here, Getting Around chapter.

Island Economy & Tourism

At the heart of Roanoke Island life is the inhabitants' desire to preserve a small-town feeling while finding ways to make a living. Islanders mostly work in tourist- and service-oriented businesses, at fishing-related jobs, as writers and artists, in local government, and in the public school system.

i In the Outer Banks economy, the largest percentages of people work in the service industries (21 percent), retail (19 percent), government (15 percent), and construction (8 percent).

Roanoke Island has history to market. The Attractions chapter describes the island's top sites: the Elizabethan Gardens, the North Carolina Aquarium, Fort Raleigh National Historic Site, the Outer Banks History Center, Roanoke Island Festival Park, the North Carolina Maritime Museum, and *The Lost Colony* outdoor drama.

The Outer Banks History Center, housed at Roanoke Island Festival Park (see the Attractions chapter), is a font of Roanoke Island lore and has old photos and area maps on display.

The main branch of the Dare County Library on US 64, just across from Manteo Elementary School, is another good source for more island information. For overall Outer Banks information, such as maps, brochures, and other local data, stop in at the Outer Banks Visitors Bureau on US 64/264. The staff is friendly and helpful, and there's even a convenient drive-through window.

Talk with some of our old-timers for some really entertaining inside information. Conversation with lifelong locals is bound to reveal a colorful tale or two. Pick up a copy of *Memories of Manteo and Roanoke Island, N.C.,* by Suzanne Tate as told by the late Cora Mae Basnight, if you're unable to make a personal connection. This oral history, from the mouth of a much-loved native (and late mother of the current president pro tem of the North Carolina Senate, Marc Basnight), is a delightful book accented with interesting photographs. Ms. Basnight, according to Tate's book, held the record for playing the same role longer than any actor in American theater, that of Agona, a Native American woman, in *The Lost Colony.* Many consider her the quintessential Agona. Another fantastic, more thorough history of the town and island is *Manteo, A Roanoke Island Town,* by Angel Ellis Khoury. It's filled with fascinating stories, anecdotes, and facts about this area.

Lots of exciting tales revolve around *The Lost Colony,* the historic outdoor drama that outlines the story of the first English settlement and its disappearance. Pulitzer Prize–winning playwright Paul Green wrote the drama, which debuted in 1937. It has played a major role in the lives of local folk ever since (see the Arts & Culture chapter). The production will celebrate its 75th anniversary in 2012.

Generations of families grew up acting in the annual play. From representing the infant Virginia Dare to playing the role of Gov. John White or Chief Manteo, many a Roanoke Island resident nurtured a love of history through the play and a love of theater as a result. Andy Griffith, who played Sir Walter Raleigh in his first acting stint, is a Roanoke Island resident.

William S. Powell's *Paradise Preserved* is the definitive source for the history of the Roanoke Island Historical Association, perpetuators of the historic play. Powell offers an exciting account of the creative endeavors of Mrs. Mabel Evans Jones, the author and producer of local pageants on Roanoke Island that predate Green's play. Evans Jones, the former superintendent of schools in Dare County, ran a summer arts camp on the island in the early 1920s. As it is with an archaeologist, the more you dig, the more you're likely to uncover something concerning Roanoke Island's roots and tales of the people who called the island home.

Boatbuilding

A description of Roanoke Island would be incomplete without a nod to a very special livelihood shared by many native islanders. Boatbuilding was and continues to be a major part of life on Roanoke Island. From the small bateau put together in a backyard shed to the 72-foot yachts constructed at major boatbuilding operations, Manteo and Wanchese share in this rich heritage.

The North Carolina Maritime Museum operates in the old George Washington Creef Boathouse on the Manteo waterfront. The museum pays tribute to the area's boat-building heritage. Here you can watch old crafts being restored and view a variety of boat exhibits.

George and Benjamin Creef operated the facility as the Manteo Machine Shop and Railways in the 19th century. The shop was built in 1884. Boats were hauled out of the water and serviced there. At this location "Uncle Wash" Creef built the first shad boat, now documented as one of the most important fishing vessels of its time because its design allowed it to effectively work nets and carry weight and still ride well in the water. Winters of the past found many fishermen holed up in shops crafting juniper vessels that took them farther from home than many had ever imagined. The Sharpie and the Shallowbag shad boat were designed and built in Manteo.

Boats are still built on Roanoke Island—huge, sleek vessels with their hulls buffed to a sun-splintering shine. Each spring these brand-new, 50-foot-plus boats emerge from private building barns and are tugged slowly down the highway to Wanchese to be put in the water for the first time. On board the boat, members of the construction crew carefully lift power lines as their vessel moves down the road, invariably delaying traffic. Smiles wreathe the faces of the crew: After six to eight months of hammering, sanding, and painting, they are ready to christen the fruit of their labor. It is a tense time, too, for no one really relaxes until everyone sees that the boat sits and moves "just right" in the water.

HATTERAS ISLAND

The sea is a strong tonic that humans often crave at the expense of security. Nowhere is this desire more obvious than on this little stretch of sand that juts precariously out into the Atlantic Ocean just off North Carolina's coast. Hatteras Island residents accept the stresses of living with a seasonal economy, storm damage, and cultural isolation as part of life in the shifting sand. The decision to live on the threshold of land and sea forges an intimate relationship with nature. Hearty islanders pulled together to rebuild hard hit areas after 2011's Hurricane Irene wreaked havoc upon northern sections of Hatteras Island.

South of Nags Head and north of Ocracoke Island, Hatteras Island measures 60 miles from Oregon Inlet to Hatteras Inlet and consists of seven small towns with a total year-round population of about 4,000 residents. Running north to south they are Rodanthe, Waves, Salvo, Avon, Buxton, Frisco, and Hatteras Village. You can enter the island from the north by car via NC 12 after crossing the Herbert C. Bonner Bridge or from the south by ferry via Ocracoke Island. As with other townships and islands of the Outer Banks, you can also reach the area by air—setting down on a small airstrip in Frisco—or by boat. (See the Getting Here, Getting Around and Fishing chapters for airfield, marina, and ferry information.)

Island Living, Economy & Tourism

Overall, Hatteras Island's residents live and work supported mostly by tourism, fishing, real estate, teaching, and government employment. Because of the seasonal economy, weather-related economic setbacks, and lack of corporations and industries that hire mass amounts of people, it's not unusual for residents to have more than one job. Cleaning rental cottages on the side provides extra money, and you may find that your waiter during the summer months is a professional from another trade altogether. Necessity also provokes creativity, and many locals sell their carvings or paintings in local shops and galleries.

Families thrive despite typical inconveniences to be expected in village living on a remote island. They pattern their living styles accordingly. You won't find a Kmart on the island, but mail-order companies get their share of business. A sense of community is evident in the packed stands at the Cape Hatteras High School basketball games (even folks with no kids attend).

It's only been during recent years that Hatteras residents have left the island in large numbers during county-mandated hurricane evacuations. More nonnatives who now live here are less likely to see out a storm. Storm danger and damage has increased due to development and tighter living quarters.

Weather plays a regular role in Hatteras life. When the island is evacuated during a hurricane warning, it's not unusual for the locals to lose a week's worth of income. This creates great financial hardship for businesses, since their annual income is made primarily during the 12 weeks of summer. Even smaller storms cause delays when the roads flood.

Despite the imposing hold nature can cast over the barrier island, visitors flock here annually to enjoy its beauty and seclusion. Today there are enough conveniences, restaurants, and diversions within reach to entertain even sophisticated vacationers. The Cape Hatteras School, with help from the local arts council, brings in cultural events for residents. There are also several noteworthy art galleries on the island (see the Arts & Culture chapter).

History tells us, though, that even without these modern additions, folks would still come to relax Hatteras-style, away from the busier pace of the towns farther up the barrier islands, to do a little crabbing, clamming, fishing, beach walking, bird watching, or chatting with the anglers who relax at the docks. Many a modern-day adult vacationer has been coming to the Outer Banks since childhood. In fact, generations of families can call Hatteras Island their summer home.

The island has two obvious drawing cards: the sea and unique landscape. Some of the best windsurfing and surfing in North America can be done in the waters along Hatteras Island (see the Attractions and Water Sports chapters). Surfers from all over the East Coast come to Hatteras Island to surf the breakers, especially during strong nor'easters. Surfers look forward to hurricane season from June through November, when big northern swells can push wave heights to 8 feet or more. National surfing championships are held in Buxton (see the Annual Events chapter).

Hatteras Island is famous as an East Coast fishing hot spot. About 40 miles offshore are the Gulf Stream, a shelf current, and the Deep Western Boundary Current, all of which cross near the continental shelf's edge. The influence of this convergence is both positive and negative. These crossing currents spawned Diamond Shoals, creating the groundwork for danger

but also supplying a rich habitat for sport fish. A wide variety of fish travel up the Gulf Stream, giving this area the reputation for being the "Billfish Capital of the World." World-record fish have been caught both offshore and in the surf at Cape Hatteras Point, where red drum and many other fish come to feed. Much of the tip of Hatteras is lined with marinas where recreational charter boats take visitors to inshore and offshore waters (see the Fishing chapter). Full-service tackle shops, staffed with knowledgeable insiders, speckle the barrier island.

North of Rodanthe and just south of Oregon Inlet is Pea Island National Wildlife Refuge, where birding is popular and rewarding. A unique maritime forest lies farther south in Buxton, with a nature trail and informative signs (see the Attractions and Natural Wonders chapters for descriptions of both).

There are three National Park Service campgrounds on Hatteras Island (at Oregon Inlet, Frisco, and Cape Point) offering more laid-back and less expensive camping than the rest of the Outer Banks' camping facilities. Several private campgrounds also are established in the island communities (see the Camping chapter).

If nature hasn't sold you on Hatteras Island's wild, raw beauty, check out the Recreation chapter for those artificial amusements that can be enjoyed by the whole family.

i The Cape Hatteras National Seashore was the first national seashore in the United States. Proposed in 1933 and authorized in 1937, it was not established until 1953 and was dedicated in 1958.

Hatteras Island Communities

Rodanthe is Hatteras Island's northernmost village, situated about 12 miles from the northern tip of the island. Rodanthe blends seamlessly with Waves and Salvo to form what is sometimes referred to as the Tri-Village area. The three towns were once one, called Chicamacomico, but by the early 1900s they had separated into three individual villages. Of the three, Rodanthe has the most commercial offerings, including restaurants, an amusement park, gas stations, a shopping center, and tackle shops, but it is primarily a residential and vacation village. Rodanthe is home to the restored 1874 Chicamacomico Lifesaving Station, a historic tourist attraction that offers many activities. It also has a popular fishing pier.

Waves is a sleepy little village of mostly vacation homes. It's hard to know when you are actually in Waves because there are no signs welcoming you. Surfers stole those so many times that the villagers finally gave up installing them. This village was known as South Rodanthe until 1939, when it got its own post office and a new name.

Salvo also has nebulous village boundaries. The locals know them, though, and that's all that matters. Salvo is vacation oriented, although there aren't many commercial enterprises. Originally called Clark, this village was reportedly named for a salvo (simultaneous firing of cannon) it was given by Union soldiers during the Civil War. At the south end of the village is a NPS day-use area that's great for soundside picnicking, swimming, windsurfing, and kiteboarding.

Avon is about 10 miles south of Salvo, separated from the northern villages by a long, beautiful stretch of undeveloped NPS property. Avon was originally called Kinnakeet, a name that is still used by many old-timers. The name changed when the village got a post office in 1883. Avon has a wealth of vacation rental homes, hotels, and commercial businesses, including the island's only large chain grocery store and movie theater. It has many shops, restaurants, water-sports rentals, a fishing pier, and a medical facility. One of the most well-known windsurfing spots in the world, Canadian Hole, is on the south end of Avon. Old Avon Village, on the west side of the island, offers a chance to see local life. Turn toward the sound at the stoplight to see the old cottages, fishing gear, boats, and villagers.

Buxton is at the widest part of the island, on a point of land that juts into the sea and is known as Cape Point. Buxton is the hub of Hatteras Island. Hotels, restaurants, shops, and small-town grocery stores line the highway. Tackle shops are abundant here because fishing at Cape Point is rightly famous, as is surfing. The black-and-white candy-striped Cape Hatteras Lighthouse is, of course, the most popular attraction. Buxton Woods, a rare maritime forest, provides protection for the village. When Buxton got its post office in 1873, it was called simply the Cape. The name changed in 1882.

Frisco, the next town heading south, is the perfect place to get away from it all, with many vacation rental homes, a couple of art galleries, a pier, some shops and restaurants, and a Native American museum. But mostly it is the fishing, uncrowded beaches, and solitude that attract people to Frisco.

Hatteras Village, at the southernmost end of the island, is a picture-book fishing village and the ferry embarkation point for Ocracoke Island. When people say they're going to Hatteras, they mean the village, not the lighthouse, the cape, or the inlet. With its proximity to the Gulf Stream, Hatteras is a world-famous fishing locale, especially renowned for its bluefin tuna fishery in winter. Several marinas and charter fishing vessels call Hatteras Village home. The village has always had a quaint, homespun appeal, with independently run restaurants and shops, small motels geared to anglers, and simple homes. In recent years Hatteras Village has seen the addition of upscale oceanfront homes, a fancy shopping complex, and the first chain hotel on the island, a Holiday Inn. Be sure to visit The Graveyard of the Atlantic Museum, at the southernmost point of the village.

OCRACOKE ISLAND

Insiders generally see Ocracoke as a tourist attraction during the warm months and romantic hideaway during the off-season, but this is a wonderful place to visit any time of the year. There's just no place like this quaint island with its pristine beaches and homey atmosphere. Nearly all development on the island surrounds Silver Lake in Ocracoke Village. The island is but a slender strip of sand, geographically much like the other Outer Banks islands. At its widest, the 16-milelong island is only about 2 miles across, narrowing in some sections to a half mile, where sound and sea are both visible from the two-lane road.

Getting Here

Access to Ocracoke Island is limited to sea and air. A free 45-minute ferry ride across the waters of Pamlico Sound transports islanders and visitors to the north end of Ocracoke from Hatteras Island. From the ferry terminal at the north end of the island, it's a 12-mile drive past undeveloped marshlands and dunes to Ocracoke Village. Two toll ferries

connect the island with the mainland. The Cedar Island and Swan Quarter ferries, each a 2½-hour ride, cost $15 per car and arrive and depart from the heart of Ocracoke Village on the southern end of the island. A small airfield allows private planes to land just outside of the village (see the Getting Here, Getting Around chapter).

Island Economy & Tourism

Vacationers flock to Ocracoke during the warm months. Once a simple fishing village where islanders primarily lived off the sea, Ocracoke now operates as a vacation resort nine months out of the year. Tourism and traffic have changed the pace of this traditional fishing village, but the influx of visitors is necessary to maintain a healthy economy.

While many Ocracokers work at tourist-related businesses, year-round residents also are employed by the National Park Service, in the local school, in the building industry, or as commercial and recreational fishermen. The island's natural beauty and easy pace act as a magnet for artists, craftspeople, and writers.

Ocracoke Island offers sightseeing options that radiate from a core village atmosphere. You can ride bikes all over the island; it's best to explore the village by foot. You can park your vehicle after arriving on the island and not use it again until you leave. Make sure to stroll through the village, which surrounds Silver Lake. Wander the back roads: Specialty shops, galleries, and old island cottages are waiting to be discovered. Casually elegant restaurants and come-as-you-are eateries offer several meal choices, and friendly islanders will make recommendations, pointing you in the right direction (we outline more than a dozen spots in the Restaurants chapter).

Sailboats moor in the protected cove of Silver Lake, and charter and commercial fishing boats fill the downtown docks. You can book half- and full-day fishing excursions year-round. All accommodations—including bed-and-breakfast inns, hotels, rental cottages, and private campgrounds—are close to the island's activity (see the Shopping, Fishing, and Accommodations chapters for details).

On the oceanside about halfway to the village from the Hatteras ferry dock, tents and camping trailers dot the secondary dunes. This popular NPS campground is open from late spring to early fall and requires advance reservations (see the Camping chapter). The Attractions chapter describes the island's historic sites in detail. Make sure you take in the British Cemetery and the stately Ocracoke Inlet Lighthouse. Come January the flow of visitors subsides, and islanders take a break from long, seven-day workweeks. Off-season tourists still can find accommodations.

GETTING HERE, GETTING AROUND

In the not-so-distant past, travel to the Outer Banks was an ordeal. Before the bridges were built, many visitors reached these barrier islands by ferry from Elizabeth City, and some people with four-wheel-drive vehicles drove down the beach from Virginia. Thankfully, we now have two bridge access points, one in Kitty Hawk, used mostly by travelers from the north, and one from Roanoke Island to Nags Head, used mostly by visitors from the south and west. North Carolina's Department of Transportation has spent considerable time and money improving state routes, making it increasingly easier to get to the bridges.

Another way to get to the Outer Banks is via long ferry rides from the North Carolina mainland to Ocracoke Island. In fact, ferry travel is still the only way to reach Ocracoke Island—outside of private motorboat or private plane—and no change is foreseeable.

But other than the state-run ferries to Ocracoke, there is no public transportation to the Outer Banks. The nearest Amtrak station is in Newport News, Virginia, and the nearest bus stations are in Elizabeth City, North Carolina, and Norfolk, Virginia. The nearest commercial airport is in Norfolk. Once you arrive by bus, train, or plane, however, you must either rent a car and drive to the Outer Banks or hire a private plane or shuttle service.

This chapter outlines the best routes for getting here by land, sea, and sky. Once you arrive, however, know that you will need some form of transportation—a motorcycle, a car, a bicycle, a scooter, or at least enough money for a cab—if you plan to venture around a bit. Don't even think of complaining about the lack of public bus transportation. Instead, while you're still unwinding from your trip, venture on down to the beach. Remove your shoes, take off your socks, and walk in the tideline. Now, are you really concerned about bus transportation? If so, you haven't walked far enough.

GETTING HERE

By Land

You can't get to any islands without spanning water, and thankfully we have several bridges. In a state of emergency, such as a hurricane evacuation, bridges are the only ways off the island. During such mass exits local officials sometimes close the bridges to incoming traffic and use all the lanes to expedite evacuation. In peak travel times (summer weekends), the bridges, especially the Wright Memorial Bridge, bottleneck, so drive cautiously.

Arriving from the North:
To the Wright Memorial Bridge

Since so many visitors are from Pennsylvania, New York, New Jersey, Connecticut, and Washington, D.C., we begin this section with directions from Richmond, Virginia, which from the north can be reached on I-95 south. If you're coming from north of the Outer Banks but south of Richmond, read through the directions and select the route nearest your location.

From Richmond, follow I-64 east to I-664 east at Hampton/Newport News and take the Monitor-Merrimac Bridge/Tunnel across the James River to I-64. The VA 168 Bypass allows you to skirt the traffic lights and congestion on Battlefield Boulevard in Chesapeake, thus easing your drive to and from the Outer Banks. From I-64, take exit 291B to VA 168 south. VA 168 becomes US 158 in North Carolina; don't worry, both names refer to the same road.

You now have two options for traveling on VA 168, but both get you to the same place. The new VA 168, linking I-64 in Chesapeake with US 158 to the Outer Banks, is known as the Chesapeake Expressway and is a faster, four-lane option, although there is a toll to use it. The second choice is to take Battlefield Boulevard. Past Chesapeake on VA 168, it's a straight shot to the Wright Memorial Bridge, which crosses the Currituck Sound to Kitty Hawk on the Outer Banks. The drive from the Virginia/North Carolina border takes about an hour, though you may wish to stop at the many antiques shops, thrift stores, and produce stands. You'll pass Mel's Diner, a 1950s-style diner in Grandy that thrives on tourism and has a loyal local following as well. If you just can't wait for some Carolina barbecue, stop at Dixie Bar-B-Q Pit in Powells Point or Saul's Cafe in Harbinger.

Another option coming from the north is to take US 17 south from I-64 in Virginia. This span of highway flanks the Intracoastal Waterway through the aptly named Great Dismal Swamp. Follow US 17 south to South Mills, where you take NC 343 to Camden, following signs to US 158 and the Outer Banks.

i Insiders make the drive from Chesapeake to the Outer Banks by traveling VA 168. Not much time is added, and tolls on the Chesapeake Expressway in Virginia can reach $6 on weekends.

Arriving from the West:
To the Washington Baum Bridge

From I-95 in North Carolina, take US 64 east toward Rocky Mount, passing through Williamston, Jamesville, Plymouth, Creswell, Columbia, over the Alligator River, and through East Lake and Manns Harbor to Roanoke Island.

The bridge over the Alligator River, part of the Intracoastal Waterway, is an old-fashioned drawbridge, opened as needed by an on-site bridge tender. If you're lucky enough to get caught by a bridge opening, get out of the car and enjoy the unique vantage of peering over the railings into the water. Yes, alligators do live in the water here. Generally, Alligator River is the most northern waterway where these creatures reside.

It is a sparse area with few stops between Plymouth and the Outer Banks, so fuel up before you leave either Williamston (approximately 1 hour and 45 minutes from Manteo) or Plymouth, especially if you're traveling at night. If you have to pull off the road, do so carefully and choose a wide shoulder if possible. In areas where canals alternate sides of the road, pull off on the side without a canal. The state Department of Transportation installed guardrails alongside the canals to make travel on this road safer.

Along this route watch for deer, black bears, red wolves, and a wide variety of birds. You'll spot an occasional blue heron wading in the roadside creeks. The state adorns the byways with colorful poppies and other wildflowers. It's tempting to pick the lush beauties, but it's illegal.

Continuing east on US 64, you'll cross the William B. Umstead Bridge, or as locals call it, the Manns Harbor Bridge, to Roanoke Island. Momentarily you'll pass through the quaint town of Manteo, which celebrated its centennial in 1999.

i The bridge spanning Croatan Sound is officially named the Virginia Dare Memorial Bridge, but it's also known as the Croatan Sound Bridge. Insiders call it "the New Bridge." All three names are recognized, but not by everyone. You may have to ask for it by three different names before you get a response.

In 2002 a bridge to the mainland opened. The Virginia Dare Memorial Bridge (known as "the New Bridge" to locals) stretches from the mainland at Manns Harbor to the Nags Head–Manteo Head Causeway, completely bypassing Roanoke Island. This 5.2-mile bridge, the longest in the state, shaves 20 minutes or so from the trip to the beaches because it avoids the two-lane bottleneck through Manteo. An Outer Banks Visitors Bureau welcome center and rest area is located at the bridge's eastern terminus. However, the old Manns Harbor Bridge remains open and should be used if you want to visit the attractions, restaurants, and shops of Roanoke Island and Manteo.

Once through Manteo, if you wish to go to the fishing village of Wanchese, turn right at the junction of US 64 and NC 345 (referred to by locals as Midway). For Outer Banks beaches, Cape Hatteras, Nags Head, and points north, veer left after passing through Manteo, remaining on US 64. Overhead signs make getting lost unlikely, but if you find yourself off your intended route, blame it on the scenery and turn back. You can't get too lost here on these islands and peninsulas! US 64 will take you across the Nags Head–Manteo Causeway and the Washington Baum Bridge.

Arriving from the West:
To the Wright Memorial Bridge

Backtrack to Williamston for an alternate route to the Outer Banks. Instead of traveling on US 64 along the southern route, you can choose to take US 17 to Elizabeth City. Both routes take about the same traveling time. From Elizabeth City follow signs on US 158 to Nags Head and Manteo, and arrive on the island from the north, crossing the Wright Memorial Bridge. US 17 seems to be the route preferred by most visiting Virginians.

Arriving from the South:
To the Ocracoke Ferries

From points south, take I-95 north to Rocky Mount, North Carolina, then US 64 east to Williamston, following the directions given earlier for arriving from the west. For an alternate southern route, follow the coastline north to Morehead City and Cedar Island, where you board a toll ferry to Ocracoke

Island. Another option is to take US 17 north from Wilmington, North Carolina, through Jacksonville and New Bern to Washington. From Washington, take US 264 east to Swan Quarter and follow signs to the Swan Quarter toll ferry, which brings you to Ocracoke Island. The route goes through the Swan Quarter National Wildlife Refuge, with gracious old cedars lining the way. From Ocracoke follow NC 12 to the Ocracoke–Hatteras ferry for passage to Hatteras Island and points north. For ferry schedules and further information, see the Ferries section of this chapter.

Crossing the Wright Memorial Bridge

No matter which route you choose, the destination is well worth the journey. Because the Wright Memorial Bridge is the main thoroughfare to and from the Outer Banks, bear in mind that summer season peak travel time (going to the island) is from noon to 6 p.m. on Saturday and Sunday. This is rush-hour traffic, Outer Banks–style. Peak travel time leaving the island is from about 8 a.m. to noon on the same days. Delays are possible from Memorial Day to Labor Day; for your convenience, travel advisories are posted on a flashing sign at the bridge.

i Cell phone service is nonexistent or sporadic in certain areas of the Outer Banks. If you must get in touch with someone (or vice versa), be sure that you have a back-up, land-line phone number.

Once you cross the bridge into Kitty Hawk, you can't miss the bigger-than-life signs that lead you to your destinations. To get to Southern Shores, Duck, Sanderling, Corolla, or Carova, turn left on NC 12 and

head north. For destinations south of Kitty Hawk, continue on US 158 to Kill Devil Hills and Nags Head. Just past 16 miles south of the bridge, the road veers right toward Roanoke Island and Manteo and branches left toward Oregon Inlet and the Cape Hatteras National Seashore. Follow NC 12 on Hatteras Island to the communities of Rodanthe, Waves, Salvo, Avon, Buxton, Frisco, and Hatteras. In Hatteras Village a ferry provides free transport to Ocracoke Island.

i The Bypass (US 158) and the Beach Road (NC 12) are marked by mileposts that originate at the Wright Memorial Bridge in Kitty Hawk and continue through MP 21 in South Nags Head. An address that reads "MP 7, Beach Road, Kill Devil Hills" is located 7 miles south of the Wright Memorial Bridge on NC 12.

At the junction of US 158 and NC 12 in Kitty Hawk is the Aycock Brown Welcome Center, which offers a wealth of information to visitors. Another great information stop is the Outer Banks Chamber of Commerce, located on 101 Town Hall Dr. about 1 block west of US 158 in Kill Devil Hills.

Crossing the Washington Baum Bridge

The Washington Baum Bridge from Roanoke Island leads to South Nags Head, where you can choose to travel north toward Nags Head, Kill Devil Hills, Kitty Hawk, Duck, and Corolla or south to Hatteras Island and Ocracoke Island. The Cape Hatteras turnoff is on the right, about a mile from the bridge's eastern terminus. At this intersection—referred to as Whalebone Junction—you bear left onto US 158 in Nags Head or go straight to connect with the Beach Road

(NC 12), either of which takes you north from Nags Head through Kitty Hawk. (Note that South Nags Head is accessed in this area via Old Nags Head Road.) A right turn at Whalebone Junction puts you on NC 12 toward Bodie Island, the Oregon Inlet Fishing Center, and points south. If you continue on NC 12 across the Herbert C. Bonner Bridge onto Hatteras Island, the road goes through Rodanthe, Waves, Salvo, Avon, Buxton, Frisco, and Hatteras Village. A ferry in Hatteras Village goes to Ocracoke Island.

By Air

Airports & Airstrips

Note to pilots: Several Outer Banks airstrips are unattended, as explained in this section. Call the state Division of Aviation at (919) 840-0112 for information not covered in the following entries.

DARE COUNTY REGIONAL AIRPORT
Airport Road, Roanoke Island
(252) 475-5570
http://darecounty.ncflyports.com
If you'd like to fly your own plane to the Outer Banks, this is the airport to call. Dare County Regional Airport's two runways measure 3,300 feet and 4,300 feet, and both are lighted. Jet-A and 100 LL fuels are available. Operating hours are 8 a.m. to 7 p.m. daily. This airport is manned, has a terminal VOR, DME, and NDB, plus automated weather updates through AWOS, which you can access at radio frequency 128.275 or by calling (252) 473-2826.

Barrier Island Aviation (252-473-4247, www.barrierislandaviation.com) and Outer Banks Air Charters (252-256-2322, www.outerbanksaircharters.com) both offer charter service to and from Dare County Regional Airport. Car rentals are available at the airport; call in advance.

FIRST FLIGHT AIRSTRIP
Wright Brothers National Memorial
US 158, MP 8, Kill Devil Hills
(252) 473-2111
Every pilot visiting the Outer Banks should sign in at least once at this historic location. At First Flight your stay is limited to 24 hours. This unattended 3,000-foot strip is maintained by the National Park Service. Since there are no lights, takeoffs and landings are permitted during daylight hours only. Reservations are not necessary, and a sign-up book is on premises. No fuel is available.

BILLY MITCHELL HATTERAS ISLAND AIRSTRIP
NC 12, Frisco
Also known as Hatteras Mitchell Field, this Hatteras Island airport is on National Park Service land. The airport is unattended. Billy Mitchell Airstrip's unlighted runway is approximately 3,000 feet long, and fuel is not available. There is a parking lot. A shelter on the premises has a phone and toilets.

OCRACOKE ISLAND AIRSTRIP
NC 12, Ocracoke Island
(252) 928-9901 (pay phone)
Another airstrip maintained by the National Park Service, this unattended facility has a 3,000-footlong runway and no lights. There is a parking lot and a pay telephone. The runway has brush and 25-foot sand dunes at either end. Listen to the weather radio or call for weather updates.

NORFOLK INTERNATIONAL AIRPORT
2200 Norview Ave., Norfolk, VA
(757) 857-3351
www.norfolkairport.com

Open 24 hours a day, Norfolk International Airport offers air service on American, Continental, Delta, Northwest, United, US Airways, and Southwest Airlines. Major rental car companies have offices at the airport. For main passenger information call the airport. For private charter information see the following entries.

Air Service
BURRIS FLYING SERVICE
(252) 986-2679
www.obxflightseeing.com

Burris Flying Service, operating from the Billy Mitchell Airport, offers air tours and aerial photography for the Outer Banks.

FLIGHTGEST
339 Audubon Dr., Corolla
(919) 840-4443
www.flightgest.com

Step up into the luxury of Flightgest flight service. An FAA carrier, Flightgest flies to most destinations east of the Mississippi. Scheduled shuttles run to and from the Norfolk International Airport in season. Flightgest flies its PC-12 Pilatus and Grand Caravan planes directly to an exclusive airstrip in Corolla or to any other Outer Banks airport.

By Water

The best way to beat the traffic—and to see some incredible scenery while you're at it—is to arrive at the Outer Banks by boat. Only very experienced boaters should attempt to navigate these tricky waters, and only with proper equipment in the best weather.

Discuss your trip with a local sailor or captain while making your plans, and be sure to pick up a copy of the *Mid-Atlantic Waterway Guide;* it provides the most detailed information available about the area's waterways. Current chart numbers from the Intracoastal Waterway (ICW) to Manteo on Roanoke Island are 12204 and 12205. Chart 12204 is a large map of the North River, and chart 12205 is a strip map that includes both the Alligator and North Rivers. Both charts cover the inlet, although 12205 provides more detail.

From the North

If you're boating from points north, you can enter the ICW in Norfolk, Virginia. The trip from Norfolk to Manteo is about 80 nautical miles. In fair weather and with a fast boat, you can make it to the Outer Banks in 5 to 6 hours; if you're sailing you may wish to spend your first night at the Coinjock Marina. Be prepared for wind, chop, and shallow waters in the Albemarle Sound. As long as you remain within the ICW markers, you won't have to worry about depth.

Any of the following three routes lead you to the Outer Banks. One takes you from Norfolk, Virginia, across the Currituck Sound to Coinjock, North Carolina, the North River, and the Albemarle Sound. From the ICW mid-sound marker, head east and look for day markers leading to the waterfront town of Manteo on Roanoke Island.

An alternate route from Norfolk leads to Deep Creek, Virginia, through the Great Dismal Swamp to Lake Drummond, North Carolina. From there, travel through South Mills to the Pasquotank River, where the ICW—locally known as the Ditch—joins the Albemarle Sound. Refer to your charts for navigating across the Albemarle Sound to the Alligator River, and then travel either the Croatan Sound or the Roanoke Sound to Manteo.

The third—and probably the easiest—route takes you from the end of the North River into the Albemarle Sound. Look for marker number 173, then bear left and follow the day markers leading behind Powell's Point. The first marker you'll come to is number 4; from there look for number 2 and then MG (the middle-ground marker). From MG head nearly due south. Look for another number 2 day marker, which takes you from the north end of East Lake toward Manns Harbor Channel, where day markers lead to the Roanoke Island Channel. (All of these markers are noted on the charts.)

From the South

If you are boating to the Outer Banks from the south, pick up the ICW between Beaufort and Morehead City, North Carolina, and follow it to the Neuse River. Take the ICW north from the Neuse River across the Pamlico River to Belhaven on the Pungo River. You may want to stop in Belhaven at the River Forest Manor, a country inn, restaurant, marina, and shipyard, where you can fuel up while touring the century-old southern plantation mansion or getting a bite to eat in its historic restaurant. Sunday brunch alone is worth the trip. An alternative stop is the new Dowry Creek Marina, with slips and fuel. After you leave Belhaven, continue north on the ICW to the Alligator River, then travel east until you spot the Roanoke Sound day markers, which lead to Manteo on Roanoke Island.

If seas aren't rough, the fastest route from the south is to go through the Pamlico Sound from either the Pamlico or Neuse River. After you pass under the Manns Harbor Bridge, look for the Roanoke Sound day markers leading to Manteo.

Roanoke Island Marinas

Manteo has several docks within walking distance to restaurants and attractions. Locations and amenities are as follows. Also see the Boating section of the Water Sports chapter.

WATERFRONT MARINA
Manteo Historic District
(252) 473-3320

The Waterfront Marina provides public docking facilities with water and power at each slip. Charges are on a per-foot basis for semiannual, annual, and transient boaters. Call ahead or radio the dockmaster on your approach to the marina. Laundry and shower facilities are available. The marina's boardwalk extends along the waterfront and is within walking distance of shops, restaurants, and other diversions. In Manteo you'll find friendly merchants and interesting sights, and several lovely inns offer a respite from your berth. A brief stroll across the bridge takes you to Roanoke Island Festival Park (see the Attractions chapter for more information).

PIRATE'S COVE MARINA
Roanoke Sound, between Manteo and Nags Head
(252) 473-3906
www.fishpiratescove.com

Open year-round, Pirate's Cove can accommodate boats from 25 to 110 feet in 195 slips. Transients are welcome, and many slips are rented year-round. Call or check the website rates, as prices vary. Slip rental includes water and electricity, showers, cable TV hookup, and laundry facilities. Pirate's

Cove offers one courtesy car that boaters can use on a limited basis to fetch supplies or other necessities. Boaters can use the tennis courts, pool, and other on-site facilities.

The on-site ship's store and restaurant are open to the public, as is the fuel dock. On the top deck of Pirates Cove Dockside Restaurant, you can have a cold drink and some steamed shrimp while getting a bird's-eye view of one of the area's most beautiful sport-fishing fleets.

Ferries

Landlubbers also can enjoy an Outer Banks arrival by boat thanks to the North Carolina Ferry System. One picturesque route is to follow US 70 east from New Bern to Havelock. Pick up NC 101, follow to NC 306, and then take the ferry to Bayview near historic Bath. Follow NC 99 to Belhaven, picking up US 264 to Swan Quarter. From here, you can take NC 94 across Lake Mattamuskeet, then US 64 to Manteo—or ride another ferry from Swan Quarter to Ocracoke Island. It sounds complicated, but signs will guide you.

An alternate route is to take US 70 through Havelock to Beaufort. US 70 continues from Beaufort to Harkers Island, following the Core Sound to NC 12, where the Cedar Island Ferry takes you to Ocracoke Island. The voyage across the Pamlico Sound is well worth the time it takes to arrive in Ocracoke. Cross Ocracoke Island from south to north via NC 12, and pick up the Hatteras Island Ferry to the upper Outer Banks.

Ferry passage is a good way to reduce your driving time if you're heading to the southern portion of the Outer Banks. It also gives you a chance to stretch and move around while still making progress. Unless you have your own boat or plane, ferry service is the only way to reach picturesque

Ocracoke Island. The ferries transport cars to the island, although we suggest that you park your car after arriving on Ocracoke and get around on foot or by bike.

Following is information on the Outer Banks ferry services. Although it is rare to have a time change, you may wish to call ahead and verify departure times. You can get more information by writing to Director, 8550 Shipyard Road, Manns Harbor, NC 27953 or by calling (800) BY FERRY. You can log on to ncferry.org and make your advance ferry reservations online. Truckers: For information about weight and size limitations, call the specific ferry location. The toll-free number is operable east of the Mississippi River only.

Hatteras Inlet (Ocracoke) Ferry

This free, state-run service links the islands of Hatteras and Ocracoke across the Pamlico Sound. The ferries accommodate 30 vehicles—including cars and large camping/recreational vehicles—and run frequently during the summer to avoid excessive delays. The Hatteras ferry does not require reservations, and the trip takes about 40 minutes. Public restrooms are at the Hatteras dock, and heads are onboard. For more information call (800) 368-8949 or (252) 986-2353.

GETTING AROUND

By Auto

We've gotten you here; now we'll get you around.

Let's get the traffic report out of the way first. The number of travelers on our roads increases dramatically during the summer. Traffic more than triples from Memorial Day through Labor Day. We realize that visitors enrich our economy, and we welcome you—cars, trucks, SUVs, and all. If you're used to big-city driving, you'll find the summer traffic tolerable. Naturally roads get very congested during hurricane evacuations, despite the advance warnings county authorities give (see the Waves and Weather: How to Stay Safe chapter for more). If you bear in mind the following tips, your drive should be a smooth one.

The northern route up NC 12 through Duck and Corolla can get bogged down on summer weekends and during weekday lunch and dinner hours. If the weather's bad, many more people shop rather than go to the beach, so expect heavier traffic when skies are gray. Allow an extra half hour or so when traveling to the northern Outer Banks on summer weekends. You may want to call the various municipalities or radio stations to see when traffic is heaviest during holidays. And if you must travel during peak traffic hours, try not to lose your cool. Relax—you're at the beach! There are plenty of places to stop for food, drinks, and shopping, though you may also want to pack some snacks, especially if you have young children.

While we do have congested areas to deal with from time to time, we have a simple road layout that makes getting lost almost impossible. These barrier islands, including Roanoke Island to the west, have only three major roadways. US 158 crosses the Wright Memorial Bridge into Kitty Hawk and winds through the center of the island to Whalebone Junction in Nags Head. This five-lane highway (the center lane is for turning vehicles only) is also called the Bypass, Croatan Highway, or the Big Road. In this book we will refer to it as the Bypass or US 158.

NC 12 runs along the beach, parallel to US 158. A two-lane road, it stretches from the southern border of the Currituck National Wildlife Refuge at the Villages at Ocean Hill development in Corolla to the ferry docks at Hatteras Island's southernmost tip. NC 12 picks up again on Ocracoke, spanning the length of the tiny island, ending in picturesque Ocracoke Village. NC 12 is also called Ocean Trail in Corolla, Duck Road in Duck and Southern Shores, Ocean Boulevard in part of Southern Shores, and either Virginia Dare Trail or the Beach Road from Kitty Hawk through Nags Head. In this book we refer to it as NC 12 (or occasionally as the Beach Road, when talking about that stretch from Kitty Hawk through Nags Head).

On Roanoke Island, US 64/264 is also called US 64 or Main Highway. This stoplight-filled road begins at the Nags Head–Manteo Causeway and runs across the Washington Baum Bridge through Manteo, across the William B. Umstead Bridge, and through Manns Harbor on the mainland. School traffic clogs US 64/264 on weekday mornings and afternoons. On rainy days in summer, this road is extremely congested with visitors headed to Roanoke Island's attractions and shops. Some congestion has been alleviated by the Virginia Dare Memorial Bridge.

US 158 and NC 12 run mainly north and south. Smaller connector streets link seaside rental cottages to year-round neighborhoods west of the Bypass.

If you truly want to relax and spend your vacation days island-style, kick off your shoes and travel on foot. You can walk for miles down the beaches, collecting shells and wading. Plenty of restaurants and fishing piers run the length of the Outer Banks, so you're usually not far from food and drink. Most spots welcome casual diners. When walking the Beach Road, watch out for vehicles with projecting mirrors—the road is narrow. It is not the best choice for biking, except in Nags Head, where there is a bike path. You can easily explore Manteo on foot, and biking is a safe alternative in that town.

By Bike

The Outer Banks boasts several paved bike paths. Running the length of Roanoke Island is a 7-mile asphalt path that has awakened the athlete in many locals, young and old, who are now regularly seen walking, riding bikes, and skating on the route. It's a wide, safe path that we are grateful to have.

An 11-mile bike path runs along NC 12 almost the entire length of the town of Nags Head. In South Nags Head the path is concrete, and in the rest of the town it is asphalt. The town of Kill Devil Hills sports a scenic asphalt route along Colington Road, running down the National Park Service property past the Wright Brothers National Memorial. Kitty Hawk's bike path begins in Martins Point, just east of the Wright Memorial Bridge. Riders can take northern paths into Southern Shores on Dogwood Trail, Juniper Trail, or Ocean Boulevard. The Ocean Boulevard segment spans the 4-mile width of Southern Shores and continues through the quaint town of Duck. Yet another Kitty Hawk route heads south from US 158 onto Woods Road and meanders through the maritime forest.

i When biking any of the paths in the area, be sure to wear proper safety gear. Sand blown along the pavement can cause your wheels to catch or skid suddenly and unexpectedly.

While pedaling these paths or biking anywhere else on the Outer Banks, please wear a helmet. You can rent bikes at several rental services, and many accommodations offer bikes and helmets as a courtesy. Watch out—the sand that blows on the road can get in your eyes as you pass the dunes and can be slippery when you brake. Follow the normal rules of the road that apply to cars, stopping at lights and stop signs and yielding to pedestrians. There is a lot of activity near the beach, so whether you're on a bike or in a car, watch out for that rolling beach ball—it is usually followed by a child.

Transportation for Hire

Even though you won't find any public transportation here, you do have a number of alternatives. Since demand for taxicabs and limousines can be great at times, make sure to call in advance.

AIRPORT SHUTTLE CONNECTION
(252) 441-5466
Airport Shuttle's sedans deliver passengers from Raleigh, Richmond, Newport News, Norfolk, and Washington, D.C., airports to any Outer Banks destination. Advance reservations are required for private cars, and a shared-ride service is available in season.

BAYSIDE CAB
(252) 480-1300, (252) 441-2500
On US 158 at MP 6, Bayside offers point-to-point service 24 hours a day.

COASTAL CAB COMPANY
(252) 449-8787
Coastal Cab offers radio-dispatched 24-hour service on the Outer Banks. Service to airports in Norfolk and Raleigh is available with advance reservations. Credit cards are accepted for out-of-town trips.

THE CONNECTION
(252) 449-2777
www.calltheconnection.com

This shuttle service operates daily between Norfolk and the Outer Banks, with door-to-door shared-ride and private service to Norfolk International Airport (other airports upon request) as well as Norfolk's bus and train stations. Full-size, air-conditioned passenger vans can accommodate groups, families, bicycles, surfboards, sailboards, etc. Drivers are fully licensed and insured. Private town cars are also available. Reservations are recommended.

ISLAND HOPPER SHUTTLE
(252) 995-6771

Island Hopper Shuttle serves Hatteras Island with transportation to and from Norfolk International Airport, plus courier service on weekdays to Kitty Hawk and Manteo.

ISLAND LIMO
(252) 441-LIMO, (800) 828-LIMO
www.islandlimo.com

If it's a stretch limo you want, Island Limo's selection suits your every need. Island Limo provides transportation to and from Norfolk International Airport via private sedan and limousine year-round.

Car Rentals

Whether you need something for getting around town or something more substantial, like a four-wheel-drive vehicle, to really explore the island, you have a number of rental options.

Cars Only
- **Dare County Regional Airport,** on Roanoke Island, off Airport Road, (252) 475-5570

- **B&R Rent-a-Car** at R. D. Sawyer Motor Company, US 64 in Manteo, (252) 473-2141
- **Enterprise Rent-a-Car** in Kill Devil Hills and Manteo, (252) 480-1838, (800) 736-8222

Cars & Four-Wheel-Drive Vehicles
- **Outer Banks Chrysler,** Plymouth, Dodge, Jeep, Eagle, US 158 at MP 5 in Kill Devil Hills, (252) 441-1146
- **Cape Point Exxon** in Buxton, (252) 995-5695

i For beach access information for April through October, check online at www.nps.gov/caha/planyourvisit/off-road-vehicle-use.htm. Information is updated weekly. Some areas close for wildlife protection, however most beaches remain open for pedestrian and off-road vehicle use.

Beach Driving

Off-road access is possible on the Outer Banks but only in designated areas and at certain times of the year. Use of a four-wheel-drive (4WD) vehicle is mandatory. Check with each township for specific rules; some places even require a permit.

Generally, tagged, licensed, and insured 4WDs are allowed on the beach in Kill Devil Hills and Nags Head from October 1 through April 30. However, permits are required in Nags Head. Southern Shores and Kitty Hawk prohibit driving on the beach at all times. As far north as Corolla and Carova in Currituck County, there are specified areas where you can drive on the beach. Hatteras Island operates under the guidance of the **National Park Service** (252-473-2111); call with any questions you have concerning off-road driving.

On Hatteras Island, driving is not allowed on the beach at Pea Island National Wildlife Refuge (the area from Rodanthe Pier north to Oregon Inlet), but farther south there are access areas marked by a sign featuring a symbol for off-road vehicles where you can travel on the beach. Obviously beach driving is not allowed at access areas that have signs with an X through the symbol. It's a good idea to stop at one of the National Park Service visitor centers or campgrounds to chat with a ranger before taking to the beach on wheels. Rangers supply up-to-date information on unusual conditions, such as eroded beach areas, that could prove hazardous to you and your vehicle.

Driving Rules & Safety Tips

The maximum speed for beach driving is 25 mph, but even that can be too fast on a crowded day. The speed limit is strictly enforced by park rangers and local law officials. Where the sand is soft, you may have to drive slower than 25 mph.

Beach drivers follow the same rules that apply when driving on asphalt: Keep to the right, pass on the left, etc. All vehicles must be street legal with valid plates, insurance, and inspection stickers, and driven by a licensed individual. Seat belts must be worn by anyone in the front seat. Standing is not allowed in any vehicle. If you are riding in the back of a pickup truck, you must sit on the bed, not on the side rail or wheel well. Jeep passengers must be seated and may not stand and hold onto the roll bar. No open containers of alcohol are allowed in vehicles.

Pedestrians have the right-of-way at all times on the beach, regardless of where they are in relation to your vehicle. Look out for children, pets, sunbathers, and anglers. Expect the unexpected. The wind often hampers hearing, so use caution when approaching pedestrians. If the wind is blowing away from them and toward you, they may not hear your approach.

When driving back to the road, keep your eye on pedestrian traffic. The edge of the Beach Road grabs the wheels a bit and can pull you to one side or another abruptly. Maintain a wide berth for anyone walking near you.

And a caution to pedestrians: Wear light clothing at night if you intend to walk near car traffic. While most drivers respect driving safety rules, some really let their hair down at the beach. Pedestrians need to be as conscientious as drivers on both sand and roadways.

> **i** Avoid parking on the pedestrian walkways that thread through the beach. A ticket will cost around $125, and you'll have to return to the Outer Banks if you want to challenge it.

Vehicle Preparation

Many, many drivers get stuck because they don't let air out of their tires before driving on the beaches. The National Park Service says its rangers generally drive with 20 pounds of pressure in their tires. This applies to vehicles of any size, from large trucks to smaller sedans. Lowering the pressure also helps prevent the engine from overheating when traveling through soft sand. Rangers advise re-inflating tires when returning to the paved roads.

Don't block the beach ramps when you lock hubs or deflate tires. We suggest pulling well off to the side of the ramp or using the parking areas found at most vehicle accesses.

Driving on Sand

Once on the beach, try to drive on the firm, wet sand below the high-tide line. If there are previously made tracks, follow them. Areas may be untracked for good reason. Watch out for areas of the beach with shell-laden, reddish sand and depressions with a bit of standing water. These can be very soft.

Restricted Areas

You are prohibited from driving on, over, or in between the dunes for any reason at any time. The dunes and their fragile vegetation create our protective barrier and are extremely vital to the delicate ecology of animal and plant life.

Please obey all the area designations on the beaches. Many portions of the beach are roped off, allowing shorebirds and turtles to nest. These areas change throughout the seasons, so areas that were open in April could be closed in August. Through traffic can be curtailed by these closings, especially at high tide. Stay alert for changes, and respect the limitations. Violations can bring substantial fines.

When driving by the waterline, always drive behind surf anglers. You don't want to snap their nearly invisible monofilament fishing line or upset their fishing activity.

WELCOME & VISITOR CENTERS

AYCOCK BROWN WELCOME CENTER AT KITTY HAWK

US 158, MP 1½, Kitty Hawk
(252) 261-4644
www.outerbanks.org

Constructed in the style of an old lifesaving station, this center is called "Outer Banks at a Glance" and includes several state-of-the-art displays, a continuously running film, and a brochure gazebo. By combining computers, photography, video graphics, period music, and sound effects, the displays offer an entertaining overview of the Outer Banks, and well-informed local staff members are ready to answer questions. Named for a 1950s photographer who has since become a local legend, this building sits a mile east of the Wright Memorial Bridge at the juncture of US 158 and NC 12. The Outer Banks Visitors Bureau operates three such welcome centers.

Resources include area maps, tide charts, ferry schedules, and brochures. Free community newspapers such as the *Coast,* published by the Virginian-Pilot, and the locally published *North Beach Sun* offer features that highlight the area.

The center is open daily from 9 a.m. to 6 p.m. from Memorial Day through Aug and 9 a.m. to 5:30 p.m. daily from Sept through Apr—except for Dec, Jan, and Feb, when the center closes at 5 p.m. It is closed Thanksgiving Day, Christmas Day, and New Year's Day. The building and public restrooms are wheelchair accessible, and the picnic area is a welcome outdoor respite for those who have been riding a long time. Contact the Outer Banks Visitors Bureau at (877) 629-4386 for more information.

OUTER BANKS CHAMBER OF COMMERCE

101 Town Hall Dr., Kill Devil Hills
(252) 441-8144
www.outerbankschamber.com

On the south side of Colington Road, near the corner of US 158 at MP 8, a wooden building with a covered porch houses the chamber of commerce in Kill Devil Hills. This center offers free information that's helpful to both visitors and permanent residents. It's a clearinghouse for written and telephone inquiries, and the friendly staff gives information on activities, accommodations, and annual events. Mail inquiries to PO Box 1757, Kill Devil Hills, NC 27948. The center is open year-round Mon through Fri from 8:30 a.m. to 5 p.m.

OUTER BANKS VISITORS BUREAU
704 US 64/264, Manteo
(252) 473-2138, (877) 629-4386
www.outerbanks.org

The Outer Banks Visitors Bureau is located near the eastern terminus of the Virginia Dare Bridge. This visitor bureau houses both the Outer Banks Welcome Center and the bureau's administrative offices. The visitor bureau provides almost any Outer Banks information requested by visitors and residents, including a huge collection of brochures, maps, and promotional materials about area offerings. Staffers also can supply information on demographics and business opportunities on the Outer Banks. The center features a rest area, toilets, and an RV dump station.

The Outer Banks Visitors Bureau is open year-round 9 a.m. to 5 p.m. every day except Thanksgiving and Christmas Day.

NAGS HEAD VISITOR CENTER AT WHALEBONE JUNCTION
Nags Head
(252) 441-6644

Operated by the Outer Banks Visitors Bureau, this welcome center is just south of the Whalebone Junction intersection on NC 12. It's open daily from 8:30 a.m. to 5 p.m. Memorial Day through Thanksgiving. It closes Thanksgiving Day, Christmas Day, and during Jan and Feb and reopens around Mar. The staff can answer all kinds of questions about southern destinations along the Outer Banks. Restrooms here are some of the few you'll find on this remote stretch of NC 12. The wooden structure also serves as a hunter contact station.

i If your vehicle becomes stuck while driving on the sand, try lowering the pressure in the tires to around 15 psi. Do not spin the wheels while trying to gain traction; accelerate gently.

PEA ISLAND VISITOR CENTER
NC 12, Pea Island
(252) 987-2394

The Pea Island Visitor Center offers information, free public restrooms, and paved parking. This facility also houses wildlife exhibits and plenty of nature-related gifts, including an excellent assortment of wildlife books for all ages. The center is open daily year-round from 9 a.m. to 4 p.m. Off-season you can visit Thurs through Sun from 9 a.m. to 4 p.m. It's closed Christmas Day. The center is staffed by volunteers, so the hours are occasionally modified. This area is an exciting stop for birders. A nature trail winds through the refuge, which is a haven for seasonal and year-round species. Pick up a free nature trail map at the center. Pea Island trails and beaches are open year-round during daylight hours.

HATTERAS ISLAND VISITOR CENTER
Off NC 12, Buxton
(252) 995-4474

About 300 yards south of Old Lighthouse Road, past the Texaco station and Cape Sandwich Co., a large wooden sign welcomes visitors to the Cape Hatteras National Seashore and Cape Hatteras Lighthouse Historic District. Turn left toward the white painted fence from the north and follow the winding road past turtle ponds and marshes. At the four-way intersection, turn left to get to the original lighthouse location, marked by a circle of granite stones etched with the names of 83 former lighthouse keepers. Or, at the four-way intersection, turn right and park the car in the parking area to explore the lighthouse in its new location. The visitor center, called the Museum of the Sea, and the bookstore, both housed in the historic former keepers' quarters, were moved to this location before the lighthouse was moved. Restrooms are located here as well. If you continue past the parking area, you'll pass the picnic area, the Buxton Woods Nature Trail, the Cape Point Campground, and off-road vehicle ramps. The beach is great for wading, sunbathing, surfing, and fishing. Four-wheel-drive vehicles are permitted along many sections of the beach year-round. Park rangers and volunteers answer questions in the visitor center and on the historic district grounds. Visitor center and bookstore hours are 9 a.m. to 6 p.m. the second Sun of June through Labor Day, and 9 a.m. to 5 p.m. the remainder of the year.

i When on Ocracoke Island, do yourself a favor and abandon your vehicle. Explore on foot and on bicycle to experience the true flavor of the island.

OCRACOKE ISLAND VISITOR CENTER
Near the Cedar Island and Swan Quarter Ferry Docks
Ocracoke Island
(252) 928-4531

This visitor center at the southern end of NC 12 is full of information about Ocracoke Island. It's located across from Silver Lake and operated by the National Park Service. If you arrive on the island from the Hatteras ferry, stay on the main road until you reach the T intersection at Silver Lake. Veer right and continue around the lake, counterclockwise, until you see the low brown building to the right. Parking is available at the visitor center.

Inside you'll find an information desk, ready staff, a small bookshop, and exhibits about Ocracoke. You can pick up maps of the winding back roads that make great bicycle paths and arrange to use the park service's docks.

The visitor center is open daily from 9 a.m. to 6 p.m. the second Sun of June through Labor Day and 9 a.m. to 5 p.m. in fall, winter, and spring. The center is closed only on Dec 25. Rangers offer free summer programs through the center, including beach and sound hikes, pirate plays, bird watching, night hikes, and history lectures. Check at the front desk for weekly schedules. Restrooms are available during peak season.

ACCOMMODATIONS

When it comes to accommodations, just like every other thing on the Outer Banks, you can have it as small and peaceful or big and busy as you choose. Visitors looking to stay a night, several days, or a week can choose from a range of family-owned seaside motels to multiple-story franchises of national lodging chains. The farther south you go, the fewer chain-owned accommodations you'll find; in fact, they almost disappear. And north of Kitty Hawk, you'll find only two hotels and two bed-and-breakfasts. In recent years elegant inns and a variety of bed-and-breakfast establishments have opened their doors—offering a little more luxury and personal attention than the traditional barrier island hotels.

OVERVIEW

A few of these motels and hotels listed in this chapter require two-night minimums on the weekends, and many require at least three-day stays for Memorial Day weekend, July Fourth weekend, and Labor Day weekend, since those are, by far, the busiest times on these barrier islands. A lot of Outer Banks hotels also have suites, efficiency apartments, and cottage units that rent by the day or week. Of course, you can stay in any room in any of these accommodations for a week or longer if you wish.

More and more, however, the Outer Banks is a vacation rental destination, where an increasing number of private homes rent by the week rather than hotel rooms renting by the night. In Dare County alone (excluding the Currituck beaches and Ocracoke), there are more than 15,000 rental cottages compared with 3,000 or so rooms or apartment-style rooms in hotels, bed-and-breakfast inns, and cottage courts. Modest cottages that offer comfort and convenience line the

ocean from Kitty Hawk through Hatteras Village. Many families and groups of friends choose to rent these cottages for a week's vacation or longer. Companies that lease these properties are included in the Weekly and Long-Term Cottage Rentals chapter.

If you're planning a summer stay on the Outer Banks, call early for reservations. Most accommodations are filled to capacity from early June through the first week of September. Sometimes you can obtain walk-in rooms during the week; however, if you know the exact week or weekend that you're planning to visit, your best bet is to book a room immediately.

Locations are indicated by milepost and town. Most of the hotels, motels, and inns are along NC 12. A few line US 158, which is also called the Bypass. Roanoke and Ocracoke Islands have several tucked beneath the trees off the beaten paths. Bed-and-breakfast inns are becoming more popular on the Outer Banks, with the largest numbers on Roanoke and Ocracoke Islands. There are now more than 180 bed-and-breakfast rooms on the Outer Banks.

Rates vary dramatically from one area of the Outer Banks to another, from oceanfront rooms to those across the highway, between in- and off-season times, and especially depending on the amenities offered with each unit. In general fall, winter, and early spring prices are at least one-third lower than midsummer rates—sometimes as little as $40 per night. The most expensive season, of course, is from mid-June to mid-August, when rates in general range from $50 a night for two people with two double beds to nearly $380 per night in some of the fancier establishments. Many hotels and motels honor AARP and other discounts and often allow children to stay free with paying adults.

i Memorial Day through Labor Day is the peak season for Outer Banks vacations, but fall and spring are becoming increasingly popular times of year to visit. Rates are lower in the spring and fall than during the summer, and there are far fewer crowds. Both of these seasons can offer remarkably warm weather and almost all of the amenities of the summer vacation—except the warmest water temperatures.

More and more accommodations providers keep their doors open all year, catering to fall fishing parties, spring visitors, and people who like the Outer Banks best in winter when few others are around. If you prefer isolation at the beach and don't mind wind and temperatures in the 40s and 50s, November through February is a wonderful time to visit. September and October, however, are our favorite months. The ocean is still warm enough to swim in, the daytime temperature seldom drops below the mid-60s, most restaurants, attractions, and retail shops remain open, yet the prices are much lower and most of the bustle is gone once school starts up again.

AREA PROFILES

Accommodations in the northern beaches are much more sophisticated than on the rest of the Outer Banks. Corolla has only two hotels that rent rooms by the night—the Inn at Corolla Light and Hampton Inn. Duck boasts two by-the-night establishments, both of them bed-and-breakfast inns, and the Sanderling Inn Resort, between Duck and Corolla, offers hotel rooms in a classic resort atmosphere. Nearly all accommodations in the northern beaches area lie along the main artery, NC 12, which is known as Ocean Trail in Corolla and Duck Road in Duck.

Kitty Hawk was one of the first Outer Banks beach towns to develop a tourist trade, and some of its hotels and motels are reminiscent of the early cottage courts. These primarily family-run businesses are small, clean, and often cheaper than nationally known hotels. There's also a Holiday Inn Express on US 158 and a couple of bed-and-breakfast inns west of the highway.

Kill Devil Hills is the most central—and most populated—place on the barrier islands. Many of its accommodations are within walking distance of restaurants, shopping, and recreational attractions. Quaint motels with fewer than two dozen rooms are common here, as are big chain establishments with oceanfront conference centers. Public beach and sound accesses abound in this town.

The Outer Banks' first resort destination was Nags Head, so here you'll find everything—a 1930s-era inn and the tallest hotel on the Outer Banks. Some accommodations retain the old-timey feel of cedar-shake cottages, while others have gone for the ultramodern, multiple-floor look complete with elevators and room service from the in-house restaurant. Like Kill Devil Hills, but a lot more spread out and slightly less populated, Nags Head has plenty of restaurants, retail shops, and recreation.

Roanoke Island's accommodations range from modest motels to fine, fabulous inns. All are just a bike ride away from the historic waterfront, and many are perfect for a romantic weekend getaway or cloistered honeymoon stay. Rental cottages aren't prevalent here because the large majority of the population, even in the summer, is made up of permanent residents; however, if you want to get away from the bustle of the beach and still be close to the sound, wetlands, and wonderful historic attractions this island has to offer, you won't have difficulty finding a room to suit your tastes.

Motels and hotels on Hatteras Island are, in general, more relaxed and simple than on other parts of the barrier islands. There are now two national chains on the island (one in Buxton and one in Hatteras), but family-owned and -operated places still dominate the accommodations. Many of these units are no-frills, without phones in the rooms or fancy furnishings, but if you are looking for an affordable place to stay along the quieter stretches of beach, don't overlook Hatteras Island's short-term room, inn, and efficiency accommodation options.

Ocracoke Island's lodgings are, in general, the most personal on the Outer Banks. Here, you'll find old inns, newer motels, upscale bed-and-breakfast inns, efficiency apartments, and a few folks who will rent you a room in their house, sometimes right next to their own.

HOW THIS CHAPTER IS ORGANIZED

Hotels in this chapter are arranged from north to south from Corolla through Ocracoke.

Price Code

The following price code is based on the average cost for a double-occupancy one-night stay in a room with two double beds during peak summer season. Extra charges may apply for holiday weekends, additional people in the room, efficiency apartments, or pets. These prices do not include local and state taxes. Unless otherwise indicated in the listing, all accommodations accept major credit cards.

$.................	**Less than $75**
$$	**$75 to $90**
$$	**$90 to $175**
$$$$	**More than $175**

ACCOMMODATIONS

Cypress Moon Bed and
Breakfast, Kitty Hawk,
$$$$, 44

Hilton Garden Inn, Kitty
Hawk, $$$$, 43

Holiday Inn Express, Kitty
Hawk, $$$, 44

Sea Kove Motel, Kitty Hawk,
$$$, 43

Kill Devil Hills

Best Western Ocean Reef
Suites, Kill Devil Hills,
$$$$, 47

The Carolina Oceanfront,
Kill Devil Hills, $$$$, 46

Cavalier Motel, Kill Devil Hills,
$$$, 46

The Clarion Oceanfront
Hotel, Kill Devil Hills,
$$$$, 48

Cypress House Bed and
Breakfast, Kill Devil Hills,
$$$$, 46

Days Inn Mariner Motel, Kill
Devil Hills, $$$, 45

Days Inn Oceanfront, Kill
Devil Hills, $$$–$$$$, 47

Miller's Outer Banks Motor
Lodge, Kill Devil Hills,
$$$, 49

Ocean House Motel, Kill
Devil Hills, $$–$$$, 49

Quality Inn John Yancey, Kill
Devil Hills, $$$$, 49

Ramada Plaza Resort and
Conference Center, Kill
Devil Hills, $$$–$$$$, 49

Sea Ranch Hotel, Kill Devil
Hills, $$$$, 45

See Sea Motel, Kill Devil Hills,
$$–$$$, 48

Shutters by the Sea, Kill
Devil Hills, $$$, 48

Travelodge Nags Head
Beach Hotel, Kill Devil
Hills, $$$, 45

Nags Head

Beacon Motor Lodge, Nags
Head, $$$, 50

Blue Heron Motel, Nags
Head, $$$, 52

Colonial Inn Motel, Nags
Head, $$$–$$$$, 50

Comfort Inn Oceanfront
South, Nags Head,
$$$$, 53

Dolphin Oceanfront Motel,
Nags Head, $$$, 53

Fin 'N Feather Waterside
Inn, Nags Head, $$$, 53

First Colony Inn, Nags Head,
$$$$, 51

Islander Motel, Nags Head,
$$$, 52

Nags Head Inn, Nags Head,
$$$–$$$$, 50

Oceanside Court, Nags
Head, $$$, 51

Owens' Motel, Nags Head,
$$$, 52

Sandspur Motel and
Cottage Court, Nags
Head, $–$$, 51

Sea Foam Motel, Nags Head,
$$$, 53

Surf Side Hotel, Nags Head,
$$$$, 51

Roanoke Island

The Cameron House Inn,
Manteo, $$$$, 55

Dare Haven Motel, Manteo,
$$–$$$, 57

Duke of Dare Motor Lodge,
Manteo, $$, 57

The Elizabethan Inn,
Manteo, $$$, 54

Island Motel & Guesthouse,
Manteo, $$–$$$, 54

Roanoke Island Inn, Manteo,
$$$$, 54

Scarborough House Bed
and Breakfast, Manteo,
$$$, 56

Scarborough Inn, Manteo,
$$–$$$, 56

Tranquil House Inn, Manteo,
$$$$, 56

The White Doe Inn, Manteo,
$$$$, 55

Wanchese

Island House of Wanchese
Bed and Breakfast,
Wanchese, $$$–$$$$, 57

Wanchese Inn Bed and
Breakfast, Wanchese,
$$$, 55

Hatteras Island

Avon Motel, Avon,
$$–$$$, 58

Breakwater Inn, Hatteras
Village, $$–$$$$, 61

Cape Hatteras Bed and
Breakfast, Buxton,
$$$–$$$$, 60

Cape Hatteras Motel,
Buxton, $$$$, 58

Cape Pines Motel, Buxton,
$$$, 61

Comfort Inn of Hatteras,
Buxton, $$$$, 60

The Croatoan Inn, Buxton,
$$$, 59

Hatteras Marlin Motel, Hatteras Village, $$$, 61

The Inn on Pamlico Sound, Buxton, $$$$, 60

Lighthouse View Motel, Buxton, $-$$$$, 59

Outer Banks Motel, Buxton, $$$, 58

Sea Sound Motel, Rodanthe, $$-$$$, 58

Ocracoke Island

The Anchorage Inn & Marina, Ocracoke, $$$-$$$$, 62

Blackbeard's Lodge, Ocracoke, $$$$, 62

The Captain's Landing, Ocracoke, $$$$, 63

The Castle Bed & Breakfast on Silver Lake, Ocracoke, $$$-$$$$, 63

The Cove Bed and Breakfast, Ocracoke, $$$$, 63

Crews Inn Bed and Breakfast, Ocracoke, $$, 64

Edwards of Ocracoke, Ocracoke, $$$, 64

Harborside Motel, Ocracoke, $$$, 64

The Island Inn, Ocracoke, $-$$$, 64

The Ocracoke Harbor Inn, Ocracoke, $$$, 65

Oscar's House, Ocracoke, $$-$$$, 65

Pam's Pelican Bed and Breakfast, Ocracoke, $$$, 66

Pony Island Motel, Ocracoke, $$$, 66

Sand Dollar Motel, Ocracoke, $$-$$$, 66

Thurston House Inn, Ocracoke, $$$, 67

COROLLA

❋THE INN AT COROLLA LIGHT   **$$$$**
1066 Ocean Trail, Corolla
(252) 453-3340, (800) 215-0772
www.corolla-inn.com

Located within walking distance of the Currituck Beach Lighthouse, the Inn at Corolla Light, open year-round, is a luxurious place where guests can plan their days around an incredible array of recreational activities available nearly at their doorstep—or they may wish simply to relax in full view of the sparkling waters of Currituck Sound and bask in the serenity of this beautifully appointed facility. This upscale development offers wooded walking, biking trails, and every leisure amenity a vacationer could dream of: an indoor sports center with an Olympic-size pool, hot tub, saunas, clay tennis courts, racquetball courts, and fitness equipment; an oceanfront complex that boasts two outdoor pools, a video game room, a restaurant, and exclusive access to the beach; soundfront pools; play areas for basketball, shuffleboard, tennis, horseshoes, and more; and terrific shops and restaurants nearby (see the Shopping and Restaurants chapters). Guests of the inn have unlimited access to all of the resort's facilities. There is a nominal fee for use of the indoor tennis courts, but all other courts are free.

Guests may also use the inn's own waterfront swimming pool, hot tub, and private 400-foot pier on Currituck Sound. The inn furnishes bicycles to guests for leisurely tours of the resort's landscaped grounds. Guests are also invited to use the complimentary video library inside.

In season parasailing, kayaking, ecotouring, and personal watercraft (Jet Skis, WaveRunners, and others) are available at a water sports-rental site on the resort. A championship golf course is nearby. A must-do is to take the proprietor's wild horse tour by a four-wheel-drive Suburban into the off-road and largely undeveloped area north of Corolla. Although sparsely inhabited, the northern beaches are rich in history, local lore, and, of course, wild horses (and plenty of other wild sights).

Some of the inn's 43 spacious guest rooms include kitchenettes, cable TVs, radios, DVD players, and private baths. Many have fireplaces and whirlpool tubs. The rooms are designed for single or double occupancy, and some are equipped with sleeper sofas, too. Guests can enjoy a free continental breakfast daily. A few rooms are pet friendly to pets weighing under 50 pounds.

The Inn at Corolla Light has two- and three-night minimum stays on weekends. Special rate packages are offered throughout the year.

HAMPTON INN AND SUITES OUTER BANKS COROLLA $$$$
NC 12, Pine Island (north of Duck)
(252) 453-6565, (800) HAMPTON
www.hamptoninn.com

Those looking for short-term lodgings on the northern Outer Banks have never had many options, but the oceanfront Hampton Inn helps fill the void. Opened in 2002, the inn has 123 sleeper rooms, a mix of guest rooms, and studio suites. Room decor has a coastal theme with ceiling fans and private balconies. Each room has a television, microwave, refrigerator, hair dryer, ironing equipment, coffeemaker, pay Nintendo, pay-per-view movies, and two two-line phones. Most rooms feature a pull-out sofa, and some have whirlpool tubs. Studio suites also feature a wet bar. The majority of rooms have an ocean view. Public areas include a heated indoor pool and whirlpool spa, an exercise room, a game room, four meeting rooms, coin-operated laundry facilities, and the Suite Shop with sundries, beach supplies, sodas, and snacks. Outdoors is a pool, kiddie pool, and a lazy river. Direct beach access is provided. Continental breakfast is served to guests each morning.

i Stay off the beach dunes! The dunes are extremely fragile and a necessary barrier from erosion. Please use the walkways and accesses provided for you.

DUCK

*SANDERLING INN RESORT $$$$
1461 NC 12, Duck
(252) 261-4111, (800) 701-4111
www.sanderlinginn.com

The Sanderling Inn Resort is situated on 12 acres of oceanside wilderness about 5 miles north of the town of Duck. The Sanderling was built in the style of the old Nags Head beach homes, with wood siding, cedar-shake accents, dormer windows, and porches on each side. Rocking chairs line the wide porches, providing a relaxing way to pass sultry afternoons while overlooking the ocean or sound.

All 87 rooms at the Sanderling are comfortable, lush, and accommodating. The inn provides guests with lounging robes, luxury soaps, toiletries, and a welcome gift. A continental breakfast and afternoon tea also come with each room.

Sanderling Inn is designed for the comfort and privacy of two guests per room, but sleeper sofas and cribs are available for an additional charge.

A separate building at the Sanderling houses conference and meeting facilities as well as the Presidential Suite, complete with whirlpool bath, steam shower, and two decks—one overlooks the ocean and the other overlooks the sound. For an additional charge, the inn's housekeeping staff provides laundry service with a 48-hour turnaround. Room service is provided by the Lifesaving Station restaurant (see the Restaurants chapter).

This is a complete resort with private beaches, a full-service spa, and state-of-the-art fitness center. The amenities continue with an indoor pool, a separate whirlpool room, locker rooms, steam rooms, an outdoor pool, tennis courts, and a natural walking or jogging trail. The Audubon Wildlife Sanctuary and the Pine Island Tennis and Racquet Club are nearby. An ecocenter offers kayaks for visitors to use. A seasonal outdoor pavilion and four three- and four-bedroom villas have been added to Sanderling's offerings. The villas are perfect for families.

The spa houses six treatment rooms and offers extended services, including manicures, pedicures, facials, massages, and more.

Full package deals are available for New Year's Eve, Valentine's Day, honeymoons, and winter escapes. Packages generally include one or more meals at the Lifesaving Station restaurant, full use of the fitness center and indoor pool, welcoming gifts, and other extras. Some seasonal discounts are available. Weekend guests must stay both Friday and Saturday nights during the summer, and a three-day minimum stay is required for in-season holidays. Wheelchair access is provided for all buildings on the property, and wheelchair-accessible rooms are available. The Sanderling Inn is open year-round. Four pet-friendly rooms are available.

KITTY HAWK

HILTON GARDEN INN $$$$
NC 12, MP 1, Kitty Hawk
(252) 261-1290, (877) 772-9444
www.hiltongardeninn.hilton.com
The Hilton Garden Inn is conveniently located on the oceanfront across from the former Kitty Hawk Pier (once open to the public for fishing, but now the activity is only available to Hilton guests). The inn offers a choice of suites and rooms with a private balcony overlooking the ocean. All rooms are equipped with high-speed Internet access and a microwave, refrigerator, and coffeemaker. Indoor and outdoor pools and a fitness area are available. A guest laundry facility, business center, and restaurant are located here. The award-winning Great American Grill serves breakfast, lunch, and dinner on-site.

SEA KOVE MOTEL $$$
NC 12, MP 3, Kitty Hawk
(252) 261-4722
This family-owned and -operated establishment rents 10 one-bedroom efficiency units, 10 two-bedroom units, and two cottages by the week only from Apr through Nov. It's across from the ocean and includes full-size kitchens and televisions in each apartment. A playground and outdoor pool also are available. No credit cards accepted.

BEACH HAVEN MOTEL $$$
NC 12, MP 4, Kitty Hawk
(252) 261-4785, (888) 559-0506
www.beachhavenmotel.com
This small motel sits across the road from its own private beach and has two buildings with a total of six efficiency units. Guests will finds all they need for a peaceful and relaxing stay. A practical, homey atmosphere

prevails at this motel, where each room has a refrigerator, microwave, hair dryer, cable TV, telephone, and porch chairs. Coffee can be brewed in each room at this uniquely groomed establishment. Beach Haven is also AAA approved.

Beach Haven is in uncrowded surroundings with natural beach landscaping that will remind visitors of a lovely oasis. Guests can loll on the elevated deck and enjoy the scenery. A grass-carpeted picnic area with tables and a gas grill is on the premises. Bike rentals are available, as are many beach accessories. You can practice your classic stroke on a putting green situated on the cashmere lawn, where you might also show off your talents in a game of croquet.

Economy rooms sleep two people, and deluxe rooms can accommodate up to four guests. Cribs are provided for infants. The decor throughout reflects a contemporary beach look with rattan and wicker furniture. Joe lives at the motel and promises to make your stay as pleasant as possible. Beach Haven is open mid-March through mid-November.

HOLIDAY INN EXPRESS $$$
US 158, MP 4¼, Kitty Hawk
(252) 261-4888, (800) 836-2753
www.hiexpress.com
Situated on the east side of US 158, Holiday Inn Express has an outdoor swimming pool and is a short walk to lifeguarded Kitty Hawk Beach, where guests can use the motel's private access and oceanfront deck. The motel's 98 rooms are spacious and have cable TV, telephones, and refrigerators. Some also have couches, and all have microwaves. Most offer two double beds and some rooms have queen-size beds.

All are attractively furnished in soft beach decor.

The inn provides a complimentary continental breakfast bar for guests each morning in the lobby. Nonsmoking and wheelchair-accessible rooms are available. Children age 17 and younger stay free if accompanied by an adult. Year-round group rates are available. This motel is within walking distance of shopping and several restaurants and is open all year.

✳CYPRESS MOON BED AND BREAKFAST $$$$
1206 Harbor Ct., Kitty Hawk
(252) 202-2731, (800) 905-5060
www.cypressmooninn.com
You'll find Cypress Moon Bed and Breakfast nestled in the maritime forest with the sound just behind. Owners Linda and Greg Hamby have furnished their home with antiques throughout the residence.

Three soundfront rooms are available at the Cypress Moon Bed and Breakfast. All rooms have a queen-size bed, entertainment centers, and refrigerators. Brunch is served daily. You can choose to be served in the dining room, in your bedroom, or on your porch. Brunch includes crab cakes or shrimp, along with a breakfast meat, fresh bread, fruit, Cypress Moon specially blended coffee, and fresh-squeezed orange juice.

If you choose to spend a day away from the beach, guests are welcome to use the kayaks or sailboards provided. A nice walkway leads to the water, and outdoor showers are available. The inn welcomes people age 18 and older and is smoke free. Cypress Moon is closed for the month of Dec. Two homes offsite are also available for vacation stays.

✳BUCCANEER MOTEL AND BEACH SUITES $$$
NC 12, MP 5½, Kitty Hawk
(252) 261-2030, (800) 442-4412
www.buccaneermotelouterbanks.com

Repeat business is the name of the game at the Buccaneer, where folks who stayed here as teenagers now bring their grandkids for visits. Owners Sandy and Dave Briggman foster the authentic Outer Banks charm that's made the Buccaneer a place vacationers return to year after year. Travelers have their choice of one- and two-bedroom units, and efficiency apartments with one to three bedrooms are available for those wishing to stay longer. Each unit has a refrigerator, coffeepot, cable TV, and microwave.

While the Buccaneer is across the highway from the beach, there are no buildings between it and the ocean, and guests only have to cross a small sand dune to reach the surf. A dune-top deck and private beach access make enjoying the Atlantic from this establishment almost as easy as if the motel were right on the ocean. Other amenities include a large, outdoor swimming pool with adjoining deck, a children's playground, a basketball court, charcoal grills, and a fish-cleaning station. The Buccaneer is open year-round. Wi-Fi is available here.

KILL DEVIL HILLS

DAYS INN MARINER MOTEL $$$
NC 12, MP 7½, Kill Devil Hills
(252) 441-2021, (800) 325-2525
www.outer-banks.com/days-mariner

Rooms and apartments include a telephone, refrigerator, and cable TV. All the rooms have a fresh, contemporary beach look.

There's easy access to the Atlantic, and the units are spacious enough to offer flexible living arrangements for families or groups. A recreation area has facilities for volleyball, and an outdoor swimming pool and showers are just off the ocean. Nonsmoking and wheelchair-accessible rooms are available. All Days Inn programs are honored, and AARP discounts are available. The Mariner is open year-round, except Christmas week, with rates discounted in the off-season.

SEA RANCH HOTEL $$$$
NC 12, MP 7, Kill Devil Hills
(252) 441-7126, (800) 334-4737
www.searanchhotel.com

Stay at the Sea Ranch for a classic Outer Banks vacation. It is locally owned and operated, with a 5-story oceanfront tower and a 2-story building that contains 50 motel-style rooms. Each unit has cable TV and free HBO, a refrigerator, microwave, coffeemaker, and telephone. About half of the hotel rooms have oceanfront views. Nonsmoking rooms are available, and the hotel is wheelchair accessible. It has a heated indoor pool. The Sea Ranch is open year-round. The Pearl fine dining restaurant is located within the hotel.

TRAVELODGE NAGS HEAD BEACH HOTEL $$$
NC 12, MP 8, Kill Devil Hills
(252) 441-0411, (888) 637-4859
www.nagsheadbeachhotel.com

This 97-room, 4-story hotel is across the highway from the ocean, so some guest rooms have views of the Atlantic, while others afford glimpses of the Wright Brothers National Memorial. Twelve of the first-floor guest rooms open directly onto the outdoor courtyard and pool. Each room has a microwave, refrigerator, color TV (with remote control, cable, and free HBO), telephone, and private balcony or patio, with nonsmoking and wheelchair-accessible rooms available. A complimentary continental breakfast featuring cereals, pastries, juices, coffee, tea, and fresh fruits is served daily in the lobby from 7 to 9 a.m. Discounts are available to AARP members. Children age 18 and younger stay free in their parents' room, and pets are welcome for a $20 per day additional charge. During summer holidays, three-night minimum stays are required. The Nags Head Beach Hotel is open all year.

THE CAROLINA OCEANFRONT $$$$
NC 12, MP 8, Kill Devil Hills
(252) 480-2600, (800) 854-5286
www.thecarolinaoceanfront.com
This 3-story property (central to Outer Banks attractions) includes 119 rooms that open along exterior corridors. They're filled with natural light and decorated tastefully. The building is T shaped, so not all rooms have views of the Atlantic; however, oceanfront units have private balconies. All rooms at this have refrigerators, microwaves, full baths, cable TV and HBO, telephones, and coffeemakers. Nonsmoking and wheelchair-accessible rooms are available. Amenities include an oceanfront pool and coin-operated laundry facilities. A complimentary breakfast is provided. Children age 18 and younger stay free with an adult. A two-night minimum stay is required on summer holiday weekends. Managers honor AARP discounts. The Comfort Inn is open all year. YMCA passes available for working out at the gym or using the outdoor or indoor pool.

> **i** If you like your accommodations and want to stay in the same place again next year, make your reservation now.

CYPRESS HOUSE BED AND
BREAKFAST $$$$
NC 12, MP 8, Kill Devil Hills
(252) 441-6127, (800) 554-2764
www.cypresshouseinn.com
This historic bed-and-breakfast inn was originally built as a private hunting and fishing lodge in the 1940s. Located 150 yards from the Atlantic Ocean, the inn, with its original tongue-and-groove cypress–paneled walls and ceilings, exudes a cozy, casual charm. Six guest rooms with queen-size beds and private shower baths are equipped with ceiling fans, cable TV, and central air. The wrap-around porch is ideal for enjoying the ocean breezes. In cold weather relax with a good book in front of a blazing fire in the common room. Early risers awake to self-serve coffee and tea on the baker's rack outside the rooms; a full gourmet breakfast is served each morning. Afternoon refreshments are also served. Bikes, beach towels, and chairs, along with an outdoor shower and a court-yard with a pergola, are available. Cypress House is smoke free. Children age 12 and older are welcome, and pets are not allowed.

CAVALIER MOTEL $$$
NC 12, MP 8½, Kill Devil Hills
(252) 441-5585
www.thecavaliermotel.com
The Cavalier has comfortable rooms with double and single beds and several one-room efficiency units with two double beds and kitchenettes right on the beach. Some rooms have full baths, while others have shower stalls. All are equipped with telephones, refrigerators, microwaves, cable TV, and free HBO. Three 1-story wings surround the adult swimming pool, the kiddie swimming pool, a volleyball court, a children's play area, and shuffleboard courts. The motel

also has 13 cottages that rent by the week. Pets are allowed in the cottages only. There is some wheelchair access here, and ramps are on the premises. Parking is available outside each room, and the covered porch with outdoor furniture is just right for relaxing with a free cup of coffee while watching the sunrise. An observation deck sits atop the oceanfront section. Children age 12 and younger stay for free in their parents' rooms. The Cavalier Motel is open year-round.

✳DAYS INN OCEANFRONT $$$–$$$$
NC 12, MP 8½, Kill Devil Hills
(252) 441-7211, (800) 325-2525
www.outer-banks.com/days-oceanfront

An oceanfront property on a wide stretch of beach, this facility opened as an Outer Banks motel in 1948. It was built to resemble an old mountain lodge and offers an inviting lobby, decorated in the nostalgia of Old Nags Head, where guests can read the newspaper and sip a cup of free coffee. The room is further enhanced by Oriental rugs on polished hardwood floors and a fireplace large enough to take away the chill on cold beach evenings during the off-season.

Guests enjoy balconies with old-fashioned furniture and nice views. The 52 rooms include singles, doubles, kings, king suites, and efficiency units that sleep six and include a living room, adjoining bedroom, and complete kitchen. All rooms have telephones, cable TV, and refrigerators. Oceanfront rooms also have microwaves. Nonsmoking and wheelchair-accessible rooms are available.

A complimentary continental breakfast is available throughout the year. Hot apple cider and popcorn are served around the fireplace during the winter, and lemonade and cookies are served in the summer. Leisure amenities include a large outdoor pool, sundeck, volleyball court, barbecue pit, and a boardwalk to the beach.

Children age 12 and younger stay for free, and AARP discounts are honored. There's a two-night minimum stay for summer holiday weekends, and Saturday check-ins are allowed only for weekly rentals. Daily and weeklong rentals are available throughout the year. This inn has won the prestigious Days Inn Chairmans award for 11 years running.

i Keep in mind that if you stay in an inn or a motel or hotel, usually household chores are taken care of by staff. If you stay in a rental cottage, household chores are your responsibility. When you leave, you are required to clean the home.

BEST WESTERN OCEAN REEF SUITES $$$$
NC 12, MP 8½, Kill Devil Hills
(252) 441-1611, (800) 528-1234
www.bestwestern.com/oceanreefsuites

All 71 one-bedroom suites in this oceanfront hotel are decorated and arranged like luxury apartments with a contemporary beach decor. The views are great, and you'll find everything you need for a truly luxurious beach vacation. Each room has a telephone, cable TV, free coffee, and a fully equipped galley-style kitchen. The bath area has a double vanity. Nonsmoking and wheelchair-accessible rooms are available. Upper-floor rooms have private balconies overlooking the ocean. Some first-floor units open onto the oceanfront pool and courtyard, while others offer a private patio. The Ocean Reef is one of the few facilities on the beach to have a penthouse suite; this one boasts a private Jacuzzi and roof-top deck.

A heated, seasonal outdoor pool and a whirlpool are available to guests in the courtyard, and the exercise room features a sauna. Other amenities include a laundry facility on the premises and year-round bar and food service. Children age 13 and younger stay free with adults. A two-day minimum stay is required on summer weekends. Ocean Reef is open all year.

SHUTTERS BY THE SEA $$$
NC 12, MP 8½, Kill Devil Hills
(252) 441-5581, (800) 848-3728
www.thecolonyivmotel.com

This modern family-owned and -operated oceanfront motel is well-maintained and offers lots of amenities, including an outdoor heated pool with a whirlpool and patio, an indoor heated pool, a dune-top gazebo, and a private beach with lifeguard. A complimentary continental breakfast is served every morning. Laundry facilities are available on the premises. Free Wi-Fi in all rooms.

The motel has 80 units, 8 of which are efficiencies. Most offer two double beds, but rooms with king-size beds are also available. Telephones, refrigerators, microwaves, TV with remote control and cable, and clock radios are provided in the units. Some rooms have direct access to the beach, while others have a small balcony overlooking the ocean. The efficiencies have an eating area and, when combined with adjoining rooms, create a good arrangement for family vacationers. Nonsmoking units are available.

Children age 17 and younger stay for free. Discounts of 10 percent are provided for AARP and AAA members. The motel is also wheelchair accessible. A two-night minimum stay is required on summer weekends. Shutters by the Sea is open year-round.

SEE SEA MOTEL $$–$$$
NC 12, MP 9, Kill Devil Hills
(252) 441-7321, (800) 635-7007
www.coverealty.com

A small, family-run motel across the street from the ocean, See Sea offers 21 rental units, including 11 motel rooms, 6 efficiencies, 3 two-bedroom apartments, and 1 three-bedroom cottage. The motel rooms and efficiencies rent by the day (the apartments and cottage require a one-week minimum stay in season). All units have a refrigerator, microwave, telephone, and cable TV. There's a pay phone on the premises. Laundry is on-site, and free coffee is provided.

Amenities include an outdoor swimming pool and a picnic area. Nonsmoking rooms are offered. See Sea Motel is open year-round.

THE CLARION OCEANFRONT HOTEL $$$$
NC 12, MP 9½, Kill Devil Hills
(252) 441-6333, (800) 424-6423
www.clarionhotel.com/hotel/nc416

This oceanfront hotel has 105 rooms, many with spectacular ocean views. Banquet and conference facilities accommodate 10 to 200 people. Amenities include an on-site restaurant and lounge, a coin-operated laundry, an outdoor pool, and a whirlpool. All rooms include telephone, cable TV with remote, free high-speed Internet access, microwave, and refrigerator. The Clarion has wheelchair-accessible rooms and two nonsmoking floors. Children age 18 and younger stay free, and AARP members receive a 10 percent discount. Weekends require minimum stays during summer. The Clarion is open all year. Pets are welcomed.

RAMADA PLAZA RESORT AND
CONFERENCE CENTER $$$–$$$$
NC 12, MP 9½, Kill Devil Hills
(252) 441-2151, (800) 635-1824
www.ramadainnnagshead.com

This 5-story, 171-room oceanfront hotel was built in 1985. It's popular with tour groups and hosts many meetings throughout the year. All rooms have a balcony or patio, cable TV with pay-per-view movies, small refrigerator, and microwave. Bellhop and room service are available here. Nonsmoking, wheelchair-accessible, and pet rooms are offered, along with guest laundry facilities and an exercise room. Meeting facilities are on the fourth floor overlooking the ocean. Several suites are available to fit a variety of conference and workshop needs. An indoor swimming pool and Jacuzzi are off the second floor atop the dunes surrounded by a large sundeck. A flight of steps takes you onto the beach where volleyball is a popular pastime. Seasonal food and beverage services are available at the oceanfront bar adjacent to the pool. Peppercorns, the hotel's fine oceanview restaurant, serves breakfast and dinner year-round and offers lunch on the deck during the summer (see the Restaurants chapter). The Ramada Plaza Resort is open all year.

OCEAN HOUSE MOTEL $$–$$$
NC 12, MP 9½, Kill Devil Hills
(252) 441-2900, (866) 536-1790
www.oceanhousemotel.com

This seaside motel is an Outer Banks favorite oceanfront spot. Rooms have been newly updated and are tasteful and comfortable. Guests can choose from rooms poolside or oceanfront. Each room comes equipped with minifridges, microwaves, and cable TV. A pool is open in season, and a playground and picnic area are also on the grounds.

*MILLER'S OUTER BANKS
MOTOR LODGE $$$
NC 12, MP 9½, Kill Devil Hills
(252) 441-7404, (877) 625-6343
www.obxmotorlodge.com

An oceanfront motel with 30 efficiency units and 8 regular rooms, Miller's rents some units only by the week during the peak season. Other units, however, are available by the day. Each room has cable TV, a refrigerator, and a microwave. Wheelchair-accessible units are available. Amenities include an on-site washer and dryer, a playground, an outdoor swimming pool, and a restaurant. Children age 12 and younger stay free here. Miller's is open from Feb through Nov.

QUALITY INN JOHN YANCEY $$$$
NC 12, MP 10, Kill Devil Hills
(252) 441-7141, (800) 367-5941
www.outerbanksnchotel.com

This family hotel is on a wide beach that's life-guarded during the summer. Shuffleboard courts, an outdoor heated pool, and a playground are on the premises.

The hotel has spacious rooms, with kings and doubles, housed in three buildings. The oceanfront units each have a balcony or patio so you can see and hear the waves from your room. Cable TV with optional in-room movies, a small refrigerator, and a telephone are in each room. Coffeemakers and coffee are provided in all rooms. Most of the rooms are nonsmoking, and this inn

ACCOMMODATIONS

offers wheelchair-accessible units. Wi-Fi is free on the premises.

Other amenities include a coin-operated laundry, and pets are welcome in some rooms. Children age 18 and younger stay free, and rollaway beds are available for an extra fee to accommodate additional kids. A two-night minimum stay is required on holiday weekends. AARP and other discounts are honored. The John Yancey is open all year. Continental breakfast is served each day. YMCA passes available to the gym or pool.

NAGS HEAD

BEACON MOTOR LODGE $$$
NC 12, MP 10¾, Nags Head
(252) 441-5501, (800) 441-4804
www.beaconmotorlodge.com

Visitors will find lots of options for seasonal and off-season stays at this family-oriented, comfortable oceanfront lodge. The James family has owned the 48-room Beacon Motor Lodge since 1970, offering one-, two-, and three-room combinations, including motel-type rooms and efficiencies, plus two cottages. All rooms are nonsmoking. Rooms are equipped with small refrigerators, phones, and cable TV with free HBO. All units also have microwaves and fridges.

Guests gather on the oceanfront patio, a grand place for enjoying the beach scene from a comfy lounge chair. Oceanfront rooms open onto a large, walled terrace, affording wonderful views of the ocean. Amenities include two children's pools, a large outdoor pool with tables and umbrellas, a playground, patios with grills, an electronic game room, and laundry facilities. Some provisions have been made for disabled guests, including a ramp for beach

access. The Beacon Motor Lodge is open late Mar through late Oct.

COLONIAL INN MOTEL $$$–$$$$
NC 12, MP 11½, Nags Head
(252) 441-7308
www.colonialinnmotel.com

At the Colonial Inn Motel you can stay in an oceanfront room, standard room, efficiency unit, or apartment—some of which accommodate as many as 10 guests. Every unit has cable TV, air-conditioning, and fridge. All are wheelchair accessible. Enjoy the beach, swim in the pool, or fish off the adjacent Nags Head Fishing Pier. Colonial Inn Motel is open for business from Mar to Dec. A nice bonus for staying at the Colonial Inn is a free pass to the Outer Banks YMCA, located nearby. Pet friendly rooms, open year-round.

NAGS HEAD INN $$$–$$$$
NC 12, MP 14, Nags Head
(252) 441-0454, (800) 327-8881
www.nagsheadinn.com

This white stucco building with blue accents and plush lawns is a tasteful contrast to the older Nags Head–style cottages nearby. Designed for family enjoyment, the oceanfront inn features a sunny lobby where greenery thrives. Guest rooms begin on the second floor of this 5-story building, and all oceanside rooms afford panoramic ocean views from private balconies. Rooms on the street side do not have balconies, but the view of Roanoke Sound from the fifth-floor rooms is notable. All rooms have small refrigerators, microwaves, satellite 32" flat screen TVs, phones, and full baths. Non-smoking rooms are available, and each floor has wheelchair-accessible rooms. A heated indoor pool and spa are available. The Nags Head Inn also features one suite with an adjoining sitting room, wet bar, and hot tub—a perfect honeymoon setting. A small conference room with adjoining kitchen/sitting area accommodates about 30 people comfortably. Tour groups are welcome. Free Wi-Fi.

OCEANSIDE COURT $$$
NC 12, MP 15½, Nags Head
(252) 441-6167
www.oceansidecourt.com
There's nothing like an oceanside stay on the Outer Banks, and that's what you'll get here. This small establishment offers four efficiencies (with cable TV and full kitchens) and seven cottages. Phones are not available in any of the units. Oceanside Court is open from Mar 1 to Dec 1. Pets are not allowed.

SANDSPUR MOTEL AND
COTTAGE COURT $-$$
NC 12, MP 15¾, Nags Head
(252) 441-6993, (800) 522-8486
www.sandspur.net
At the Sandspur you can choose from a room, efficiency, or cottage. All rooms feature two double beds, cable TV, ceiling fans, refrigerators, and microwaves. The efficiencies also have stoves. The rooms have no phones, but a pay phone is on the premises. The motel has a coin-operated washer and dryer. The Sandspur closes in Dec and reopens Mar 1.

SURF SIDE HOTEL $$$$
NC 12, MP 15½, Nags Head
(252) 441-2105, (800) 552-7873
www.surfsideobx.com
This attractive 5-story hotel is situated on the oceanfront, rooms facing north, south, and east have ocean views. Some rooms have views of Roanoke Sound as well. All rooms have private balconies and are decorated attractively in muted beach tones. Refrigerators, cable TV, hair dryers, coffeemakers, microwaves, irons and ironing boards, and phones are standard in all rooms. The honeymoon suites feature king-size beds and private Jacuzzis. An elevator provides easy access, and wheelchair-accessible rooms are available; so are nonsmoking rooms. An adjacent 3-story building offers rooms and efficiencies with either ocean or sound views. A continental breakfast is provided each morning, and the staff hosts an afternoon wine and snacks social hour for guests. You can choose between an indoor pool and hot tub that are open all year and an outdoor pool for swimming in warm weather. The Surf Side is open all year.

✳FIRST COLONY INN $$$$
US 158, MP 16, Nags Head
(252) 441-2343, (800) 368-9390
www.firstcolonyinn.com
Back in 1932 this gracious old structure was known as Leroy's Seaside Inn. The landmark hotel was moved and refurbished, but it's still a favorite for those who like the ambience of a quiet inn. The old Nags Head–style architecture, resplendent under an overhanging roof and wide porches, has been preserved and is listed in the National Register of Historic Places. The First Colony received a historic preservation award from the Historic Preservation Foundation of North Carolina.

The Lawrence family, with deep roots in the area, rescued the hotel from demolition in 1988. The building was sawed into three sections for the move from its oceanfront location to the present site. The interior was completely renovated and now contains 26 rooms, all with traditional furnishings and modern comforts.

In the sunny breakfast room, you can enjoy a complimentary continental breakfast and afternoon tea. Upstairs, an elegant but cozy library with books, games, and an old pump organ is a favorite place to read the paper or meet other guests. A great selection of jazz as well as classical music wafts throughout the reception area.

Each room is appointed in English antique furniture. Special touches, such as tiled baths, heated towel bars, English toiletries, telephones, TVs, iron with ironing board, individual climate control, and refrigerators, are standard. Some rooms have a wet bar, kitchenette, Jacuzzi, DVD player, and private balcony; some rooms include an additional trundle bed or daybed for an extra person. The first floor is wheelchair accessible, and one room is designed for disabled guests. Smoking is not permitted in the inn.

Guests are invited to relax at the 55-foot swimming pool and sundeck behind the inn or to follow the private boardwalk across the street to the oceanfront gazebo. This magnificent year-round inn provides easy access to the ocean and is close to many shops and restaurants. The inn has a policy of Thursday night free for stays of five weeknights or longer (must include consecutive Sun, Mon, Tues, Wed, and Thurs stays).

ISLANDER MOTEL $$$
NC 12, MP 16, Nags Head
(252) 441-6229
www.islandermotel.com

The Islander is a small, popular oceanfront property featuring an attractive landscape and well-maintained rooms. Most rooms have an ocean view, and all have either a balcony or patio, although some of the first-floor units tucked behind dunes do not offer ocean views. All have sitting areas, coffeemakers, and refrigerators. Some first-floor units offer kitchenettes. Guests enjoy the pool and private dune walk to the ocean. This property is convenient to Nags Head restaurants, shops, recreational outlets, and attractions. The Islander is open Apr through Oct. Free Wi-Fi.

BLUE HERON MOTEL $$$
NC 12, MP 16, Nags Head
(252) 441-7447
www.blueheronnc.com

The Blue Heron Motel is considered one of the Outer Banks' best-kept secrets among the small motels in the area. The family-owned facility provides a year-round indoor swimming pool, a spa, and outdoor pools. The Gladden family lives on the premises and pays careful attention to the management of the property. It's in the midst of fine Nags Head restaurants and offers plenty of beach for those who come to relax. All units have a full kitchen, cable TV, phones, and shower/tub combinations. A wheelchair-accessible room is available. Second- and third-floor rooms offer private balconies. The Blue Heron Motel is open all year and offers weekly rates. YMCA passes are available.

OWENS' MOTEL $$$
NC 12, MP 16, Nags Head
(252) 441-6361
www.owensmotel.com

The Owens family has owned and operated this attractive motel, one of the first on the beach, for 60 years. Adjacent to the family's famous restaurant (see the Restaurants chapter), this property across the highway from the ocean is well maintained. This 3-story oceanfront property includes efficiencies with large, private balconies. Each efficiency has a tile bath and shower, cable

TV, and a full kitchen. Thirty-one additional rooms are located just across the street from the beach. Rooms are all tastefully furnished. Most have two double beds; four rooms have kings. All rooms include a refrigerator and a microwave. The motel swimming pool on the west side of the property provides an alternative to the ocean. There is easy access to Jennette's Pier, and a comfortable oceanfront pavilion with rocking chairs is enticing. Owens' Motel is open Apr through Oct.

SEA FOAM MOTEL $$$
NC 12, MP 16½, Nags Head
(252) 441-7320
www.seafoam.com

This attractive oceanfront motel offers a choice of rooms, efficiencies, and cottages. Efficiencies accommodate two to four people, and cottages sleep up to six comfortably. The efficiencies and cottages rent weekly. Rooms are tastefully decorated, and some have washed-oak furniture. All rooms have cable TV with HBO, refrigerators, microwaves, and phones. Some have king-size beds, and each has a balcony or porch. Some units in the 1- and 2-story buildings have ocean and poolside views. Children are welcome, and they will enjoy the playground. Other features include a large heated outdoor pool, children's pool, sundeck, shuffleboard area, and a gazebo on the beach for guests' pleasure. Sea Foam Motel is within walking distance of several restaurants. Children younger than age 12 stay free with parents. Sea Foam Motel is open Mar through mid-December. Pets are not allowed.

DOLPHIN OCEANFRONT MOTEL $$$
NC 12, MP 16½, Nags Head
(252) 441-7488, (800) 699-1962
www.dolphinmotel.net

The Dolphin offers rooms and efficiencies. Some rooms have an ocean view. The breezeway to the beach and an outdoor pool add special touches. All rooms and efficiencies have fridges and cable TV. Nonsmoking rooms are available. The Dolphin opens the last Fri in Mar and closes the last Sat in Oct. Pets are allowed. Families particularly enjoy the picnic area with charcoal grills, picnic tables, and children's playground. Free Wi-Fi.

**COMFORT INN OCEANFRONT
  SOUTH** $$$$
NC 12, MP 17, Nags Head
(252) 441-6315, (800) 334-3302
www.choicehotels.com

The Comfort Inn Oceanfront South, a 7-story oceanfront hotel, is the tallest building on the Outer Banks. The light peach-and-teal exterior gives this hotel a clean, contemporary beach look. The 105-room hotel has deluxe oceanfront rooms with magnificent views from private balconies; oceanside and streetside rooms are available, too. Each room has a cable TV, phone, refrigerator, and microwave. Nonsmoking rooms are available. A honeymoon suite with a hot tub is popular, as are rooms with king-size beds. One wheelchair-accessible room is available. Corporate meeting rooms accommodate groups of 350 people. The oceanfront pool and deck are favorite places. Other amenities include a game room and a playground. A complimentary continental breakfast is offered in the lobby. The inn is open all year. Pets accepted in some rooms.

FIN 'N FEATHER WATERSIDE INN $$$
Nags Head–Manteo Causeway,
Nags Head
(252) 441-5353, (888) 441-5353
www.finnfeatherwatersideinn.com

A charming motel along the water's edge, the Fin 'N Feather is popular with anglers and hunters. If you're planning to come in the fall or spring, call well in advance for reservations. This motel's proximity to Pirate's Cove Yacht Club is convenient for anyone headed out for a day on the open seas. The motel also has its own boat ramp. Housekeeping units are available year-round at Fin 'N Feather and feature double-bed efficiencies. Each efficiency has a stove, a refrigerator, and cooking utensils. The rooms are clean and comfortable. Large windows open onto the water from either side and offer stunning views of the sound. All rooms are nonsmoking, and dogs are welcome. Free Wi-Fi.

ROANOKE ISLAND

Manteo

**✳ISLAND MOTEL &
GUESTHOUSE** $$–$$$
US 64, Manteo
(252) 473-2434
www.theislandmotel.com

In the heart of Manteo, convenience is a hallmark at this neat little motel. Most of the 14 rooms have their own microwave or full kitchen, cable TV, air-conditioning, and two double beds. Foldaway beds are available for children. Daily, weekly, and monthly rates are offered. Amenities include courtesy bikes, fishing poles, other sports equipment, and surfing lessons. Nonsmoking rooms are available, and smoking is not allowed in the main house. Dogs are allowed for a nominal fee. This motel is open all year. The Island Motel also operates three adorable theme cottages located 1 block away. In-season rates start at $200 per night. These cottages are nonsmoking and do not allow pets.

THE ELIZABETHAN INN $$$
US 64, Manteo
(252) 473-2101, (800) 346-2466
www.elizabethaninn.com

The Elizabethan Inn is a year-round resort facility with spacious shaded grounds, country-manor charm, and Tudor architecture reflecting the area's heritage. The hotel consists of three buildings providing more than 80 rooms, efficiencies, and apartments, plus a spa and an on-site restaurant. Nonsmoking and wheelchair-accessible rooms are available. All rooms have cable TV with HBO, refrigerators, and direct-dial phones. Rooms are available with a king-size bed or two queen-size or double beds, and two rooms have whirlpool baths. All have coffeemakers.

The inn's Nautics Hall Health & Fitness Complex is available for guests (see the Recreation chapter). Guests may also use the outdoor pool and a heated, competition-size indoor pool.

ROANOKE ISLAND INN $$$$
305 Fernando St., Manteo
(252) 473-5511, (877) 473-5511
www.roanokeislandinn.com

With the sparkling Roanoke Sound and quaint Manteo waterfront just a stroll away, you'll find yourself easing into the relaxed village pace the moment you step up to this attractive inn. The distinctive white clapboard with dark green shutters distinguishes a gracious, restored residence with the comforts of a small, well-designed bed-and-breakfast. The furnishings are handsome, reflecting the meticulous care of the owner, designer-architect John Wilson IV.

Each of the inn's eight rooms features a private entrance, private bath, TV, and phone. Guests may choose to stay in the bungalow behind the inn, which is complete with antique tub and furnishings, wet bar, and refrigerator. Browse through a collection of Outer Banks–related books and artwork in the lobby. A light breakfast is offered in the butler's pantry. The private grounds are landscaped with gardenia, fig bushes, and native plants. Relax by the picturesque pond complete with koi and sweet-smelling lotus plants. Dip nets are provided so guests can net crabs along the bay's edge. Bicycles are furnished for touring the town and nearby historic attractions, including the *Elizabeth II* and the Outer Banks History Center. For a more adventuresome vacation, guests may rent a house on their own private island in the sound. Guests must provide their own boat to make the 10-minute journey to the home, available May through September. Guests must provide their own cell phone. Reed Hill is another choice rental located on the oceanfront in historic Nags Head. The home can be rented by the week through Roanoke Island Inn. Roanoke Island Inn is open from Apr through Oct.

THE WHITE DOE INN   **$$$$**
Sir Walter Raleigh Street, Manteo
(252) 473-9851, (800) 473-6091
www.whitedoeinn.com
In a restored 1898 home, the White Doe Inn retains its turn-of-the-century charm and offers guests an elegant escape in its rooms and hideaways. It is one of the few Dare County houses listed on the National Register of Historic Places. The inn offers several guest rooms, each with a private bath and fireplace. Honeymoon suites are available. Lounge on the large wraparound porches; guests also have full use of the library, formal parlor, foyer, and dining room of this stately old home. Afternoon tea, coffee, and desserts are served, as is evening sherry.

The inn serves a full southern-style, four-course breakfast every morning, a time for guests to read the newspapers, enjoy the fine food, and prepare for a day of exploring historic Manteo and Roanoke Island. This is a nonsmoking establishment, but smoking is allowed on the porch. Bicycles and beach equipment are provided, and as well as croquet and bocce ball sets. Special events for up to 50 people, including weddings, reunions, or retreats, can be accommodated. Check the website for special-interest weekend packages. The inn is open all year, and off-season rates are available. Spa and concierge service is available.

✷THE CAMERON HOUSE INN   **$$$$**
300 Budleigh St., Manteo
(252) 473-6596, (800) 279-8178
www.cameronhouseinn.com
Comfort and elegance are the hallmarks at this well-appointed inn. Some rooms feature fireplaces, soaker tubs, or down-stuffed sofas, and all have luxurious tiled bathrooms. All rooms are nonsmoking and all have Internet access. A big breakfast is set out each morning, usually offering homemade muffins and breads, quiches, fresh fruit, granola, juices, coffee, and tea. Afternoon treats perk you up after a long day on the beach or visiting attractions, especially if you also take a moment to relax on the antique front porch swing or in the comfy wicker chairs. The inn is in historic downtown Manteo, where restaurants, attractions, and shopping are all just a few minutes' walk away.

The Cameron House Inn also offers some of the best advice on what to see and do while you are on the Outer Banks—advice not easily matched. The website also has an extensive area calendar of events. The Cameron House is frequently the site for conferences, retreats, and business meetings.

i Nothing feels better on your skin than the Atlantic Ocean at the Outer Banks, but beware! Sharks are everywhere. Stay behind the breakers in shallow water where you can see through the water to the sandy bottom. Flat beaches far from fishing piers and surf fishermen are the safest.

SCARBOROUGH INN $$–$$$
524 US 64, Manteo
(252) 473-3979
www.scarborough-inn.com

This small inn is a delightful and friendly place to stay. The 2-story structure was modeled after a turn-of-the-20th-century inn. Each of the guest rooms is filled with authentic Victorian and pre-Victorian antiques and other interesting furnishings, mostly family heirlooms.

The inn's main rooms are set away from the street and offer cable TV, phone, microwave, private bath, small refrigerator, and coffeemaker. A light continental breakfast is delivered the night before, an especially nice treat for early risers.

Rooms in the 2-story inn have exterior entrances and open onto a covered porch. The annex has four units: two suites with queen bedrooms and sitting rooms and two regular queen rooms. The barn has two king rooms. All six units in the annex and barn are equipped with wet bars and small storage spaces for kitchen utensils and miscellaneous items. Pets are not allowed. Complimentary bicycles are available for guests age 18 and older. Scarborough Inn is open year-round.

✳TRANQUIL HOUSE INN $$$$
405 Queen Elizabeth Ave., on the waterfront, Manteo
(252) 473-1404, (800) 458-7069
www.1587.com

This lovely 25-room country inn on Shallowbag Bay was modeled after an old hotel that stood on this site. Richard Gere and Diane Lane stayed at the Tranquil House in 2007 while filming the movie *Nights in Rodanthe*. Although the inn looks authentically aged, it is enhanced by up-to-date conveniences: TVs, telephones, and private baths. Two of the 25 rooms are one-bedroom suites that feature a queen-size bed and a separate sitting room with sofa and two TVs.

Large rooms on the third floor have high ceilings. Nonsmoking rooms are available, and the inn has one room equipped for disabled guests. A ramp to the first floor makes rooms on that level accessible to all.

The spacious second-floor deck faces east toward the bay. The *Elizabeth II*, the flagship attraction of Roanoke Island Festival Park, is docked across the water. Shops along the waterfront are a few steps away, and the marina behind the inn is convenient for those arriving by boat. The inn's restaurant, 1587, specializes in gourmet cuisine and offers an extensive selection of wines (see the Restaurants chapter). Guests have free use of bicycles. The inn is open all year.

SCARBOROUGH HOUSE BED AND
BREAKFAST $$$
Fernando and Uppowac Streets, Manteo
(252) 473-3849
www.scarboroughhouseinn.com

The Scarborough House, owned by Phil and Sally Scarborough, opened in 1995. Each of the four guest rooms has its own refrigerator, microwave, and private bath. Nonsmoking rooms are available. A romantic loft room has a king-size bed and a whirlpool bath. This inn is appointed with period antiques and other fine furnishings. A continental breakfast is served daily. Everything about these accommodations reflects the owners' care and personal touch. The Scarborough House is open year-round.

DUKE OF DARE MOTOR LODGE $$
US 64, Manteo
(252) 473-2175

On the main street and only a few blocks from the Manteo waterfront, this 57-room family motel provides the basics in accommodations: clean rooms with full baths, cable TV, and phones. Wheelchair-accessible rooms are available. The lodge also has an outdoor pool. The Duke of Dare is close to shopping, restaurants, and attractions. It is open all year.

DARE HAVEN MOTEL $$–$$$
US 64/264, Manteo
(252) 473-2322
www.darehaven.com

The Dare Haven, a family-run motel suited to the cost-conscious vacationer, is toward the north end of Roanoke Island and is a favorite place for families and fishing enthusiasts—there's enough room here to park your own boat and trailer. Visitors planning to attend *The Lost Colony* or visit any of the other Roanoke Island attractions and historic sites of Fort Raleigh find this location convenient. The motel-style rooms are basic, clean, and comfortable, and have cable TV and telephones. Most are decorated in traditional Outer Banks style, with paneled walls

and wraparound porches. All are ground level. Call for special rates for groups and extended stays. The motel is open all year, and some rooms are pet friendly. A large dog run is on-site.

Wanchese

ISLAND HOUSE OF WANCHESE
BED AND BREAKFAST $$$–$$$$
104 Old Wharf Rd., Wanchese
(252) 473-5619, (866) 473-5619
www.islandhouse-bb.com

This old home, built in 1902, was converted into a bed-and-breakfast several years ago. Furnished in period antiques, with Oriental rugs and cabana fans, the small but cozy establishment offers many comforts, including private baths, cable TV, clock radios in every room, beach towels and chairs, and a hot tub for guests. Each of the four rooms and one suite has a double bed.

Island House offers a breakfast buffet often including casseroles, grits, fresh fruit, sweets, and juice. Evening tea is served with snacks. A guest pantry is open 24 hours a day. This is a nonsmoking establishment, but smoking is allowed on the porch. Kids 8 and up are welcome, as are small pets. Island House is open year-round.

WANCHESE INN BED AND
BREAKFAST $$$
85 Jovers Ln., Wanchese
(252) 475-1166, (252) 473-0602
www.wancheseinn.com

Dock your boat just behind this quaint bed-and-breakfast. Nestled in the heart of Wanchese, this delightful inn serves a full breakfast each day. Pets are not allowed; and the inn is open all year.

ACCOMMODATIONS

HATTERAS ISLAND

Rodanthe

SEA SOUND MOTEL   **$$–$$$**
Sea Sound Road, Rodanthe
(252) 987-2224
www.seasoundmotelobx.com
Sea Sound is between NC 12 and the ocean and offers efficiencies and regular motel-style rooms. The efficiencies have fully equipped kitchens including microwaves. Motel rooms feature either one double or two queen-size beds. All accommodations have heat and air-conditioning, color TV, and phones, and coffeemakers. An outdoor pool is available. Sea Sound also features an outdoor grill, picnic area with table, and small basketball court. It's open Mar through mid-December. This motel is nonsmoking, and free Wi-Fi is available.

Avon

AVON MOTEL   **$$–$$$**
NC 12, Avon
(252) 995-5774
www.avonmotel.com
This 45-unit establishment has been in business for more than 50 years and offers oceanside motel rooms and a handful of efficiency apartments. Motel rooms come with either two double beds or one queen-size or one king-size bed, and each has a microwave, compact refrigerator, and coffeemaker. The efficiencies have either two or three rooms with a variety of bed setups along with fully equipped kitchens. All rooms and efficiencies have air-conditioning, cable TV with free HBO, and in-room phones. Wi-Fi is free. Anglers will appreciate the lighted fish-cleaning station at the motel and the guest laundry.

The motel is located near tackle shops, a fishing pier, four-wheel-drive beach accesses, windsurfing and beach shops, restaurants, and gift stores. The Cape Hatteras Lighthouse is 6 miles away. The Avon Motel is open Mar through Dec.

Buxton

CAPE HATTERAS MOTEL   **$$$$**
NC 12, Buxton
(252) 995-5611, (800) 995-0711
www.capehatterasmotel.com
Cape Hatteras Motel's efficiency units and motel rooms are popular with anglers, surfers, and folks who enjoy Hatteras Island's beaches. Sailboarders especially like this facility because it is near Canadian Hole, one of the best windsurfing spots on the East Coast (see the Attractions chapter). Efficiencies sleep up to six comfortably, offer double beds as well as queen-size and king-size beds, and have full kitchens (they rent weekly, but nightly rentals also may be available). The newer, more modern town houses and apartments have a great view of the beach. The motel has an outdoor swimming pool and spa, and its position at the north end of Buxton is convenient not only to pristine, uncrowded beaches but also to restaurants and services. The Cape Hatteras Motel is no smoking and is open year-round.

OUTER BANKS MOTEL   **$$$**
NC 12, Buxton
(252) 995-5601, (800) 995-1233
www.outerbanksmotel.com
Situated next to the Cape Hatteras Motel, this establishment offers beachfront motel-style rooms, efficiency units, and two- and three-bedroom cottages. Units accommodate up to eight people comfortably, and some of the units provide an ocean view.

Rooms and the efficiency offer enclosed porches with sliding windows and screens for a relaxing evening listening to the ocean. The pine-paneled rooms have tiled baths, microwaves, toasters, and small refrigerators. All units have cable TV and telephones.

The owners also have additional cottages in Buxton Village, a mile from the ocean, near Connor's Market. Because these units are not oceanfront, rental rates are lower. If you rent one of these cottages, you are welcome to use the motel pool and beach facilities. The cottages are clean, simply furnished, and provide the basics for family vacationers, including cable TV. The motel has a coin-operated laundry, a fish-cleaning station, and a guest freezer to store your big catch. If you enjoy crabbing or you just want to paddle around on Pamlico Sound, the motel has several rowboats that guests may use free of charge. This motel is open year-round.

LIGHTHOUSE VIEW MOTEL $-$$$$
NC 12, Buxton
(252) 995-5680, (800) 225-7651
www.lighthouseview.com
Lighthouse View is easy to find on the big curve in Buxton, where the Hooper family began serving vacationers in the 1950s. Located within a mile of the Hatteras Lighthouse, the motel has more than 85 units including motel rooms, efficiencies, duplexes, villa units, and cottages. Most units are oceanfront, and all are oceanside. The complex has an outdoor pool and hot tub. Surfers, sailboarders, and anglers enjoy the proximity to ocean and sound.

Rooms have cable TV, phones, full baths, and daily maid service. Efficiencies accommodate two to six people and are equipped with complete kitchens. The oceanfront villas offer balconies on both the oceanside and soundside, so you can enjoy sunrises and sunsets. The six duplexes offer two decks and sleep up to six people each. Efficiencies and villas usually rent on a weekly basis, and there is a three-night minimum stay, but they can be rented nightly when available. Note that there is no daily maid service for the villas, efficiencies, and duplexes, but linens can be exchanged. Cottages are rented by the week only. Efficiencies, duplexes, villas, and cottages are fully furnished. Wheelchair-accessible, one-room efficiencies are also available. Lighthouse View is open year-round.

THE CROATOAN INN $$$
46854 NC 12, Buxton
(252) 995-5968, (800) 635-6911
www.thecroatoaninn.com
Falcon's traditional Outer Banks–style rooms appeal to family-oriented guests who appreciate moderate prices, accommodations with character, and the peaceful environment of Hatteras Island. Attention to detail is important at the Croatoan, which is apparent in the clean, well-maintained rooms and grounds.

This motel includes 30 rooms and two fully-equipped apartments all at ground level. All rooms and apartments have daily maid service. Nonsmoking rooms are available. The rooms include cable TV with HBO, and many have a refrigerator and microwave. All rooms have wooden deck chairs on a wide, covered porch. Call ahead for reservations.

Guests have use of the swimming pool and complimentary bikes. You'll also find a shaded picnic area with barbecue grills amid mature oak trees, away from the road. The landscaping includes martin and bluebird houses, palm trees, and planted shrubs and flowers that attract the local bird population.

*THE INN ON PAMLICO SOUND $$$$
NC 12, Buxton
(252) 995-7030, (866) 995-7030
www.innonpamlicosound.com

This welcoming inn showcases the Pamlico Sound with awe-inspiring views from its numerous decks, porches, and docks, and from many of its rooms. No need to bring along beach towels or chairs; both are provided for guests. Kayaks and bicycles are also on-site for guest use. A swimming pool overlooks the sound.

A 14-seat home theater room is a great spot to watch your favorite team or movie in high definition. All guest rooms have large televisions with DVD players. A movie library with over 1,200 titles gives viewers plenty to choose from, and a book lending library offers some great reading choices. No charges are included to guests to use any of these amenities. Free Wi-Fi is offered as well.

Rooms offer either king- or queen-size beds and are located with a sound view or a garden view. Fresh baked goodies and beverages are provided in the afternoons. Stocked guest beverage refrigerators, snack baskets, candy, and chocolate dishes are located throughout the inn. A fine restaurant is also located within this establishment.

Well-behaved children over the age of 8 are welcomed. Pets are not allowed.

COMFORT INN OF HATTERAS $$$$
NC 12, Buxton
(252) 995-6100, (800) 432-1441
www.outerbankscomfortinn.com

The Comfort Inn is in the heart of Buxton, close to the beach and shops. The 60 units and one suite with exterior access are standard motel-style rooms with king-size or double beds. Rooms are decorated in attractive, soft beach colors; all have cable TV with HBO, refrigerators, direct-dial phones, and microwaves. Nonsmoking and wheelchair-accessible rooms are available. Free ice and guest laundry are available. A complimentary continental breakfast is served in the lobby. Guests have use of the outdoor swimming pool, gazebo, and 3-story watchtower, the latter two providing panoramic views of the ocean, the sound, and nearby Cape Hatteras Lighthouse (see the Attractions chapter). AARP and AAA discounts are honored. There is ample parking for boats and campers. The Comfort Inn is open year-round.

*CAPE HATTERAS BED AND
   BREAKFAST $$$–$$$$
46223 Old Lighthouse Rd., Buxton
(252) 995-6004, (800) 252-3316
www.capehatterasbandb.com

A short walk to the beach makes this bed-and-breakfast inn popular with sailboarders as well as beach lovers, lighthouse enthusiasts, honeymooners, surfers, and couples who just want to get away. The 2-story inn offers several styles of accommodations. Each has its own entrance opening onto a covered porch running the length of the building. Rooms offer a wide variety of options. Call or check the website for availability. All units have cable TV and private baths. A large sundeck with comfortable chairs, a gas grill, and a table are available for guests' use.

Amenities include a common dining and living area upstairs (where a complimentary full breakfast is served), flatscreen cable TV, gas grill, and hot and cold outdoor showers. Beach gear, coolers, bicycles, and beach toys are available along with lockable storage for surf- and sailboards. Daily maid service is provided. Weekly rentals are available, with special accommodations available for honeymooners. The inn is open Apr through mid-December. Guests may use nearby Spa Koru for workouts at no extra charge. Wi-Fi is free.

CAPE PINES MOTEL $$$
NC 12, Buxton
(252) 995-5666, (866) 456-9983
www.capepinesmotel.com

Cape Pines Motel, a mile south of the Cape Hatteras Lighthouse, is a 1-story facility with private exterior entry to each room. Each of the 26 rooms offers cable TV and a full bath. Furnishings have a contemporary beach look. Some rooms have queen-size beds, and all rooms are nonsmoking. Cape Pines Motel has three apartments, each offering separate bedrooms, a living room, and a full kitchen. In the summer season the apartments rent on a weekly basis only. Deluxe rooms are available with microwaves, coffeemakers, and refrigerators. The owners like to say that the Cape Pines is so clean, you'd think your mother works here!

Stretch out and relax around the pool and the lawn, which has picnic tables and charcoal grills. Fish-cleaning tables and a pay phone are on the premises. Wi-Fi is free. Cape Pines is close enough to walk or bike to shopping or attractions. The motel is open year-round and is pet friendly.

Hatteras Village

BREAKWATER INN $$–$$$$
NC 12, Hatteras Village
(252) 986-2565
www.harbormotel.com

This beautiful new inn is in the heart of Hatteras Village. Convenient to restaurants, shops, and services, it's adjacent to the Hatteras charter boat fleet. Visitors park their cars and walk or bike to most places in this community. Breakwater Inn has 21 new rooms with 2 queen-size beds and a kitchenette and 2 oversize king suites with living area, full kitchen, a king-size bed, and a whirlpool tub. These rooms have a spectacular view of the Hatteras harbor. The 12 rooms in the Fisherman's Quarters are standard hotel rooms, and one large efficiency is located there also. All rooms have cable TV, microwaves, refrigerators, and telephones. Daily maid service and fresh linens are provided. Guests enjoy the in-ground pool and kiddie wading pool and the long, shaded porches. Pets are allowed in some rooms for a onetime $30 fee.

HATTERAS MARLIN MOTEL $$$
NC 12, Hatteras Village
(252) 986-2141, (866) 986-2141
www.hatterasmarlin.com

The recently renovated Hatteras Marlin Hotel is in sight of the harbor fishing fleet, restaurants, and shops. The 39 units are divided among three buildings and consist of standard motel rooms with king- or double-size beds and one-bedroom efficiencies. A newer building near the back of the property away from the road offers a pair of two-bedroom suites with combined living, kitchen, and dining areas.

All rooms have cable TV, microwaves, refrigerators, and coffeemakers. Accommodations sleep one to six people comfortably and rent weekly or nightly, depending upon availability. The motel has an in-ground swimming pool and sundeck. Hatteras Marlin Motel is open all year, except for Christmas.

OCRACOKE ISLAND

THE ANCHORAGE INN & MARINA $$$–$$$$

NC 12, Ocracoke
(252) 928-1101
www.theanchorageinn.com

The Anchorage Inn overlooks Silver Lake and the village. Besides 35 motel-style rooms, the inn has a marina and fishing center, recreational amenities, an outdoor cafe, and gift shops nearby. The attractive 4-story redbrick building with white trim has elevator access to each floor. Accommodations offer some of the best bird's-eye views available of the harbor and Ocracoke Village, especially from upper-floor rooms. Most of the rooms have some view of Silver Lake Harbor. Each of the rooms has a king- or queen-size bed or two double beds, full bath, direct-dial phone, and cable TV with Showtime and Cinemax. The fourth-floor units are nonsmoking rooms and have king-size beds. Wheelchair-accessible rooms are available. Pets are allowed in some rooms for a $25 fee. This is also the only hotel in Ocracoke with an elevator.

The Anchorage Inn offers its guests a complimentary continental breakfast, a private pool with a sundeck situated on the harbor, and an on-premises boat dock and ramp. The gazebo at Silver Lake is a perfect place to watch a sunset. Guests can walk to restaurants, shops, and the historical sites on Ocracoke Island. Bike rentals are available. Fishing charters, which depart from the dock across the street, can be booked with the marina's dockmaster. The inn is open Mar through Nov. Free Wi-Fi.

BLACKBEARD'S LODGE $$$$

Back Road, Ocracoke
(252) 928-3421, (800) 892-5314
www.blackbeardslodge.com

Ocracoke's oldest hotel, Blackbeard's Lodge, was built in 1936 by local entrepreneur, developer, and visionary Robert Stanley Wahab. The building's first floor originally housed Ocracoke's only movie theater on one side and skating rink on the other. "Rooms for hire" occupied the second floor and often accommodated visiting dignitaries, movie stars, and well-heeled types who flew their planes to the island, landed on the barren sand flats, and taxied right up to the front door. A subsequent owner added some rooms to the gabled third floor and stretched the building out with additional rooms in the wing now called the annex.

In January 2007, Chip and Helena Stevens purchased the lodge. Chip is the great-grandnephew of the original proprietor, Robert Stanley Wahab, bringing Blackbeard's Lodge back into the family.

This is a family-oriented property during the vacation season that changes focus to accommodate "outdoors and sporting types" and those wanting to quietly get away from it all during the fall, winter, and spring. Blackbeard's units range from a room with one double bed to a room that sleeps eight with a full kitchen and dining area. All rooms have television. Some rooms feature whirlpool baths, while others may include a kitchenette, king-size bed, refrigerator, or wet bar. Several pet-friendly rooms are available; call ahead to reserve.

A game room complete with pool table, foosball, and electronic games is available for inclement days or for nights when friendly competition is in order. A fleet of bicycles are for rent. The lodge has a heated swimming pool with sundeck, wraparound porch with rockers, fish-cleaning table, and free water access for rinsing the salt and sand off your vehicle if surf fishing or beach driving is your passion. Blackbeard's Lodge is open all year long. In the off-season a complimentary hot breakfast is served from 8 to 10 a.m. Free Wi-Fi in the common area.

THE CAPTAIN'S LANDING $$$$
324 NC 12, Ocracoke
(252) 928-1999
www.thecaptainslanding.com

Breathe in the fresh sea air and feel the soft ocean breeze while you stay at the Captain's Landing on scenic Silver Lake in Ocracoke. Luxury suites and a penthouse apartment provide panoramic views of the lighthouse, the village, and harbor life. The first and second floors offer suites with queen-size beds, one-and-a-half baths, a sleeper sofa in the living area, a fully equipped kitchen, and a spacious private deck. The penthouse has a queen-size bed in the master suite and a guest room with two double beds. A sleeper sofa is located in the office. The penthouse has two full baths, a laundry room, expansive dining and living areas, and a well-stocked gourmet kitchen. Enjoy spectacular sunsets from the decks, which are accessible from most rooms. There's free Wi-Fi, and bikes are available to take out for a spin.

✳THE CASTLE BED & BREAKFAST ON SILVER LAKE $$$–$$$$
155 Silver Lake Rd., Ocracoke
(252) 928-3505, (800) 471-8848
www.thecastlebb.com

Among the finest accommodations on Ocracoke Island, the Castle has been part of the local scenery and part of the island's rich history for more than 50 years. Each of the 11 bedrooms, which have been extensively renovated and redecorated, are furnished with antiques and offer a private bath, television, small refrigerator, and phone. The house has a large living room with a surround-sound entertainment system, central air-conditioning, and a custom 9-foot pool table. A full country breakfast is served from 8:30 to 9:30 a.m. (Breakfast is for bed-and-breakfast guests only.) Children age 12 and older are welcome.

The top of the Castle has a cupola, private to the Lighthouse Suite, that overlooks Silver Lake, with panoramic views from the sound to the ocean. A large deck extending from the cupola may be used for sunning, relaxing, or watching the sunset. The pier on Silver Lake offers large and small boat dockage in slips up to 50 feet. Dockage is available on a complimentary first-come basis for all guests.

In addition to the Castle Bed & Breakfast, courtyard and villa suites are available. One-, two-, and three-bedroom suites are available, each with large whirlpool tubs, full kitchens, and spacious, comfortable living areas. Studio bedrooms are also available with kitchenettes.

Everyone who stays at any of the Castle properties may use the heated pool, steam showers, sauna, bicycles, and the conference room.

THE COVE BED AND BREAKFAST $$$$
21 Loop Rd., Ocracoke
(252) 928-4192
www.thecovebb.com

The Cove is a beautiful beach home located within walking distance of Ocracoke's many shops and restaurants. It is a large place—more than 5,000 square feet—and is within view of the sound and Ocracoke's lighthouse. Rooms come equipped with cable TVs and hair dryers. Each room has its own balcony and bath and free Wi-Fi. Full breakfasts are served each day in the large common area. A large screened porch beckons you to sit a while and absorb the wonderful, clean Ocracoke air at the end of a beach day.

The inn is a nonsmoking establishment; children age 15 and older are welcome, but pets are not. A public boat dock for launching a kayak or small craft is nearby. Complimentary bicycles are available for touring around town. Transportation is provided to and from the airstrip.

CREWS INN BED AND BREAKFAST $$
Back Road, Ocracoke
(252) 928-7011
www.ocracokers.com

The Crews Inn is a place to get away from it all. No phones or TVs will disturb your privacy in this vintage 1908 island home. Three rooms have private baths, and two share a bath. All have double beds. The wraparound porch is an especially nice spot for guests to gather, for the building is surrounded by large live oaks and is far enough away from traffic for easy chatting. This is a nonsmoking establishment. The inn serves mostly a continental but occasionally a full breakfast. Crews Inn is open year-round. Children over the age of 10 are welcome. No pets please.

EDWARDS OF OCRACOKE $$$
Pony Island Road, Ocracoke
(252) 928-4801, (800) 254-1359
www.edwardsofocracoke.com

This charming motel, away from the center of Ocracoke and off the main route near the Back Porch Restaurant, consists of eight motel rooms, three efficiencies, six apartments, and two cottages. Most of the units have screened porches and phones. Some open onto a veranda. All have cable TV. Cottages rent weekly during the summer, and efficiencies require a three-day minimum stay. Some have refrigerators. The

price code above pertains to nightly rentals of the motel rooms only. The motel offers inexpensive accommodations in a family setting with a carefully landscaped green lawn, flower beds, and pine trees. The motel is open mid-March through Thanksgiving and for New Year's Eve.

HARBORSIDE MOTEL $$$
Across from Silver Lake Harbor Ocracoke
(252) 928-3111
www.ocracokeharborside.com

This Ocracoke island getaway offers 18 rooms and 4 efficiencies, all well kept and comfortable with cable TV, phones, and refrigerators. Most rooms offer two double beds; one has three double beds, and two have one double bed. Guests can use the waterfront sundeck, docks, and boat ramp across the street. Nonsmoking rooms are available. Harborside has its own gift shop offering clothing, books, gourmet foods, and small gifts. Other shops and restaurants of Ocracoke Village are within walking distance. The Swan Quarter and Cedar Island ferry docks are nearby. The same family has owned this property since 1965, and their hospitality and service are firmly established. A complimentary breakfast of homemade muffins, coffee, juice, and tea is provided. The motel is open Easter through mid-November. AAA members receive a discount.

THE ISLAND INN $–$$$
NC 12, Ocracoke
(252) 928-4351, (877) 456-3466
www.ocracokeislandinn.com

The Island Inn, owned by the Newell and Storrs families, provides a variety of accommodations suitable for single adults, couples, and families with children. Originally built from shipwreck wood as an Odd Fellows

Lodge in 1901, the main building has served as a school, a dance parlor, and an army barracks during World War II. It was restored by former owners and has been recognized in *Country Inns of the Old South, Southern Living, Cuisine,* and the *Saturday Evening Post.*

The main building is a nonsmoking establishment. Many of the 28 rooms reflect the inherently romantic style of this country inn. The main building houses individual rooms and suites, all uniquely furnished with antiques and quilts. The adults-only rooms and suites accommodate a wide range of needs. If you're looking for a contemporary feel, ask for the Crow's Nest, which offers spectacular views of the postcard-pretty village.

Across the street a much newer 3-story structure includes two rooms with king-size beds. Families with children find these casual accommodations a welcome retreat. The third floor has one- and two-bedroom luxury villas overlooking the heated pool. Each beautifully furnished villa has a kitchen, living and dining area, washer and dryer, plenty of windows, and a whirlpool tub. The inn also rents a number of cottages, some of which accommodate pets with a $25 fee attached, and has a heated swimming pool that is kept open as long as weather permits. Cable TV with free Showtime is available in every room. The inn has an on-site restaurant (see the Restaurants chapter), a large lobby for lounging, and a covered porch with rocking chairs. Island Inn closes for a few weeks in Jan but otherwise is open year-round. Nonsmoking and free Wi-Fi.

THE OCRACOKE HARBOR INN $$$
On Silver Lake Harbor, across from the Coast Guard Station, Ocracoke
(252) 928-5731, (888) 456-1998
www.ocracokeharborinn.com

This lovely 16-room, 7-suite inn overlooks picturesque Silver Lake Harbor. The inn's private decks with Adirondack chairs are a great place to kick back, relax, and enjoy the view. Each room features either two queen-size beds or one king-size bed and includes a minifridge, cable TV, coffeepot, hair dryer, and climate control. The suites have two-person whirlpool tubs and kitchenettes. Suites are studio-style or one bedroom. Three three-bedroom island homes and a two-bedroom apartment are also offered. All rooms are nonsmoking, and wheelchair-accessible rooms are available. A complimentary continental breakfast is served each morning. Also available are complimentary boat docking, outdoor showers, barbecue grills, bicycle rentals, and lots of outdoor decks. The Ocracoke Harbor Inn is open year-round. Pets are not allowed. Free Wi-Fi.

OSCAR'S HOUSE $$–$$$
1 block from Silver Lake Harbor, Ocracoke
(252) 928-1311
www.oscarsbb.com

Oscar's House was built in 1940 by the keeper of the Ocracoke Lighthouse and was first occupied by the World War II commander of the Ocracoke Naval Base. Stories abound about Oscar, who lived and worked on the island for many years as a fisherman and hunting guide. This guesthouse has operated as a bed-and-breakfast since 1984. It is managed by Ann Ehringhaus, a massage therapist, local fine-art photographer, minister, and the author of *Ocracoke Portrait.*

The house retains the original beaded-board walls, and all four guest rooms are delightfully furnished. One upstairs bedroom has a loft creating a comfortable setting. Two baths, one upstairs and one down, accommodate guests, as does an outdoor shower (with dressing room). The house has central heating and central air-conditioning and is comfortable and welcoming. The large kitchen with a big table is available to guests; however, the stove is off-limits. Ann serves a complimentary full breakfast to all guests and will gladly adhere to special preferences for vegetarian or macrobiotic meals. Smoking is not allowed, nor are pets. You can treat yourself to one of Ann's therapeutic massages. In spring and fall Ann offers workshops in photography and therapeutic bodywork. Call for details.

Oscar's House has a deck area complete with barbecue grills. Meals are eaten inside or outdoors. Oscar's House is within walking distance of all village shops and restaurants, and bicycles are free for guests. Ann also gladly transports guests to and from the Ocracoke Airport, which is open to single- and twin-engine planes. This bed-and-breakfast is open from Apr to Oct.

**PAM'S PELICAN BED AND
  BREAKFAST**   **$$$**
Across from fire station, Ocracoke
(252) 928-1661, (888) 773-5422
www.pamspelican.com
Built originally as a lodge, Pam's Pelican captures the feel of laid-back Ocracoke style that many vacationers seek while staying on the island. The four rooms are spacious, bright, and cheerful and have private baths. Amenities include cable TV, an in-room fridge, a small pool, and free use of bicycles. Pelican Lodge also operates Pelican Airways, which includes sightseeing flights, flight training, and charter services. See the Getting Here, Getting Around chapter for more details. The lodge is open year-round. Pam's Pelican is pet friendly, however no smoking inside.

PONY ISLAND MOTEL   **$$$**
NC 12, Ocracoke
(252) 928-4411
www.ponyislandmotel.com
At the edge of Ocracoke Village, a short distance from Silver Lake Harbor, Pony Island Motel offers 54 rooms, efficiencies, and suites and 4 cottages. The grounds are spacious and inviting. The inn hosts families and couples in search of peace and solitude on Ocracoke Island. Most of the units have either single or double occupancy, but the motel offers some rooms that accommodate up to five people. Each room has a telephone, refrigerator, cable TV, and wireless Internet. The efficiencies have fully equipped kitchens. Rooms are refurbished regularly but maintain a traditional decor. Nonsmoking rooms and one wheelchair-accessible room are available. A newer 23-unit, 3-story addition overlooks the pool. Rooms have a kitchenette. Suites have a full kitchen and whirlpool tubs. The motel is within walking distance of the Ocracoke Lighthouse and other island attractions. Bike rentals and boat docking are available. The pool and spacious lawn with picnic tables and grills offer plenty of room for family activities. The Pony Island Restaurant, a local favorite, is next door (see the Restaurants chapter). Pony Island Motel is open year-round.

✳SAND DOLLAR MOTEL   **$$–$$$**
Sand Dollar Lane, Ocracoke
(252) 928-5571, (866) 928-5571
www.sanddollarmotelocracoke.com
This establishment is in the heart of Ocracoke Village behind the Back Porch Restaurant (there are no street signs). Fresh flowers welcome guests to the lobby. You're likely to be greeted by Roger Garrish, the property's former owner and an Ocracoke native, who is a

great source of island information. The Sand Dollar has 11 rooms and a two-bedroom cottage. Two of the rooms are efficiencies with small microwaves and coffeemakers; all rooms have refrigerators and cable TV. Bedding options include queen- and double-size beds. One special room is connected to the pool and has a private deck and a king-size bed. The Sand Dollar is a nonsmoking establishment. Pets are not allowed. Guests enjoy a dip in the pool. Repeat visits are common at this neat little place, so book your stay early. The inn is open from Apr 1 to mid-November.

THURSTON HOUSE INN $$$
NC 12, Ocracoke
(252) 928-6037
www.thurstonhouseinn.com

The Thurston House Inn was built in the 1920s. The former home of Capt. Tony Thurston Gaskill is now on the Register of Historic Places in North Carolina. It was renovated in 1996 by the captain's granddaughter, Marlene Mathews, and her husband, Randal. An addition was completed next to the inn in 1999. Today, Donna Boor runs the inn alongside her mother, Annie. The inn offers six rooms, each with a private bath. A phone is available in the hallway, and each room has cable TV and wireless high-speed Internet. All rooms are heated and air-conditioned and have private decks and porches with either king- or queen-size beds.

Guests enjoy relaxing on the covered porches and deck, which connects the inn's two buildings. A continental breakfast is part of the package. Children older than age 12 are welcome. This is a nonsmoking establishment, but smoking is allowed on the porches. The inn is within walking distance of Silver Lake, Ocracoke Lighthouse, and various stores, restaurants, and historic sites. Local airport pickup is available. Reservations are recommended. The inn is open Mar 1 through Nov.

WEEKLY & LONG-TERM COTTAGE RENTALS

If your idea of the perfect vacation is to settle down with all the comforts of a home away from home, the Outer Banks is a perfect choice. By far the most popular accommodations here are private beach cottages. More than 13,500 rental cottages are available in Dare County, and that's not including the thousands of cottages available in Corolla in Currituck County or on Ocracoke Island in Hyde County. From the unique off-road beaches of Carova just south of the Virginia line to the removed island of Ocracoke, accessible only by plane, boat, or ferry, you'll find a tremendous variety in price, location, and character. Although most vacationers stay for a week, longer- and shorter-term rentals are available throughout the year.

OVERVIEW

Most beach cottages are owned by individuals and are represented by a property management firm. Usually these cottages reflect the individual tastes and preferences of their owners. Although property management firms or rental companies will set their own minimum standards for the homes they represent, beach homes vary widely in design, decor, and the amenities they offer. You can rent anything from a palatial nine-bedroom oceanfront mansion with a private pool, home office, and media room to a cozy little saltbox on the sound side.

Rental companies compete rigorously to secure the greatest possible number of bookings for their owners, and the trend is to add more amenities, thus encouraging guests to return again and again. In recent years many companies have encouraged their cottage owners to add greater value to

a week's vacation by including, as standard, amenities that used to be luxuries. Whirlpool baths, hot tubs, appealing interior decorating, book and video libraries, fireplaces, baby cribs, and playpens are becoming increasingly common, particularly in the newer properties. Veteran visitors to the Outer Banks are accustomed to bringing their own linens and towels as only a few property management firms require their owners to provide linens.

Of course, you'll pay more for these luxuries. Rental prices are based primarily on the season, the cottage's proximity to the ocean, the number of occupants it "sleeps," and the amenities it offers. The peak, most expensive, season runs from mid-June through the end of August. Substantial discounts are offered in the fall and spring, considered "mid-season" by most companies, and, of course, the best bargains are from late November to late March. More vacationers are discovering the joys of the Outer Banks during seasons other than summer: With its temperate climate, the Outer Banks offers a great variety of outdoor activities to enjoy, even if the weather is too cold for ocean swimming or lounging on the beach.

LOCATION, LOCATION, LOCATION!

An "oceanfront" cottage is one that sits directly on the beach with no cottages or lots to the east facing the ocean. Some, but not all, have private walkways to the ocean, an especially convenient and important feature if the cottage sits behind a dune. (Dunes are fragile and need protection. It's against the law to climb them.) If your cottage doesn't have a private walkway, you'll have to use the community or public access; check on this when you make your reservation. Also, although most oceanfront cottages offer spectacular vistas, some have tall dunes obstructing the view from one or more levels. Oceanfront cottages without views are more the exception than the rule, but you won't encounter any disappointing surprises if you double-check at the time of rental.

There's no underestimating the convenience of an oceanfront cottage. You don't have to schlep the beach equipment very far, and when the little ones get cranky, you can sun yourself on your deck or patio and listen to the pounding surf while they nap inside.

The next best thing to oceanfront is "semi-oceanfront," which usually means one lot back from oceanfront. The distance to the ocean varies, but many

semi-oceanfronts still offer good views of the water and reasonable beach-going convenience. In some areas, especially Kitty Hawk, Kill Devil Hills, and Nags Head, you'll have to cross the Beach Road (NC 12) to get to the surf.

When a cottage is described as "between the highways," it is located between the Beach Road and US 158. Actual distances from the beach vary, but you can expect a 5- to 15-minute walk. Cottages identified as "westside" are located west of US 158 in Kitty Hawk, Kill Devil Hills, and Nags Head. Those west of NC 12 in Corolla, Duck, and Southern Shores are referred to as "soundside." Of course, "soundfront" cottages are those with no houses or lots between them and the sound.

Westside or soundside cottages tend to be among the last to book and can offer a very affordable and pleasant alternative to costlier oceanside cottages. Many communities offer pools, tennis courts, hiking trails, and other amenities on the soundside to enhance rentals. Some vacationers have come to prefer the soundside areas for their tranquility and the convenience of certain water sports, such as windsurfing and canoeing. Finally, many soundfront cottages offer views as spectacular as those on the ocean. It's the place to be if you prefer the sunset to the sunrise. (See the Real Estate chapter for more information on individual communities.)

Most rental companies identify, either in terms of number of lots from the beach or distance measured in feet, how close (or far) cottages are to the ocean, so you should get an idea when you make your reservation how long a trek you can expect.

WHEN & HOW TO RESERVE YOUR COTTAGE

As you might imagine, properties closest to the ocean are snatched up quickly. Many rental companies offer returning guests the opportunity to make advance reservations for the next year as they check out, so cottages in prime locations will often have several weeks reserved even before the New Year. Expect to make your reservation in January or February if you have your heart set on a particular cottage on the ocean. Otherwise you'll still have a good variety from which to choose if you reserve by the end of March. Don't despair, however, if you can't make a decision until later. You might have to call around, but you can usually find something to rent, possibly even at the last minute. (One caveat: The pickings will be slim for spur-of-the-moment trips in summer months.)

Nearly all rental companies publish a color brochure or catalog describing their properties; the new editions typically are available after Thanksgiving. You'll find photos and property descriptions not only in a company's brochure but on its website as well. Online availability and reservation booking capabilities are often the easiest way to complete the process.

The rental company's catalog or website will almost certainly cover the essential elements of the lease. Make sure you read these thoroughly before making your reservation, and form a list of questions you want to ask the reservationist. You'd be surprised at how familiar many reservationists are with the properties they rent. This is also the right time to discuss any special needs anyone in your party may have. You'll typically be asked to secure your cottage with a deposit—usually 50 percent, with the balance due 30 days in advance of your visit.

i "Cottage" is the traditional beach name for a vacation rental house on the Outer Banks. A "cottage" may be a tiny saltbox, of which there are only a few, or a mansion with numerous bedrooms, bathrooms, and Jacuzzis or hot tubs. Take your pick! Either way, it's a "cottage" to insiders.

AMENITIES

Rental companies list the amenities offered at each cottage on their websites and in their catalogs. In addition, most companies require their owners to supply certain amenities as standard. Typical standard items include air-conditioning, telephone, television, DVD player, washer and dryer, barbecue, microwave—most appliances and items you'd expect to find in the typical home. Still, don't take anything for granted. Read the descriptions and your lease thoroughly to avoid misunderstanding.

Unless the lease stipulates that your rental is equipped with linens and towels, bring your own. The cottage listing will tell you the sizes and number of beds in the home. You'll also need to supply your own toiletries, paper products, and cleaning supplies such as laundry and dishwashing detergents, sponges, and paper towels. It's a good idea to arrive with enough of the basics to get you through a half day so you won't need to visit the grocery store immediately.

If you don't feel like hauling a lot of extra stuff to the beach, you can rent just about anything you need, including linens, towels, beach equipment, bicycles, outdoor furniture, and recreational equipment. At the end of this chapter is a list of companies you can call in advance; many will deliver the items you request right to your cottage.

MINIMUM STAYS

During the mid- and off-seasons, you'll of course have more options than in peak season, when occupancy runs at close to 100 percent. During the summer it's very difficult to find a cottage to rent for less than a week. Most rent from Saturday to Saturday or Sunday to Sunday. Some families enjoy renting for two or even more consecutive weeks, but don't expect a price break.

You'll have better luck finding a shorter-term rental during slower seasons. Most companies offer what they call "partial" rentals from September through May or June. Some charge a flat fee for a three- or four-day period; others charge a nightly fee. Make sure you understand how the fee is determined. In the off-seasons many rental companies get creative to increase bookings. That's the time to look for special getaway packages. As you might expect, the mid- and off-seasons offer some excellent bargains and are especially popular with vacationers who don't have school-age children in tow. If you have the option of enjoying the Outer Banks during the slower seasons, you'll be delighted with the meandering pace and quiet. Most restaurants and shops now stay open at least through Thanksgiving, and more and more are extending their operating times well beyond that. Visiting the Outer Banks during off-season holidays is becoming increasingly popular.

ADVANCE RENTS

Expect to pay an advance rent, typically 50 percent of the full lease amount, soon after you make your reservation. It's usually due within 10 days. Personal checks are commonly accepted if the reservation is made in plenty of time for the check to clear. Some companies allow credit-card transactions, but be aware that some will charge an additional fee to cover the extra costs charged by the bank that handles the card. In most cases the balance of the lease amount is due 30 days prior to arrival. If payment is accepted at check-in, it's usually required in the form of a certified check or cash. Most rental companies will not accept a personal check upon arrival.

i Before making your cottage reservation, check online to see if the homes you're interested in offer a virtual tour. If so, you'll be able to view several rooms within each home before making your choice.

SECURITY DEPOSITS

Besides advance rents, most rental companies also require their guests to pay a security deposit. This, of course, is for the owner's protection. The amounts required vary depending upon the company's policies. Cottages are typically inspected between check-ins to make sure everything is in order. If you notice any damage in a cottage just after arriving, inform your rental company immediately. A little extra caution on your part will help prevent any misunderstanding about who caused the damage. Remember that rental companies are anxious to please you, but they also answer to their owners.

If anything is damaged during your stay or is determined missing after you leave, expect to have an amount deducted from your security deposit. Cottages that allow pets usually require an extra deposit for possible pet damage and a standard fee for flea extermination after you and your pet depart.

HURRICANE EVACUATION REFUNDS

Most rental companies now offer insurance with each reservation made. In accordance with North Carolina's Vacation Rental Act, if a guest buys vacation insurance, or if a guest is offered insurance but declines the offer, the real estate company is not required to reimburse that guest for any rental days that he or she loses as a result of hurricane evacuation. Each rental company sets its own policy governing refunds in the event of a hurricane. The few remaining companies that do not offer insurance generally may issue a partial or full refund in the event of a mandatory evacuation. Each area's local government officials are ultimately responsible for issuing evacuation orders. The County of Currituck has jurisdiction over Corolla and the four-wheel-drive beach areas, Hyde County has jurisdiction over Ocracoke, and Dare County governs every place in between.

The island of Ocracoke is usually evacuated before all other areas because access and egress is only by ferry or boat, and the rough waters stirred up by a hurricane even hundreds of miles away will make passage difficult or impossible as the storm approaches. Hatteras Island also tends to evacuate early because sections of NC 12 quickly flood when waters rise. If a mandatory evacuation of your area is ordered, comply.

Most rental companies will not issue refunds for days you don't occupy the property once reentry is permitted. Most Ocracoke property managers make exceptions for refunds in case the ferries aren't operating. These policies do vary from business to business, so make inquiries along with your reservation.

Consider buying travel insurance, which will protect your vacation investment in a variety of unexpected scenarios.

HANDLING/INSPECTION FEES & TAXES

Some rental companies charge a handling fee for processing information and an inspection fee for cottage inspection following your checkout. This is a nonrefundable fee assessed in addition to other charges.

In Dare County a combined 12.75 percent tax is added to all rents and fees. The taxes in Currituck County total 13.75 percent.

PET RULES & COSTS

Some cottage owners allow guests to bring pets, within certain limits, but you'll be assessed extra fees for the privilege. You can usually count on an extra cleaning and extermination fee and a higher security deposit. Rental companies will often restrict the size of the pets accepted (for example, dogs up to 75 pounds), but if your pet does not conform to the restrictions, ask the rental manager if it's possible to make an exception. Many companies will contact the cottage owner in an attempt to accommodate a reasonable request. Be aware, too, that some cottages will allow dogs but not cats and vice versa. Whatever you do, don't bring a pet "illegally"—this is almost always grounds for eviction without a refund.

CHECK-IN & CHECKOUT TIMES

Of course you're anxious to begin your vacation, but you'll save yourself (and others) aggravation if you respect check-in and checkout times. Rental companies need this time to clean and inspect cottages and perform minor maintenance.

Checkout is usually by 10 a.m.; check-in is usually at 4 p.m., give or take an hour. (These standard times account for the heavy traffic on Saturday and Sunday mornings and afternoons.) Most companies allow you to occupy your cottage earlier if it has been serviced properly, but don't arrive expecting this. If you want to travel during off-peak hours in the summer and plan to arrive several hours before check-in, head for one of the beach access areas that has showers and changing facilities, and just plan to spend the time relaxing. If you plan to check in after the rental company's office closes, most will make arrangements to leave your keys and cottage information in an outside box for pickup.

Be prompt when you check out. This is a courtesy to the rental company and the next guest. You might be assessed an extra fee if you overstay your welcome!

OCCUPANCY

The number of people your cottage can accommodate is listed in the description of the property in the rental brochure. This is determined by the number and type of beds and the septic and water capacity. Do not exceed the maximum occupancy or you could risk eviction. Most rental companies rent to family groups only and will not rent to minors. Any violation of this policy could result in a ruined vacation—and no refund.

MAIL, TELEPHONE, WI-FI & FAX SERVICES

When you make a reservation, you can request the cottage's phone number to leave with those back home who may need to reach you. Often the cottage's physical address and telephone number are printed on your lease, which you'll receive after making your initial payment. Almost all cottages have telephones these days, although a few of the older ones do not (and with the proliferation of cell phones, this may not be a problem for you). At any rate, the caveat once again is to know exactly what you're renting. Of course, you'll be required to pay for long-distance calls, and many home owners have a block on their lines to prevent direct-dialed long-distance calls. Either bring along a calling card or buy a prepaid phone card, but don't make calls from your cottage that will be charged to the home owner.

If you expect to receive mail while on vacation, ask the reservationist for the proper mailing address and make sure you tell your correspondents to mark the envelope clearly with your name and cottage identification. The same common sense applies if you expect to receive faxes while you're on vacation. Most rental companies either have a fax machine set aside for guest use or will let you use theirs, but a fee is almost always charged. If you're expecting something important, it's a good idea to instruct the sender to call you when the fax has been sent to be sure it arrives. Rental companies are exceptionally busy during summer and peak holiday times, so your fax might be one of a few dozen that comes in over the course of a day.

If wireless Internet access is important to you while staying on the Outer Banks, be sure to check your rental cottage description. It will be listed, if the home offers this service. Most real estate companies offer this search option to help choose a home.

TRASH PICKUP & RECYCLING

Rental companies usually supply information on designated trash pickup days in the check-in packet. When you check out, bag your refuse securely and make sure the receptacle sits beside the road, ready for pickup.

Recycling is with few exceptions the renter's responsibility. Some communities provide recycling service and the proper bins, but in most areas you'll need to carry your recyclables to one of the collection points. Ask your rental company for the location nearest your cottage and for sorting instructions.

Many beach access areas now have recycling bins in addition to trash cans to keep the beach litter free.

EQUIPMENT RENTALS & RELATED SERVICES

If you'd rather not take everything with you to the beach, Outer Banks equipment rental companies from north to south can provide almost anything you need or want, including baby furniture, beach chairs, umbrellas, bicycles, linens, fishing gear, grills, and more. You can also rent recreational equipment such as personal watercraft, boogie boards, surfboards, and kayaks. Check the Water Sports chapter for companies that specialize in these. The following listings cover companies that supply the widest variety of equipment and services.

AT YOUR SERVICE
(252) 261-5286
www.atyourserviceobx.com

Serving the needs of vacationers on the Outer Banks since 1988, At Your Service takes on such tiresome chores as running errands and buying groceries by acting as your personal concierge. The service has babysitters (it's the oldest babysitting and elder-care service on the Outer Banks). It can also help in stocking your vacation cottage with groceries and other necessities before you arrive, providing linens and cleaning service, arranging in-house personal chef service, and seeing to details to make a vacation run smoothly. At Your Service has a well-trained and competent staff. For more information, see the Education and Child Care chapter.

OCEAN ATLANTIC RENTALS
Corolla Light Town Center, Corolla
(252) 453-2440, (800) 635-9559
www.oceanatlanticrentals.com

Ocean Atlantic combines quality equipment with reasonable rates and full service to give you the best values in rental ware on the beach. All baby items meet federal safety standards, and Ocean Atlantic uses well-known brand-name equipment. Beach umbrellas and chairs, bikes, cribs, TVs, DVD players, kayaks, linens, grills, the latest videos and DVDs, and water sports equipment are among the items Ocean Atlantic offers. Surfing lessons for all skill levels are taught out of their four locations. Ocean Atlantic also has a full-service wedding rental package complete with dance floors and tents. Other locations are at: Duck Road, Soundfront, Duck, (252) 261-4346; US 158, MP 9.75, Kill Devil Hills, (252) 441-7823; and NC 12, Avon, (252) 995-5868.

MONEYSWORTH BEACH HOME EQUIPMENT RENTALS
947 West Kitty Hawk Rd., Kitty Hawk
(252) 261-6999, (800) 833-5233
www.mworth.com

With Moneysworth, all items are delivered to your vacation home on your check-in day and picked up after you check out. This company has a wide assortment of beach and sports equipment, TVs, DVD players, grills, baby items, linens and bicycles. And the best part is you do not have to be present for delivery or pickup service. They'll deliver whatever you need from Ocean Hill to Hatteras Village.

JUST FOR THE BEACH RENTALS
501 Old Stoney Rd., Corolla
(866) 629-7368

Delivery is available from Nags Head to Corolla, or you can stop in the store to browse through numerous items. Beach equipment, bikes, baby supplies, linens, fishing rods, and beach wheelchairs are among the items this company leases. Another location is at NC 12, MP 9, Kill Devil Hills, (252) 441-6048.

METRO RENTALS
US 158 and Colington Road, MP 8, Kill Devil Hills
(252) 480-3535, (866) 490-3535
www.metrorentalobx.com

This company specializes in wedding and catering needs, party supplies and tents, heavy equipment, and beachcombing devices such as metal detectors. Delivery to anywhere on the Outer Banks.

BEACH OUTFITTERS
NC 12, Ocracoke
(252) 928-6261
www.ocracokeislandrealty.com

Beach Outfitters, at Ocracoke Island Realty, is open all year and accepts reservations. Free delivery and pickup are available on Ocracoke Island with an order of more than $100. Available rental items include beach chairs and umbrellas, towels and linens, bikes, rollaway beds, baby equipment, TVs, DVD players, steamer pots, and kitchen appliances.

COTTAGE RENTAL COMPANIES

Many rental companies have more than one office, so check the listing to see which areas they serve. Listings proceed from north to south.

A company's inventory of cottages can change from year to year, but almost all companies offer some accommodations that allow pets, a few wheelchair-accessible cottages, and partial-week rentals in the mid- and off-seasons. In the following listings, we concentrate on which areas companies cover and approximately how many cottages they represent. We recommend that you contact companies directly for comprehensive information. Nearly all will supply you with a free brochure or catalog of their rental properties.

Corolla

TWIDDY & COMPANY REALTORS
1127A Schoolhouse Ln., Corolla
(252) 457-1100, (800) 489-4339
www.twiddy.com

Twiddy & Company offers exceptional Outer Banks vacation rentals from Carova to Southern Shores. Special event and wheelchair-accessible homes are available, as are homes from the oceanfront to the sound. Weddings, corporate retreats, and other functions can be accommodated. Many of Twiddy's choice homes include private pools and spas; pets are allowed at some accommodations.

SUN REALTY
1135 Ocean Trail, Corolla
(252) 453-8822, (888) 853-7770
www.sunrealtync.com
Sun Realty is one of the largest realty companies on the Outer Banks, with more than 25 years of making Outer Banks vacationers' dreams come true. Sun Realty prides itself on providing the highest level of customer service and lists the largest selection and variety of homes on the Outer Banks. A concierge is available within each Sun Realty location to help plan special events.

COROLLA CLASSIC VACATIONS
1196 Ocean Trail, Corolla
(866) 453-9660
www.corollaclassicvacations.com
Corolla Classic Vacations manages vacation homes in the Corolla area, including Pine Island, Ocean Sands, Ocean Lake, Crown Point, Ocean Hill, and Corolla Village. Many of the homes are equipped with elevators and are wheelchair accessible. Properties with access to golf, tennis, private pools, and hot tubs are available, and some units allow pets. Beds are made and bath towels are ready upon your arrival.

ÉLAN VACATIONS
Hunt Club Dr., Currituck Club Center, Corolla
(866) 760-ELAN
www.elanvacations.com
Élan Vacations is a full-service travel company representing luxurious vacation homes along the Outer Banks. Élan Vacations likes to provide a relaxing and fun-filled experience with highly personalized service to guests

and owners. A concierge is available who can reserve anything from maid service to hang-gliding lessons to dinner reservations at your favorite restaurant. Élan guests are greeted with an assortment of gifts, including select North Carolina wine, coffee, and other Élan products.

RESORTQUEST OUTER BANKS VACATION RENTALS
(800) 962-0201
www.resortquest.com/vrp/destinations/outerbanks
ResortQuest Outer Banks Vacation Rentals offers an outstanding choice of rental homes and rental condos with luxurious space, multiple rooms, fully appointed kitchens and baths, and other thoughtful details of home. Close to these rental homes are some of the country's most unforgettable beaches, golfing, fishing, and more. ResortQuest Outer Banks has rental homes from Kill Devil Hills to the Villages at Ocean Hill in Corolla.

KARICHELE REALTY
TimBuck II Shopping Village
66 Sunset Blvd., Corolla
(252) 453-4400, (800) 453-2377
www.karichele.com
Karichele Realty manages properties in Corolla and the four-wheel-drive area. During the off-season, weekend packages are available. Pets allowed in some units. Wheelchair-accessible cottages also are available.

STAN WHITE REALTY & CONSTRUCTION INC.
812 Ocean Trail, Corolla
(252) 453-9619, (800) 338-3233
www.outerbanksrentals.com
This is the northern beaches location for Stan White Realty, renting properties from

Whalehead to Nags Head. This location serves as the check-in office for rentals in and around Corolla.

VILLAGE REALTY

501B Hunt Club Dr., Corolla
(252) 453-9650, (877) 546-5362
www.villagerealtyobx.com

The northern beaches' location of Village Realty represents oceanfront, soundfront, and in-between homes in Pine Island, Ocean Sands Whalehead, Corolla Light, and the Currituck Club, the only golf community on the Currituck Outer Banks. Rentals at the Currituck Club include use of the pool, fitness center, and other amenities. Ask about golf packages.

Duck

SUN REALTY

1187 Duck Rd., Duck
(252) 261-7911, (888) 853-7770
www.sunrealtync.com

Sun Realty is one of the largest realty companies on the Outer Banks, with seven locations. Sun Realty prides itself on providing a high level of customer service and lists the largest selection and variety of homes on the Outer Banks. A concierge is available within each Sun Realty location to help plan special events.

CAROLINA DESIGNS REALTY

Village Square, 1197 NC 12, Duck
(252) 261-3934, (800) 368-3825
www.carolinadesigns.com

Carolina Designs manages weekly rentals ranging from one-bedroom condos to eight-bedroom estates, with linens included. Properties are primarily from Corolla to Southern Shores and Nags Head. Many of the homes have pools and allow pets and most offer wireless Internet.

DUCK'S REAL ESTATE A STAN WHITE COMPANY

1232 NC 12, Duck
(252) 261-4614, (800) 992-2976
www.outerbanksrentals.com

Duck's Real Estate manages weekly rentals from Corolla to Southern Shores. Three-day golf packages also are available. Pets are accepted in some units. Some cottages are wheelchair accessible.

TWIDDY & COMPANY REALTORS

1181 NC 12, Duck
(252) 457-1100, (800) 489-4339
www.twiddy.com

Twiddy & Company manages rental properties from Carova to Southern Shores and offers several specialty properties that accommodate weddings, corporate retreats, and other special functions. A special-events coordinator can be recommended. All of the company's cottages include linen and towel service as a standard amenity. A number of cottages allow pets. Many include private pools and spas.

Southern Shores

SOUTHERN SHORES REALTY

5 Ocean Blvd., Southern Shores
NC 12, Kitty Hawk
(252) 261-2111, (800) 334-1000
www.southernshores.com

Southern Shores Realty manages year-round and weekly rentals throughout the Outer Banks. Weekend packages also are available year-round. Dogs are accepted in some units. Ramps and elevators are offered in some cottages.

Kitty Hawk

ATLANTIC REALTY

US 158, MP 2½, Kitty Hawk
(252) 261-2154, (800) 334-8401
(252) 453-4110, (800) 669-9245 in
Corolla
www.atlanticrealty-nc.com

This company manages rental homes and condominiums from Corolla to South Nags Head for year-round and seasonal rental. Pets are accepted in some units.

KITTY DUNES REALTY

US 158, Kitty Hawk
(252) 261-2326, (800) 334-DUNE
www.kittydunes.com

Kitty Dunes manages rental properties from Corolla to South Nags Head. Most properties rent by the week, but long-term rentals are offered in Colington Harbour. Three-night weekend packages are often available, even during the summer. Pets are accepted in many units, and a few cottages are wheelchair accessible. Some properties include private pools and spas.

JOE LAMB JR. & ASSOCIATES

US 158, MP 2, Kitty Hawk
(252) 261-4444, (800) 552-6257
www.joelambjr.com

This company manages properties ranging from 2-bedroom cottages to 13-bedroom homes and year-round rentals from Corolla to South Nags Head. Three-night packages are offered during the off-season. Pets are accepted in some cottages. Wheelchair-accessible rentals are also available. Units in some developments include pool access. Many have private pools.

SEASIDE VACATIONS

1070D Ocean Trail, Corolla
(252) 255-5500, (888) 685-9581
www.outerbanksvacations.com

Seaside Vacations offers the best service possible for every guest. The company represents a select group of vacation rental accommodations. Properties range from Corolla to South Nags Head and include condominiums, cottages, and palatial oceanfront estates. Staff members have personally visited every property and can make the best recommendations for a property based on a guest's needs. Another location is at 5727 South Croatan Hwy., MP 13.8, Nags Head.

PRUDENTIAL RESORT REALTY

3608 North Croatan Hwy., Kitty Hawk
(252) 261-8282
www.resortrealty.com

Prudential Resort Realty manages weekly rental properties from Corolla to South Nags Head. Some three-night packages are available with a maximum of five days' notice. Some cottages allow pets. Renters leasing a special resort club home can check in as early as 11 a.m. Other locations are at: 791-A Sunset Blvd., TimBuck II Shopping Village, Corolla, (252) 453-8700; 1248 Duck Rd., Duck, (252) 261-8888; and 5129 South Croatan Hwy., Nags Head, (252) 441-5000, (800) 458-3830.

WRIGHT PROPERTY MANAGEMENT (WPM)

US 158, MP 4¾
3719 North Croatan Hwy., Kitty Hawk
(252) 261-2186, (800) 276-7478
www.wpmobx.com

Wright Property Management offers cottages and condominiums for weekly, partial-week, or year-round rentals from Duck to South Nags Head. Some WPM units offer swimming pools, tennis facilities, hot tubs, and private pools; many units will accept pets. Rentals can be booked tentatively on the website or from 9 a.m. to 5 p.m. by telephone. Wright Property Management specializes in affordable cottage rentals for Outer Banks vacationers.

Kill Devil Hills

BEACH REALTY & CONSTRUCTION/ KITTY HAWK RENTALS
US 158, MP 6, Kill Devil Hills
(252) 441-7166, (800) 635-1559
(252) 261-6605 in Duck
(252) 453-4141 in Corolla
www.beachrealtync.com
This company manages properties from Ocean Hill to South Nags Head. Some are available for year-round rental, but most rent by the week. Several of the properties are wheelchair accessible, and pets are accepted in some other units.

GATEWAY REALTY
William E. Wood Building, Kill Devil Hills
(252) 480-0093, (800) 633-4491
www.gatewayobx.com
Gateway specializes in sales, long-term rentals, and property management from North Currituck beaches to South Nags Head. Gateway currently manages more than 130 long-term and summer/student rentals.

SUN REALTY
US 158, MP 0, Kitty Hawk
(252) 261-1152, (800) 346-9593
www.sunrealtync.com

Sun Realty offers the largest inventory of rental properties on the Outer Banks from Corolla through Hatteras Island. Weekly, monthly, and year-round rentals are available. A special program for disabled guests is offered. Pets are accepted in some units. Check out Sun Realty's Guest Advantage rewards program. Other locations are at: US 158, MP 9, Kill Devil Hills, (252) 441-7033, (800) 334-4745; NC 12, Salvo, (252) 987-2766, (800) 345-0910; and NC 12, Avon, (252) 995-5865, (800) 345-0910.

Nags Head

OUTER BANKS RESORT RENTALS
Croatan Centre, MP 13½
Nags Head
(252) 441-2134
www.outerbanksresorts.com
Ronda Williams manages the sales and rentals of time-shares from Duck to South Nags as well as a few in Hatteras. Sixteen time-share resorts are represented.

i If you're traveling in Kitty Hawk, Kill Devil Hills, or Nags Head and the Bypass is congested, try driving along NC 12. Although the speed limit is 35 mph, it can actually get you to your destination more quickly on higher-traffic days.

COVE REALTY
Between NC 12 and US 158
MP 13½, Nags Head
(252) 441-6391, (800) 635-7007
www.coverealty.com
Cove Realty manages properties in Old Nags Head Cove and South Nags Head for year-round, weekly, and student rental. Pets are accepted in some units. Weekend packages are available during the off-season. Guests

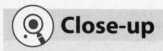

Close-up

Old Nags Head: Authentic Outer Banks Architecture

For much of the 19th century, Nags Head was a getaway for the wealthy; a place to relax and recuperate; a safe haven from disease and so-called toxic vapors that doctors believed promoted illness. Summer after summer, growing families and networks of friends made this then-isolated beach one of the East Coast's most popular resort communities.

The Nags Head of yesteryear is still evident in a milelong row of cottages that line the oceanfront east of Jockey's Ridge. Weathered and stately, about a dozen homes built between 1860 and 1940 best characterize the unique Nags Head–style architecture that has become one of the Outer Banks' signatures. State historians say the Nags Head Beach Cottage Row Historic District is one of the few turn-of-the-20th-century resort areas remaining on the Eastern Seaboard that has maintained its original character.

For the last few Septembers, Preservation North Carolina, a private nonprofit historic preservation group, has opened up many of the Nags Head cottages, with the owners' cooperation, for public tours. Scores of people eagerly took the group up on the offer, strolling from house to house and meeting the owners, some of whom spent almost every summer of their lives in the family's Nags Head oceanside retreat.

The beach cottages were designed to be functional and practical. Most notable for large porches lined with windproof built-in benches that wrap around three, even four, sides, the houses feature unpainted wooden siding, weathered by salt air to a deep brown, and angled porches and roofs. Shuttered windows offer ready shelter from sun and wind, but they are easily propped open with an attached stick. Pilings boost the floors away from encroaching waves. And if the ocean came a little too close for comfort, the houses were made to be moved easily. Some already have been moved away from the surf four times.

Most of the homes are 1- or 2-stories and have three or four bedrooms. Stairwells to upper floors are narrow and the steps are creaky and often uneven. In some places on the first floor, you can see through cracks to the scrubby plants and sand beneath the house. All houses now have flush toilets, rather than employing the former outhouses, but many still depend only on the original outdoor shower installed away from the living quarters. Former servants' quarters have been changed into spare bedrooms, offices, or storage areas. Most cottages now have new kitchens in former breezeways, which separated the original kitchens from living space for heat and safety reasons.

What hasn't changed is the remarkable airiness and light that the rooms are effused in—and the way the steady heaving and sighing of ocean waves dominate the background sounds. The homes were all designed to foster air circulation; many cottage owners find no need for air-conditioning. Seabreezes flip and billow curtains away from bedroom windows, opening to spectacular oceanfront vistas.

Although there was already a thriving resort community near what is now Soundside Road in Nags Head, no one dared build near the Atlantic until 1866, when Dr. William Gaskins Pool erected the first beachfront house on the Outer Banks. According to historical documents, Pool paid $30 for 50 acres of land along the Atlantic. In the interest of securing companionship, he gave 130-foot-wide lots away to friends, who built their own homes. Eventually others followed, and one of the oldest beachfront settlements in the state took hold. The 13 original Nags Head cottages were built between the end of the Civil War and World War II's onset.

Some cottages that have been part of the Preservation North Carolina tours include:

The Windemere
Erected by well-known builder S. J. Twine, who constructed many of the cottages in the historic district, this 1-story house was completed in the 1930s.

Fred Wood Cottage
This 2-story house, also constructed by Twine, has two gable-end chimneys and a covered porch surrounding all four sides.

Whedbee Cottage
One of the few Civil War–era homes, this 2-story frame home was finished in 1866.

Badham-Kittrell Cottage
Another house built by Twine, this 1928 home is one story with an L-shaped wing extending from the back of the house. The second level perches over the main living area.

Miss Mattie Midgett's Store
Moved from the soundside in 1933, this 1914 store supplied vacationers and locals with groceries, mail, and the area's only telephone. It still houses the booty from years of beachcombing by Miss Mattie's daughter, Nellie Myrtle.

Martha Wood Cottage
This 2-story house was likely built in 1870 or earlier. Possibly the oldest of the historic district's remaining cottages, it is distinguished by two projecting dormers on the beach side and a small, L-shaped addition in the rear.

The Silver Cottage
This home was built in 1883 when its original owner paid $6.06 in annual taxes. For more information about future tours, please call **Preservation North Carolina** at (252) 832-1651 in Raleigh or (252) 482-7455 in Edenton.

have access, for a small fee, to a swimming pool as well as to tennis courts in Old Nags Head Cove.

NAGS HEAD REALTY

US 158, MP 10½, Nags Head
(252) 441-4315, (800) 222-1531
www.nagsheadrealty.com

Nags Head Realty manages weekly rentals from the Crown Point development in the northern beaches to South Nags Head. Three-day rentals are offered during the off-season. Some units accept pets.

RENTALS ON THE OCEAN

US 158, MP 16½, Nags Head
(252) 441-5005
www.rentalsontheocean.com

Do you want to reserve your spot on the beach and bring Fido, too? Rentals on the Ocean may have just what you're looking for. They offer cottages for families of all sizes from 2 to 26, and all their cottages accept pets. Every cottage is either oceanfront or oceanview. Rentals on the Ocean offers cottages year-round.

STAN WHITE REALTY & CONSTRUCTION INC.

US 158, MP 10½, Nags Head
(252) 441-1515, (800) 338-3233
www.outerbanksrentals.com

Stan White Realty likes to find the perfect rental home for families, renting from Whalehead to Nags Head. Weekly and year-round rentals are available. Pets are allowed in some of the weekly rentals. Wheelchair-accessible units are available. Two other Stan White offices are on the northern beaches, one in Corolla and one in Duck, called Duck's Real Estate.

VILLAGE REALTY

US 158, MP 14½, Nags Head
(252) 480-2224, (800) 548-9688
www.villagerealtyobx.com

You are in good hands when you choose to rent from Village Realty. Properties from Nags Head to Corolla are available. Linens and towels are provided for every stay. Beds are made for clients before check in. Special weekend and golf packages are available. Some cottages allow pets. Some have elevators and can accommodate disabled vacationers. Complimentary 24-hour holds are offered while you and your party are making your rental home decision. Village Realty has a second office at the Currituck Club in Corolla.

Roanoke Island

PIRATE'S COVE REALTY

Nags Head–Manteo Causeway, Manteo
(252) 473-6800, (888) 314-5795
www.pirates-cove.com

Pirate's Cove Realty manages properties in the Pirate's Cove Resort for weekly rentals. Two-night weekends also are offered during the off-season. Some cottages accept pets. All units include access to an outdoor swimming pool, tennis courts, playground, and free boat slips. Pirate's Cove Realty also manages properties at the Shallowbag Bay Club, a nearby development on the water closer to downtown Manteo. These one- to three-bedroom luxury waterfront condominiums are in an upscale marina. Several secluded waterfront properties are also offered in downtown Manteo.

Hatteras Island

AVON COTTAGES
NC 12, Avon
(252) 995-4123
www.avoncottages.com

Each of Avon Cottages' rental homes has a magnificent view of the Atlantic Ocean. Eight are oceanfront, 7 are semi-oceanfront, and 11 are oceanside, ranging from one to five bedrooms. All cottages have a large combination living room/dining room/kitchen, plus central heat and air, a microwave oven, and remote color TV with HBO. Fully equipped kitchens include plates and utensils; you may bring your own sheets and towels or rent them on-site. Laundry facilities, outside showers, and fish-cleaning tables are provided. Parking is also available.

COLONY REALTY CORP.
NC 12, Avon
(252) 995-5891, (800) 962-5256
www.hatterasvacations.com

Colony handles affordable weekly units and long-term rentals in Avon, Buxton, Frisco, and Hatteras. Most of the units, which are single-family cottages or condos, will accept pets. Three-day minimum stays can be arranged in the off-season. Several wheelchair-accessible units are available. Colony Realty specializes in reasonably priced Cape Hatteras family vacations.

DOLPHIN REALTY
NC 12, Hatteras Village
(800) 338-4775
www.dolphin-realty.com

This company manages properties, including homes and one-room efficiencies, throughout Hatteras Island. Some are available for year-round rental. Pets are accepted in some units.

HATTERAS REALTY
NC 12, Avon
(252) 995-5466, (800) 428-8372
www.hatterasrealty.com

Hatteras Realty manages properties on Hatteras Island for weekly rental only. Units may be rented by partial weeks during the offseason. Pets are accepted in some units. Wheelchair-accessible cottages are available. Every guest has free access to the pool and tennis courts at Club Hatteras. Vacationers have depended on Hatteras Realty for their accommodations since 1983. A fee-based kid's program for ages 4 to 12 both entertains and educates the little ones.

MIDGETT REALTY
NC 12, Hatteras Village
(866) 348-8819
www.midgettrealty.com

Midgett Realty manages properties from Rodanthe to Hatteras Village for weekly rentals. Three-night rentals are available during the off-season, and some units accept pets. Several wheelchair-accessible units are offered. Serving Hatteras Island has been a family tradition for more than 100 years.

OUTER BEACHES REALTY
NC 12, Avon, Waves and Rodanthe
(800) 627-1850
www.outerbeaches.com

Outer Beaches Realty manages a large selection of rental cottages from Rodanthe to Hatteras Village. Weekly and three-day rentals are available. A few allow pets. Some wheelchair-accessible properties also are offered. Dedicated exclusively to Hatteras Island, Outer Beaches Realty offers the island's largest selection of vacation rental cottages. Upon check-in you'll find a starter amenities bag inside your cottage. Concierge services are available, as well as luxurious signature Elite homes.

i What's the weather like? During summer, of course, expect hot days and balmy nights. In spring and fall temperatures can range from the 80s to the 40s. Winter weather fluctuates from warm (70s) and sunny to starkly cold (30s and 40s), with averages in the 50s. Bring a variety of clothing for maximum comfort.

SURF OR SOUND REALTY
NC 12, Avon
(252) 995-5801, (800) 237-1138
www.surforsound.com
Surf or Sound Realty offers almost 500 cottages on Hatteras Island. Pets are accepted in some units. Wheelchair-accessible rentals also are available. You can make reservations on the website.

Ocracoke Island

OCRACOKE ISLAND REALTY INC.
NC 12, Ocracoke Village
(252) 928-6261, (877) 646-2822
www.ocracokeislandrealty.com
Ocracoke Island Realty manages weekly rental properties on Ocracoke. Three-night packages are available during the off-season. A few of these cottages allow pets.

YEAR-ROUND RENTALS

It can be quite a challenge to find a suitable property for long-term residential rental. However, it's not terribly difficult to find what most people on the Outer Banks call a "winter rental," a time period that usually refers to late fall through early spring, when the cottage is not usually booked for weekly rentals. If you're looking for year-round residential or seasonal accommodations during summer, you'll need to begin your search as soon as possible.

Some rental companies deal lightly in long-term rentals, but few make it a specialty. It's worth some phone calls to the companies that specialize in the areas in which you're interested, but a better bet is probably to check the classifieds in the local newspapers. If you plan to spend the summer working on the Outer Banks, ask your employer for suggestions. Some smart businesspeople are beginning to help their seasonal workers by offering housing.

Good places to look for long-term rentals are in Colington Harbour, on Roanoke Island, and between the highways in Nags Head, Kill Devil Hills, and Kitty Hawk. Southern Shores has a large year-round community. Currituck County, just north of the Wright Memorial Bridge, also offers some affordable options.

The following companies manage year-round rentals: Atlantic Realty, Colony Realty Corporation, Cove Realty, Dolphin Realty, Gateway Realty, Jim Perry & Company, Joe Lamb Jr. & Associates, Kitty Dunes Realty, Kitty Hawk Rentals/Beach Realty & Construction, Seaside Vacations, Southern Shores Realty, Stan White Realty & Construction, Sun Realty, and Wright Property Management. These companies are listed in greater detail earlier in this chapter or in the Real Estate chapter.

CAMPING

Imagine drifting off to sleep on a bed of soft sand with the murmur of waves gently kissing the sandy shoreline. A whispering breeze ruffles your tent, ushering in the sounds of nocturnal creatures and the salt-laden air. Now imagine waking up to a spectacular sunrise over the ocean as gulls begin to wheel and turn above the waves and dolphins play just off the beach. Welcome to an experience you won't soon forget—camping on the Outer Banks. From spring through autumn, lovers of the outdoors make their way to the numerous campgrounds that line these barrier islands to experience nature. Whether choosing to bed down with nothing more than a tent and a sleeping bag or deciding to "camp" in a recreational vehicle, opportunities abound.

OVERVIEW

More than 100,000 people frequent the National Park Service campgrounds for their home away from home each year, while thousands of other nature lovers set up camp at privately owned campgrounds. Some private campgrounds only open during the summer season, offering few creature comforts besides cold showers, but others are year-round establishments providing electric and water hookups, sewage disposal, laundry facilities, swimming pools, game rooms, bathhouses, and cable television. Some campgrounds rent furnished RVs. All have well-maintained roads and drive-up sites that accommodate any type of vehicle. Note that taxes are not included in any of the prices quoted.

National Park Service campgrounds operate under the same rules and regulations and charge the same fees. NPS campgrounds do not take reservations (except the Ocracoke Campground between Memorial Day and Labor Day) and accept payment in cash or credit cards upon arrival. Sites operate on a first-come, first-served basis. The National Park Service provides lifeguards at Coquina Beach, Cape Hatteras Lighthouse, south of the Frisco Pier at Sandy Bay, and on Ocracoke Island. For more information on any of the local NPS campgrounds, call (252) 473-2111, and check the NPS website for the most up-to-date information on the opening and closing dates of each campground: www.nps.gov/caha.

Camping on the beach is prohibited, as is wilderness camping in open areas, including Nags Head Woods, Kitty Hawk Woods, and Buxton Woods. But there is one spot where wilderness camping is allowed— Portsmouth Island. This now-uninhabited island is accessible only by boat.

Remember, these islands are home to a variety of wildlife, locals included. Please respect their homes by not littering or disturbing the environment in any way. We want to keep it just the way it is so you can enjoy camping again next year.

NORTH OF OREGON INLET

JOE & KAY'S CAMPGROUND
Colington Road, Little Colington Island
(252) 441-5468

About a mile west on Colington Road, before you get to the first bridge, Joe & Kay's Campground has 70 full hookup sites rented on a yearly basis. An additional 15 tent sites are also available from April through November. Call for rates. Reservations aren't accepted, so sites are secured on a first-come, first-served basis. Credit cards and personal checks are not accepted.

OREGON INLET CAMPGROUND (NPS)
NC 12, Bodie Island
(252) 473-2111
www.nps.gov/caha

The northernmost National Park Service campground on the Outer Banks, this facility offers 120 sites along the windswept dunes just north of Oregon Inlet. If you're arriving from the north, look for the campground entrance on the east side of NC 12 just before crossing the Bonner Bridge. It is located on the ocean almost directly across from the Oregon Inlet Fishing Center. Water, cold showers, modern toilets, picnic tables, and charcoal grills are available here. There aren't any utility connections, but dumping stations are nearby. Most of these sites are in sunny, exposed areas on the sand. Park rangers suggest that campers bring awnings, umbrellas, or other sources of shade. You may need mosquito netting and long tent stakes. Oregon Inlet Campground is open Apr through Oct. Campers

are limited to a two-week stay. Reservations are not accepted, and sites are assigned on a first-come, first-served basis. Fees begin at $20 per night. Golden Age Passport holders receive a 50 percent discount. This campground accepts cash, credit cards, and personal checks.

HATTERAS ISLAND

CAPE HATTERAS KOA
NC 12, Rodanthe
(252) 987-2307, (800) 562-5268
www.koa.com

A large campground approximately 14 miles south of the Bonner Bridge across Oregon Inlet, Cape Hatteras KOA has about 300 sites, including one- and two-room "Kamping Kabins." These units feature locking doors, ceiling fans, electricity, and picnic tables, and each has a porch. Ask about wheelchair-accessible units. Friendly, attentive staff greet campers as they arrive at this well-equipped campground. The campground is open Mar 1 through Nov and accepts reservations.

Besides hot showers, drinking water, and bathhouses, Cape Hatteras KOA offers campers a dump station, laundry facilities, two pools, a hot tub, a playground, a game room, a restaurant, and a well-stocked general store. Campers can even take in a round or two of miniature golf or a whirl on the campground's "Fun Bike"—a low-slung three-wheeler ridden inside the park. The ocean is just beyond the dunes for fishing and swimming, and the sound is the perfect place to fish, crab, or watch spectacular sunsets. The campground's recreation program offers varied activities in the summer. Rates are extremely variable according to proximity to the beach, season, and accommodations.

Call or check the website for details. Significant savings are available in the off-season, from Dec 1 through Mar 1. Prices do not include tax.

RODANTHE WATERSPORTS AND SHORELINE CAMPGROUND
NC 12, Rodanthe
(252) 987-1431
www.watersportsandcampground.com

This soundfront campground is open year-round for recreational vehicles and tents. Sail-boarders and kiteboarders especially enjoy this campground because they can sail right to some of the campsites. Other campers enjoy swimming, boating, and fishing in the sound. The water sports business next door rents kayaks, sailboats, Wave-Runners, surfboards, and bicycles (see the Water Sports chapter). But what really keeps campers coming back are the spectacular, unobstructed sunset views.

Hot showers, picnic tables, and a few grills are on-site. If you'd rather not cook, you can grab a pizza from Lisa's Pizzeria right next door (see the Restaurants chapter). Pets are allowed. Reservations are recommended. Personal checks and credit cards are accepted. Call for nightly rates. When you pay for six nights, the seventh night is free.

NORTH BEACH CAMPGROUND
NC 12, Rodanthe
(252) 987-2378

In the village of Rodanthe, North Beach Campground sits alongside the ocean south of the Chicamacomico Lifesaving Station. Here 110 sites, all with water and electric hookups, offer campers both tent and RV accommodations and a wide range of amenities. Bathhouse, hot showers, picnic tables, a laundry facility, an outdoor swimming pool, and a pump-out station are available. There aren't any grills here, and open fires aren't allowed, so bring your own grill or camp stove if you want to cook. North Beach Campground's grocery store sells fuel and convenience-store items. Pets are allowed on leashes. Reservations are accepted. The campground is open from Mar through Nov.

CAMP HATTERAS
NC 12, Rodanthe
(252) 987-2777
www.camphatteras.com

A 50-acre campground, Camp Hatteras is a complete facility open year-round, offering many amenities. The site includes 1,000 feet of ocean and sound frontage. Nightly and monthly reservations are accepted. All of Camp Hatteras's 400-plus sites have full hookups, concrete pads, and paved roads. Tent sites, laundry facilities, hot showers, full bathhouses, and picnic tables are also available. Camp Hatteras has expanded soundside with 92 paved full hookups.

For recreation this campground provides three swimming pools, a clubhouse, a pavilion, a marina, three stocked fishing ponds, two tennis courts, a nine-hole miniature golf course, volleyball, basketball, kayaks, sailboards, and shuffleboard. The jumping pillows, outdoor cinema theater, and an express train create more opportunities for all-ages fun. A free boat ramp for campers is available. Sports and camping areas are separate, so sleeping outdoors is still a quiet experience—even if you nap midday.

Call or go on the website for details about rates. Personal checks and credit cards are accepted. Pets are allowed on leashes for an additional fee. Wireless Internet is available.

OCEAN WAVES CAMPGROUND
NC 12, Waves
(252) 987-2556
www.oceanwavescampground.com

Open Mar 15 through Nov 15, Ocean Waves Campground is a seaside resort with sites for RVs and tents. Of 68 spaces, most offer full hookups and concrete pads. Each has its own picnic table. Three bathhouses, hot showers, and laundry facilities are available. Campers enjoy the game room and outdoor pool. Asphalt roadways are well maintained. Wi-Fi and a gameroom are available.

SANDS OF TIME CAMPGROUND
North End Road, Avon
(252) 995-5596
www.sandsoftimecampground.com

This year-round campground has 51 full hookup sites and 15 tent sites, some with full shade. Hot showers, flush toilets, laundry facilities, a dump site, picnic tables, and a pay telephone are offered to all Sands campers. Visitors enjoy swimming, fishing, and sunbathing at the nearby beach. The infamous Canadian Hole is just 2½ miles away, making this a great spot to stay for your kiteboarding or windsurfing vacation. Grills aren't provided, and open fires are not allowed. Bring your camp stove to cook. Pets are allowed on leashes. Reservations are accepted and recommended for summer and fall. Credit cards are not accepted.

CAPE WOODS CAMPGROUND
Buxton Back Road, Buxton
(252) 995-5850
www.capewoods.com

Clean, quiet, and green best describe this campground. Scattered throughout the pine, live oak, and ash trees are 125 sites, some for tents, some with water and electricity, and some with full hookups. Cape Woods is open year-round and gladly accepts reservations. This full-service campground provides fire pits, grills, and picnic tables, as well as hot showers in two bathhouses, one of which is wheelchair accessible and one of which is heated for winter campers. An outdoor swimming pool, a playground, a small game room, a volleyball court, and a horseshoe pit are also available. Children and grown-ups can freshwater fish in the surrounding canals. Laundry facilities are available, and ice and propane gas are for sale. Discounts are honored. It is open Mar through Dec.

CAPE POINT CAMPGROUND (NPS)
Off NC 12, Buxton
(252) 473-2111
www.nps.gov/caha

The largest National Park Service campground on the Outer Banks, Cape Point is about 2 miles south of the Cape Hatteras Lighthouse, across the dunes from the Atlantic. This campground has 202 sites—none with utility connections. It's open from Memorial Day through Sept but does not accept reservations.

Flush toilets, cold showers, drinking water, charcoal grills, and picnic tables are provided. Each site has paved access. A wheelchair-accessible area is available, and a dumping station is nearby.

The campground is a short walk from the ocean. Most of these sites sit in the open, exposed to the sun and wind. Bring some shade, long tent stakes, lots of bug spray, and batteries. Cost is $20 a night; pets are allowed on leashes.

✳FRISCO WOODS CAMPGROUND
Frisco Woods, off NC 12, Frisco
(252) 995-5208, (800) 948-3942
www.thefriscowoodscampground.com
This 30-acre soundside campground boasts abundant forest and marshland beauty and at least 150 sites in a wooded wonderland. Electricity and water are available at 122 campsites. Full hookups are offered at 35 other sites, and there are 100 tent sites. Cabins have air conditioning and electricity. Amenities include an in-ground swimming pool, picnic tables, hot showers, free Wi-Fi, a coin laundry, a small country store, propane gas, and public phones. Sailboarders like this campground because they can sail directly from the sites onto Pamlico Sound. This spot is definitely an insider favorite. Crabbing, fishing, kayaking, and wandering through the woods are also readily available to campers staying at Frisco Woods. Frisco Woods is open Mar 1 through Dec 1, and reservations are accepted. Pets are allowed on leashes. Weekly, monthly, and seasonal rates are available on request, and special event and group rates also are offered.

FRISCO CAMPGROUND (NPS)
NC 12, Frisco
(252) 473-2111
www.nps.gov/caha
Frisco Campground is operated by the National Park Service and sits about 4 miles southwest of Buxton. Just off the beach, next to ramp 49, this is the area's most isolated and elevated campground. Its undulating roads twist over dunes and around small hills, providing privacy at almost every site. Some tent areas are so secluded in stands of scrubby trees that you can't see them from where you park your car.

Frisco Campground has 127 no-frills sites, each with a charcoal grill and picnic table. Flush toilets, cold-water showers in bathhouses, and drinking water are available. There aren't any hookups here, but RVs are welcome. A wooden boardwalk crosses from the campground to the ocean.

Reservations aren't accepted; payment may be made with cash, credit cards, or personal checks. Call for rates. Pets are allowed on leashes. Frisco Campground is open Apr through Oct. Golden Age discounts are honored.

OCRACOKE ISLAND

TEETER'S CAMPGROUND
British Cemetery Road, Ocracoke Village
(252) 928-3135, (800) 705-5341
Near the heart of Ocracoke Village, tucked in a shady grove of trees, Teeter's Campground offers 2 full-hookup sites, 12 sites with electricity and water, and 10 tent sites. Hot showers are available. Six charcoal grills are installed at tent sites, and each site has a picnic table. There aren't any public laundry facilities on Ocracoke, so don't plan to machine wash any of your clothes. Call for rates. Teeter's Campground is open Mar 1 through Nov. Reservations are recommended on holiday weekends. Credit cards are not accepted.

BEACHCOMBER CAMPGROUND AND OCRACOKE STATION
NC 12, Ocracoke Village
(252) 928-4031
Less than a mile from Silver Lake and the nearest beach access, Beachcomber Campground has 29 sites with electricity and water and 7 tent sites.

Hot showers and fully equipped bathrooms are available, as are picnic tables and grills. A deli on the premises offers fresh sandwiches. Gourmet groceries and a large wine selection are available, as well as beach supplies, souvenirs, and T-shirts.

Leashed pets are allowed at Beachcomber. The campground is open year-round. Reservations are recommended for summer camping. Call for rates.

OCRACOKE CAMPGROUND (NPS)
NC 12, Ocracoke Island
(800) 365-CAMP (reservations)
www.nps.gov/caha

An oceanfront campground 3 miles east of Ocracoke Village just behind the dunes, this National Park Service campground maintains 136 campsites. No utility hookups or laundry facilities are available, but there are cold showers, a dumping station, drinking water, charcoal grills, and flush toilets. As at all NPS campgrounds, stays are limited to 14 days. The facility is open May through Sept.

Since most of these sites sit directly in the sun, bring some sort of shade. Long tent stakes help to hold down tents against the often fierce winds that whip through this campground. The breeze, however, is a welcome relief from summer heat. Bug spray is a must in the summer.

Ocracoke is the only campground on the island operated by the National Park Reservation Service. Call or visit the website from mid-May through mid-September to make reservations. Major credit cards are accepted. Sites are assigned on a first-come, first-served basis. All sites cost $23 per night.

Even though it looks like an inviting spot, camping on the beach is not permitted. Local officers and National Park Service personnel patrol the areas regularly and will ask you to leave.

RESTAURANTS

When you visit the Outer Banks, be sure to bring your appetite. In this seemingly remote area of the world, we have the basic ingredients from which world-class cuisine is created. We have bounty from the mainland, the sounds, and the ocean. We have innovative, educated, experienced chefs and restaurateurs. And we have an atmosphere that lends itself to an eclectic variety of hip, funky, chic, laid-back, comfortable, rustic, family-style places. In short we have cutting-edge cuisine and we know how to serve it.

OVERVIEW

Just across the Wright Memorial Bridge on the Currituck mainland grow the vegetables found on many Outer Banks menus: Silver Queen sweet corn, Red Bliss potatoes, sugar snap peas, luscious tomatoes, brightly colored bell peppers, slender green beans. And we can't forget about the fields of strawberries and melons or the orchards of trees laden with succulent peaches and figs. The source of smoke-cured country hams and the largest peanuts you've ever eaten lies farther inland. Wanchese Produce on Roanoke Island plays a starring role on a daily basis, supplying restaurants with herbs. Organic lettuce, mesclun mix, and bunches of fresh basil, thyme, rosemary, lemongrass, dill, and edible flowers are just a few of the fragrant wonders delivered to the back doors of kitchens all along this sandy bar.

And then there's the seafood. So much tuna is caught in the warm waters of the Gulf Stream that the tiny fishing village of Wanchese exports literally thousands of tons each year. In addition to tuna, local menus sport mahimahi, wahoo, and mako shark from the Gulf Stream. From inshore ocean waters and our sound waters come fresh flounder, Spanish and king mackerel, bluefish, black grouper, drum, striped bass (locally known as rockfish), speckled trout, gray trout, oysters, clams, mussels, shrimp, and crabs. Along Colington Road and the streets of Kitty Hawk Village, you can easily spot the long wooden shedder beds, brightly lighted all night long, where soft-shell crabs are gathered as soon as they molt.

Big-city purveyors supplement our local seafood and produce; while the grocery stores carry mainly the basics, our restaurants pride themselves on offering daring ingredients.

Wine has become one of our restaurants' biggest drawing cards. Wine dinners abound during the off-season, and many are attended by the vintners themselves. Wine-loving restaurateurs are happy to accommodate a variety of tastes, as evidenced by the increasing number of wines by the glass that we see cropping up on lists. Lists of bottled wines lengthen each season, and restaurants along the northern beaches sometimes offer 100 or more varieties of the world's finest wines. A surprising number of Outer Banks restaurants have received coveted awards of excellence from *Wine Spectator* for their wine selections and for their pairing of wine with food.

Many area restaurants serve alcoholic beverages, at least for dinner; however, those in Southern Shores and those on Colington, and Ocracoke Islands are forbidden to offer mixed drinks and serve only beer or wine. Some establishments allow brown bagging, which means you can bring in your own liquor.

Restaurants are opening earlier in the spring and staying open longer into the fall each year. The shoulder seasons have become popular times to dine out. Most eateries open by March and don't close their kitchens until after Thanksgiving. Some open briefly for the holidays. A few are busy enough to stay open year-round.

Dinner isn't the only meal to eat out, of course. Bakeries, diners, and even seafood restaurants serve big breakfasts, lunches, and weekend brunches. A few welcome bathing suit–clad customers just off the beach. The majority of restaurants, however, require you to wear shirts and shoes. Many cooks will package meals to go and some eateries deliver, with menus offering much more than just pizza.

If you're eating an evening meal out, feel free to dress as comfortably as you desire. Even most of the expensive, elite establishments welcome sundresses, sandals, and shorts. Restaurant managers say everything from evening gowns and suits to jeans and T-shirts is acceptable at their tables.

Reservations aren't taken at many restaurants. Others, however, suggest or even require them. The Blue Point, the Left Bank, and Elizabeth's Cafe in Duck; Ocean Boulevard in Kitty Hawk; Colington Cafe on Colington Island; and 1587 in Manteo all get so booked up during summer that it's best to call at least three days ahead to secure a table. The fare at these fabulous places is well worth the advance planning.

If sticking to a budget is a concern, you can have homestyle meals from tuna steaks to North Carolina barbecue for less than $8 in many Outer Banks family-style restaurants. Sure, you'll find a few of the nationally popular fast-food chains, complete with drive-through windows, uniformed employees, and a known commodity, but if you want something ranging from a little bit different to extraordinary, read on. With our diversity of restaurants, you're bound to find something to suit any appetite.

Price Code

The following price code is based on the cost of main courses for one person and does not include appetizers, dessert, and alcoholic beverages. Many area eateries have senior-citizen discounts and children's menus. Most entrees include at least one vegetable or salad and some type of bread. Here's our breakdown: Prices do not include the 8.75 percent sales tax or the gratuity, which should be 15 to 20 percent, depending on the quality of service. Some restaurants offer early-evening dining discounts to encourage patrons to avoid peak dining hours. Most have at least two or three daily specials that change according to the availability of food and the whims of the chef.

$.................	Less than $12
$$	$12 to $22
$$$	$22 to $38
$$$$	More than $38

HOW THIS CHAPTER IS ORGANIZED

Restaurants in this chapter are arranged from north to south from Corolla through Ocracoke.

Seasons and days of the week each place is open are included with every profile. Unless otherwise noted, these eateries accept MasterCard and Visa, and many accept other major credit cards as well.

We've included some primarily carry-out and outdoor dining establishments that offer quick, cheap eats, cool ice-cream concoctions, and perfect items to pack for a picnic or offshore fishing excursion.

RESTAURANTS

Poor Richard's Sandwich Shop, Roanoke Island, Manteo, $, 121

Hatteras Island

Atlantic Coast Cafe, Waves, $–$$, 123

Avon Cafe, Avon, $$, 124

Breakwater Island Restaurant, Hatteras Village, $$, 126

Bubba's Bar-B-Q, Frisco, $$, 126

Bubba's Too, Avon, $$, 124

Capt'n Rolo's Raw Bar & Grill, Frisco, $$, 126

Diamond Shoals Restaurant, Buxton, $$, 125

Dinky's Waterfront Restaurant, Hatteras, $–$$, 127

Dirty Dick's Crab House, Avon, $–$$, 124

Dolphin Den, Avon, $, 124

Down Under Restaurant & Lounge, Rodanthe, $$, 123

Fish House Restaurant, Buxton, $$, 125

Gingerbread House Bakery, Frisco, $, 126

Good Winds Seafood & Wine, Waves Island, $$–$$$, 123

Leonardo's Pizza, Rodanthe, $, 122

Lisa's Pizzeria, Rodanthe, $, 122

Oceana's Bistro, Avon, $–$$, 124

Orange Blossom Cafe and Bakery, Buxton, $$, 125

Quarterdeck Restaurant, Frisco, $$, 125

Rusty's Surf and Turf, Buxton, $$–$$$, 125

Top Dog Cafe, Waves, $, 123

Ocracoke Island

The Back Porch Restaurant, Ocracoke Village, $$$, 129

Cafe Atlantic, Ocracoke Village, $$, 130

Capt. Ben's, Ocracoke Village, $$, 130

Creek Side Cafe, Ocracoke Village, $, 131

Daijo Restaurant, Ocracoke Village, $$, 132

Flying Melon, Ocracoke Village, $$, 129

Howard's Pub & Raw Bar Restaurant, Ocracoke Village, $–$$, 130

Island Inn Restaurant, Ocracoke Village, $$, 131

Jason's Restaurant, Ocracoke Village, $, 127

Jolly Roger Pub & Marina, Ocracoke Village, $$, 132

Ocracoke Coffee & Island Smoothie, Ocracoke Village, $, 131

Pony Island Restaurant, Ocracoke Village, $$, 128

Smacnally's Raw Bar and Grill, Ocracoke Village, $–$$, 127

Thai Moon, Ocracoke Village, $, 129

COROLLA

COROLLA PIZZA & DELI $
Austin Complex, NC 12, Corolla
(252) 453-8592

This takeout-only deli serves hot and cold subs and sandwiches, Philly cheese steaks, and pizza by the pie or slice for lunch and dinner. Each pizza is made to order on hand-tossed dough. Regular red sauce and gourmet white pizzas, including the ever-popular chicken pesto pizza, are available. During the summer season Corolla Pizza offers free delivery after 5 p.m. You can walk in or call ahead to have your order waiting. Corolla Pizza is open seven days a week in summer. Call for off-season hours.

NICOLETTA'S ITALIAN CAFE $$$
Corolla Light Town Center
NC 12, Corolla
(252) 453-4004

A cornerstone of fine dining on the northern Outer Banks. White linen tablecloths and a view of the Currituck Beach Lighthouse please the eye as sounds of classical jazz mix with Sinatra and friends to set the mood in the dining room. Nicoletta's menu features fresh seafood, pork, and a wide selection of gourmet pasta combinations, all prepared in the Italian tradition with a creative touch. An extensive wine list with more than 30 selections complements the fare, and sinful desserts end the meal satisfactorily. Nicoletta's has been a frequent winner of the *Wine Spectator* award. Children can create their own pasta dish by selecting from three pastas, three sauces, and meatballs.

Nicoletta's is open for dinner year-round. In season it is open seven days a week; call for off-season hours. Dress is casual, and reservations are requested. Catering and private parties are available.

TOMATO PATCH $
Monteray Plaza, NC 12, Corolla
(252) 453-4500

The Tomato Patch is a warm, welcoming restaurant offering pizza, seafood, sandwiches, and classic Italian fare. Amazing gourmet pizzas—like the Seafood Sensation with shrimp, crab, tomato, pesto, and mozzarella—will please any palate. A fully stocked bar, known as Dr. Unks Oasis, is located here. Live music is featured in season. Open for lunch and dinner and late night throughout the season.

BACCHUS WINE & CHEESE $
Monteray Plaza, NC 12, Corolla
(252) 453-4333,
(252) 453-2429 to fax orders
www.bacchuswineandcheese.com

Bacchus Wine & Cheese carries an enormous selection of domestic and imported wines and beer plus some fantastic deli sandwiches, subs, and tortilla wraps. You can eat in the shop or at an outside table or get anything to go. Available for take-home preparation are custom cut-to-order steaks

and Maine and Caribbean lobster tails. Bacchus is open for lunch and dinner daily in season; call for off-season hours.

SUNDOGS SPORTS BAR AND
GRILL $-$$
Monteray Plaza, NC 12, Corolla
(252) 453-4263

Sundogs is the top sports-viewing facility in Corolla. It has the traditional decor of a sports bar and the features you would expect—a long bar, a pool table, video games, and TVs. If there's a game on, customers like to sidle up to the bar, drink a few beers, and chow down on jumbo buffalo wings served with ranch or blue cheese dressing, beer-battered onion rings, mile-high nachos with tricolor tortillas, or personal flat-bread pizzas. A steam bar offers shrimp, crab legs, and more. For meals try hearty sandwiches like the Black Angus burger or the Carolina crab cake sandwich. Fish-and-chips are available along with a 12-inch Coney Island hot dog. There is a children's menu, a late-night menu, and a full bar. Sundogs is open year-round. In season Sun-dogs has live entertainment seven nights a week, including a comedy night. You must be 21 or older to enter after 10 p.m.

NORTH BANKS RESTAURANT &
RAW BAR $$
TimBuck II Shopping Village
NC 12, Corolla
(252) 453-3344

This 50-seat restaurant and raw bar serves lunch and dinner all year. Lobster, shrimp, oysters, clams, and mussels are available as well as filet mignon, fresh locally caught fish, grilled beef, chicken, and sandwiches. Diners enjoy the waterside view from this upscale but casual restaurant that boasts 28-foot vaulted ceilings. North Banks also offers desserts and appetizers as well as imported and domestic beers and wine. Order a flaming martini for an exciting start to your meal.

i Does a gourmet meal cooked in your rental cottage sound like a winning option? Call At Your Service at (252) 261-5286 or (800) 259-0229 to arrange in-house personal chef service.

*MIKE DIANNA'S GRILL ROOM $$
TimBuck II Shopping Village
NC 12, Corolla
(252) 453-4336
http://grillroomobx.com

Mike Dianna's Grill Room prides itself on creating an unforgettable dining experience and wants dining here to become a tradition in your family. Steaks, veal, lamb, ribs, chicken, and seafood are all cooked over a mesquite grill, bringing you aromatic wood cooking at its best. The homemade French bread that accompanies the meals is excellent. Four or five different fish specials are offered each night. The Grill Room is also known for its broad selection of international wines. The restaurant serves dinner nightly during the summer; call for off-season hours. A kid's menu is available. Live music is scheduled every Thursday evening in season. Private parties of up to 150 people may be held here. Beverages and sushi served until 2 a.m. most nights in season.

STEAMER'S SHELLFISH TO GO $
TimBuck II Shopping Village
NC 12, Corolla
(252) 453-3305
www.steamersshellfishtogo.com

Steamer's Shellfish To Go is Corolla's version of the popular New England–style clambake.

This gourmet seafood market offers full take-out of the best the Outer Banks has to offer presented in a refreshingly different fashion. Gourmet lunch and dinner entrees (grilled fish, chicken, baby back ribs, and vegetarian lasagna, to name a few), fantastic homemade soups, salads, and desserts are served here. Steamer Pots To Go are made to order and layered with seafood, Red Bliss potatoes, yellow onion, and corn on the cob with cocktail sauce, butter, lemon, and claw crackers. Take home your Steamer Pot To Go, place it on the hot stove, add a cup of water, and in 30 to 45 minutes you'll have a seafood feast like no other. Steamer's Shellfish To Go is open in season for lunch and dinner, Apr 1 through Columbus Day weekend. The waterfront deck is perfect for outdoor dining.

*NORTHERN LIGHTS BAKERY $
Corolla Light Town Center
NC 12, Corolla
(252) 453-0201

Got a sweet tooth that needs satisfying? Stop in at this adorable bakery and pick up delightful pastries, cupcakes, and sugary concoctions. Cakes are also available and can be made to order. Northern Lights also offers smoothies, coffees, and teas.

BAD BEAN TAQUERIA $
TimBuck II Shopping Village
NC 12, Corolla
(252) 453-4380

This casual eatery serves fresh, authentic Mexican cuisine. Inspired by the many taquerias along the Pacific coast, their motto is "the only good bean is a bad bean." Try the mahimahi fish tacos for a delicious south of the border meal. A large selection of Mexican beers and Bad Bean margaritas are offered. Patrons can eat in or takeout. Catering is available.

ROUTE 12 STEAK & SEAFOOD CO. $$
TimBuck II Shopping Village
NC 12, Corolla
(252) 453-4644
Route 12 pleases diners with one of the best kid's menus in Corolla, tempting nightly dinner specials, an outstanding wine list, and a fully stocked bar. Open seven days a week in season. Lunch is served in season from 11:30 a.m. to 3 p.m. and dinner from 5 to 9 p.m. Call for off-season hours. Reservations are recommended in summer months.

SMOKEY'S RESTAURANT $
Ocean Club Centre
NC 12, Corolla
(252) 453-4050
www.smokeysrestaurant.com
This down-home, family-style restaurant opened in 1991 and is a Corolla original. Its specialties include house-prepared barbecue true to the original North Carolina recipe, delicious baby back ribs, half-pound burgers, southern fried chicken, fresh yellowfin tuna steaks, homemade Currituck crab cakes, fried and steamed shrimp, and fried clams accompanied by all the trimmings, from coleslaw and baked beans to hush puppies, biscuits, and onion rings. Smokey's offers a children's menu and will package most of its items for takeout. Desserts, wine, and beer are also available. Open for lunch and dinner, Mar through Dec, Smokey's serves seven days a week in season. Call for off-season hours.

*METROPOLIS $–$$
Ocean Club Centre
NC 12, Corolla
(252) 453-6167

Creativity reigns at this chic and urban tapas and martini restaurant. Diners return often to this contemporary and stylish dining experience. The menu at Metropolis is ever changing, using only the freshest ingredients available. Favorites include roasted red pepper and feta dip and tuna sashimi. Black and blue tenderloin medallions are served in the cooler months, along with the spicy shrimp taco. A full martini list includes 30-plus choices. Wine, liquor, and microbrew beers are served here as well. This Corolla hotspot is open until 2 a.m.

i A great time to eat out on the Outer Banks is Sunday night. Many folks have just checked into their cottage and don't go out for dinner. Often you can get seated more quickly and have a wider choice of where to eat on Sunday evening.

DUCK

THE LIFESAVING STATION AT THE
SANDERLING $$$
NC 12, Sanderling
(252) 449-6654
www.thesanderling.com
The Lifesaving Station, part of the Sanderling Resort north of Duck, is one of the Outer Banks' loveliest restaurants, housed in a restored 1899 lifesaving station that is a National Historic Landmark. The dining rooms reflect turn-of-the-20th-century coastal architecture and are enhanced with rich woods and brass, nautical antiques, and original artifacts of the lifesaving station. Contemporary American cuisine emphasizing local seafood is the specialty here. The restaurant serves breakfast, lunch, and dinner every day to everyone, not only guests of the resort.

The restaurant has an award-winning wine list and a full bar. The upstairs Swan Bar and Lounge are good places to relax before or after you eat. A children's menu is available. Dinner reservations are highly recommended. All three meals are served seven days a week year-round.

THE LEFT BANK $$$$
NC 12, Sanderling
(252) 261-8419
www.thesanderling.com

Part of the Sanderling resort complex, the name "Left Bank" takes its inspiration from the Left Bank of Paris and also refers to the restaurant's location on the Outer Banks. The Left Bank offers panoramic vistas of Currituck Sound and marsh grasses through a half-moon-shaped window wall. The interior is sublimely chic, like nothing else on the Outer Banks, with leather banquettes, mohair chairs, a bar top of blonde onyx lit from underneath—all backgrounded by the spectacular view. The emphasis is on the freshest regional foods available. The wine list is a careful selection of boutique wines, and the martinis are a house specialty. Dinner is served Tues through Sat Apr through Dec, and Thurs through Sat Jan through Mar. Reservations are recommended. Men should be aware that long pants and covered footwear are required, as well as a collared shirt.

i It's not vacation if you spend the whole time in the kitchen. If you've got a houseful of people, consider hiring a personal chef. You can choose a chef who cooks all three meals in your house or one who just drops off dinner every evening. Ask your rental company for suggestions.

FISHBONES SUNSET GRILLE AND RAW BAR $$
NC 12, Duck
(252) 261-3901
www.fishbonessunsetgrille.com

Sister restaurant to the popular Fishbones Raw Bar & Restaurant, Fishbones Sunset Grille and Raw Bar has become another favorite Duck dining spot. The restaurant sits by the Currituck Sound and is the village's prime sunset-watching spot. It is patterned after the older Fishbones, with Caribbean-influenced entrees and appetizers, moderately priced food, a fun atmosphere, and good service for locals and visitors alike.

Fishbones Sunset is known for its extensive drink menu. Specialty drinks are served in novelty vessels, like a tiki god, a monkey, or a pineapple. The full bar list is available upstairs at a stunning horseshoe-shaped bar covered with coral tiles, downstairs at another bar and raw bar, and outside at a tiki bar. Meals are served upstairs or down or outside on the deck. Dinners focus mostly on seafood, and the blackened fish and conch fritters are standouts. The raw bar serves all the freshest Outer Banks favorites. For lunch, seafood, sandwiches, and burgers are served. Lunch and dinner are served every day year-round.

Fishbones Sunset also offers breakfast, daily in season and on weekends in the off-season. Breakfast choices include omelets, skillet dishes, smoked salmon bagels, and a wonderful cinnamon french toast served with a guava-banana syrup. Lunch and dinner entrees are equally outstanding, with a wide range of chowders, freshest fish, sandwiches, and steaks. It is a popular nighttime hangout, with live music four or five nights a week in the summer and one or two nights in the off-season (see the Nightlife chapter).

Fishbones Sunset offers catering and site rental for weddings and large parties.

ELIZABETH'S CAFE & WINERY $$$
Scarborough Faire, NC 12, Duck
(252) 261-6145
www.elizabethscafe.com

Well-known across the nation for its wine and exceptional cuisine—and perfectly matched combinations thereof—Elizabeth's is a perennial *Wine Spectator* award winner and for years Elizabeth has swept the fine-dining awards.

The restaurant is small, warm, and casual inside, with a fireplace that's usually lit on chilly evenings. Service is always excellent. If you have trouble selecting a wine from the extensive wine list, owner Leonard Logan is more than happy to help you choose a bottle to complement any meal. Leonard loves a celebration and is always ready to pop open a bottle of champagne.

Besides the regular menu offerings, which include country French and California eclectic, two prix fixe dinners (six- or seven-course meals and accompanying wines) are available every night. All the dishes are made with fresh ingredients, from seafood and steak to unusual pastas. A pastry chef creates different desserts daily.

Elizabeth's Wine Gallery is an area of the restaurant where shoppers can choose from more than 1,650 selections. Tastings of reasonably priced, featured wines are offered before you make your purchase. The wine bar is open in the afternoon, and if you choose to savor a glass, you may do so inside the gallery, outside on the porch, or in the adjacent garden.

FISHBONES RAW BAR & RESTAURANT $$
Scarborough Lane Shoppes
NC 12, Duck
(252) 261-6991
www.fishbonessunsetgrille.com

Specializing in locally caught seafood, this raw bar and grill has been a crowd pleaser since 1995. Fishbones won the Outer Banks chowder cook-off with an original recipe during its first year in business. Lunch items include sandwiches, crab cakes, fried seafood, and creamy soups such as tomato conch and, of course, chowder. Dinner entrees feature such Caribbean cuisine favorites as calypso eggplant and coconut shrimp, as well as pastas with fresh clam sauce, lobster tails, crab legs, and more than a dozen raw bar selections. The hot crab dip, barbecue shrimp, and conch fritters are outstanding appetizers. This is a casual place with a full bar, five types of beer on tap, 50 bottled beers from all over the world, a wine list, and several microbrews. Fishbones serves lunch and dinner seven days a week year-round, and specials change daily for both meals. Takeout is available for all menu items. Reservations are not accepted.

*THE BLUE POINT BAR & GRILL $$$
The Waterfront Shops, NC 12, Duck
(252) 261-8090
www.goodfoodgoodwine.com

This beautifully renovated and expanded bistro is one of our favorite places to dine on the Outer Banks. It's been open for dinner since 1989 and consistently receives rave reviews from magazines such as *Southern Living, Gourmet,* and *Wine Spectator.* Here regional southern cooking takes on a cosmopolitan flair.

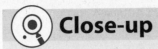

Close-up

OBX Catch

Encompassing Currituck, Hyde, Tyrell, and Dare counties, OBX Catch is a branding campaign designed to help consumers identify which restaurants and seafood retailers are selling locally harvested seafood. Eighty percent of all seafood served nationally is imported and only two percent is FDA inspected. As part of a larger "local food" movement, OBX Catch is aimed at educating both locals and visitors about the benefits of requesting locally harvested, fresh seafood.

A diverse group of local fisherman, restaurants, seafood markets, grocers, and community members launched OBX Catch in 2010. The program uses a logo to identify which restaurants and retailers are providing local seafood—a Gold membership indicates more than 50 percent of seafood on the menu is locally provided, and a Silver membership indicates up to 50 percent. Individual dishes should bear the OBX Catch logo as well, insuring diners of the local origin of the catch.

The unique Atlantic coast ecosystem produces one of the most diverse year-round selections of fish and shellfish available, and it provides the greatest fishing revenue in North Carolina. But while our local seafood is plentiful, it is also highly seasonal. Summer is the time for softshell crabs and shrimp, flounder is best in the fall, and winter is better for oysters and sea trout to name a few. Looking for the OBX logo at your seafood retailer will insure that your meals are fresh, in season, and locally caught by our native watermen.

The Blue Point's menu is contemporary southern cuisine and changes seasonally. Starters range from Hatteras tuna to fresh tomato-mozzarella stacks, each artistically arranged and flavored with a fresh combination of seasonings. Entrees include jumbo lump crab cakes served with Currituck corn on the cob, homemade soups, unusual seafood dishes, steaks, salads, and perfect pastas. Desserts, like warm Kentucky bourbon pecan tart with caramel ice-cream or key lime pie, are divine.

It's open for dinner, and reservations are highly recommended; in summer dinner reservations are required. The Blue Point is open for lunch Tues to Sun from 11:30 a.m. to 2:30 p.m. and for dinner seven days a week in season; call for off-season hours.

AQUA RESTAURANT $$–$$$
NC 12, Duck
(252) 261-9700
www.aquaobx.com

Aqua is Duck's most sassy waterfront dining hotspot. Located on the sound, this restaurant serves lunch and dinner. Sophisticated regional cuisine is topped off by a glorious water view. Ingredients used here are organic and locally grown whenever possible. An extensive wine list is offered. The staff is well trained by one of the owners, who is a certified sommelier. Truly spoil yourself and complete your visit with a facial or massage at the Aqua Essence Day Spa located on the second level.

ROADSIDE RAW BAR & GRILL $$
NC 12, Duck
(252) 261-5729

Occupying a renovated 1932 cottage, this restaurant is warm and homey, with hardwood floors inside and a patio with umbrella-shaded tables out front. Live jazz is performed here some evenings in season (see the Nightlife chapter).

A casual, fine-dining establishment, Roadside offers half pound Angus burgers, fresh fish sandwiches, meat loaf, and a variety of salads and sandwiches for lunch. The Roadside clam chowder is chock-full of shellfish, and you can choose from steamed and seasoned shrimp by the pound or half pound and steamed clams by the dozen. In addition to mixed greens and Caesar salads is our favorite: a warm salad of bay scallops, black beans, corn, and red bell peppers with sesame-soy dressing. Weather permitting, enjoy your meal on the patio while watching the summertime foot traffic in downtown Duck. The restaurant serves lunch and dinner year-round; call for off-season hours. Reservations are not accepted. Patrons enjoy live jazz on the outdoor patio on some evenings in the summer.

DUCK DELI $$
NC 12, Duck
(252) 261-3354

This casual deli on the east side of the highway opened in 1987 primarily to serve lunch. Since then Duck Deli has expanded to offer breakfast, lunch, and dinner seven days a week, year-round. Barbecued pork, beef, chicken, and ribs are the specialties here.

TOMMY'S GOURMET MARKET
AND WINE EMPORIUM $$$
NC 12, Duck
(252) 261-8990, (800) 692-2168
www.tommysmarket.com

Tommy's is an intimate family-owned gourmet market that is famous for its Angus steaks, aged for 21 days and cut to order. The market also offers fresh-baked goods and a deli that features roasted ham and chicken, shrimp, sandwiches, fresh salads, and daily luncheon specials. Tommy's also will prepare dinner for you. Preset menus or items a la carte can be carried out ready to eat. In addition to providing a full range of groceries, Tommy's has an extensive wine selection and carries imported beer. The market is open Mar through New Year's.

*DUCK PIZZA $$
Scarborough Lane Shoppes
NC 12, Duck
(252) 255-0099
www.duckpizza.com

Duck Pizza offers yummy specialty pizzas, subs, wraps, wings, strombolis calzones, and more. Beer is served in the cafe. Free delivery is offered to Southern Shores, Duck, and Pine Island.

RED SKY CAFE $$$
NC 12, Duck
(252) 261-8646
www.redskycafe.com

The Red Sky Cafe features local foods and an eclectic style of preparation. The casual atmosphere helps deliver a memorable dining experience. The lunch menu lists tasty offerings like the seafood quesadilla with blackened shrimp and crab, black bean spread, and Monterey Jack and cheddar cheeses all wood-fired in a jalapeño tortilla.

Dinner temptations include the bruschetta fresh catch, wood-fired fish topped with tomatoes and fresh mozzarella. A children's menu is available. An extensive wine and beer list rounds out the menu. The Red Sky is open Mar through Dec for lunch and dinner.

SOUTHERN SHORES

COASTAL PROVISIONS WINE BAR AND CAFE $$
Southern Shores Crossing
NC 12, Southern Shores
(252) 480-0023
www.coastalprovisionmarket.com
At Coastal Provisions, it's about taste, service, and pleasure. Diners are sure to be pleased with the combination of a chef's market, artisan cheese and deli, prepared meals to go, fresh and prepared local seafood, wine bar, and table service by candlelight. Coastal Provisions also caters and can accommodate small intimate celebrations as well as upscale events.

KITTY HAWK

HIGH COTTON BBQ $$
NC 12 MP ½, Kitty Hawk
(252) 255-2275
www.highcottonbbq.com
For a flavorful taste of outstanding regional cooking, try High Cotton. These Tarheel natives prepare their barbecue by cooking it long hours over smoking hickory coals, producing Outer Banks barbecue at its very best. Ribs, beef brisket, and smoked or fried chicken are also available. Order with the traditional sides and some sweet tea, and you're in High Cotton. A kid's menu is available, and beer is served on premise. High Cotton is a popular choice to cater parties and weddings. Open Mar through Dec.

✳RUNDOWN CAFE $$
NC 12, MP 1, Kitty Hawk
(252) 255-0026
Open since 1993, this Caribbean-style cafe has been a big hit with locals, offering spicy, unusual alternatives to traditional Outer Banks seafood. Named for a Jamaican stew, Rundown serves island entrees flavored with African and Indian accents.

There's a full bar, and the bartenders can come up with some pretty potent concoctions. Guinness stout, Bass, Pyramid, and Harp beers are on tap. The upstairs bar is a great place to soak in the sunset, catch a few rays, or linger over a cool cocktail after a hot day in the sun. The downstairs dining area is smoke free. Lunch and dinner are served seven days a week. A kid's menu is available, and takeout orders are welcome. Rundown is closed in Dec and Jan.

SOUTHERN BEAN $
Dunes Shoppes, US 158, Kitty Hawk
(252) 261-JAVA
This comfortable, gourmet coffee shop caters to folks looking for healthful light meals with a great cup of java. Three types of just-brewed coffee always simmer, filling the air with tantalizing aromas. They serve every type of specialty coffee drink imaginable, from espresso and cappuccino to iced lattes—even in decaf varieties. More than 30 flavors of freshly roasted coffee beans are sold by the pound. Inexpensive fresh lunch items are served throughout the day. Southern Bean is also one of the few places on the Outer Banks where you can get freshly squeezed juices and a wide variety of fruit smoothies. Open daily year-round from 7 a.m. to 8 p.m. in the summer, and from 7 a.m. to 6 p.m. in the off-season.

✱SEASIDE GOURMET TO GO $

Dunes Shoppes, US 158, Kitty Hawk
(252) 261-2546
www.seasidegourmet.com

This takeout restaurant is tucked away within the Dunes Shoppes. Finding it will be worthwhile because insiders try their fresh locally originated food and always return. Seaside makes healthy and delicious food convenient and affordable. Vegetarian and seafood entrees are available as well as sandwiches, wraps, and kid-friendly foods. Menu items are original and healthy. Seaside is open for lunch and dinner.

OCEAN BOULEVARD $$$

NC 12, MP 2, Kitty Hawk
(252) 261-2546
www.obbistro.com

This cozy, upscale eatery gives you a great feeling from the moment you walk into the gold-walled dining room until you leave after a fabulous meal. It opened in 1995 and quickly became one of the most popular places on the Outer Banks.

Ocean Boulevard's wine list, which has won the *Wine Spectator* Award of Excellence, contains more than 100 selections. Microbrewed beer is available, and the bar specializes in martinis.

Dessert offerings include a white chocolate crème brûlée and a macadamia nut torte with caramel ice cream. A full line of coffee drinks and herbal teas tops off your dining experience.

This elegant eatery will please even the most discriminating diners. It's open year-round for dinner only. During summer, doors are open seven days a week. Call for off-season hours. Reservations are highly recommended.

JIMMY'S SEAFOOD BUFFET $$$

US 158, MP 4, Kitty Hawk
(252) 261-4973
www.jimmysbuffetobx.com

Jimmy's Seafood Buffet specializes in food and fun. Some say that the only thing more exciting than the food is the atmosphere. Start your evening off on the open-air thatched-roof porch, where the bar offers eight frozen drinks with a souvenir glass. "Kiddie cocktails" are available for the younger set.

Inside this all-you-can-eat tropical paradise you'll find all of your favorite seafood and all you'll want of it! Choose from crab, shrimp, oysters, clams, and lobster. Landlubbers can opt for barbecued ribs, chicken, and prime rib, among more than 100 selections. There's also a soft-serve ice-cream bar.

Jimmy's is open nightly for dinner starting at 2:30 p.m. in season; call for off-season hours and for info on the $100 cash drawing for early birds.

CAPT'N FRANK'S $

US 158, MP 4, Kitty Hawk
(252) 261-9923

Capt'n Frank's is an institution on the Outer Banks, serving all-beef Oscar Mayer hot dogs with a variety of accompaniments. If "going to the dogs" doesn't appeal to you, Capt'n Frank's also offers barbecue sandwiches and addictive nacho fries—french fries with chili, cheese, hot peppers, and sour cream. Steamed shrimp is served nightly in season. Wash down the tasty morsels with a cold beer. Capt'n Frank's serves lunch and dinner daily Memorial Day through Labor Day. Off-season the restaurant is open every day for lunch except Sun.

i Very few restaurants on the Outer Banks serve dinner past 8:30 or 9 p.m. During the lively summer season, however, you may be able to get a late dinner from one of the carry-out restaurants on the islands.

HURRICANE MO'S RESTAURANT & RAW BAR $$
NC 12 and East Kitty Hawk Road,
MP 4, Kitty Hawk
(252) 261-0215

Hurricane Mo's has roared into Kitty Hawk. Formerly located at Pirates Cove, this restaurant serves traditional fresh seafood, steaks, pasta, and many island inspired creations in a cozy Tuscan-inspired dining room. Vegetarians have a wide selection, and there is a kid's menu. Seafood lovers enjoy the steamed and raw shellfish bar. This eatery has a full bar including wine and beer.

*BLACK PELICAN OCEANFRONT CAFE $$
NC 12, MP 4, Kitty Hawk
(252) 261-3171
www.blackpelican.com

This casual restaurant is in an old Coast Guard station and features an enclosed deck overlooking the Atlantic. It's roomy and wide, with three separate levels and a huge bar with several TVs (see the Nightlife chapter). Hardwood floors, tongue-and-groove appointments, light gray accents, burgundy carpeting, and black bentwood chairs all add to the comfortable ambience of this moderately priced eatery. Gourmet pizzas are cooked in a wood-hearth oven. Try the steamed shellfish fresh from the sea. An extensive selection of appetizers is made from scratch. Dinner offerings include pasta and seafood specials, grilled or blackened to

suit your taste. A children's menu is also available. Black Pelican serves lunch and dinner seven days a week year-round.

LONGBOARDS ISLAND GRILL $$
US 158, MP 4, Kitty Hawk
(252) 261-7833

Entrees include traditional Outer Banks fish, great crab cakes, and shrimp jambalaya. Specials change daily. A children's menu is available at this kid-friendly restaurant. Dinner is served seven days a week. Open year-round; call for off-season hours. Pool table, games and a large bar round out the offerings,

JOHN'S DRIVE-IN $
NC 12, MP 4¾, Kitty Hawk
(252) 261-6227

Home of the planet's best milk shakes, John's has been an Outer Banks institution for years. Folks have been known to drive 2 hours from Norfolk just to sip one of the fruit and ice-cream concoctions, which are often so thick they won't flow through the straw. Our favorite is the chocolate, peanut butter, and banana variety, but you'll have to sample a few first and create some of your own combinations before making that call for yourself.

Besides the milk shakes and ice-cream-sundae treats, John's serves delicious mahimahi, trout, and tuna sandwiches or boats with the fish crispy-fried alongside crinkle fries. Dogs love this drive-in, too. If your pooch waits patiently in the car, the worker behind the window probably will provide him or her with a free "puppy cup" of soft-serve vanilla ice cream. We can't think of a better doggie treat on a hot summer afternoon.

John's Drive-In is open from May through Sept or Oct for lunch and early dinner. It's closed Wed. No credit cards are accepted.

LA FOGATA MEXICAN RESTAURANT $
US 158, MP 4½, Kitty Hawk
(252) 255-0934

A traditional Mexican restaurant, La Fogata gets its name from the Spanish word for "campfire." For the price, La Fogata serves the best ethnic food on the beach. People wait in line to eat here on weekend nights. You'll see a lot of locals in this colorful spot year-round.

Airy, bright, and decorated with Mexican art and photographs, the interior of this ultra-casual eatery usually hums with Latin tunes. The waiters bring baskets of crispy tortillas and bowls of homemade salsa as soon as they distribute the menus. All entree portions are generous, so save room for the main course. Recommended appetizers include the hot queso (cheese) dip and stuffed jalapeño peppers.

Specialties are fajitas, beef and chicken tacos, enchiladas, and chiles rellenos. The cooks make the dishes hot or mild, depending on your desire. Selections come in every possible combination, vegetarian varieties, and a la carte if you want to try one of everything. (Actually, that's impossible here. The menu has more than 36 dinner selections, many starting at $6.50.) A full bar offers Mexican, American, and imported beer. Mixed-drink and margarita prices are among the lowest on the beach. La Fogata is open for lunch and dinner year-round, seven days a week.

OUTER BANKS TACO BAR $
US 158, MP 4½
Ocean Plaza, Kitty Hawk
(252) 261-8226
www.obxtacobar.com

House-made corn tortillas and a free salsa bar are just two reasons to stop at Outer Banks Taco Bar. The quesadillas and burritos are delicious. Try a mojito or a margarita to round out your meal. Burgers are also served, and catering is available.

HENRY'S RESTAURANT $
US 158, MP 5, Kitty Hawk
(252) 261-2025

Everyone loves a trip to Henry's. Easy on the purse, this local favorite serves waffles, pancakes, sausage, and other hearty breakfast favorites until 1 p.m. each day. Lunch is also satisfying here with sandwiches and burgers among the most popular entrees. Dinner includes fresh fish, soups, and salads. A children's menu is available.

KILL DEVIL HILLS

✳CHILLI PEPPERS COASTAL GRILL $$
US 158, MP 5, Kill Devil Hills
(252) 441-8081
www.chilli-peppers.com

World fusion with a southwestern twist describes the cooking at this fun, award-winning restaurant. Adventuresome diners are wowed by the chefs' wild concoctions. Most dishes have some type of chili in them. If you prefer a milder meal, they can do that and still tickle some untapped taste buds. The menu here changes frequently, with daily lunch and dinner specials sometimes stunning even the regulars. Weekly Tapas Nights, which feature little plates of dishes from a chosen cuisine, are held on Thursday night in fall, winter, and spring. One week you might taste samples of German food, the next Italian, the next Moroccan, and so on. This is a big hit with the locals. Sushi nights are also popular.

✳FRONT PORCH CAFE $
US 158, MP 6, Kill Devil Hills
(252) 449-6616
www.frontporchcafe.net
The Front Porch Cafe sources top-quality coffee beans from all over the world, then roasts each batch by hand in their store. Owners Paul Manning and Susannah Sakal enjoy chatting with customers in their friendly, relaxed community coffeehouse. Freshly baked cinnamon rolls, scones, and muffins are available every day. Customers can also select from the wonderful varieties of teas on hand.

AWFUL ARTHUR'S OYSTER BAR & RESTAURANT $$
NC 12, MP 6, Kill Devil Hills
(252) 441-5955
www.awfularthursobx.com
Awful Arthur's is a comfortably casual place where you won't mind peeling seasoned shrimp or picking the meat from succulent crab legs with messy fingers. Seafood is the specialty. You'll find scallops, oysters, clams, mussels, homemade crab cakes, and daily entree specials. The bartenders are some of the fastest shuckers in town. Bass ale and several other varieties of beer are on tap, or order from a full line of liquor and specialty drinks. For landlubbers, several nonseafood sandwiches are served. At night Awful Arthur's is usually packed. A late-night menu is available. Awful Arthur's T-shirts are seen all over the world and are local favorites. This popular eatery is open seven days a week year-round for lunch and dinner.

CAROLINA SEAFOOD $$$
NC 12, MP 6¼, Kill Devil Hills
(252) 441-6851

For an elaborate, all-you-can-eat seafood buffet where "fried has died," try Carolina Seafood. Here adults can enjoy more than 30 items for one price: salad, soups, hush puppies, garlic crabs, crab legs, scallops, stuffed shrimp, and several types of fish served baked, broiled, blackened, steamed, or sautéed. Roast beef is cut to order, and a variety of desserts are included in the price. If you're not feeling hungry enough to tackle the buffet, Carolina Seafood serves crabs, scallops, shrimp, and other seafood by the basket. A children's menu is available. This restaurant is open at 4:30 p.m. seven nights a week from Apr through Nov. Call for off-season hours.

i If you're heading out for a day on the sand, Stop 'N' Shop Convenience and Deli on the Beach Road in Kill Devil Hills is a great place to stock up. It has one of the best delis on the beach, an excellent selection of wine and beer, everything you'll need for a successful day's fishing, and all the latest water toys, too.

JOLLY ROGER RESTAURANT $$
NC 12, MP 6, Kill Devil Hills
(252) 441-6530
Serving some of the locals' favorite breakfasts, this lively restaurant is open for three meals a day 365 days a year. Besides the usual eggs, pancakes, sausage, bacon, and toast, Jolly Roger's bakery cooks up some of the biggest muffins and sticky buns you've ever seen. For lunch choose from sandwiches, local seafood, or daily specials. Dinner entrees include homestyle Italian dishes, steaks, broiled and fried fish, and a popular $9.95 prime rib special each Friday. All the desserts are homemade, and special orders are accepted for items to go. The food isn't

fancy, but the portions are enormous. You'll have no excuse if you leave here hungry. Jolly Roger also steams spiced shrimp in the separate bar area each afternoon and is the karaoke headquarters of the Outer Banks seven nights a week.

MAKO MIKE'S $$
US 158, MP 7, Kill Devil Hills
(252) 480-1919

This is the most outrageously decorated dining establishment on the Outer Banks. The fluorescent shark fins outside, decorated with swirls, stripes, and polka dots, don't give even a glimpse into what you'll see once you step inside. Some patrons compare it to an underwater experience. We think it's almost like visiting an octopus's garden complete with three separate levels of dining, fish mobiles dangling overhead, painted chairs, bright colors exploding everywhere, and murals along the deep blue walls.

The menu is impressive and varied. Dinner offerings are seasoned with Mediterranean, Cajun, Asian, and other exotic spices and include nine varieties of fresh pasta, seven wood-fired pizzas, several varieties of fresh blue-water fish, beef, pork, vegetarian stir-fries, mixed grills, scallops, shrimp, and dozens of other options.

This huge restaurant caters to couples, families, and large groups. A small meeting room is available for private parties. A separate bar serves frozen drink specials in addition to dozens of bottles of beer and wine. A children's menu is provided. Dinner is served seven days a week year-round. Call for winter hours. Mako Mike's owner, Mike Kelly, also operates Kelly's Restaurant & Tavern and is part owner of Pamlico Jack's Pirate Hideaway, both in Nags Head.

GOOMBAYS GRILLE & RAW BAR $$
NC 12, MP 7, Kill Devil Hills
(252) 441-6001
www.goombays.com

This island-style eatery is light and bright inside with lots of artwork, an outrageous fish tank, and a wall-size tropical mural in the dining room. The ambience is upbeat and casual, with wooden tables and chairs and a bare tile floor. The horseshoe-shaped bar, which is separate from the eating area, is a great place to try some of the delicious appetizers or drink specials.

Everything here is reasonably priced and flavorful. A raw bar is open until 1 a.m., serving steamed shrimp, oysters, vegetables, and other favorites. Key lime pie is always a smart choice for dessert. In season Goombays has live music every Wednesday. Goombays is open for lunch and dinner seven days a week in summer. Call for off-season hours. Goombays closes for Dec and Jan.

i The soft-sculpture ceiling at Goombays Grille & Raw Bar is an amazing work of art. While sitting in the dining room, you can look up and imagine you're seeing what a fish sees when it glances up toward the ocean's surface.

PORT O' CALL RESTAURANT &
GASLIGHT SALOON $$$
NC 12, MP 8½, Kill Devil Hills
(252) 441-7484
www.outerbanksportocall.com

This antiques-adorned restaurant offers fresh seafood cuisine with entrees including an array of seafood, veal, chicken, pasta, and beef. Blackboard specials change nightly. Each dinner comes with fresh-baked bread, starch of the day, and salad. The soups and chowders are hot and succulent, and all the desserts are luscious. A children's menu is offered. Special early-bird dinners are served from 4:30 to 6 p.m. Live entertainment is offered in a large, separate saloon (see the Nightlife chapter). Port O' Call is open from mid-March through Dec.

THE THAI ROOM $$
Oceanside Plaza, NC 12, MP 8½,
Kill Devil Hills
(252) 441-1180

The Thai Room has been an insiders' favorite for years. Jimmy, the fast-talking, fast-moving owner, lets his patrons choose their own level of spice—from mild to gasping hot. When he asks, "Very hot?"—think twice before you say yes. He means it. Besides the daily specials, an in-season buffet dinner allows you to sample several of the wonderful choices. Try the deep-fried soft-shell crabs when they're in season; they're perfectly crunchy and beyond description. To complete your meal choose from more than a dozen American-style desserts. The Thai Room is open for lunch and dinner year-round. All items are available for take-out. The restaurant also has a full bar where you can indulge in exotic drinks and Thai beer while you wait for a table or take-out order.

OUTER BANKS BREWING STATION $$
US 158, MP 8½, Kill Devil Hills
(252) 449-BREW
www.obbrewing.com

Everything about the Outer Banks Brewing Station is first class. Fine handcrafted brews, inspired cuisine, and noble yet subtle decor all work together to provide a sublime culinary experience. Customers who expect standard brewhouse pub fare will be pleasantly surprised to find contemporary, cutting-edge cuisine prepared by schooled chefs. The signature beers are always in demand. Ölsch is always on tap, and five other brews change according to the season, the brewer's whim, or the alignment of the stars.

The owners say they believe that fine brewing deserves to be paired with revolutionary cuisine, and they certainly have the goods to prove it. The food is outstanding.

The specials are always appealing, but the jerk-basted wahoo over jasmine rice with pineapple beurre blanc is astounding. Desserts are extremely tempting; so is a glass of tawny port. The restaurant also has an excellent wine list.

The Outer Banks Brewing Station occupies a unique, church/barnlike building built especially for this use. Two silos anchor the building, prompting the owners to advertise their location as "between the silos in Kill Devil Hills." The serpentine bar stretches into the back of the restaurant, where a crowd gathers for drinks until the wee hours (see the Nightlife chapter). The Brewing Station is a year-round restaurant. Lunch and dinner are served daily, and a kid's menu is available. Check out the sleek new 93-foot wind turbine. The power it generates will pay for itself in about 15 years.

✳JK'S $$$
US 158, MP 9, Kill Devil Hills
(252) 441-9555
www.jksrestaurant.com

Fine-dining insiders love JK's selection of mesquite-grilled meats. JK's serves western beef shipped directly from Nebraska, lamb and veal from Summerfield Farms in Virginia, and ribs from the Midwest. A seasoned, professional staff fits right in with the classy, comfortable dining room and bar. Three to four varieties of fresh fish are offered nightly. The menu varies according to the best meats available, but generally it has a prime rib chop, porterhouse steak, New York strip, Kansas City strip, top sirloin, veal rib chop, and lamb loin chops. Ribs and chicken are dry marinated with JK's special seasoning and are then mesquite grilled. JK's has a full bar and an excellent wine list with some really good values. Dinner is served from 5 p.m. year-round; takeout is available.

BOB'S GRILL $
US 158, MP 9, Kill Devil Hills
(252) 441-0707
www.bobsgrillobx.com

Bob serves big, cheap breakfasts all year, seven days a week, until 2:30 p.m.—and that's hard to find around here. The blueberry pancakes are big enough to cover the entire plate. Eggs are made any way you want, and the hash browns flavored with onions and peppers are some of the best around.

For lunch a hamburger, tuna steak, or one of several traditional hot and cold sandwiches will fill you. Owner Bob McCoy cooks much of the food himself. A hot lunch special is available every day. You can't leave town without trying Bob's No. 1 seller—Philly steak and cheese. Dinners feature the biggest cuts of prime rib on the Outer Banks, Cajun beer batter–dipped shrimp, and fresh mahimahi caught just offshore. The salads are also good. Save room for the hot fudge brownie dessert. Bob's is closed from 2:30 to 5 p.m. daily, but it's open for three meals a day every day all year.

THE PIT SURF SHOP, BAR AND GRILL $
US 158, MP 9, Kill Devil Hills
(252) 480-3128
www.pitsurf.com

The Pit is the favorite counterculture hangout of the beach. It's the prime après-surf spot, where the food is good and cheap, the staff has personality, and board-sport videos are always shown. The hallmarks of Pit dining are economy and portion size; the West Coast–style wraps are big and filling. Beans, meats, cheese, veggies, and even mashed potatoes are blended into a variety of creative wraps. The Pit makes a mean quesadilla, hot sandwiches, salads in a fresh tortilla bowl, appetizers, fries, rings, wings, and more. Drinks run the gamut from alcohol to up-to-the-minute SoBe flavors and everything in between. Food is served continuously from 11:30 a.m. until 9 p.m., and delivery is offered on weekdays in the off-season. People always hang around the Pit, killing time and meeting friends. See the Nightlife and Water Sports chapters for more about the Pit.

DARE DEVIL'S AUTHENTIC PIZZERIA $
NC 12, MP 9, Kill Devil Hills
(252) 441-6330, (252) 441-2353

This pizza parlor has been in business for more than a decade and is known for its superb stromboli and hand-tossed pizzas. You can also order any item for takeout. Dare Devil's is open 7 days a week for lunch and dinner from Mar through Nov.

MEXICALI BREWZ $
NC 12, MP 9, Kill Devil Hills
(252) 480-0069

The vivacious colors of the outside of Mexicali Brewz invite you to a gratefully good dining experience. The inexpensive menu offers surprisingly great choices. Overstuffed fish burritos and mildly spicy chipotle chicken, both served with black beans and rice, are two of the delicious choices. A full bar specializes in beer and margaritas. This kid-friendly spot is open Mar through Oct. If you like to spend time outside, live music is offered occasionally in the side courtyard. Corn hole is played while patrons enjoy the Outer Banks summer nights.

MAMA KWAN'S GRILL AND TIKI BAR $$
US 158, MP 9½, Kill Devil Hills
(252) 441-7889
www.mamakwans.com
Mama Kwan's is a favorite surf-style hangout in Kill Devil Hills, a haven of good food sandwiched between McDonald's and Pizza Hut on French Fry Alley in the cedar-shake building. The atmosphere is laid-back and fun, with classic and current surf videos and occasional Elvis movies playing on TVs. Children are welcomed with a special menu and crayons.

Mama's features local seafood, land food, and veggies with touches from some of the world's best surf spots. The full bar serves beer, wine, and specialty frozen drinks in novelty glassware. Lunch and dinner are served daily. This is a popular nighttime hangout, and a late-night menu is served every night in season and on weekends in the off-season (see the Nightlife chapter).

AMERICAN PIE $
NC 12, MP 9½, Kill Devil Hills
(252) 441-3332
For some mouthwatering fresh-baked pizza with a hand-tossed crust, step into American Pie. This restaurant serves only the freshest ingredients on their New York–style pizzas. Homemade stromboli, calzones, subs, and salads round out the menu. The homemade ice cream is a must to round out your meal. Patrons may dine indoors, outdoors, or order to take out. Delivery is also available.

PEPPERCORNS $$
Ramada Plaza Resort, NC 12, MP 9½, Kill Devil Hills
(252) 441-2151
With a wide-open dining room overlooking the Atlantic Ocean, Peppercorns has a traditional family menu with something for everyone. Chef Greg Sniegowski prepares many Outer Banks favorites, including locally caught shrimp and crab cakes. The soup du jour is always filling and delicious. Entrees include chicken stuffed with crab meat, andouille sausage, and smoked Gouda cheese and jerk mahimahi served with a mouthwatering pineapple sweet-and-sour sauce. Vegetarian entrees are always provided. There's a full bar and a children's menu. Peppercorns provides take-out food and room service for Ramada guests. This restaurant is open daily year-round for breakfast, lunch, and dinner. There's nightly entertainment in season on the outdoor tiki deck and in the lounge. Peppercorns is a popular spot for banquets and wedding receptions.

PIGMAN'S BAR-B-QUE $
US 158, MP 9½, Kill Devil Hills
(252) 441-6803
www.pigman.com
Richard and Topr are the owners of Pigman's, known for its delectable food. At this counter-service eatery you can get beef, pork, chicken, and barbecue. Try the low-fat creations: catfish, turkey, and tuna barbecue. The sweet potato fries here are spectacular. Catering is available. Pigman's is open for

lunch and dinner seven days a week year-round. Piggy Lou's Little Squealers is a special menu for those younger than age 10 or older than age 65.

FLYING FISH CAFE $$
US 158, MP 10, Kill Devil Hills
(252) 441-6894
www.flyingfishcafeobx.com

This delightful restaurant serves an array of American and Mediterranean dishes. Chefs at Flying Fish make their own pasta daily and offer seafood, vegetarian entrees, and a variety of unusual grains and starches. Gourmet potpies, eggplant Parmesan, at least four types of fresh fish, and exceptional beef dishes are always on the menu. All entrees come with a starch of the day, vegetables, and just-baked bread, including focaccia. At dessert time can you resist the Grecian Urn, a waffle filled with ice cream and topped with glazed fresh fruit and whipped cream?

The Flying Fish Cafe has won several *Wine Spectator* Awards of Excellence. More than 40 types of wine are served either by the bottle or by the glass. A children's menu is available. Early-bird dinner specials are served from 5 to 6 p.m. The Flying Fish is open for dinner every day year-round. Reservations are recommended.

COLINGTON ISLAND

COLINGTON CAFE $$
Colington Road, 1 mile west of US 158,
Kill Devil Hills
(252) 480-1123
www.colingtoncafe.com

Step back in time at this cozy Victorian cafe, nestled among live oaks on Colington Road. This popular restaurant is only a mile off the Bypass, but once you've arrived you'll feel worlds away from the busy beach. This restored old home set high on a hill is tranquil and absolutely lovely. Three small dining rooms are adorned in tasteful decor. Nightly specials may include wonderful pasta dishes, a mixed grill with hollandaise, game fish, and tender filet mignon. Seafood entrees depend upon what's just been caught. Only fresh herbs and vegetables are used in cooking and as side dishes.

Owner Carlen Pearl's French heritage permeates her restaurant's delicious cream sauces, and she makes most of the irresistible desserts herself—from blackberry cobbler to chocolate tortes and crème brûlée. Restaurants in Colington may serve only beer or wine by law, but you'll have plenty of choices at Colington Cafe. Check out the reserve wines and be sure to save room for a glass of port with dessert. Colington Cafe is open for dinner seven days a week, Apr through Nov, and for the Christmas holidays. Call for off-season hours. Reservations are highly recommended, and a children's menu is available.

OUTER BANKS EPICUREAN $–$$
Colington Road
(252) 480-0005
www.outerbanksepicurean.com

Amy Huggins believes in cooking slow food for busy people. Local wild caught seafood and meats that are hormone and antibiotic free are always on the menu at Outer Banks Epicurean. Take-home meals are fully cooked and refrigerated—just reheat. Cooking classes for kids and adults are offered, as are kayak tours of crab shedders. Check the website—Amy is brimming with creative and fun ideas. Open Mon through Fri from 10 a.m. until 8 p.m. and Sat from noon until 8 p.m.

NAGS HEAD

RED DRUM GRILLE AND TAPHOUSE $$
NC 12, MP 10, Nags Head
(252) 480-1095

Since opening in 1998, the Red Drum Grille and Taphouse has been carving out its niche on the Outer Banks. The handsome redbrick exterior presents an apt introduction to the tasteful decor: Glossy, deep rust-colored tables and cozy oak booths give the room a warm, inviting feel.

The menu has something for everyone. Lunch fare from the steamer menu includes crab legs, shrimp, vegetables, clams, and oysters. Large burgers, a chicken sandwich with Smithfield ham and Havarti cheese, fish-and-chips, and a fish burrito are some of the locals' favorites.

At dinner Red Drum offers simple country fare. You'll find apple-glazed pork chops, ribs, steaks, a mixed grill of the day, and lots of fresh seafood, including seafood pasta with large shrimp and scallops and a mixed seafood platter. Grilled or fried fresh fish, pasta, and vegetarian dishes are also available. The Red Drum Grille and Taphouse serves lunch and dinner from Feb through Nov and has a kid's menu.

KELLY'S OUTER BANKS
RESTAURANT & TAVERN $$$
US 158, MP 10½, Nags Head
(252) 441-4116
www.kellysrestaurant.com

Kelly's is an Outer Banks tradition and one of the most popular restaurants. This is a large, upscale eatery and a busy place. The decor reflects the area's rich maritime heritage. The tavern is hopping seven nights a week (see the Nightlife chapter).

Dinner is the only meal served here, and it's offered in several rooms upstairs and downstairs. Kelly's menu offers fresh seafood dishes, chicken, beef, pastas, and a raw bar for those who enjoy feasting on oysters and other steamed shellfish. An assortment of delicious homemade breads accompanies each meal. Kelly's sweet potato biscuits are succulent—we usually ask for a second basket. Desserts are flavorful, filling, and homemade. A separate children's menu is available, complete with crayons and special placemats for coloring. Kelly's also caters private parties, weddings, and any style event imaginable. The restaurant and lounge are open year-round.

DIRTY DICK'S CRAB HOUSE $$
US 158, MP 10½, Nags Head
(252) 480-3425
www.dirtydickscrabs.com

The litany of crab choices at Dirty Dick's Crab House reminds us of Bubba's roster of shrimp in *Forrest Gump*. There are snow crab legs, soft-shell crab sandwiches, spiced crabs, crab cakes, and steamed crabs, plus steamed shrimp, clams, clam chowder, gumbo, jambalaya, and Cajun Creole. The popular Dick Burger is a crab and shrimp patty with Cajun sauce. There are sandwich platter specials and offerings for the kids. You can purchase Dick's special spice and famous Dirty Dick's T-shirts. Crustaceans are cooked to order for takeout. Dirty Dick's has a sister Outer Banks location on NC 12 in Avon, by the Avon Pier. Two other locations are open in Panama City, Florida, and Myrtle Beach, South Carolina. All locations are open seasonally; call for hours.

FIREFLY $$
US 158, MP 10¾, Nags Head
(252) 480-0047

The bright yellow building on the west side of the bypass is home to one of the newer restaurants on the Outer Banks. Firefly serves good southern cuisine at an affordable price. This family atmosphere restaurant offers butter knife tender filets, slow-cooked ribs, seafood, and special creations like bacon lobster mac and cheese. This restaurant is open for both lunch and dinner 7 days a week in season. Kids have their own menu and can order the special "Bug Juice" drink, which comes with its own light show. Wine, beer, and a full bar are available.

TORTUGAS' LIE SHELLFISH BAR AND GRILLE $
NC 12, MP 11, Nags Head
(252) 441-RAWW
www.tortugaslie.com

A locals' favorite on the Outer Banks, this small, upbeat eatery is housed in a turquoise cottage across from the ocean near a great surf break. Tortugas' features an enclosed porch furnished with handmade wooden booths, table seating, and an expanded bar that seats more than two dozen people. The creatively concocted food is good, and the atmosphere inside is fun and casual, with turtle-themed batiks hanging from the white walls.

The menu offers quick-fried fish bites, supersize fish and black bean burritos, sandwiches, seafood flavored with outrageous spices, and a full raw bar. The french fries are among the best on the Banks. Dinner entrees include pork medallions, steak stir-fries, just-off-the-boat tuna steaks, succulent shrimp, and pasta plates. The daily specials are tempting; sushi is served on Wednesday night, and the place usually is packed with locals. Desserts are delicious and change daily.

The full bar offers loads of specialty drinks. This hip, laid-back eatery is open seven days a week for lunch and dinner from Feb through Dec. Call for winter hours. (See the Nightlife chapter.)

PIER HOUSE RESTAURANT $
Nags Head Fishing Pier, NC 12, MP 12, Nags Head
(252) 441-5141
www.nagsheadpier.com

With an amazing ocean view on the beach, this family-style restaurant allows patrons to sit right above the ocean. You can feel the salt spray if you dine on the screened porch, and from inside the air-conditioned building, you'll notice that waves sometimes crash beneath the wooden floor's slats. This is a great, easygoing place to enjoy a big breakfast before a day of fishing or to take a break from angling on a hot afternoon. The Em Special is an insiders' favorite for breakfast. Lunch includes sandwiches, soups, and seafood specials. Dinner entrees include local fresh seafood, steaks, and chicken. All-you-can-eat dinners are popular picks, accompanied by coleslaw, hush puppies, and french fries. You can have your fish grilled, broiled, or fried. And, if you hook 'em, they cook 'em. Free sightseeing passes come with supper so you can stroll down the long pier after your meal and watch the anglers and surfers. Pier House Restaurant is open seven days a week from Mar through Nov. Breakfast, lunch, and dinner are served until mid-October, and the restaurant has all liquor permits.

i Clean the fish you catch, and the Pier House Restaurant in Nags Head will broil or fry it right up for you.

AUSTIN FISH COMPANY $
US 158, MP 12½, Nags Head
(252) 441-7412
www.austinfishcompany.com

A visit to Nags Head isn't complete without visiting Austin Fish Company, across from

Jockey's Ridge. The store stocks an extensive seafood collection—including crabmeat, steamed crabs, shrimp, oysters, clams, fish, scallops, and tuna—for customers to take home and cook. Even selective locals drive out of their way to purchase Austin's fresh seafood. If you've enjoyed a good day fishing, Austin's will vacuum pack your catch and ship it home for you.

JOCKEY'S RIBS $$
NC 12, MP 13, Nags Head
(252) 441-1141
For dining in or for takeout, Jockey's Ribs has been serving finger-licking barbecue ribs and more for over 20 years now. Entrees include lean and meaty slabs of pork ribs, hot and spicy barbecued chicken wings, roasted chicken, steaks, chops, chicken and rib combos, and seafood. The seafood is always a favorite. A children's menu is available. Dinner is served nightly from 5 to 10 p.m. in season. Call for off-season hours.

MULLIGAN'S $$
US 158, MP 13, Nags Head
(252) 480-2000
www.mulligansobx.com
Mulligan's can lay claim to serving some of the best burgers on the beach. The burgers are big, juicy, and tasty and come with a variety of toppings. Mulligan's also serves steak, seafood, and an array of pasta entrees for lunch and dinner. A new steam bar, upstairs and downstairs dining rooms, and two full bars make this hopping restaurant a great place to visit when you are hungry and don't want to wait forever on your food. Mulligan's is located in a bright yellow building across the street and just south of Jockey's Ridge. The interior is colorful and fun. A children's menu is available. The restaurant is open

year-round and has gone green, recycling glass, oyster shells, and more. Evening entertainment includes poker on Tuesday night and karaoke on Thursday and Friday.

COUNTRY DELI $
Surfside Plaza, NC 12, MP 13,
Nags Head
(252) 441-5684
www.countrydeliobx.com
Strictly a take-out place, Country Deli offers breakfast breads plus some of the biggest sandwiches on the beach. You can create your own sandwich or choose from several popular menu items. Side salads of macaroni, pasta, potato, and vegetables also are served. Pick from several types of chips; sour pickles come free with every option. Brownies and cheesecake are tempting dessert selections. Country Deli is open for lunch and dinner seven days a week during the summer and offers free delivery to Nags Head and parts of Kill Devil Hills. No credit cards accepted.

GRITS GRILL $
US 158, MP 14, Nags Head
(252) 449-2888
Just north of the Outer Banks Mall is Grits Grill, which has a strong local following. The restaurant offers a standard-fare breakfast and lunch menu plus fresh bakery items and fresh Krispy Kreme donuts. If you can't live without your Krispy Kremes, make sure you get to Grits early in the morning, because they sell out quickly. Grits specializes in takeout orders and is open all year from 6 a.m. to 3 p.m.

LA FOGATA MEXICAN RESTAURANT $
US 158, MP 14, Nags Head
(252) 441-4179

RESTAURANTS

Across from the Outer Banks Mall, La Fogata joins its original Kitty Hawk sister restaurant with the same name and some delicious Mexican food at affordable prices. These restaurants boast a strong Outer Banks following. The mall location has the same menu and similar decor as the Kitty Hawk restaurant (see the listing under Kitty Hawk for more information).

TAIKO JAPANESE RESTAURANT AND SUSHI BAR $$
Outer Banks Mall, US 158, MP 14, Nags Head
(252) 449-8895

This Outer Banks restaurant serves sushi all day, for lunch and dinner. Taiko's sushi is top-notch, rolled tightly and cut into perfect, bite-size pieces. Our favorite is the spicy tuna roll, with fresh raw tuna, a kick of spices, and a hint of crunch. The miso and clear soups are refreshing, as are the udon and soba noodle dishes and the seaweed salad. Japanese-style entrees include steak teriyaki, shrimp tempura, and chicken sukiyaki. Lunch boxes combine sushi or sashimi with seaweed, rice, and a shrimp dumpling.

The dining room is peaceful and serene, with soft music and tasteful, understated Asian decor. Japanese beer, sake, plum wine, green tea, and many other beverages are served. Everything at Taiko is available for takeout. Taiko is open year-round, serving lunch and dinner daily in season. Call for off-season hours.

PAMLICO JACK'S PIRATE HIDEAWAY $$
US 158, MP 16, Nags Head
(252) 441-2637
www.pamlicojacks.com

Formerly known as Penguin Isle, Pamlico Jack's is the latest restaurant in the local Kelly family host of eateries. This family-style restaurant has a killer deck and view of the Pamlico sound. Food is deliciously prepared by local star Chef Lee Miller, and the food is island inspired. Legend has it that Pamlico Jack traveled from the Caribbean to the Keys, and then the Outer Banks and back again! And the food samples the finest from each area. Adults will enjoy the Rum Jumper Bar, and the kids will find plenty to rave about. Open nightly. In-house artists provide caricatures for a fee.

THE DUNES $–$$
US 158, MP 16½, Nags Head
(252) 441-1600
www.thedunesrestaurant.com

When a large crowd or big family is gathering for a meal, this beautifully renovated restaurant accommodates all in its three huge dining rooms. Breakfast at the Dunes is a Nags Head tradition—you can tell by the packed parking lot—where every early-morning entree in every imaginable combination is offered. A popular breakfast bar is available or order off the extensive menu. Lunches include great burgers and homemade crab cakes served with fries and coleslaw. The rib-eye steak sandwich is also a good choice.

Dinners feature local, well-prepared seafood moderately priced and a huge salad bar. All-you-can-eat specials are popular. There are also plenty of desserts to choose from if you're not already too full. The Dunes' R Bar is a full-service cocktail lounge. The service is fast and friendly at this nonsmoking establishment. The Dunes serves every day except in late Dec and most of Jan. A children's menu is offered,

OWENS' RESTAURANT $$$
NC 12, MP 16½, Nags Head
(252) 441-7309
www.owensrestaurant.com

The oldest Outer Banks restaurant owned and operated continuously by the same family, Owens' is a local legend. This eatery has thrived for more than 60 years.

Clara and Bob Owens first owned a small hot dog stand in Manteo. In 1946 they opened a 24-seat cafe in Nags Head on the deserted strip of sand that's now filled with hotels, rental cottages, and thousands of vacationers who arrive each summer. The Owenses reared their two children, Bobby and Clara Mae, in the restaurant, serving breakfast, lunch, and dinner during those early days. This food-loving family serves some of the best traditional Outer Banks–style seafood in the area.

Owens' Restaurant now seats more than 200 people and offers only evening meals. The atmosphere is still homey yet upscale; the food is still fresh and made from scratch; the large lobby overflows with memorabilia of the barrier islands and Owens family heritage.

Locally caught seafood, often fresh off the boat, is broiled, fried, sautéed, or grilled each evening. Coconut shrimp, "Miss O" crab cakes, and pasta are among the most popular entrees. There's a mixed grill for patrons who prefer prime rib with their fish. Live Maine lobsters, plucked from the tank, are steamed just before serving. Owens' soups, including Hatteras-style clam chowder and lobster bisque, are delicious. All of the homemade desserts are well worth saving room for.

A full bar upstairs in the Station Keepers' Lounge serves beer, wine, mixed drinks, and special coffee concoctions. Light fare is also available upstairs. Owens' is open from mid-March through New Year's Eve. Dinner is served seven days a week. Reservations are not accepted.

✳SAM & OMIE'S $$
NC 12, MP 16½, Nags Head
(252) 441-7366
www.samandomies.net

Begun as a place for early-morning anglers to indulge in a big breakfast before the Oregon Inlet charter fishing fleet took off, Sam & Omie's is one of the oldest family restaurants on the barrier islands. In fact, the famed *Lost Colony* production and Sam & Omie's have both been around since the 1930s. Omie Tillett retired his boat, *The Sportsman,* and he long ago sold this little wooden building at Whalebone Junction. The restaurant, however, retains its old beach charm and continues to produce hearty, home-style food based on traditional local recipes for breakfast, lunch, and dinner.

This is a very casual place with wooden booths and tables and a full-service bar. Local fishermen congregate to contemplate the day's catch, and families flock to enjoy the low-priced, filling meals. Photographs of famous Gulf Stream catches line the walls, and the TV usually is tuned in to some exciting sporting event. For breakfast, omelets are a favorite. We like to make a meal of the rich she-crab soup and red chili poppers for lunch. Salads, sandwiches, hamburgers, fish fillets, turkey clubs, and daily specials also are served. A steamer has been added for healthy vegetables and fish. For dinner try a soft-shell crab sandwich in season or select fish or chicken entrees. Sam & Omie's is open from early Mar through Nov, at least. Call for winter hours.

SUGAR CREEK SOUNDFRONT SEAFOOD RESTAURANT $$

Nags Head–Manteo Causeway,
Nags Head
(252) 441-4963
www.sugarcreekseafood.com

Sugar Creek is one of the most popular places on the beach for lunch and dinner. Eat at the full-service bar in this casual restaurant or sit at a table in one of the soundfront dining rooms. The seafood stew is extremely tasty and overflowing with shrimp and scallops. Marinated tuna is a must for fish lovers. Prices are reasonable, and the atmosphere is lively and fun. Sugar Creek is open from Mar through Thanksgiving seven days a week. Next door at the Sugar Shack, you can eat at one of the tables or order great take-out food including pizza.

*THE BRINE AND BOTTLE $–$$

Caribbean Professional Building,
Nags Head-Manteo Causeway,
Nags Head
(252) 715-1818
www.thebrineandbottle.com

Inspired by old Nags Head and the things that owners Andrew and Ashley love, this dining destination is a treasure of a find. You'll find the menu to be delightful and unusual with pickled eggs and homemade pimento cheese offered, as well as soups that are out of this world. Local regional cuisine is served in a small plate format. The Brine and Bottle won the coveted 2011 Chef's Choice award at the Taste of the Beach. If you enjoy a killer sound view with your wine or beer then this is the place for you. Dine inside or out on the glorious deck. Be sure to put a stop at Bottle and Brine on your list of places to visit. Wide selection of choice wines for retail sale available.

TALE OF THE WHALE $$

Nags Head–Manteo Causeway,
Nags Head
(252) 441-7332
www.taleofthewhalenagshead.com

Family-operated and -owned for more than two decades, Tale of the Whale is situated on Roanoke Sound. You can enjoy the delightful views either looking through the expansive windows inside while savoring dinner or on the 75-foot deck and gazebo while sipping a refreshing cocktail.

Tale of the Whale serves the freshest available food in generous portions. Seafood, lots of pasta, steaks, chicken, and prime rib are menu staples. Specials are offered daily, and early-bird specials are available from 5 to 6 p.m. in season. Combination platters are prepared fried or broiled. Desserts are made on the premises. Tale of the Whale is open daily for dinner from Apr through Nov. A children's menu is available, and seniors receive a 10 percent discount on their entree.

BASNIGHT'S LONE CEDAR CAFE $$

Nags Head–Manteo Causeway,
Nags Head
(252) 441-5405
www.lonecedarcafe.com

The Basnight family of Manteo operates this casual, upscale eatery where diners wearing everything from shorts to suits are welcome. In fact, it's not unusual to see the former president pro tem of the state senate himself, Marc Basnight, talking with guests and removing dinner plates. Check out the mural of local boats completed by family members. This restaurant is one of very few in the state to be named a certified green restaurant. Shedders along the soundfront area of the restaurant provide a scenic spot for crabs to shed their shells and provide soft shell crabs for diner. No chemicals are used at this toxic free restaurant.

Appetizers are plentiful, ranging from onion straws to clam chowder, seafood bisque, clam and oyster fritters, hot crab balls, and hot crab dip plus soups and other specials of the day. Lunch entrees start at $8.99. and include sandwiches and fresh local seafood. For dinner try Black Angus beef, homemade pasta, sliced duck breast, fried or broiled seafood, or order any of the evening specials. Choose a beverage from the full bar and an extensive wine list. Desserts, home-baked daily, include pumpkin and pecan praline cheesecakes; pecan, peanut butter, lemon, or key lime pie; banana fritters; and 16-layer chocolate cake.

This cafe offers a view of the water from every table and is open for lunch and dinner daily year-round. Vegetarian and children's offerings are available. Reservations are not accepted.

ROANOKE ISLAND

Manteo

GARDEN DELI & PIZZERIA $
US 64, Manteo
(252) 473-6888
Shaded by pine trees, this tiny restaurant has a breezy outdoor deck perfect for summer dining. The cheerful, hometown crew has watched this Garden grow into one of the most popular lunch spots for the working crowd in Manteo. Here New York–style stone-oven pizzas are cooked to order and packaged to go, if you wish. The Philly cheese steaks, panini, burgers, gyros, and a wide assortment of deli sandwiches, homemade salads, and antipasto salads are wonderful. Fresh tuna and chicken salad plates are just right for a light lunch or dinner. Garden Pizzeria delivers evenings to Roanoke Island. The restaurant is open for lunch and dinner Mon through Sat year-round. Call about delivered boxed lunches for charter boat trips. Garden Deli specializes in party-boat catering.

i Celebrate Oktoberfest on the Outer Banks at the Weeping Radish Brewery & Bavarian Restaurant in Manteo each September. There's a German oompah band among others, traditional dancing, beer, food, and activities for the whole family.

BIG AL'S SODA FOUNTAIN & GRILL $
US 64/264, Manteo
(252) 473-5570
www.bigalsobx.com
You can't miss Big Al's, across from the Christmas Shop in downtown Manteo. Originally planned as an ice-cream parlor, this spot has expanded into a full-blown soda fountain and family restaurant. It's definitely a place to take the kids. With '50s decor and memorabilia, Big Al's is a great place to kick back and enjoy some good ol' American food and fountain treats. Plus you can get fish so fresh, it's literally off the boat. Children's meals are reasonably priced. Kids can have fun in the game room, with a pinball machine, video games, and a jukebox. There's even a dance floor. Big Al's serves lunch and dinner daily.

DARRELL'S RESTAURANT $$
US 64, Manteo
(252) 473-5366
This down-home restaurant started as an ice-cream stand in 1960 and has been a favorite

family-style eatery for the past two decades. It's common knowledge that the fried oysters at Darrell's are among the best in town. Menu items such as popcorn shrimp, crab cakes, grilled marinated tuna, and fried scallops are served with french fries, coleslaw, and hush puppies to provide more than enough to fuel you through the day. Meat eaters will be satiated by steaks, barbecued minced pork, and grilled marinated chicken. Daily seafood specials are served for dinner; a children's menu is available. The hot fudge cake is a must for dessert. Beer and wine are served. Darrell's is open for lunch and dinner year-round but is closed Sun.

HUNGRY PELICAN $
The Waterfront Shops, Manteo
(252) 473-9441

Deli sandwiches are the specialty of the house at the Hungry Pelican. Sandwiches are piled high with a variety of meats including ham, salami, turkey, roast beef, and more. The aroma of their fresh-baked bread fills the air. Soups, salads, and several side dishes are offered. The homemade desserts are delicious. Seating can be found outdoors or inside with a gorgeous Manteo waterfront view.

ADRIANNA'S RESTAURANT $$-$$$
The Waterfront Shops, Manteo
(252) 473-4800

Overlooking Shallowbag Bay and the state ship *Elizabeth II*, this is a favorite Manteo eatery for watching boats on the water or a romantic summer moon. It's a picturesque and relaxing restaurant with good service and equally admirable food. Formerly the Waterfront Trellis, this restaurant has been completely redesigned. Intended primarily as a wedding reception site complete with a waterfront view, this also makes a romantic

reservations-only dining experience. Locals and visitors reserve Adrianna's for wedding receptions, family parties, or reunions. Since this restaurant is less than a 10-minute drive from *The Lost Colony,* it's a good place to take in an early meal before the outdoor drama begins. Beer, wine, and champagne are available. Lunch and dinner are served seven days a week from Mar through Dec.

FULL MOON CAFE & GRILL $$
Creef's Corner Queen Elizabeth Avenue, Manteo
(252) 473-MOON

This eclectic eatery consistently overflows with local and visiting patrons. The innovative cuisine has a nouveau American flair. Most of the entrees and specials (which usually involve creative takes on pasta and seafood) are so unusual we haven't seen them anywhere else on the Outer Banks. Hummus spread, baked Brie, and mushroom caps stuffed with shrimp are succulent appetizers. Lunch specials include gourmet sandwiches to satisfy everyone's tastes, vegetarian offerings, seafood, chicken, and homemade soups, such as Hungarian mushroom, curried spinach, and spicy tomato. Each entree is served with corn chips and Full Moon's own salsa. The dinner menu features enticing seafood dishes, stuffed chicken breasts, roasted eggplant with other vegetables in marinara sauce and provolone cheese, and a beef dish with portobello mushrooms and a Gorgonzola cheese sauce. Daily pasta specials are also available as a half serving with a side salad. All the desserts are delightful. Beer (including some microbrews) and a good selection of wine are available. You can eat inside the dining room or dine outdoors in the courtyard if you take any meal to go. Reservations are accepted for parties of six or more. Full Moon is open for lunch and dinner seven days a week in summer. Hours are reduced off-season, so call for specific schedules. The Full Moon Brew Pub is located conveniently next door.

POOR RICHARD'S SANDWICH SHOP $
The Waterfront, Manteo
(252) 473-3333
www.poorrichardsmanteo.com
With half the workforce in Manteo making a beeline to Poor Richard's every day, this casual eatery is a local gathering spot for reasonably priced food with fast counter service and interesting offerings. Try the cucumber sandwich with cream cheese—a cool meal that surprises your palate. Cold and grilled sandwiches are made to order, and specials are offered daily. Homemade soups, meatless chili, hot dogs, salad plates, cookies, and ice cream are also available. Breakfast includes scrambled egg and bacon sandwiches, bagels and cream cheese, and fresh fruit. Steamed shrimp is available for lunch and dinner. Poor Richard's is a worthy filling station. You can eat inside at a roomy booth or take your meal out on the back porch and enjoy the waterfront view. Poor Richard's is open daily in the summer for breakfast, lunch, and dinner. Occasionally the restaurant hosts live music in the evenings. Though it's open year-round, call for off-season hours. Poor Richard's After Hours is located in front of the restaurant, serving wine and beer. Live music is offered in season Thursday through Saturday.

1587 $$$
Tranquil House Inn
405 Queen Elizabeth St., Manteo
(252) 473-1587
www.1587.com

The owner of this critically acclaimed restaurant can make your mouth water just by reading his menu aloud. The offerings are unusual, upscale, cosmopolitan, and some of the most ambitious on the Outer Banks. Ambience is elegant and romantic: The soft glow of intimate lighting, a gleaming copper-topped bar in a separate lounge area, and polished wood and mirrors reflect the lights sparkling off boats anchored in Shallowbag Bay. The constantly changing menu is always as fresh and fabulous as the food.

Soups prepared each day might include Mediterranean mussels and crayfish with spring vegetables and feta cheese in a light tomato broth. Salads, served a la carte, offer mixed greens with pecan-encrusted goat cheese, tossed with a mango vinaigrette with dried cherries, toasted pumpkin seeds, and sweet onions.

Dinner entrees range from crispy cornmeal orange accompanied by roasted vegetable risotto and whole-grain mustard cream, finished with white-wine-sautéed shrimp and vegetables, to Asiago risotto with sea scallops, shrimp, and vegetables surrounded by crawfish gumbo.

A children's menu offers simpler dishes for younger tastes. Vegetarian requests are welcome. The exquisite dessert creations are delicious and are so beautiful that you may want to take a snapshot before digging in!

*THE ORTEGA'Z GRILL $
Sir Walter Raleigh St., Manteo
(252) 473-5911
www.ortegaz.com
Bring some spice to your life at The Ortega'z Grill. Located in the former Green Dolphin, Ortega'z serves delicious southwestern cuisine. Everything here is prepared fresh

in-house; even the tortillas are homemade. Three main choices for the Latin entrees are delicately roasted chicken, tender beef, and pulled pork. The pulled pork tacos are a popular and satisfying choice. Sandwiches are also served, and dinner entrees are available in the evenings. Open 11 a.m. to 9 p.m. Mon through Sat, Ortega'z serves beer and wine. Takeout is available, and there is a menu just for the smaller tykes in your party.

i If you're going to watch the entertainment under the stars at Illuminations Summer Arts Series at Roanoke Island Festival Park, Manteo restaurants and caterers will provide boxed picnics to take with you. Call Festival Park at (252) 475-1500 for information.

THE COFFEEHOUSE ON ROANOKE ISLAND $
106-A Sir Walter Raleigh St., Manteo
(252) 475-1295
Here is the perfect coffeehouse atmosphere: sofas, newspapers, local chatter, tables inside or on the deck, and a friendly owner who handles the busiest of morning rushes with aplomb. The coffee is just right, not overly strong, and the espresso and cappuccino drinks are expertly prepared. A selection of loose teas is available. Iced coffees are good for summer days, and the chai milk shake beats everything. Milk shakes and smoothies are large, and the staff will give you the leftovers if they make one that's too big for your cup. The Coffeehouse serves heavenly cinnamon oat and blueberry scones, muffins, bagels, cinnamon bread, pastries, biscotti, granola, and fruit. You can have your granola with

soy milk or yogurt, if you'd like. The Coffeehouse is open every day for breakfast, light lunches, and snacks.

LA CABANA $
US 64, Manteo
(252) 473-9364
Tony Calvio brings you Latin flavor from Central America—and it's the newest insiders favorite. Fried plantains, tamales, coconut rice, beans, and more are offered at this popular eatery.

HATTERAS ISLAND

Rodanthe, Waves & Salvo

LISA'S PIZZERIA $
NC 12, Rodanthe
(252) 987-2525
Specialty pizzas, deli sandwiches, subs, calzones, chicken parmigiana, and salads are among the most popular items at this restaurant. Lisa's also serves breadsticks, hot wings, and garlic and cheese bread. Beer and wine are available, and there's a separate children's menu. Lisa's serves lunch and dinner seven days a week beginning at 11 a.m. from early Apr through Nov. All items can be eaten inside the restaurant, carried out, or delivered. Call for off-season hours.

LEONARDO'S PIZZA $
NC 12, Rodanthe
(252) 987-6522
Located beside Reef, Leonardo's Pizza has delicious pizza, calzones, and subs. Pizzas are prepared in the traditional thin-crust Sicilian style. Sauces and dough are homemade daily, and only the freshest ingredients are used. Salads and antipasto and a wide variety of nonalcoholic drinks round out Leonardo's offerings. Delivery is free

within Rodanthe, Waves, and Salvo villages. At lunch pizza by the slice is available, along with subs and calzones. Leonardo's is open in season every day from 11:30 a.m. until 9 p.m. and from 11:30 a.m. until 9 p.m. Tues through Sat in the off-season.

GOOD WINDS SEAFOOD & WINE $$–$$$
NC 12, Waves Village Kiteboarding Resort
(252) 987-1100
www.goodwindsrestaurant.com
Overlooking the Pamlico sound from its second floor location in the Kiteboarding resort, Good Winds offers the familiar and the not-so-familiar. Excellent local seafood is featured along with specialties like alligator burgers and conch fritters. Breakfast, lunch, and dinner are served here, alongside an incredible view of the sound and kiteboarders riding the wind and waves.

ATLANTIC COAST CAFE $–$$
NC 12, Waves
(252) 987-1200
http://atlanticcoastcafe.com
For breakfast, lunch, or dinner, stop into Atlantic Coast Cafe—your taste buds will be glad you did! This spot, across from the KOA campground, serves breakfast starting at 7 a.m. Lunch and dinner include choices like the shrimp Reuben, fish wrap, burgers, and seafood. Crab cakes and other choices are available for dinner. Sides include potato salad and mac 'n cheese, a surefire kid pleaser. Frozen coffee, chai teas, and smoothies are available all day. Eat inside or outdoors on their cool soundside deck. Half-price burgers are served from 4 to 6 p.m. each evening in season. Free Wi-Fi.

TOP DOG CAFE $
NC 12, Waves
(252) 987-1272
www.topdogcafeobx.com
Specializing in burgers that weigh up to one-and-a-half pounds, Top Dog Cafe also serves steamed seafood, Philly-style steak subs, shrimp and oyster baskets, all-beef hot dogs, salads, and appetizers. The owners Joe and Pat offer a casual atmosphere, and diners can choose to eat on the shady screened porch or on the sundeck. This establishment has a kid's menu and sometimes live music. Beer and wine are served. Open for lunch and dinner; call for hours and days.

DOWN UNDER RESTAURANT & LOUNGE $$
NC 12, Rodanthe
(252) 987-2277
www.downunderrestaurant.com
This Australian-style restaurant is family friendly and offers wonderful views of the sound. Decorated with authentic Australian art and memorabilia, Down Under is one of a kind on the Outer Banks. Lunch specialties include the Great Australian bite, similar to an Aussie burger, made with hamburger, a fried egg, grilled onions, cheese, and bacon. Spicy fish burgers, Vegemite sandwiches, and marinated chicken sandwiches are good authentic options, too. Kangaroo, a delicious meat that is very popular at Down Under, is imported from Australia for 'roo stew, 'roo burgers, and kangaroo curry. Try the stuffed jalapeños served with Down Under's famous sweet chili sauce or the vegemite.

Dinner selections include the INXS platter catch of the day. Enjoy a side order of the foot-high onion rings and a Foster's lager or Cooper's stout. Parents will appreciate the children's menu, and kids will like the extraordinary decor. Everyone will enjoy the view. Down Under is open seven days a week for lunch and dinner from Apr through early Oct. The restaurant is wheelchair accessible. Large parties are welcome.

Avon

DIRTY DICK'S CRAB HOUSE $–$$
NC 12, Avon
(252) 995-3425
www.dirtydickscrabs.com

Located near Food Lion in Avon, Dirty Dick's serves an incomparable selection of crabs, including snow crab legs, soft-shell crabs, spiced crabs, crab dip, crab cakes, and steamed crabs. The steamed, spiced crabs are superb, and Dick's sells its special spice. The menu also includes steamed shrimp, clams, clam chowder, gumbo, jambalaya, and Cajun and Creole dishes. Sandwich platter specials and other offerings satisfy the kids. The tasty Dick Burger is a crab and shrimp patty with Cajun sauce. Order any of the menu items and steamed crabs for takeout. Dirty Dick's has two other Outer Banks locations, as well as one in Virginia Beach and in Panama City. Dirty Dick's is open for lunch and dinner in season and closes for a couple of months in the winter. Call for off-season hours.

AVON CAFE $$
NC 12, Avon
(252) 995-7866
www.avoncafe.com

Avon Cafe is all about good times, great friends, exceptional food, and the spirit of rock 'n' roll. Chef Laney brings a taste of zest to your plate with fresh locally inspired dishes. Hereford beef, fresh caught fish, and other items are offered on the varied menu. There is a great kid's menu that includes

mashies. The retail portion of Avon Cafe sells Laney guitars, handmade by the chef.

OCEANA'S BISTRO $–$$
NC 12, Avon
(252) 995-4991
www.oceanasbistro.com

Oceana's Bistro, located across from the Avon Pier, is known as the place to be with a menu that will please any palate. Appetizers range from bruschetta with mozzarella to sesame seared tuna. Quesadillas, sandwiches, and overstuffed potatoes are offered, too. For a fuller meal the menu has offerings like prime rib and pasta specialties. Homemade soups and desserts are served daily. Breakfast, lunch, and dinner are all available here.

DOLPHIN DEN $
NC 12, Avon
(252) 995-7717

Fine and fresh are the key components to the great lunches and dinners at the Dolphin Den. The coconut shrimp is a crowd favorite. Fried and broiled seafood platters are offered, as well as seafood linguine, crab cakes, and other yummy entrees. Open at 11 a.m. for lunch and 4 p.m. for dinner, the Dolphin Den also offers take-out family meals.

BUBBA'S TOO $$
NC 12, Avon
(252) 995-4385

For lip-smackin', finger-lickin' barbecue, Bubba's is the place on Hatteras Island. Meeting undeniable success, Bubba opened his second location next to the Food Lion many years ago. Bubba's fame has survived him, as have his eateries. Customers relish the ribs, sandwiches, Bubba's original barbecue sauces, and mouthwatering desserts. Eat at the restaurant or take the food out. Either way, have plenty of napkins and a big appetite ready. Bubba's is open for lunch and dinner Apr through Oct.

Buxton

DIAMOND SHOALS RESTAURANT $$
NC 12, Buxton
(252) 995-5217

The parking lot at this eatery, which is within walking distance of several Buxton motels, always seems to be crowded around breakfast time. Here you'll find one of the best breakfasts on Hatteras Island, featuring all your early-morning favorites. Diamond Shoals is also open for lunch and dinner, with plenty of local seafood choices, a salad bar, and some good nightly specials. Steaks and other landlubber specials are available.

A remarkable 200-gallon saltwater aquarium is stocked with tropical and Gulf Stream sea life. Diners can get an up-close-and-personal look at corals, anemones, and a variety of fascinating marine creatures. Diamond Shoals is open from Mar through Dec and weekends throughout the winter.

*ORANGE BLOSSOM CAFE AND BAKERY $$
NC 12, Buxton
(252) 995-4109
www.orangeblossombakery.com

The Orange Blossom starts the day with delicious baked goods for breakfast. The famous Apple Uglies—huge apple fritter–style pastries piled high with fruit—are favorite early-morning treats. This restaurant is open year-round, except for a spell during the winter, for takeout or eat in. Open Wed through Sun for breakfast 6:30 to 11 a.m. An array of organic coffees is also available here.

RUSTY'S SURF & TURF $$–$$$
NC 12, Buxton
(252) 995-4184
www.rustyssurfnturf.com

Chef and owner Rusty Midgett brings global styles of preparation to local seafood. Located between Natural Art Surf Shop and the ABC Store, this fun and cheerful restaurant has local artwork adorning the colorful walls. Delicious burgers, fish, and barbecue sandwiches please diners of all ages. Beer and wine served on premise.

FISH HOUSE RESTAURANT $$
NC 12, Buxton
(252) 995-5151

Can you tell that this always-bustling eatery occupies a former fish house? If the simple wooden architecture and wharf-front location didn't give it away, you might notice something fishy when you glimpse down and see the concrete floors sloped for easy washing so the fish scales flow back into the sound. The Fish House is now a comfortable restaurant where everything is casual and easygoing. Overlooking Buxton Harbor, it serves some of the best Outer Banks seafood prepared with traditional, local recipes. The tilefish is a popular choice, as are the home-made crab cakes. Everything is served on disposable plates with plastic utensils. Beer and wine are served. Fish House is open for lunch and dinner daily from Mar through Thanksgiving. A kid's menu is available.

Frisco

QUARTERDECK RESTAURANT $$
NC 12, Frisco
(252) 986-2425

Fresh local seafood served broiled or fried, crab cakes packed with jumbo lump meat, and Hatteras or New England clam chowder are among the most popular offerings here. Crab puffs and stuffed flounder are house specialties. The Quarterdeck has an 18-item salad bar. For dessert the coconut cream, lemon meringue, and key lime pies are delicious. Beer and wine are available, as is a children's menu. This low-key spot occupies a 70-year-old building that housed Hatteras Island's original bar. Since 1978, the same family has owned and operated the Quarterdeck, which is open for lunch and dinner daily (except on Sat, when it is not open for lunch) from mid-March through late Nov.

GINGERBREAD HOUSE BAKERY $
NC 12, Frisco
(252) 995-5204

From this tiny cottage flanked by gingerbread-style fencing, breakfast and dinner are served Monday through Saturday in season. To start the day sample egg biscuits, french toast, omelets, or waffles. If you'd rather indulge yourself in delicious baked goods, try a frosted doughnut, cookie, or freshly made bagel. By early evening you can order a gourmet pizza made on the bakery's own dough. Crusts range in thickness from hand tossed to pan depth and are offered in white and whole wheat varieties with 30 toppings to choose from. Ice cream, brownies, and sweet breads all are great dessert options. During the summer the Gingerbread House also delivers from Buxton to Hatteras Village, and its bakers make super specialty cakes on a day's notice for any occasion. No credit cards accepted.

CAPT'N ROLO'S RAW BAR & GRILL $$
NC12, Frisco
(252) 995-3663

Capt'n Rolo's serves generous portions of local seafood. Homemade soups, barbecue, and fish tacos are featured items on the menu. A kid's menu is offered. Occasionally live music is scheduled for evenings. Full bar, beer, and wine. Open Tues through Sun.

BUBBA'S BAR-B-Q $$
NC 12, Frisco
(252) 995-5421
www.bubbasbbque.com

If you're in the mood for some genuine Carolina barbecue, just follow your nose to this acclaimed roadside joint. The hickory fires start early so the pork, chicken, beef, ribs, and turkey can cook slowly over an open pit. The late Larry "Bubba" Schauer and his wife, Julie, brought their secret recipe from West Virginia to Hatteras Island more than 20 years ago—and the food has been drawing locals and tourists to their eatery ever since. Homemade coleslaw, baked beans, french fries, and corn bread round out the meal.

Bubba's has a children's menu and a nice selection of beer and soft drinks. Bubba's Sauce is a hot commodity with barbecue fans and is sold at retail and specialty shops across the Outer Banks. Bubba's is open daily for lunch and dinner from 11 a.m. to 9 p.m. during the summer; call for winter hours. You'll find a second Bubba's, Bubba's Too, farther north on NC 12 in Avon, next to the Food Lion.

Hatteras Village

BREAKWATER ISLAND RESTAURANT $$
NC 12 at Oden's Dock, Hatteras Village
(252) 986-2733
www.breakwaterhatteras.com

If dining in a comfortable atmosphere with a stunning view of Pamlico Sound or relaxing with some live music on a deck at sunset sounds good, then this restaurant is the place for you. A second-story dining room, deck, and bar overlook a small harbor and stone breakwater, providing a unique feel to this locally loved outpost.

The dinner menu features fresh, innovative seafood dishes, prime rib, veal, and pasta, all served in generous portions. Live entertainment is performed atop the deck on select evenings in summer. Dinner is served every day but Tues during the season. A good selection of beer and wine is available. Children's items are also offered. Check for winter hours.

DINKY'S WATERFRONT
RESTAURANT $–$$
Village Marina, NC 12, Hatteras
(252) 986-2020
www.villagemarinahatteras.com
A fabulous view of the sound accompanies each meal at Dinky's, which is located on the second floor of Village Marina. Diners can choose from the delicious daily specials or order fresh seafood, hand-cut steaks, chicken, or pasta. Excellent desserts and good beer and wine lists complete the offerings at Dinky's, where families are welcome. Open for dinner from 5 to 8:30 p.m. year-round.

OCRACOKE ISLAND

JASON'S RESTAURANT $
NC 12, Ocracoke Village
(252) 928-3434
www.jasonsocracoke.com
On the north end of the village, Jason's has a casual, come-as-you-are atmosphere that welcomes islanders and vacationers alike. You can sit outside on the spacious screened porch or hang at the bar and watch the chefs at work. Standouts on the menu are pizzas and Italian specialties, including lasagna and vegetarian

lasagna, spaghetti with meatballs, chicken parmigiana, and fettuccine Alfredo. Salads, sandwiches, and subs, plus dinner entrees such as New York strip steak, Jamaican jerk chicken, and seafood add to the list of goods. If you just want a few munchies to get you by, try an appetizer. We liked the spinach and artichoke dip and shrimp quesadillas. To wash it down, choose from beers, including several on tap, and wines. Carryout is available for all menu items. Lunch and dinner are served daily year-round 11:30 a.m. until 10 p.m.

SMACNALLY'S RAW BAR
AND GRILL $–$$
On Silver Lake, NC 12, Ocracoke Village
(252) 928-9999
www.smacnallys.com
sMacNally's is smack in the middle of the village action, at the Anchorage Inn Marina, and is a popular gathering spot on the island. It's an outdoor establishment, on the docks, with the smell of salt and fresh-caught fish coming off the water and charter boats tied up practically to the bar. Fishermen walk off the boats and have a beer in their hand before they can say "Budwei . . ." sMacNally's claims to serve the coldest beer on the island. Patrons hang around the raw bar and at tables on the dock. The raw bar serves fresh local seafood, including oysters, clams, and shrimp. A grill cooks burgers and the like. Lunch and dinner are served daily in the warm season, through Nov. A children's menu is offered. The bar stays open until midnight and is an occasional music venue. It's closed in the colder months. Steamed seafood buckets and boxed lunches are sold to go.

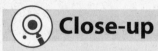 **Close-up**

Outer Banks Brogue

If you're lucky enough to get off the beaten path and meet some real Outer Banks natives, you'll be treated to a dialect known as Outer Banks Brogue. Related more closely to Welsh English and some coastal New England dialects than a typical southern drawl, Outer Banks Brogue is characterized by its distinct long "I" sound—locals were once known as "high tiders," pronounced something like "hoigh toide." In addition to the distinct pronunciations, Outer Banks Brogue boasts some unique vocabulary as well:

Dingbatter: a mildly derogatory name for anyone not from the Outer Banks; an outsider. "That dingbatter just asked me, 'When does the four o'clock ferry leave?'"

Pizer: a porch. "Let's go out and sit on the pizer."

Whopperjawed: anything built that isn't square, true or plumb; anything misaligned. "The pizer leans terrible off the house—it's all whopperjawed!"

Mommucked: when one is worked to excess; beaten up from overwork. "I been out shrimpin' all noight—like to been mommucked to death!"

Slick cam: dead calm; when there is no wind at all and the water surface is glassy. "Ain't a breath of air moving—it's dead slick cam."

Drime: a mild explicative indicating that something isn't true, especially when doubting someone's story. "Drime! That ain't roight!"

Meehonky: a game of hide-and-seek. "The young'uns a playin' meehonky."

Quamish: feeling sick, particularly to the stomach. "Smellin' them bad oysters made him quamish."

Calm of day: dawn. "The waves were really breaking at the calm of day."

Chunk: to throw. "Macon chunked a rock at the sheriff."

Findings: salvage from a shipwreck. "Wynn tol' me he got his findings from that Four-Master."

Swarp: to kill. "Horace says he swarped them trout with a wire."

PONY ISLAND RESTAURANT　　**$$**
NC 12, Ocracoke Village
(252) 928-5701

A casual, homey place that people have come back to time and again since 1960, this restaurant features big breakfasts of biscuits, hotcakes, omelets, and the famous Pony Potatoes—hash browns covered with cheese, sour cream, and salsa. Dinner entrees include interesting fresh local seafood creations, pastas, steaks, and salads. The kitchen will even cook your own catch of the day for you, as long as you've cleaned the fish first. Beer and wine are served, and homemade desserts finish the tasty meal. The Pony Island Restaurant is adjacent to the Pony Island Motel. Breakfast is served from 7 to 11 a.m. The restaurant closes during lunchtime and reopens nightly for dinner from late Mar through Nov. Take-out orders are welcomed. Children's and senior's menu available.

FLYING MELON $$
NC 12, Ocracoke Village
(252) 928-2533

The Flying Melon has a unique decor and yummy food to tempt any palate. Brunch is served from 9 a.m. to 2 p.m. and includes fresh fruit, biscuits, and New Orleans–style french toast. On its lunch menu the Melon has a portobello sandwich, a Philly cheesesteak, hamburgers, and more. The dinner entrees are often Louisiana-inspired dishes made with fresh ingredients and local seafood. The Flying Melon offers imported beer and a full wine list, and there is a menu for the wee ones in your party. Reservations are not necessary. Smoking is allowed on the porch but not within the building. Open year-round, serving Tues through Sun in season and Wed through Sun in the off season.

✳THE BACK PORCH RESTAURANT $$$
1324 Country Rd., Ocracoke Village
(252) 928-6401

Whether you dine on the wide screened-in porch or eat in the small nooks or open dining room of this well-respected restaurant, you'll find that dinners at the Back Porch are some of the most pleasant experiences on the Outer Banks. This older building was renovated and refurbished to blend with the many trees on the property. It's off the main road, surrounded by waist-high cacti, and is a quiet place to enjoy appealing entrees and comfortable conversation. Overall it's one

of our favorite restaurants on the 120-mile stretch of barrier islands and well worth the 2-hour trip from Nags Head.

Advertising "original dishes with a personal touch," the menu is loaded with fresh vegetables and local seafood and changes seasonally to offer the freshest ingredients. All sauces, dressings, breads, and desserts are made in the restaurant's huge kitchen and each piece of meat is hand cut.

All the desserts are divine. Freshly ground coffee is served here, and the wine selections and imported beer are as ambitious as the menu. If you get hooked—like we are—you can try your hand at some of the restaurant's recipes at home by buying a copy of *Back Porch Cookbook*. Dinner is offered nightly in season. Call for off-season hours.

The Back Porch Lunchbox, next to the Pony Island Motel, offers homemade bag lunches or picnics for the beach or ferry. Sandwiches, cold steamed shrimp, baked goods, drinks, and fruit are available. Call (252) 928-3651.

THAI MOON $
Spencer's Market, NC 12,
Ocracoke Village
(252) 928-5100

Here's something different on Ocracoke Island: ethnic food, which is a refreshing change of pace on the Outer Banks. Thai Moon offers authentic Thai specialties for takeout only. Chicken, pork, beef, and vegetarian options are available. Pad Thai and fried rice with shrimp, chicken, or bean curd are specialties. Thai Moon is open for lunch and dinner Tues through Sat and for dinner only on Sun and Mon. Call for off-season hours. Cash only. Note the sushi and Asian grocery next door supplying all of your Southeastern Asian cooking needs.

CAPT. BEN'S $$
NC 12, Ocracoke Village
(252) 928-4741

Serving Ocracoke locals and guests since 1970, Capt. Ben's is a casual restaurant. Owner and chef Ben Mugford combines southern tradition with gourmet foods. Ben is especially revered for his crabmeat, prime rib, and seafood entrees. He serves a mean Caesar salad and comes up with some good pasta and chicken creations. Sandwiches, crab cakes, and shrimp salad are good for lunch; each comes with chips or fries. Dinners come with soup, baked potato, and salad. And all the desserts are delicious. A large variety of domestic and imported beer is available, and the wine list complements the menu. The decor in this family eatery is nautical and friendly. The lounge and sundeck are comfortable places to relax if you have to wait for a table. Lunch and dinner are served daily from Apr through mid-November. Call for off-season hours. Children have their own menu at Capt. Ben's.

✴HOWARD'S PUB & RAW BAR
RESTAURANT $-$$
NC 12, Ocracoke Village
(252) 928-4441
www.howardspub.com

Fun loving and casual, Howard's Pub has continued to expand its menu diversity. Don't be misled by the selection of more than 200 imported, domestic, and microbrewed beers. The crew at Howard's Pub has established its "little corner of paradise" as the choice hangout for families, couples, and individuals alike. The restaurant's various areas—including the long wraparound bar, the main floor and game area, the large screened porch, and the ocean-to-sound-view deck—provide plenty of room for your group.

Howard's Pub & Raw Bar Restaurant is the only Outer Banks place we know that can boast that it has opened every day since 1991—including Thanksgiving, Christmas, Easter, and hurricane evacuations! This place has become a must-stop for everyone visiting Ocracoke, with great local flavor and guaranteed good times. (See the Nightlife chapter for more on Howard's Pub.)

The restaurant boasts the only year-round raw bar on the island and is home to the spicy Ocracoke Oyster Shooter. We love these raw oyster, hot sauce, pepper, and draft combinations, especially when washed down with an unusual or hard-to-find imported beer. Wine is available by the bottle.

The upstairs deck affords breathtaking views of the ocean, sound, salt marshes, and sand dunes. On a clear day you can even see Portsmouth Island! There are big-screen TVs and many smaller ones for viewing any number of events from just about anywhere in the restaurant. Board games, darts, a pool table in the off-season, and coloring books for the wee ones, plus live music and a 17-speaker sound system, guarantee that you can party to your heart's content. The full menu and drinks are served Sun through Thurs from 11 a.m. to 10 p.m. and Fri and Sat from 11 a.m. until midnight.

CAFE ATLANTIC $$
NC 12, Ocracoke Village
(252) 928-4861

Cafe Atlantic operates in a traditional beach-style building. There's not much that's traditional about their innovative, fantastic food, however. Views from the dining room look out across marsh grass and dunes. The gallerylike effect of the restaurant is created with hand-colored photographs and watercolors.

Dinner is served at this upscale yet casual eatery each day but Tuesday in season. The Sunday brunches are among the best on the Outer Banks. Brunch menus change weekly, but champagne and mimosas are always served.

All of the soups, dressings, sauces, and desserts are made from scratch. Dinner entrees include fresh Atlantic seafood, beef, pastas, and vegetarian entrees. A children's menu is available, and the restaurant has a nice selection of wine and beer. Cafe Atlantic is open from early Mar through Oct. Lunch openings may vary off-season, so call for hours. This nonsmoking cafe, though isolated on tiny Ocracoke, is certainly among the best dining experiences the Outer Banks has to offer.

OCRACOKE COFFEE & ISLAND SMOOTHIE $
Back Road, Ocracoke Village
(252) 928-7473

Ocracoke Coffee is the neatest place on the island to take care of caffeine and sugar cravings. The aromatic eatery offers bagels, pastries, desserts, brewed coffee drinks, espresso, shakes, whole-bean and ground coffees, and loose tea. The shop is nestled under tall pines on Back Road, within an easy walk of almost anything in the village. We know you'll find your way here in the morning (everyone does), but why not walk in after dinner for something sweet as well? The shop's feel is way hip, but it's also cozy and inviting, and the folks frothing your concoctions are friendly as can be. Look for more than 10 varieties of smoothies

for a cool respite from the summer heat. Ocracoke Coffee is open daily from 7 a.m. to 9:30 p.m., and live music plays during summer evenings on the deck. The shop closes Dec through Mar.

ISLAND INN RESTAURANT $$
Lighthouse Road, Ocracoke Village
(252) 928-4351
www.ocracokeislandinn.com

This family-owned and -operated restaurant at the Island Inn is one of the oldest establishments on Ocracoke. Its main dining room and airy porch are furnished in a traditional country style, with blue and white china to dine on and bright, nautical touches throughout. The owners welcome everyone; you don't have to be a guest at the inn. Standard breakfast fare, such as pancakes, eggs, and hash browns, is available. The cook also comes up with some unusual creations, such as oyster omelets with spinach and bacon and shrimp omelets loaded with melted Jack cheese, green chiles, and salsa. For dinner locally landed seafood and shellfish entrees are grilled, fried, or broiled to your liking. Beef, pork, lamb, pasta, and stir-fry dishes also are available, as are vegetarian offerings. All the breads and soups are made daily at this restaurant, and homemade pies are perfectly delicious. Beer and a selection of wines are served here, and a children's menu is available. Reservations are needed for large groups; the owners are happy to accommodate private party requests. The Island Inn Restaurant is open for breakfast and dinner daily except in the dead of winter. Call for off-season hours.

CREEK SIDE CAFE $
NC 12, Ocracoke Village
(252) 928-3606
www.ocracokecreekside.com

RESTAURANTS

Overlooking Silver Lake Harbor from a second-story vantage point, this restaurant offers wonderful views. A covered porch that wraps around two sides of the wooden building has ceiling fans and breezes to cool afternoon diners. Inside, the eatery is casual and friendly, serving brunch items daily and lunch and dinner from a single menu from Apr to early Nov. Soups, salads, seafood, and pasta dishes are the afternoon and evening fare here. Beer and wine are available, and four champagne drinks offer unusual alcoholic creations.

*JOLLY ROGER PUB & MARINA $$
NC 12, Ocracoke Village
(252) 928-3703

Jolly Roger is the perfect place to kick back and relax on Ocracoke Island. Although a roof, canopy, and umbrellas cover many of the dining tables, the entire restaurant is open, with tables on large decks overlooking the harbor. There's nothing fancy here—wooden tables, paper plates, and plastic cutlery—but the service is good, the beer is cold, and the food is wonderful. The menu features homemade soups, sandwiches, salad plates, local seafood, and daily specials. Stop in for live entertainment at sunset; you'll hear the music wafting down the street as you stroll through the village. Beer and wine are served, and there's a good-size bar on premises. Jolly Roger serves lunch and dinner daily in season.

DAJIO RESTAURANT $$
NC 12, Ocracoke Village
(252) 928-7119
www.dajiorestaurant.com

Doug and Judy Eifert bring affordable dining to the heart of Ocracoke Village, serving only the finest local ingredients whenever possible. Breakfast, lunch, and dinner are served here, along with a special shrimp hour from 3 to 5 p.m. each day. Music is often enjoyed by patrons in the bar area.

ATTRACTIONS

The Outer Banks' biggest attraction is, of course, the water. Nine hundred square miles of water surround these islands, providing a huge, liquid playground for swimmers, boaters, sailors, surfers, anglers, waders, and divers. For those who don't want to get wet, just being on these narrow islands with 175 miles of Atlantic Ocean beaches and views of sparkling blue from every angle is enough.

Nature is so stark and apparent on the Outer Banks that no man-made attraction could ever compare with its glory. But we also have an abundance of stellar man-made attractions, many the sole reason people travel to the Outer Banks. These attractions satisfy history buffs, nature lovers, arts aficionados, and thrill seekers.

OVERVIEW

Some of the Outer Banks attractions were created by men and women out of pride for the significant historic events that took place here, such as the Wright brothers' first flight and the first attempted English settlement in the New World. Others, like *The Lost Colony* outdoor drama, are themselves as much a part of history as the events they portray.

If you're accustomed to metropolitan-area prices, you're in for a real treat. Local attractions are affordable, with most costing less than $10 and many open for free. The priciest attractions are worth every penny and still affordable compared with city prices. Most places offer special family, child, or senior discounts. While some of the attractions stay open year-round, many close in the winter months or strictly curtail their hours. Call ahead.

The Outer Banks is not just the home of two of the most significant events in the nation's history—the first English-speaking colony and the first powered flight—it's also gifted with an extraordinary coastline.

Between lighthouses, lifesaving stations, wild horses, and shipwrecks, visitors can get lost in our long, lively history.

Wide-open wildlife refuges spread across the islands, and fluorescent-lighted fish tanks glow at the state aquarium. You can dive into history by boarding a reproduction 16th-century sailing ship or scuba dive into the Atlantic to explore a Civil War shipwreck. There's never enough time to see everything the Outer Banks has to offer.

In this chapter we highlight our favorite attractions. Many others are there to be discovered; insiders often share their own secret spots. Many of these places have free admission or request nominal donations. We begin with the northernmost communities and work southward. Each area has its own section, so pick your pleasure.

Also, read the Recreation, Shopping, Arts & Culture, Water Sports, Fishing, Kidstuff,

Natural Wonders, and Nightlife chapters for more exciting, educational, and unusual things to do and places to play on the Outer Banks.

COROLLA

HISTORIC COROLLA VILLAGE SCHOOLHOUSE AND COROLLA VILLAGE LANES
Corolla Village
(252) 453-3341

Though everyone refers to the whole Currituck Outer Banks as "Corolla," technically Corolla is the small village center on the unpaved road behind the lighthouse. Few people realize that Corolla was a thriving community that began to grow in 1875 after the lighthouse was built. In 1890, at the peak of the area's waterfowl-hunting market, 200 residents lived in the village. The village population declined during World War II and the following years. Only a few residents lived in Corolla well into the 1980s, when a paved public road was opened to the area and development of the Currituck Outer Banks began. The faces of the Currituck Outer Banks and Corolla Village have changed dramatically, but you can still get a sense of the old village by walking on the dirt road on the west side of NC 12 behind the lighthouse. In the shade of the oaks and pines, it is easy to imagine the life of the early residents.

A few of the historic buildings from the old village remain and have been restored to look as they did when they were built. A walking-tour map is available at many of the shops in the area or at Twiddy & Company Realtors, whose owners took charge of restoring the buildings. The restored Corolla Schoolhouse is on the tour, though you can't go inside. The charming schoolhouse, on the

corner of Schoolhouse Lane and Corolla Village Lane, was built in the mid- to late 1890s and finally closed in 1958. Also on the tour are several restored historic homes that have been converted into shops, so you can go inside, including the Lewark and Parker residences. A new building was built to look like Callie Parker's store. The walking tour will also take you past the 1878 US Lifesaving Station that was moved to the village, the Currituck Beach Lighthouse and Lightkeeper's Residence, and the historic Whalehead Club.

COROLLA WILD HORSE FUND
Corolla Village Road, Corolla
(252) 453-8002
www.corollawildhorses.com

The Corolla Wild Horse Fund is located in the historic Corolla schoolhouse, lovingly restored by Twiddy & Company Realtors. The Corolla Wild Horse Fund houses educational and interactive displays informing visitors about the delightful wild horses that roam the Outer Banks. Visitors are drawn to the beautiful photographs lining the walls. An interactive educational display interests adults and children. Call about special events held throughout the summer. The events for children are educational and usually involve a craft. A small fee is charged for the activities, but entrance into the building is free. Donations are greatly appreciated, and 100 percent of proceeds benefit the wild horse fund. A second location is housed in the Corolla Town Center.

KILL DEVIL HILLS LIFESAVING STATION
Off NC 12, Corolla

Built in 1878, the Kill Devil Hills Lifesaving Station is now the setting for Outer Banks Style, a specialty shop in Corolla (see the Shopping chapter). The interior doesn't look anything like the old outpost, but the exterior appearance, a peaked roof and crossed timber frame, remains relatively unchanged.

The US Lifesaving Service was established in the late 19th century, and stations were built every 7 miles along the Outer Banks. Crews lived in the wooden structures throughout winter months, patrolling the beaches for shipwrecks and survivors. This station, which was moved almost 30 miles north of its original location, is especially significant because it was frequented by the Wright brothers during their several sojourns to the barrier islands. The Kill Devil Hills Lifesaving Station crew assisted Orville and Wilbur with their early experiments in flight, and some crew members witnessed the world's first powered airplane soar over the sand dunes.

This lifesaving station was brought from Kill Devil Hills to Corolla in 1986, where it was restored and renovated. History buffs are welcome to visit Outer Banks Style and the lobby of Twiddy & Company Realtors (behind the station), where a collection of memorabilia used by the lifesaving service and the Wrights is on display. This unique, hand-wrought structure is at the foot of the Currituck Lighthouse on the west side of NC 12 in historic Corolla Village.

✳ THE WHALEHEAD CLUB
Currituck Heritage Park, NC 12, Corolla
(252) 453-9040
www.whaleheadclub.com
Overlooking the windswept wetlands of Currituck Sound, this grand dame of days gone by was once the Outer Banks' biggest, most modern structure. Today the Whalehead Club is one of the area's most magnificent attractions and affords a romantic trip back

in time to an era of lavish accommodations and elaborate ornamentation.

The house was built as a private residence between 1922 and 1925, when the Currituck Outer Banks was in its heyday as a waterfowl-hunting paradise. The owners, a wealthy northerner named Edward Collins Knight and his wife, Marie Louise LeBel Knight, originally called their home Corolla Island because the house was situated on an islandlike mound that was created when a circular canal was dug around the lot. The Knights spent their winters and hunted at Corolla Island from 1925 to 1934.

The 21,000-square-foot house has seen many uses since then. It sat empty for years, as relatives of the Knights were not interested in the remote location. In 1969 the house was sold to Ray Adams of Washington, D.C., for a reported $25,000. It was Adams who named the home the Whalehead Club. This grand and beautiful home sat empty for nearly 25 years, suffering significant vandalism.

The house, on the National Register of Historic Places, is now owned by Currituck County and has been restored to the way it looked in 1925. The multimillion-dollar restoration project began in 1999 with the replacement of the copper roof. The exterior was painted its original canary yellow. The interior has been completely restored, down to the paint, cork floors, Tiffany glass, and art nouveau details. A team of researchers and restoration specialists has tracked down as much information as possible to make the restoration as accurate as possible.

Visitors are welcome and can take a guided tour of the house. Tours begin on the half hour and include a self-guided exhibition on display in the basement gallery. A special "behind the scenes" tour is offered

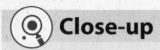 **Close-up**

The Wild Horses of Corolla

Corolla's wild horses are part of the mystique of the Outer Banks: a symbol of the roots, endurance, and resilience of an isolated land and its tough inhabitants. They are also the symbol of the toll taken by breathtaking growth in Corolla.

Visitors to the northernmost stretches of barrier beach no longer see pastoral views of horses grazing on golf courses or newly planted lawns. They no longer see the majestic beasts loping on oceanside sands. They won't even see close-ups of the few that were once corralled at the Currituck Beach Lighthouse.

There are no horses left in Corolla. They are now fenced in the Currituck National Wildlife Refuge. Believed by many to be descendants of Spanish mustangs, the wild horses have the compact, stocky conformation and, according to one scientist, the genetic markers of the Barb horses that were brought to the Outer Banks as early as 1523 by Spanish explorers. One native Outer Banker who has studied the "Banker ponies" said they may be the oldest breed of horse in North America. Though the horses have Spanish origins, they are of a breed all their own, due to nearly 400 years as an isolated species. The horses are recognized as a significant cultural and historical resource by the state of North Carolina.

Before development in Corolla intensified in the mid- and late 1980s, wild horses ranged freely among the sea grasses and dunes of the northern barrier islands. A late discovery for developers, the area didn't have electricity until 1968, telephone service until 1974, or a public paved road until 1984. Tourists driving on the new road were charmed that undomesticated horses milled freely in plain view. Less than 10 years later, horses were lounging in shade under rental cottage decks, nosing through garbage cans, and strolling nonchalantly through the grocery store's automatic door.

Tourists took to feeding and petting them—or attempting to. Close calls with horse bites and kicks became part of the local lore. But as the area grew, the interaction between horses and humans became more dangerous. After the road

---

daily (by reservation only). Guides are very knowledgeable about the home as well as the history of the area. The museum shop stocks tasteful merchandise that is unique to the Whalehead Club, including handcrafted jewelry, picture frames, ornaments, and birdhouses made from the original copper roof shingles. The Whalehead Club is situated on 39 acres known as Currituck Heritage Park. It offers an ideal location for picnics, leisurely walks, fishing, or enjoying a beautiful Outer Banks sunset.

The Whalehead Club is open from May 1 through Oct 31 and during the weeks of the Easter, Thanksgiving, and Christmas holidays (not on the actual holidays themselves). House tours take place daily in season beginning at 9 a.m. The last tour begins at 4 p.m. The tours last 45 minutes. Cost is $9 for adults and free for children age 8 and younger. A variety of themed tours are offered, most geared toward specific interests and age groups. Call or check the website for details.

between Duck and Corolla was made public in 1984, 17 horses were killed in vehicle accidents in just four years. A group of local citizens established the Corolla Wild Horse Fund in 1989 to protect the animals after three pregnant mares were killed. The group rallied public support, managing to have the county pass an ordinance to help protect the horses from harm. The wild horses, in fact, became the area's most popular attraction.

Still, horse-fund volunteers and staffers were unable to protect their charges. After a poll revealed that most people wanted to preserve the horses in their own environment instead of relocating them, the fund erected a mile-and-a-half-long fence, stretching from sound to sea near where the pavement ends in Corolla. The idea was not to enclose the wild animals but to allow them to roam freely—but safely—in the more than 1,600 acres of public and private land north of the fence. On March 24, 1995, the horses were herded behind the fence. But the Corolla wild-horse story was not yet over.

Like clever children, some of the herd, which numbered 100 by then, strayed around the fence up to Virginia, where they were not welcome. Other horses, led by a particularly stubborn stallion, began sneaking back into Corolla Village. They were always herded back home, but the few recalcitrant horses always found a way out. In 1999 the Corolla Wild Horse Fund took the wandering horses to the private Dews Island in Currituck Sound, where they had 400 acres to graze. Today there are no horses on Dews Island, but 65 horses stay behind the fence and roam the vast area between the off-road ramp and Carova.

The horses are better protected than ever. The staff at the Corolla Wild Horse Fund is responsible for overseeing the health and safety of the herd. Volunteers are needed to help with activities such as a census, marking the horses, and taking health samples. The Corolla Wild Horse Fund Office is on Corolla Village Road. The office phone number is (252) 453-8002. The mailing address is PO Box 361, Corolla, NC 27927, or you can visit www.corollawildhorses.com.

*OUTER BANKS CENTER FOR WILDLIFE EDUCATION
Currituck Heritage Park, NC 12, Corolla
(252) 453-0221
www.ncwildlife.org

Located between the historic Whalehead Club and the Currituck Lighthouse, the 22,000-square-foot center is devoted to teaching the history of wildlife of North Carolina's northeastern coastal region. A self-guided tour through the diorama of the marsh educates visitors about the regional ecology. Regional history is explored through the boating, hunting, and fishing heritage. Salt marsh ecology can be experienced first-hand. A wonderful film, *Currituck, Life by Water's Rhythms,* shows regularly in the theater. Special events for adults and children are regularly scheduled; call or check the website for dates and times. Admission is free for most programs. A gift shop is on the premise.

✳CURRITUCK BEACH LIGHTHOUSE
Off NC 12, Corolla
(252) 453-4939
www.currituckbeachlight.com
Visitors can climb the 214 steps to the top of the lighthouse, coming eye to eye with the 50,000-candlepower lamp that still flashes every 20 seconds and can be seen for 18 nautical miles. The climb up the narrow, winding staircase is not for the faint of heart, but a panoramic view of the Currituck Outer Banks is your reward.

Inside, at the base and on the first two landings, are lighthouse exhibit panels installed in 2001. They cover the broad history of coastal lighthouses, including all of the North Carolina lighthouses, and give an in-depth history of the Currituck Beach Lighthouse and its buildings. The Fresnel lens is explained, and there is a special exhibit on the former Currituck Beach Lighthouse keepers.

The Lightkeepers' Residence, a beautiful Victorian dwelling, was constructed of precut, labeled materials and was shipped for assembly on-site by the US Lighthouse Board. The residence was abandoned when the lighthouse was automated in 1939 and keepers were no longer needed on-site (though they still visited once a week to change batteries and perform maintenance). The residence, on the National Register of Historic Places, fell into serious disrepair but was restored by a group known as Outer Banks Conservationists starting in 1980. It is not open for tours, except by appointment during the first two weeks in Nov.

Today the keeper's main duties, among many others, are keeping the lighthouse open for tourists, overseeing preservation work, and hiring volunteers and staff. In 2005 the Currituck Beach Lighthouse celebrated its 130th anniversary as a working lighthouse. Be sure to visit the on-site museum shop.

Visitors climb the lighthouse for a fee of $6, cash or check only. Children younger than age 8 climb for free. School groups and other large groups are offered a discounted rate. The lighthouse is open daily from Easter through Thanksgiving. Climbing hours are 10 a.m. to 6 p.m. during eastern standard time and to 5 p.m. during daylight saving time. If you're climbing you must go up at least 15 minutes before closing time. During periods of lightning or high winds, the lighthouse tower may be closed to climbers.

COROLLA CHAPEL
Old Corolla Village Road, Corolla
(252) 453-4224
The Corolla Chapel, built in 1885, is one of Corolla's most-treasured historic structures. Snuggled into the soundside village, 2½ blocks behind the lighthouse, the chapel served generations of native Corollans in its small sanctuary.

In its early years the church was used primarily by Missionary Baptists, although originally it was supposed to be interdenominational. Catholic Masses were first said at the church in 1917 and continued on a sporadic basis through the world wars for Coast Guard personnel stationed nearby. In 1938 the Baptists dropped Corolla from their circuit, saying it was too remote, and the church became interdenominational. In the 1960s Corolla's population reached its all-time low, and the church was no longer used. It lay idle for 25 years.

The last living trustee of the chapel was John Austin, and when he died, the church passed to the hands of his son, Norris Austin, who still lives in the village. In 1987, as

Corolla began to grow again, Austin invited Pastor John Strauss to be the minister of the chapel. Strauss led a restoration, adding a vestibule, bathroom, and storage area in 1992. With regular interdenominational services, he also began to develop a following.

The church outgrew its small chapel. In the summer months the village chapel that seats only 100 would have that many (or more) people standing outside. On Easter 2001 Pastor Strauss offered communion to 2,000 people during four services. This led to construction of a new church building across the road from the original chapel. The old Corolla Chapel was then moved across the street and melded into the new sanctuary to form the shape of a cross. The new sanctuary has the same tongue-and-groove beaded-board paneling and details as the old one, so that the two blend seamlessly together, inside and out. The new facility was designed to hold 200 to 250 worshipers. Today, Pastor Rick Griffis leads services at the Corolla Chapel.

The best way to see the Corolla Chapel is to attend a service. Interdenominational services are held year-round on Sun at 10 a.m. From Memorial Day through Oct, an additional Sun service is held at 8:30 a.m. Four interdenominational services are held on Easter; one is a sunrise service on the beach.

PINE ISLAND AUDUBON SANCTUARY
NC 12, between Duck and Corolla
Set between remote villages of sprawling vacation rental cottages, Pine Island Audubon Sanctuary is a secluded, outdoor enthusiast's paradise and a major resting area for birds along the great Atlantic flyway. Ducks, geese, rabbits, deer, fox, and dozens of other animals make their home in this 5,400-acre wildlife refuge on the northern Outer Banks.

Hundreds of other species fly through during spring and fall migrations.

Live oaks, bayberry, inkberry, pine, yaupon, holly, and several species of marsh grass grow naturally in this wild, remote wetland habitat. The Pine Island Clubhouse and grounds are privately owned, but if you're a member of the Audubon Society, tours are available.

Hikers, bikers, and strollers can park at Sanderling Inn to access a 2.5-mile clay trail through a portion of the sanctuary. The maintained path is open year-round.

DUCK

US ARMY CORPS OF ENGINEERS FIELD RESEARCH FACILITY
NC 12, Duck
(252) 261-6840, ext. 401
www.frf.usace.army.mil
Set on a former navy weapons test site, the Waterways Experiment Station of the US Army Corps of Engineers has helped scientists study ocean processes since 1977. This 173-acre federally owned scientific mecca has gained a reputation as one of the premier coastal field research facilities in the world. Just north of Duck Village, the site includes state-of-the-art equipment to monitor sand movement, wave forces, water currents, temperatures, and sedimentation. Its 12 full-time employees regularly host dozens of scientists from around the globe to conduct experiments on sand movement, beach erosion, and coastal dynamics. In 1997, during the world's largest near-shore research experiment, 250 coastal engineers gathered at the research facility to study the near-shore zone of breaking waves to determine the dynamics of beach erosion.

The public is invited to tour the research facility from mid-June through mid-August. One free tour is held each day, Mon through Fri, at 10 a.m. Reservations are not necessary, and the tour is held rain or shine, except in lightning. The tours last about an hour and a half, sometimes longer, and include an eco-lecture about how the sound and ocean waters coexist, barrier island environments, and ocean currents. Researchers lead the tours onto the beach, into the observation tower, and into the research facility. The public is not allowed on the pier because of the great amount of research equipment there. Since part of the tour is outside on a sandy trail and on the beach, participants should be prepared for a strenuous walk.

Besides the 1,840-foot pier, the US Army Corps of Engineers' experiment station owns a 125-foot observation tower and a 35-foot-tall Coastal Research Amphibious Buggy, the CRAB, which carries people and equipment from the shore into the sea. The corps works in cooperation with the US Army and Navy and the National Oceanic and Atmospheric Administration, using the latest technically advanced equipment to improve the design of coastal navigation projects. Research conducted at the station could eventually alter the way engineers design bridges, help people pick sites for beach nourishment projects, improve projections about where the shoreline might erode, determine how and why sandbars move, and predict what effect rock jetties might have on Oregon Inlet.

✳**DUCK TOWN PARK**
(252) 255-1286
www.townofduck.com
Native soundside plants provide the backdrop for the grassy gathering space. A playground and parking lot are on the premises,

and the gazebo and amphitheater house performing acts. Cultural and community events are held throughout the summer and fall. Regularly scheduled events include a children's story hour, a summer evening music series, and *The Lost Colony* show highlights. The popular annual Duck Jazz Festival is held in mid-October. Check the website for details, or call the events hotline at the number listed above.

A soundside boardwalk, nature trails, a public kayak and canoe launch, a picnic pavilion, and a gazebo are also open to the public.

i Scotch bonnets, the North Carolina state shell, are rarely found on the Cape Hatteras National Seashore beaches but are often found on the remote beaches of Portsmouth Island. Whole sand dollars can be found there, too.

KITTY HAWK

MONUMENT TO A CENTURY OF FLIGHT
Off US 158 Bypass, behind the Aycock Brown Welcome Center, Kitty Hawk
(252) 441-6584
www.monumenttoacenturyofflight.org
This sculptural garden was conceived by local artist Glenn Eure and brought to fruition by the nonprofit group Icarus International. It features stainless-steel pylons placed in ascending order by height, symbolizing the steps humans have taken to reach the heavens. Adorning the pylons are black granite slabs that name 100 of the most important moments in the history of flight. The courtyard contains 5,000 bricks, each engraved with a personal message.

KILL DEVIL HILLS

✳WRIGHT BROTHERS NATIONAL MEMORIAL
US 158, MP 8, Kill Devil Hills
(252) 441-7430
www.nps.gov/wrbr

Set atop a steep, grassy sand hill in the center of Kill Devil Hills, the trapezoidal granite monument to Orville and Wilbur Wright is within easy walking distance of the site of the world's first powered airplane flight. Below where this lighthouse-style tower now stands, on the blustery afternoon of December 17, 1903, the two bicycle-building brothers from Dayton, Ohio, soared over a distance of more than 852 feet, staying airborne for an unheard-of 59 seconds in their homemade flying machine.

The monument was erected to honor Orville and Wilbur Wright in 1932. In the low, domed building on the right side of the main drive off US 158, the National Park Service operates a visitor center, gift shop, and museum. Here you can view interpretive exhibits of humankind's first flight and see displays on later aviation advancements. Exhibits about the Wright brothers' struggles to fly include parts of their planes, engines, and research notes. Reproductions of their gliders are displayed in the flight room, and rangers offer free guided historical tours year-round.

The visitor center is itself an attraction. Opened in the early 1960s, it is recognized as a significant example of modernist architecture. It's one of only a handful of examples of modernist architecture built in eastern North Carolina during the 20th century, mainly because the National Park Service was one of a few groups in the region that had the financial resources to hire architects from outside the region.

The Philadelphia architectural firm of Ehrman Mitchell and Romaldo Giurgola designed the building to reflect the natural environment of the Outer Banks and symbolically portray flight in static form. The horizontal roof with a shallow concrete dome reflects the surrounding landscape of beach and dunes, while the overhang of the dome represents the soaring possibilities of flight. The National Historic Register–listed structure is considered a key work in the Philadelphia school of expressive modernist architects.

The 100th anniversary celebration of the first flight was held in December 2003. An olive-shaped, domed Centennial Pavilion was added for the celebration. The Centennial Pavilion houses a US Air Force exhibit, NASA exhibit, and exhibits from the Cirrus Corporation and the Wright Experience. The Wright Experience details the story of replicating the original Wright *Flyer*. In a nearby temporary facility, one of the two Wright Flyer replications is stored. The facility is open occasionally for viewing, but not at regularly scheduled times. Harry Combs, deceased Wright brothers historian and aviator, donated more than $1 million to build and replicate the *Flyer* housed here.

Outside the exhibit center four markers set along a sandy runway commemorate the takeoff and landing sites of each of Orville and Wilbur's December 17 flights. Reconstructed wooden sheds replicating those used at the Wrights' 1903 camp and hangar also are on the grounds and open to visitors. These sheds are furnished with tools, equipment, and food canisters similar to those the brothers used.

A short hike takes you from the visitor center to the monument hill, but if you'd rather drive or ride, parking is available closer to the base of the hill. Paved walkways make access easy. The grass is filled with cacti and sand spurs, so you're advised to stay on the paths. Also, be aware that the walk up the monument hill is longer and more strenuous than it looks. On a hot summer day, consider visiting the site in the morning or late afternoon, when the sun is not as strong.

At the bottom of the south side of the monument hill, a sculpture added for the 100th anniversary celebration of flight is displayed. It re-creates Orville flying the plane, with Wilbur running alongside and local John Daniels taking the historic photo of the event.

Besides tours, the exhibit center at the Wright Brothers National Memorial offers a variety of summer programs. Grounds and buildings are open to vehicles from 9 a.m. until 5 p.m. Labor Day through Memorial Day. Hours are from 9 a.m. to 6 p.m. in the summer. Thirty-minute flight-room talks are given by rangers every hour on the hour, year-round. Expect the entire tour to take about 1 to 2 hours. Add an additional 30 minutes if you'd like to attend a program.

Cost for entry at the guard gate is $4 for adults ages 16 and older, and admission is good for seven days. Persons age 15 and younger get in free, as do seniors with Golden Age Passports and other passports, which are available at the gate.

NAGS HEAD WOODS ECOLOGICAL PRESERVE
Ocean Acres Drive, Kill Devil Hills
(252) 441-2525
www.nature.org
If you've had a little too much sun, or if you'd like to spend time in a secluded forest on a part of the Outer Banks few people get

to see, allocate an afternoon for the Nature Conservancy's Nags Head Woods Ecological Preserve, west of US 158. The maritime forest itself is well hidden, and many rare plant and animal species live within this protected landscape. It's one of the most tranquil settings on the Outer Banks.

The Nature Conservancy, an international, nonprofit conservation organization, oversees this maritime forest. Nags Head Woods is not a park—it is an example of a successful private-public partnership between the Nature Conservancy, the towns of Nags Head and Kill Devil Hills, and private landowners.

More than 5 miles of trails and footbridges wind through forest, dune, swamp, and pond habitats as well as graveyards and farm sites from the 19th and 20th centuries. Trails are open to visitors on weekdays from 10 a.m. to 3 p.m., while members of the Nature Conservancy are welcome during any daylight hours. No camping, firearms, picnicking, or alcoholic beverages are allowed in the preserve. Bicycling, pets on leashes, and other activities that might damage the trails are restricted to the Old Nags Head Woods Road, which winds from north to south through the woods.

For more information, write to the Nature Conservancy at 701 West Ocean Acres Dr., Kill Devil Hills, NC 27948. All donations are welcome, and memberships start at $50. Monies support the preserve's environmental education and research programs.

NAGS HEAD

✳JOCKEY'S RIDGE STATE PARK
US 158, MP 12, Nags Head
(252) 441-7132
www.jockeysridgestatepark.com

The East Coast's tallest sand dune and one of the Outer Banks' most phenomenal natural attractions, Jockey's Ridge has long been a favorite stop for tourists. In the early 1970s bulldozers began flattening the surrounding dunes to make way for a housing subdivision. A Nags Head woman, Carolista Baum, singlehandedly stopped the destruction and formed a committee that saved Jockey's Ridge.

State officials made the sand hill a protected park in 1975, but the dunes are unruly. Since then the steepest side of the hill has shifted more than 1,500 feet to the southwest. Jockey's Ridge is also getting shorter. At the turn of the 20th century, the highest mound was estimated at 140 feet. In 1971 it was about 110 feet tall.

Today the 1.5-mile-long, 420-acre-plus dune—which varies from 90 feet to 110 feet in height—is open to the public year-round until sunset. It's a popular spot for hang gliders, summer hikers, small children who like to roll down the steep slopes, and teenagers who delight in sandboarding or flinging and flipping themselves down the sandy hills. Sandboarding is allowed only from Oct 1 through Mar 31. More than one million people visit Jockey's Ridge each year.

Park headquarters is near the northern end of a parking lot off the west side of US 158. You'll notice an entrance sign at MP 12, Carolista Drive, in Nags Head.

A visitor center, museum, and gift shop are near park headquarters. The free museum features photo displays of the history and recreation at the dune and a diorama of the animals that inhabit the area. Information panels of plants and animals and an auditorium where slide shows and videos are shown are also at the facility. Maps available from the park ranger indicate walking areas.

Two trails—the Soundside Nature Trail, a very easy 45-minute walk, and Tracks in the Sand, a 1.5-mile trek—are open to hikers looking for a change of scenery. Jockey's Ridge State Park offers natural history programs throughout the summer, including stargazing and wildlife discovery evening hikes and early-morning bird watching and natural history discovery adventures. Fantastic educational programs for kids are also offered, but rangers warn that they fill up fast, and many require advance registration. Call for program schedules. Sheltered picnic areas are available for lunches.

It's a long hike to the top of the ridge. Bring shoes or boots. Don't try it barefoot in summer; you'll burn your feet. Also, some lower areas around the dune are covered with broken glass. At the top of Jockey's Ridge, you can see both ocean and sound. Cottages along the beach look like tiny huts from a miniature train set. Kite-flying and hang-gliding enthusiasts catch the breezes that flow around the steep summit, shifting the sand in all directions. (See the Recreation chapter for information on hang gliding.)

If your mobility is impaired, a 360-foot boardwalk affords wheelchairs and baby strollers a slightly sloping incline onto a wooden platform overlooking the center of the dune. For the visually impaired, audio guides are available at the park office. Park rangers can also provide a ride on a four-wheeler to the top of the dune if you call 24 hours in advance.

The park opens at 8 a.m. every day except Christmas. Closing time depends on the season: Nov through Feb, 6 p.m.; Mar and Oct, 7 p.m.; Apr, May, and Sept, 8 p.m.; and June through Aug, 9 p.m.

This is sunset-watching central, especially in the summer months, when hundreds of people may climb the dunes to watch the sun sink into Roanoke Sound. A soundside access is on the southwest side of Jockey's Ridge. This also provides access to a great beach on the gentle sound waters.

NAGS HEAD BEACH COTTAGE ROW
Historic District, NC 12, MP 12–13, Nags Head

The long row of rustic, weatherworn cottages on the ocean in Nags Head around mileposts 12 and 13 is famously known as the "Unpainted Aristocracy." The homes have been on the National Register of Historic Places since 1977. They feature the Nags Head–style cedar siding grayed in the wind and salt, wraparound porches, propped-open shutters, dormers, and gabled roofs. Although Nags Head was a vacation destination earlier, it wasn't until 1855 that an Elizabeth City doctor built the first house on the oceanfront. He was lonely, so he sold the land around him to other people who vacationed in the wooded area by the sound. By 1885 13 homes sat at the ocean's edge.

Many of the cottages are still in the original families. Nine of the original 13 are still standing. Two were replaced with similar structures, one was destroyed by fire, and one was razed. Several other cottages scattered between mileposts 12 and 13 have interesting histories, although they are not considered part of the Unpainted Aristocracy. The land around these homes is private, and the homes are occupied. Feel free to drive by or walk by and admire, but please respect the owners' privacy and don't trespass on their property.

OUTER BANKS BEACHCOMBER MUSEUM
Historic District, NC 12, MP 13, Nags Head

Built on the sound in 1914, this simply structured general store for years provided the area with groceries, mail, and the only telephone in town. Rolled to its current location in 1933, it later became the home of Nellie Myrtle Pridgen, the cantankerous daughter of Mattie Midgett. Nellie was renowned for her feverish protection of Nags Head beaches. For most of her 74 years, Nellie was also a passionate beachcomber. She would quickly stride the beach and sound each day, regardless of weather. She picked up anything and everything of interest and cataloged it. Nellie passed away in 1994, and her extensive collection of findings has been opened to the public by her daughter. Beach glass, war items, buttons, fulgurite (sand fused by lightning), rare shells, and more are on display in this treasure trove of history.

i Virginia Dare, the first child born to the colonists on Roanoke Island, was born on August 18. Each year on that day a wonderful celebration is held at the Elizabethan Gardens. Madrigal singers fill the air with their beautiful songs, and a 45-minute play is performed at this free event. The play changes each year.

ROANOKE ISLAND

Roanoke Island brims with attractions. Anyone visiting the Outer Banks should definitely come over for the day, although with many new bed-and-breakfasts, restaurants, and shops in town, it's becoming more of an overnight destination in its own right.

If you're planning to visit many of the attractions on Roanoke Island, a Roanoke Island Attractions Pass or Queen's Pass will save you up to 25 percent of the admission fees. The Attractions Pass combines admission to the North Carolina Aquarium, the Elizabethan Gardens, and Roanoke Island Festival Park. The Queen's Pass allows admission to the same three attractions, plus *The Lost Colony*. Children younger than age 5 can visit all of these attractions except *The Lost Colony* for free. The passes are good for one calendar year and are available at the local attractions and the Outer Banks Visitors Bureau.

✳THE ELIZABETHAN GARDENS
Off US 64, Roanoke Island
(252) 473-3234
www.elizabethangardens.org
Created by the Garden Club of North Carolina Inc. in 1960 to commemorate the efforts of Sir Walter Raleigh's colonists at establishing an English settlement, these magnificent botanical gardens offer an exquisite, aromatic environment year-round. They include 10.5 acres of the state's most colorful, dazzling flora. The flower-filled walkways contrast with the windblown, barren Outer Banks beaches.

Six full-time gardeners tend more than 1,000 varieties of trees, shrubs, and flowers in the Elizabethan Gardens. The tree-lined landscape is divided into a dozen gardens, where translucent emerald grass fringes marble fountains, and beauty blooms from every crevice.

Visitors enter at the Gate House into formal gardens along curving walkways carefully crafted from brick and sand. The bricks were handmade at the Silas Lucas Kiln, in operation during the late 1800s in Wilson, North Carolina.

Although this botanical refuge is breathtakingly beautiful all year, vibrant with seasonal colors and fragrances, it is perhaps the most striking in spring. Azaleas, dogwood, pansies, wisteria, and tulips bloom around every bend. Rhododendron, roses, and lacecap and other hydrangea appear in May. Summer brings fragrant gardenias, colorful annuals and perennials, magnolia, crape myrtle, Oriental lilies, and herbs. Chrysanthemums and the changing colors of leaves signal the beginning of fall, and camellias bloom from fall through the winter.

In the center of the paths, six marble steps down from the rest of the greenery, sits the crown jewel of the Elizabethan Gardens: a sunken garden, complete with Roman statuary, tiered fountains, and low shrubs pruned into geometric flower frames. The famous Virginia Dare statue nearby is based on an Indian legend that says Virginia, the first English child born in America, grew up among Native Americans (see the Roanoke Island section of the Area Overview chapter).

Special events include the spectacular WinterLights holiday display. The entire gardens are illuminated and the glow is bound to put any Scrooge into the spirit of the season. Other events include Flute Frenzy, Easter Eggstravaganza, gardening classes, kids' summer camps, cooking classes, art classes, and more.

The gardens are closed Thanksgiving Day, Christmas Eve, Christmas Day, and New Year's Day. From Mar through Nov the gardens open at 9 a.m., and closing time varies depending on the season (between 5 and 7 p.m.). The gardens are open daily from 10 a.m. to 4 p.m. in Dec, Jan, and Feb. When *The Lost Colony* is running, the gardens stay open until 8 p.m. so that visitors can tour the gardens then head next door to see the outdoor drama. Season and daily passes are available.

Wheelchairs are provided. Most paths are wheelchair accessible. Some plants are for sale in the garden gift shop. A meeting room is available for a fee to community groups up to 100 people. The gardens also are a favorite wedding locale.

FORT RALEIGH NATIONAL
HISTORIC SITE
Off US 64, Roanoke Island
(252) 473-5772
www.nps.gov/fora
When you visit Fort Raleigh, don't expect to see a fort. What exists on the site is a small earthworks fortification. It is not a daunting barricade but a lovely spot drenched in American history. On the north end of Roanoke Island, near the Roanoke Sound's shores, Fort Raleigh marks the beginning of English settlement in North America. Since this attraction is next to the Elizabethan Gardens and *The Lost Colony*'s Waterside Theatre, many people combine a trip to all three.

Designated as a National Historic Site in 1941, this more than 500-acre expanse of woods includes the "outerwork"—an area built intentionally away from living space—along with a soundside beach, the National Park Service's Cape Hatteras National Seashore headquarters, the Fort Raleigh Visitor Center, and nature trails.

The Fort Raleigh Visitor Center offers interpretive exhibits in a small museum. The museum is not particularly interesting to children, though adults will be fascinated by the story of the colonists who attempted the first English settlements in the New World. A 17-minute video provides an introduction to the historic site. Also, a 400-year-old Elizabethan room from Heronden Hall in Kent, England, is on display. It was removed from an authentic 16th-century home. The

room gives visitors a feel for the type of accommodations the aristocratic English were used to at the time of the attempted settlements. A gallery inside displays artifacts excavated from the site and copies of watercolors by John White, governor of the Roanoke colony.

Outside, Fort Raleigh has a variety of options for experiencing the history of Roanoke Island. Behind the visitor center is the earthworks, which is not very impressive but gives you an idea of the original. The Thomas Hariot Nature Trail, named for the scientist who accompanied one of the voyages, winds through the woods behind the visitor center. Hariot's descriptions of the New World are quoted on interpretive signs along the trail. The pine-needle path leads to the sandy shores of Roanoke Sound.

Self-guided tours and tours led by park service personnel are available at this archaeologically significant site. Interpretive programs on African-American history, European colonial history, Native American history, and Civil War history are offered in the summer. Fort Raleigh National Historic Site is open year-round from 9 a.m. to 5 p.m. seven days a week. Hours are extended in the summer. The grounds of Fort Raleigh provide a place for a picnic, especially under the huge live oaks on the grass median of the parking lot. Restrooms are on-site.

FREEDMEN'S COLONY SITE, WEIRS
POINT, AND FORT HUGER
Roanoke Island
(252) 473-5772
At the northernmost end of Roanoke Island, on the east side of the Manns Harbor bridge, are several historic landmarks that are part of the Fort Raleigh National Historic Site. You can access these sites by the Freedmen's

Trail, a 2-mile, self-guided trail that starts near the Elizabethan Gardens entrance. You can get there by car and park in the sizable lot or ride a bike along the Manteo Bike Path, which ends at this site. Weirs Point is an attractive public beach on Croatan Sound. The beach is wide enough to allow for a picnic or game of Frisbee, and the sound water is warm and shallow. Picnic benches, a Dare County information kiosk, and restrooms are provided at Weirs Point. Watch for stumps and broken stakes in the water. The tide creeps up quickly, so keep blankets out of its encroaching flow.

Next to the beach is an exhibit about the Freedmen's Colony, a community for runaway slaves between 1862 and 1867. During the Civil War Roanoke Island was seized by Union soldiers in 1862. After that, runaway slaves were welcomed on the island, given food, and allowed to settle in the Union camp. Slaves from all over northeastern North Carolina flocked to the safe haven. Male freed slaves worked for the Union forces for $10 a month plus rations and clothing. Women and children were paid $4 a month. In 1863 the colony was officially established, and the freed slaves were given land and agricultural tools. Many of the freed slaves joined the Union effort, but the ones who remained behind were given health and education services. By 1866, however, most of the freedmen were forced to leave. Exhibits at the site explain the story.

In 1901, from a hut on Weirs Point beach, one of the unsung geniuses of the electronic age began investigating what was then called "wireless telegraphy." Reginald Fessenden held hundreds of patents on radiotelepathy and electronics, but he died without any credit for many of them. In a letter dated "April 3, 1902, Manteo," Fessenden tells his patent attorney that "I can now telephone as far as I can telegraph. . . . I have sent varying musical notes from Hatteras and received them here with but 3 watts of energy." Thus, the world's first musical radio broadcasts were completed on this soundside sand of the Outer Banks.

About 300 yards north of Weirs Point, under 6 feet of water, lay the remains of Fort Huger. This was the largest Confederate fort on the island when Union troops advanced in 1862. The island migrated quite a bit in the past 145 years; the fort formerly sat securely on solid land.

> **i** Backstage tours at *The Lost Colony* are offered within the season for only $5 per person. Get an up-close look at the theater, costume shop, and prop rooms. The tours are held Monday through Saturday at 6:30 p.m. and take a maximum of 50 people. Call (252) 473-3414, ext. 225, to reserve a spot.

THE LOST COLONY
**Off US 64, Waterside Theatre,
Roanoke Island
(252) 473-3414, (800) 488-5012
www.thelostcolony.org**

The nation's longest-running outdoor drama has been running for over 70 years. This historical account of the first English settlement in North America is a must-see for Outer Banks visitors. It's almost as legendary as the story it depicts. Pulitzer Prize–winning author Paul Green brought the history of English colonization to life through an impressive combination of Elizabethan music, Native American dances, colorful costumes, and vivid drama on a soundside stage in 1937. His play continues to enchant audiences today at Waterside Theatre, near Fort Raleigh, on Roanoke Island.

The Lost Colony is a theatrical account of Sir Walter Raleigh's early explorers, who first settled on the shores near the present-day theater in 1585. (Andy Griffith got his start playing Sir Walter Raleigh for several seasons.) Children and adults are equally captivated by the performers, staging, and music; many locals see the show every year and always find it spellbinding. If you have youngsters, come early and have them sit in the front row by the stage. The closer you sit to the stage, the more you'll enjoy the show.

In 2001 *The Lost Colony* got a boon when Tony Award–nominated Broadway actor Terrance Mann agreed to direct the show. Mann, who has held principal roles in *Cats, Les Miserables, Beauty and the Beast,* The Addams Family, and *The Scarlet Pimpernel,* performed in *The Lost Colony* as a dancer and in the role of Old Tom before making it big on Broadway. Mann made many changes to the play, returning many of the nostalgic nuances of the glory days of the show. Another famous name associated with the show is William Ivey Long, who won a second Tony Award in 2001 for his costume design work on *The Producers.* Long has been the costume designer for *The Lost Colony* for more than 15 years and has been associated with the show since he was a young boy, when his parents worked on *The Lost Colony.*

Just after the season in late summer of 2007, a fire broke out during the night at the Waterside Theatre. The costume shop burned to the ground, and had it not been for an eagle-eyed Nags Head resident, more of the theater would have suffered damage. Help reached the theater in time to control the fire from spreading; however, around 95 percent of the costumes were lost in the fire.

The costumes that did survive were on display at a museum or being cleaned. Following Long's designs, costumes were remade both locally and in New York. Outstanding community support made funding possible. Now, *The Lost Colony* is fortunate to have an almost entirely new wardrobe.

It can get chilly in the evenings when the wind blows off the sound, so we recommend sweaters, even in July and August. Mosquitoes at this outdoor drama can be vicious, especially after a rain, so bring plenty of bug repellent. The theater is wheelchair accessible and the staff is glad to accommodate special customers.

Once you arrive, settle back and enjoy a thoroughly professional, well-rehearsed, technically outstanding show. The leads are played by professional actors. Most of the backstage personnel are pros—and it shows. Supporting actors are often locals, with some island residents passing from part to part as they grow up. On August 18 four local infants are chosen to participate in the play in honor of Virginia Dare's birthday.

The Waterside Theatre is well designed, and all of the seats are pretty good. Tickets begin at $20. Seats in the Producer's Circle offer the most panoramic view of the show and cost slightly more. Group discounts are available for 20 or more people. Group reservations must be made in advance.

The show begins at 8:30 p.m. and runs six nights a week (closed Sun) from the end of May through late August. This is probably the most popular summertime event on the Outer Banks, so we recommend that you make reservations, though you can try your luck at the door if you wish. Make paid mail reservations by writing *The Lost Colony,* 1409 US 64/264, Manteo, NC 27954; or reserve tickets by phone. Tickets are available online, by phone, or at several Outer Banks businesses. If a production is rained out, ticket holders can exchange their passes for another night or get a refund.

Check the website or call the Waterside Theatre box office for details on upcoming events. This season's *Pirate's: A Boy At Sea* will be performed at 2 p.m. at Waterside Theatre on Wed and Thurs in season. Tickets are $12. Check the website for more detailed information.

i **Insiders call the box office before attending a show at Waterside Theatre and reserve a backstage tour and a Waterside sunset picnic to create a memorable experience.**

*NORTH CAROLINA AQUARIUM AT ROANOKE ISLAND
374 Airport Rd., Roanoke Island
(252) 473-3494
www.ncaquariums.com

The North Carolina Aquarium on Roanoke Island is an outstanding facility. Its 68,000 square feet of space includes a $16 million expansion that was completed in 2000. The theme of the aquarium is Waters of the Outer Banks, and visitors get to see a variety of marine communities: coastal freshwaters, wetlands, estuaries, roadside ditches, the Gulf Stream, and the Graveyard of the Atlantic on the ocean floor.

A major attraction is the Graveyard of the Atlantic tank, holding 285,000 gallons of salt water, or about 2.35 million pounds. It takes 209 pilings sunk about 35 feet into the ground to support the weight of this enormous tank. The tank's highlight is a 53-footlong replica of a Civil War ironclad, the USS *Monitor*. Expert scuba divers who have seen the real *Monitor* wreck say the

replica is extremely accurate. Scuba divers give educational presentations from the tank and answer spectators' questions while inside. Also in the tank are sea turtles and nearly 1,000 other sea creatures, including sharks, cobia, tarpon, jack crevalle, bluefish, and black and red drum.

Wetlands on the Edge is another favorite exhibit. In this tree-filled atrium, river otters swim and play in a clear pool of river water, while visitors watch through a glass screen. Also here are several American alligators, who bask in the sunlight near their pond. You'll also see turtles.

The Coastal Freshwaters exhibit explores freshwater marine animals and habitats. From ponds and lakes to the Albemarle Sound, this exhibit displays turtles, sunfish, gars, and bowfins. The Croatan Sound tank showcases the fish that local anglers catch. Marine Communities features nine tanks representing environments from grass flats to the Gulf Stream, displaying blue crabs, summer flounder, puppy drum, lobster, a porcupine puffer, and much more. Close Encounters is the touch tank area, where kids can touch horseshoe crabs and other creatures. Staff members are on hand to answer questions.

Walk outside, behind the aquarium, and you're right on the banks of Roanoke Sound. Rest on a bench or walk along a path through the trees. Bleached-white whale bones form a natural sculpture garden. Along the short path interactive exhibits tell the story of the area's birds and plant life.

The aquarium offers educational films, lectures, and classes year-round. Field trips to nearby salt marshes and fishing areas are available for a fee. For information about daily programs or special activities, such as crabbing classes, cooking classes, crafting with seaweed, gyotaku (fish printing), and more, call (252) 473-3494, ext. 242. The gift shop is a real treasure, with a multitude of toys that teach children to think and become environmentally aware. Posters, stuffed animals, gifts, souvenirs, puzzles, games, T-shirts, and more are top quality and based on a natural theme.

Open year-round from 9 a.m. to 5 p.m. daily, except Christmas and New Year's Days. Prices are $8 for adults ages 13 to 61, $7 for seniors and active military personnel, and $6 for children age 3 to 12. Kids age 2 and younger are admitted free.

OLD SWIMMING HOLE
Airport Road, Roanoke Island
(252) 473-1101, ext. 313
Go for a swim after a visit to the aquarium. Right next door, the county facility maintains a beach, picnic tables, grills, picnic shelter, kids' playground, sand volleyball court, and restrooms. The beach is lifeguarded from 10 a.m. to 6 p.m. from Memorial Day to Labor Day. Families with small kids love the sound waters.

KITTY HAWK AERO TOURS
Main Terminal, Airport Road Manteo
Airport, Manteo
(252) 441-TOUR, (877) 359-8447
For a bird's-eye view of the Outer Banks and a shocking perspective on how fragile the barrier islands really are, take a 30-minute air tour over the land and ocean in a small plane.

Pilots will gear tours to passengers' wishes but usually head south to Bodie Island Lighthouse and back. Bring your camera for this high-flying cruise. Rates begin at $60 per flight.

Biplane flights in an open-air-cockpit authentic 1941 Waco are also available from the same site beginning at $80 per flight. These 5- to 7-minute trips take you back in time, complete with goggled leather helmets. Longer trips are also offered. Air tours are offered year-round, weather permitting. Advance reservations are accepted.

ELIZABETH R/BLOODY MARY AND THE VIRGIN QUEEN/SHEPHERD OF THE OCEAN
The Elizabethan Gardens and Roanoke Island Festival Park
(252) 475-1500
www.elizabethr.org
Adding to the cultural delights of Roanoke Island are the finely crafted short plays *Elizabeth R*, *Bloody Mary and the Virgin Queen*, and *Shepherd of the Ocean*. Performed by the acclaimed Barbara Hird, these three dramatic performances give insight into the life of Queen Elizabeth I. *Elizabeth R* is an internationally acclaimed one-woman show that examines the private life of Elizabeth Tudor, or Queen Elizabeth I. During the hourlong performance, the queen, dressed in her full regalia, reveals the private details of her life, including her likes and dislikes, the reasoning behind her decisions, and information about the people around her. Elizabeth R is suitable for ages 14 and over. Performances are held on select weekday summer afternoons at 3 p.m. on the indoor Roanoke Island Festival Park stage.

Bloody Mary and the Virgin Queen is a humorous musical farce based on the relationship between Queen Elizabeth I and her half sister, Mary Tudor. The two absolutely loathed one another, yet they're buried in the same tomb in London's Westminster Abbey. Through fast-paced dialogue of bantering, arguing, cajoling, singing, crying, and laughing, the two actors teach a history lesson in a most entertaining way. Barbara Hird plays Elizabeth, and Marsha Warren plays Mary. The performance is about an hour long. While the dialogue is witty and interesting for adults, there really isn't enough action for young attention spans. *Bloody Mary and the Virgin Queen* is recommended for ages 10 and up. *Shepherd of the Ocean* comically examines the relationship between Queen Elizabeth I and Sir Walter Raleigh. *Shepherd of the Ocean* is suitable for ages 14 and over. Call (252) 475-1500 for reservations to any of these shows.

MOTHER VINEYARD
Off Mother Vineyard Road, Roanoke Island

The oldest-known grapevine in the United States grows on Roanoke Island. When the first settlers arrived here, the Outer Banks were covered with wild grapes. Arthur Barlowe wrote to Sir Walter Raleigh in 1584: "Being where we first landed very sandy and low toward the water side, but so full of grapes as the very beating and surge of the sea overflowed them, of which we found such plenty, as well there as in all places else, both on the sand and on the green soil, on the hills as in the plains, as well on every little shrub, as also climbing toward the tops of high cedars, that I think in all the world the like abundance is not to be found."

The Mother Vine is one of those grapevines, so old that it may have been planted even before Europeans arrived in the New World. Certainly it was already old in the 1750s, as records attest, and scuppernong grapevines do not grow swiftly. Another story is that this vine was transplanted to Roanoke Island by some of the Fort Raleigh settlers. Whichever story is true, the Mother Vine is more than 400 years old, and it's still producing fine, fat, tasty grapes. In fact, for many years a small winery owned by the Etheridge family cultivated the vine on Baum's Point, making the original Mother Vineyard wine until the late 1950s.

Mother Vineyard Scuppernong, the Original American Wine, is still produced by a company in Petersburg, Virginia. It is a pink wine, quite sweet, similar to a white port.

The Mother Vine is on private property and a bit out of the way. To find it, drive north from Manteo on US 64. About 0.75 mile past the city limits, turn right onto Mother Vineyard Road. Go less than a half mile, where the road makes a sharp turn to the right at the sound. About 300 feet past the turn, on the left, the patient old vine endures beneath a canopy of leaves, twisted and gnarled, ancient and enduring. Please stay on the road if you're sneaking a peek.

✳DOWNTOWN MANTEO
Off US 64; Queen Elizabeth Avenue and Budleigh and Sir Walter Raleigh Streets, Manteo

Named for a Roanoke Island Native American who accompanied English explorers back to England in the 16th century, Manteo is one of the oldest Outer Banks communities and has long been a commercial and governmental hub for the area.

When Dare County was formed in 1870, this area along Shallowbag Bay became the county seat. Roanoke Island provided a central location that everyone could reach by boat. It wasn't until 1873, when a post office was established here, that the county seat became known as Manteo. In 1899 Manteo incorporated and became the Town of Manteo. Today hundreds of permanent residents

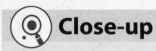 **Close-up**

North Carolina's Best of the Bunch

Long before the English came to the fair shores of the Outer Banks, native dwellers were enjoying the delicious fruits of the muscadine grape that grows only in eastern North Carolina. The earliest English notation of this wild grape is found in Giovanni de Verrazzano's logbook from 1524, noted while exploring the Cape Fear River Valley. The muscadine grape to this day evokes a strong personal association for native North Carolinians.

America's first cultivated grape was used to create the best-selling wine in the country, at one time. One of the most popular varieties of the bronze to black muscadine grape is the scuppernong. Thomas Jefferson is reported to have claimed three wines as favorites—two were imported from Europe, and the third was scuppernong! Southerners love to make wine, grape hull pies, and jellies from the scuppernong grape, named for the region in which it was found. This particular variety has been cultivated for over 400 years and is known as the "big, white grape." This wine eventually became so popular, production couldn't match demand, and vintners began producing watered-down or poorer quality scuppernongs. For a time thereafter, the name scuppernong became synonymous with cheap jug wine.

As recent studies of the muscadine varieties in general have revealed excellent health benefits, interest in scuppernongs and muscadine grapes has recently resurfaced. These grapes, although tough-skinned, are very sweet and candylike and contain a unique and extremely strong blend of antioxidants. According to North Carolina State University researchers, the muscadine boasts 40 times the health benefits of any other grape. The grapes (and wines, pies, and jellies) are winning back fans, due to the news on health benefits, better-tasting vintages, and their colorful history. North Carolina scuppernong is a popular state wine and 14 wineries produce the wine.

The grapes are plentiful over most of the Outer Banks. They are easy to spot in September and through mid-October. Manteo's legendary Mother Vine is the nation's oldest cultivated grapevine, according to North Carolina's Wine and Grape Council. This vine may be the source of all cultivated scuppernongs in the United States. Read more about this specific historical vine on page 151.

make this Roanoke Island town their home, and many more county residents commute from other towns to work. On Budleigh Street, many of the county and town offices are scattered in older office buildings. Manteo's bed-and-breakfast inns, restaurants, and shops beckon tourists, and thousands of visitors arrive each summer to explore this historic waterfront village. (See the Roanoke Island section of the Area Overview chapter.)

On the docks of Manteo's waterfront, 53 modern dockside slips with 110- and 220-volt electrical hookups offer boaters overnight or long-term anchorage. A comfort station with restrooms, showers, washers, and dryers also serves vessel crews and captains. Shop and dine within walking distance in Manteo—or better yet, bike. This is a town to enjoy on two wheels.

Across the street from the waterfront, in the center of the downtown area, independently owned shops, eateries, and businesses offer everything from handmade pottery to books to clothing, all in a 4-square-block area.

Around the southeast point of the waterfront, the town's American Bicentennial Park is wedged between the courthouse and a 4-story brick building housing shops and condominiums. Picnic benches afford a comfortable place to rest and enjoy the view across the bay to Roanoke Island Festival Park, where the state's replica 16th-century sailing ship *Elizabeth II* rocks gently on small sound waves. A wood-plank boardwalk leads along the town's waterfront. One end bustles with kayak and boat tours coming and going, boaters docking in the harbor, and tourists strolling along the docks or exploring shops and restaurants. Around the corner is a gazebo for resting and a long pier for fishing or crabbing. A children's playground with equipment is on the corner, as are picnic tables. At the far end of the docks, you'll find a bit of serenity, where the activity diminishes and the only company you'll have is a few cattails.

If, as most visitors do, you reach the Banks via US 158, you can get to Manteo by traveling south until you reach Whalebone Junction. Bear right onto US 64 at the traffic light near RV's restaurant. Continue across the causeway and high-rise bridge past Pirate's Cove, then bear right at the intersection, turning onto US 264 Business. Turn right at either of the town's first two stoplights to go downtown.

✳ROANOKE ISLAND FESTIVAL PARK AND *ELIZABETH II*
1 Festival Park, Manteo
(252) 475-1500,
(252) 475-1506 (24-hour events line)
www.roanokeisland.com

An expansion of the *Elizabeth II* Historic Site, Roanoke Island Festival Park is one of the largest attractions on the Outer Banks. This vibrant history, educational, and cultural arts complex opened in 1998, with top-quality facilities that add a tremendous variety to the year-round interests on Roanoke Island. Visitors explore the evolution of Roanoke Island and the Outer Banks from the late 16th century to the early 1900s through living-history interpretation, exhibits, film, and visual and performing arts programs.

The site includes the 8,500-square-foot Roanoke Adventure Museum, where interactive displays allow you to touch, see, and hear the history of the Outer Banks. In the Film Theater, *The Legend of Two Path,* a 45-minute film developed especially for the site by the North Carolina School of the Arts, tells the story of the first English landing on Roanoke Island from the Native American point of view. There's an outdoor performance pavilion that offers classical and popular concerts on lush pastoral lawns; a gallery, with art shows that change monthly; a small theater where special films and plays are held in an intimate setting; and a museum store bursting with treasures.

Porches, lawns, and boardwalks add charm, and you're just as likely to encounter an Elizabethan settler there as you are inside. The Children's Performances, held daily in the summer months in the Film Theater, are excellent. Many special events are held at Festival Park year-round, such as a fishing rodeo, beach music festivals, and a Civil War encampment.

See the website or call for details, and also see the Annual Events chapter.

The *Elizabeth II*, designed as the centerpiece for the 400th anniversary of the first English settlement in America, is a representative sailing ship similar to the one that carried Sir Walter Raleigh's colonists across the Atlantic in 1585. Interpreters clad in Elizabethan costumes conduct tours of the colorful 69-foot ship.

Although it was built in 1983, the *Elizabeth II*'s story really began four centuries earlier, when Thomas Cavendish mortgaged his estates to build the *Elizabeth* for England's second expedition to Roanoke Island. With six other vessels, the original *Elizabeth* made the first colonization voyage to the New World in 1585 and landed on the Outer Banks.

There wasn't enough information available about the original vessels to reconstruct an exact replica, so shipbuilders used the designs of vessels from 1585 to build the *Elizabeth II*. Constructed entirely in a wooden structure on the Manteo waterfront, the completed ship slid down hand-greased rails into Shallowbag Bay in front of a crowd of enthusiastic dignitaries and locals in 1983.

Stretching 69 feet long and 17 feet wide and drawing 8 feet of water, *Elizabeth II* was funded entirely through private donations. Her decks are hand hewn from juniper timbers. Her frames, keel, planking, and decks are fastened with 7,000 locust wood pegs.

Every baulk, spar, block, and lift of the ship is as close to authentic as possible, with only three exceptions: a wider upper-deck hatch for easier visitor access; a vertical hatch in the afterdeck to make steering easier for the helmsman; and a controversial pair of diesel engines that were installed in the *Elizabeth II* in 1993. The 115-horsepower motors help the grand sailing ship move under its own power,

instead of relying on expensive tugboats. Now the vessel can cruise up to 8 knots per hour with no wind and travel for up to 40 hours without refueling its two 150-gallon tanks. The state ship stays on the Outer Banks most of the year, but during the off-seasons it sometimes travels to other North Carolina ports, serving as the state's only moving historic site.

Explore the grounds and you'll discover the Settlement Site, a recreation of the first English military establishment on North American soil. Try on armor, learn how nails were made, and more at this staffed camp.

The newest addition to Roanoke Island Festival Park is American Indian Town. Explore coastal Algonquian culture and history. This exhibit takes visitors on a journey to a native community as it would have been in the 1500s, when the English first stepped foot onto this faire soil.

Roanoke Island Festival Park is open year-round. Hours vary according to season. Admission is $8 for adults, $5 for students, and free for children younger than age 5. Group rates are available. Call ahead for a schedule of events.

i First Friday on Roanoke Island is held from 6 to 8 p.m. on the first Friday of each month, beginning in April. Discover the magic of historic downtown Manteo. Locals and visitors mingle at this special night, which offers music, shopping, and dining. For more information call (252) 473-5121.

ROANOKE ISLAND FESTIVAL PARK PERFORMING ARTS SERIES
Roanoke Island Festival Park Pavilion,
1 Festival Park, Manteo
(252) 475-1500
www.roanokeisland.com

The outdoor pavilion at Roanoke Island Festival Park provides an idyllic setting for the cultural arts performances of students from the University of North Carolina. Visitors are invited to spread out blankets or set up folding chairs on the expansive, lush lawn facing the pavilion. Performances include dance, children's shows, classical music, drama, film, and jazz. Picnics are welcome. The pavilion has an open back, so you often can see the waters of the Roanoke Sound flowing behind the performers, making an especially tranquil setting. Check the website or call for details.

OUTER BANKS HISTORY CENTER
**Roanoke Island Festival Park,
1 Festival Park, Manteo
(252) 473-2655**
Adjacent to the visitor center at Roanoke Island Festival Park, the Outer Banks History Center is a remarkable repository of North Carolina state and regional history. The North Carolina State Archives, Division of Archives and History, Department of Cultural Resources, administers this Outer Banks treasure.

Opened in 1988, the history center collection includes 100,000 manuscript items, 35,000 books, 35,000 photographs, 1,500 periodical titles, a large collection of important maps, hundreds of audio and video recordings, microfilm, and ephemera. Some of the more than 700 maps in the collection are more than 400 years old. The collection also includes items relating to lighthouses and other Outer Banks architecture, local history about towns, shipwrecks, the US Lifesaving Service, Civil War artwork, and *The Lost Colony* outdoor drama records and memorabilia.

Materials are housed in closed stacks to ensure security and the climate control needed for preservation. However, staffers at the history center are knowledgeable and happy to help anyone access the facility's vast resources. Journalists, authors, history buffs, students, scientists, genealogists, and casual tourists find the stop worthwhile.

A special gallery features archived materials and photographs, and traveling exhibits are displayed from time to time. The reading room and gallery are open year-round from 9 a.m. to 5 p.m. Mon through Fri and 10 a.m. to 3 p.m. on Sat. The Outer Banks History Center is a public facility and is free of charge.

PIONEER THEATRE
**113 Budleigh St., Manteo
(252) 473-2216**
This nostalgic movie house is the best place to see movies on the Outer Banks and the oldest theater continuously operated by one family in the United States. The original Pioneer Theatre, opened in 1918 by George Washington Creef, was located a block over and showed silent films accompanied by a local pianist. The current Pioneer Theatre opened in 1934 and is now run by Creef's grandson, H. A. Creef.

This movie house is a family gathering place for Manteo locals. All of the movies are first run and usually family oriented (G, PG, or PG-13), and people come regardless of whether they're interested in the show. Friday night the place is overrun with school kids, so it's best to avoid that night unless you're one of them. This theater is definitely old-fashioned in its prices at $5 a ticket and you won't get gouged at the candy counter either. One movie is shown every night at 8 as long as there are at least three people in the theater. Listings change weekly, without fail, on Friday. Check the billboard on the highway in Manteo, or call the theater for the current listing and a brief synopsis of the movie.

NORTH CAROLINA MARITIME MUSEUM ON ROANOKE ISLAND
104 Fernando St., Manteo
(252) 475-1750

In 1998 the vintage George Washington Creef Boathouse in downtown Manteo was revitalized as an outpost of the North Carolina Maritime Museum in Beaufort. This effort breathed new life into the old boathouse that has stood on the Manteo waterfront since 1940.

The museum is dedicated to North Carolina's place in boatbuilding history. The crew at the museum, many of them volunteers, stay busy refurbishing and rebuilding wooden boats. Inside, a number of crafts represent the region's maritime history. There's an 1883 original Creef shadboat, a variety of sailing skiffs, a Davis Runabout speedboat, and a multimedia presentation on the construction of the *Elizabeth II*, which was built on this site. This is also a working boat shop, where visitors observe staff and volunteers working on a variety of repair and building projects. If you're interested in becoming a volunteer, talk to the curator.

Before the boathouse, this site was home to much of Manteo's extensive boatbuilding history. A boatyard and repair railway were here from the 1880s until 1939, when nearly everything on the Manteo waterfront burned in a devastating fire. George Washington Creef Jr. constructed this boathouse in 1940 to build shallow-draft freight boats and repair the shadboats invented and built by his father, George Washington Creef Sr. The shadboat is now the North Carolina state boat. The boathouse was later used to build rescue craft for the military and world-record-holding speedboats.

The museum is worth the trip to Manteo for those interested in boats and boatbuilding of the past and present. It is open Tues through Sat. Hours vary with the season.

MILL LANDING
NC 345, Wanchese

Near the end of a winding 5-mile road, past a long expanse of wide, waving marshlands overflowing with waterfowl, Wanchese is well off the beaten path of most visitors (see the section on Roanoke Island in the Area Overview chapter) and remains one of the most unspoiled areas on the barrier islands. At the very end of NC 345, one of the most picturesque and unchanged areas of the Outer Banks is often overlooked: Mill Landing, which embodies the heritage of the Outer Banks. Here active fishing trawlers anchor at the docks, their mesh still dripping seaweed from the wide roller wheels. Watermen in yellow chest waders and white rubber boots (known locally as Wanchese wingtips) sling shark, tuna, and dolphin onto cutting-room carts. Pieces of the island's past float silently in the harbor, mingling with remade boats that are still afloat and sunken ships that have long since disappeared.

The fish houses at Mill Landing include Wanchese Fish Company, Etheridge's, Jaws Seafood, Quality Seafood, and Moon Tillett's. These houses ship seafood to restaurants in Hampton Roads, Baltimore, New York, Boston, and Tokyo. Scallops, shrimp, fish, and crabs are available here in season.

WANCHESE SEAFOOD INDUSTRIAL PARK

615 Harbor Rd., Wanchese
(252) 473-5867

A 69-acre industrial park on a deep harbor at Wanchese, this state-supported facility was built in 1980 with $8.1 million in state and federal funds. It was designed to attract large-scale seafood-processing companies to set up shop on the secluded Roanoke Island waterfront. After federal promises about stabilizing Oregon Inlet failed to materialize, few deep-draw fishing trawlers could keep risking the trip through the East Coast's most dangerous inlet.

Oregon Inlet continued to shoal terribly through the 1980s, and the seafood park remained largely vacant until 1994, when some smaller area businesses and fish-processing plants began establishing themselves there. Unpredictable weather patterns still affect the channel's navigability.

The industrial park is an educational attraction for anyone interested in the maritime world of boatbuilding and sea harvesting. Visitors are welcome to drive or walk through and visit the boat docks. Stop by the office if you have questions.

PIRATE'S COVE YACHT CLUB

Nags Head–Manteo Causeway, Manteo
(252) 473-3906, (800) 367-4728
www.fishpiratescove.com

If you're interested in what the boats are catching in the Gulf Stream, head over to Pirate's Cove Yacht Club between 4 and 5 p.m. When the charter boats return to their slips, the catches of the day are thrown out on the docks to be picked up by the fish cleaners. Visitors are welcome to stroll along the boardwalk and watch. You might see tuna, wahoo, dolphin (the fish, not the mammal), cobia, or any of a number of fish. This is especially exciting for kids, who may not have seen such big fish before. If you would rather see the fish on the end of your own line, charter opportunities are available at Pirate's Cove. See the Fishing chapter for more information.

DARE COUNTY MAINLAND

WOLF HOWLS

Alligator River National Wildlife Refuge, Dare County Mainland
(252) 473-1131, ext. 243
www.fws.gov/alligatorriver

Go to the Alligator River National Wildlife Refuge to hear the red wolves howl. After sunset you meet a refuge staff person at Creef Cut Wildlife Trail at the intersection of US 64 and Milltail Road on the Dare County mainland. After a brief talk about the red wolves, you are led (in vehicles) about 6 miles back into the dark refuge. On the way you might even see some bears. In the dark woods, you get out of your car and listen as the staff person howls to elicit howls from the wolves. The wolves' response will give you goosebumps. You can't see the wolves, which makes them even more mysterious and adds to the allure of this experience. The 2-hour howl tours are held every Wed at 7:30 p.m. June through Sept 2. This experience costs $5, and preregistration is required. Call (252) 796-5600 to register. Free Howls are also held on Earth Day, April 22, at 7 p.m., in Oct during National Wolf Awareness Week, and again in Oct for Howl-o-ween. Join the Holiday Howl in Dec. Call to obtain the starting times and alternate dates.

A threatened species, red wolves have made a comeback in northeastern North Carolina due to careful management since the early 1980s. There are 10 wolves in captivity at the Alligator River National Wildlife Refuge and nearly 100 roaming free over about one million acres in northeastern North Carolina, including the refuge. For more information, see the Natural Wonders chapter. Check the website for other fun outings.

BODIE ISLAND

CAPE HATTERAS NATIONAL SEASHORE
Bodie, Hatteras, and Ocracoke Islands
(252) 473-3111
www.nps.gov/caha

Cape Hatteras National Seashore is a tremendous treasure for the residents and visitors of the Outer Banks. Here you will find the Outer Banks' most captivating open spaces, where long reaches of rugged dunes, windblown brush, wide beaches, and soundside wetlands are protected from development. Established in 1953 by the National Park Service and dedicated in 1958, the Cape Hatteras National Seashore includes part of Bodie Island and most of Hatteras and Ocracoke Islands, except for the village centers and Pea Island National Wildlife Refuge. The northern boundary begins south of Whalebone Junction in Nags Head, and the southern boundary is on Ocracoke Island. This was the very first national seashore in the nation. It consists of some of the narrowest land inhabitable by humans—skinny stretches of sand often less than a half mile wide. The national seashore provides miles-long stretches where there is not one simple structure obscuring the view. Wildlife, waterfowl, and seabirds are abundant in the national seashore, including the American oystercatcher and the threatened piping plover. Sea turtles survive here, too, as they often come ashore to lay eggs on the beaches in summer. Designated shorebird and sea-turtle sanctuaries are well marked for protection on the beaches.

The Cape Hatteras National Seashore beaches are some of the cleanest and least crowded on the East Coast. If you're looking for solitary recreational space or simple peace and quiet, you'll find it here. Most of the beaches do not have lifeguards, however, so make sure you know swimming safety precautions before going in. Lifeguards are stationed in summer at Coquina Beach on Bodie Island, at the beach near the Cape Hatteras Lighthouse, and at the Ocracoke Guarded Beach. Numerous access points are offered all along NC 12, the highway that threads through the seashore. Three of the Outer Banks' four lighthouses are located within this national seashore, and there are four campgrounds in the Cape Hatteras National Seashore (see the Camping chapter). Camping is prohibited on the beach.

Three visitor centers are established in the national seashore. The Bodie Island Visitor Center (252-441-5711) is on NC 12, in Nags Head heading south. The Cape Hatteras Visitor Center (252-995-4474) is in Buxton next to the Cape Hatteras Lighthouse. The Ocracoke Island Visitor Center (252-928-4531) is near the Cedar Island ferry dock. All provide extensive information on camping and activities in the national seashore.

The Cape Hatteras National Seashore is dedicated to community outreach and has summer programs to help visitors learn more about the natural surroundings. The National Park Service provides guided beach walks, bird walks, campfires, fishing trips, history tours, dozens of kids programs, snorkeling trips, turtle talks, and much more. The schedules are lengthy, so the best way to find out about programs is to pick up the information at one of the visitor centers or call ahead and have it mailed to you.

Driving on the beach is allowed in the Cape Hatteras National Seashore at certain access points only. Four-wheel-drive vehicles may enter only at designated ramps. Sound-side off-road travel is permitted on established roads or trails. Off-road access ramps are available at the visitor centers. Beach bonfires require a permit. Several day-use areas are available throughout the area, and nature trails provide visitors with an up-close look at the seashore environments. Personal watercraft like Jet Skis and WaveRunners are prohibited in Cape Hatteras National Seashore.

BODIE ISLAND LIGHTHOUSE AND
KEEPERS' QUARTERS
West of NC 12, Bodie Island
(252) 441-5711

This black-and-white beacon with horizontal bands is one of four lighthouses standing along the Outer Banks. It sits more than a half mile from the sea, in a field of green grass, closer to the sound than the ocean. This site, 6 miles south of Whalebone Junction, is one of the most picturesque on the Outer Banks. Photographers are drawn to the immaculately kept, spacious lawns, the charming double keepers' quarters and oil house, and the proud tower.

The lighthouse itself is not open for climbing, but the setting is worth the trip. The keepers' quarters has exhibits about the lighthouse and a small bookshop. The grounds are perfect for a picnic, and nature trails lead into the wide expanses of marshland behind the tower, through cattails, yaupon, and wax myrtle. The trails end up at Roanoke Sound, offering a view of the

private camp on Off Island. The slough that rushes through the water between Bodie and Off Islands is a popular fishing hole, and anglers often line the banks.

The current Bodie Island Lighthouse is the third to stand near Oregon Inlet, which opened during a hurricane in 1846. The first lighthouse was built south of Oregon Inlet in 1847 and 1848 and was the only one in the 140 miles between Cape Hatteras and Cape Henry, Virginia. The lighthouse developed cracks and structural damage within 10 years and had to be removed and rebuilt. The second light was also built south of Oregon Inlet. It was complete and lighted in 1859. Confederate forces destroyed the second tower during the Civil War so that it wouldn't fall into Union hands. The 170-foot lighthouse that stands today was built in 1872, this time north of Oregon Inlet because the inlet was moving south at a steady pace. Wanchese resident Vernon Gaskill served as the last civilian lightkeeper of the Bodie Island Lighthouse. The US Coast Guard operated the light for many years, and it was transferred to the National Park Service in 2000. The NPS hopes to restore the lighthouse so that it will one day be open to the public, but the price tag on the restoration work is $1 million. The first-order Fresnel lens will be of particular interest to visitors. The visitor center is open from 9 a.m. until 5 p.m. every day except Christmas. The grounds are always open.

COQUINA BEACH
NC 12, Bodie Island

Though not as broad as it once was due to storms, Coquina Beach is still one of the widest beaches on the Outer Banks and a favorite getaway. Just 6 miles south of Whalebone Junction, this beach has half the crowd but all the amenities you need: a lifeguard in the summer, a bathhouse, restrooms, outdoor showers, and lots of parking. Part of the allure of this remote area is that it's miles away from any business or rental cottage, making it a superb spot to sunbathe, swim, fish, and surf. The sand is almost white, and the beach is relatively flat.

Drawing its name from the tiny butter-fly-shaped coquina clams that burrow into the beach, at times almost every inch of this portion of the federally protected Cape Hatteras National Seashore harbors hundreds of recently washed-up shells and several species of rare shorebirds. Coquinas are edible and can be collected and cleaned from their shells to make a chowder. Local brick makers also have used the shells as temper in buildings.

LAURA A. BARNES
Coquina Beach, NC 12, Bodie Island
One of the last coastal schooners built in America, the *Laura A. Barnes* was completed in Camden, Maine, in 1918. This 120-foot ship was under sail on the Atlantic during a trip from New York to South Carolina when a nor'easter drove it onto the Outer Banks in 1921. The *Laura A. Barnes* ran aground just north of where it now rests at Coquina Beach. The entire crew survived. In 1973 the National Park Service moved the shipwreck to its present location, where visitors view the remains of the ship behind a roped-off area that includes placards with information about the *Laura A. Barnes* and the history of lifesaving.

✳OREGON INLET FISHING CENTER
NC 12, Bodie Island
(252) 441-6301, (800) 272-5199
www.oregon-inlet.com

Sportfishing enthusiasts, or anyone remotely interested in offshore angling, must stop by this bustling charter-boat harbor on the north shore of Oregon Inlet. Set beside the US Coast Guard station on land leased from the National Park Service, Oregon Inlet Fishing Center is owned by a group of 18 stockholders, most of them local fishermen. All vessels charge the same rate. A day on the Atlantic with one of these captains may give rise to a marlin, sailfish, wahoo, tuna, or dolphin on the end of the line. (See the Fishing chapter for details.) An exciting afternoon activity is to head to the boat docks at Oregon Inlet Fishing Center between 4 and 5 p.m. When the charter boats return to the docks, you'll have an opportunity to see a variety of Gulf Stream creatures as the mates unload the boats and hurl the huge fish on the docks. In summer the docks are crowded with spectators. Next to the fishing center store is a display case housing a 1,152-pound blue marlin, caught in 1973 and brought back to this fishing center. The store stocks bait and tackle, supplies, hot dogs and snacks, T-shirts and hats galore, and more. The fishing center has an air-fill tank for putting air back into your tires after driving on the beach (there's a four-wheel-drive access across the street). The boat ramp at the fishing center provides easy access to some of the best fishing grounds on the East Coast. There is plenty of parking, and restrooms are on-site.

OREGON INLET COAST GUARD
STATION
NC 12, Bodie Island
In the 19th and early 20th centuries, the federal government operated two lifesaving stations at Oregon Inlet. The Bodie Island station was on the north side of the inlet. The

Oregon Inlet station was on the south. Both of these original facilities are now closed. The Oregon Inlet station sits perilously close to the migrating inlet, the victim of hurricanes and decades of neglect. It is weatherworn and bedraggled, a testament to the ravages of salty winds and storms. Yet this building is a picturesque reminder of the history of the Outer Banks and how quickly changes occur. There is plenty of parking next to the station, and you can walk around the grounds and out to the jetties, but you can't go inside the building. This is also a popular and lucrative fishing spot. You can fish from the rock jetties, wade out into the deep cove, or walk the catwalk on the south end of the Bonner Bridge.

The Bodie Island station has been replaced by the Oregon Inlet Coast Guard station, which includes a 10,000-square-foot building, a state-of-the-art communications center, maintenance shops, an administrative center, and accommodations for the staff. Coast Guard crews have rescued dozens of watermen off the Outer Banks. They also aid sea turtles and stranded seals by helping the animals get back safely to warmer parts of the ocean.

OREGON INLET AND THE BONNER BRIDGE
NC 12, Oregon Inlet

The view from the crest of the Herbert C. Bonner Bridge has to be the most beautiful vista on the Outer Banks. If only there was a place to pull over and enjoy it more fully! As you drive over you get a sweeping glimpse of this infamous inlet and all its surrounding shoals, sandbars, and spoil islands. Sea captains call this the most dangerous inlet on the East Coast—and with good reason. Since 1960 at least 30 lives and an equal number

of boats have been lost at Oregon Inlet. The current through the inlet is dangerously swift and reckless, and shoals form alarmingly fast, causing boats to run aground.

The only outlet to the sea in the 140 miles between Cape Henry, in Virginia Beach, and Hatteras Inlet south of Hatteras Island, Oregon Inlet lies between Bodie Island and Pea Island National Wildlife Refuge. It is the primary passage for commercial and recreational fishing boats based along the northern Outer Banks. Even though it's often dredged, the inlet is sometimes impassable by deep-draft vessels.

Although a safe inlet is crucial to the commercial and recreational fishing industries, federal officials have refused to authorize or fund construction of jetties, rock walls that some scientists say would stabilize the evershallowing inlet. Oregon Inlet was created during a hurricane in September 1846, the same storm that opened Hatteras Inlet between Hatteras Village and Ocracoke Island. It was named for the side-wheeler *Oregon*, the first ship to pass through the inlet.

In 1964 the Herbert C. Bonner Bridge was built across the inlet. This two-lane span finally connected Hatteras Island and the Cape Hatteras National Seashore with the northern Outer Banks beaches. Before the bridge was built, travelers relied on ferry boats to carry them across Oregon Inlet.

Hurricane-force winds blew a dredge barge into the bridge in 1990, knocking out a center section of the span. No one was hurt, but the more than 5,000 permanent residents of Hatteras Island were cut off from the rest of the world for four months before workers could completely repair the bridge.

Wear and tear due to time, use, and climate conditions has taken its toll on this bridge. In 1997 the Bonner Bridge was recommended to be repaired and replaced by 2004. The project costs more than the North Carolina DOT can afford. Its budget would be completely wiped out for several years if North Carolina footed the bill. Federal funds have already been allocated to build a new bridge; however, approval for the project has been held up many times. For the latest information on building a new bridge, go to www.replacethebridgenow.com.

Four-wheel-drive vehicles can exit NC 12 on the northeast side of the inlet and drive along the beach, even beneath the Bonner Bridge, around the inlet. Fishing is permitted along the catwalks of the bridge and on the beach. Free parking and restrooms are available at the Oregon Inlet Fishing Center. There are also parking and portable toilets on the southern end of the bridge. This trip is especially beautiful at sunset or sunrise.

HATTERAS ISLAND

PEA ISLAND NATIONAL WILDLIFE REFUGE
NC 12, Pea Island
(252) 987-2394

Pea Island National Wildlife Refuge begins at the southern base of the Herbert C. Bonner Bridge and is the first place you come to when entering Hatteras Island from the north. The beach along this undeveloped stretch of sand is popular with anglers, surfers, sunbathers, and shell seekers. On the right side of the road, heading south, salt marshes surround Pamlico Sound, and birds seem to flutter from every grove of cattails.

Founded on April 12, 1938, the Pea Island refuge was federally funded as a winter preserve for snow geese. President Franklin D. Roosevelt put his Civilian Conservation Corps to work stabilizing the slightly sloping dunes, building them up with bulldozers, erecting long expanses of sand fencing, and securing the sand with sea oats and grasses. Workers built dikes near the sound to form ponds and freshwater marshes. They planted fields to provide food for the waterfowl.

With 5,915 acres that attract nearly 400 observed species of birds, Pea Island is an outdoor aviary. Few tourists visited this refuge when Hatteras Island was accessible only by ferry. After the Bonner Bridge opened in 1964, motorists began driving through this once isolated outpost.

Today Pea Island is one of the barrier islands' most popular havens for birders, naturalists, and sea-turtle savers. Endangered species, from the loggerhead sea turtle to the tiny piping plover shorebirds, inhabit this area. Pea Island's name comes from the "dune peas" that grow all along the now grassy sand dunes. The tiny plant with pink and lavender flowers is a favorite food of migrating geese.

Four miles south of the Bonner Bridge's southern base, the Pea Island Visitor Center offers free parking and easy access to the beach. If you walk directly across the highway to the top of the dunes, you'll see the remains of the federal transport *Oriental*. Its steel boiler is all that remains of the ship, which sank in May 1862.

On the sound side of the highway, in the marshes, ponds, and endless wetlands, whistling swans, snow geese, Canada geese, and 25 species of ducks make winter sojourns in the refuge. Savannah sparrows, migrant warblers, gulls, terns, herons, and egrets also alight in this area from fall through early spring. In summer American avocets, willets, black-necked stilts, and several species of ducks nest here.

Bug repellent is a must on Pea Island from Mar through Oct. Ticks also cause problems. Check your clothing before getting in the car, and shower as soon as possible if you hike through any underbrush.

NORTH POND TRAIL
NC 12, Pea Island

A birder's favorite, this wheelchair-accessible nature trail begins at the visitor center parking area and is about a mile long. The trail runs along the top of a dike between two man-made ponds that were begun in the late 19th century and completed by the Civilian Conservation Corps in the 1930s. The walkway includes three viewing platforms, marshland overlooks, and mounted binoculars.

Wax myrtles and live oaks stabilize the dike and provide shelter for scores of songbirds. Warblers, yellowthroats, cardinals, and seaside sparrows land during biannual migrations. The quarter-mile Salt Flats Trail starts at the north end of the North Pond Trail.

The US Fish & Wildlife Service manages Pea Island refuge's ecosystem. Workers plant fields with fescue and rye grass to keep the waterfowl coming back. Pheasants, muskrats, and nutria live along these ponds year-round.

PEA ISLAND VISITOR CENTER
NC 12, Pea Island
(252) 987-2394

A paved parking area, free public restrooms, and the Pea Island Refuge Headquarters are 4 miles south of the Oregon Inlet bridge on the sound side of NC 12. Refuge volunteers staff this small welcome station year-round and are available to answer questions. Visitors see exhibits on wildlife, waterfowl, and

bird life and browse the small gift shop. In summer the facility is open seven days a week from 9 a.m. to 4 p.m. In the off-season the center is open Thurs through Sun from 9 a.m. to 4 p.m. It's closed Christmas Day. Free nature trail maps are available, and in summer months special nature programs are offered, such as bird walks, turtle talks, and guided canoe tours.

Hunting, camping, and driving are not allowed in the refuge. Open fires are also prohibited. Dogs must be kept on leashes on the east side of the highway. Firearms are not allowed in the refuge; shotguns and rifles must be stowed out of sight even if you're just driving straight through Hatteras Island. Fishing, crabbing, boating, and other activities are allowed in the ocean and sound but are prohibited in refuge ponds.

About 3 miles farther south on NC 12, a kiosk just beyond the refuge headquarters marks the site of the remains of the nation's only African-American lifesaving station.

CHICAMACOMICO LIFESAVING STATION
NC 12, Rodanthe
(252) 987-1552
www.chicamacomico.net

With volunteer labor and long years of dedication, this once-decrepit lifesaving station is beautifully restored and open for tours. Its weathered, silvery-shingled buildings sparkle on the sandy lawn, surrounded by a perfect picket fence. Even the outbuildings have been brought back to their former uses. Today the nonprofit Chicamacomico Historical Association oversees and operates the lifesaving station. Volunteers set up a museum of area lifesaving awards and artifacts in the main building and have recovered some of the lifesaving equipment for the boathouse.

Volunteers take school groups on tours of the station, showing how the britches buoy helped rescue shipwreck victims and explaining the precise maneuvers surfmen had to follow on shore.

The station is open from Easter weekend through the Sat after Thanksgiving, Tues through Sat from 9 a.m. to 5 p.m. Various programs have been added to the roster and are offered every open day in the summer and on Wed, Thurs, and Fri in the off-season. At 2 p.m. programs might include a guided tour, a knot-tying class, or a storytelling hour. All programs are suitable for all ages. The guided tour gives more details on the site, the lifesaving service, and the equipment used. Group tours can be accommodated with advance notice. Admission is free, although donations are welcome and are greatly needed to further the restoration and expand the programs at this site. Call for additional program information.

i The shipwreck site of the *USS Monitor* was the first site in the United States to be designated a National Underwater Marine Sanctuary. The *Monitor,* a Civil War ironclad, sank in 240 feet of water about 16 miles off Cape Hatteras in a storm on New Year's Eve of 1862. The sanctuary is federally protected, and divers can visit only if they have a federal permit.

SALVO POST OFFICE
NC 12, Salvo

If you're heading south on NC 12 through Hatteras Island, slow down as you leave Salvo to spot a tiny whitewashed building with blue and red trim on the right side of the road. That's the old Salvo Post Office, which was the country's smallest post office until an arsonist burned about half of it down in 1992. It sat atop low rails in the postmaster's front yard. Over the years villagers moved it to the front yard of each new postmaster's house. The wooden structure had beautiful gilt post boxes surrounding the small glass service window, but it didn't have a bathroom, air-conditioning, or a wheelchair-accessible ramp. Although community volunteers rallied and rebuilt their little post office quickly, the federal government refused to reopen the outpost, which was originally erected in 1901. Today Salvo residents drive to Rodanthe to pick up their mail, and this tiny charmer sits empty by the road.

CANADIAN HOLE
NC 12, Avon

If a breeze is blowing, pull off the west side of the road between Avon and Buxton (1.5 miles south of Avon) into the big parking lot on the sound. Known as Canadian Hole, this is one of America's hottest windsurfing spots—and a magnet for visitors from Canada. Whether you ride a sailboard or not, this sight is not to be missed. On windy afternoons more than 100 sailboarders and kiteboarders spread out along the shallow sound, their brightly colored butterfly sails gently skimming into the sunset. There's a nice bathing beach here, so bring chairs and coolers and plan to watch the silent wave riders, some of whom are famous in windsurfing circles. The state recently expanded the parking area here. See the Water Sports chapter for more details.

✳CAPE HATTERAS LIGHTHOUSE
Off NC 12, Buxton
(252) 995-4474
www.nps.gov/caha

The Cape Hatteras Lighthouse is one of the most beloved and famous lighthouses in the nation, especially after it survived a move of more than 1,600 feet in 1999. The nation's tallest brick lighthouse at 208 feet, this black-and-white striped beacon was shown the world over as it was precariously jacked up and moved along roll beams to its new location away from the encroaching sea. The monumental relocation project was named the 2000 Outstanding Civil Engineering Achievement by the American Society of Civil Engineers. The lighthouse now stands the same distance from the Atlantic Ocean as it did when it was first built in 1870.

The original Cape Hatteras Lighthouse was built in 1803. The tower sat near Cape Point and was only 90 feet tall. Lit with whale oil, it was barely bright enough to be seen offshore. Erosion weakened the structure, and in 1861 Confederate soldiers removed the light's lens. The current Cape Hatteras Lighthouse was erected in 1870 with more than one million bricks and 257 steps. A special Fresnel lens that refracts light increased its visibility. The lighthouse was 1,600 feet from the ocean when it was built, but by 1987 it was only 120 feet from the crashing waves. After years of study, the National Park Service came to the conclusion that it had to "move it or lose it." The lighthouse was moved 1,600 feet back from the shore in just a few weeks, from June 17 to July 9, 1999. About 20,000 visitors a day watched. It reopened to the public on May 26, 2000. Its 800,000-candlepower beacon, rotating every seven-and-a-half seconds, can be seen 18 miles out to sea.

The view from the top of the Cape Hatteras Lighthouse is surreal and unforgettable. Try to make the climb while visiting the historical site.

The visitor center, called the Museum of the Sea, and the bookstore, both housed in the historic former keepers' quarters, were moved to this location before the lighthouse was moved. Restrooms are located here. If you continue past the parking area, you'll pass the picnic area and the Buxton Woods Nature Trail. If you continue on, you'll come to the Cape Point Campground and off-road vehicle ramps. The beach here is famous for swimming, sunbathing, surfing, and fishing, and you can take four-wheel-drive vehicles along many sections of the beach year-round. Park rangers and volunteers willingly answer questions and can be found in the visitor center and on the historic district grounds. Visitor center and bookstore hours are 9 a.m. to 6 p.m. daily in season, 9 a.m. until 5 p.m. off season, closed only Christmas Day.

In Buxton, signs along NC 12 lead you to the lighthouse. To the left you can visit the original lighthouse location, marked by a circle of granite stones that are etched with the names of 83 former lighthouse keepers. To the right are a parking area and the lighthouse's new location.

THE *ALTOONA* WRECK
Cape Point, Buxton

Four-wheel-drive motorists may enter the beach at the end of Cape Point Way on ramp 44. Here the Outer Banks juts out into the Atlantic in a wide elbow-shaped curve near the Cape Hatteras Lighthouse. The beaches in this area offer some of the barrier islands' best surf fishing. Two rules of the beach: Do not try to drive on the beach in anything but a four-wheel-drive vehicle, and be sure to let the proper amount of air out of your tires before traversing sand (see the Getting Here, Getting Around chapter for more information).

For those not driving on the beach, park on solid ground near the road and walk over the ramp to a foot trail. The path begins at the base of the dune. At the edge of a seawater pond, you'll catch a glimpse of the remains of the shipwreck *Altoona*. Built in Maine in 1869, the *Altoona* was a two-masted, 100-footlong cargo schooner based in Boston. It left Haiti in 1878 with a load of dyewood bound for New York. On October 22 a storm drove it ashore near Cape Point. Lifesavers rescued its seven crew members and salvaged some of the cargo, but the ship was buried beneath the sand until uncovered by a storm in 1962. The sea has broken the big boat apart since then, but you can still see part of the bow and hull beneath the waves.

DIAMOND SHOALS LIGHT
In the Atlantic Ocean, off Cape Point, Buxton

You can only visit this attraction in private boats, but you can see this unusual light tower from the eastern shore of Cape Point and from the top of the Cape Hatteras Lighthouse. Its bright beacon blinks every two seconds from a steel structure set 12 miles out in the sea.

Diamond Shoals once held a lighthouse, but waves beat the offshore rocks that held the structure so badly that federal officials gave up the project. Three lightships have been stationed on the shoals since 1824. The first sank in an 1827 gale. The second held its ground from 1897 until German submarines sank it in 1918. The third beamed until 1967, when it was replaced by the current light tower.

Diamond Shoals, the rocks around the tower, are the southern end of the treacherous near-shore sandbars off Hatteras Island.

BUXTON WOODS NATURE TRAIL
Cape Point, Buxton

Leading from the Cape Point Campground road about 0.75 mile through the woods, the Buxton nature trail takes walkers through thick vine jungles, across tall sand dunes, and into freshwater marshes (see the Natural Wonders chapter). Small plaques along the fairly level walkway describe the area's fragile ecosystems. People who hike this trail learn about the Outer Banks' water table, the role of beach grass and sea oats in stabilizing sand dunes, and the effects salt, storms, and visitors have on the ever-changing environment.

Cottonmouths seem to like this trail, too, so beware of these unmistakable snakes. They are fat, rough scaled, and stubby looking in brown, yellow, gray, or almost black. If you see a cottonmouth, let it get away—don't chase it. If it stands its ground, retreat.

This hike is not recommended for all, but picnic tables and charcoal grills just south of the nature trail provide a welcome respite for everyone. The walk is fine for hardy nature lovers who don't mind mingling with the outdoor elements.

FRISCO NATIVE AMERICAN MUSEUM
NC 12, Frisco
(252) 995-4440
www.nativeamericanmuseum.org

This enchanting museum on the sound side of NC 12 in Frisco is stocked with unusual collections of Native American artifacts gathered since the 1930s, plus numerous other fascinating collections. The museum boasts one of the most significant collections of artifacts from the Chiricahua Apache people and has displays of other Native American tribes' works from across the country, ranging from the days of early humans to modern time. Hopi drums, pottery, kachina dolls, baskets, weapons, and jewelry are displayed in homemade cases.

The museum property includes outdoor nature trails through 3 acres of woods, with a screened-in pavilion, a large pond, and three bridges on the land. Hours are 11 a.m. to 5 p.m. Tues through Sun, year-round. Admission is $5 per person or $15 per family. Seniors are charged $3. Group rates are available. The museum and trails are also designed to accommodate the vision impaired.

HATTERAS–OCRACOKE FERRY
NC 12, Hatteras Village NC 12, Ocracoke Island
(252) 986-2353, (800) BY FERRY
The only link between Hatteras and Ocracoke Islands, this free state-run ferry carries passengers and vehicles across Hatteras Inlet daily, year-round, with trips from 5 a.m. to midnight. A fleet of 10 ferry boats, some 150 feet long, carry up to 30 cars and trucks each on the 40-minute ride. (See the Getting Here, Getting Around chapter for the full schedule.)

You can get out of your vehicle and walk around the open decks or stay inside the car. A passenger lounge a short flight of steps above the deck offers cushioned seats and wide windows. On the lower deck telescopes give people a chance to see seagulls and passing shorelines up close for a quarter. Free restrooms also are on the deck; however, there's no food or drink to be found on this 5-mile crossing, so pack your own picnic. Beware if you decide to break bread with the dozens of birds that fly overhead; after they eat they, too, look for free bathrooms. And they'll follow—overhead—all the way to Ocracoke. The experience is exciting but can be messy.

A souvenir shop is located at the Hatteras ferry docks; it sells everything from coloring books and Frisbees to sweatshirts and coffee mugs. Drink and snack machines are on-site.

A day trip to Ocracoke is a must for every Outer Banks visitor, whether you're staying in Corolla or on Hatteras Island. (See the Ocracoke section of the Area Overview chapter for more about Ocracoke.) The free ferry is the only way to get there besides by private boat or airplane. On summer days more than 1,000 passengers ride the flat ferries.

A 12-mile stretch through open marshlands and pine forests lies between the ferry and Ocracoke Village. NC 12 picks up at the ferry docks and continues to the southern end of the island. On the left, wide-open beaches await avid four-wheelers and those who like to have a piece of the seaside to themselves.

A National Park Service oceanfront campground is to the left before you get to the village. Ocracoke is a quaint fishing village that has recently grown into a popular tourist destination. Over 700 people live on Ocracoke Island year-round. Boutiques, seafood restaurants, craft shops, and other retailers line the quiet, twisting lanes, but most are open only in the summer. We recommend that you park your car somewhere near the waterfront and rent a bicycle to tour this picturesque, isolated island.

GRAVEYARD OF THE ATLANTIC MUSEUM
NC 12, Hatteras Village
(252) 986-2996
www.graveyardoftheatlantic.com
The Graveyard of the Atlantic Museum showcases the maritime history and heritage of

the Outer Banks and its people, from the earliest exploration and colonization to the present day. Particularly emphasized are the years from 1524 to 1945. The museum is still in the process of being completed, but several rooms and exhibits are open to the public.

Exhibits include artifacts from historical shipwrecks, unique "beach finds," and locally carved ships' models; there is a special exhibit on Billy Mitchell in Hatteras. Admission is free, and donations are gratefully accepted.

OCRACOKE ISLAND

OCRACOKE PONY PENS
NC 12, Ocracoke Island

The Ocracoke Pony Pens are one of the most popular attractions on Ocracoke Island. The National Park Service maintains a herd of about 30 horses in a 180-acre pasture located off NC 12, about 6 miles south of the Hatteras–Ocracoke ferry docks. Visitors can walk up to the pens to view these once-wild horses. An observation platform allows a good view of the ponies.

Ocracoke ponies have played a large role in the history of the island. At times the herd's population ranged from 200 to 500, all of the animals roaming free on the island.

No one is really certain how the horses arrived at the island, but legend says they swam ashore from Spanish shipwrecks off the coast. The horses adapted well to a diet of marsh grasses and rainwater. The locals used this natural resource for work and recreation, and even the Coast Guard and US Lifesaving Service employed the ponies.

The pen is free to visit, but donations are certainly welcome. Though not running wild, the ponies are not tame, and they may try to kick or bite if you try to climb into the pen or feed or pet them.

Ocracoke ponies have distinctive physical characteristics: 5 lumbar vertebrae instead of the 6 found in other horses, 17 ribs instead of the 18 found in other horses, and a unique shape, posture, color, size, and weight. For more information see the Ocracoke Island section of the Area Overview chapter.

HAMMOCK HILLS NATURE TRAIL
NC 12, Ocracoke Island

A 0.75-mile nature trail north of Ocracoke Village, Hammock Hills covers a cross-section of the island. The 30-minute walk begins near the sand dunes, traverses a maritime forest, and winds through a salt marsh. Hikers learn how plants adapt to Ocracoke's unusual elements and the harsh barrier island weather. Bring your camera on this scenic stroll. We highly recommend bug repellent in spring and summer months. Watch out for snakes in the underbrush. The well-marked trailhead is on NC 12 just across the road from the National Park Service campground.

OCRACOKE ISLAND VISITOR CENTER
NC 12, Ocracoke Village
(252) 928-4531

The National Park Service's Ocracoke Island Visitor Center, at the southern end of NC 12, is full of information about the island. It's in a small building with a large lawn next to the Cedar Island ferry docks. If you're arriving on the island from the Hatteras ferry, stay on the main road, turn right at Silver Lake, and continue around the lake counterclockwise until you see the low brown building on your right. Free parking is available at the visitor center.

Inside there's an information desk, helpful staff, a small bookshop, and exhibits about Ocracoke. You can arrange to use the park service's docks here and pick up maps of the winding back roads that make great bicycle paths.

The visitor center is open Mar through Dec from 9 a.m. to 5 p.m. Hours are extended in the summer. Rangers offer free summer programs, including a beach walk, a walk through the village, turtle talks, a pirate play, snorkeling, an evening campfire, kids programs, and more. Programs last from 30 to 90 minutes and offer a fun way to learn more about the history and ecology of the island. Check at the front desk for changing weekly schedules. Restrooms are open to the public in season.

OCRACOKE ISLAND MUSEUM AND PRESERVATION SOCIETY
Silver Lake, Ocracoke Village
(252) 928-7375

A visit to the Ocracoke Island Museum provides a wonderful peek into Ocracoke as it once was. The home of Coast Guard Capt. David Williams, the historic, 2-story house was moved to this location in 1989 and restored to its former early-19th-century glory by the Ocracoke Preservation Society. The original wainscoting, floors, staircases, and wood-burning stove are still intact. Inside, a bedroom, living room, and kitchen are set up with period furnishings donated by local families. Original photographs of island natives are throughout. Exhibits about fishing and seafaring are especially interesting, as is the exhibit on the island's traditional brogue.

Upstairs, the museum has a small research library that the public can use with the museum personnel's permission.

Admission is free, and the museum is open from Easter through the end of Nov. In summer hours are 10 a.m. to 5 p.m. Mon through Fri and 11 a.m. to 4 p.m. on Sat. Off-season hours are 10 a.m. to 4 p.m. Mon through Fri and 11 a.m. to 4 p.m. on Sat.

✳OCRACOKE VILLAGE WALKING TOUR
West end of NC 12, around Ocracoke Village

The easiest ways to explore Ocracoke are by bicycle and on foot. The narrow, winding back lanes weren't meant for cars. And you miss little landmarks and interesting areas of the island if you drive through. People on Ocracoke are generally friendly, and you'll get a chance to chat with more locals if you slow down your touring pace through this picturesque fishing village.

No matter where you are in Ocracoke Village, just start walking and you'll find something interesting. One nice tour of the northeast side of the village starts at the Ocracoke Island Visitor Center. Park in the lot opposite the visitor center. Turn left out of the lot and walk down NC 12 around the shores of Silver Lake, past the sleepy village waterfront. You'll pass many small shops, boutiques, and some large hotels. Keep walking until you see a small brick post office on your right.

Opposite the post office, a sandy, narrow street angles to the left. This is Howard Street. It winds through one of the oldest and least changed parts of the village. Note the humble old homes, the attached cisterns for collecting rainwater, and the detached kitchens behind these historic structures.

Continue walking past or stop in Village Craftsman, a gallery. After about 400 yards Howard Street empties onto School Street. Turn left and you'll see the Methodist church and K–12 public school that serves all the children on Ocracoke. With graduating classes of fewer than a dozen students, this is the state's smallest public school.

The church is usually open for visitors, but use discretion if services are in progress. And please wipe your feet as you go in. On entering, note the cross displayed behind the altar. It was carved from the wooden spar of an American freighter, the *Caribsea*, sunk offshore by German U-boats in the early months of 1942. By strange coincidence, the *Caribsea*'s engineer was Ocracoke native James Baugham Gaskill, who was killed when the boat sank. Local residents say that several days later a display case holding Gaskill's mate license, among other things, washed ashore not far from his family home.

Ocracoke has had a Methodist church since 1828. The current one was built in 1943 with lumber and pews salvaged from older buildings. A historical-sketch pamphlet is available in the vestibule for visitors.

On leaving the church, walk around the north corner of the school, past the playground, onto a narrow boardwalk. This wooden path leads to a paved road beyond it. Turn left. This was the first paved road on the island and was constructed by Seabees during World War II.

After walking less than a mile down this road, turn right at the first stop sign. A few minutes' walk along this narrow, tree-shaded street brings you to the British Cemetery, where victims of World War II are buried far away from their native soil. (See the subsequent listing in this section.) It's on your right, set back a bit from the road and shaded by live oak and yaupon. The big British flag makes it easy to spot.

To return to the visitor center, walk west until you reach Silver Lake, then turn right. You'll pass craft shops and several boutiques along the way. (See the Shopping chapter for details.) If the weather's nice, we suggest a stop for an outdoor drink at the waterfront Jolly Roger, the Creek Side Cafe upstairs above the bicycle stand, or Howard's Pub on the highway before heading back to the ferry docks.

Some people prefer to take this tour on their own; others like to go with a guide. Village Craftsmen offers a ghost and historic walking tour. Either way, wear comfortable shoes. Tours through Village Craftsmen are $12 for adults and $6 for children. Call (252) 928-5541 or go to www.villagecraftsmen.com.

i On Tues and Fri at 7:30 p.m. (7 p.m. in the off-season), meet at the Village Craftsmen on Howard Street in Ocracoke Village. Local storyteller Philip Howard will take you on a 90-minute tour of the area, complete with ghost stories and historical information. Space is limited, so call ahead: (252) 928-5541. The cost is $12 for adults and $6 for children ages 6 to 12.

OCRACOKE LIGHTHOUSE
Southwest corner of Ocracoke Village

The southernmost of the Outer Banks' four lighthouses, this whitewashed tower is the oldest and shortest. It is the second-oldest lighthouse in the nation. It stands 77.5 feet tall and has an askew iron-railed tower set on the top. The lighthouse is not open for tours or climbing, but volunteers occasionally staff its broad base, offering historical talks and answering visitors' questions. Inquire about possible staffing times at the visitor center or National Park Service offices.

Ocracoke's lighthouse still operates, emitting one long flash every few seconds from a half hour before sunset to a half hour after sunrise. It was built in 1823 to replace Shell Castle Rock Lighthouse, which was set offshore closer to the dangerous shoals in Ocracoke Inlet. Shell Castle Light was abandoned in 1798 when the inlet shifted south.

The beam from Ocracoke's beacon rotates 360 degrees and can be seen 14 miles out to sea. The tower itself is brick, covered by hand-spread, textured white mortar. The walls are 5 feet thick at the base.

On the right side of the wooden boardwalk leading to the lighthouse, a 2-story white cottage once served as quarters for the tower's keeper. The National Park Service renovated this structure in the 1980s. It now serves as the home of Ocracoke's rangers and the structure's maintenance supervisor.

To reach the light, turn left off NC 12 at the Island Inn and go about 800 yards down the two-lane street. You can park near a white picketed turnoff on the right. Visitors must walk the last few yards down the boardwalk to the lighthouse.

BRITISH CEMETERY
British Cemetery Road, Ocracoke Village

Beneath a stand of trees, on the edge of a community cemetery, four granite gravestones commemorate the crew of the British vessel HMS *Bedfordshire*. This 170-foot trawler was one of a fleet of 24 antisubmarine ships that British prime minister Winston Churchill loaned the United States in April 1942 to stave off German U-boats. On May 11 of that year, a German submarine torpedoed and sank the British ship about 40 miles south of Ocracoke.

All four officers and 33 enlisted men aboard the *Bedfordshire* drowned. US Coast Guard officers stationed on Ocracoke found four of the bodies washed ashore three days later. They were able to identify two of the sailors. Townspeople gave Britain a 12-by-14-foot plot of land and buried the seamen in a site adjacent to the island's cemetery.

Since then Coast Guard officers have maintained the grassy area within a white picket fence. They fly a British flag above the graves, and each year, on the anniversary of the sailors' deaths, the local military establishment sponsors a ceremony honoring the men who died so far from their own shores.

DEEPWATER THEATER
School Road, Ocracoke
(252) 928-4280
www.molassescreek.com

Deepwater Theater is the home of Ocracoke's most famous band, Molasses Creek. This high-energy acoustic folk-fusion band plays bluegrass and ballads and rolls everything together with a wacky sense of humor. Gary Mitchell, Kitty Mitchell, and fiddler Dave Tweedie compose the band, which has a loyal following in the United States and abroad. Based on the island, they play here all summer and at other times of the year. Molasses Creek performs all over the nation, and it was featured on National Public Radio's *A Prairie Home Companion* with Garrison Keillor. In season on Monday Deepwater Creek has on its bill Philip and Amy Howard with Fiddler Dave in *You Ain't Heard Nothin' Yet,* telling tales of Ocracoke Island. Each Wednesday Ocrafolk Opry picks and grins and warms your soul. On Thursday Molasses Creek performs in a show appropriate for the whole family.

Tickets go on sale 30 minutes before each show, shows begin at 8 p.m. Pricing varies with shows; details are listed on the website.

PORTSMOUTH VILLAGE
South of Ocracoke Island, by private
boat access, Portsmouth Island
(252) 728-2250
www.nps.gov/calo

The only ghost town on the Eastern Seaboard, Portsmouth Village is about a 20-minute boat ride south of Ocracoke Island and was once the biggest town on the Outer Banks. Today the 23-milelong, 1.5-mile-wide island is owned and managed by the National Park Service as part of Cape Lookout National Seashore. Wilderness camping, hiking, shelling, fishing, and other activities are available on the wide beach. Free, self-guided walking tours of the village are a fascinating way to see how islanders lived in the 19th century.

Visiting Portsmouth Village is utterly surreal. Many of the former homes and village buildings are intact and restored, but they sit hollow, yet hopeful, as if waiting to come to life. Peeking into the windows of some of the unrestored buildings, you'll see remnants of the families who once lived there—curtains, unmade beds, upturned old chairs, broken frames—as if they left in a hurry and never came back.

There is a visitor center on-site, staffed by volunteers who commit to living on the island for extended periods of time. You can see the old post office, the church, the old Coast Guard station, and other buildings. Some of the homes are private, their owners granted extended leases in exchange for restoration work. Portsmouth Island is a rugged adventure, and there are few conveniences. Restrooms are provided in the visitor center, and there's a comfort station (toilets only) on the other side of the village. You must bring your own water, food, insect repellent, and sunscreen. Mosquitoes are notorious in the summer and fall.

You can get to the island by private boat or with a charter service. Capt. Rudy Austin runs round-trip boat trips to the island, daily in summer and by appointment in the off-season. Call at least one day in advance for reservations, (252) 928-4361 or (252) 928-5431. Portsmouth Island ATV Excursions, (252) 928-4484, leads guided tours of the village and island on ATVs from Apr through Nov. Call for reservations and information.

NIGHTLIFE

For many of us who live here—and for many visitors as well—the best evening entertainment is watching the sun set over the sound waters. Soundfront decks, piers, gazebos, and public beaches are perfect spots to toast your friends and the setting sun. It's not uncommon for us to rush home in the evening, call our friends, and arrange for a rendezvous spot at which to watch the sunset. Many locals sail or motor their boats out into the sound in anticipation of our favorite entertainment, provided free each day. Moonrise over the ocean is pretty spectacular, too, and under a Carolina moon, just about anything is possible.

OVERVIEW

The Outer Banks after hours isn't like other resort areas. So many families—and early-rising anglers—come here that many people bed down for the evening early. We don't have the huge strips of late-night entertainment joints that you find in many other vacation destinations, but a number of bars and dance floors are scattered across the barrier islands.

Families enjoy a variety of early-evening entertainment options here. Miniature golf, go-kart tracks, movie theaters, bumper boats, and a bowling alley are listed in the Recreation chapter. And don't forget *The Lost Colony* outdoor drama; that's detailed in the Attractions chapter.

There are plenty of places to shoot pool, catch sporting events on big-screen TVs, play interactive trivia, throw darts, listen to some quiet music, or boogie the night away to a live band.

Outer Banks musicians play everything from blues to jazz to rock to alternative and country tunes. Both local and out-of-town bands take the stage often during the summer season. Several area nightclubs assess nominal cover charges at the door, usually ranging from $1 for dueling acoustic guitar duos to $10 or more for the national acts that grace these sands between mid-May and Labor Day. Many acoustic acts, however, are heard for free.

If live music is what you're listening for, the *Virginian-Pilot's* weekly *Coast* supplement—available free at area grocery and convenience stores and motels—has up-to-date listings plus music scene information in the "After Dark" column. (See the Annual Events and Arts & Culture chapters for more nighttime possibilities.)

Alcoholic beverages are available at most Outer Banks lounges until around 2 a.m. Beer and wine are offered throughout the barrier islands. In Southern Shores and on Colington, Roanoke, Hatteras, and Ocracoke Islands, it is illegal to serve mixed drinks. However, with the exception of Colington Island, state-run ("ABC") stores sell liquor in each of these areas. Most nightclubs in areas that serve only wine and beer allow brown bagging, which means customers may bring in their own alcohol for the evening. Call ahead to make sure that brown bagging is allowed where you're going.

Several restaurants on the Outer Banks offer late-night menus or at least raw and steamed bar food until closing. Every nightclub operator will be glad to call a cab to take you home or to your hotel or rental cottage after an evening of imbibing. Beware: The legal drinking age in North Carolina is 21, and the blood-alcohol content level for a drunken-driving arrest is only 0.08. Law enforcement is strict.

Check the Restaurants chapter for sunset entertainment options. Several spots also feature outdoor acoustic music until dark—but this section is for those who like to stay out late.

COROLLA

SUNDOGS SPORTS BAR AND GRILL
Monteray Plaza, NC 12, Corolla
(252) 453-4263
Sundogs is a sports bar, so expect a lot of people hanging out watching Monday Night Football and the like. But it's also a gathering spot, where people linger at the bar until the late hours. A pool table and video games provide other entertainment. Sundogs also has a comedy night each week.

DR. UNKS OASIS
Monteray Plaza, Corolla
(252) 453-0053
Dr. Unks offers late-night music, a full bar, and even a late-night menu. It shares a

building with the Tomato Patch Restaurant. Live music is offered on some summer evenings.

METROPOLIS
Ocean Club Centre, NC 12, Corolla
This cosmopolitan restaurant and bar stays open until the wee hours—2 a.m. The full bar that specializes in martinis is a nice spot to enjoy an evening out.

DUCK

FISHBONES SUNSET GRILLE AND RAW BAR
NC 12, Duck
(252) 261-3901
www.fishbonessunsetgrille.com
Situated right on Currituck Sound across from the entrance to Barrier Island Station, Fishbones Sunset Grille and Raw Bar is the only place in Duck to see live bands. During the summer Fishbones has live music every night except Sunday and Monday. In the off-season there's live music at least twice a week. The house band is Jah Seed, which plays at least once a week. Other bands, including blues, rock, and a Jimmy Buffett-style act, play here as well. In season the raw bar and sushi bar are open until 10 p.m. or later, so you can get a bite before the bands really kick in.

FISHBONES RAW BAR & RESTAURANT
Scarborough Lane Shoppes, NC 12, Duck
(252) 261-6991
This raw bar and restaurant is one of Duck's most popular evening hangouts. Open daily, it features a full bar with five beers on tap, 50 international bottled beers, various microbrews, and a wine list.

ROADSIDE RAW BAR & GRILL
NC 12, Duck
(252) 261-5729

Low-key, casual, and serving great food, Roadside is a favorite early-evening hangout for locals and tourists alike. This 1932 restored cottage with hardwood floors exudes a cozy, homey feeling. On the outdoor patio you can hear live jazz on Tuesday and Thursday evenings in summer months. Appetizers and cocktails are served outside during the music. Roadside is open year-round, but call for off-season hours.

KITTY HAWK

OCEAN BOULEVARD
NC 12, Kitty Hawk
(252) 261-2456
www.obbistro.com

Friday and Saturday nights are hopping at Ocean Boulevard with acoustic performers on the outdoor patio. On Friday evenings around 10 or so, the restaurant hosts a band indoors. Many locals swing by on Friday night to catch up at the end of the week. This is a popular spot, and the music is always good.

LONGBOARD'S ISLAND GRILL
US 158, MP 4, Kitty Hawk
(252) 261-7833

A popular nightspot for locals year-round, this restaurant features a large, three-sided bar and beautiful terrariums and aquariums throughout the dining area. It's open seven days a week and has karaoke on Wednesday through Saturday nights year-round. Once a month or so, a live band appears on Saturday nights. Longboard's is popular all year with the 30-plus crowd. It's open until 2 a.m. in season and has a late-night munchies menu.

i For up-to-date nightlife listings, the *Coast,* a free tabloid published by the *Virginian-Pilot,* is the most comprehensive place to look. You'll find it in racks everywhere.

BLACK PELICAN OCEANFRONT CAFE
NC 12, MP 4, Kitty Hawk
(252) 261-3171
www.blackpelican.com

With 12 TVs and an enclosed porch overlooking the ocean, this Kitty Hawk hangout is a fun place to catch up on sporting events or relax at the bar. It's in a former Coast Guard station and still features hardwood floors, tongue-and-groove appointments, and light gray accents reminiscent of days gone by. In the evenings its upbeat atmosphere is anything but antique. Gourmet pizzas are a great treat for late-night munchies. Takeout is available, too. The Black Pelican is open year-round.

BAREFOOT BERNIES
NC 12, MP 4½, Kitty Hawk
(252) 261-1008
www.barefootbernies.com

Late night music is offered at this hotspot all through the summer months. An enormous bar accommodates large parties easily in this classy yet casual spot. Reggae, rock, and cover bands perform here throughout the season. Check the regularly updated website for details on performances during your visit.

KILL DEVIL HILLS

CHILLI PEPPERS COASTAL GRILL
US 158, MP 5, Kill Devil Hills
(252) 441-8081
www.chilli-peppers.com

This restaurant's bar area always teems with partying people who often come here to eat and stay late, especially on sushi nights (Wednesday and Friday year-round) and tapas nights (Thursday in the off-season). Seven nights a week you can enjoy fresh fruit margaritas, a nice wine selection, and dozens of domestic and imported beers from the full bar. Bartenders also serve nonalcoholic beers and fruit smoothies. The outdoor patio invites you to sip your drinks under the stars. Steamed seafood and vegetables are served until closing.

i A good source for entertainment schedules on the Outer Banks and in nearby cities is 99.1 the Sound radio station, which airs daily updates on who's performing where and when. This information is also on the web at www.991thesound.com.

JOLLY ROGER RESTAURANT
NC 12, MP 6, Kill Devil Hills
(252) 441-6530
www.jollyrogerobx.com
Adorned with hanging plants and colorful lights, the lounge is separate from the dining area at this mainstay restaurant. The bar is open seven nights a week. Every night Jolly Roger hosts karaoke or offers interactive TV with games covering sports, movie trivia, and more. Both draw a regular audience, and prizes are even awarded to some of the big winners. Locals love this place. People from their early 20s to late 60s enjoy relaxing and dancing in this lounge.

GOOMBAYS GRILLE & RAW BAR
NC 12, MP 7, Kill Devil Hills
(252) 441-6001
www.goombays.com

This popular nightspot is packed with tourists and locals and is open seven nights a week. It's fun and colorful with a tropical island flair and flavor. Goombays is Caribbean and casual, where you feel right at home even if you've never visited the Outer Banks. On Wednesday live bands play for "Locals Night" year-round beginning at 10:30 p.m. A horseshoe-shaped bar is set to the side of the dining area, so you can lounge on a stool or high-backed chair in the bar area or have a seat at a nearby table after the dining room closes at 10 p.m. Goombays serves imported and domestic beer, wine, and mixed drinks until 2 a.m. Try some of the special rum, vodka, and tequila combos that come with toys to take home. Steamed shrimp and veggies are served until 1 a.m.

PORT O' CALL RESTAURANT & GASLIGHT SALOON
NC 12, MP 8½, Kill Devil Hills
(252) 441-7484
http://outerbankspocrestaurant.com
One of the area's most unusual places to hang out—and one of the few local nightclubs that attracts national bands in the summer—the Gaslight Saloon is decorated in an ornate Victorian style complete with overstuffed armchairs, antique wooden tables, and a long mahogany bar. The dance floor is a good one and an upstairs lounge (with separate bar) overlooks the stage. Port O' Call hosts live entertainment seven nights a week in season and every weekend while the restaurant is open from mid-March through Dec. There's usually a cover charge here. Cover may be waived for diners. In recent years Port O' Call has hosted such national acts as Southern Culture on the Skids, Leon Russell, Fishbone, Molly Hatchet, and an array of first-rate reggae

artists. Beer, wine, and liquor are served until 2 a.m.

✳OUTER BANKS BREWING STATION
US 158, MP 8½, Kill Devil Hills
(252) 449-BREW
www.obbrewing.com

Outer Banks Brewing Station is one of the hottest restaurants and nightspots on the beach. Outside, it looks like a big white barn with silos at either end (the silos are for making beer). Inside, it's absolutely inviting and city chic, with a stretch-length bar, high ceilings, warm wood tones, an open kitchen, innovative house-made beer, well-chosen wines, and sublime food. The brew is a big draw, with selections like a Hefeweizen wheat beer, Mutiny Pale Ale, and Kölsch summer brew. After dinner hours the Brewing Station stays open late, treating a crowd of lingerers to "righteous music"; blues, jazz, and funk bands and sometimes acoustic acts play all year. Both regional bands and national acts are booked here, and the Sunday open-mike and sushi night is very popular. Expect large crowds on band nights. Live entertainment is held Friday and Saturday in season. You can also expect music most every night in the summer. The Brewing Station is open until 2 a.m. seven nights a week. Call or check the website for entertainment schedules.

THE PIT SURF SHOP, BAR AND GRILL
US 158, MP 9, Kill Devil Hills
(252) 480-3128
www.pitsurf.com

The Pit is a conglomerate surf shop, hangout, restaurant, cybercafe, bar, band venue, and teen scene. It's a popular, casual hangout spot all day and all night and was named one of the best bars in the world for 2003 in *Men's Journal* magazine. Every summer night, and most off-season nights, something fun happens at the Pit. Thursday night is Mug Night with a DJ, when you pay $5, bring your own mug, and drink beers for as little as a buck. Bands play twice a week in season, and the Pit consistently gets the biggest names in talent. Burning Spear, the Wailers, 2 Skinnee J's, the Connells, All Mighty Senators, and Everything are just a few of the bands that play here. The Pit serves food until 9 p.m. and has pool tables, foosball, videos, Internet access, and boardsport videos to keep you otherwise entertained.

The Pit is one of the only places on the beach welcoming the under-21 crowd. Underage revelers have three summer nights of their own—Mon, Wed, and Fri—(once in a while in the off-season) with no alcohol served. These nights feature DJs or occasionally a band. Cover charges vary.

PEPPERCORNS RAMADA PLAZA
   RESORT
NC 12, MP 9½, Kill Devil Hills
(252) 441-2151

Enjoy a breathtaking ocean view from the plate-glass window wall while visiting with friends and listening to acoustic soloists or duos in the Ramada's intimate lounge area. Live music is performed daily throughout summer and often starts earlier here than elsewhere on the Outer Banks—sometimes they get started at 8 p.m. This is an open, laid-back place with booths, tables, and a full bar. The music is never too loud to talk over. But if you'd rather listen, some of the best guitar talent on the beach shows up here in season.

MAMA KWAN'S GRILL AND TIKI BAR
US 158, MP 9½, Kill Devil Hills
(252) 441-7889
www.mamakwans.com
This retro-Hawaiian restaurant and bar is always packed late with young partiers. It's often the place local restaurant workers go when they get off work. On Friday nights a DJ keeps things hoppin'. Tiki lights create an island atmosphere. The bar's specialty is frozen drinks served with surprises. It's open every night until 2 a.m.

NAGS HEAD

RED DRUM GRILLE AND TAPHOUSE
NC 12, MP 10, Nags Head
(252) 480-1095
Red Drum pours 18 beers on tap, including hard-to-find brews like Sierra Nevada, J. W. Dundee's Honey Brown, Woodpecker Cider, Black Radish, and Pyramid Hefeweizen. You can get wine by the glass or the bottle. Red Drum also serves liquor from its beautiful long, redwood-colored bar.

BEACH ROAD GRILL
NC 12, MP10½, Nags Head
(252) 480-2228
This restaurant offers a full bar and can really get hopping on the weekends. Live entertainment is offered on Friday and Saturday nights most of the year. This is a fun place for fun people, with an occasional cover charge.

KELLY'S OUTER BANKS RESTAURANT
   & TAVERN
US 158, MP 10½, Nags Head
(252) 441-4116
www.kellysrestaurant.com
Probably the most consistently crowded tavern on the Outer Banks, Kelly's offers live bands five nights a week in season and an open-mike fest with a lip-synch contest and cash prizes on Tuesday. During fall and winter, rockin' bands take the stage, and fun people always fill this place. A full bar serves suds, shots, and everything in between. Folks often line up around its three long sides two or three people deep. The big dance floor is usually shaking after 10 p.m. If you're in the mood just to listen and watch, secluded booths surround the dance floor a few steps above the rest of the lounge, and tables are scattered throughout the tavern. A dartboard and fireplace adorn the back area. Featuring a tasty variety of foods served late into the night, a lounge menu offers appetizers and steamed shellfish. An old-fashioned popcorn popper provides free munchies served in wicker baskets throughout the evening. Singles particularly enjoy this tavern.

i Parents looking for some alone time without the children should ask their vacation rental company about babysitting services and children's programs in the area. These types of services are growing in popularity on the Outer Banks.

✳TORTUGAS' LIE SHELLFISH BAR AND
   GRILLE
NC 12, MP 11, Nags Head
(252) 441-7299
www.tortugaslie.com
Our favorite place to meet friends for a laid-back evening—or to hang out with long-lost local pals—Tortugas' offers probably the most comfortable atmosphere you'll find on the Outer Banks most of the year. The bar winds around a corner to allow at least a half dozen more stools to slide under the refurbished

countertop. Old license plates are perched on the low, wooden ceiling beams, and the sand volleyball court remains ready for pickup games out back all summer. Bartenders serve black and tans in pint glasses—that's right, Tortugas' has Guinness and Bass ale on tap. Beer is served by the longneck bottle or by the iced-down bucket. Shooters, mixed drinks, and tropical frozen concoctions are sure to please any palate. The steamer is open until closing, so you can satisfy late-night appetites with shellfish or fresh vegetables. Whether you're visiting or here to stay, Tortugas' is one place you won't want to miss. Most nights it remains open until 2 a.m. Tortugas' closes for a brief spell in Dec and Jan.

MULLIGAN'S
US 158, MP 13, Nags Head
(252) 480-2000

Mulligan's is heralded as a popular evening hot spot and maintains its image as the Outer Banks' own version of TV's *Cheers*. Mulligan's serves microbrewed beer on tap or in iced-down bottles. Wine and liquor are available. Acoustic music plays on weekends in the off-season and on Wed, Fri, and Sat in summer.

HATTERAS ISLAND

AVON CAFE
NC 12, Avon
(252) 995-7866
www.avoncafe.com

Avon Cafe offers occasional late night bands. Check the website for details.

FROGGY DOG RESTAURANT & BAR
NC 12, Avon
(252) 995-5550
www.froggydog.com

Late-night acoustic music plus karaoke singers take the stage at this casual Hatteras Island nightspot. The Froggy Dog is open nightly in season, serving beer and wine and entertainment on most Sundays; call for schedule.

OCRACOKE ISLAND

HOWARD'S PUB & RAW BAR RESTAURANT
NC 12, Ocracoke Village
(252) 928-4441
www.howardspub.com

This is our absolute favorite place to hear live bands. Featuring the friendliest crowd of locals and visitors around, Howard's Pub has an atmosphere and feeling all its own. Once you've visited you'll plan to stop at this upbeat yet casual place at least once during every visit to Ocracoke. Howard's is open late nights—and is a great spot to mingle with locals.

The pub serves more types of beer than any place we know—more than 200 varieties are available. There's a second-floor outdoor deck with breathtaking, ocean-to-sound views, perfect for catching sunsets or falling stars. A huge, screened porch—with booths and table seating for relaxing in the evening breezes—borders an entire side of the spacious wooden building. The dance floor has more than doubled in recent years. Two big-screen TVs and numerous smaller ones offer sports fans constant entertainment. Howard's has a dartboard, a pool table in the off-season, board games, and card games available free for playful patrons. The full menu, including pizza, sandwiches, hamburgers, and raw bar items, is offered until closing time.

NIGHTLIFE

Bands play most nights during summer season and on weekends during winter. Music covers rhythm and blues, bluegrass, jazz, rock, and originals. The occasional open-mike and karaoke nights are favorites for locals and visitors alike. Howard's Pub never charges a cover, and even when electricity fails the rest of the island, this place is equipped with a generator so the crew keeps cooking—and the beer stays cold.

JOLLY ROGER PUB & MARINA
NC 12, Ocracoke Village
(252) 928-3703

A waterfront eatery with an open bar overlooking Silver Lake, this pub has a huge outdoor deck that's covered in case of thunderstorms. Local acoustic guitarists perform Caribbean and country music with no cover charge Thursday and Friday nights. Jolly Roger serves beer, wine, and great food throughout the warm summer months.

SHOPPING

S hopping on the Outer Banks is a unique pursuit—and a busy one on rainy days when attention shifts from the beach to the stores. Still, rain or shine, there's so much to explore and to be found on side streets in quiet villages or between the Beach Road (NC 12) and the Bypass (US 158), not necessarily visible from the road. So take your time. Consider it a treasure hunt.

OVERVIEW

Many shops have seasonal hours, and most close from December to March. During the height of the summer season, the majority are open seven days a week (some with extended evening hours). A good many shops in Southern Shores, Kitty Hawk, Kill Devil Hills, and Nags Head are open year-round, though not every day. Corolla and Hatteras shopping tends to be more seasonal, but some businesses keep their doors open through the fall and winter.

This chapter lists of some of our favorite shopping spots on the Outer Banks, organized by community, beginning at the northern reaches of Corolla and Duck and running south through Ocracoke Island. Outer Banks retailers offer service, goods, variety, and a hometown greeting that's second to none. And just to show how much Bankers appreciate your business, we'll share an insiders' secret: There are unbeatable sales on the Outer Banks during our shoulder seasons.

COROLLA

Corolla, about 10 miles north of Duck, offers convenient and novel shopping along NC 12. We begin at the northernmost point. Most Corolla shops close in the off-season.

i The MacArthur Center is an enormous megamall in nearby Norfolk, Virginia, and its big-name stores (Nordstrom, Dillards, Restoration Hardware, and the like) lure shoppers from all over North Carolina and Virginia. If you're a serious shopper, this is the place for you, only an hour and 15 minutes from the Outer Banks.

AUSTIN BUILDING
NC 12, Corolla
Winks of Corolla is the anchor of this shopping center near Historic Corolla Village. Winks has been around since before NC 12 was opened to the public. Winks sells gas, sundries, groceries, snacks, drinks, toiletries, and any other convenience items you'll need. Recently, Winks added a gift area and a tackle section to its variety of offerings. Next door is the Corolla Post Office, Corolla Pizza, and an ice-cream store.

HISTORIC COROLLA VILLAGE

This off-the-beaten-path section of town, which is really Corolla proper, was the original town center in the days of old Corolla. Today you see remnants of old Corolla by walking down the dirt roads north of the lighthouse. New stores have been built here, but in a vintage style that gives visitors the feeling of how things looked in old Corolla. Shop owners are proud to bring vitality back to this historic area and share the histories of their buildings with visitors. A walking-tour map also gives historic information. You can easily walk from the Whalehead Club to the lighthouse to the shops in Historic Corolla Village.

LIGHTHOUSE GARDEN

Corolla Village and Schoolhouse Roads, Corolla
(252) 453-0171
www.lighthouse-garden.com
Lighthouse Garden is located in the former Helen Parker House (ca. 1920). The home has been restored to its original charm. The Lighthouse Garden brings the spirit of outdoor living with decor for porches, gardens, and homes. Silk flowers and topiaries, concrete statuary, botanical prints, locally crafted iron works, birdbaths, mosaic furniture, and candles are among the great finds. Many items are one of a kind, so insiders return often.

OLD COROLLA TRADING COMPANY

Corolla Village Road, Corolla
(252) 453-9942
Just north of Lighthouse Garden, this store occupies a new cedar-sided building inspired by local historic architecture. The shop has a nautical theme, with antiques, prints, pillows, lanterns, telescopes, and more. It's not just nautical: It sells frames, weather vanes, vintage posters, gifts, and Bauer International furniture, featuring refined leather, mahogany, and wicker items.

SPRY CREEK DRY GOODS

Corolla Village Road, Corolla
(252) 453-0199
Spry Creek is a fun and funky shop. One step inside and you may think you're in Tuscany or the Mediterranean. Bright yellow walls are a perfect backdrop for the Spanish, Mexican, and Portuguese pottery and ceramics on sale. Shoppers will delight in the jewelry, artwork, and decoys produced by local artisans. Mouth-blown glassware from Mexico, pampering soaps and linen sprays, and vivid stained-glass pieces round out the eclectic offerings.

*THE ISLAND BOOKSTORE

1130 Corolla Village Road, Corolla
(252) 453-2292
This shop is built on the site of Callie Parker's old general store. John Wilson IV (who has designed many of Manteo's historical reproductions) designed this new building, reminiscent of a mercantile in the 1930s. Bill and Ursula, the owners of Island Bookstore, bring more than 35 years of bookselling experience to Corolla. Best sellers are discounted, and books are available on just about any subject matter imaginable. Southern and regional books are well represented in this atmospheric bookshop.

A GREENER SHADE OF YOU

1130 Corolla Village Rd., Corolla
(252) 453-6644
www.agreenershadeofyou.com
Located just behind Island Bookstore, A Greener Shade of You brings eco-friendly

style to shoppers with a conscience. Designer fashions made from organic cotton, bamboo, hemp, and more will brighten your wardrobe. Organic accessories and bath and skin products round out the offerings.

LORENZ FINE PHOTOGRAPHY
Corolla Village Road, Corolla
(800) 646-5812
www.blorenz.com

Master photographer Bruce Lorenz creates unique and exquisite portraits. With over 30 years of experience, Lorenz will attend an event or come to your home to photograph you, your family, your pet, or whatever you prefer. Call to arrange an appointment. Many examples of this talented photographer's work can be viewed on the website.

COROLLA LIGHT TOWN CENTER
NC 12, Corolla

The shops of Corolla Light Town Center are clustered outside the entrance to the Corolla Light development. Dining, shopping, and convenience items are found within.

Ocean Threads specializes in swimwear for the entire family and features maternity, mastectomy, and long-torso suits. This shop is packed with lots of sportswear for men and women, including name brands such as Billabong, Airwalk, Rusty, Arnette, Oakley, Emeric, Janco, Roxy, Quicksilver, Rusty Girl, and more. The shop also carries hats, stickers, and incense.

Ocean Atlantic Rentals offers bikes, strollers, cribs, bedding, beach chairs, umbrellas, water sports gear—you name it. For anglers **Corolla Bait and Tackle** has it all, including rods and reels, live bait, tackle and lures, advice, charter booking, and a friendly dog sitting by the door.

Island Revolution is the only surf shop in town with its own killer skateboard park located just outside. Island Revolution stocks a full line of surfboards, skateboards, and all the accessories and beach items you'll need, such as boogie boards and leashes and sunglasses. Adult and kid's clothing from O'Neill, RVCA, Colt, and other hot name brands are sold here. Island Revolution holds surf and skateboard clinics in season; call for times.

Northern Lights Bakery is worth a stop all on its own. Delightful pastries, donuts, cupcakes, and all things sweet are created here from scratch. Coffee and smoothies are also available. Cakes are kept in stock and can also be made to order.

Kites, accessories, puzzles, and games can be found at **Flying Smiles.** Jeep fans will enjoy shopping for gear and clothing at **Jeep Clothing Company. The Village Fisherman** delights with whimsical gifts, garden accessories, and local artwork. **Mustang Sally's** offers stylish wear for men, women, and children. Mustang Sally's also stocks gifts, artwork, fine silver jewelry, and more.

i Bargain hunter's alert: The best time to shop on the Outer Banks is during the off-season. You'll find deals on many things from swimsuits to sunglasses to surfboards. Retailers offer their greatest deals around Thanksgiving and Christmas, right before they close their doors for the winter.

FARMER'S DAUGHTER
NC 12, Corolla
(252) 453-9116

In the same building as Stan White Real Estate, the Farmer's Daughter adds country charm to your home. Choose from home accessories, crafts, decoys, collectibles (such as Department 56, Boyds Bears, and Byers' Choice babies), and gift items such as T-shirts, lighthouses, statues, and Christmas decorations. Local artisans' work is for sale, as is the world's first and only supply of saltwater fudge. This location is open year-round.

MONTERAY PLAZA
NC 12, Corolla

The plaza is anchored by **Food Lion** and speckled with several locations to buy ice cream or other goodies to taste between stops on your shopping excursion. The plaza has public restrooms and plenty of parking. This shopping center is the home of RC Theatres' Corolla location (see the Recreation chapter).

Gray's Department Store is an Outer Banks clothing tradition for men and women. Celebrating more than 50 years of business, Gray's offers name-brand swimwear and sportswear, top-quality T-shirts, sweatshirts, and everyday shoes. **Carolina Outdoors** is an outfitter for hiking and climbing clothing and offers T-shirts, ladies' wear, and children's clothing, plus jewelry and souvenirs. This sporting goods business is operated by Kitty Hawk Kites and features an outdoor climbing wall in the courtyard. Kayak tours and hang-gliding lessons are available.

Do the whole family a favor and check out **Corolla Surf Shop & Corolla Surf Museum.** Great gear and boards are stocked here, and you can sign up anyone age 9 or older to learn to surf. Teaching now for over 11 years, the experts here can quickly get you up on the board and having fun in the waves Corolla Surf Shop also carries skateboarding equipment. The museum houses classic boards, surf memorabilia, and photography. **Surfside Casuals** offers a wide range of surfwear for men, women, and children.

TW's Bait and Tackle has everything you'll need to catch the big one, plus sunglasses and T-shirts. The delightful aroma of fresh coffee beans greets you at the door of **Alice's Craft Gallery.** Stocking artisan pottery from North Carolina and beyond, this store offers truly tempting wares.

Birthday Suits/OBX Gear is a beach-wear boutique carrying casual sportswear and accessories for the entire family. The store is packed with an extensive line of swimwear for men, women, and children. Check out the selection of sunglasses, shoes, accessories, and swim goggles. **Bacchus Wine & Cheese** carries one of the most extensive selections of domestic and imported wines on the Outer Banks as well as wine accessories and delicious deli sandwiches. **Dockside North Seafood Market,** on the other end of the plaza from Bacchus, sells fresh fish, scallops, shrimp, clams, crabmeat, and oysters in season.

TIMBUCK II SHOPPING VILLAGE
785 Sunset Blvd., NC 12, Corolla
(252) 453-9888
www.timbuckii.com

TimBuck II is a shopping, dining, and entertainment village with more than 60 shops and restaurants. The entire family could spend a day here, with everyone happily entertained. Shops are geared to all interests, restaurants abound, and the entertainment factor is high. While you shop, you can drop the kids off at the **Corolla Raceway** for go-karting and bumper boating, or the **Golf Links** for miniature golf. ✳**Kitty Hawk Kites** offers kite-flying lessons, and ✳**Kitty Hawk Surf Company** offers parasailing, kayaking, Jet Skiing, and more. Everyone can meet for a meal at one of many restaurants.

Ground-level parking, covered decks, public restrooms, a recreation area, and playground are features. The shopping center is open daily from Memorial Day to Labor Day from 10 a.m. to 9 p.m. During the rest of the year, individual shop schedules may vary, and only some shopkeepers stay open year-round. Operating hours in the shoulder seasons vary from store to store.

Fashionistas will want to visit *Beach Braids.** Have your locks professionally braided or get an all natural henna tattoo. A mehndi artist is on staff for customers who would like a more traditional design, or choose from the many designs on display. **Tar Heel Trading Co.** carries American handcrafted decorator items, accessories, serving pieces, puzzle boxes, pottery, wind chimes, and designer jewelry. This popular business has several locations. At the Corolla shop look for contemporary cottage decor, including art for the walls and exquisite blown glassware. **Good Vibes** video rents DVS movies and Nintendo rentals. Blank 8 mm tapes, digital cards, and more are also stocked here.

Corolla Book, Card and Gift Gallery has beautiful gifts and items for the entire family—posters, candles, Corolla souvenirs, greeting cards, florals, Jelly Bellies, jewelry, Beanie Babies, and local T-shirts and hats. A large children's department sells hats, shirts, toys, books, and games. And the store offers a wide selection of local books and best sellers in hardcover and paperback. It's open from Easter through Thanksgiving.

Michael's Gems & Glass is a fun shop for kids of all ages. It offers rocks and minerals, fossils, marbles, and other toys plus sterling silver jewelry.

Cotton Gin offers quality clothing and gifts, including Department 56 collectibles and Tom Clark gnomes, decoys, and carvings. The store's primary location is a sprawling barn-red building on US 158 on the Currituck mainland. The Corolla shop features gifts, unique bedding, and bath and kitchen supplies.

Coastal Karma is an original gift shop featuring music, sarongs, carved tikis, and lots more good stuff. Everything here is fun, funky, and fresh. **Eclectic Treasures** sells fine arts, crafts, and gifts. **Ocean Treasures** offers artworks and gifts from famous artists like Wyland, Greg Harvey, and Dan Mackin.

Dolphin Watch Gallery offers fine art, pottery, carvings, mosaics, Pandora jewelry, and more. **Just for the Beach** stocks beach essentials: chairs, clothing, swimwear, sunscreen, and more. **DogNutz** is a shop for dogs and people who are nutz about them. Gifts featuring over 300 breeds will wow any dog fancier. OBK9 beach gear for your dog is sold here, and you can also pick up something for your special cat or horse. No visit to the Outer Banks is complete without driving through a **Brew Thru.** Beer, wine, ice-cold sodas, and T-shirts abound here; you can even fill your tank at this location.

Try My Nuts sells gourmet nuts and candies, Try My Nuts apparel, and Wall of Fire sauces and nuts, which are so hot the owners say they'll hurt your feelings. Don't believe it? Free samples are offered daily. **Paisley the Perfect Giftdom** offers insulated bags and totes, foldable tub coolers, adult slushies, shore shoes, and personalized beach towels.

Gray's Department Store is huge, selling the largest selection of Tommy Bahama and Fresh Produce sportswear on the Outer Banks. Gray's sells T-shirts, sweats, hats, sportswear, and swimwear for the whole family. A northern location of **Nags Head Hammocks** sells handcrafted rope hammocks and swings.

Corolla Candles and Fun at Bathtime is a candle lover's dream come true. Hundreds of fragrances, colors, and styles of candles are available. Bath bombs and an amazing hand dipping wax activity can also be found here. Spend some time in **Miss Kitty's Old Time Photo** studio. Choose from 3,000 costumes and several settings to produce old-time photos. Once you select your costumes, whether a Civil War hero, a 1920s flapper, or a cowgirl, it only takes three minutes to see the results. Antique-style frames are available.

Mystic Jewel brightens and calms your mind, body, and spirit with its eclectic offerings. Unique candles, semiprecious jewelry, and home accents help make up the incredible selection. **Mustang Sally's** offers clothing, jewelry accessories, and gifts for creative people. **Kitty Hawk Surf Company** carries Reef, Rainbow, and other brand-name sandals. Choose from a wide selection of rash guards, bodyboards, and other fun items. Brand-name surf wear, like Quicksilver, Volcum, Roxy and Billabong, is also available at this happening store.

Corolla Wine Cigar Gourmet Shop is located in a new soundfront location. Formerly North Banks Wine Shop, this jewel of a shop offers specialty beers, a diverse wine selection, gourmet food, and gift items. The walk-in humidor is sure to please cigar aficionados. The whole family will enjoy a stop at **Kitty Hawk Kites.** Follow Outer Banks tradition and pick up a kite to fly on the beach—there are plenty here to pick from, and the staff is quite knowledgeable. T-shirts and beach toys are also available at this location. Sign up for hang gliding lessons or dolphin tours here as well. Treat your feet to a stop in ✳**Soundfeet Shoes.** With popular, comfortable shoes in stock, shoppers will find name

brands like Naot, Uggs, Merrill, Sperry, Crocs, Dansko, and more. The **Corolla ABC store** stocks packaged liquor. The **Corolla Visitors Center** is located within this mall.

If you're hungry after all that shopping, you're at the right place. TimBuck II has more than 10 places to eat at, including ice-cream shops, a pizza parlor, a deli, a Subway, a fudge shop, and sit-down restaurants. See the Restaurants chapter for some of the options.

DUCK

Duck is a shopper's best friend—and a budget's nemesis. People from all over the Banks come here for spending sprees. This small village is packed with shopping centers tucked into small nooks on the waterfront or in the trees.

Duck is walkable; in fact walking is preferable to maneuvering a vehicle around all the SUV-filled parking lots and on the crowded two-lane road. A paved bike path runs the length of the village, making it safe to walk from place to place. Parking is at a premium in Duck, so once you find a space, hold on to it. Remember, the sound of rain is every shopper's battle cry, so if you want to avoid crowds, don't go on a rainy day.

DUCK WATERFRONT SHOPS
NC 12, Duck

These shops provide all kinds of shopping opportunities. **Sunset Ice Cream** is just the spot to sip or slurp a refreshment. Entertainment is provided by dozens of mallards and other web-footed friends paddling around in the Currituck Sound shallows just below the railings. It's open Easter through Thanksgiving. At **Duck's General Store** you'll find great gifts including finely crafted sterling silver jewelry; a wide selection of T-shirts, sweatshirts, and hats; postcards and humorous greeting cards; and books on North Carolina and the Outer Banks. It's open year-round.

Islands By Amity offers stylish clothing from such lines as Juicy Couture, Three Dot, and Seven Jeans. Islands has a large aromatherapy section with lotions, soaps, and candles. You'll also see lots of artistic gifts and jewelry, including sterling silver baby gifts, music, picture frames, and stuffed animals. It's open year-round. **Barr-ee Station** features name-brand men's and women's clothing, shoes, and accessories—priced up to 50 percent off the regular retail price. And **Barr-ee Station Swimwear Outlet,** inside the same shop, sells discounted name-brand swimwear at up to 50 percent off.

For one-of-a-kind clothing for women and children, visit **Donna Designs,** a shop featuring hand-painted artwork—crabs, fish, turtles, flowers, and frogs, to name a few subjects—on cotton T-shirts including tees for adults and children, sweatshirts, sundresses, and French terry. A line of gifts and home decor items are available and Donna also carries Jantzen clothing. **North Beach Outfitters** sells outdoor clothing for men and women and adventure gear, including kayaks. Names include Patagonia, the North Face, Royal Robbins, Horny Toad, Columbia, Naot, Teva, Reef, Ocean Kayak, and Necky. High-end sunglasses, such as Oakley, Revo, and Costa del Mar, and rack sunglasses are available. **Candy and Corks** offers wines and yummy sweets. Fudge, taffy, chocolate, and some classic candies are available.

In a newer section of this building are several exciting shops. **Dazzles** is a magical shop with mobiles, hanging glass lanterns, whimsical plant stakes, chimes, jewelry,

unique cards, frames, doormats, candles, and many more items. **Gray's** sells clothing for men, women, and children, including a large selection of Tommy Bahama and Fresh Produce. The **Kid's Store** has kites, toys, games—something for all ages. **Sea Dragon Gallery** offers exquisite American-made crafts, with local, North Carolina, and national artists represented. Shop for colorful and quality furniture at the locally owned Outer Banks Furniture Outpost, a sister store to the larger Outer Banks Furniture located in Nags Head. **Life's a Beach, A Lily Pulitzer Shop** stocks fun, colorful dresses and clothing for women and girls plus shoes and accessories. Lily fans were happy to see this shop come to Duck. Be sure to stop in **Duck's Cottage** in the Waterfront Shops parking lot. Inside this inviting building you'll find best-selling books and a great choice of more eclectic reads. Tempting pastries, coffees, and teas round out the offerings.

TOMMY'S GOURMET MARKET AND WINE EMPORIUM
NC 12, Duck
(252) 261-8990
www.tommysmarket.com

At Tommy's pick up delicious, fresh-baked goods such as pastries, turnovers, breads, bagels, and doughnuts. The deli features roasted ham and chicken, ready-to-eat spiced shrimp, sandwiches, fresh salads, fresh-baked pies, and daily luncheon specials. Tommy's is famous for its Angus steaks, aged for 21 days and cut to order. Tommy's maintains an extensive wine selection and carries imported beers in addition to a full range of groceries. It's open Mar through New Year's.

WEE WINKS SQUARE & VICINITY
NC 12, Duck

Wee Winks, across the street from Wee Winks Square, is a practical stop for a wide variety of needs, such as last-minute food and gas purchases or a newspaper. An ABC package store is in the vicinity.

Stop by **Beach Essentials,** open Mar through Oct, for boogie boards, lotions, rafts, and lots more. Children are fascinated by the shop's hermit crabs, and ladies are taken with the Larimar jewelry direct from the Caribbean. At **Lady Victorian** you'll find contemporary styles for today's woman. Outfits and suits are the emphasis here, in cotton, silk, and linen, plus quality dresses, evening wear, intimate apparel, travel accessories, and personal items such as bath products, soaps, and powders. Lady Victorian is open year-round.

Kitty Hawk Kites stocks a remarkable selection of toys for all ages. Shoppers can choose from kites, wind chimes, pirate treasures, water toys, and even T-shirts and sweatshirts. Nearby at **Kitty Hawk Surf Company,** all types of beach-lifestyle clothes are available. Swimsuits, sandals, pants, dresses, and jackets are just some of the trendy items on hand. Surfboards, kayaks, and all kinds of water equipment are sold here.

NAGS HEAD HAMMOCKS
NC 12, Duck
(252) 261-1062
www.nagshead.com

Tucked into the trees on the waterfront, this shop is huge, with plenty of display space for the hammocks, footstools, and porch swings made by this company. These are quality, handmade hammocks durable enough to last for years. Nags Head Hammocks has numerous Outer Banks locations.

LOBLOLLY PINES SHOPPING CENTER
NC 12, Duck

Loblolly Pines is a complex of shops and eateries where you can purchase anything from decals to precious gems. Whet your appetite with an ice-cream cone or sweet treat as well. **Yesterday's Jewels** carries an interesting collection of old and new jewelry, including gold and sterling silver. **Outer Banks Running Company** sells running shoes in trusted brands, and the staff is very helpful with fittings. The shop also sells running wear and workout clothes and has information on local races. **The Glass Bead** has a great selection of beads from all over the world. Unique and custom jewelry is sold at this location as well. Sample the many scents at **Southern Candle and Gifts,** where soy and locally made candles are sold.

OSPREY LANDING
NC 12, Duck

Osprey Landing is a smaller shopping area overlooking the sound.

Sarah De Spain jewelry designer and goldsmith creates original and custom jewelry. This store also carries designs by other specially selected jewelry designers. Pandora bracelets are available here. **SunScents** offers more than 30 brands of candles and unique locally produced seashell candles. Spa products can be found here as well.

Just north of Osprey Landing are two other spots. **Soundfeet Shoes** sells the biggest selection of shoes on the Outer Banks, including Birkenstock, Naot, Dansko, Nike, Reebok, and more. A branch of **Ocean Atlantic Rentals** is also here; it rents any items you might have left behind, such as linens, towels, cribs, baby items, bikes, and water sports gear.

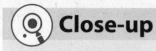 **Close-up**

Sticking with OBX

Chances are if you've looked into any aspect of the Outer Banks, you've run into its alter-ego designation: OBX. This seemingly official shorthand has made its way into print and websites everywhere, and most people seem to understand what it means . . . but it wasn't always that way. In fact, sales of the first Euro-style OBX stickers were usually preceded by an explanation of what OBX meant.

The oval Euro-decal phenomenon itself had its beginnings in 1969 with none other than the United Nations. Most license plates at the time looked the same regardless of the country of origin, so the UN developed codes for the oval stickers, and they were issued in addition to license plates. The stickers eventually made their way into US pop culture first as status symbols for imported cars and later as a way to identify preferred vacation spots, like MV for Martha's Vineyard.

In 1994 Outer Banks local Jim Douglas, owner of Chilli Peppers restaurant, was sitting at a cafe on Nantucket Island and noticed people buying oval stickers with the letters ACK. He thought the Outer Banks ought to have something similar. Jim's plan was to sell a few thousand oval stickers with OB for a small profit, but when the X was added, the little stickers caught on. Not only did the X act to make OB plural, it subliminally borrowed from everything X in our culture, from Generation X to the X Games and all things X-treme. And what started as a small venture for Jim gradually mushroomed into a true phenomenon.

The first stickers were sold at the Stop 'N' Shop in Kill Devil Hills in 1994, and partners Jill and Greg Bennett started selling OBX clothing items at their swimsuit shop, Birthday Suits/OBX Gear, in 1996. With any good idea will come imitators, so Jim and company formed OBX Stock Inc. and, after a four-year battle, successfully registered OBX as a legal trademark. OBX Gear is the headquarters for all things OBX, and only authorized dealers may sell the trademarked merchandise. As the OBX designation has taken on a life of its own, the entrepreneurs have lent the three letters to everything from surf contests and hang-gliding competitions to charity fund-raisers and art shows.

Since the Euro-decal phenomenon has matured, the multiletter designations can be for anything from "anytown USA" to political statements. Some oval stickers have become as arcane as personalized license plates, with casual observers trying to puzzle out just what the letters might mean. If parody is a compliment, the OBX oval sticker gets high marks. A recent spoof has the letters OBX in a black rectangle with small letters below stating: Think Outside the Oval.

SCARBOROUGH LANE SHOPPES
NC 12, Duck

Scarborough Lane features amenities you won't find elsewhere in Duck Village, including covered parking, sheltered walkways, and public restrooms. Most of these shops are open part of the week Mar through Dec; in summer they tend to stay open late, seven days a week.

Outer Barks is a must-stop for dog and cat lovers. Kevin and Robyn offer fun stuff for your favorite pets. Ample parking at the rear of Scarborough Lane makes an easy walk into this captivating store. Check out the terrific selection of jewelry, ceramics, art, clothing, and pet accessories. This shop even offers life preservers for your beloved pooch. Bring Fido along and he'll get his picture mounted on Outer Barks's wall of fame. Once a week in the afternoon, your best friend can enjoy complimentary doggie daiquiris at Yappy Hour. Arf d'hoeuvres are served, and pooches can create a paw painting. Call Outer Barks, (252) 261-6279, for the Yappy Hour schedule. Outer Barks is open Mar through the end of Dec.

Look to the **Island Trader** for sterling silver jewelry and a variety of gifts, plus home and garden accessories. Here you'll find baskets and candles, kitchen linens, and North Carolina food products with a flair—hot sauces, chutneys, and barbecue sauces.

At **Tar Heel Trading Co.,** you'll see silver and gold jewelry and elegant items handcrafted in America by local and national artists. Tar Heel is known for its collection of wooden puzzle boxes and museum-quality wildlife art. Different items are available at the store's other two locations, in Sea Holly Square in Kill Devil Hills and TimBuck II in Corolla. **Confetti Clothing Company** has stylish wear for women. **Toy-rific** features top-of-the-line playthings for infants, toddlers, and school-age kids, including stuffed animals, puzzles, beach toys, and kites. *✹The Wooden Feather** offers something really different in Duck for decorators, decoy collectors, and wildlife enthusiasts. Even if you don't think you are one of those people, you should stop by this gallery. Handmade decoys, wildlife sculptures, art furnishings, prints, fish carvings, birdhouses, and collectibles with a natural theme fill this charming shop. Stylish gifts that will appeal to any nature lover are stocked here.

Birthday Suits/OBX Gear is a favorite local store specializing in bathing suits for adults and children; it also has hip clothes for men and women, sandals, jewelry, hats, and more. Many visitors return to this shop every year for a new suit. Be sure to check out the annual sale in January.

Diane Strehan, owner of **Diane's Lavish Linens,** will help you add just the right touch to your beach cottage or help you pick out a special gift, maybe for yourself. The shop has embroidered towels, face cloths, lace tablecloths, curtains, and body luxuries, like specialty soaps and lotions. Vera Bradley products are available, as are window coverings and gifts for little ones. Go home with professionally created braids after a visit to **Beach Braids.** Custom braids can last up to 3 months. Also available are natural henna tattoos, and a mehndi artist is on hand to create authentic henna designs.

Christmas lovers will delight in a trip to the **Christmas Mouse.** Stunning ornaments and holiday decor abound here. The mind, body, and spiritual powers of gemstones are celebrated at the **Mystic Jewel.** Shoppers will find jewelry to love year-round. **Nail Trix** will give your hands and toes a bit of uplifting color. Waxes are done here as well.

Beach Petites isn't just for petite wear. Betsy carries great lines like Tribal, Sacred Threads, and Lanalee. Pop into **Duck Pizza** for a delicious calzone or pizza. For some great snacks to take home for gifts, stop in at **Try My Nuts.** Sauces, chocolates, and other treats are sold here, too.

SCARBOROUGH FAIRE
NC 12, Duck
Scarborough Faire features a series of boutiques and businesses in a garden setting. The facade is reminiscent of the architecture

of old-time lifesaving stations. The buildings are set into a grove of trees, and the shops are connected by a walkway through the woods, creating one of the shadiest spots in Duck in midsummer.

The **Island Bookstore** sells established works of fiction, discount hardcover best sellers, a wide variety of nonfiction, children's books, and specialty selections. The collection of works by southern authors is extensive, and you also can find audio books and jazz and blues on compact disc. Visit the upstairs addition, which features expanded offerings in many subjects, including travel, art, war, sports, and cooking. It's a book lover's dream. Special orders are welcome. The shop is open year-round.

Solitary Swan Antiques features cherry, pine, and walnut furniture and accessories such as porcelains, glassware, and pewter, plus traditional crafts and outdoor garden pieces, decoys, and folk art. The shop is open all year. **Ocean Annie's** sells handmade pottery. Some of it is functional, some decorative, and it's all beautiful. Gift items include wooden boxes, chimes, clocks, jewelry, and frames. The gourmet coffee beans smell so good you'll want a cup, but you'll have to get the beans to go and make yourself a cup at home. The **Culinary Duck** has everything for the kitchen—cookbooks, utensils, pots and pans, sauces, and more. A visit to **Rub A Dub Duck Bath Shop** will set you up with everything you need to pamper yourself, including soaps, bath oils, aromatherapy products, and more.

The refreshing **Urban Cottage** offers home furnishings and gifts that you won't find anywhere else. It's a home-decor boutique with everything from sofas and beds to candles and glasses. Fabulous furniture pieces are handmade and can be custom ordered to suit your needs. You'll swoon over the Sandra Drennen bedding and pillows, which are handcrafted from antique and European linens and dish towels. Housewares, lamps, rugs, mirrors, wall art, candles, unique gifts, and hand-painted peppermills and glassware are just some of the other things you'll find here. If you need help putting it all together, the friendly, talented ladies at this shop offer interior design services.

Got walls? **Beach Gallery** will help you decorate them with their oil prints and picture frames. Within the walls of **Mango's Boutique** are fine women's fashions and great shoes, along with jewelry and accessories. Everyone deserves a little **Luxury.** Stocking loungewear, this gift and boutique store specializes in beauty, romance, and bridal lingerie. **The Fudgery** bakes and serves scrumptious hand-turned fudge in many flavors. **Sooey's BBQ and Rib Shack** is a great stop for some yummy pork. Check out the handpainted oils and watercolors at **Affordable Art. Sand Reflections** carries Waterford crystal, high end jewelry, and home decor. Occasional wine tastings are held at this store.

Gray's Department Store outfits shoppers with shoes, clothing, hats, and more. Tommy Bahama, Fresh Produce, and OBX apparel can be found at this popular Outer Banks store.

DUCK VILLAGE OUTFITTERS
NC 12, Duck
(252) 261-7222

This funky shop looks like it should be on a Caribbean island, but here it is in the heart of Duck, next to the Burger King and a gas station. DVO sells surfwear for all four seasons as well as surfboards, wetsuits, kayaks and kayaking gear, bikes and bike-related stuff, skateboards and the accompanying hard goods, shoes, and sunglasses. You can rent sports gear and bikes, too.

DUCK SOUNDSIDE SHOPPES
NC 12, Duck

To add country charm to your home, visit the **Farmer's Daughter,** which sells home accessories, crafts, decoys, collectibles (such as Department 56, Boyds Bearstones, and Byers' Choice babies), and a variety of gift items such as lighthouses, statues, T-shirts, and Christmas decorations. This shop is open year-round.

Plum Crazy is a fabulous women's boutique where every item is unique and creative. Clothing by designers like Seven Jeans, XOXO, and She-Bible and jewelry, handbags, and even furniture are featured here.

A location of **Surfside Casuals** offers thousands of swimsuits by names such as Roxy, Raisins, Jantzen, Quicksilver, Billabong, Rusty, Roxanne, and others. There are eight locations of this store on the Outer Banks. **Bob's Bait & Tackle** is Duck's only tackle shop. Come here for live bait, lures, tackle, rods and reels, charter information, and advice.

GREENLEAF GALLERY
NC 12, Duck
(252) 261-2009

On the southern end of the village, Greenleaf Gallery is considered the classiest gallery on the Outer Banks. You'll find the work of several accomplished local artists, including painter Rick Tupper, who owns the gallery with his wife, Didi. Didi sets a high mark for inclusion in her gallery, so everything here is finely crafted and one of a kind. Glass, wood, oil, watercolor, fiber, pottery,

and sculpture are among the mediums featured. See the Arts & Culture chapter for more information.

SOUTHERN SHORES

THE MARKETPLACE
US 158, MP 1, Southern Shores

The Marketplace in Southern Shores is the large shopping center on the north side of US 158 at MP 1. A **Food Lion** grocery store and a **CVS Pharmacy** are its anchor stores. The following are the specialty shops that fill out the Marketplace selection.

The **UPS Store** provides 26 business communication and postal services all under one roof, including packaging, shipping, copying, faxing, and mailbox rental. If you've bought too much on vacation to easily cart home, owner Bart Smith will ship it for you.

A realty company, a pizza parlor, a bagel shop, a dry cleaner, **Rita's Ice,** a Starbucks, and a Chinese restaurant add to the offerings at the Marketplace.

SOUTHERN SHORES CROSSING
1 Ocean Blvd., Southern Shores

This fun shopping center is tucked behind Southern Shores Realty, just past the traffic light on Ocean Boulevard.

Diva's Day Spa & Salon is a full-service day spa offering massages, facials, and nail care in a friendly, upscale environment. You can find catalog clothing and antique furnishings at **Barr-ee Station.** ✳**ARTspace** is a working art gallery. Stop in and view the works of Katy Caroline and other resident artists. Great taste is evident at **Coastal Provisions Market.** Chef-prepared takeout is available for lunch and dinner. Both specialty and everyday groceries can be found at Coastal Provisions, including fresh seafood and produce and fine cheeses and wine.

SANDY RIDGE CENTER
US 158, Southern Shores

This mall is an easy stop off where US 158 and the beach road connect. **Tropical Smoothie** offers healthy smoothies and freshly made sandwiches. Put the final touches on your suntan at **Surfside Tans. Interspaces** offers the latest in style with ceramic tile, hardwood flooring, and other items to finish your remodel or new home.

KITTY HAWK

CENTRAL GARDEN CENTER & NURSERY
US 158, MP ¼, Kitty Hawk
(252) 261-7195

This family-owned and -operated business has been serving the area for more than 40 years. The garden center sells indoor plants, shrubs, and trees plus annuals and perennials. Landscape services are available, and you'll find Christmas trees and wreaths at the holidays. It's open year-round.

ISLANDER FLAGS
US 158, MP ¼, Kitty Hawk
(252) 261-6266
www.flagfinder.com

Islander Flags specializes in custom flags. The professionals here can help you design a flag to suit your needs, or they can turn a logo or artwork into a flag. This is a big store, and you'll be surprised at all the flags in stock—decorative flags, military flags, national and state flags, marine flags, and more. This shop is next to Coastal Auto Mart and is open all year.

THE SHORESIDE CENTER
US 158, MP 1, Kitty Hawk

This center features **Wal-Mart, Subway,** and **McDonald's.** The shops are open year-round. **Natural Creations Fine Jewelry** is a locally owned shop selling contemporary and traditional jewelry. **Harris Teeter** is a large grocery store with a terrific bakery, deli, and salad bar. Harris Teeter has an extensive selection of cheeses and wines as well as other gourmet foods not always available in other supermarkets on the Outer Banks. An outstanding floral department is located here. This store is open year-round.

CARAWAN SEAFOOD
US 158, MP 1, Kitty Hawk
(252) 261-2120

Situated on the lot in front of the Shoreside Center, locally owned Carawan Seafood sells fresh local fish and shellfish in season plus flown-in fish, seafood, and live lobsters. We know quite a few insiders who frequent this shop several times a week. The store carries a small selection of wine and beer, gourmet food items, seashells, lures, and tackle. An area next to the seafood shop sells a few Southwestern crafts, including jewelry and gift items. Caravan is open year-round.

OCEAN CENTRE
NC 12, MP 1½, Kitty Hawk

This inviting band of shops is located across the road and south of the former Kitty Hawk Pier. **Salon Swank** is a full-service salon offering the latest hair styles. **Island Art Supply** stocks anything your inner artist desires.

Kitty Hawk Tobacco has a complete selection of tobacco accessories, cigarettes, and cigars. **Duck Donuts** has the yummiest doughnuts in town. **High Cotton BBQ** is a southern barbecue fan's delight, serving lunch and dinner complete with iced tea. **Outer Banks Yoga and Pilates** offers expert instruction throughout the day and evening.

AMBROSE FURNITURE
US 158, MP 2, Kitty Hawk
(252) 261-4836

Ambrose Furniture is a family-owned and -operated furniture showroom that has conducted business in the area for more than 50 years. The store has a free design service and a qualified staff to assist you with your selection of furniture, blinds, and housewares. The store is open year-round.

WINKS GROCERY
NC 12, MP 2, Kitty Hawk
(252) 261-2555

Winks is what shopping is supposed to be like at a beach store—a sometimes-sandy floor, beach music filling the air, and an easy feeling. Winks has a deli, lots of edibles, beach supplies, beer, wine, and deli sandwiches, plus sweatshirts and T-shirts, toys, and gag gifts. The shop is open all year.

✳WAVE RIDING VEHICLES
US 158, MP 2½, Kitty Hawk
(252) 261-7952
www.waveridingvehicles.com

Wave Riding Vehicles is the largest surf shop on the Outer Banks. WRV stocks beach fashions, swimsuits, and gobs of T-shirts in the popular brands (see the Water Sports chapter for surfing equipment information). It also offers snowboarding equipment and apparel. It's open year-round.

HOTLINE PINK
US 158, MP 3½, Kitty Hawk
(252) 261-8164

In the hot pink building next to Ace Hardware, this community thrift shop functions to benefit the local women's shelter. You'll see books, furniture, clothes, and household items. Remember this place when you're spring cleaning—donations are needed.

KITTY HAWK PLAZA
US 158, MP 4, Kitty Hawk
(252) 261-8200

Daniel's Homeport is the largest store in this complex. Daniel's specializes in housewares and accessories such as candleholders, dried flowers, picture frames, wine racks, rugs, bedding, lamps, wicker and outdoor furniture, and much more. A full window-treatment department supplies curtains and shades, blinds, and shutters (some on order). In the same shopping center you'll find **Red's Army Navy,** a military surplus supply store, **Soundfeet Shoes** outlet shop, **Major Party,** festive goods, and the **Children's Hospital of the King's Daughters Thrift Store,** where frugal folks find all sorts of used goods.

BUCCANEER'S WALK
US 158, MP 4, Kitty Hawk

Right next to Capt'n Frank's hot dog restaurant is Buccaneer's Walk, an attractive shopping complex fashioned after 19th-century fishing and whaling villages and coastal places the owners have visited. **Capt'n Frank's Peanut Shop** sells, of course, peanuts, in addition to candy, Carolina stuff, candles, linens, and gifts.

   Tar Heel Trading Co. stocks fine American handicrafts, artwork, and gift items.

Puzzles Pranks & Games stocks a huge variety of brainteasers and fun family-time games.

Lilly's Closet stocks cool clothing, adorable shoes, and accessories for girls and boys. The **Cook Shop** offers delightful cookware, glassware, and cutting boards. **Lotus Day Spa** is an intimate spot offering reflexology, massage, facials, and more. **Island Nautical** supplies you with a bounty of sea-inspired gifts, artifacts, and books. While away an afternoon browsing through the bounty of treasures at **☀B & B Antiques.** You never know what you'll stumble across in this delightful store, and you'll want to make it a must-see on your list of fun places to stop on your trip.

OCEAN PLAZA
US 158, MP 4, Kitty Hawk

Outer Banks Taco Bar is a tastefully good find. Delicious burritos and tacos are made to order with only the freshest ingredients. Sandwiches prepared with locally caught seafood are served here and made with locally grown produce. Wine, beer, and yummy sangria are available. Catering is offered. Check the board for daily sandwich specials, like the insiders' favorite soft shell crab sandwich. **The Wine Specialist** stocks wines for all budgets and tastes. Free wine tastings on Wednesday. **OBX Romance Store** offers bachelorette party supplies and more.

THE BREAD COMPANY BUILDING
US 158, MP 4½, Kitty Hawk

The ever-popular **Island Bookstore** is housed here. This full-service bookstore stocks cookbooks, best sellers, business books, local interest titles, audio books, and a great children's selection, including specialty toys. A big draw is the magazines, many of which are generally hard to find. This is a great spot to while away an afternoon. Bill is especially good at offering books for every interest and taste. There is an outstanding children and teen's section here as well. **Knuckle Up** is a community fitness center offering personal training, fitness kickboxing, boxing, and spinning. **Health-A-Rama** is a well-stocked health food store. Organic produce and meats, whole food vitamins, pet supplies, and beauty supplies are just a few of the items found here.

DIAMONDS 'N DUNES
US 158, Harborside Shops, MP 4¾, Kitty Hawk
(252) 255-0001

Diamonds 'n Dunes jewelry store will dazzle your senses. The store celebrates the visual wonders of the area with a beautiful mural of mermaids and wild horses adorning a wall. Owners Ken and Eileen like to say that they sell jewelry and happiness. The main area serves traditional clients with a variety of jewelry lines including Pandora, Kabana, and Eileen's own designs. Upstairs is the bridal jewelry salon where clients can privately select their rings. Diamonds 'n Dunes strives for superb customer service.

KILL DEVIL HILLS

SHORE FIT SUNWEAR
US 158 and East Helga Street, MP 5½, Kill Devil Hills
(252) 441-4560
www.yoursuit.com

You're sure to find a suit to fit at Shore Fit, where the mission is to find a suit for the hard-to-fit woman. This swimwear boutique stocks swimsuits in sizes from 8 to 28, many that will enhance or flatten your curves. The store carries maternity suits, suits for women who've had mastectomies, athletic suits, cover-ups, sarongs, swim dresses, and more. The staff is very helpful, and you can order suits from the website. The boutique closes in the off-season.

SEAGATE NORTH SHOPPING CENTER
US 158, MP 5½, Kill Devil Hills

At the north end of Kill Devil Hills, Seagate North offers a variety of shopping experiences.

Black Tie Affair sells wedding formal dresses, wedding accessories, formal-wear rentals, gifts, and more. The latest, most stylish wear is available through Black Tie, and they offer dependable service for your big day. **Gold-N-Gifts** has gold, silver, diamond, and gemstone jewelry for sale; baby gifts and John Perry figurines are also in stock. **Sun Shack** is a tanning and clothing salon. **Cyber Dog** is a holistic pet food and supply store. **A Penny Saved Thrift & Consignment** has gently used goods for sale.

In the parking lot of Seagate North is one of our favorite produce stands, **Tarheel Too.** You'll find fruits and vegetables, locally grown when possible, as well as some of the best mesclun mix around. Homemade baked goods and jellies are delicious.

MILEPOST 6
Plaza US 158, MP 6, Kill Devil Hills
(252) 480-0519

Glazin' Go Nuts is a paint-your-own pottery studio that everybody loves, especially on a rainy day (see the Kidstuff chapter). Glazin' Go Nuts shares a space with **Front Porch Cafe,** a coffee shop that makes heavenly coffee drinks and baked goods and roasts its own coffee.

For the widest choice of beer or wine on the Outer Banks, a stop at **Chip's Wine and Beer Market** is required. Discount prices, a hand-picked selection, and educated, friendly service make shopping at Chip's a pleasure. Next door at the **Chip's Tasting Room,** regularly scheduled classes help customers untangle the mystery of wine—without any snobbery. The **Music Store** offers music supplies and instruments. **Bangs** hair salon rounds out the offering.

AWFUL ARTHUR'S BEACH SHOP
NC 12, MP 6, Kill Devil Hills
(252) 449-2220

This is a haven for Awful Arthur's paraphernalia inspired by the popular oyster bar next door. You'll find T-shirts, sweatshirts, golf shirts, hats, beach towels, and glassware bearing the eatery's infamous logo. Shop for beach needs, including beer and groceries, beach chairs and umbrellas, fireworks, seashells, tackle, coolers, and hermit crabs. Bad Barracuda's merchandise is available here, too. Awful Arthur's Beach Shop is open year-round.

THE DARE CENTRE
US 158, MP 7, Kill Devil Hills

This center is anchored by **Belk's** department store, which stocks clothing and shoes for men, women, children, and babies. There are large shoe, accessory, jewelry, makeup, perfume, lingerie, and home-decor departments. **Food Lion,** a national chain grocery store, is also here. Other stores include **Atlantic Dance and Boutique,** an Outer Banks dance studio. The boutique sells dancewear for adults and children. **Fashion Bug** offers discount fashions, and **Dollar Tree** has everything under the sun for $1. Kids love this store, but there are also good deals on toiletries and household items. The **Outer Banks Sports Locker** specializes in sporting goods, sportswear, and fitness apparel and equipment. **Cold Stone Creamery** has delicious ice cream in several flavors for a wonderful afternoon treat. **Beach Express** stocks all types of toys, beach wear, and beach supplies.

New **York Bagels** has fresh, yummy bagels every day for breakfast and lunch. **Little Caesar's Pizza** is here, as are **Subway** for sandwiches and **China King** for take-out Chinese.

NORTH CAROLINA BOOKS
US 158, MP 7½, Kill Devil Hills
(252) 441-2141

In the Times Printing building, North Carolina Books is chock-full of secondhand paperbacks and reduced-price hardcover books. Bring in your old paperbacks and use them as credit toward the purchase of other secondhand books from the store. The store also has new books and tapes and is open year-round.

✳STOP 'N' SHOP CONVENIENCE AND DELI
NC 12, MP 8½, Kill Devil Hills
(252) 441-6105

Insiders consider this little treasure trove a hidden gem. More than your average gas and goodies store, the Stop 'N' Shop offers an upscale convenience alternative. The store is jam-packed with tempting items. The deli (which starts serving fresh bagels, hot coffee, and breakfast sandwiches at 6:30 a.m. year-round) uses Boar's Head meats, and the store boasts gourmet food products and one of the best selections of wine and microbrewed beer on the beach. There are large selections of beach and fishing equipment;

the store sells boogie boards, sand chairs, and umbrellas, and it sells and rents rods and tackle. Prices here often beat the competition. The variety of daily newspapers is impressive. During the summer season, the store is open until midnight, 11 p.m. in the off-season.

THE TRADING POST
NC 12, MP 8½, Kill Devil Hills
(252) 441-8205

Here's a good general store to buy things for the beach. It carries T-shirts, souvenirs, swimwear, and convenience grocery items. A branch post office functions here. It's closed from late Nov through early Mar.

✳KDH COOPERATIVE GALLERY AND STUDIOS
US 158, MP 8½, Kill Devil Hills
(252) 441-9888
www.kdhcooperative.com

This gallery, a cooperative of numerous local artists, provides an eclectic mix of artworks that creates an interesting shopping experience. Upstairs, several artists work in their studios. See the Arts & Culture chapter for more information.

THE BIRD STORE
US 158, MP 9, Kill Devil Hills
(252) 480-2951

The Bird Store carries a complete line of antique and new decoys produced by local carvers. Antique fishing gear, fish prints, and original art are also on display. It's open Easter through Christmas.

THE PIT SURF SHOP, BAR AND GRILL
US 158, MP 9, Kill Devil Hills
(252) 480-3128
www.pitsurf.com

The Pit's surf shop is huge and stocks a selection of surf and skate wear and gear, plus sunglasses, shoes, women's clothing, and more. See the Water Sports chapter for more information.

COMPASS ROSE
US 158, MP 8¾, Kill Devil Hills
(252) 441-9449
Compass Rose sells a unique blend of gift items imported from Thailand, Vietnam, and Indonesia from their bright pink building. You'll find candles, ornately carved furniture, fine paper, frames, jewelry, chimes, and much more. Be sure to check out the pots out front. Some great deals can be found.

LIFESAVER SHOPS
NC 12, MP 9, Kill Devil Hills
Lifesaver Rent Alls fills rental needs and offers thrifty bargains—these folks rent it all! Look for beach umbrellas, chairs, TVs, DVD players, baby equipment, cottage supplies, portable radios, microwaves, charcoal grills, and blenders. Linen service complete with sheets, pillowcases, and bath towels is offered. Sports items abound, too—look for surfboards, ocean kayaks, boogie boards, snorkel and fishing equipment, and bikes galore. It's open Mar through Nov. **Crabby Fries,** next door, offers delicious sandwiches. This is a great spot to pick up a picnic lunch. They also offer free delivery. Call (252) 441-9607 for details.

NAGS HEAD HAMMOCKS
US 158, MP 9½, Kill Devil Hills
(252) 441-6115, (800) 344-6433
www.nagshead.com
You can't miss the setting, with its palm trees and lush landscaping. At the shop you'll find the famous, durable, high-quality handmade hammocks; single- and double-rope rockers, footstools, and bar stools; single and double porch swings; "slingshot" swings; captain's chairs; and double recliners. You can also purchase items via mail order all year.

T-TOPS RACING
US 158, MP 9½, Kill Devil Hills
(252) 441-8867
For everything NASCAR under the sun, make a pit stop at T-Tops. This is a licensed NASCAR store with merchandise covering all NASCAR drivers. The main selling items are die-cast cars, but there are also NASCAR-inspired jackets, sweatshirts, T-shirts, hats, clocks, wallets, jewelry, and more in this 4,000-square-foot store. It's one of the largest NASCAR stores in the nation and is open year-round.

THE BIKE BARN
Wrightsville Avenue, MP 9½,
Kill Devil Hills
(252) 441-3786
The Bike Barn, located behind Taco Bell between the Beach Road and the Bypass, sells a wide variety of bikes, parts, and accessories. Skilled mechanics are on staff to service all types of bikes. The shop rents 18-speed and 21-speed hybrids, gear bikes, and beach cruisers and is open year-round.

ISLAND DYES
NC 12, MP 9½, Kill Devil Hills
(252) 480-0076
Island Dyes offers T-shirts and a full line of women's clothing, reggae and Grateful Dead T-shirts, and tobacco accessories. Adventurers get hairwraps and henna tattoos here, too. Call for store hours or more information.

BEACH BARN SHOPS
US 158, MP 10, Kill Devil Hills

On the west side of the Bypass, the Beach Barn Shops is the place to stop. It houses **Birthday Suits/OBX Gear,** a popular swimsuit and sportswear shop. *Southern Living* magazine wrote, "Everybody goes to Birthday Suits for a new bathing suit." For women, there's an unbelievable selection of cute suits in all styles, including mix-and-match separates, bra-size tops, and maternity, mastectomy, athletic, and long-torso suits. Women also love the contemporary sportswear, a fine selection of dressy dresses (including some by Betsey Johnson), and accessories—purses, shoes, hats, luggage, and pajamas. Men find trunks and briefs and a whole selection of sportswear and Hawaiian surf shirts. Kids' and babies' suits are adorable.

ROANOKE PRESS AND CROATAN BOOKERY
US 158, MP 10, Kill Devil Hills
(252) 480-1890

This shop is owned by the same folks who publish the *Coastland Times* newspaper and operate Burnside Books in Manteo. Here you'll discover secondhand and new books; both bookstores carry an extensive line of books about North Carolina and the Outer Banks. This one is open all year.

NAGS HEAD

Nags Head is a shopper's mecca, with its boutiques along the Beach Road, US 158, and the Nags Head–Manteo Causeway, and larger shopping destinations such as the Outer Banks Mall and the Tanger Outlet Stores on US 158.

BEN FRANKLIN
US 158, MP 10, Nags Head
(252) 441-7571

Across the street from the Food Lion Plaza, Ben Franklin carries clothing for all ages and everything you need for the beach. There are some great buys on ladies' dresses. It is open Easter through mid-November.

SOMETHING FISHY
NC 12, MP 10½, Nags Head
(252) 441-9666

Here's a fun shop swimming with fish. You'll delight in the fish-print clothing made by owner Sherrie Lemnois, who has been creating these masterpieces for years. Clothing, jewelry, toys, home decor, and gifts are available with a fishy theme. Also in the shop are Asian-inspired items, prompting the owner to say she sells everything from "fish to feng shui." Lucky Bamboo home-decor products are best sellers.

GALLERY ROW
Gallery Row and Driftwood Street,
Nags Head

Around MP 10 are numerous art galleries that are collectively referred to as "Gallery Row." If you're shopping in Nags Head, you'll want to see these wonderful art galleries situated between the highways. See the Arts & Culture chapter for a complete listing.

THE CHRISTMAS MOUSE
US 158, MP 10½, Nags Head
(252) 441-8111

This holiday-oriented shop brims with Christmas collectibles, Cairn Gnomes, papier-mâché Santas, Snow Babies, porcelain dolls, unique ornaments, and nautical- and midwestern-themed trees. Sixty decorated trees get you in the spirit. It is open year-round.

SHOPPES AT 10.5
US 158, MP 10.5, Nags Head

Food Lion anchors this small mall. The **Front Porch Cafe** offers wonderful coffees and teas from all over the globe. Fresh pastries are always on hand, and a comfy room is available to hang out and use the free Wi-Fi. **Foxy Flamingo** offers colorful and fun clothing. Order custom designer clogs at **Chameleon Clogs.** Artist Rabiah will help you design a pair of clogs that reflects the fashionable fun in your personality. A nail salon and a Chinese take-out restaurant round out the offerings.

GULF STREAM GIFTS
NC 12, MP 10½, Nags Head
(252) 441-0433

Gulf Stream features contemporary nautical gifts, jewelry, and lighthouse and dolphin memorabilia. The store is open from Easter until Thanksgiving.

ATLANTIC WIND SHOPS
US 158, MP 10½, Nags Head

This newer mall includes **Forbes Candies,** where you can purchase famous Outer Banks saltwater taffy, high-end chocolates, and general beach needs. ✳**Lil' Grass Shack** is a fun women's and children's wear clothing boutique. Swimwear, accessories, sandals, luggage, and Roxy clothing are featured. Top off your shopping trip with an artisan-roasted cup of coffee and a cinnamon bun at the **Morning View Coffee** cafe.

✳THE FRENCH DOOR
US 158, MP 11, Nags Head
(252) 441-4042

Insiders all love The French Door. This locally owned store inspires shoppers with colorful and creative gifts, home decor, and unique jewelry. Everything is hand selected by the owner/artist Donna Greenlee, and her personality shines through her selections. Donna has a great eye for the fun and the fabulous. The French Door is hip and stylish and has something for everyone.

CENTRAL SQUARE
US 158, MP 11, Nags Head

This weathered cottage-style complex of shops has come to house a conglomeration of antiques shops. **Edith Deltgen's Gallery** is owned by local artist Edith Deltgen, and some of her unique sculptures and creations are housed here. She also offers antiques, including furniture, estate jewelry, and household items. **Mystic Antiques** sells true antiques, including furniture, dressers, and beds. These shops make for great browsing. **Southern Soldier Antiques** features both fun and meaningful memorabilia and antiques. **Shooters at the Beach** is a full-service photography studio. **Electric Beach Tanning Salon** gets your skin beach ready.

PIRATE'S QUAY
US 158, MP 11½, Nags Head

Boutiques, stores, offices, and eateries carry tobacco, jewelry, crafts, and clothing in this shopping center.

Cloud Nine is an adventure in clothing, accessories, and other discoveries from around the world. Owner Ginny Flowers has beads and lots of them. Other finds include recycled sea glass, Grateful Dead merchandise, T-shirts made by locals and visitors, beautiful batiks, and treasures from Africa and Nepal. Cloud Nine also carries gold and silver jewelry. Bring in your sea glass and have a custom necklace made. It's open

Easter through Thanksgiving. **A-New-U** is a full-service hair salon.

AUSTIN FISH COMPANY
US 158, MP 12½, Nags Head
(252) 441-7412

Austin is a Nags Head fixture near Jockey's Ridge. It's a full-service seafood store that also serves as a gas station with some of the lowest prices on the beach. The store stocks crabmeat, steamed crabs, shrimp, oysters, clams, fish, scallops, live lobsters, and more. If you would like your catch shipped home, the staff will vacuum pack and freeze it for you. Austin's is open May through Nov. In the parking lot outside is the Nags Head Produce Stand where you'll find fresh local produce and flowers.

JOCKEY'S RIDGE CROSSING
US 158, MP 13½, Nags Head

At this complex, **Kitty Hawk Kites** sells kites, windsocks, and banners, as well as quality men's and women's sportswear and outerwear, sandals, T-shirts, and sweatshirts. This year-round shop also offers a large selection of toys. (See the Water Sports chapter for exciting sporting opportunities offered by these folks.)

Also open year-round, **Kitty Hawk Surf Company** carries popular name-brand clothing, boogie boards, accessories, and sunglasses plus windsurfing and kayaking gear. It offers all sorts of sporting opportunities (see the Water Sports chapter).

How Sweet It Is is the place to stop for homemade ice cream, tasty deli sandwiches, and delicious ice-cream cakes. To satisfy a yearning for fudge, stop by the **Fudgery.** A stop in **Miss Kitty's Old Time Photos** will send you on your way with a memorable picture of your group. **Life on a Sandbar**

provides hair wraps and temporary tattoos to vacationers hoping to go home with a new look. Sand art and windchimes are sold here as well. Choose your own bear and watch it be stuffed at the **Outer Banks Bear Factory,** where children enjoy having birthday parties. Pups love **Salty Paws** and the homemade, all-natural dog treats sold there. All types of pet accessories are available. Choose from hundreds of beads at **The Glass Bead** for all of your jewelry making needs.

SURFSIDE PLAZA
US 158, MP 13, Nags Head

Surfside Casuals has more swimsuits than just about any other store on the beach and an extensive line of casual wear for men and women. All of Surfside's many Outer Banks shops are open Easter through Thanksgiving. If you're hungry, the **Country Deli** has delicious, huge, and inexpensive sandwiches for lunch.

Find outlet-priced T-shirts, sunglasses, jeans, footwear and more at the **Nags Head Harley-Davidson** shop. **Blue Moon Beach Grill** serves lunch and dinner year-round and is becoming a quite popular eatery. One of the three popular **Beach Braids** is located in the Surfside Plaza. Get a great new look with braids in your hair that can last up to 3 months. That's what we call a long lasting souvenir!

CROATAN CENTRE
US 158, MP 14, Nags Head

This fun group of shops features gifts, fine jewelry, CDs, and shoes. Halloran & Co. offers sterling silver jewelry, 14-karat gold and gemstones, and unique wares. **Sound Feet Shoes,** open year-round, offers men's, women's, and children's casual and fancy shoes and sandals, including popular sports shoes by Reebok and Nike.

If you're looking for new and used CDs, look no further than **SSR Music,** which offers music for all tastes. Located inside Radio Shack, SSR also sells music videos, T-shirts, posters, and accessories. If they don't have something in stock, ask them to special order it for you; they can usually turn such requests around in a couple of days at no extra charge. The store is open all year.

Ocean Threads has T-shirts, shorts, and boardshorts for guys and gals—lots of stylish flip-flops and sunglasses, too. **Island Tobacco** offers cigars, tobacco products, and smoking implements. **Rock-A-Bye Baby** sells gently used goods such as clothes, cribs, toys, and high chairs.

OUTER BANKS MALL
US 158, MP 15, Nags Head

The Outer Banks Mall is open year-round and is home to shopping, service, entertainment, and dining businesses. The north wing of Outer Banks Mall is predominantly food oriented. **Outer Banks Cleaners** is also here.

On the south wing of Outer Banks Mall, **West Marine** offers boating hardware, gear, cleaning and repair supplies, Mercury engines, life jackets and safety equipment, marine electronics, and more. West Marine also sells fishing equipment, including gear, coolers, rods, reels, tackle, and lures. **Outer Banks Furniture** is a huge home-furnishings store with sofas, chairs, beds, dining tables, rugs, home accessories, and much more.

The **Cottage Shop** sells items that will give your home or cottage a relaxing, warm feeling. Everything from trendy welcome mats to functional backyard grills is

stocked here. **Perfect Image Hair Salon** offers stylish affordable cuts. Need just the right card or gift? Try the **Hallmark** located here.

Dare Jewelers offers sea life and nautical jewelry along with traditional fine jewelry. Locally created stained-glass items are also showcased. **Professional Opticians** will fill all your eyewear needs.

> **i** In the front parking lot of Seagate North is an insiders' favorite— the Tarheel Too produce stand. You'll find fruits and veggies, locally grown when possible. Prices are great, and the homemade baked goods and jellies are delicious.

FORBES CANDY & GIFT SHOP
US 158, MP 15½, Nags Head
(252) 441-7293

You can't come to the beach without picking up a box of saltwater taffy. Forbes, an Outer Banks tradition, has it here. Stop in for a box or three of the company's famous homemade gooey goodies. The shop, which is open year-round, also features a gift and souvenir selection.

CAHOON'S
NC 12, MP 16½, Nags Head
(252) 441-5358

Cahoon's is a large, family-owned grocery and variety store operating for more than four decades. It's a nice change of pace from chain supermarkets. Dorothy and Ray Cahoon bought the store shortly before the Ash Wednesday storm of 1962 and, despite what must have been a rather wild start, continue to stock everything you'll need for your visit to the beach, including good meats that butcher Robert Heroux cuts to perfection. The store is open Mar through Thanksgiving.

TANGER OUTLET CENTER
US 158, MP 16½, Nags Head
(252) 441-5634

Tanger is a discount-outlet shopping center brimming with great buys in all sorts of merchandise, from clothes to dishes to shoes. Once you park you'll wander for hours here. Bring plenty of cash!

All shops in the Tanger complex are open year-round. At **Rack Room Shoes** you can outfit the entire family with quality discounted tennis shoes and casual and dressy year-round footwear. **Michael's Gems & Glass** sells jewelry, rocks, minerals, and glass of all kinds.

Hot stores recently added to the Tanger Mall are **J. Crew, Aeropostale, Gymboree,** and **Merrell.** We've found fashionable short leather boots at **Nine West Outlet** that really last, plus lots of dressy and casual shoe selections for women only. The **Dress Barn** has sweaters (dressy, sporty, and casual dressy) for women and some super tops for all occasions.

No visit to Tanger Outlet Center is complete without a stop at **Gap Outlet,** where bargains are abundant. Locals stop in every week to pick up fun fashions at great prices.

Other store names you'll recognize include Polo/Ralph Lauren, Eddie Bauer Outlet, Coach, Tommy Hilfiger, Izod, Kitchen Collection, Wilson Leather Outlet, Van Heusen, Bass, Simply Read, Hanes Brands, and Sunglass Hut.

WHALEBONE SEAFOOD MARKET
US 158, MP 16½, Nags Head
(252) 441-8808

Whalebone is run by the Daniels family, known locally for their commercial-fishing roots. The full-service seafood market sells whatever's in season. It's open Easter through Oct.

ROANOKE ISLAND

The town of Manteo is thriving. There is so much to see, do, and buy now in Manteo that parking can be a challenge, but that just means you'll need to park on a side street and walk a few blocks. Or you can park in the Roanoke Island Festival Park lot, where you'll find space almost any time of year, and take a pleasant stroll over the Cora Mae Basnight Bridge to shop and eat.

We start with the shops along US 64, where you can find bargains as well as unusual gifts. Then we move on to downtown Manteo.

MANTEO

PIRATE'S COVE SHIP'S STORE
Pirate's Cove Yacht Club,
Nags Head–Manteo Causeway, Manteo
(252) 473-3906

This marina store has a selection of active sportswear, including Kahalas, a Hawaiian line of beautifully hand-screened and batik clothing. The shop also carries gifts, picture frames, windup crabs, marina supplies, and groceries as well as a line of 14-karat gold jewelry with a fishy flair. It's open year-round.

✳SILVER BONSAI GALLERY
905 US 64/264, Manteo
(252) 475-1413
www.silverbonsai.com

In a restored home on the main highway, Silver Bonsai is a gallery owned by local artists Ben Stewart and Kathryn Holton-Stewart.

The Stewarts are silver- and goldsmiths and bonsai artists. Their work fills the gallery along with the work of many local artists. One of the artists is often at work in the studio. The artwork and gifts in Silver Bonsai are distinctive. You'll find paintings, sculpture, candles, soaps, exquisite jewelry, copper items, quilts, furniture, Japanese pottery and local pottery, and more. See the Arts & Culture chapter for more information. This store is worth a stop just to admire the incredible Etch A Sketch drawings.

ISLAND PRODUCE
US 64/264, Manteo
(252) 473-1303

Island Produce offers fresh seasonal vegetables and fruits as well as flowering plants for the garden and home, including beautiful lilies, pumpkins, and Christmas trees in season. Statuary and fountains to adorn your garden are here, too. It's open Apr until Christmas.

CHESLEY MALL
US 64/264, Manteo

Food-A-Rama holds down the fort at this year-round shopping venue. **Island Pharmacy** is an old-fashioned store where you can buy prescription and over-the counter medicines, sundries, film, and gifts, and use the UPS and Airborne Express services in the back of the store. Island Pharmacy also sells gift items, including glass and china knickknacks and some stuffed animals. One of the best selections of gift cards on the beach can be found here, too.

The **Hallmark Shop** carries party supplies, religious products, candy (try the spicy jelly beans), cards, stationery, and photo albums. **Subway** and **Top China** offer options for quick meals. **Family Dollar** is a good stop for the budget shopper.

THE CHRISTMAS SHOP/ISLAND GALLERY
US 64/264, Manteo
(252) 473-2838
www.outerbankschristmas.com

Welcome to sparkle land! When Edward Greene closed down the historic Christmas Shop, both visitors and locals were amazed. The place had been a local landmark for around 40 years. Luckily, Mr. Greene decided about 2½ years after shutting the doors, to reopen with more magic and even more Christmas. All new, the Christmas Shop will inspire you to new levels of Christmas creativity, offering fine gifts, music boxes, jewelry, toys, decorations, and more. The Island Gallery has also returned. New are the 6 antiques shops, the Glass Spinner, and History Island. Reserve an afternoon to explore the labyrinthine interior. Kids of all ages love visiting here.

BURNSIDE BOOKS
US 64/264, Manteo
(252) 473-3311

Burnside carries office and art supplies and a selection of historical and children's books. Upstairs you'll find used hardback and paperback books and a North Carolina book section. It's open all year.

HOTLINE THRIFT SHOP
US 64/264, Manteo
(252) 473-3127

West of the Dare County Public Library, Hotline Thrift is a fund-raising shop for Outer Banks Hotline, a crisis intervention service that operates a shelter for battered women and their children. Hotline may be the most popular secondhand store on the Outer Banks. The bargain-priced inventory includes furniture, toys, books, knickknacks, and clothing for men, women, and children. It's open year-round.

Downtown Manteo

WANCHESE POTTERY
107 Fernando St., Manteo
(252) 473-2099

This artistic shop is a small business near the Waterfront on Fernando Street, where customers watch local potters Bonnie and Bob Morrill at work (see the Arts & Culture chapter). The shop is known locally for its beautiful, useful art, and it also features handmade baskets and fresh cooking herbs. It's open year-round, but call for winter hours.

FINE YARNS AT KIMBEEBA
Budleigh St., Manteo
(252) 473-6330
www.kimbeeba.com

Located beside the Pioneer Theatre, Kimbeeba stocks all types of yarns. Knitting, crocheting, felting, spinning, weaving—Kimbeeba has it all. Offering inspiration and guidance for your creativity, this shop is a find for the crafter with style.

MANTEO FURNITURE
209 Sir Walter Raleigh St., Manteo
(252) 473-2131

Manteo Furniture stocks a large selection of home and cottage furnishings ranging from traditional to contemporary. The store, which has been in operation more than 50 years, offers down-home friendly service. Allow yourself plenty of time to browse through the many rooms of this 48,000-square-foot showroom/warehouse. The company sells a full line of GE appliances and offers financing and free delivery. It's open year-round.

OUTER BANKS QUILTS AND ANTIQUES
108 Sir Walter Raleigh St., Manteo
(252) 473-4183

This large store carries the goods of more than 12 antiques and collectibles dealers. It's also the Outer Banks' only official quilt shop, with handmade quilts and quilting supplies.

MANTEO BOOKSELLERS
105 Sir Walter Raleigh St., Manteo
(252) 473-1221

Housed in charming quarters dotted with wing chairs, cozy corners, and quaint antiques, Manteo Booksellers is a must-browse for every reader. Three rooms are packed with books ranging from literary classics to delightful children's stories. The Outer Banks and Latin American sections (they also have books in Spanish) are excellent, as are the historical, self-help, Civil War, and North Carolina fiction areas. The cookbook selection is extensive.

The bookstore has a busy calendar filled with book signings and free readings by authors, poets, and storytellers. Manteo Booksellers is open year-round.

MY SECRET GARDEN
101 Sir Walter Raleigh St., Manteo
(252) 473-6880

Next door to Manteo Booksellers, My Secret Garden features Tiffany-style lamps, custom wreaths and swags, unique garden accessories and statuary, handmade birdhouses, and mermaid items. This shop offers hand-painted furniture, including mirrors, lamps, dressers, and servers, plus indoor fountains, collegiate items, pirate and mermaid gifts, and pottery. This is a charming shop with lots of gift ideas. It's open year-round.

OLD CREEF'S CORNER
Corner of Queen Elizabeth and Sir Walter Raleigh Streets, Manteo
Full Moon Cafe & Grill serves delicious and affordable food. It also sells T-shirts, inexpensive toys and candy for the kids, and small gift items. Next door is **Full Moon Brewery** where you can enjoy crafted beers.

CENTENNIAL SQUARE
Sir Walter Raleigh, Queen Elizabeth, and Fernando Streets, Manteo
This beautiful square of buildings offers interesting shops on the first level with apartments above. On the Sir Walter Raleigh Street side, you'll find **Art by Locals,** which has the artwork of Scott Geib, Emily Terrell, and more. Around the corner is **Muzzie's Antiques,** which offers an assortment of antiques and treasures. Estate and heirloom jewelry and garden statuary are just a few of the items. There are also furnishings, mosaic tables, painted furniture, lamps, trinket boxes, pillows galore, cards, and bath products.

THE WATERFRONT SHOPS
Queen Elizabeth Street, Manteo
Along the Manteo Waterfront sits this 4-story complex with businesses, restaurants, residential space, and covered parking.

Charlotte's is a quality women's boutique that features traditional and contemporary fine and casual clothing, accessories, gifts, and a beautiful sweater collection, including ones by designers Lisa Nichols and Michael Simon. The store is open year-round.

Island Accent Gifts showcases fine gifts and jewelry, often with a sea or nautical theme. If you're looking for locally produced items, stop in at **Roanoke Marshes Trading Company.** They offer such items by Outer Banks artists as shell candles, hand-painted glassware, and nautical wall decor. **Washed Ashore** displays handpainted landscapes, portraits, and artisan crafts.

MAGNOLIA MARKET SQUARE
Queen Elizabeth Street, Manteo
This group of shops is across from the Tranquil House Inn. **His Shells by Brenda** offers home decor and furniture decorated with shells. All pieces are guaranteed for life. **Nest** is an elegant and eclectic store brimming with good things for your home. Linens, jewelry, artisan fragrances, and clothing are just a few of the offerings here. **Theraroma** carries therapeutic organic essential oils at their aroma bar.

ENDLESS POSSIBILITIES
105 Budleigh St., Manteo
(252) 475-1575
This shop recycles, gives back to the community, and offers stylish accessories for sale all at once. Clothing specially selected from Hotline, a community thrift store, is shredded into strips. The fabric is then handwoven on looms into colorful boas, pocketbooks, rugs, and hats. Volunteers do the weaving, and proceeds benefit the Outer Banks Crisis Intervention and Prevention Center. Every item is custom made and one of a kind. You can pay a fee and weave your own item, if you are feeling creative. Open Mon through Sat from 10 a.m. to 5 p.m.

PHOENIX SHOPS
Between Budleigh and Ananias Dare Streets, Manteo
This strip of shops faces an inner courtyard instead of the street. **Something Special** is just that. Brimming with items from the

world over, you'll find unique gifts sure to please. **Inspired by the Sea** sells hand-painted furniture and decor pieces. Lighthouses and seascapes are often painted on their work.

ℹ️ On high traffic days making a left turn in your vehicle on US 158 (the Bypass) can be challenging. If you don't have the benefit of a traffic light, try an "Outer Banks left." Take a right turn and continue until you find a traffic light, then make your left. At that point you can either make a couple of turns and be back on US 158, or you can just take the beach road. It's faster and a lot safer to use the Outer Banks left strategy when traffic is clogged.

SLEEPING IN, LTD.
101 Fernando St., Manteo
(252) 475-1971
Surround yourself in luxury with goods from Sleeping In. High quality linens and fine loungewear are impossible to resist in this well appointed store. Shoppers also find lovely gifts, accessories, and lotions here.

NANCYWARE POTTERY
402 Queen Elizabeth St., Manteo
(252) 473-9400
www.nancywarepottery.com
In a building across from the Tranquil House Inn, this is the pottery studio of artist Nancy Hase. The potter's wheel is on display, and you can see her work from time to time. She also offers classes on the wheel. In this year-round shop you'll find Nancy's pottery, jewelry, and tile work. The pottery is high-fire functional stoneware that is dishwasher, microwave, and oven safe. Kitchen items include deep-dish fluted pie plates,

colanders, three-piece child dining sets that can be personalized, vases, dishes, and spoon rests.

400 BUDLEIGH ANTIQUE MALL
Budleigh Street, Manteo
(252) 473-9339
This mall features more than 25 rooms filled with antiques, furniture, and more. Vintage Christmas decorations and collectible kitchenware are among the popular items for sale.

THE MUSEUM SHOP
Roanoke Island Festival Park, Manteo
(252) 475-1500
This Museum Shop at Roanoke Island Festival Park goes beyond what you'd expect at a museum store. This store is huge, packed with historically themed gifts and items for the home. Inspired by Roanoke Island life and history, sections include Elizabethan, Civil War, nautical, and Native American themes. In the book section books about the Outer Banks are extensive, and there are handsome leather-bound blank journals and a wide range of music. In the Elizabethan section you'll find teapots, tea, biscuits, and other English items. The nautical section has books, telescopes, tide clocks, old maps, models, and more. The toys include hats, swords, and capes for playing dress-up. Jewelry, candy, food, games, gifts, and home decor items are all here.

Wanchese

After you cross Roanoke Sound westbound on the Nags Head–Manteo Causeway and pass Pirate's Cove, turn left at the next intersection onto NC 345 and head toward Wanchese. **In Season Out of Season** is a fun shop in Wanchese that carries nautically inspired items. Beaded jewelry, inspirational pieces, and metalwork pieces are some of just a few of the gift items this shop carries.

NATURE'S HARMONY
Shipyard Road, Manns Harbor
(252) 473-3556
www.naturesharmonynursery.com

Nature's Harmony is a full-scale nursery with three greenhouses specializing in herbs, perennials, and wildflowers. It offers a plant-maintenance service for your office or home. This store sells pottery and garden-related accessories plus fertilizers and mulches. Landscaping services are available. It's a lovely, peaceful spot that's open from Feb through Christmas.

HATTERAS ISLAND

Rodanthe

Rodanthe has several general stores where you can find groceries, camping and fishing supplies, bait, and seafood—the vacation necessities—and arty shopping experiences.

PAMLICO STATION SHOPS
NC 12, Rodanthe
(252) 987-1080

This 2-story shopping center is located on the east side of NC 12 in Rodanthe. **Moon Over Hatteras Gift Shoppes** has a great selection of gift items. **Hatteras T-Shirts** stocks T-shirts, hats, and accessories, plus hermit crabs. Bathing suits fill the **Surfside Casuals** shop, located on the first level. This store offers a great selection of clothing to make your shopping quest on Hatteras Island a success. The **Glass Bead/Beach Mugs** is a great spot where crafty types can

enjoy a Danish and a cup of tea or coffee while creating a new necklace or enjoying the free Wi-Fi.

THE ISLAND CONVENIENCE STORE
NC 12, Rodanthe
(252) 987-2239

This is one-stop shopping for groceries, rod and reel rentals, bait and tackle, propane gas, gasoline, and deli items, including breakfast biscuits, sandwiches, hand-dipped ice-cream cones, and fried chicken. You can take your food with you or eat at the tables. The store also carries souvenirs, gifts, and beach supplies and offers 24-hour wrecker service and auto repair. It's open year-round.

RODANTHE SURF SHOP
NC 12, Rodanthe
(252) 987-2412

Rodanthe Surf Shop has been the place to get your custom surfboard or really happening clothing for men, women, and kids for over 15 years.

SEA CHEST
NC 12, Rodanthe
(252) 987-2303

Calling all sea lovers to this treasure trove of souvenirs and collectibles. Antiques, kites, and more are all housed here under one roof.

REEF
NC 12, Rodanthe
(252) 987-2821

All your beach needs can be found in one stop at Reef. Stocking sunglasses, toys, towels, chairs, rash guards, and more, you'll be fully outfitted for the beach by the time you leave the store.

HATTERAS JACK
NC 12, Rodanthe
(252) 987-2428

All types of quality brand name fishing equipment can be found at Hatteras Jack's. Custom rods and reels are fine tuned to give fishermen the edge to catch the big one. Bait and tackle are available here. If you'd like some free friendly expert advice, this is definitely the place to come.

PIRATES OF CHICAMACOMICO
NC 12, Rodanthe
(252) 987-2402

Arrrgggghh. All things pirate spoken here. Toys, gifts, and more await.

OCEAN GOURMET AND GIFTS
NC 12, Rodanthe
(252) 987-1166

Just north of Camp Hatteras, this is the place to come for fresh fudge, ice cream, and candy. Other vacation necessities are available, too, such as hermit crabs, fireworks, bathing suits, beachwear, and nautical gifts and lighthouses.

Waves

Waves is home to only a few businesses, including **Hatteras Island Surf Shop** (see the Water Sports chapter) and **Michael Halminski's Photography Gallery** (see the Arts and Culture chapter for details). **Kitty Hawk Kites** is a traditional stop when visiting the Outer Banks. Find kites, toys for all ages, and outdoor wear for the adventure minded. **St. Waves Seafood and Produce** provides fresh seafood, angus steaks, homemade desserts, and more.

WAVES VILLAGE

Waves Village is the newest addition for the adventure minded kiteboarding fans and their families. Nine luxury condos are located on the sound, with shopping areas on site. **Kitty Hawk Kites** offers much more than kites. Find great T-shirts, jewelry, shoes, toys, and more at this Outer Banks legendary institution. **Route 12 Coffee and Teas** stocks coffee, teas, and pastries. **Life Is Good** offers a line of clothing and adventure wear. **Forbes Candies** will satisfy any sweet tooth.

Salvo

Salvo is a sleepy little village, so don't expect much in the way of shopping.

THE BLUE WHALE
NC 12, Salvo
(252) 987-2335

The Blue Whale offers a mix of the usual beach items (T-shirts, groceries, beach supplies) and the unusual (gourmet coffees and hot sauces). The Blue Whale imports beer and wine and specializes in jams, jellies, and salad dressings. Crafts created by Jeanette and Laura are sold here.

ISLAND TATTOO/ISLAND DYES
NC 12, Waves
(252) 987-2465

Four artists are available to give you a permanent souvenir of your Outer Banks vacation. Body piercing is available too. Next door at Island Dyes, get your groove on with tie-dye shirts and loads of fun accessories.

HOME PORT GIFTS
NC 12, Waves
(252) 987-1550

Home Port Gifts is one of the loveliest upscale gift shops on the Outer Banks. Original artwork, crafts, and exquisite jewelry in fine silver and 14-karat gold (much of it with a nautical theme) will tempt you. You'll find quality accessories for the home and nautical antiques, including Tiffany-style stained-glass pieces, nautical sculptures, handcarved decoys, terra-cotta sculptures, and sea candles by Sally Knuckles. The work of about 120 artists is on display.

FISHIN' HOLE
NC 12, Salvo
(252) 987-2351

The Fishin' Hole is best known as a general tackle shop, but the shop, open Apr through mid-Dec, also sells beach supplies and groceries.

PEA ISLAND ART GALLERY
NC 12, Salvo
(252) 987-2879

Housed in a beautiful building suggesting an old lifesaving station, Pea Island Art Gallery represents local and regional artists. Stop in for a browse and know that a portion of any purchase will benefit Pea Island Wildlife Refuge or Chicamacomico Life Saving Station.

Avon

ISLAND SHOPPES
NC 12, Avon

This small shopping center houses two of the Outer Banks' most popular stores—**Sawgrass Gallery** and **Kitty Hawk Kites.** Kitty Hawk Kites is a sports store selling kites and offering kayak ecotours, kiteboarding lessons, and parasailing. It's also an outfitter, selling sporty outdoor clothes and gear for all your adventures.

SANDCASTLES
NC 12, Avon
(252) 995-7171
www.sandcastlesavon.com

Sandcastles is a store made from dreams and sand. Local art, unique jewelry, windchimes, and hand-made kaleidoscopes offer a dreamy shopping experience.

THE FISHERMAN'S DAUGHTER
NC 12, Avon
(252) 995-6148

The Fisherman's Daughter offers clothing from the Brighton collection, items from Vera Bradley, and other popular name brands, along with Pandora jewelry. Filled with one of a kind finds, it carries OBX and HI products, Yankee Candles, and Cat's Meow. Check out the souvenir and gift area upstairs.

MILL CREEK GIFTS
NC 12, Avon
(252) 995-3188

This true Hatteras Island shop, owned by a real local, is filled with delightful gifts. Mermaids, fairies, and angels abound, and lighthouse collectibles and candles, seashells, and souvenirs wait on the shelves. Wind chimes catch the constant breeze, while fish mobiles and stained glass twinkle in the sun.

AVON SURF SHOP
NC 12, Avon
(252) 995-4783

No attitude here, just a good selection of surfboards, skateboards, and accessories. Surfwear is available here for men, women, and little ones. Surf lessons and board rentals are offered here as well. Newtons Surfboards from local shaper Mark Newton are available here.

ISLAND SPICE AND WINE
NC 12, Avon
(252) 995-7750
Island Spice and Wine is a little bit of wine heaven. Specializing in California, Italian, and French wines, it has some tasty accompaniments, including gourmet coffees, foods, and cheeses. How about a gourmet gift basket? You can sneak in some neat kitchen gadgets or cute cookie cutters. There are wine racks, serving ware, barbecue tools, Gourmet Kitchen cooking supplies, and cookbooks. A selection of specialty beer and Asian food products includes sushi-making supplies. An expanded gift section carries North Carolina food products, such as delicious sauces and preserves and organic North Carolina cooking wine flavored with basil, tarragon, and rosemary. Check out the line of collectibles, huge mug selection, angel items, and whimsical salt and pepper shakers. The store is open year-round.

NAGS HEAD HAMMOCKS
NC 12, Avon
(252) 995-3744
www.nagshead.com
Here's another branch of the Outer Banks' legendary hammock shop. Nags Head Hammocks are known for their sturdiness. Select from traditional hammocks, hammock porch chairs, hammock tables, hammock swings, or hammock stools. Fitted pillows make them even more comfortable.

DAIRY QUEEN SHOPPING CENTER
NC 12, Avon
Take a break from the sun and while away an afternoon in the Dairy Queen Shopping Center. The **Glass Bead** has all the supplies for jewelry making, including a fabulous selection of beads. Crystal beads, handmade

beads, and semiprecious stones make up just a part of the selection. The painting and photography of artist Zofia Lategano is featured in **Zofia's Art Gallery.** Art classes for kids are offered, too. If shopping for windsurfing gear is on your list, stop in at **Sailworld,** with its complete range of windsurfing and kiteboarding accessories.

✳ASKINS CREEK STORE
NC 12, Avon
(252) 995-6283
Askins Creek is the southernmost shopping spot in Avon. Askins Creek is a well stocked store offering tackle, beach items, books, and grocery needs. Check out the jewelry too! Out back, you can wash the salt air off of your vehicle or boat in the carwash.

COUNTRY ELEGANCE
Harbor Road, Avon
(252) 995-6269
As you head south, if you turn right on Harbor Road at the only stoplight south of Whalebone Junction, you'll come across this store in Old Avon Village. It features birdhouses, aromatherapy oils, lighthouses, handpainted shirts, antique quilted heirlooms, whimsical art, designer dolls, and baskets. There are also wood crafts, cake candles, and lots and lots of lace. This shop is open Easter through mid-November.

DOCKSIDE HATTERAS
NC 12, Avon
(252) 995-5445
Dockside Hatteras carries gifts, furnishings, and home accents. Shoppers will find home necessities like mattresses, dishes, and pots and pans. Dockside Hatteras also carries high-density deck furniture. Free setup and delivery are offered from Ocracoke to Corolla.

HATTERAS ISLAND TOY STORE
NC 12, Avon
(252) 995-7171

Toys for kids of all ages are stocked at the Hatteras Island Toy Store, including popular toys like Groovy Girls and Thomas the Tank Engine, plus educational toys, art supplies, puppets, puzzles, and games.

VILLAGE GROCERY
NC 12, Avon
(252) 995-4402

The Village Grocery is a one-stop shop that carries everything a regular grocery store does while catering to your specialty needs. Boar's Head deli meats, certified Angus beef, organic foods, and gourmet cheeses are just some of the finer items. A convenient salad bar and delicious Boar's Head sandwiches, wraps, and panini are available for a quick lunch or dinner. Open year-round. Located next to Kinnakeet Corner.

HATTERAS ISLAND BOARDSPORTS
NC 12, Avon
(252) 995-6160
www.hiboardsports.com

The island-style decor in this shop invites you to enter and browse clothing and equipment or get serious about surfing, windsurfing, and kitesurfing. Buy or rent equipment, have a lesson, and see Hatteras Island from a different perspective on a kayak tour in Pamlico Sound.

HATTERAS PLAZA
NC 12, Avon

This Avon plaza is anchored by **Food Lion** and an **Ace Hardware** store. **Jewels By the Sea** showcases local and Hawaiian jewelry. Jewels also carries sunglasses, Italian handbags, and designer perfumes. **Ocean**

Threads and **Surfside Casuals,** right next door to each other, have similar offerings—surfwear by Billabong, Roxy, and others plus bathing suits, T-shirts, sandals, sunglasses, and stickers. On the other end of the plaza is **Island Cycle,** which rents, repairs, and sells bicycles. **Beach Pharmacy** sells an assortment of arts and crafts supplies besides the usual drugstore items. **Try My Nuts** has yummy treats of all types, including, of course, nuts. Chocolates, candy, popcorn, and even T-shirts are sold here. Dining choices include **La Fogata Mexican Restaurant, Chinatown** Chinese restaurant, and **Cafe 12. Sweet N Simple Pleasures** sells fudge alongside jewelry and gifts. ✳**This Little Cottage** has all the best for your home, like Pine Cone Hill, Matteo, and Serena and Lily.

If you'd like to keep the rest of the family entertained while you shop, drop them off at **RC Theaters.** The theater has four showings daily of first-run films during summer.

Buxton

A 5-mile drive south of Avon through Cape Hatteras National Seashore brings you to the village of Buxton, where your discoveries will range from a general store and bait and tackle shop to specialty boutiques. Buxton's market, **Conner's,** offers groceries and basic supplies year-round.

DAYDREAMS
NC 12, Buxton
(252) 995-5548

Daydreams has earned a reputation for having stylish clothing and a selection of top name brands such as Patagonia, Dansko, and Birkenstock. The shop, open Mar through Christmas, carries clothing for men, women, and children, plus accessories and jewelry.

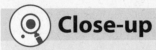 **Close-up**

Native American Outer Banks Place Names

The original inhabitants of the Outer Banks were Croatan "Indians," a part of the Algonquin tribe, and their tribal name lives on as the name of the Croatan Sound. As a result of their interactions with the early explorers and the famous "Lost Colony," many place names from the native language were adopted, and some are still in use today.

Two local tribal chiefs, Manteo and Wanchese, lent their names to the two towns on Roanoke Island, and Roanoke itself is an early Algonquin name. Hatteras is an English rendition of a Native American word that meant "there is less vegetation"—on the early maps it was 'Hattorask' and referred to an area north of modern day Hatteras. The town of Avon was originally Kinnakeet, meaning "that which is mixed," and "Chicamacomico" was the early name for the area that is now Rodanthe, Waves, and Salvo. Anyone who has pulled off the road there and gotten stuck might guess the Native American meaning of Chicamacomico: "place of sinking down sand." Ocracoke is another derivation of an Algonquin name, written on early maps as "Woccocon" and "Ococcock." Currituck comes from the early name "Cortank" meaning "wild goose," and another spelling, "Caratoke," is the name for route 158 in Currituck county. Other Native American names in the area include Chowan and Mattamuskeet.

DILLON'S CORNER
NC 12, Buxton
(252) 995-5083

This bait and tackle shop carries fishing rods, including custom-built ones. It is also jammed with gifts, Yankee Candles, jewelry, pottery, lighthouse replicas, T-shirts, and a bevy of Beanie Babies. Gas is available as well. It's open year-round.

THE COTTAGE SHOP
NC 12, Buxton
(252) 995-3960

A bright yellow building serves as a beacon for those interested in functional and imaginative decor. Inside the Cottage Shop shoppers find items for the kitchen, bedroom, porch, and garden and pretty much the rest of the home. Rental-cottage packages are offered to outfit your entire home.

NATURAL ART SURF SHOP
NC 12, Buxton
(252) 995-5682

Natural Art is owned by Scott and Carol Busbey, serious surfers who love the sport and the lifestyle. During the 25-plus years the shop has been in business, it has gained a reputation for being "the surfer's surf shop," specializing in surfing only. Scott, who has his own line of boards called In The Eye, manufactures custom boards and does repairs. Carol makes clothing (her hand-sewn women's and men's tops and children's shirts and dresses are unique and colorful). The shop rents surfboards, boogie boards, swim fins, wet suits, and surf videos and sells surfing gear, clothing, T-shirts, and sweatshirts. It's open Mar through Dec. (See the Water Sports chapter for more information.)

i Brew-Thru convenience stores are a must-stop for visitors to the Outer Banks. Nothing's better on a hot summer day than driving through one of these five well-placed stores for a cold beverage. Sodas, water, beer, T-shirts, and more are delivered to your car door, and you never have to get out of the car. Most everyone stops at Brew-Thru, even if just for the novelty of this fun place.

OSPREY SHOPPING CENTER
NC 12, Buxton

Osprey is behind Natural Art Surf Shop and Rusty's Surf and Turf Restaurant and has an ABC package store. **Ocean Notions Gift Shop** has a selection of gifts, including candles, bath products, and nautical trinkets as well as women's and men's clothing and a small selection of children's apparel. Look no further for beach supplies and a selection of gold and silver jewelry. It's open Mar through mid-December.

BUXTON VILLAGE BOOKS
NC 12, Buxton
(252) 995-4240

Comfortably nestled in what was once the summer kitchen of an island house, Buxton Village Books has been a village landmark since 1984. This charming space is packed with lots of good reads, including all the current best sellers, sea stories, hard-to-find southern fiction, kids' books, and saltwater fly-fishing titles. In a room overlooking Pamlico Sound, you can browse over a delightful selection of notecards and stationery. The owner, Gee Gee, is an avid reader and willing to discuss literature. The shop has a public fax machine; ask about the shop's mail-order catalog. It's open year-round.

Frisco
ISLANDER GIFTS
NC 12, Frisco
(252) 995-5427

An incredible selection of gifts and souvenirs awaits you at Islander Gifts. Shoppers can purchase anything from a seashell to Christmas ornaments. You'll also find home decor pieces, pirate toys, and bird carvings.

INDIAN TOWN GALLERY AND GIFTS
NC 12, Frisco

Nestled in the woods, Indian Town represents artists from the local villages. Many of the paintings have an Outer Banks offshore-fishing theme. The gallery also features pottery, chimes, cards, gifts, lighthouses, and jewelry. Artist Wayne Fulcher is often at work right in the store. A coffee shop is on site, and free Wi-Fi is available.

RED DRUM POTTERY
NC 12, Frisco
(252) 995-5757

Accomplished potters Rhonda Bates and Wes Lassiter moved their studio from Edenton, North Carolina, to Frisco in 2001. Watch them as they turn their wonderful creations at the wheel. These are well-crafted, artistic pieces, whether intended for functional or decorative use. It's definitely worth a stop to see their bowls, pitchers, vases, vessels, platters, teakettles, miniatures, and fabulous fish- and crab-imprinted hanging wall tiles. In late afternoons these hospitable potters invite customers to paint a piece of pottery and fire it raku-style. The gallery is open seven days a week year-round.

SCOTCH BONNET FUDGES
NC 12, Frisco
(252) 995-4242

The sweetest spot on Hatteras Island has homemade fudge (more than 20 varieties, including sugar free), ice cream, bulk taffy, Jelly Belly jelly beans, and other sweet treats. Scotch Bonnet also carries T-shirts, sweatshirts, jewelry, gifts, hermit crabs, and accessories. Don't miss the hermit crab races every Friday during the summer. The homemade fudge here is so good that it has been featured on the Food Network.

ALL DECKED OUT
NC 12, Frisco
(252) 995-4319, (800) 321-2392
www.obxoutdoorfurniture.com
Owner Dale Cashman and his crew handcraft outdoor furniture such as picnic tables, Adirondack chairs, benches, wooden recliners, and hammocks, and they ship anywhere in the United States. Stop by and try a seat. It's open year-round with the exception of two weeks at Christmas. Call for a free catalog.

HATTERAS TRADING COMPANY
NC 12, Frisco
(252) 995-9990
www.hatterastradingcompany.com
The perky pink building invites you to come inside and explore the island-style furnishings stocked within. Home, patio, and Tiki bar items along with handmade wood and metal art can be purchased here. Pick up beach items, Hawaiian shirts, hula wear, and the popular windblocks, too.

FRISCO ROD & GUN
NC 12, Frisco
(252) 995-5366
www.friscorodgun.com
Frisco Rod & Gun is directly across from the entrance road to ramp 49 and Billy Mitchell Air Field. Frisco Rod & Gun specializes in fishing and hunting equipment, including offshore, inshore, and surf-fishing equipment, as well as fly-fishing equipment, guns, ice, bait, tackle, and one of the best selections of knives we've seen anywhere. The local owners carry camping supplies, namebrand outdoor apparel, Sperry Topsiders, Woolrich, Hook & Tackle, foul weather gear, and T-shirts, and offer free air for your tires. They are open year-round.

Hatteras Village

Hatteras Village offers a mixture of services, including a pharmacy, grocery store, and other shops. The ferry terminal's **Ship's Store,** located in the lobby, offers T-shirts, coffee mugs, coloring books, and souvenirs.

STOWE ON TWELVE
NC 12, Hatteras Village
Stowe on Twelve houses several upscale stores worth venturing into. **Beach Diva** brings West Coast clothing, accessories, and footwear to the extreme East Coast. The look here is fashion forward, and the owner will help shoppers find just the right look. **Hwy 12 PhotoArts** sells a selection of photographs and more. **Fox Watersports** has the latest in surf fashion. **Family Jewels** offers jewelry from Pandora and Sweet Romance. The owner's custom handmade jewelry is a must-have. Signature billfish images designed with a chuckle in mind are offered at **Karen Rhodes Billfish Art.** Karen has billfish images on just about anything you can imagine—T-shirts, flip-flops, tiles, and more. She offers a humorous take on the life of a billfish. **Sally Newell Interiors** is a wonderful home furnishings shop. Sally offers design services; please call for an appointment.

BEACON SHOPS
NC 12, Hatteras Village

At the north end of Hatteras Village, this group of tempting shops will brighten anyone's day. **Sandy Bay Gallery** showcases Outer Banks artists. Filled with original paintings, local photography, pottery, and jewelry, this shop can ship any item you purchase. Find Flax clothing alongside the Kiko line, Click, and April Cornell at **Izabelle's Closet.** Pick up some great food items at the **Salty Gourmet.**

BURRUS' RED & WHITE SUPERMARKET
NC 12, Hatteras Village
(252) 986-2333

A Hatteras Village tradition, Burrus' Red & White has been serving locals and visitors since 1866. It carries seafood and freshly cut meat and has a full-service deli and salad bar. You'll also find gourmet and Eight O'clock coffee, fresh produce, frozen foods, dairy products, and health and beauty aids. This market, a locals' favorite and a welcome respite from chain grocery stores, is open year-round.

HATTERAS HARBOR MARINA STORE
Hatteras Marina, NC 12, Hatteras Village
(252) 986-2166

The marina store has jewelry, name-brand sportswear, fishing supplies, unique gifts, deck shoes, and other items. Geared to please visitors, it's open year-round and caters to charterboat fishermen and their families.

LEE ROBINSON GENERAL STORE
NC 12, Hatteras Village
(252) 986-2381
www.obag.com

The original Lee's opened in 1948 but was replaced by a replica several years ago. We're glad it kept the old look, including the wide front porch and the wooden floors.

Lee Robinson carries items you need for a vacation at the beach, plus something you wouldn't necessarily expect to find at a beach general store: a great selection of fine wine. The store carries groceries (including gourmet items), chocolates, fudge, books and magazines, T-shirts, sweatshirts, jewelry and gifts, plus sundries such as film, lotions, boogie boards, and hats. Don't miss the upstairs gift gallery. It's a good place to buy a Coke in a glass bottle and something to snack on for the ferry ride to Ocracoke. It's open year-round.

HATTERAS LANDING
NC 12, Hatteras Village
(252) 986-2205

Right next to the Hatteras–Ocracoke ferry docks at the southern end of Hatteras Village, this spiffy shopping center means you'll never again have a boring wait for the ferry. The only problem is that people get carried away with shopping and are late for boarding.

Birthday Suits/OBX Gear is an Outer Banks favorite, carrying fashionable swimwear for the whole family. For hard-to-fit women, there are bra-size tops that can be mixed with separate bottoms, plus long-torso suits and maternity suits. Men's sizes range from 28 to 4XL and include competition briefs and volleyball and surf trunks. Kids' swimwear ranges from size 2 to preteen, as well as swim diapers. Birthday Suits has a huge selection of OBX gear and contemporary sportswear for women, men, and children.

Farmer's Daughter brings a country-casual look to your home. Gifts and collectibles are the hallmarks of this store, which is an Outer Banks favorite. There are also original artworks by Outer Banks artisans, and the world's first and only supply of saltwater fudge. **Parrot Bay** offers seashores gifts, tropical decor, and beach apparel for the whole family.

Kitty Hawk Kites/Carolina Outdoors is an outdoor store selling kites, toys, outdoor apparel, sunglasses, sportswear, and more. This location has a rock-climbing wall right in the middle of the shopping center.

OCRACOKE ISLAND

Shopping in Ocracoke is casual, interesting, and easily managed on foot. Small shops are scattered throughout the village and along the main street, on sandy lanes, and in private homes. You'll discover that some dockside stores have the feel of a general store. Ocracoke Village shops offer local crafts, artwork, quality accessories for the home, antiques, beachwear, books, music, and magazines as well as the ubiquitous T-shirts and even a few souvenir mugs. An ABC package store is adjacent to the Ocracoke Variety Store.

OCRACOKE VARIETY STORE
NC 12, Ocracoke
(252) 928-4911
Ocracoke Variety is on NC 12 before you enter the village from the north. Shop for groceries and fresh meat, beer, wine, T-shirts, beachwear and accessories, ice, gifts, books, magazines, camping and fishing supplies, household items, health and beauty aids, and even a few art supplies. **True Value Hardware** is conveniently located next door. There's a bulletin board posted at the front entrance featuring menus of the local restaurants and community information. Open all year.

PIRATE'S CHEST GIFTS AND T-SHIRTS
11 Back Rd., Ocracoke
(252) 928-4992

Peruse the variety of merchandise sold here: T-shirts, souvenirs, jewelry, local shells, books, scrimshaw, coral, lighthouse prints, 14-karat gold jewelry, Joan Perry sculptures, and more. Look for the shell-filled boat in the parking lot. The store is open Mar through Nov.

✴ISLAND RAGPICKER
NC 12, Ocracoke
(252) 928-7571
Island Ragpicker will catch your eye with an attractive mixture of bells, baskets, and hand-woven rugs displayed on the porch and everywhere inside. This exciting and imaginative store offers fine quality crafts (some by local craftspeople), handmade brooms, rugs, cards, decoys, pottery, dishes, jewelry, and casual cotton apparel. Look for local and nature books, short story collections, and self-help books along with an amazing assortment of easy-listening music. The Ragpicker has great cards. The shop is open Mar through Dec.

SPENCER'S MARKET
School Road and NC 12, Ocracoke
This shopping complex houses the **Gathering Place,** featuring nautical decor along with gifts, art, and impressive folding knives. Pick up some stylin' shades at the **Sunglasses Shop. Zillies Island Pantry** stocks needs for your dining creations. Takeout from **Thai Moon** is always delicious.

DEEPWATER POTTERY & BOOKS TO BE RED
School Road and NC 12, Ocracoke
(252) 928-7472 (Deepwater Pottery),
(252) 928-3936 (Books to Be Red)
On the corner of School Road and NC 12, a lovely historic home under a canopy of trees houses these two wonderful shops.

Deepwater Pottery is a working pottery studio and gift shop, carrying handmade stoneware, candles, and glass; surprising home and garden accents; and a special bath section, which is filled with soaps and other great-smelling bath luxuries. The bath section carries Burt's Bees products. Books to Be Red has a wonderful selection of books by local authors, New Age journals, magazines, cards, and a paperback section of fiction, nonfiction, and children's books. There's a section of gently used books. The shop is open Mar 1 through Christmas.

NATURAL SELECTIONS HEMP SHOP
School Road, Ocracoke
(252) 928-HEMP
Natural Selections, the Ocracoke Island Hemp Shop, offers a great selection of products made from hemp and other natural fibers. Natural Selections is a socially and environmentally conscious shop, committed to the belief that the use of hemp will save the planet from herbicides, pesticides, fertilizers, and deforestation. Once you feel the natural fibers, you'll want to wear the pants, dresses, shirts, jackets, and hats sold here. Natural Selections also sells bags, hemp home accessories, natural cosmetics, jewelry, and gifts.

CAPTAIN'S LANDING
NC 12 on Silver Lake, Ocracoke
Just past the Jolly Roger Pub and Marina is this little conglomeration of shops, not really connected but clustered around the post office. **Downpoint Decoys,** a small rustic shop under an old oak tree, sells decoys both old and new, and the local carver/proprietor is available to talk to. He also sells lures, painted oars, and wildlife art.

*MERMAID'S FOLLY
Irvin Garrish Highway, Ocracoke
(252) 928-RAGS
At this shop you'll find finely crafted works of art. The clothing, T-shirts, hats, bags, and jewelry are imaginative and casual, making this store a fun place to shop. It also has furniture, trunks, lamps, and home accessories.

THE COMMUNITY STORE
Ocracoke Waterfront, Ocracoke
(252) 928-3321
Operating since 1918, the Community Store is the place to shop for essential items in the heart of Ocracoke Village. Walking through the door is like stepping back in time. There's a cooler full of ice cream and frosty-cold sodas and beer.

HARBORSIDE GIFT SHOP
NC 12, Ocracoke
(252) 928-3111
Harborside is one of the many pleasant surprises for visitors to Ocracoke. Quality sportswear for the family, a gourmet food section, gift basket service (some ready-mades are available), teas, cooking items, pottery, books, and magazines share the shop with an interesting collection of T-shirts and—look up!—a model train that chugs along overhead throughout most of the store. You'll also find domestic and imported wine and beer. It's open Easter through Thanksgiving.

VILLAGE CRAFTSMEN
Howard Street, Ocracoke
(252) 928-5541, (800) 648-9743
Village Craftsmen is an Ocracoke landmark—it's been in business more than 30 years—but it isn't as easy to find as, say, the lighthouse. The shop is on the narrow dirt

lane known as Howard Street, a bit of a walk from the main street. Here you'll discover an abundance of North Carolina crafts, pottery, rugs, books, locally made soaps, candles, and jewelry. You can buy stoneware, tie-dyed dresses, and T-shirts, too.

Owner Philip Howard, a seventh-generation Ocracoke Island resident, sells his pen-and-ink and watercolor prints in his shop. A fine selection of cassettes and CDs features Celtic, blues, jazz, and bluegrass music. Musical instruments, such as catpaws and strum-sticks, help set a creative mood at this out-of-the-way place. The instruments are lightweight and simple to play. You can pick up a mail-order catalog at the shop or have one mailed to you. Village Craftsmen closes for the month of Jan.

i Walk in any direction in the heart of Ocracoke, and soon you'll notice little signs that point down narrow lanes to marvelous galleries and shops. Some are tucked into the woods; others are in garages or little buildings behind artists' houses. Each one is a treasure in itself.

✳OVER THE MOON
British Cemetery Road, Ocracoke
(252) 928-3555

Over the Moon is a wonderful shop filled with handmade contemporary crafts. More than 100 artists and craftspeople provide work such as jewelry, porcelain, and Story-People—Brian Andreas's books, prints, and sculptures with insights written on the work. There are pins and magnet cards, Metamorphicards, and hammock chairs. Pace yourself; this is a place to linger. It is open Easter through Thanksgiving.

ISLAND ARTWORKS
British Cemetery Road, Ocracoke
(252) 928-3892

A brightly colored little shop across from Over the Moon, Island Artworks is a fun place to browse. It's a contemporary craft gallery with colorful jewelry by local artist Kathleen O'Neal; fused glass and mosaics by Libby Hicks; photography, watercolors, pottery, woodworking, sculpture, mosaics, birdbaths, garden stakes, and more.

TEACH'S HOLE
Back Road, Ocracoke
(252) 928-1718
www.teachshole.com

Come listen to the tales of the notorious Edward Teach—better known as Blackbeard the Pirate—at Teach's Hole. The "piratical pirate-phernalia," as George and Mickey Roberson call their collection, includes a gift shop and exhibit. More than 1,000 pirate items, including a life-size re-creation of Blackbeard in full battle dress and artifacts from the 17th and 18th centuries, form the exhibit. One exhibit features "Blackbeard's Doom" on an eight-minute video viewed for a fee. Items in the gift shop include pirate toys, music boxes, movies, and more than 100 pirate book titles, plus maps, flags, hats, T-shirts, costumes, ship models, and treasure coins. For more information see the Kidstuff chapter. Teach's Hole is open Easter though Thanksgiving from 10 a.m. to 6 p.m., Mon through Sat.

OCRACOKE RESTORATION CO.
NC 12, Ocracoke
(252) 928-2669
www.ocracokerestoration.com

Formerly known as Roadhouse Stained Glass Co. of Ocracoke, Ocracoke Restoration carries antique English stained glass, wrought-iron gates, and other decorative items. Most of their glass decorates windows and doors, though smaller stained-glass pieces, many originally from porch lanterns, can be found here. You can find such imports as lamps and garden pieces, plus an occasional armoire or table. The store is open from Mar through Jan. Shipping is available anywhere.

*RIDE THE WIND SURF & KAYAK
NC 12 and Silver Lake, Ocracoke
(252) 928-6311
www.surfocracoke.com

Open Apr through Christmas, Ride the Wind Surf & Kayak offers complete surfing equipment and gear, swimsuits, ladies' and men's clothing, shoes, sandals, handbags, suntan lotions, sunglasses, watches, and jewelry. See the Water Sports chapter for surf and boogie board rentals as well as kayak tour information.

OCRACOKE ISLAND TRADING COMPANY
NC 12, Ocracoke
(252) 928-7233

This Aussie outfitter sells casual clothing. T-shirts range from size small to XXXL, adorned with "Ocracoke" or funny sayings. The store also stocks sportswear, hats, dresses, fishprint clothing, shorts, and more. If you're looking for gift items and souvenirs, look here.

BELLA FIORE POTTERY
109 Lighthouse Rd., Ocracoke
(252) 928-2826

Talented artist Sarah Fiore creates colorful handmade pottery in this working artist studio and gallery. She also features natural body products, lampworked hair picks, and other art pieces.

VILLAGE DIVA
NC 12, Ocracoke
(252) 928-2828

Step into Village Diva and marvel at the incredible selection of women's clothing. Lines like CP Shades and Flax are sold here. Village Diva also carries home accessories and garden accents.

*SILVER LAKE TRADING CO.
Back Road near British Cemetery Road, Ocracoke
(252) 928-3086

Silver Lake Trading Co. is one of the best gift shops on Ocracoke Island, with goods that are eccentric, fun, and fashionable. You'll find things for your home and garden, including Christopher Radko ornaments, Asian-inspired pottery, locally made pottery and wooden bowls, picture frames, funky lamps, Sandra Drennen linens, pillows, candles and soaps, garden statues, and even plants. Other goods include off-the-wall refrigerator magnets and poetry kits, lunch boxes, unique toys, naughty but hilarious cards and cocktail napkins, and Dirty Girl soap and bubble bath.

KIDSTUFF

The beach is always a popular lure for children. They can play tag with the waves, build whimsical sandcastles, fly a kite, play volleyball, or dig for treasure they just know has been left. The Outer Banks is a large sandy playground, with opportunities for exploration that are only limited by your imagination. For kids this means the possibilities are infinite, especially on sunny days at the beach. Be sure to check out the Waves and Weather chapter so your children have a safe vacation at the beach. If the skies are overcast or the temperature too cold to play by the shore, they'll need a little more help from you (and us!) to entertain themselves.

Read the chapters on Recreation, Attractions, and Water Sports for a more complete listing of activities children will enjoy. Kidstuff takes a look at the not-so-obvious as well as some favorites.

KIDS' FAVORITE THINGS TO DO

The Beach

They dig for coquinas, those tiny crablike creatures that burrow frantically into the wet sand when the surf pulls away from the beach. They chase sand crabs and sandpipers and poke at jellyfish with sticks. They draw in the sand, construct structures both simple and intricate, and cover themselves and others with sand, making you grateful that so many Outer Banks accommodations have outdoor showers so you can wash off at the end of the day. (As a convenience to visitors, some townships and villages offer public restrooms and shower facilities at one or more beach access areas.)

Little kids who aren't old enough or confident enough to immerse themselves in the ocean still find endless ways to enjoy the beach. They need adults to keep them safe (more on that shortly), keep them fed and watered, and then get out of the way of their creativity unless they make you the object of it.

An inflatable baby pool makes a day shoreside more pleasant for infants and toddlers. Set it up under a big umbrella and toss in some floating toys. Buckets and shovels and boogie boards are essential equipment for slightly older kids. Even if they're not old enough to ride the waves, little kids like to sit or lie on boogie boards at the very edge of the water. Older kids tend to gravitate to more expensive props such as body boards and surfboards.

At the risk of stating the obvious, here are a few things to remember about kids on the beach: Keep your young ones slathered in sunscreen, reapplying it frequently. Never take your eyes off them at the ocean or the sound, and stay within close range. The surf, even where it is most shallow, is rough; undertows and currents are insidious. There are sudden drop-offs and deep holes in the ocean and the sound. Keep kids away from the water when the red warning flags are flying.

Please read carefully about beach safety, and choose a section of the beach that is served by lifeguards. A list of guarded beaches is provided in the Waves and Weather chapter.

If you have very young children, a soundside beach is a more tranquil alternative to the ocean. The gentle waters are perfect for children, enabling them to build their confidence and their swimming skills.

i **If skimboarders are playing in the surf, don't let your tot get too near the action. Skimboards travel fast and are very sturdy. An out-of-control board can cause onlookers a painful ankle injury.**

Fishing or Crabbing

Soundside Beaches, Docks & Piers

Many a grown-up's most cherished childhood memories involve fishing at the Outer Banks. It's a wonderful way for you and your kids to share special time together.

You can rent or buy equipment at a tackle shop (see the Fishing chapter) or at a pier. Along with your equipment, get some advice on what's biting, what to use to catch it, and where to find it. Stake out a spot at the surf or head to one of the piers.

For a unique experience treat the family to an excursion on a headboat, which offers per-person rates for half-day charters. Rookie anglers get plenty of help with their rods and reels, which are supplied, from experienced mates. Many passengers go along

for the ride and spectacular scenery. Either way it's a comfortable and affordable way to experience the Outer Banks from the water, which insiders consider an essential part of the Outer Banks experience. Check the Fishing chapter for more information on the headboats that operate in the area. Also refer to the Recreation chapter for information on sunset and moonlight cruises.

Crabbing can be particularly memorable. If you dig in the early morning or late afternoon, you'll probably have more crabs to steam at the end of the day. Head west to the sounds. Try the soundside beaches or the soundside piers in Kitty Hawk on Kitty Hawk Bay (off West Tateway and Windgrass Circle) and in Kill Devil Hills (on Orville Beach between Durham and Avalon Streets). In Corolla there are some good crabbing spots near the Whalehead Club. One of the most popular locations is on Big Colington Island, below the second bridge on Colington Road near the firehouse. On Hatteras Island, crab in the sound at any quiet soundside location in the national seashore.

Part of the fun of crabbing is rigging the simple equipment. You don't need to invest in crab traps or special bait. Fishing line, chicken necks, a net, and a deep bucket or cooler will do just fine. Tie a chicken neck to the end of your string, dangle it in the water, and wait for the crabs to come. Then scoop them up (quickly) with the net. It'll take a few tries, but you'll get the hang of it. Grown-ups or older kids can wield the net for the little ones. To free the crab from the net, don't use your hands; dangle the net over the cooler and wiggle it free. Tell the kids to keep their fingers out of the bucket!

If your catch measures 5 inches or less at the widest part of the shell, you have to throw it back. (Not only is this the law, but it will help ensure another batch of crabs for next year's visit.) Keep only "keepers," the ones that measure more than 6 inches.

The best part of crabbing, like fishing, is feasting on what you've caught. Steam the crabs with your favorite spice, pile the steamed crabs on a picnic table spread with newspaper, and serve with melted butter and lemon.

Hunt for Buried Treasure

Anywhere

What could be more exciting than finding a pirate's map leading to a treasure chest full of gold and silver and jewels? After all, some of history's most famous and feared pirates, including the notorious Blackbeard, frequented these shores.

This adventure doesn't leave it to chance. Create the treasure and map for the little kids to find. Recruit older kids to help set up the treasure hunt—but make sure they can keep a secret. This adventure requires some planning and preparation, but it's well worth it. For maximum excitement, talk about pirates and tell pirate stories—or, better yet, schedule a trip to Teach's Hole (see subsequent entry)—a day or two before.

WHAT YOU'LL NEED:

- A book about pirates (geared to the appropriate age for your children: *Blackbeard the Pirate,* by Robert E. Lee, is packed with information, or buy one of the many coloring books on the subject, which you'll find at drugstores, gift shops, and bookstores)
- A bag full of bright and colorful baubles (fake gold coins, plastic jewelry)
- Silver and gold spray paint
- A lot of small rocks and pebbles

- A wooden box to serve as a treasure chest
- Parchment paper
- Pretty shells

Turn the rocks and pebbles into precious metals by spraying them with the gold and silver paint. When they're dry, heap them into the treasure chest along with the baubles, leaving a few handfuls to scatter around the burial site. Stake out a likely spot to bury your treasure. Don't make it too difficult to find, but don't make it too easy, either! Somewhere close to your cottage will do. Draw the treasure map. Be creative with your route and clues. You can crumple the paper, smudge it, rub it in the dirt, and char the edges to make it look old. Remember "X" marks the spot. Now somehow you've got to have the good fortune to "accidentally" stumble upon this authentic pirate treasure map with the kids. Help them find their way to the buried treasure, and enjoy their excitement.

Take in a Show

SUMMER CHILDREN'S SERIES
Roanoke Island Festival Park, Manteo
(252) 475-1506
www.roanokeisland.com
Roanoke Island Festival Park offers excellent children's programming with its Summer Children's Series. In June, programs are held Tues through Thurs at 10:30 a.m. and change weekly. Past performances have included puppet and marionette shows, storytellers, and plays. Christmas programs, such as Shoreline Entertainment's Christmas Show/Musical Review, are also held. The usual fee is waived if you have paid for park admission. Programs are held in the Film Theater, which seats about 200 people.

THE LOST COLONY CHILDREN'S THEATRE
(252) 473-2127

Performers and technicians with *The Lost Colony* are staging an imaginative selection for kids. The show plays each Wed and Thurs June through August at 2 p.m. at Roanoke Island Festival Park. The cost is around $12 per ticket.

Race a Hermit Crab

SCOTCH BONNET FUDGES
NC 12, Frisco
(252) 995-4242
www.scotchbonnetfudges.com

And they're off! Every Friday in season, hermit crabs race to the finish line at Scotch Bonnet Fudges. For lots of family fun, bring your crab or rent one at the store and get set to race. Crabs take off in separate contests to win prizes for their sponsors. Join the Scotch Bonnet crowd under the tent on Friday afternoon for free soft drinks and prizes.

Curl Up with a Good Book

MANTEO BOOKSELLERS
105 Sir Walter Raleigh St., Manteo
(252) 473-1221
www.manteobooksellers.com

Rediscover the pleasures of a bookstore that exists because its proprietor loves books.

Kids are welcome here. Little readers can plant themselves in little chairs in the children's section and browse an extensive selection of the very best books for kids. If you haven't already discovered the Crabby and Nabby series by author Suzanne Tate and artist/illustrator James Melvin, do yourself and your child a favor and start collecting. They introduce children to a variety of friendly indigenous creatures whose adventures afford a perfect opportunity to learn something about the Outer Banks.

The place stays lively throughout the year with author signings, readings, children's storytelling, and other special events. Check calendar listings in local newspapers or call for more information.

SUMMER STORIES FOR KIDS
Corolla Library, 1123 Ocean Trail, Corolla
(252) 453-0496

The storytelling hour is every Wed at 10 a.m. from late June through early Aug at the library. If you need to check out a book, the library is open year-round, Mon through Wed from 10 a.m. to 3 p.m. and Thurs from 3 to 7 p.m. You need a picture ID to check out books.

STORYTIME AT THE DARE COUNTY LIBRARY
Manteo (252) 473-2372
Kill Devil Hills (252) 441-4331
Hatteras (252) 986-2385

Preschool story hours are held at the libraries to acquaint young kids with the library and help them enjoy books at an early age. Story hours include games, songs, puppets, stories, and plays, sometimes with guest storytellers. Programs last 30 to 45 minutes and are held once a week at each of the library locations: Tuesday in Hatteras, Wednesday in Manteo, and Thursday in Kill Devil Hills. Separate programs are held for 2-year-olds, 3- to 5-year-olds, kindergarten to first graders, and second graders to fifth graders.

KIDS' FAVORITE PLACES TO GO

Miniature golf, waterslides, "dollar stores," movie theaters, and more attractions and gifts from nature than you could explore in two weeks' time provide an abundance of places to delight the most discriminating kid visitor. Here are some favorites. See the Recreation and Attractions chapters for more ideas.

ISLAND REVOLUTION SKATE PARK
Corolla Light Town Center
(252) 453-2440

This killer skate park rocks. Two bowls with a mini-ramp-spine street course offer 5,000 feet of island fun. Open every day from 10 a.m. until 8 p.m. in season and Mon through Fri from 2 p.m. until dark in the off-season. Private parties can be booked here.

Creation Stations

Do your kids have creative energy to burn? For hands-on fun, try one of these stores.

Duck Duck Art: The kids or the whole family can create memorable works of art and more under the guidance of the artists at this space, located upstairs in the Savvy Home shop. NC 12, Duck; (252) 261-0092.

Island Art Supply: Classes in painting, drawing, sculpting, and more for kids age 5 and older. North Carolina Highway 12, MP 1, Ocean Centre, Kitty Hawk; (252) 255-5078.

Home Depot: On the first Sat of each month from 10 a.m. to noon, kids can build a project using hammers and nails. US 158 MP ½, Wal-Mart shopping complex, Kitty Hawk; (252) 261-4115.

THE WHALEHEAD CLUB
Currituck Heritage Park, NC 12, Corolla
(252) 453-9040
www.whaleheadclub.com

In season Mon through Fri at 10 a.m. and 4 p.m., the Whalehead Club hosts a kids' search and find tour for ages 10 to 13. There is a small fee. A children's treasure hunt for ages 6 to 9 is also held. Each child receives a prize. To participate, it costs $5 per child plus an adult admittance ticket. History, art, environmental awareness, geography and navigation, and many other subjects are covered. Also offered is a children's art time held at 10 a.m. for ages 6 to 9. The art time is $5 and adults are expected to purchase an admittance ticket as well. A ghost tour is offered in season the first Sat of each month. The tour is held at 7:30 p.m. and costs $14 for people 8 and over and $7 for those under 8.

OUTER BANKS EPICUREAN
Colington Road, Kill Devil Hills
(252) 480-0055

Amy Huggins inspires creativity in young chefs with Outer Banks Epicurean cooking classes. The emphasis here is on slow healthy delicious food, and the kids will love cooking (and eating) with Amy. Perhaps they'll come home with some leftovers, too!

JOCKEY'S RIDGE STATE PARK
US 158, MP 12, Nags Head
(252) 441-7132
www.jockeysridgestatepark.com

Jockey's Ridge is the tallest sand dune on the East Coast, and there's no better location for kite flying. Kids have plenty of room to run without getting their lines crossed or caught in a tree. See the Kite Flying section of the Recreation chapter.

Scrabbling around in the sand is a joy unto itself. Clamber to the top of the dune and enjoy the expansive ocean-to-sound views. If you make arrangements in advance, a park ranger will drive a physically challenged visitor up the dune in a four-wheel-drive vehicle. From October through May, you can pick up a free permit at the park's offices for sandboarding, but you don't need any equipment to enjoy a good old-fashioned roll down the huge sandy hill.

Check local newspapers and at the park office for a current schedule of programs offered by the state park rangers. These are wonderful opportunities to stimulate and satisfy curious young minds. What could be more enchanting to a child than to climb the ridge at night and gaze at constellations or learn about animal tracks in the sand or net fishing in the sound?

Rinse off at the soundside beach at the park's southwest corner, which also has picnic tables and parking. Be sure to wear shoes.

The park headquarters is north of the dune and west of US 158 on Carolista Drive.

THE PROMENADE
US 158, MP 0, Kitty Hawk
(252) 261-4400

The Promenade is one huge family fun center, with an outdoor play park for kids, an indoor arcade with everybody's favorite games, an 18-hole miniature golf course, a chip and putt, an ice-cream parlor, and a driving range. The water-sports division offers parasailing, sailing, boating, and personal watercraft. You could spend the whole day and eat at the restaurant, snack bar, and picnic tables on-site. The Promenade is open every day in the summer and closes Oct through Mar.

GLAZIN' GO NUTS AND GARDEN OF BEADIN'
US 158, MP 6, Kill Devil Hills
(252) 449-2134

Glazin' Go Nuts, a paint-your-own-pottery studio, is a favorite place for kids and adults to spend a creative afternoon. Studio time costs $7 per painter for the day. You buy the pieces you want to paint for an additional charge, from $4 to $40, with most pieces averaging around $15. After you've painted, leave your masterpiece to be fired. It takes about three or four days for the turnover. The studio will ship your works to you if you go home before then.

Next door is a sister shop called **Garden of Beadin'.** It is a full-line bead store with glass, semiprecious stones, and unique specialty beads. The Garden is open year-round, and classes are held in the summer months. Call for days and times.

KITTY HAWK KITES
US 158, MP 13½, Nags Head
(252) 441-4124
www.kittyhawk.com

Just across the street from Jockey's Ridge State Park, Kitty Hawk Kites is a fun store for kids to visit. It has all sorts of kites, a rock-climbing wall, and toys galore, and store personnel lead kayak tours that kids are welcome to join. Family Fun Day takes place every summer Wed from 10 a.m. to 2 p.m., with activities for children and adults. Call to inquire about kite-making workshops, where kids make their own kites and fly them. Kitty Hawk Kites sponsors many family-friendly events on Jockey's Ridge and at other locations. See the Annual Events chapter or call for information.

NAGS HEAD BOWLING CENTER
US 158, MP 10, Nags Head
(252) 441-7077

Nags Head Bowling offers fun for kids, but parents bowl peacefully here while their children are totally enthralled. This facility sports kiddie bumpers running the length of the lane, so even barely walking tykes can knock down pins every time. Games cost $4.95 each; shoes rent for $3.50. Nags Head Bowling is open from noon until midnight daily. If you're sensitive to smoke, bowl early in the afternoon. See the Recreation chapter for evening specials.

Select from many video games in the entrance, including Tekken 2, Ultimate Mortal Kombat, Ms. Pac-Man, Stargate pinball, and air hockey. You must be 21 to play pool in the on-site bar unless accompanied by an adult. Yes, there is a snack bar!

JENNETTE'S PIER
US 158, MP 16½, Nags Head
(800) 832-3474
www.jennettespier.net

In 2011, Jennette's Pier grandly reopened under the auspices of the North Carolina Aquarium. Three wind turbines adorn the pier, and a stop inside the pierhouse is worth the trip. Many children's programs are available such as science camps, fishing workshops, surfing lessons. and more.

TEACH'S HOLE
Back Road, Ocracoke
(252) 928-1718
www.teachshole.com

This Ocracoke stop fascinates the younger crowd. The pirate shop features a historical exhibit about Edward Teach (aka Blackbeard) that includes a short video, weapons, old bottles, Blackbeard in full battle dress, and dioramas for the kids. There is a small fee to view the exhibit, but children younger than age 6 get in free. The gift shop, a must for all ages, is filled with everything imaginable related to pirates and piracy. Teach's Hole is open Easter through Thanksgiving.

WOLF HOWLS
Alligator River National Wildlife Refuge, Dare County Mainland
(252) 216-9464
www.fws.gov/alligatorriver

Kids love hearing the red wolves howl eerily in the refuge at night. The staff leads a guided trip deep into the refuge, and a leader can usually get the wolves to howl. Sometimes kids get to howl to see if the wolves respond. Howls are held once a week in the summer and at other times during the year. See the Attractions chapter for more information.

THE FISHING DOCKS
At the end of the day, kids love to go to the fishing docks to see the fish caught on the charter boats. Take the kids to the docks between 3 and 5 p.m. to see tuna, dolphin, wahoo, and more. This is a spectator event only. Head to Pirate's Cove Yacht Club in Manteo, Oregon Inlet Fishing Center south of Nags Head, or Hatteras Harbor Yacht Club or Oden's Dock in Hatteras Village.

Kids' Camps

NORTH CAROLINA AQUARIUM AT ROANOKE ISLAND
(252) 473-3493
www.aquariums.state.nc.us/ri

The aquarium leads the Aquatic Adventures Summer Camp for students ages 6 to 7, 7 to 9, and 10 to 12. The camps last for five half days, with children learning about the Outer Banks waters and habitats through many hands-on activities and field trips. Each weeklong camp for the 10- to 12-year-olds concludes with a sleepover at the aquarium. Also, the aquarium can be rented for sleepover parties among the fishes and sharks.

ELIZABETHAN GARDENS
Off US 64, Roanoke Island
(252) 473-3234
www.elizabethangardens.org

Families savor this oasis of serenity and fun. Kids love the Scratch 'n Sniff workshop offered throughout the year. Etiquette classes for young people are available, and children's camps run throughout the summer months.

OUTER BANKS FAMILY YMCA
US 158, MP 11, Nags Head
(252) 449-8897

The YMCA has weeklong day camps for all ages. Full-day camps are for ages 5 to 12. Each week has a special theme, and kids do activities related to the theme in addition to going to the pool and ocean and on field trips. The YMCA also hosts several sports camps in beach volleyball, girls field hockey, soccer, basketball, and junior ocean rescue. Day passes are available for the superb skate park. Call for information.

SUMMER ART CAMPS
KDH Cooperative Gallery
502 US 158, MP 8½, Kill Devil Hills
(252) 441-9888

The KDH Cooperative Gallery offers arts camps for kids in the summer. Each session rewards kids with art and craft projects they take home at the end of the week. Painting, drawing, sculpting, and printmaking are some of the classes taught by professional artists. Camps are held from 10 a.m. to noon for five days. The gallery also offers workshops for all ages.

JOCKEY'S RIDGE STATE PARK
US 158, MP 12, Nags Head
(252) 441-2588
www.jockeysridgestatepark.com

A wide range of educational nature programs are offered for kids. Take a dune hike and learn about the animals and plants in the area. Choose from a soundside hike, sunset on the ridge, crabby clinic, birding on the sound, and lots more. All programs are free and open to the public.

DARE COUNTY PARKS AND RECREATION
(252) 473-1101, ext. 313
www.darenc.com/depts/parks_rec

Parks and Rec offers sports camps in basketball, soccer, cheerleading, gymnastics, triathlon training, and fishing. These weeklong camps, held Monday through Friday, are usually about 5 hours per day. There's also an Adventure Camp, where participants go on a weeklong camping trip. Toddler Camps for ages 3 to 5 last about 2 hours. Call for information.

i Learning to surf while staying on the Outer Banks is a popular and exciting pastime. When choosing a surf school, ask if the instructor is first aid certified and confirm that only beginner boards are used (soft or soft top boards).

4-H CAMPS
Dare County Cooperative Extension
(252) 473-1101, ext. 442

In the summer 4-H offers weeklong day camps for elementary school children at four sites in the county: Kitty Hawk Elementary, First Flight Elementary, Manteo Elementary, and Munchkin Academy in Buxton. Camps last from 7:30 a.m. to 5:30 p.m. and include educational and fun activities and a field trip based on a particular theme. The Support Our Students is for middle-school students and alternates between Manteo and First Flight Middle Schools. This is a day-tripper's program, with off-site educational field trips. One-week camps away from home, in which campers travel to one of five 4-H camps in the state, are also held. You must preregister for all these camps. Call for information.

OCEAN ATLANTIC RENTALS SURF SCHOOL
Corolla Light Town Center, Corolla
(252) 453-2440, (800) 635-9559
www.oceanatlanticrentals.com
Kids and adults can learn to catch waves in the Ocean Atlantic Rentals Surf School. Classes are taught by a professional out of each of the four Ocean Atlantic locations,

and the instructors will teach students of all skill levels. Other locations are at: Duck Road, Soundfront, Duck, (252) 261-4346; NC 12, MP 10, Nags Head, (252) 441-7823; and NC 12, Avon, (252) 995-5868.

CLUB HATTERAS KIDS
NC 12, Avon
(252) 995-4600
www.hatterasrealty.com
Kids ages 4 to 12 come to Hatteras Realty to participate in fee-based programs, giving their caretakers time on their own. Club Hatteras Kids takes young ones to the soundside beach to crab and play in the water. They also play basketball, volleyball, miniature golf, croquet, and tennis and go for hikes. In quieter moments they enjoy crafts and storytelling. The morning session includes lunch, and the evening session includes dinner; each program is $25. Hatteras Realty runs Club Hatteras Kids during summer months.

ARTS & CULTURE

The Outer Banks is the kind of place where many artists envision spending their days painting the beauty that surrounds them or sculpting forms wrought by visions brought forth by the ocean. For many this dream has come to fruition, and the beach has become a haven for artists of all kinds. The powerful influence of the ocean and wetlands appears in many works of art, as do the abundant wildlife and spirit of the residents as they work and play. Our historic landmarks provide inspiration for an artistic appetite. The relative isolation of our barrier islands, though seen by some as a drawback to year-round living, is a real plus to the artist, especially in the off-season. This is the time to contemplate and study, then commune with the muse and put insights into a tangible piece of art. When a nor'easter blows on a gray February day, the muse may be an artist's only visitor! Take the time to visit our many galleries and talk with some of our local artists and writers. Through their eyes you are sure to gain more appreciation of this special area.

OVERVIEW

You can get a feel for this fascinating visual arts arena, which runs the gamut from conceptual art to classical painting, by attending several annual events. One of the longest running of these is the Dare County Arts Council's Frank Stick Memorial Art Show, which was started back in 1978. The show is held at the Ghost Fleet Gallery in Nags Head every February and features more than 150 artworks (see the Annual Events chapter for more information).

For some family fun of the artistic kind, set aside the first weekend in October for the arts council's annual Artrageous Art Extravaganza, which features hands-on creative booths with cookie decorating, hat creations, weaving, face painting, and much more. Fashion shows, food, live music,

art collaborations, and local art and craft booths highlight the two-day event. During an elegant Sunday auction, fine art by adults and children is put on the block. Dedicated volunteers who coordinate the weekend event outdo themselves year after year. (See the Annual Events chapter for more information.)

Another must-see is the New World Festival of the Arts each August on downtown Manteo's waterfront, an ideal site for showcasing the talents of approximately 80 local and national artists and artisans. Look for painting, photography, jewelry, pottery, and an assortment of handcrafted items. If you would like to show your work or need more information, call the phone number listed in the Annual Events chapter entry.

Private visual art studios are scattered from Corolla to Ocracoke for art seekers. Many local artists offer lessons, mostly in watercolor and other painting techniques. We do have many landscape painters here, but our 50 or more commercial art/craft galleries are packed with expressions as individualistic as grains of sand.

The Outer Banks has become a bona fide art community. Artists living here and in the surrounding areas are a close-knit group, sharing tips and encouraging each other in their endeavors. Perhaps because of the lifestyle here, our artists are eager to meet visitors. Since 1997 the Town of Nags Head has purchased more than 90 pieces of art by local and regional artists. The collection, selected by the town's artwork selection committee, includes paintings, sculpture, photographs, wood carvings, etchings, mobiles, found-object art, and more. The public is invited to view this collection during town hall operating hours.

Local theater groups present plays, comedies, and dramas both seasonally and year-round. Music streams from some nightclubs, and standup comics perform summer stints. Symphonies, vocal groups, and individual classical, folk, and pop artists enliven our local auditoriums throughout the year. What we can't generate ourselves in the way of cultural experiences, we import with the help of volunteer-based nonprofit organizations. Thanks to the efforts of the Dare County Arts Council, Outer Banks Forum, the Theater of Dare, the Roanoke Island Historical Association (producers of The Lost Colony), the North Carolina School of the Arts, and Roanoke Island Festival Park, insiders on the Outer Banks enjoy exposure to local, regional, and national cultural opportunities.

We begin with a description of major arts organizations and follow with a north-to-south excursion through the Outer Banks' eclectic galleries and other creative venues. Please see the Annual Events chapter for arts events.

ORGANIZATIONS

DARE COUNTY ARTS COUNCIL
Old Courthouse, Manteo
(252) 473-5558
www.darearts.org
The Dare County Arts Council supplies the Outer Banks with a wide variety of creative opportunities with the help of countless volunteers, generous patrons and members, and some state and county support. This nonprofit group has a permanent office/gallery in downtown Manteo at the address above. The gallery hosts visual arts shows, and visitors are encouraged to stop by to view these shows or to gather information on arts and cultural events in the area. Office hours are 10 a.m. to 5 p.m. Mon through Fri and occasional weekends when volunteer staff is available.

The council is affiliated with the North Carolina Arts Council as the local distributing agency of the state's Grassroots funds. The DCAC also subsidizes other area arts organizations, such as Theater of Dare, the Writers' Group, the Outer Banks Forum, and Icarus International, which hosts an art exhibition honoring humankind's first powered flight each December at two Nags Head galleries (see the Annual Events chapter).

DCAC sponsors several cultural programs in the community and local schools every year. For example, DCAC has brought in performances from the Shady Grove Band, the African American Dance Ensemble, and the New York Chinese Folk Dance Company.

DCAC operates on funds from grants, fund-raisers, and annual memberships. Memberships generally range from $25 and up. This is a great way to support the arts in the community.

ELIZABETH R & COMPANY
(252) 473-1500
www.elizabethr.org

Elizabeth R & Company sponsors scholarly research projects centered on North Carolina history and professional films, audio presentations, and performances that interpret history. Three of its popular interpretive performances are staged on Roanoke Island every summer—*Elizabeth R, Bloody Mary and the Virgin Queen,* and *Shepherd of the Ocean. Shepherd of the Ocean* is a whimsical comedy about Queen Elizabeth I and Sir Walter Raleigh, starring Barbara Hird and Chris Chappell. *Elizabeth R* portrays the life of Queen Elizabeth I. *Bloody Mary* tells the story of Queen Elizabeth I and her half sister Mary Queen of Scots in a hilarious farce. For more information, see the Attractions chapter.

OUTER BANKS FORUM FOR THE
LIVELY ARTS
(252) 202-9732
www.outerbanksforum.org

The Outer Banks Forum organizes six lively arts performances a year, bringing world-class performers to this remote stretch of the world. Since 1983 the forum has scheduled these performances from Oct through Apr, making the off-season months brighter for many folks. The forum seasons are filled with interesting and varied selections, including bluegrass, opera, and folk tales. All performances are held in the First Flight High School auditorium. Starting time is at 7:30 p.m. Season subscriptions cost $95.

ROANOKE ISLAND FESTIVAL PARK
1 Festival Park, Manteo
(252) 475-1500,
(252) 475-1506 (24-hour events line)
www.roanokeisland.com

Roanoke Island Festival Park blends art, history, and education in celebration of Roanoke Island's role as birthplace of English-speaking America. The state park is on its own small island across from the Manteo waterfront, also the home berth of the *Elizabeth II.* Completed in 1998, the park features a variety of cultural opportunities year-round. The park's art gallery is a beautiful space that holds monthlong art shows. At receptions for these shows on Sunday afternoons, arts-minded folk meet. The Film Theater's house film is *The Legend of Two Path,* a 45-minute film depicting the English landing on Roanoke Island from the Native Americans' point of view; other top-notch cultural arts performances and films are also staged in the theater year-round.

The outdoor pavilion, which seats up to 3,500 people on the lawn, is a marvelous place to watch cultural arts performances. University of North Carolina students perform here on select evenings, as do visiting symphonies and musicians. Also on-site are an 8,500-square-foot Adventure Museum, which has 400 years of Outer Banks history, a museum store, and the Outer Banks History Center. For more information, see the Attractions chapter.

ROANOKE ISLAND HISTORICAL
ASSOCIATION
1409 US 64/264, Manteo
(252) 473-2127
www.thelostcolony.org

The Lost Colony, a unique outdoor drama, is staged throughout the summer in a waterside theater on Roanoke Island (see the Attractions chapter). Each year *The Lost Colony* entices 125 actors and crew across the nation to answer the casting call for the symphonic drama that chronicles the fate of the first English settlement in America.

Many of *The Lost Colony* thespians try out for the Lost Colony's Children's Theater that wows junior audiences during the summer months with classics such as *Sleeping Beauty and Pirates: A Boy At Sea*. Others take on roles as time-warped sailors for hilarious and educational interpretive tours of the *Elizabeth II*.

A full day of special events, including free children's theater selections, interpretive park tours, and special performances, takes place on Virginia Dare's birthday, August 18. Call the Lindsey Warren Visitor Center at Fort Raleigh (252-473-5772) for a schedule.

If you're interested in joining the Roanoke Island Historical Association and supporting *The Lost Colony*, write to the address listed above (zip code 27954) or call. Contribution details vary. You may become a member and/or contribute to the annual fund or the endowment fund.

THE THEATRE OF DARE
(252) 261-4064
www.theatreofdare.org

The Theater of Dare was established in 1992 with a grant from the Outer Banks Forum. Its members bring quality live theater to the Outer Banks by taking part in all phases of production, such as directing, set design, and performing. The Theatre of Dare produces three main stage productions a year from fall to spring. TOD embodies the true spirit of community theater by welcoming amateur and professional thespians alike. The organization thus far has produced hits such as *Arsenic and Old Lace, Steel Magnolias,*

The Odd Couple, Peter Pan, Bell Book and Candle, The Gin Game, and Little Women. The Theatre of Dare performances are held at COA in Manteo. Adult tickets are usually around $13 and kids are around $8. For more information about membership, volunteering, auditions, or production dates, call Mike Hunter at the number listed here.

ICARUS INTERNATIONAL
(252) 441-6584
www.monumenttoacenturyofflight.org

Icarus International was founded in 1993, purposely a decade before the centennial of flight in 2003, with the goal of celebrating flight through the arts. The organization has been widely successful in its efforts to raise the awareness of the history of flight. Each year Icarus International holds an international visual arts competition and a literary competition based on a flight-related theme. Literary entries are published annually. Icarus International also sponsors an annual portrait commission for inductees into the First Flight Shrine at the Wright Brothers National Memorial. In 2003 the group completed the $1 million Icarus Monument, celebrating 100 years of flight. The monument is located at MP 1 in Kitty Hawk behind the Aycock Brown Welcome Center. Icarus International has created a book called *Pioneer Aviators of the World*. It tells the story of the first pilots from 100 countries.

GALLERIES

Corolla

DOLPHIN WATCH GALLERY
TimBuck II Shopping Village Ocean Trail, Corolla
(252) 453-2592
www.dolphinwatchgallery.com

Dolphin Watch Gallery features the works of owner/artist Mary Kaye Umberger. This artist creates hand-colored etchings on handmade paper drawn from scenes indigenous to the Corolla area, including wildlife, ducks and other waterfowl, seascapes, and lighthouses. Other art pieces here include pottery, stoneware, carvings of marine life, and wax sculptures (candles shaped by hand, with flower petals molded by the artist's fingertips). The gallery is open year-round; call for off-season hours.

Duck

GREENLEAF GALLERY
1169 NC 12, Duck
(252) 261-2009
www.outer-banks.com/greenleaf

Greenleaf Gallery offers exquisite fine crafts and paintings from nationally, regionally, and locally known American artists. Approximately 300 artists and artisans are represented at Greenleaf. Featured are one-of-a-kind handcrafted jewelry, ceramics, wood, glass, and furnishings, plus sculpture, acrylic and watercolor paintings, etchings, lithographs, and mixed-media pieces. Expect to find both the delightful and the serious at Greenleaf, anything from a huge, whimsical praying mantis to the works of some of the nation's finest glass artisans. One of the best things about visiting Greenleaf is seeing the sublime paintings of Outer Banks artist Rick Tupper, who owns the gallery with his wife. Call for a schedule of artists' exhibitions. The gallery is closed on Sun and from Jan through mid-Mar.

THE WOODEN FEATHER
Scarborough Lane, NC 12, Duck
(252) 261-2808
www.woodenfeather.com

The Wooden Feather proudly showcases the best of American ingenuity and creativity with award-winning handcarved decoys and shorebirds as well as driftwood sculptures. The gallery features an outstanding collection of antique decoys. Garden accessories, jewelry, and gifts are sold here as well. The store is open seven days a week from Mar through Dec, with longer hours during the summer season.

Kitty Hawk

ARTSPACE
NC 12, Southern Shores Crossing,
Southern Shores
(252) 261-2787
www.obxartspace.com

ARTspace is working artists, studio space, art shows, classes, and a fun space. A visit here is worthwhile and enlightening.

Kill Devil Hills

FIRST FLIGHT SHRINE
Wright Brothers National Memorial
Visitor Center, US 158, MP 8,
Kill Devil Hills
(252) 441-7430
www.nps.gov/wrbr

While the First Flight Shrine is not a commercial art gallery, it has a body of portraiture that deserves recognition. Every year for more than 30 years, the First Flight Society has inducted into the shrine one or more individuals who have accomplished an outstanding "first" that has enhanced the development of aviation. Hanging in the same room as a replica of Wilbur and Orville Wright's first *Flyer* are more than 55 faces of great aviators, such as Amelia Earhart, Adm. Richard E. Byrd, Neil Armstrong, and Col. Edwin Aldrin. The portraits, which are donated by Icarus International, are produced annually and exhibited through a partnership with the National Park Service at the Wright Brothers National Memorial Visitor Center (see the Attractions chapter for more about the memorial).

KDH COOPERATIVE GALLERY AND STUDIOS
US 158, MP 8½, Kill Devil Hills
(252) 441-9888
www.kdhcooperative.com

This is an artist-operated cooperative, the dream and reality of artist and owner Julie Moye. It's a centralized place to see the work of 29 local artists. The juried members of this cooperative show their work and assist in running the gallery. Oil, acrylic, watercolor, pastels, pen and ink, ceramics, jewelry, fiber, furniture, candles, pottery, glass, and metal are featured. Each member serves on panels to hang and display art, jury, organize shows, and assist customers during daily business hours. Upstairs is the Artists Attic, a lively studio space and classrooms. Several artists have set up studios upstairs and often work during business hours. Visitors are welcome upstairs to talk with the artists and watch them work. The other half of the upstairs is classroom space, where classes are held year-round for children and adults. Pottery, drawing, photography, stained glass, mosaic, candle making, blacksmithing, and basket making are some of the classes offered, or you can design your own class and pitch it to the staff. KDH Cooperative offers art classes for kids, including creative writing, drawing, and comic strip drawing, as well as summer art camps and classes on school holidays.

Nags Head

A treasure trove of art galleries is tucked into Nags Head's Gallery Row. Seven galleries and a consignment shop are within a block of one another, and three more galleries are in the vicinity. This little art mecca is a great place to spend an entire afternoon, poking in and out of each gallery and chatting with the owners. Gallery Row is around MP 10 at Gallery Row and Driftwood Streets. Park at any of the galleries and walk to the others. This is a low-traffic, laid-back area so don't feel rushed to get out of your parking space. Nearby on the Beach Road are the Seaside, Anna Gartrell, and Yellowhouse art galleries.

SALLY HUSS GALLERY
Gallery Row, 300 East Driftwood St., Nags Head
(252) 441-8098
www.sallyhussobx.com

Sally Huss Gallery features the upbeat original art and prints of the California artist of the same name. Huss creates impressionistic paintings in bold colors featuring childlike scenes. Her designs, coupled with cheerful sayings, are transferred onto mugs, gift wrap, T-shirts, cards, and key chains. Adults and kids alike get a kick out of her lighthearted creations that are dotted with toucans, mermaids, elephants, hearts, and sailboats. You'll also want to see the original ceramics. In addition to Huss's art, this gallery features unique home decor, gifts, and work from local potters. The gallery is open all year.

MORALES ART GALLERY
207 East Gallery Row, Nags Head
(252) 441-6484, (800) 635-6035
www.prints-r-us.com

Mitchell and Christine Lively at the Morales Art Galleries have made financial success a personal reality for many struggling artists by showcasing their work and producing fine-art prints shown at their three gallery locations on the Outer Banks.

Morales Art Gallery is the oldest art venue on Gallery Row; the late Jesse Morales first opened the doors in 1971. Today the Morales galleries and Fine Art Print Shop carry fine original local, regional, and nationally known art. Showcased here are the works of Larry Johnson, Pat Williams, Dennis Lighthart, Pat Troiani, Tony Feathers, and Anda Styler. Expect to find limited-edition prints by the Greenwich Workshop, Mill Pond Press, Hadley House, Somerset Publishing, and Wild Wings. If you want to view a major collection of original seascapes, this is the place.

Mitchell has been framing and publishing art for more than two decades. The couple's dedication to the arts has been felt community-wide, especially in their generosity to the Dare County schools. A member of the Professional Picture Framers Association, Morales Art Gallery offers a wide variety of choices in custom framing. It is open year-round.

GLENN EURE'S GHOST FLEET GALLERY
**Gallery Row, 210 East Driftwood St.,
Nags Head
(252) 441-6584
www.angelfire.com/on2/ghostfleet**
Glenn and Pat Eure, owners of the Ghost Fleet Gallery, run an original art establishment that primarily features Glenn's work. A printmaker, Glenn creates in a variety of forms including etching, wood cutting, colligraphy, serigraphy, and relief carving in addition to drawing, wood carving, and oil, acrylic, and watercolor painting. His oeuvre includes a series of collagraphs (thin collages run through a printing press) honoring Wilbur and Orville Wright's first flight. The fine-art prints, each hand-pulled by the artist, contain flight imagery from da Vinci's time to the present. Glenn specializes in large canvases that bulge out from their frames—irregular shapes that are painted in a nonobjective style. He also produces lighthearted watercolors that feature boat scenes.

The Eures rotate other artists' work in the West Wing Gallery and the Second Dimension gallery located a flight up. In the off-season Eure hosts several community shows: the Icarus International Art Show in December, the Frank Stick Memorial Art Show in February, and a county public school art show. Poetry readings also are held year-round at the gallery (see the Annual Events chapter). The Ghost Fleet Gallery is open year-round. Hours are cut back some in Jan and Feb.

JEWELRY BY GAIL, INC.
**Gallery Row, 207 Driftwood St.,
Nags Head
(252) 441-5387
www.jewelrybygail.com**
Gail Kowalski is a designer-goldsmith who has won national recognition for her creations in precious metals and stones. Her pieces have been regularly spotted on Hollywood's elite on the red carpet. Most of the jewelry designed and made here falls into the "wearable art" category. Check out Selections by Gail, a department of very high-quality but moderately priced handmade jewelry from all over the world. Kowalski personally selects each piece exhibited here. The Charming Lights sterling and gold lighthouse jewelry collection is a favorite. Images of the four local lighthouses are fashioned into earrings, pendants, and charms. The gallery is open Mon through Sat and is closed in Jan.

SEASIDE ART GALLERY
NC 12, MP 11, Nags Head
(252) 441-5418
www.seasideart.com
Original etchings and lithographs by Picasso, Whistler, Rembrandt, and Renoir are among the thousands of original works of art on display at Seaside Art Gallery. Sculptures, paintings, drawings, Indian pottery, fine porcelains, Mexican silver jewelry (including the work of William Spratling), seascapes, and animation art from Disney and Warner Bros. are spread throughout numerous rooms in this sprawling gallery. Seaside is a Gold Circle dealer for Disney Classic Figurines. Prints by David Hunter are meticulously rendered and range from biblical portraiture to peaceful coastal scenes.

The gallery hosts several competitions annually, including an International Miniature Art Show (see the May listings in the Annual Events chapter) and the Icarus International Art Show. Printmaking workshops are held here each year by David Hunter. The gallery is open year-round.

YELLOWHOUSE GALLERY AND ANNEX
NC 12, MP 11, Nags Head
(252) 441-6928
www.yellowhousegallery.com
Yellowhouse Gallery houses one of North Carolina's largest collections of antique prints and maps. Thousands of original old etchings, lithographs, and engravings are organized for browsing in several rooms of one of Nags Head's older beach cottages. Established in 1969, the gallery features Civil War prints and maps; prints of botanicals, fish, shells, and birds; and old views and antique maps and charts of the Outer Banks. Yellowhouse Gallery also offers a huge selection of decorative and fine-art prints and

posters as well as souvenir pictures and maps of the Outer Banks. If the picture you want is not in stock, Uncle Jack, the proprietor, will order it for you.

Roanoke Island

SILVER BONSAI GALLERY
905 US 64/264, Manteo
(252) 475-1413
www.silverbonsai.com
Silver Bonsai Gallery, nestled in one of the island's original homes, is a distinctive art gallery. Owners Ben and Kathryn Stewart, both metalsmiths and bonsai artists, sell their own creations here, as well as the works of other artists, and can often be seen at work in the studio at the back of the gallery. The Stewarts create simple yet elegant silver and gold jewelry and sculpture and design special pieces upon request. The gallery sells a broad range of fine art by local artists, including paintings, wood, glass, sculpture, quilts, and more. Silver Bonsai is open seven days a week, but closes for the month of Jan.

WANCHESE POTTERY
107 Fernando St., Manteo
(252) 473-2099
Customers can watch local potters Bonnie and Bob Morrill at work in their studio in downtown Manteo. This shop is known for its beautiful, useful art graced with delicate, lead-free glazes. One savvy insider bought a handsome mug here that holds a generous amount of coffee, sits easily without wobbling, and has an exquisite glaze that turns a morning routine into an artistic awakening. Choose dinnerware, oil lamps, hummingbird feeders, mugs, bowls, and pitchers among other items. The shop also features some handmade baskets and fresh cooking herbs.

Wanchese Pottery is open all year. Winter hours are 1 to 5 p.m. Thurs, Fri, and Sat.

NANCYWARE POTTERY
402 Queen Elizabeth St., Manteo
(252) 473-9400
www.nancywarepottery.com
This is the pottery studio of artist Nancy Hase. The potter's wheel is on display and you can see her working from time to time. She also offers classes on the wheel. The pottery is high-fire functional stoneware that is dishwasher, microwave, and oven safe. The variety of kitchen items, including deep-dish fluted pie plates, colanders, and three-piece child dining sets, can be personalized, as can the vases, dishes, and spoon rests.

ROANOKE ISLAND FESTIVAL
Park Art Gallery Manteo
(252) 475-1506
www.roanokeisland.com
Roanoke Island Festival Park's Art Gallery is the finest arts exhibition space on the Outer Banks. The gallery is vast and uncluttered, allowing much room for appreciating the works of art hanging in the exhibitions. Gallery shows change monthly, featuring the works of an individual artist or sometimes groups of artists. In late 2007, Pocosin Arts Folk School exhibited traditional crafts and artwork influenced by eastern North Carolina and the Pocosin area. The Priceless Pieces Past & Present Quilt Extravaganza is a popular show, held every year in Mar, with dozens of quilts made or owned by locals. The Dare County Arts Council's Mollie Fearing Art Show is another popular show held here. Each monthly show has an opening reception on a Sun afternoon. Roanoke Island Festival Park is closed in Jan and part of Feb.

HUBBY BLIVEN, WILDLIFE ART
543 Ananias Dare St., Roanoke Island
(252) 473-2632
Bliven runs a full-service frame shop and wildlife art gallery featuring his own work. He also operates a museum on the premises that includes Civil War, World War I, World War II, and Native American artifacts. Bliven's shop is the place to go if you're looking for lighthouse photos that include all eight North Carolina sentinels framed together or as individual prints. This group includes the Prices's Creek lighthouse in Southport, a rare find. Bliven is very fortunate to have been given access to photograph this structure on private property. His shop is open year-round.

Hatteras Island

GASKINS GALLERY
NC 12, Avon
(252) 995-6617
The Gaskins Gallery focuses on original local art and custom framing. Artists and owners Denise and Elizabeth Gaskins feature exclusively original family art, including their own watercolors and those of their octogenarian grandmother, who began painting several years ago. The paintings generally are coastal scenes or florals. You'll also find pottery, decorator prints, and posters. The Gaskins Gallery is open year-round.

i Early Christmas shoppers love a summer outdoor art show. The New World Festival of the Arts in Manteo in August welcomes 80 artists from the Outer Banks and all along the East Coast. You'll find pottery, paintings, metalwork, photography, basketry, painted tiles, and so much more. This show is held midweek. For more information, see the Annual Events chapter.

INDIAN TOWN GALLERY AND GIFTS
NC 12, Frisco
(252) 995-5181
Nestled in the woods in Frisco, Indian Town represents artists from local villages. Many of the paintings have an Outer Banks theme. The offshore-fishing theme paintings are stunning. The gallery also features pottery, chimes, cards, gifts, lighthouses, and jewelry. Artist Wayne Fulcher is often at work in the store.

RED DRUM POTTERY
NC 12, Frisco
(252) 995-5757
Accomplished potters Rhonda Bates and Wes Lassiter work in this studio, and you can watch them as they turn their wonderful creations at the wheel. These are well-crafted pieces, whether they are intended for functional or decorative use. It's definitely worth a stop to see their bowls, pitchers, vases, vessels, platters, teakettles, miniatures, and fabulous fish- and crab-imprinted hanging wall tiles. Do you raku? Come try it in the early evening—call for an updated schedule. The gallery is open seven days a week year-round.

SANDY BAY GALLERY
NC 12, Hatteras Village
(252) 986-1338
This gallery features original fine art and crafts with an emphasis on Outer Banks artists. Sandy Bay is filled with original watercolor and acrylic paintings and photography, as well as crafts by potters, jewelers, glass artisans, and paper, wood, stained-glass, and fiber artists. The hand-carved decorative waterfowl, including egrets, blue herons, sandpipers, and dowitchers, have grace and personality. Glass boxes with silver trim by Mary Anne feature a geometric collage of colored and clear glass reminiscent of Mondrian's paintings. You also can choose from a selection of prints. The gallery is open Mar through Christmas Eve.

Ocracoke Island

VILLAGE CRAFTSMEN
Howard Street, Ocracoke
(252) 928-5541, (800) 648-9743
www.villagecraftsmen.com
The artwork in this well-known gallery includes North Carolina pottery, handmade wooden boxes, jewelry, and other original items. The focus is on excellent craftsmanship and variety. Owner Philip Howard also sells his pen-and-ink and watercolor prints here. See the Shopping chapter for more about this local landmark, open year-round except the month of Jan.

ISLAND ARTWORKS
British Cemetery Road, Ocracoke
(252) 928-3892
www.islandartworks.com
Owner-artist Kathleen O'Neal has lived on Ocracoke for more than 25 years. "Art jewelry" aptly describes most of the finds here. O'Neal does all the copper enameling and silver- and goldsmithing work herself. The gallery also features local and North Carolina artwork such as large, contemporary-style watercolors of island scenes by Debbie Wells and the fused glass work of Libby Hicks. Local photography, sculptural assemblages created by O'Neal, glass art, hand-carved wooden boxes, and mixed-media art are just some of the exciting discoveries at Island Artworks. It's a real fine-art experience. This colorful shop is open from mid-March until Christmas.

OVER THE MOON
British Cemetery Road, Ocracoke
(252) 928-3555
www.overthemoongiftshop.com

Over the Moon features handmade contemporary crafts from 150 artists across the nation. Shop for jewelry, porcelain, and Brian Andreas's StoryPeople—books, prints, and sculptures adorned with insightful sayings. See the Shopping chapter for other items found here. Over the Moon is open from Easter through Thanksgiving.

STUDIOS

These are private studios that can be visited by appointment only.

Southern Shores & Kitty Hawk

RUSSELL YERKES
(252) 261-6947
www.yerkesworks.com

One of the Outer Banks' most popular artists is Russell Yerkes, probably best known for his vibrant "fish" paintings, though his subject matter encompasses much more than fins. This nationally recognized watercolorist creates imaginative images of aquatic scenes and accepts commissions.

The Greenleaf Gallery in Duck (see the separate listing under Galleries) carries a nice selection of Yerkes's work. Yerkes also shows at festivals all over the East Coast. Check the website for a schedule.

W. E. (ELLIE) GRUMIAUX JR.
120 South Dogwood Trail,
Southern Shores
(252) 255-0402

One of the most recognized artists on the Outer Banks, Grumiaux, who works in watercolor, specializes in portraying the buildings, boats, and landscapes that typify this resort area, as well as the lesser-known places in the surrounding towns. Grumiaux is also the one to call for a portrait of your cottage or boat. His work is found in local churches, homes, and galleries such as Greenleaf Gallery in Duck and Seaside Gallery in Nags Head (see separate entries under Galleries).

Kill Devil Hills

E. M. (LIZ) CORSA
(252) 480-0303

Think Beatrix Potter. Throw in some sophistication and humor, and you have an idea of the depth and delight of E. M. Corsa's work. Referred to as a "watercolor wordsmith," her original watercolors and prints feature both wild and domestic animals with an attitude, presented in an anthropomorphic style. Corsa's inspiration comes from nature and family and is coupled with her unique sense of humor. She's a published writer of humorous magazine essays who combines images and titles in a thought-provoking and fresh manner. Her work can be viewed at Greenleaf Gallery in Duck. To view her work or find out where her next showing is, call the artist.

CAROL TROTMAN
(252) 441-3590

Painter Carol Trotman specializes in floral watercolors. Her complicated garden scenes as well as poetic profiles of single blossoms are exceptional. You can purchase reproductions on cards or original full-size work by calling the artist for an appointment or by visiting Greenleaf Gallery in Duck or Sandy Bay Gallery in Hatteras Village.

SUSAN VAUGHAN
(252) 480-3301
www.wellsvaughan.byregion.net

Vaughan paints in a folk-art style, producing town portraits in acrylics that are very popular on the Outer Banks. Available prints include her representations of Manteo, Kill Devil Hills, Duck, Elizabeth City, and Corolla. Vaughan also paints local scenes, and she welcomes commissions. Call for commission information.

Nags Head

MARSHA CLINE
(252) 441-5167
www.marciacline.com

Marsha Cline, a longtime resident of the Outer Banks, is well known for her dedication and versatility. Her medium constantly changes and expands, yet her style remains distinctive. People have come to recognize the vivid color and warm spirit in Cline's work. A passion for painting and love of life is evident in her local Outer Banks scenes, travel-inspired works, and latest passion to be captured on the canvas. Her work is on display in many popular local restaurants, such as the Rundown Cafe, Southern Bean, and Tortuga's Lie. Her work is also on display at the KDH Cooperative Gallery, in area businesses, and in homes from coast to coast. She also paints by commission and welcomes contact by appointment at her home studio in Nags Head.

RAY MATTHEWS PHOTOGRAPHER
(252) 441-7941
www.raymatthews.com

Ray Matthews has been living on the Outer Banks for more than 25 years, during which time he has developed a love for nature that is presented masterfully in his prints.

Matthews is a consummate custom-slide printer as well as a commercial photographer. His work is shown at Outer Banks Style in Corolla. Call for an appointment. He is available year-round. Look for his Outer Banks calendar in finer retail stores.

Roanoke Island

THE HAT LADY
(252) 473-1850

At her working studio Genna Miles creates fine-art wearable hats in one-of-a-kind designs. Miles employs spinning and crochet techniques with natural, hand-dyed fibers and trinkets to set off these artistic creations that will warm heads and hearts. Her baby bonnets crafted in 100 percent cotton are precious. The Hat Lady specializes in spinning animal hair into yarn. Bring in your dog or cat's shedded hair, and she'll make it into a hat for you. Miles accepts commissions. You can see her work in many of the annual Outer Banks art exhibitions, where she has been known to break away from headwear and create fiber and mixed-media sculptures that reflect her love for nostalgic items and thrift-store treasures.

NICK SAPONE
292 The Lane, Wanchese
(252) 473-3136

Local decoy carver Nick Sapone produces hand-carved, hunting-style decoys. He makes both wooden decoys and the traditional Outer Banks–canvas style. He welcomes visitors to his home studio by appointment.

Hatteras Island

MICHAEL HALMINSKI STUDIO
Midgett Way, Waves
(252) 987-2401
www.michaelhalminski.com

Outer Banks seascapes and landscapes dominate the photography collection displayed at this studio. The bird photos are inspiring, especially Halminski's egret pictures. His fine collection of cards is stunning. Call for an appointment.

JURIED ART EXHIBITIONS

The Outer Banks offers several juried art exhibitions each year. While the traditional definition of "juried" implies that work is selected for showing by judges, most shows here have an open-entry policy, and the work is judged for excellence and originality. Entry fees generally average $10 to $15.

Here we've listed the major shows in the area; for detailed information, call either the galleries mentioned or the Dare County Arts Council (252-473-5558). New shows are always cropping up, so keep in touch with the arts council. See the Annual Events chapter for more art activities.

Nags Head

FRANK STICK MEMORIAL ART SHOW
**Glenn Eure's Ghost Fleet Gallery,
Gallery Row, 210 East Driftwood St.,
Nags Head
(252) 473-5558
www.angelfire.com/on2/ghostfleet**
This late January show is open to Dare County residents and Dare County Arts Council members. All genres of art are welcome; some restrictions (including the size of the work) apply.

INTERNATIONAL MINIATURE ART SHOW
**Seaside Art Gallery, NC 12, MP 11,
Nags Head
(252) 441-5418
www.seasideart.com**
Any artist may enter this May show held at Seaside Art Gallery. Work entered cannot exceed 40 inches. The show features mini-paintings, drawings, sculpture, wood-turned bowls, collages, and more.

MOLLIE FEARING MEMORIAL ART SHOW
**Roanoke Island Festival Park, Manteo
(252) 473-5558
www.darearts.org**
The Dare County Arts Council puts on this annual art show, held at the beautiful Festival Park Art Gallery. Dare County Arts Council members and Dare County residents are invited to enter this show, which is held in May. Call DCAC at the number above for information.

ICARUS INTERNATIONAL ART SHOW
**Nags Head
(252) 441-6584**
Open to any artist, the Icarus International Art Show is held in December at Glenn Eure's Ghost Fleet Gallery and the Seaside Art Gallery (see listings under Galleries). The theme always revolves around flight, as the show was created to pay annual homage to the Wrights' first powered flight.

ANNUAL EVENTS

The beach isn't just for summer anymore. The Outer Banks has become a favorite destination for visitors year-round, providing those vacationing during less crowded times with a selection of activities to enjoy when life slows a bit.

When it comes to annual events on the Outer Banks, the environment and history are on our side. We have our time-honored cornerstones that draw national audiences, including the festivities each December commemorating the anniversary of humankind's first powered flight and the annual celebrations that revolve around Virginia Dare's birthday. Our environment is the calling card for national surfing championships, windsurfing and kiteboarding competitions, hang-gliding events, and world-class fishing tournaments.

The Outer Banks Forum (252-202-9732) offers musical performances, dramas, and comedies in the off-season. Look to the Theatre of Dare (252-473-1825) for comedy and drama performances in the off-season. The Dare County Arts Council (252-473-5558) sponsors a variety of performing and visual arts events throughout the year. Check out the Arts & Culture chapter for other options.

Check www.outerbanks.org/events for recently added activities.

JANUARY

OUTER BANKS WEDDING EXPO
First Flight High School, Kill Devil Hills
www.outerbanksweddingassoc.org
The largest wedding event on the Outer Banks takes place every year in early to mid-January. More than 1,000 brides and families attend the Sunday exhibit and meet with many of the businesses on the beach that cater to the local wedding industry. Foods can be sampled from caterers, photographers display their work, and musicians play samples of their music throughout the day. A fashion show and a drawing for an all-expenses-paid wedding tops off the event.

DARE COUNTY SCHOOLS ANNUAL ART SHOW
Glenn Eure's Ghost Fleet Gallery
210 East Driftwood St., Gallery Row, Nags Head
(252) 441-6584
For one week in mid-January, the Dare County Schools put together an art show that showcases works by kids from seven public schools, grades K–12. If you like children's art, this is the show for you. The works range from delightful watercolors to wild chairs crafted after such artists as Georgia O'Keeffe and Picasso. This show is primarily for viewing—it's difficult to wrestle work away from

parents. Don't expect to make any purchases, although some high-school students may be more inclined to sell for some pocket money. The show's reception is on a Sunday, generally at 2 p.m. Call for more information. Admission is free, and you can't beat the brownies and other goodies they serve.

FRANK STICK MEMORIAL ART SHOW
Glenn Eure's Ghost Fleet Gallery
210 East Driftwood St., Gallery Row,
Nags Head
(252) 473-5558

This art show has been held in late January through early February every year since 1978 and features the work of more than 160 artists. If you want to submit work, you must be at least 18 years old and a Dare County resident or a member of the Dare County Arts Council, which sponsors the show. The evening reception is eagerly anticipated, and local artists and patrons flock to the gallery to view the newest offerings from the art world. But don't be shy; the event welcomes visitors to partake of the sights, sounds, and tastes of the evening. If you can't make the reception, stop by during the month of February and view this always exciting and innovative exhibit. This is the best venue to see what area artists have been producing of late. Many artists go out on a limb, introducing new styles. It's a fun show, and the reception becomes an annual get-together for locals and visitors alike.

FEBRUARY

ELIZABETHAN RENDEZVOUS CABARET
Pamlico Jack's Pirate Hideaway
(252) 473-1061

This seven-course gourmet feast includes musical entertainment and dramatic interpretations. Tickets are about $100 per person and include food, wine, and beer.

MARCH

CIVIL WAR LIVING HISTORY WEEKEND
Island Farm
US 64, Roanoke Island
(252) 473-6500
www.theislandfarm.com

At Island Farm's living history site, travel back to 1862 when Union troops entered Croatan Sound and occupied Roanoke Island. Island Farm recreates the aftermath of the battle. See camp and officers' quarters, military drills, and hearth cooking demonstrations, and listen to a freed slave's perspective. $10 per person ages 6 and up.

PRICELESS PIECES PAST & PRESENT
QUILT EXTRAVAGANZA
Roanoke Island Festival Park Art Gallery,
Manteo
(252) 475-1500

If you love quilts and the fabric arts, you'll love this popular annual show. The show features old and new quilts made by or belonging to Dare County residents. There are also demonstrations. It's held throughout the month of Mar.

POLAR PLUNGE
(252) 449-8897

The Polar Plunge raises money for the "We Build People" campaign to help impoverished people on the Outer Banks attend programs at the Outer Banks YMCA. Child care, the swimming pool, and summer camp programs are also supplemented by taking the plunge. Refreshments are served before and after the event, which takes place on the beach at the Ramada Inn in Kill Devil Hills.

ST. PATRICK'S DAY PARADE
NC 12, Nags Head
(252) 441-4116
The St. Patrick's Day Parade is held the Sunday before St. Patrick's Day every year. The parade begins at the Nags Head Fishing Pier at MP 12 on the Beach Road and proceeds north to about MP 10. Reputed to be one of the largest parades of its kind in North Carolina, the event is fun for the whole family. Float participants throw candy, so wear something with pockets! Kelly's serves free hot dogs and sodas after the parade and celebrates with an evening of live entertainment. All events are free.

TASTE OF THE BEACH
Hilton Garden Inn, Kitty Hawk
(252) 202-8837
www.obxtasteofthebeach.com
Four days of food, dining, and fun. At the finest independent restaurants all over the beach, partake in wine tastings, cooking classes, and more. Top notch eateries compete for awards, and the event culminates in a grand tasting. This event grows each year and has become quite popular. Get tickets early, check the website for details.

APRIL

FIRE AND ICE GALA
Wright Brothers Memorial Pavilion
(252) 473-2127
www.thelostcolony.org
Enjoy a deviously good time at the annual Lost Colony fund-raiser. Eat delicious food; cast a bid for your favorite art work, vacation package, or other items in the silent auction; and dance into the evening at this dressy event. Tickets are $100 each.

KELLY'S MIDNIGHT EASTER EGG HUNT
Kelly's Outer Banks Restaurant & Tavern
US 158, MP 10½, Nags Head
(252) 441-4116
Adults enjoy searching for treats by flashlight. It's free fun. Anyone 21 or older may participate in this late-night egg hunt on the restaurant premises. The event's exact date depends on when Easter falls. Participants find eggs that may be empty or contain prizes such as gift certificates, free drink coupons, or free T-shirt coupons.

ANNUAL EASTER EGGSTRAVAGANZA
Kitty Hawk Kites
US 158, MP 12, Nags Head
(252) 441-4124, (800) FLY-THIS
www.kittyhawk.com
This event is held at Kitty Hawk Kites in Nags Head, with the specific date dependent on when Easter falls. Kids enjoy chalk coloring contests, a variety of games, and an Easter candy dig on the premises. Small fries get a kick out of meeting KHK's fuzzy brown mascot, Wil-Bear Wright. All activities are free.

EASTER EGGSTRAVAGANZA
Elizabethan Gardens
US 64, Roanoke Island
(252) 473-3234
Spring over to the Elizabethan Gardens and participate in this festive event. Hundreds of Easter eggs are hidden among the 40,000 blooms. Bunnies, Easter hat competitions, and more.

THE OUTER BANKS SENIOR GAMES
Thomas A. Baum Senior Center
300 Mustian St., Kill Devil Hills
(252) 441-1181
Dare County seniors age 55 and older are eligible to compete in the Outer Banks

Senior Games, a competition involving shuffleboard, billiards, spin casting, golf, bowling, horseshoes, table tennis, and much more. All ages are welcome to watch and cheer for the competitors in this late Apr event, which has been happening every year since 1988.

A modified version of the games is offered for disabled seniors. Volunteers work with each individual needing assistance. Games for this group can include door basketball and rubber horseshoes.

The local group of seniors sends hundreds of competitors to state competitions every year. Some have gone on to the national contest. Festivities include dinner at a local restaurant. The registration fee is $10 to participate in four events including the arts competition (see next listing) and includes lunch on opening day and track and field day.

THE OUTER BANKS SILVER ARTS COMPETITION
Thomas A. Baum Senior Center
300 Mustian St., Kill Devil Hills
(252) 441-1181

This is the art component of the Outer Banks Senior Games, featuring an exhibition of talent and craftsmanship in the visual, literary, heritage, and performing arts. The events last for several days, culminating in a free evening performance at the Kitty Hawk Elementary School. The $10 games registration fee covers entry into the arts competition.

ANNUAL OUTER BANKS BIKE WEEK
Kitty Hawk Harley-Davidson
8739 US 158, Harbinger
(252) 491-2901

NAGS HEAD HARLEY-DAVIDSON
US 158, MP 13, Nags Head
(252) 255-5922
www.outerbanksbikeweek.com

Rumbling into town, motorcyclers explore the Outer Banks for bike week every April. More than a few riders comb the area on their bikes during the festivities. Included in the fun are poker runs, bike shows, beauty contests, beer belly and tattoo contests, music, and official party sites named for each night.

INNER-TRIBAL POWWOW "JOURNEY HOME"
Cape Hatteras School, Buxton
(252) 995-4440
www.nativeamericanmuseum.org

For something truly special come to the Inner-Tribal Powwow put on by the folks at the Frisco Native American Museum and Natural History Center. The Inner-Tribal Powwow gathers 75 to 100 members of many different tribes for a weekend of celebration on the ancestral grounds of Hatteras Island. Tribal representatives come from all over North Carolina, the East Coast, and from as far away as Canada, Ohio, Washington State, and Arizona. It's a family event, with emphasis on the sharing of cultures. Many of the Native Americans dress in full regalia. Storytelling, drumming, and dancing are all part of the celebration. You'll get to sample Native American food, buy Native American wares, and watch Native craftspeople at work, as vendors often craft their wares. Demonstration dances and friendship dances (in which the public joins) make this an exciting cultural event, as does the Saturday-night bonfire. Recent additions to the festivities include workshops, pottery, weaving demonstrations, drumming, totem pole carving, and lots more. Small admission fees are charged either by the day or for the entire weekend, and children, seniors, and families are discounted.

EARTH DAY CELEBRATION
North Carolina Aquarium at Roanoke Island
(252) 473-5121
Admission to the aquarium is free on Earth Day (April 22). From 11 a.m. until 3 p.m.

OCEAN RODEO KITEBOARDING HATTERAS CREW GATHERING
NC 12, Frisco
(877) FLY-THIS
www.kittyhawk.com
Wind lovers enjoy this weeklong gathering featuring free demos. Kiteboarding reps bring the latest equipment. Part of the fun is the dinner at Good Winds restaurant, and everyone loves the swag bags.

MAY

HATTERAS VILLAGE OFFSHORE OPEN BILLFISH TOURNAMENT
Hatteras Harbor Marina, NC 12,
Hatteras Village
(252) 986-2555, (888) 544-8115
www.hatterasoffshoreopen.com
Anglers contend for cash prizes as they fish to catch and release the biggest billfish. A meat fish category is included for the largest tuna, dolphin, and wahoo caught daily. The three-day fishing tournament is sponsored by the Hatteras Village Civic Association. This is a Governor's Cup–sanctioned event, and it's the kickoff tournament in the Governor's Cup challenge. All competitors must enter Level 1 for $700; three additional levels— Level 2 at $800, Level 3 at $500, and Level

4 at $1,000—are not mandatory. Fishing begins at 8 a.m., and lines come out of the water promptly at 3 p.m. Festivities with food and drink are usually held each evening, and the event closes with an awards banquet. The tournament is open to the public.

MOLLIE FEARING MEMORIAL ART SHOW
Roanoke Island Festival Park, Manteo
(252) 473-5558
www.darearts.org
This exhibition, sponsored by the Dare County Arts Council, is open to all artists, and cash awards are given. It is held throughout the month of May and is open for public viewing. Call for membership, reception, and entry information.

BRITISH CEMETERY CEREMONY
British Cemetery Road, Ocracoke Island
(252) 928-3711
This ceremony commemorates the 1942 sinking of a British ship. On May 11 of that year, the HMS *Bedfordshire,* a trawler stationed off Ocracoke to protect our shores during World War II, was torpedoed and sunk by a German submarine. All on board perished, and only four bodies were recovered. Island residents buried these men, and every year on May 7 the US Coast Guard holds a service to honor them. The service is free. (See the Attractions chapter for more information.)

MARCH OF DIMES FOR BABIES WALK
Roanoke Island Festival Park, Manteo
(800) 732-7097
This fund-raising walk benefits the March of Dimes. The walk starts at Festival Park, winds through downtown Manteo, and ends back

at Festival Park. Music and refreshments are offered after the walk.

HANG GLIDING SPECTACULAR
Jockey's Ridge State Park, US 158, MP 12, Nags Head
(252) 441-4124, (800) FLY-THIS
www.kittyhawk.com

Spectators and participants cover the dunes at the park every year to attend the longest-running hang-gliding competition in the country (nearly 40 years), Pilots from all over the world compete in a variety of flying maneuvers, including an aerotow competition. Beginner hang-gliding lessons are given. The event is sponsored by Kitty Hawk Kites, and a complementary street dance and an awards ceremony add icing to the cake. Annual inductions to the Rogallo Hall of Fame (Southern Shores local Francis Rogallo was the beloved father of the Flexible Wing Flyer—the prototype for the modern hang glider) close the ceremony. Hang-glider pilots who have achieved their Hang One are welcome to compete. The public is invited to view the event for free. Participants pay an entry fee.

YUENGLING NAGS HEAD WOODS 5K RUN
Nags Head Woods Ecological Preserve
Ocean Acres Drive, Kill Devil Hills
www.active.com

Folks from all walks of life run side by side through Nags Head Woods in this annual event, held on the second Saturday in May. The run is limited to the first 400 runners registered. For entry fees and tickets, call the number listed.

i If you want to enter an art show sponsored by the Dare County Arts Council but you aren't a Dare County resident, simply join the arts council and you'll qualify to enter. You'll have a chance to win a cash prize, show your work, and help support the arts with your entry fee.

INTERNATIONAL MINIATURE ART SHOW
Seaside Art Gallery, NC 12, MP 11, Nags Head
(252) 441-5418, (800) 828-2444
www.seasideart.com

Artists from all over the world compete for cash prizes in this exhibition of miniature art. Past shows have seen more than 600 works from 38 states and 12 countries. The work includes paintings, sculpture, and drawings of all styles. The art is on view for the month of May.

JUNE

DARE DAY FESTIVAL
Downtown Manteo
(252) 475-5629

This is the quintessential small-town family event. Dare Day, held the first Saturday of June, is a much-loved local tradition that celebrates the wonderful county of Dare. You'll find locals, visitors, politicians, children, and just about everybody you can think of coming out to enjoy the day in downtown Manteo. Dare Day features arts and crafts booths, lots of food (including in-season soft-shell crabs), national and local musical entertainment, kids activities, games, rides, and much more. A free concert is held at Roanoke Island Festival Park in the pavilion. All of Festival Park's sites, including the

Elizabeth II, are free on this day. For a taste of real local culture, don't miss this event.

ROGALLO KITE FESTIVAL
Jockey's Ridge State Park, US 158,
MP 12, Nags Head
(800) 334-4777
www.kittyhawk.com
This two-day annual; festival celebrates kites of all sizes and shapes. Fly a kite on the dunes and enjoy nightly entertainment at Kitty Hawk Kites. Exhibitions, demonstrations, and kid's activities are all a part of this event.

i Before you leave home, check www.outerbanks.org/calendar_ of_events for recently added happenings on the Outer Banks. It's a great resource for new celebrations happening on the islands.

HATTERAS MARLIN CLUB BILLFISH TOURNAMENT
Hatteras Marlin Club, off NC 12,
Hatteras Village
(252) 986-2454
www.hatterasmarlinclub.com
The Hatteras Marlin Club Billfish Tournament, going strong since 1959, offers a week of competition fishing and entertainment to participants and their guests. Teams head for offshore waters looking to catch the biggest billfish or meat fish, including blue marlin, tuna, dolphin, and wahoo. Evenings are filled with socials that include entertainment, cocktails, appetizers, and dinner. The tournament is for members and anglers invited by the tournament committee. Call for registration fee information.

BLOODY MARY AND THE VIRGIN QUEEN
Roanoke Island Festival Park, Manteo
(252) 475-1506
www.roanokeisland.com
This farce is based upon the tempestuous relationship between Queen Elizabeth I and Mary Tudor. General admission to the park includes the performance; however, tickets must be reserved in advance. Appropriate for ages 14 and older. Performed select weekdays at 3 p.m. in the film theater.

SHEPHERD OF THE OCEAN
Roanoke Island Festival Park, Manteo
(252) 475-1506
www.roanokeisland.com
Shepherd of the Ocean is a whimsical comedy inspired by the relationship between Sir Walter Raleigh and Queen Elizabeth I. Moments before Sir Walter Raleigh is set to be executed, he looks back upon his time with the beloved queen. General admission to the park includes the performance; however, tickets must be reserved in advance. Appropriate for ages 14 and older. Performed select weekdays at 3 p.m. in the film theater.

TEA WITH THE QUEEN
Waterside Theatre, Roanoke Island
(252) 473-2127
www.thelostcolony.org
Have an audience and enjoy tea with Queen Elizabeth I and her royal court at Waterside Theatre, the same spot where *The Lost Colony* performs in the evenings. A backstage tour is included. Advance reservations required. Ticket prices are adults $22, children 7 to 18 $11.

JULY

SAND SCULPTURE CONTEST
On the beach north of Ocracoke Village
(252) 928-7689

This artistic endeavor kicks off Fourth of July festivities on the island. Kids and adults are welcome to participate in the early-morning event. You can work alone or in groups. Past events have seen sand transformed into turtles, jumping dolphins, pirates, mermaids, and ships. The contest is free. Call for times and location.

INDEPENDENCE DAY PARADE AND FIREWORKS DISPLAY
Ocracoke Village
(252) 928-7689

This festive parade featuring a half dozen floats makes its way through the streets starting around 3 p.m. on July 4. Local shopkeepers and residents create floats for what's dubbed the village's biggest annual event. The parade moves down NC 12 through Ocracoke Village. The evening ends with a gala fireworks display at Lifeguard Beach. Ocracokers say it's the best Fourth of July celebration on the Outer Banks.

DUCK ANNUAL 4TH OF JULY PARADE
Duck
(252) 255-1234
www.townofduck.com

This parade is often held on July 3rd, so traffic will not be stopped (call ahead). At 9 a.m. the parade winds its way from Scarborough Lane, up Clover Way to Christopher Drive. After the parade, there is entertainment at Duck Town Park.

MANTEO INDEPENDENCE DAY CELEBRATION
Manteo
(252) 473-1101

Activities run from 1 to 9 p.m. and include a Wacky Tacky Hat Contest, children's games, food and other concessions, musical entertainment, and a street dance from 6 to 9 p.m., when a fireworks display begins. The event is free.

FIREWORKS FESTIVAL AND FAIR
The Whalehead Club, NC 12, Corolla
(252) 453-9040

The historic hunt club is the backdrop for the fireworks and fair that begin at 6 p.m. and run to 11 p.m. The Currituck County Board of Commissioners and the Corolla Business Association host this event. Expect fun, food, live musical entertainment, and, of course, pyrotechnics galore. Admission is free.

ANNUAL EVENING UNDER THE STARS WITH THE NORTH CAROLINA SYMPHONY
Outdoor Pavilion, Roanoke Island
Festival Park
(252) 473-2138
www.roanokeisland.com

Bring a lawn chair, a blanket, and a picnic if you like. Great music under the stars enhances a romantic evening. Event begins at 8 p.m.; however often other entertainment begins around 6 p.m. Free.

ANNUAL WRIGHT KITE FESTIVAL
Wright Brothers National Memorial
US 158, MP 8, Kill Devil Hills
(252) 441-4124, (800) 334-4777

This mid-July family event involves kite flying for all ages and also includes free kite-making workshops, stunt kite demos, and children's games. The event, sponsored by Kitty Hawk Kites and the National Park Service, has been held every year since 1978. You can watch for free. Adults are invited to participate in kite contests. Call for fees.

OBX SUMMER ARTS FESTIVAL
Hilton Garden Inn, Kitty Hawk

Held July 15 from 10 a.m. until 7 p.m. and July 16 from 10 a.m. until 5 p.m., this free event features many fine artworks.

AUGUST

HATTERAS ISLAND ARTS AND CRAFTS GUILD CRAFTS SHOW
Cape Hatteras High School
NC 12, Buxton

This craft show, held in early August, features pottery, dolls, clock making, shellwork, and countless other goodies. Hours are 10 a.m. to 4 p.m. both days, and admission is free.

ANNUAL KITTY HAWK KITES OCEAN GAMES & SURF KAYAK COMPETITION
Ramada Plaza Beach, Kill Devil Hills
(252) 441-4124
www.kittyhawk.com

In late August, spend a fun day at the beach with Kitty Hawk Kites. Kids can build sandcastles, watch kite demos, and fly a kite. A 5-mile kayak race tops off the event.

ANNUAL HERBERT HOOVER BIRTHDAY CELEBRATION
Manteo Booksellers
Sir Walter Raleigh Street, Manteo
(252) 473-1221

On August 10 browse through this superb bookstore, taste three cakes (each one inscribed with "Happy," "Birthday," or

"Herbie"), sip some famous "Herbert Sherbert" punch, and chat with Hoover fans at this tongue-in-cheek free event. The reason for the fun? It's purely for the sake of having a celebration. The day includes a book signing. Look for a special display of Hoover memorabilia. Come eat, drink, and think Herbert Hoover!

ANNUAL SENIOR ADULTS CRAFT FAIR
Thomas A. Baum Center
300 Mustian St., Kill Devil Hills
(252) 441-9388

Local senior citizens provide the crafts for this community project sponsored by the Outer Banks Women's Club. It's been a tradition for more than 25 years. Admission is $1.

ALICE KELLY MEMORIAL LADIES ONLY BILLFISH TOURNAMENT
Pirate's Cove Yacht Club
Nags Head–Manteo Causeway, Manteo
(252) 473-6800, (800) 367-4728
www.fishpiratescove.com

The tournament, sponsored by Pirate's Cove since 1989, honors the memory of local fishing enthusiast Alice Kelly, who died in her 30s from Hodgkin's disease. Kelly was a high-spirited woman whose love for fishing inspired many local women to try (and fall in love with) the sport. Women form teams and arrange for charter boats to carry them out to sea. The tournament occurs in mid-August. The entry fee is $400.

ANNUAL PIRATE'S COVE BILLFISH TOURNAMENT
Pirate's Cove Yacht Club
Nags Head–Manteo Causeway, Manteo
(252) 473-6800, (800) 367-4728
www.fishpiratescove.com

All Summer Long . . .

The Lost Colony
Waterside Theatre, Manteo
(252) 473-3414; www.thelostcolony.org
The Lost Colony is a theatrical presentation of a 400-year-old mystery performed on the actual location of the historical event. It is presented May 29 through Aug 20 at 8 p.m. Backstage tours and picnics are available with a reservation before the show. Call the box office or visit the website for details. Other presentations are performed at 2 p.m. on Wed and Thurs. More information appears in the Attractions chapter.

First Friday
Downtown Manteo
www.roanokeisland.net/recreation/by_night/firstfriday
Visit the waterfront and downtown Manteo the first Friday of the month Apr through Dec. The waterfront comes alive with music, artisans, magicians, and more. 6 p.m. until 9 p.m.

Real Night School, Real Watersports Waves
(252) 987-6000; www.realkiteboarding.com
Free kiteboarding classes are held Tuesday nights at 6 p.m. Kiteboarding pros and celebs often are available to give advice and answer questions.

Hatteras Realty Programs
Avon
(252) 995-5466, (800) 428-8372; www.hatterasrealty.com
Held June through August, Hatteras Realty is a center for fun. Kinnakeet Sound Safari is held Tues through Fri from 9:30 a.m. to 2 p.m. for ages 4-12. Kids travel and study the unique estuary known as the Pamlico Sound. $25. Tuesday night is Kid's Night Out. Traditional Mexican activities, a brief Spanish lesson and tacos are included in the evening. 6 p.m. until 10 p.m. Kids ages 4-12. $25. Carolina Coastal Cooking is held on Wed from 7 until 9 p.m. The resident chef combines the latest trends with the classic Outer Banks recipes. Reservations required. $5. Hatteras Heroes is a storytelling time. Danny Couch gives an exciting multimedia presentation. 7 p.m. Free, reservations recommended.

Chicamacomico Lifesaving Station
NC 12, Rodanthe
(252) 987-1552
Summer programs at the Chicamacomico Lifesaving Station run June through August. Tues evenings at 7:30 p.m. there is a beach bonfire program. The program lasts 1 hour. Guests hear detailed stories about three dramatic rescues that occurred in the area. No hot dogs or marshmallows allowed! Beach chairs, flashlights, and bug spray are recommended. A

1-hour porch program held each weekday at 2 p.m. offer a variety of programs Lifesaving stations were the cultural, social, and educational centers of the community in times past, making the Lost Colony story a perfect fit for this quaint setting.

Roanoke Island Festival Park Performing Series
Roanoke Island Festival Park, Manteo
(252) 475-1506; www.roanokeisland.com

Starting in late June and running through mid-August, Roanoke Island Festival Park stages wonderful cultural activities almost every day of the week. Students from the University of North Carolina perform on select nights in the pavilion. You'll see dance, jazz, children's shows, classical music, and drama. See the Attractions and Arts & Culture chapters for more about this series.

Duck Town Park
NC 12, Duck
(252) 255-1286; www.townofduck.com

Throughout June, July, and August, a variety of programs are held at Duck Town Park. Check the website or call the above number for more information on these programs. Bring a hat and a blanket or beach chair to this lovely setting.

Whalehead Club Wednesday Wine Festival
Corolla
(252) 453-9040

Held July, August, and September, come enjoy North Carolina wines and wines from around the world each Wed. A $20 admission fee not only admits you to the sampling areas, but you also may keep the souvenir glass, listen to popular local musical groups, sample food from local vendors, and take a complimentary tour of the Whalehead Club. 3 until 7 p.m.

Kitty Hawk Kites Kids Day
Corolla, Nags Head, Waves, Hatteras
(252) 441-4124; www.kittyhawk.com

This free event is held on Tuesday (except in Waves, on Wed) June through August. Kids can make and fly a kite, try their hands at yoyos, have their faces painted and—best of all—demo the latest toys.

Summer Concerts on the Lawn
Currituck Heritage Park, Corolla
(252) 453-9040

Thursday evenings from 6:30 until sunset July through August, relax at Currituck Heritage Park. Musicians from the N.C. School of the Arts and local musicians entertain with the sounds of jazz, blues, folk, and classic rock. Bring a beach chair or a blanket. Snack concessions available. Free. Leashed pets welcome.

Pirate's Cove Yacht Club has hosted a billfish release tournament every August since 1983. Contenders fish for several days to catch and release the largest billfish. A meat fish (tuna, dolphin, and wahoo) category, in which a prize is awarded for the largest catch, adds to the fun. The tournament is an official part of the N.C. Governor's Cup Billfish Series and occurs mid-month. Call for entry fee information.

NEW WORLD FESTIVAL OF THE ARTS
Manteo
(252) 473-2838
This mid-August event brings downtown Manteo alive with art every year. The outdoor two-day show features more than 80 artists showcasing fine art and crafts, including pottery, jewelry, paintings, and more. Outdoor booths and tents line the historic waterfront, attracting visitors who return each year looking for their favorite artists; free admission.

VIRGINIA DARE BIRTHDAY CELEBRATION
Fort Raleigh National Historic Site Visitor Center
US 64/264, Roanoke Island
(252) 473-2127
This event, held August 18, commemorates the birth of Virginia Dare, the first English child born in the New World. The celebration features a daylong series of special happenings. Past events featured performances by members of the cast of *The Lost Colony* and demonstrations of arms from that period in history. Call the National Park Service for details. This event is free. The Elizabethan Gardens, right next to Fort Raleigh, honors Virginia Dare's birthday by offering free admission to the gardens on this day and a free play about Queen Elizabeth and Sir Walter Raleigh.

VIRGINIA DARE NIGHT PERFORMANCE OF *THE LOST COLONY*
Waterside Theatre US 64/264, Roanoke Island
(252) 473-3414, (800) 488-5012
www.thelostcolony.org
On August 18 *The Lost Colony* celebrates Virginia Dare's 1587 birth by casting local infants in the role of baby Virginia. This makes for a special and spontaneous performance; usually baby Virginia is played by a doll. (For details on the famous outdoor drama, see the Attractions chapter.)

NATIONAL AVIATION DAY
Wright Brothers National Memorial
US 158, MP 8, Kill Devil Hills
(252) 441-7430
www.nps.gov/wrbr/
Explore planes galore at this free mid-August event. Aviation enthusiasts enjoy viewing about 25 different types of single-engine aircraft ranging from the antique to modern-day models. The schedule is not firm until a few days before the event so weather conditions can be taken into consideration. Past events have included a flyover with US Air Force and Navy planes, jets from Langley Field, and the Blue Angels. The day's festivities include free admission to the memorial

SEPTEMBER

OUTER BANKS PIRATE FESTIVAL
Kitty Hawk Kites
MP 12½, Nags Head
(252) 441-4124
www.kittyhawk.com
Hark, all ye little buccaneers! Aaaaarrgh, it's pirate week on the Outer Banks in mid-September. Community events throughout the week culminate at the Nags Head Kitty Hawk

Kites location. Entertainment, reenactments, games, stories, and pirate appearances top off the week.

HATTERAS VILLAGE CIVIC
   ASSOCIATION SURF FISHING
   TOURNAMENT
Hatteras Village Civic Center
NC 12, Hatteras Village
(252) 986-2579
Since 1982 surf-fishing fans have met the third week in September for this tournament. Anglers fish for eligible species including drum, bluefish, trout, and more. Call for registration fees and information.

DAY AT THE DOCKS—A CELEBRATION
   OF HATTERAS WATERMEN
Hatteras Village
www.dayatthedocks.org
In mid-September, visit Hatteras Village to view the commercial and charter fleets anchored in the Hatteras waters. Displays, boat skills, demonstrations, and competitions kick off the day. Maritime games for kids will be available throughout the day, and fresh local seafood will be featured in the chowder cook-off and cooking demonstrations. Local musicians will perform throughout the day. The event takes place from 10 a.m. until 5 p.m.

ESA EASTERN SURFING
   CHAMPIONSHIPS
Location varies
(800) 937-4733
www.surfesa.org
Competition is open to Eastern Surfing Association members only, but it's an exciting and free spectator event. Watch as surfers grab their boards and head to the ocean to pit their skills against the waves and their

fellow competitors. For more information write to Box 400, Buxton, NC 27920.

OBX TRIATHALON
www.obxmarathon.org
This event, held in early September, brings athletes to compete in this unique coastal environment. The event features half distance, sprint, and Olympic distance challenges.

WAVE RIDING VEHICLES HURLEY
   OUTER BANKS PRO SURF
(252) 261-7952
www.waveridingvehicles.com
Talent from all over the world competes at one of the largest pro surfing events on the east coast. $30,000 purse.

OCTOBER

NORTH CAROLINA BIG SWEEP
Dare County beaches
(800) 27-SWEEP
www.ncbigsweep.org
This is a local waterway cleanup that's hooked into a statewide and national event. Trash picking runs from 9 a.m. to 1 p.m. on the first Sat in Oct. Folks have cleaned the waterways since 1986, performing their civic duty. Obviously, it's free. Call the above number for more information.

ARTRAGEOUS ART EXTRAVAGANZA
   WEEKEND
Dare County Arts Council
Dare County Recreation Park
Mustian Street, Kill Devil Hills
(252) 473-5558
www.darearts.org
Artrageous, started in 1990, is a community art festival and auction sponsored by the Dare

County Arts Council the first weekend in Oct. Children and adults are invited to spend Saturday painting, weaving, and creating various arts and crafts. All art supplies are provided. Listen to local musicians young and old, eat tasty food, and witness art in the making by professionals. Artists sell their wares. Collaborative paintings by children are auctioned on Saturday; a more formal adult auction, complete with hors d'oeuvres and cocktails, takes place on Sunday. Saturday's events do not require an admission fee. Average price for booth activities is $1. The Sunday evening auction is held at varying locations; call for details.

NAGS HEAD SURF FISHING CLUB INVITATIONAL TOURNAMENT
Nags Head
(252) 441-5464

The Nags Head Surf Fishing Club's tournament will celebrate 60 years in 2010. Team fishing can be booked solid for years. But participants are welcome to fish the individual tournament on Sat from 8 a.m. to noon. Call for details.

OUTER BANKS HOMEBUILDERS ASSOCIATION'S PARADE OF HOMES
Homes from Corolla to South Nags Head and Manteo
(252) 449-8232
www.obhomebuilders.org

The OBHA opens new and remodeled homes to the public for this event being held early October. It costs $10 to tour about 32 participating homes. Proceeds are donated to local charities.

ANNUAL JAZZ FESTIVAL
Duck Town Park
(252) 255-1286
www.townofduck.com

Join the town of Duck at the second annual jazz festival held at the town park. Several jazz bands will perform at this free festival held October 11 from 11 a.m. until 5 p.m. Bring a blanket and enjoy some great music.

OUTER BANKS STUNT KITE COMPETITION
Wright Brothers Memorial
MP 8, Kill Devil Hills
(252) 441-4124, (800) FLY-THIS
www.kittyhawk.com

Entrants compete on the Eastern League Circuit of the American Kiting Association. The program features novice, intermediate, and expert challenges as well as workshops and demos. Kids enjoy making kites. Music, kite ballet competitions, and team train competitions highlight the sanctioned event. Registration and competition fees are charged to competitors.

RED DRUM TOURNAMENT
Frank and Fran's Fisherman's Friend
NC 12, Avon
(252) 995-4171

Two hundred anglers fish the surf and try to catch the largest red drum during this late October event, sponsored by the popular Avon tackle shop. Fees are about $100 per person. Limited space is available for this three-day tournament.

KELLY'S/PAMLICO JACK'S CHARITY GOLF TOURNAMENT
US 158, MP 15, Nags Head
Currituck Club, Corolla
(252) 441-4116

Six-person teams play 18 holes for charity during late October. Proceeds benefit the Outer Banks Community Foundation. Fees per team generally run around $500.

TEACH'S LAIR SHOOTOUT KING MACKEREL TOURNAMENT
Teach's Lair Marina, NC 12
Hatteras Village
(252) 986-2460

In this Hatteras Village tournament, anglers try their luck in capturing the largest king mackerel at the end of October or early November. Entry fees range from $300 to $350. The tournament is open to the public.

NOVEMBER

WINGS OVER WATER FESTIVAL
Many Outer Banks locations
(252) 216-9464
www.wingsoverwater.org

Wings Over Water is a six-day celebration of the Outer Banks' wonderful wildlife and wildlands. It offers a number of activities for those who want to learn more about this enchanting natural area. You select the field trips, programs, and seminars that interest you the most and then get an inside look at the various ecological settings and wildlife of the Outer Banks. For example, go on guided bird-watching trips at Pea Island National Wildlife Refuge, kayak or canoe into a salt marsh, or motor out to the waters of the Gulf Stream. There is such an enormous list of activities that this is only the tip of the iceberg. All programs charge a moderate fee. For information or to register for the event, call the number above or visit the website, where there's an online registration form.

MOUNT OLIVET UNITED METHODIST CHURCH BAZAAR
300 Ananias Dare St., Manteo
(252) 473-2089

For this event the church is filled with all sorts of goodies, including books, kitchenware, antiques, and baked treats. Get there early—this is a very popular event. Browse table after table covered with exciting finds—something old, something new. The day features a late afternoon/early evening auction. There's no charge. This event is held the first Sat in Nov.

MANTEO ROTARY ROCKFISH RODEO
Roanoke Island Festival Park, Manteo
(252) 473-4268
www.rockfishrodeo.com

Whether you call them rockfish, striped bass, or stripers, the fish can win you big money and help a good cause in this tournament. Participants fish in the sound or ocean from 6 a.m. to 3 p.m. and bring one fish back to the weigh station. Trophies are given to the top four winners in the ocean and sound categories, and the top winner can win up to $5,000. All nonfishing events and the weigh-in are held at Roanoke Island Festival Park. Registration, a social hour, and an anglers' rule meeting are held Friday night. Saturday it's fishing, the weigh-in, and an awards dinner. Manteo Rotary, the sponsor of this event, uses the profits to give college scholarships to local youth, and they have granted more than $170,000 to students because of this tournament.

OBX MARATHON AND HALF MARATHON
Kitty Hawk and Jockey's Ridge State Park
www.obxmarathon.org

The second Sun in Nov brings runners from all over the country to the OBX Marathon. Runners begin in Kitty Hawk and journey by the Wright Brothers National Memorial, through Nags Head Woods maritime forest, and across the scenic Washington Baum Bridge to finish on Roanoke Island.

Participants in the half marathon will take off at Jockey's Ridge State Park and follow the same route from that point. Four thousand slots are available, and the total purse for both events is $25,000. Prizes, music, food, medals, and T-shirts follow the event.

CAPE HATTERAS ANGLERS CLUB INDIVIDUAL SURF FISHING TOURNAMENT
Buxton
(252) 995-4253
The Cape Hatteras Anglers Club sponsors a one-day individual surf-fishing tournament in mid-November. Registration is held at the Cape Hatteras Anglers Club in Buxton, and fishing takes place from 8 a.m. to noon. Prizes are awarded.

HATTERAS ISLAND ARTS AND CRAFTS GUILD HOLIDAY SHOW
Cape Hatteras High School
NC 12, Buxton
(252) 995-4673
This craft show held in late November includes pottery, dolls, shellwork, and woodworking. Hours are 10 a.m. to 4 p.m. each day. Admission is free.

ALL SAINTS EPISCOPAL CHURCH CHRISTMAS BAZAAR
40 Pintail Trail, Southern Shores
(252) 261-6674
www.allsaints-eastcarolina.org
Expect to be wowed on the Friday and Saturday before Thanksgiving, when All Saints Episcopal Church becomes a Christmas shopper's paradise. Fine art, hand-painted home accessories, custom jewelry, artful Christmas decor, and more are available at this annual event. Delicious baked goods are prepared just in time to serve

for Thanksgiving. You'll find truly wonderful gifts in all price ranges. This event is not to be missed!

ADVICE 5K ANNUAL TURKEY TROT
Duck
(252) 255-1050
www.advice5.com
Pump up your Thanksgiving Day appetite with an early-morning 5K run. This annual, nonsanctioned 3.1-mile run starts behind Scarborough Lane Shops in Duck and ends at the Red Sky Cafe/Village Wine Shop, where everyone gathers for a raffle and to see the winners. The top male and female runners win a pumpkin pie. This is a lively event. Walkers and runners are welcome, and no one is expected to take it too seriously. Register early by calling the number above, or register in person at the Red Sky Cafe on the Wed before Thanksgiving Day. There is no race-day registration.

ISLAND FOODWAYS
US 64, Roanoke Island
(252) 473-6500
During the weekend after Thanksgiving, Island Farm interprets fall food traditions and shares how Roanoke Islanders prepared for winters during the 1850s. Activities such as hearth cooking, food preservation, oxdrawn wagon, corn shucking, and shelling are demonstrated. Bring a nonperishable food item for the food pantry and receive $1 off admission.

KITES WITH LIGHTS
Jockey's Ridge State Park, Nags Head
(252) 441-4124
Stunt kites are strung with lights, creating a magical, multicolored nighttime scene. The kites fly sky high, dancing to traditional

Christmas carols. Climbing up Jockey's Ridge at night is fun, especially when you're treated with a show like this at the top. Christmas carols, hot apple cider, and cookies make it more fun. This event is held in late Nov. It's free and begins at sunset.

CHICAMACOMICO LIFESAVING STATION CHRISTMAS LIGHTING
Rodanthe
(252) 987-1552
This classic lifesaving station looks absolutely stunning when decorated for the holidays with lights, greenery, and ribbons. In late Nov when the building is decorated in its finery, the folks at Chicamacomico have a daylong celebration and open house.

DECEMBER

LIGHTING OF THE TOWN TREE AND CHRISTMAS PARADE
Manteo
(252) 473-2133
Manteo and Dare County get ready for the holidays over the first weekend in December with events for the whole family. On Friday the big town tree, right on the waterfront next to the Tranquil House Inn, is lit about 6:30 p.m. The event is accompanied by carols, a Yule log, cake, and hot chocolate. It's a good place to gather and get in the holiday spirit.

On Saturday morning a hometown parade rambles through the streets of downtown Manteo. Kids love watching the floats, bands, dancers, local organizations, and, of course, Santa. Afterward, celebrate with food, holiday crafts, entertainment, and a chance to visit with Santa at the waterfront. We like to go to the parade then early Christmas shop in downtown Manteo.

CHRISTMAS AT ROANOKE ISLAND FESTIVAL PARK
Manteo
(252) 475-1506 (24-hour events line)
This beautiful cultural center is alive in December with plenty of good cheer. Expect concerts, sing-alongs, children's performances, and a sale in the Museum Store. Call the events line for holiday offerings.

OUTER BANKS HOTLINE'S FESTIVAL OF TREES
(252) 473-5121
Since 1988 this popular auction and fundraiser has taken place in early December. Businesses and individuals donate fully decorated Christmas trees and other holiday items to be auctioned and delivered to buyers. Proceeds benefit Hotline's crisis intervention program and needy families in the area. Past trees have been decorated with Beanie Babies, handwoven tapestry wear and accessories, and CDs. The festive event includes several days of celebrations. Call the Hotline office for location and ticket information.

HOLIDAY TOUR OF HOMES
Historic Manteo
(252) 473-5548
Get an inside peek at some of Manteo's finest homes on this festive tour. The Elizabethan Gardens and the Island Farm are included on the route. This magical event is sponsored by the Manteo Preservation Trust.

MAN WILL NEVER FLY MEMORIAL SOCIETY INTERNATIONAL ANNUAL SEMINAR AND AWARDS PROGRAM
Comfort Inn South
NC 12, MP 17, Nags Head
(800) 334-4777

This tongue-in-cheek organization tries to prove every year that man never really flew and abides by the motto "Birds Fly, Men Drink." The banquet is held annually the night before the anniversary of the first flight and is open to the public. The food is prepared buffet-style and features meat as well as seafood. Call for ticket and reservation information.

WRIGHT BROTHERS ANNIVERSARY OF FIRST FLIGHT
Wright Brothers National Memorial
US 158, MP 8, Kill Devil Hills
(252) 441-7430, (800) 334-4777
On December 17, 1903, Wilbur and Orville Wright made their first successful flights before a handful of local residents. This event is celebrated every year on December 17, in the exact place where those flights occurred. Bands play and planes fly as the monumental events of the Wright brothers are recalled. Speakers generally include military personnel, local dignitaries, and individuals who have dedicated their lives to the advancement of flight technology. A portrait of the year's induction to the First Flight Society is unveiled. There is no charge.

SEASIDE ART GALLERY
NC 12, MP 11, Nags Head
(252) 441-5418
This international art show, started in 1993, carries the theme of the mystery and beauty of flight. Each year a specific flight-related theme is chosen, and artists submit original art in all genres to compete for a multitude of top-dollar prizes. The art is displayed through the month of December at two Nags Head galleries. A children's component is included at another location. Call the listed numbers to get on the mailing list. Children enter for free. Adult entries run between $10 and $15. A commission is taken for sold work by Icarus International, a nonprofit group. A literary competition is held on the same theme as the visual arts competition every year. The chapbook of juried entries is published in December.

GRAND ILLUMINATION AT ELIZABETHAN GARDENS
Off US 64, Roanoke Island
(252) 473-3234
www.elizabethangardens.org
The first weekend in December is a time of wonderment and magic in the Elizabethan Gardens. Teams of designers light the gardens into a glowing paradise of winter wonderment. Hot chocolate, fire pits, and entertainment create an atmosphere certain to put any Scrooge into the spirit of the holiday.

NATURAL WONDERS

To become a true Outer Banks insider, you must develop a relaxed attitude and deep respect for nature, especially the weather. Outer Bankers' lives are ruled by nature's temperaments. From the calm, humid, and sunny days of early summer to the windy days of autumn and the raw days of winter nor'easters, you'll marvel at the variable weather conditions. And then spring, both warm and cold, sunny and rainy, comes around again.

The interplay of sand, land, water, and wind is the primal force that drives life on these barrier islands. During your visit, even if you're not inclined toward contemplation, slow down and spend some time getting acquainted with your temporary habitat and with what makes it unique.

OVERVIEW

Bounded by the Atlantic Ocean on the east and a vast expanse of sound waters to the west, and connected in between by waterways and wetlands, the Outer Banks is among the most fascinating and complex habitats in North America. The Gulf Stream and the continental shelf's edge influence us from a mere 37 miles away. Cradled within our boundaries are several unusual maritime forests, and Cape Hatteras marks the dividing line for northern and southern animal and plant species.

Because of our geographic location and environmental offerings, animal lovers from the world over come to the Outer Banks to sight rare pelagic birds, breaching humpbacks, and nesting waterfowl. Even manatees and harbor seals have visited our shores. Anglers ply the waters for anything from the humble flounder to the majestic blue marlin. Botanists study our ancient live oaks. Writers hole up in wooden beach cottages

and ponder how poetically the wind howls. Families return year after year, generation after generation, to splash among the waves, explore tidal zones for sealife, and canvass the shores for colorful shells.

While the old-timers rightfully argue that things have changed dramatically here since the 1970s, there's always been a constant: We are at the mercy of the forces of nature. Our dependency is clear: Nature feeds us, creates and crumbles livelihoods, offers unlimited free entertainment, is the artist's muse, and sends us scurrying for shelter at a whim.

In this chapter we'll introduce you to the land and its wonders, shaped by our bountiful waters and our crazy Outer Banks weather.

Insiders have self-imposed, state, and national restrictions on game fishing. We support tag-and-release programs and escort infant loggerhead sea turtles off the sand and into the water. Young and old alike participate annually in a nationwide coastal cleanup. All we ask of our visitors is that you treat the area's fragile ecosystem with care. This vacation paradise is home not only for us but also for our less vocal friends who thrive on the air, sea, and land.

THE LAND

It doesn't take long to realize that the Outer Banks' barrier island system—a narrow stretch of sand—contains vast variety in topography. Geologists refer to the Outer Banks and similar land forms as "barrier islands" because they block the high-energy ocean waves and storm surges, protecting the coastal mainland. Winds, weather, and waves create the personality of the slender strips of sand. Inlets from the sounds to the sea are ever shifting, opening new channels to the ocean one century or decade, and closing off primary passageways the next.

Sand forms a partnership with the sea to create a wonderland that sweeps from Carova down through the Cape Hatteras National Seashore onto Ocracoke Island. At Jockey's Ridge State Park in Nags Head, huge migrating dunes heralded as the largest sand hills on the East Coast create one of the most popular attractions on the Outer Banks (see the Attractions chapter). It is an amazing sight to see the sand moving ribbonlike as the wind whips across the dunes. Human forms dot the landscape, insignificant against the towering backdrop as they climb the dunes to fly kites, hang glide, or simply view the sound and ocean.

At sunset the visual drama intensifies. The forms coming and going become stark silhouettes. Come nightfall the dunes are silent, but wildlife exists. Foxes roam the area,

as do deer and opossum, and vegetation thrives in the sand. Wild grapes, bayberry, black cherry, and Virginia creeper live along the park trail.

Sand is a challenge and a blessing. It thwarts seaside gardeners who replace their sandy land with mainland soil to grow vegetables. Outer Bankers have a long-standing love/hate relationship with the gritty stuff: We play in it, pour it out of our shoes daily, and constantly suck it into vacuums, but we know that this movable earth has played a vital role in the formation of our natural habitat.

The next time you stroll along the shore, notice vegetation such as sea oats and spartina climbing the sloping dunes. Windblown sand collects behind these pioneer plants, which often grow in otherwise barren soil. With the right combination of currents and breezes, a dune can grow large enough to protect areas that lie behind them, forming tall barriers against the salty sea spray, hence allowing the birth of maritime forests. Our habitat has generated several such phenomena that interest the naturalist and layperson alike.

i Incredible photos can be taken just at sunset. The light on the Outer Banks becomes ethereal, making photographs works of art.

Nags Head Woods

Lo and behold! A maritime forest that seemingly defies nature flourishes on the Outer Banks. Normally, vegetation that is constantly battered by salt and wind is stunted and minimal. In the Nags Head Woods Ecological Preserve, 1,400 acres of maritime forest contain a diversity of flora and fauna that's very unusual in a harsh barrier island climate. This forest has been able to thrive due to a ridge of ancient sand dunes, some 90 feet high, that has shielded the land from the effects of the sea. The woods also owe their diversity to freshwater supplied by the high dunes that absorb and slowly release rainwater into the underlying aquifer, swamps, and dozens of year-round and seasonal ponds.

Botanists have identified more than 300 plant species in the forest, with a mixture of northern and southern varieties. This combination is rare, existing in only four places in the world. In fact, Nags Head Woods is classified as globally rare. The oldest tree in the woods is thought to be a 500-year-old live oak, but woody plants have been growing in this area for thousands of years.

Plant lovers appreciate the woods throughout the year. The forest is lush with ferns, pines, oaks, red bay, blueberry, grasses, bamboo, sassafras, gums, and hundreds more species. Several species rare to North Carolina thrive in the forest, including the wooly beach heather, water violet, southern twayblade, and mosquito fern.

Arguably the most diverse population of reptiles and amphibians on the Outer Banks has found a permanent home in Nags Head Woods. These include 5 species of salamanders, 14 species of frogs and toads, more than 20 species of snakes, and multiple species of lizards and turtles. This unusual forest provides nesting spots for more than 50 species of birds and is home to a wide variety of mammals, including raccoons, river otters, gray fox, white-tailed deer, and opossum.

Insiders like to visit the forest in the fall and spring. Cooler weather and fewer mosquitoes make the trek more appealing, and there are plenty of visiting birds and waterfowl. The great blue heron and green heron are common to the woods. Several species

of songbirds may serenade you as you walk: Carolina chickadees, great crested flycatchers, many thrushes, and numerous warblers.

More than 5 miles of trails are available to hikers. Center Trail is a quarter mile long and features scenic pond overlooks. The Sweetgum Swamp Trail takes hikers through rolling hills of forests, dunes, and ponds. The Blueberry Ridge Trail connects to the Sweetgum Swamp Trail for a total length of 3.5 miles. To head toward the sound, take the Roanoke Trail past the farm site and cemetery of the Tillett clan—allow about an hour for the 1.5-mile round-trip. And the Discovery Trail provides a quick quarter-mile view of the ponds, swamps, and dune ridges found on the longer trails.

Dogs on leashes, four-wheel-drive vehicles, and bikes are allowed on the road that runs through Nags Head Woods, but they are not allowed in other parts of the preserve. Visitation hours are 10 a.m. to 3 p.m. Mon through Fri during the off-season and Mon through Sat during the summer. Members of the Nature Conservancy may tour the preserve during any daylight hours. These limitations help preserve the natural habitats of this rare ecosystem. There is no fee to enter, but a donation is requested.

The Nags Head Woods Ecological Preserve (252-441-2525) is overseen by the Nature Conservancy, an international nonprofit conservation organization. If you wish to contribute to the Nature Conservancy, you can send a donation to 701 West Ocean Acres Dr., Kill Devil Hills, NC 27948 or call (252) 441-2525 for membership information.

Buxton Woods Coastal Reserve

Buxton Woods on Hatteras Island is the largest maritime forest in North Carolina. The 3,000-acre forest measures 3 miles wide and

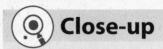

Close-up

Beach Nourishment—An Ongoing Debate

The Outer Banks' most important resource by far is its beaches. With more and more scientific evidence pointing to an increasing rate of global warming, rising sea levels, and the possibility that warmer sea surface temperatures will lead to increased frequency and intensity of hurricanes, perhaps no topic here is as important, or controversial, as beach nourishment.

Simply put, beach nourishment is the importation of sand to an area of the beach threatened by increasing erosion. The idea seems simple enough: Take sand from an area where it's not needed (a choking inlet, for example) and pump it onto a shrinking beach. Navigation through the inlet is improved, beachfront properties are protected, and the beach itself is preserved for everyone, including the fragile ecosystems closest to the ocean. How could such a win-win scenario be controversial? The devil is in the details.

The barrier islands that make up the Outer Banks beaches are phenomenally complex systems, and the beaches themselves are in constant motion. The Outer Banks is slowly rolling over itself, gradually retreating toward the mainland. Left alone the beach would continue its migration, and the complex processes that move sand up and down the beach, cut inlets, and rearrange geography would continue as well. The only problem with this natural migration process is people. When buildings were built close to the ocean, our modern erosion problems began.

There are perhaps only three solutions to the problem of beach erosion: stabilization, retreat, or to do nothing. Doing nothing was the strategy of choice for many years, even as recently as the 1980s. Structures were left to face the retreating beach, and when they inevitably succumbed to the sea, they were declared hazardous and demolished. Retreating, or moving away from the shoreline, is also problematic as a long-term strategy. If we decide to move threatened structures away from the rising sea, where will we move them? As a result of these unpalatable options, most coastal communities are relying on beach nourishment as their strategy to combat the inevitable process of erosion.

Wide flat beaches protect oceanfront property by absorbing wave energy more effectively than short steep ones. Some areas along the East Coast have tried to stabilize their beaches with hardened structures, such as seawalls and jetties, with sometimes disastrous results. Jetties interrupt longshore currents that transport sand down the coast, and the beaches down the coast can suffer much higher erosion rates as a result. Seawalls tend to reflect the wave energy back onto the beach, again leading to higher-than-average erosion rates. Beach nourishment seems to be the best way to ensure a wide beach, but it is not without its own problems.

50 feet high at the tallest ridge. This landmass has the capacity to act as a storage area for freshwater. Only 900 acres are owned by the National Park Service. The state of North Carolina bought an additional 800 acres to protect as the North Carolina Coastal Reserve. The county also designates Buxton Woods as a special environmental district.

One common problem with beach-nourishment projects is the sand itself. Not only is an ample supply needed, not just any sand will do. In fact, the quality of the sand to be pumped onto a beach is one of the biggest factors in determining how long the nourishment will last. Without careful control, the sand can contain gravel, stones, or even crushed shell, leaving the beach not only more susceptible to continued erosion but ill suited for recreation. Even worse, a poorly nourished beach can be an ecological nightmare. One nourished beach in southern North Carolina, for example, contained so many large stones that sea turtles could no longer nest there. Where the sand is taken from has to be carefully considered as well. If inlets are dredged, the change in flow can create erosion problems for the inlets and the beaches in their immediate vicinity. If the continental shelf is harvested for sand, the wave action along the immediate coast may be altered, changing the flow of sand and leading to even more erosion.

Even when a nourishment plan is well thought through and an ample supply of the proper quality sand is located, who pays for all this? Beach nourishment is famously expensive—these long-term projects have price tags into the multiple hundreds of millions and can go on for decades. Currently, the federal government pays about 65 percent of the costs, with the remainder being paid for by state and local governments. How the state and local money is raised is an area of contentious debate. Some say that as public "land," the beaches should be paid for by everyone. Others will say that such expenditures benefit only the elite who own oceanfront property and point to nourishment sites with little or no public access.

While most would agree that the beaches are priceless, careful valuations are necessary to fund such a huge undertaking as beach nourishment. Not only are the beaches valuable as protection from the ocean during storms, but they are directly or indirectly responsible for a huge percentage of the local economy, from the property taxes of oceanfront lots (houses with wide beaches are simply worth more than those with short steep ones) to the jobs and revenue provided by the tourism industry. Exactly how the calculations are made that put a dollar value on the beaches is yet another area of contentious debate.

If beach nourishment is to be part of a long-term solution to the geologic reality of a retreating shoreline, open communication and cooperation among federal, state, and local governments is essential. Local populations have the responsibility to stay well informed about decisions affecting the beaches and about who is making the decisions and why. By all accounts beach nourishment is both temporary and expensive.

Whenever human engineering attempts to manipulate complex natural processes, the outcome can be problematic. Only with local support and careful, long-term planning can an undertaking as expensive and complex as beach nourishment be successful.

Buxton Woods is a simpler ecosystem than Nags Head Woods because it sticks out 30 miles farther into the ocean and doesn't have the protection that the Nags Head forest has; however, compared with surrounding land at the Cape Hatteras National Seashore, Buxton Woods holds incredible diversity. A bird's-eye view shows an overall ridge and lowlands throughout the area.

The woods lie at the meeting place for several northern and southern species and have a viable population of dwarf palmetto and laurel cherry. A mix of wetlands and forests combines both northern deciduous maritime forests and southern evergreen maritime forests. Nowhere else on Hatteras Island is the mammal population so diverse as in Buxton Woods. The woods are home to white-tailed deer, gray squirrels, eastern cottontail rabbits, raccoons, and opossum. In the woods is Jennette's Sedge, one of the largest, most highly developed and diverse freshwater marsh systems found on a barrier island in North Carolina. See the Attractions chapter for more information on Buxton Woods.

Alligator River National Wildlife Refuge

On the mainland to the west of Roanoke Island is the Alligator River National Wildlife Refuge, covering parts of Dare, Hyde, and Tyrrell Counties. The refuge encompasses 150,000 acres of wetlands, wooded fields, and pocosin habitat. Pocosin is the Native American word for "swamp on a hill." These swamps are characterized by high organic content soils with deep peat deposits that hold vast quantities of water. In dry weather pocosins are highly susceptible to wildfire.

The refuge is home to black bears, white-tailed deer, gray fox, bobcats, raccoons, mink, beaver, squirrels, opossum, river otter, nutria, alligators, and its most-talked-about residents—red wolves.

Red wolves are a critically endangered species because of hybridization and public fear of large carnivores in most habitats. In the early 1970s the US Fish and Wildlife Service declared the species extinct in the wild because they had been eradicated in nearly every segment of their southeastern United States range. Fish and Wildlife captured the remaining red wolves and bred them until a location was found to bring them back into the wild. The location they found was Alligator River National Wildlife Refuge, chosen because it is within the red wolf's historical range, the human population is of moderate size and density, prey species are abundant, and the area is surrounded by water on three sides (which, it was hoped, would restrict some movement by the wolves). The area had very few coyotes, which would lessen the chance that the wolves would hybridize.

In 1986 a five-year experiment to rebuild a self-sustaining red wolf population in the wild began. During this experiment red wolves proved that they could adapt to life in the wild, find food, and avoid people. Today close to 100 red wolves roam free in the five-county area of northeastern North Carolina. There are also free-ranging wolves on three islands off the coasts of South Carolina and Florida. The refuge staff offers a unique program called "Wolf Howls" during which you can go into the refuge at night with a ranger and listen to the wolves howl. See the Kidstuff chapter or call (252) 473-1131 for information.

Mackay Island National Wildlife Refuge

On Knotts Island in both North Carolina and Virginia, Mackay Island contains 8,646 acres of important wildlife habitat and wintering grounds for waterfowl. Mackay Island offers walking and driving trails that provide wildlife observation opportunities. Hunting and fishing are allowed at Mackay Island Refuge.

To get there, take the free, short ferry ride from the Currituck mainland to Knotts Island and follow the signs. You'll see signs for the ferry as you drive on US 158.

Currituck National Wildlife Refuge

Just north of Corolla on the Currituck Outer Banks, this refuge was established in 1984. It consists of 3,213 acres managed by the Mackay Island staff. The refuge lacks public facilities but is open to the public during daylight hours. Visitors mostly look for wildlife and take photographs. The wild horses that used to roam in Corolla now roam here, along with deer, wild boar, and other wildlife.

Audubon Wildlife Sanctuary at Pine Island

Audubon is a 5,000-acre wildlife sanctuary at Pine Island and a protected habitat for deer, birds, rabbits, and a huge variety of plant life. There is an unmarked 2-mile trail you can walk, but the sanctuary is not really a park for people. The land is primarily soundside marshland with pine trees and waterfowl. The sanctuary runs 3 miles long north to south and is approximately 200 yards wide from east to west.

Cape Hatteras National Seashore

The Outer Banks should get a medal for firsts. Not only do we claim First Flight and the first English pioneers to colonize in the New World, but Cape Hatteras was the first seashore in the United States to become a national seashore (in 1953). The park covers 85 percent of Hatteras Island, which stretches south of the Bonner Bridge for 33 miles to Hatteras Inlet.

The beaches are clean and uncrowded. Subtle beauty abounds in the park. The swaying sea grasses, shifting sands, and tenacious vegetation appear monochromatic at first glance. A closer study reveals pleasant surprises. Lush purple flowers and delicate white-petaled flowers with scarlet centers grow entwined in the roadside brambles. In the marshes sea lavender, morning glories, and marsh aster add color. In the early morning or late afternoon, you can usually see dozens of brown marsh rabbits nibbling grasses. All along the seashore ghost crabs burrow in the sand and scurry about by day and night—a pure delight for children. One of the more spectacular sights is the occasional glow of phosphorus visible in the waves breaking on shore during a dark night. Sometimes the crabs glow eerily.

The park offers visitors a respite from the busyness of a resort community. It's a peaceful ride down NC 12 and always a welcome one except when the ocean washes away the dune and claims the road. There are several attractions within the park borders that appeal to the nature lover, including the **Pea Island National Wildlife Refuge,** with more than 5,000 acres of wildlife habitat. The refuge is both a year-round and seasonal home for nearly 400 species, including the snow goose, Canada goose, and whistling swan. During the fall you can watch large flocks of snow geese ascend from their watery resting places. This section of the park may be one of the most poetic spots on the Outer Banks. The waterfowl are just far enough away to appear untouched by the human element. You can get up-close views through binoculars and a camera's lens. Photographers also enjoy this stretch for the interesting tree lines and sunsets on the salt marsh. Plan to stop and bird watch at the platform just off the road.

The **North Pond Trail,** on Pea Island, is another birder's destination. The **Ocracoke pony pens** and **Hammock Hills Nature Trail** across from the Ocracoke Campground are two more hot spots in the Cape Hatteras National Seashore. See the Hatteras Island section in the Attractions chapter for more information on these sites; the Waves and Weather chapter for lifeguard information within park boundaries; and the Getting Here, Getting Around chapter for more about off-road driving.

In Buxton, at a jutting tip of Cape Hatteras, is an area of beach accessible only by four-wheel-drive vehicles. Locals call this "the Point," and it serves as a well-used haven for surf casters. The sea is powerful at this spot, marked by strong currents, deep holes, shoals, and opposing waves crashing into each other. Wildlife writers and anglers alike call it heaven. The bottom topography—created by strong shoaling and the Point's proximity to the Gulf Stream and its spinoff eddies—justifies calling this wet and sandy area a real Outer Banks natural wonder. (See the Fishing chapter for more about the Point.)

Whale watching is an exciting activity for park visitors, though sightings are not restricted to the park boundaries. There are more species of whales passing by the coast of North Carolina than anywhere in eastern North America. Mostly groups of small- to medium-toothed whales make passage both far offshore and in sight of the beach. Deeper offshore is the migration path for killer and blue whales.

The three largest species are the sperm whale, humpback, and fin whale. Sperm whales make their way past our coast in the springtime. In the winter you can see both humpback and fin whales. Humpbacks are particularly visible from shore. They can be seen breaching and lunge feeding. In the latter action, the whale blows a bubble net to corral fish, then leaps through it open-mouthed to gulp in everything.

Pilot whales can be seen offshore year-round. Even the most endangered species, the northern right whale, was identified while scratching its head on an Outer Banks sandbar. We've also had rare washups of the dense beaked whale. Offshore sightings have been made of the Cuvier's beaked whale, and the first live sighting of the True's beaked whale was 33 nautical miles southeast of Hatteras Inlet.

Visitors to the park delight in filling all available pockets and pails with shells. Hatteras Island is one of the farthest points out on the Eastern Seaboard. Its steep beaches cause high-energy wave action, so unbroken shells rarely make it to the shore. But the sea tosses up lovely blue mussels, quahog, jack-knife clams, slipper shells, baby's ears, jingle shells, and oysters. A good time to search for shells is at changing tides, after high tide, or following a storm. If you are seeking whole shells, continue south to Ocracoke Island, where the beaches have gentle slopes.

THE WATER

Estuary, Sound & Salt Marsh

Fly over the Outer Banks in a small plane and it becomes clear that this string of islands is more an offspring of the sea than the land. With more than 2.2 million acres of sounds and bays between its barrier islands and mainland, North Carolina ranks behind only Alaska and Louisiana in estuarine acreage. With 2 million acres covered by the vast Currituck-Albemarle-Pamlico sound system, the Outer Banks region ranks second in size

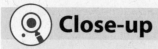

Close-up

The Glowing Ocean

If you are out on the beach after dark and the ocean seems to shimmer and glow, you may be seeing a natural occurrence known as bioluminescence. Tiny pinpoints of greenish light in the ocean occur occasionally on moonless nights. Most often they appear as waves break onto the shore or in your footprints along the edge of the water. According to Pat Raves at the North Carolina Aquarium on Roanoke Island, this phenomenon can be credited to incredibly small plants, called *Noctiluca,* that produce light when disturbed. Mole crabs also can be seen glowing; the crabs feed on *Noctiluca,* which sometimes stick to their backs.

Predicting when the ocean will glimmer with *Noctiluca* is difficult; no one seems to know exactly when this phenomenon will happen. So stroll outside on a moonless night: You may be lucky enough to witness bioluminescence; if not, you will still enjoy a beautiful walk.

only to the Chesapeake Bay in terms of water surface area. Each day more than 15 billion gallons of water pass into the barrier islands' estuaries. The bulk of it flows into the Pamlico Sound and then to the Atlantic through four major Outer Banks inlets.

The Albemarle Sound, the mouth of which sits west of Kitty Hawk, is fed by seven major rivers and is the largest freshwater sound on the East Coast. The Currituck Sound, also freshwater, lies northeast of the Albemarle. Due south of these bodies of water are two brackish sounds, the Roanoke and the Croatan. Farther south is the saltwater Pamlico Sound. Nestled in the crook of this sound, where Cape Hatteras indents toward the sea, is the famous Canadian Hole, one of the nation's top windsurfing spots (see the Water Sports chapter).

The Outer Banks landscape is also defined by its salt marshes. The marshes shelter the barrier islands from the sounds, and cord-grass and other vegetation break much of the wave action and act as safe havens for marine life. The wetlands are nursery grounds for many of the fish we enjoy dining on. Ninety percent of all commercial seafood species must spend at least part of their life cycle in the salt marsh. They spawn offshore and release their eggs into the inlets, where currents carry them into the marsh. Oysters, crabs, shrimp, and flounder flourish in the calmer waters of the marsh, which offer places to hide and lots of food. The salt marsh is also attractive to waterfowl and other bird species, which find food here.

The Sea

Perhaps the sea in its entirety is too huge for the human mind to comprehend, but it is only through trying to understand her that you come to appreciate the Outer Banks fully. The ocean dominates the islands, influencing their weather, land, flora, fauna, and the lifestyle of the people. Scientists work daily at the US Army Corps of Engineers Field Research Facility in Duck studying currents to understand erosion. Outer Banks history is steeped in harrowing accounts of lifesaving efforts, and the economy is heavily based in sea-oriented tourism, the commercial sea-food industry, and recreational fishing.

The position of Cape Hatteras, jutting into the Atlantic, puts us near the continental shelf's edge, which is approximately 37 miles southeast of Oregon Inlet and near the junction of three ocean currents: the Deep Western Boundary Current, Gulf Stream, and Shelf Current. These physical combinations create a nutrient-rich habitat for sea life, resulting in world-renowned offshore fishing and a wonderland for pelagic birds.

The Gulf Stream

A forceful flow of water in the Atlantic Ocean passes off the Outer Banks' shores every day. The Gulf Stream is a swift ribbon of blue sea that has been flowing by since time immemorial. It is powered by forces arising from the earth's rotation and the influence of the winds, and the energy and warmth it emits has had a profound effect on humankind. While the stream's course is influenced somewhat by gales, barometric pressure, and seasonal changes, the general flow remains fairly constant, creating a dichotomy: While the stream is ever present, its contents are ever changing. Millions upon millions of tons of water per second are carried along this ancient path. Swept along are fish, microscopic plants and animals, and gulfweed that originates in the Sargasso Sea.

Gulfweed lines the edge of the stream, creating a habitat for baitfish. You can easily scoop a handful of vegetation and find it teeming with life. The weed offers protection to infant fish, turtles, crabs, sea horses, and the most peculiar sargassumfish. Endangered loggerhead sea turtles less than two weeks old, their egg beaks still intact, have been spotted in the weed.

Flying fish are always fun to watch, although what we see as antics is actually the fish's sprint for life as it glides about 200 to 300 yards to escape a predator. The offshore life cycle is fascinating, and nowhere is it more evident than at the Gulf Stream.

BIRD WATCHING

With ocean beaches, sand dunes, scrub thickets, marsh, pocosins, black-water swamps, and maritime and inland forests, the Outer Banks and surrounding inland regions are rich in waterfowl and other birds. Nearly 400 species of birds have been sighted within Cape Hatteras National Seashore and its surrounding waters. Many birds choose the area because of the diverse habitats and because it's a convenient stop along the eastern flyway. But occasionally a vagrant will blow in with strong winds or storms. Accidental species spotted on the Outer Banks are numerous, including the pacific loon, western grebe, white-winged dove, snowy owl, western tanager, cerulean warbler, sandhill crane, and many others.

Though birding is always exciting on the Outer Banks, the greatest variety of species occurs during the spring and fall migrations. Good numbers of migratory shorebirds can be seen on inlet tidal flats, the ponds at Pea Island and Bodie Island, and the salt ponds at Cape Hatteras Point. Land-bird observations occur in the shrub thickets along the dikes at Pea Island and in the maritime woods. Herons, egrets, terns, skimmers, and other birds that breed locally are best seen in the warmer months. These birds frequent both salt- and freshwater areas. Winter ducks, geese, and swans usually concentrate on ponds at Pea Island and Bodie Island and on Lake Mattamuskeet.

In the marshes herons, egrets, ibises, waterfowl, rails, and shorebirds are visible. These birds can be seen in the marshes all over the Outer Banks, but an easy access point into the marsh is the trails behind the Bodie Island Lighthouse.

Pea Island National Wildlife Refuge is one of the top birding sites on the whole East Coast. Impoundments, salt flats, and ponds house snow geese, Canada geese, willets, tundra swan, and several species of ducks. The live oaks house songbirds during fall migration. On the beaches shorebirds, gulls, terns, and pelicans keep busy. Nesting birds may include piping plover, American oystercatcher, terns, and skimmers.

Other great birding areas to visit include Nags Head Woods, Buxton Woods, Alligator River National Wildlife Refuge, Currituck National Wildlife Refuge, Jockey's Ridge State Park, and Ocracoke Island.

> **i** Great stargazing can be enjoyed on Outer Banks beaches—especially at Pea Island. Sound accesses and sound piers offer a nice stargazing experience as well.

Pelagic Bird Watching

You don't have to be a bird lover to realize you have entered a unique bird-watching area as you tool down NC 12 through the national seashore. Off in the distance, in the wetlands, a variety of species feed and sun. What is not so obvious is the goldmine of pelagic species offshore, where birders witness both common and rare birds that never come to shore.

Local fishing headboats have been taking birders to the deep water for years. In fact, the sightings are so fruitful that a good part of Capt. Allan Foreman's charter

boat business involves these trips. Foreman's *Country Girl* (252-473-5577), which fishes out of Pirate's Cove Yacht Club on Roanoke Island, is a 57-foot headboat built to carry large parties offshore. Down in Hatteras, Capt. Spurgeon Stowe runs bird-watching excursions aboard the 72-foot *Miss Hatteras* (252-986-2365) from Oden's Dock (see the Fishing chapter for more information on these boats). Bird enthusiasts spend the day searching for more than two dozen species that live on the water.

The petrel and shearwater families are the largest groups of birds visible here. Traveling from the Caribbean and the coast of Africa, these species summer off the Outer Banks.

Among the petrels, the black-capped petrel is probably one of the most common to North Carolina waters. Twenty-five years ago this species was believed to be on the verge of extinction, and still today several varieties are a conservation concern. No one knew where the birds were. Scientists now say that the world's population lives in the Gulf Stream off the Outer Banks area. For comparison's sake, Florida birders may see one or two black-capped petrels per trip, whereas trips departing from the Outer Banks can yield as many as 100 sightings on a good day.

What's exciting about these trips is the chance to view species that are rarely, if ever, seen on land. These birds are highly adapted for life on the sea. They could be mistaken for gulls or ducks, but as a group they are unique. Their tubular nostrils allow them to drink salt water then expel the salt.

A much rarer bird sighted off North Carolina is the white-faced storm petrel. In a good year one or two sightings are recorded. This bird shows up in the late summer or early fall and is difficult to spot anywhere else in the world.

While bird watching off the Outer Banks, Mike Tove, a biologist from Cary, North Carolina, discovered two species of petrel that were rarely seen near North America. One of them, called the herald petrel, until recently was known from only a handful of recordings going back to the 1920s.

"In 1991 boats started venturing offshore farther than usual," Tove said. "We started finding them. It's now a bird we see a half-dozen times a year. People come great distances looking for them."

Tove officially presented to discovery another rare species in May 1991. "I had a bird that was identified as a Cape Verde petrel," he said. Prior to Tove's sighting, resurrected field notes revealed only three other recorded sightings of the bird. This species was entirely unknown in the United States and is extraordinarily rare anywhere in the world. "And we're seeing them with almost predictable regularity in late spring in very deep offshore waters past the edge of the continental shelf," he said. Tove's sightings form the baseline data for research. All the birds have been well documented with photographs.

You don't have to have a doctorate, as Tove does, to enjoy bird watching. If you want to glimpse offshore species, here are a few tips:

- Bring fairly low-power, waterproof binoculars (Zeiss or Leitz 7X or 8X are excellent).
- Don't bother to bring your spotting scope; if you're a photographer, bring a telephoto lens to help document rarities.
- Constantly scan the horizon and wave tops for birdlife, and call out your sighting with the boat as reference; for example, six o'clock is directly off the stern.
- Don't wait to try to identify the bird before calling it out; your fellow watchers will aid in that. Identification is often very difficult, and to do it accurately you must have a great deal of field experience and ability to interpret flight and molt patterns, which can be even more difficult during heavy seas.
- Expect long periods where no birds are seen, but be prepared for the appearance of a good number and variety. Always take good notes on any unusual species before consulting your field guide. Describe and sketch exactly what you saw without allowing outside influences to color your recollection.
- Offshore bird watching can be an exciting new adventure. If you haven't spent any time on the water, don't allow your fears to get the best of you. Captains won't take you out if the weather is too risky, and you can follow our tips on preventing seasickness (see the Fishing chapter).

Happy bird watching!

i Visiting on an overcast day and yet you want to see the sunset? Often on overcast days on the Outer Banks, the sunset will appear for a brief time, just before the sun sinks into the horizon. Sky watchers may still want to take in a viewing just before sunset— the sun may peek out and surprisingly give a spectacular show.

WEATHER

By the end of this guidebook, you may well be tired of the word "variety." It aptly describes not only the above-mentioned natural wonders but our weather as well. We find the weather to be changeable on the Outer Banks. Business owners who specialize in outdoor attractions are plagued by phone calls when the skies turn dark.

We tell our visitors that because the weather is so mercurial, wait 10 minutes and those dark clouds very possibly may be gone. There's variation from town to town. It may be pouring in Corolla, but Manteo has sunny skies. Torrential rains could send beachgoers scattering at noon, but 20 minutes later sunshine pours down from the heavens.

It seems to rain less in winter, while late-summer evenings hold their share of window-rattling thundershowers. The good part is that the skies are usually clear during the day.

The Atlantic Ocean, which is slow to warm and cool and heats to a maximum of about 80 degrees in the summer, affects air temperatures. Our nearness to the sea keeps summer air temperatures about 10 degrees cooler than our mainland counterparts. In the winter, disregarding the windchill factor, our air temperatures do just the opposite. Air flowing over the Gulf Stream toward us warms the winter air.

Nor'easters, occurring most often in the fall and winter, plague homeowners and fishermen alike. The high winds keep boats at the docks, sometimes knocking out three to seven workdays. These same winds wreak havoc on precariously perched oceanfront property. If the high winds coincide with the high tide and—heaven forbid—the full moon, powerful storm waves cover the land and cause beach erosion, structural damage, and both oceanside and soundside flooding.

March has seen a few nasty storms, too, including the infamous Ash Wednesday storm that struck on March 7, 1962, and the March storm in 1993, when winds were clocked at 92 mph. The sound waters rose 8 to 10 feet, causing great damage. Year-round residents see all this nasty weather as a trade-off for living in such a paradise. While we tend to highlight the more extreme weather patterns here, there are far more absolutely gorgeous days occurring year-round.

The wind blows most of the time at an average of 8 to 10 mph. Occasional gale-force winds range from 30 to 35 mph. In summer the wind blows predominantly out of the southwest, often increasing in the late afternoon. Southwest winds are warm, and if you're on a beach facing east, they create a generally flat ocean but stir up the sound. The wind frequently comes out of the northeast, which is a colder wind. Old-timers say that the wind always blows out of the northeast for an odd number of days— one, three, or five—before switching around again. Northeast winds create a rough ocean on east-facing beaches and are more predominant in fall and winter. Northwest and southeast winds are less common, but of course they do occur, usually as the wind is about to switch to northeast or southwest.

The weather is endlessly fascinating on the Outer Banks, something that almost every resident watches with vigilance. Surfers and anglers and anyone else who works or plays outside watch the Weather Channel (channel 16) for information. Many restaurants and bars even keep a TV tuned into the Weather Channel. Hurricanes, of course, are a whole different ballgame. See the Waves and Weather: How to Stay Safe chapter for information on what to do in case a hurricane threatens.

WAVES & WEATHER: HOW TO STAY SAFE

The Outer Banks is known for its sparkling, clean beaches. Sun worshipers from all parts of the world come to the Outer Banks to delight in the surf. But the ocean is fickle and can change its mood in the blink of an eye. Each beach is different, and to stay safe you need to follow a few rules. Store these tips along with your seashells to help make your stay a comfortable and safe one.

THE OCEAN

Most of the time you don't even notice the bare flagpoles dotting the dunes up and down our coast. But when the ocean is too rough for swimming, there's no way you can miss the red flags hoisted all along the beach. *If red flags are flying, do not go into the water.*

Not only is the ocean too dangerous for swimming or wading, it is also against the law to swim during a red-flag warning. You will be fined for going into the water.

The flags signify not only dangerous waves but also deadly rip currents. Churning water can easily knock you down, and reports of broken bones are not uncommon. Rough water also produces floating debris—such as ships' timbers—that seems to come from nowhere. We've seen adult men wading in knee-deep water knocked down by powerful waves and dragged by rip currents on red-flag days. In short, even if you see surfers in the water, stay out while the flags are flying, and caution children to keep well away from the tide line. Keep in mind, too, that if you go into the water while the flags are flying and need rescuing, you are jeopardizing not only your life but also the lifeguard's life when he or she has to come in after you.

i Wear sunscreen! Sand, water, and concrete surfaces can reflect 85 percent of the sun's rays. Don't be fooled by a cloudy day: 90 percent of the sun's rays penetrate the clouds. Dermatologists say that nearly half of the damage to skin occurs in childhood and early adolescence. Everyone should wear waterproof sunscreen of SPF 15 or higher.

Water Sense

- Never swim alone.
- Never swim at night.
- Observe the surf before going in the water, looking for potentially dangerous currents.
- Nonswimmers should stay out of the water and wear life jackets if they're going to be near the water.

- Swim in areas with on-duty lifeguards, or use extreme care.
- Keep nonswimming children well above the marks of the highest waves.
- Keep an eye on children at all times; teach them never to turn their backs on the waves while they play at water's edge.
- Don't swim near anglers or deployed fishing lines.
- Stay 300 feet away from fishing piers.
- Watch out for surfers and give them plenty of room.

Losing Control in the Waves

If a wave crashes on you while surfing or swimming, and you get tumbled in bubbles and sand like a sheet in a washing machine, don't try to struggle to the surface against it. Curl into a ball, or go limp and float. The wave will take you to the beach, or you can swim to the surface when it soon passes.

Currents

A **backwash current** on a steeply sloping beach can pull you toward deeper water, but its power is swiftly checked by incoming waves. To escape this current, swim straight toward shore if you're a strong swimmer. If you're not, don't panic; wait and float until the current stops, then swim in.

The **littoral current** is a "river of water" moving up or down the shoreline parallel to the beach. It is created by the angled approach of the waves. In stormy conditions this current can be very powerful due to high wave energy.

Rip currents often occur where there's a break in a submerged sandbar. Water trapped between the sandbar and the beach rushes out through the breach,

sometimes sweeping swimmers out with it. You can see a rip; it's choppy, turbulent, often discolored water that looks deeper than the water around it. If you are caught in a rip, don't try to swim against the current. Instead, swim across the current, parallel to the shore, and slowly work your way back to the beach at an angle. Try to remain calm. Panic will only sap the energy you need to swim out of the rip.

When a wave comes up on the beach and breaks, the water must run back down to the sea. This is **undertow**. It sucks at your ankles from small waves, but in heavy surf the undertow can knock you off your feet and carry you offshore. If you're carried out, don't resist. Let the undertow take you out until it subsides. It will only be a few yards. The next wave will help push you shoreward again.

Sharks

To reduce your risk of shark bites, take the following precautions:

- Do not swim alone; sharks are more likely to attack a solitary individual.
- Do not wander from shore.
- Avoid the water at dawn or during twilight hours when sharks are most active and have a competitive sensory advantage for hunting.
- Don't wear bright clothing or reflective jewelry that attracts the attention of sharks and other fish.
- Be especially wary if you're bleeding or menstruating, since shark's olfactory senses are acute.
- Avoid thrashing about wildly—excessive splash can appear to be shark prey. For this reason it is advised that you not swim with pets.
- Do not swim near fishing action.

- Stay away from inlets, fishing piers, and, if possible, steep drop-offs and the areas between sandbars—these are favorite hangouts for sharks.
- If you see a shark, calmly leave the water as quickly and quietly as possible.

Jellyfish

Watch for jellyfish floating on the surface or in the water. While some can give little more than an annoying stinging sensation, others can produce severe discomfort. The Portuguese man-of-war is sometimes blown onto Outer Banks beaches and can be recognized by its distinctive balloonlike air bladder, often exhibiting a bluish tint. Man-of-war stings can be serious. Anyone who is stung by the tentacles and develops breathing difficulties or generalized body swelling should be transported to the nearest emergency facility for treatment. In extreme cases death can result from anaphylactic shock associated with man-of-war toxin exposure.

BEACH SERVICES

Emergency Assistance

Many areas of the Outer Banks don't have lifeguards or flag systems warning you when to stay out of the water. Keep in mind that help can be a long way off, and an emergency is not the time to learn about ocean safety. Water conditions here call for unusual vigilance. We are vigilant about hanging red warning flags, but sometimes they are stolen by souvenir-seeking scavengers. It's always best to listen to local radio stations or call municipal headquarters for daily water conditions anytime you plan to enter the ocean, despite the season. The Weather Channel also posts rip-current warnings. Accidents can and do occur. If you have an emergency and need the rescue squad, dial 911 for help. Please remember that this number is for emergencies only.

i Check out the following websites for information on water safety: www.usla.org and www.kittyhawkfd .com/oceanrescue.html.

Lifeguards

Lifeguard services are at fixed sites throughout Dare and Currituck Counties.

Corolla Ocean Rescue (252-453-3242) provides guards from 9:30 a.m. to 5:30 p.m. from Memorial Day weekend through Labor Day at the following Corolla beaches: Ocean Hill, Corolla Light, Bonito Street (Whalehead), Ocean Sands at Buck Island and sections P, O, F, and D, and Pine Island at the South County Beach Access. Lifeguards also patrol the beaches from Pine Island to the Penny's Hill area of the off-road area.

Kitty Hawk Ocean Rescue (252-261-2666, www.kittyhawkfd.com/oceanrescue .html) operates two stands, one at Byrd Street and one at the Kitty Hawk Bathhouse. The stands are staffed from Memorial Day to Labor Day, 10 a.m. to 6 p.m. Roving lifeguards also patrol the beaches of the town. From Labor Day through mid-October, a supervisor stays on the beach.

In **Kill Devil Hills** (252-480-4066), lifeguard stands are at the following beaches: Helga Street, Hayman Boulevard, Fifth Street, Fourth Street, Second Street, First Street, Asheville Street, Woodmere Street, Carlow Street, Ocean Bay Boulevard, Oregon Street, Clark Street, Martin Street, Atlantic Street, Calvin Street, Ocean Acres Beach Access, and Lake Drive. There are also patrolling guards.

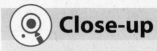

Close-up

What's the Signal? The Manteo Weather Tower

Way back in 1904, just a year after the Wright Brothers successfully enjoyed a powered flight, the US Weather Bureau built a weather station in Manteo. Local dignitary Alpheus W. Drinkwater was placed in charge of communicating the weather from the station. He flew signal flags from the station tower to warn mariners of the changing winds or of upcoming stormy weather. When evening fell, a series of flashing lights began signaling the forecast. The local weather news was also transmitted elsewhere by telegraph. Mariners weren't the only folks to put good use to the flag system. Local landlubbers also would refer to the flags to know how to plan their days. Drinkwater, who lived from 1875 until 1962, saw many exciting changes throughout his life. He holds the honor of sending news by telegraph of the Wright Brothers' flying successes onto the continental United States.

Recently, the town of Manteo has refurbished the tower. The weather flags are flying again. Reportedly, only five towers like this are in active use across the nation. People on land and sea can again tell at a glance when to come to port or don their raingear.

Guards are on duty from 9:30 a.m. to 5:30 p.m. in the summer.

Surf Rescue places guards on the beaches in Duck and on Roanoke Island from Memorial Day weekend through Labor Day weekend. Hours are 9:30 a.m. to 5:30 p.m. Duck lifeguard locations change according to where the greatest population of swimmers is in any given year. Duck has four fixed but movable stands and two roaming lifeguards. On Roanoke Island a guard is at the Old Swimming Hole on the sound between the airport and the aquarium.

Nags Head Ocean Rescue Services (252-441-5909) are provided by the town of Nags Head to its beaches. This service is also provided to Southern Shores through a contracted arrangement. Guarded beaches are available daily beginning Memorial Day weekend through Labor Day, 10 a.m. to 6 p.m. Nags Head Ocean Rescue stands are located at the following beaches:

- In Southern Shores: Hillcrest and Chicahauk, plus two roving vehicles.
- In Nags Head: Albatross Street, Bonnet Street, Enterprise Street, Espstein Street, Forrest Street, Gray Eagle Street, Hargrove Street, and Juncos Street. There are also seven roving vehicles and two trucks.

Within the Cape Hatteras National Seashore, lifeguards are on duty from Memorial Day through Labor Day at Coquina Beach on Bodie Island, at the Cape Hatteras Lighthouse Beach, and at the Ocracoke Lifeguard Beach (use the first access road past the airport).

ALCOHOL

The effects of alcohol are amplified by the heat and sun of a summer afternoon, so be aware. It's illegal to operate boats or motor vehicles if you've had too much to drink, and enforcement officers keep an eye out for violators, so practice moderation. Alcohol and swimming is a potentially deadly combination. Even small amounts of alcohol can give you a false sense of security.

SAFETY IN THE SUN

It's amazing how many red-bodied people we see lying on the beach, limping into restaurants or, worse yet, waiting in medical centers while visiting the Outer Banks. The sun feels so good. Combined with the sea air, it seems to have a rejuvenating effect. Actually any form of tan or burn is now considered damaged skin. While we can't stop visitors and insiders alike from toasting themselves, these tips will help keep you comfortable.

- Start out with short periods of sun exposure when you first arrive. It seems as if most visitors initially overdo it and have to be careful for the rest of their stay. The summer sun is intense, and you'd be surprised how much of a burn your skin can get in 20 or 30 minutes on an afternoon in July.
- Use ample sunscreen (SPF 15 or higher) whenever you're in the sun for any length of time. Put an extra coat on nose, cheeks, lips, and any other high-exposure spots. For maximum benefit apply sunscreen at least 20 minutes before going out, since it can take a while for it to become fully effective.
- Avoid the hottest parts of the day, from 10 a.m. until 2 p.m., when the sun's rays are the strongest. Explore some of the other fun things listed in this guide.

i Purchase a beach umbrella anchor for long days on the shore. The anchor will keep your umbrella from blowing away as the afternoon breeze picks up.

- Don't hesitate to cover up on the beach. Healthy, protected skin is a sign of good sense.

Pets

Dogs must be on a leash unless they are in the water. Park Service rangers and lifeguards patrol the beaches, and they will fine you if your dog is running free. Voice command control is not enough. Fines are around $50. Some communities do not allow pets on the beach at all from mid-May through mid-September. Heed local signs. Not only are unleashed pets a nuisance to non–pet owners, but also they can damage turtle and bird nests and the fragile dune systems.

i Hot summer days are physically stressful for dogs, who lack sweat glands to cool themselves down. Avoid having your dog on the beach in the hottest part of the day, and make sure your dog has plenty of fresh water to drink. If your dog shows signs of heat stroke or exhaustion, spray him with cool water, get him to a shaded area, and call a vet.

Litter

We shouldn't even have to say it, but, believe it or not, there are people who leave trash behind at the beach. If you're getting ready to throw down a soda bottle or candy wrapper, remember that while you may only be visiting the Outer Banks, you are littering in a year-round community, not to mention destroying natural beauty. Inevitably what is tossed in one backyard winds up littering the lawn of another due to the wind factor. Secure all trash and trash bags carefully and carry them to a trash receptacle. Feel free to pick up any stray trash. It's not uncommon to see locals doing just this.

HURRICANES

June through November marks hurricane season. Basically, the whole shoreline of the East Coast is threatened when a hurricane visits, but because of our low elevation, lack of shelter, and our situation in the ocean, these barrier islands are especially vulnerable to storms. Forecasters and almanac writers state that a significant hurricane strikes the Outer Banks approximately once every nine years. After Hurricane Isabel of 2003, visitors and locals alike were reminded of the dangers these storms bring. It's wise to be prepared by packing a hurricane kit in advance. See the sidebar in this chapter for a list of items to include in such a kit.

When Dare County officials order an evacuation, everyone must leave the Outer Banks. This includes vacationers who have already paid for their week's stay and permanent residents who are sometimes hesitant to leave their homes. Newspapers and radio and television stations keep the public notified about evacuations as well as reentry information. Make plans early especially if you have pets or elderly people with you. The Weather Channel issues early warnings or signs of an approaching storm. By all means, stay off the beaches and out of the water. More information about our emergency procedures can be gleaned by calling Dare County at (252) 473-3355, Currituck County at (252) 232-2115, or Ocracoke at (252) 928-1071.

Tornadoes spawned by hurricanes are among the worst weather-related killers. When a hurricane approaches, listen for tornado watches and warnings. (A tornado watch means conditions are favorable for tornadoes to develop. A warning means a tornado has been sighted.) When a warning is issued, seek shelter immediately, preferably in an inside room away from windows. If you are outside at the time and a tornado is headed your way, move away from its path at a right angle. If you feel you don't have time to escape, lie flat in a ditch or ravine.

Hurricane watches mean a hurricane could threaten the area within 24 hours, but evacuation is not necessary at this point. If a warning is issued, however, visitors should leave the islands and head inland using US 64/264 or US 158 and following the green and white Hurricane Evacuation Route signs.

Here are some guidelines to help you stay safe if a hurricane threatens.

- The most important safety tool is common sense. Use it and stay aware and observant to have a safe and enjoyable vacation.
- By late May recheck your supply of boards, tools, batteries, nonperishable foods, and other items you may need during a hurricane.
- Listen regularly to the latest weather reports and official notices. This will give you advance notice, sometimes before watches and warnings are issued. Keep a battery-powered radio on hand in case the power goes out.
- If your area comes under a hurricane watch, continue normal activities but stay tuned to the Weather Channel or to a local radio station and ignore rumors.
- If your area receives a hurricane warning, stay calm. Leave low-lying areas that may be swept by high tides or storm waves. If there's time, secure mobile homes before leaving for more substantial shelter. Move

Hurricane Kit

Be sure to include these items in your hurricane kit:
- AM/FM radio with extra batteries
- Baby supplies, if necessary
- Bar soap
- Can opener
- Cash
- Change of clothing for each member of the family
- Eating utensils
- First-aid kit
- Flashlights and extra batteries
- Food (nonperishable) and water, enough for three days for the entire family
- Hygiene items: toilet paper, toothpaste, etc.
- Ice chest or cooler
- Important documents: birth certificates, medical records, insurance papers, etc.
- Matches
- Plastic bags for waste
- Plywood for windows
- Prescription medications, glasses, etc.
- Sleeping bags and blankets
- Spare key for home and vehicles

And don't forget your pets during a storm. They need special attention since they can't take care of themselves. Animals are barred from public shelters for health reasons, so make plans for evacuating your pet before the storm strikes by finding out which hotels and motels in safe areas allow pets. Have an up-to-date identification tag on your pet's collar, a current photograph, and current medical/vaccination records with you. Make sure your pet is properly restrained with a carrier or leash, since even the calmest animals become frightened in a storm. Bring a week's worth of food as well as any medications your pet might need, and don't forget a litter pan and litter if you have a cat.

automobiles to high ground as both sound and sea can flood even central spots on the Outer Banks.

- Moor boats securely or haul them out of the water to a safe place.
- Board up windows or protect them with storm shutters. (Though some people recommend using tape on windows, many experts and most locals will tell you tape isn't strong enough, and it's very difficult to remove.) Secure outdoor objects that might blow away, such as garbage cans, outdoor furniture, tools, etc., that may become dangerous missiles in high winds. If the items can't be tied down, bring them inside.
- Store drinking water in clean bathtubs, jugs, or bottles because water supplies can become contaminated by hurricane floods.
- Be sure you have lots of flashlights, batteries, and emergency cooking facilities.
- Keep your car fueled since service stations may be inoperable for several days following a storm.
- Stay indoors during a storm, and keep your pets inside. Do not attempt to travel by foot or car. Monitor weather conditions and don't be fooled by the calm of the hurricane's eye—the storm isn't over yet!

- Stay out of disaster areas unless you are qualified to help. Your presence might hamper rescue work.
- If necessary, seek medical attention at the nearest Red Cross disaster station or health center.
- Do not travel except in an emergency, such as transporting someone who is injured. Be careful along debris-filled streets and highways. Roads may be undermined and could collapse under the weight of the car. Floodwater could hide dangerous holes in the road.
- Avoid loose and dangling wires. Report them to the power company or the police.
- Report broken sewer or water mains to the county or town water department.
- Be careful not to start fires. Lowered water pressure may make firefighting difficult.
- Stay away from rivers and streams.
- Check roofs, windows, and outdoor storage areas for wind or water damage.
- Do not let young children or your pets outside immediately after a storm. There are numerous dangers like fallen power lines and wild animals that have been disoriented because of the storm.

RECREATION

From early on these barrier islands have lured sunbathers, swimmers, surfers, and outdoor enthusiasts in search of excellent sportfishing and waterfowl hunting. The appeal has since widened to include more outdoor activities: windsurfing, hang gliding, parasailing, scuba diving, biking, golf, tennis, and in-line skating, just to name a few. And for a respite from these more strenuous workouts, you can choose among sight-seeing cruises, ATV excursions, and beach-combing. We have entire chapters covering water sports, fishing, and golf. In this chapter we list some other recreation options.

OVERVIEW

Not all activities involve a fee. You can spend an afternoon walking the wide beaches searching for shells and pieces of sea glass or buy a kite and send it soaring atop the wafting winds. Bird-watching opportunities abound in the wildlife refuges along the Outer Banks; see the Natural Wonders chapter. Nags Head Woods offers both a shady respite during the heat of summer and a great place to take secluded hikes through one of the most marvelous preserved maritime forests on the Atlantic Seaboard. Bike paths line roads along the sounds and the sea, through towns, and along the Wright Brothers National Memorial. If you need to get to sea for a while and enjoy the Outer Banks from a different vantage point, ride the free state ferry to Ocracoke Island.

When you've had a little too much fun in the sun, there are indoor activities such as bowling alleys, movie theaters, roller rinks, and noisy, state-of-the-art video arcades. Don't forget to check out the Kidstuff chapter for additional activities geared toward children.

If you're looking for parks, the **Dare County Parks and Recreation Department** has several throughout the county, some with playgrounds, tennis courts, picnicking sites, and ball fields. Call (252) 473-1101, ext. 313, to find the one nearest you. See the Playgrounds section of the Kidstuff chapter for the best playgrounds.

AIRPLANE TOURS

Even people who have lived on the Outer Banks for years are awestruck when they first view this stretch of islands from the air. Small planes offer tours daily most of the year from Corolla through Ocracoke. Pilots are always pleased to dip their passengers over a school of dolphins frolicking in the Atlantic, circle one of the four lighthouses beaming from these beaches, or cruise around the Wright Brothers National Memorial, where Wilbur and Orville flew the world's first successful heavier-than-air craft. Bring your camera, for these adventures provide great photo opportunities of both sea and sound shores and otherwise inaccessible wetlands.

Reservations are strongly recommended at least a day in advance of takeoff. All flights depend on the wind and weather. For information on charter flights to Norfolk and other destinations off the Outer Banks, refer to the air service section in the Getting Here, Getting Around chapter. Several services offer flight instruction to obtain a pilot's license and certification.

Roanoke Island

KITTY HAWK AERO TOURS
Main Terminal Airport Road, Roanoke Island
(252) 441-TOUR, (877) 274-2461
www.kittyhawk.com
Based at the Manteo Airport, these air tours fly half-hour trips in Cessna aircraft year-round. Flights take you soaring south over Oregon Inlet, flying above the waves to see shipwrecks, over Jockey's Ridge and Roanoke Island, and back to circle the Wright brothers monument. Prices begin at $60. Tours are offered from 10 a.m. to 5 p.m. in the off-season, and from 9 a.m. to sunset during summer.

If you're up for more high-flying excitement, try a trip in a 1941 Waco biplane, with its open cockpit. Twenty-minute trips take two passengers around the central Outer Banks. Leather helmets and old-fashioned Red Baron–style goggles are included in the price. Biplane tours are offered May through Sept from 9 a.m. until sunset. Reservations are preferred for both types of flights.

Hatteras Island

BURRIS FLYING SERVICE
Frisco Shopping Center
NC 12, Frisco
(252) 986-2679
Burris Flying Service offers sightseeing tours of Hatteras Island and the surrounding areas.

The short tour, about 30 minutes, takes you around Cape Hatteras and the lighthouse, while the longer tour, about an hour, can go either north to Rodanthe or south to Ocracoke Island. Both short and long tours fly two or three passengers. Additional trips are available, including a summer sunset tour. This is unparalleled opportunity for aerial photography. Tours are offered daily from May 1 through Oct 31. Advance reservations are recommended.

ALL-TERRAIN VEHICLE, 4WD & HORSE TOURS

Whether you're cruising along the beach or chasing a sunset up the marshy sounds on an all-terrain vehicle (ATV), you're limited to 15 mph, and you can't ride on the dunes. These tours are available only on the northern Outer Banks north of Corolla.

Corolla

COROLLA OUTBACK ADVENTURES
Wee Winks Shopping Center NC 12, Corolla
(252) 453-4484
www.corollaoutback.com
This outpost on the northernmost area of the Outer Banks has been operating for more than 20 years and conducts guided tours with Land Cruisers. Customers are transported by truck north of where the pavement ends to the four-wheel-drive area, where a convoy of self-driven vintage Land Cruisers cruise along the beaches and through protected wildlife refuges. Even though the area is becoming more populated, you can still catch a glimpse of wild horses, rare waterfowl, wild boars, and feral hogs. Tours are 2 hours.

RECREATION

BACKCOUNTRY OUTFITTERS AND GUIDES
Corolla Light Town Center, Corolla
(252) 453-0877
www.outerbankstours.com
Backcountry Outfitters and Guides offers Wild Horse Safari Tours that head to Carova, near the North Carolina border, looking for the famous wild horses—and they find them. Two-hour tours are led in Chevy Suburbans that hold up to 10 people. After the 15-mile drive up the beach to the horses' stomping grounds, passengers unload from the vehicle and take a few photos, while the guide educates everyone about the horses. Along the tour you'll see other wildlife, plus the elements of the Outer Banks ecosystem. These tours take place year-round. Corolla Outback Adventures also offers four-wheel-drive/kayak expeditions. All tours and rentals are weather dependent. Backcountry fans can also choose Segway Safari Tours or Kayak Adventures.

Ocracoke Island

PORTSMOUTH ISLAND ATV EXCURSIONS
NC 12, Ocracoke Village
(252) 928-4484
www.portsmouthislandatvs.com
A Portsmouth Island ATV Excursion allows you to ride the shoreline of one of the most beautiful and remote beaches in the world on an island famous for its shorebirds, sea turtles, and seashells. Excursions begin with a 20-minute boat ride from Silver Lake Harbor in Ocracoke Village. Once on the island, you will discover the historic deserted village of Portsmouth, a settlement that in 1860 was a thriving port town with more than 685 residents. Now owned by the National Park Service, Portsmouth Island is home to the only ghost town on the East Coast (see the Day Trips and Attractions chapters for more details). As part of the tour, you will be guided through the village's US Lifesaving Station, the Methodist church, the post office and general store, and the village visitor center.

i Beach glass is anything but trash on the Outer Banks. Beachcombers compete to find it. One of the best spots to find these colorful tumbled treasures is on the beaches in the town of Nags Head.

ATHLETIC CLUBS

Despite all the outdoor activities the Outer Banks has to offer, many locals and visitors still crave vigorous indoor workouts at traditional gyms and health clubs. During the heat of the summer and the cold winds of winter, they're a good choice for strenuous exercise. These fitness centers are open year-round and include locker room and shower facilities. They are open to the public for annual, monthly, weekly, and walk-in daily membership rates.

SANDERLING
Pine Island Racquet Club
NC 12, Sanderling
(252) 453-8525
www.thesanderling.com
Pine Island Racquet Club is an integral part of the Sanderling Inn Resort and Conference Center, a 12-acre luxury resort located 5 miles north of Duck. The fitness center is located 3 miles north of the conference center and is a fully equipped facility. State-of-the-art exercise equipment and the latest in cardio machines are available for use, along with three tennis courts and a pro

shop. Walk-in charges are $20 and weekly charges are $60.

Kitty Hawk

BARRIER ISLAND FITNESS CENTER
US 158, MP 1, Kitty Hawk
(252) 261-0100

Barrier Island Fitness Center (located behind Wal-Mart) is a complete, full-service health club. It has a full line of free weights, circuit-training equipment, and an assortment of cardiovascular equipment, including elliptical trainers, treadmills, stair climbers, recumbent cycles, and Airdynes. Certified aerobics classes, including aquafit, are offered.

The staff includes fitness instructors, two personal trainers, and two massage therapists. Other amenities at the center include tennis courts, saunas, steam rooms, tanning beds, and an indoor pool. Parents rejoice: There is on-site babysitting and a cybercade with computer games for the kids. The cybercade is complete with high-speed Internet and e-mail access.

The facility is open to the public (age 18 and older) Mon through Fri 6 a.m. to 9 p.m., Sat 9 a.m. to 7 p.m., and Sun 9 a.m. to 5 p.m. The pool is open until 10 p.m. daily. Drop-in rates are $15 a day or $45 a week.

i Traveling on two wheels? Pick up a Dare County bicycle trails map published by the North Carolina Department of Transportation. It's free at the Outer Banks Visitors Bureau.

Nags Head

OUTER BANKS FAMILY YMCA
US 158, MP 11, Nags Head
(252) 449-8897
www.obxymca.org

This facility includes a fitness room with weight and cardiovascular equipment. A wood-floored exercise room is available for activities like aerobics, yoga, Pilates, and karate. The 7,000-square-foot gymnasium is marked for both basketball and volleyball and can be used for indoor soccer. An 8,000-square-foot indoor pool, 25 meters long with six lanes, is one highlight of the YMCA. Swim lessons, water aerobics, and lap times are available. A hot tub can accommodate up to 10 people. Another highlight is the outdoor skate park: With more than 14,000 square feet of quarter pipes, bank ramps, pyramids, and a "tot lot" for little tikes, this is a challenging, state-of-the-art skate park. A concrete bowl section with a snake run completes the park. Day passes and week passes are available for the skate park. The Y also has an outdoor water park that features two swimming pools. The upper pool is known as the deep well pool, with a depth of 12 feet and a 1-meter platform diving board.

An area in this 150-gallon pool is designated for water sports like water polo and volleyball. The lower pool is known as the family pool and has a zero-grade entry. Two 25-yard lap lanes are available for recreational swimming. There's also a hydrotherapy area, as well as a very fun 20-foot waterslide.

Wellness programs and family programs, such as Parents Night Out, are available, as is a nursery where children are actively stimulated while parents work out. Children and youth sports leagues include soccer, hockey, basketball, volleyball, and wrestling, and there are adult basketball and volleyball leagues. Call for membership rates. No day passes are issued for most of the facility, except to members of other YMCAs who have a membership card with them. Other YMCA members are charged a fee, and access is limited in summer. The one area of the Y to which passes are sold to the general public is the skate park. A day pass is $15; a 10-day flex pass is $75.

Roanoke Island

NAUTICS HALL HEALTH & FITNESS COMPLEX
US 64, Manteo
(252) 473-2101

A competition-size, indoor heated pool is the centerpiece of this health club at the Elizabethan Inn, where water aerobics, swimming lessons, and lap times are offered throughout the year. There's a workout room with Nautilus and Paramount equipment, free weights, Stair-masters, treadmills, and an aerobicycle. Low-impact and step aerobics instruction is available daily. Other amenities include an outdoor pool, a hot tub, a racquetball court, sundecks, a sauna, and massage therapy on the premises. Nautics Hall is open from 6:30 a.m. to 9 p.m., Mon through Fri, and from 9 a.m. to 9 p.m. on summer weekends. On Sunday during the off-season, hours are 9 a.m. to 5 p.m. Monthly memberships cost $50 per person.

BIKING & SKATING

The flat terrain on these barrier islands is quite a treat for cyclists. But be forewarned that NC 12 is well-trafficked with fast-moving vehicles. Cyclists need to be skilled enough to ride without swerving and to anticipate the actions of car drivers, who, as many bikers know, often don't even see bicycles on the road or yield any sort of right-of-way to cyclists. It is unwise to allow children to ride their bikes on NC 12 and especially on US 158, where drivers often swerve out of their lanes as they're scoping the sights or looking for a business. It's best to restrict children to side streets or to the designated bicycle paths. These side streets and paths are also the best places to in-line skate. All roadways are either dusted or covered with sand.

- Corolla: extended shoulder along NC 12 on the Currituck Outer Banks, some separate paths in private developments
- Duck: separate bike path along NC 12 from Martins Point to Sanderling
- Southern Shores: separate bike path along NC 12 from Town Hall to Duck
- Kitty Hawk: separate bike path starting at Kitty Hawk Elementary School on US 158 south to Kitty Hawk Road
- Kill Devil Hills: separate bike path from the end of West First Street, along Colington Road, ending at NC 12
- Nags Head: separate bike path along NC 12 from MP 11½ to MP 21
- Roanoke Island: separate bike path running the entire length of the island along US 64/264 from the base of the Washington Baum Bridge at Pirate's Cove to the Manns Harbor Bridge
- Hatteras Island: extended shoulder along NC 12
- Ocracoke Island: extended shoulder along NC 12

While there is little crime on the Outer Banks, bicycles do disappear. Lock up carefully, and never leave your bike parked overnight in a front yard or in an easily accessed spot. If your bike is stolen, call the local police. Sometimes bikes are taken on nocturnal joy rides and later found by police, so call them before you panic. It's also a good idea to record your bike's serial number for identification purposes.

Since vehicular traffic is very heavy during summer months, and many of the drivers are unaccustomed to the roads, arm yourself with the following safety tips. If you have children who will be biking, make sure that they understand the rules of the road before they leave the driveway.

- Use designated bike paths when available.
- Wear safety helmets.
- Ride on the right side of the road with the flow of traffic.
- Always maintain a single file.
- Obey all traffic rules.
- Cross US 158 at a stoplight whenever possible.
- Use hand signals for stops and turns.
- Don't double up unless the bike is designed for more than one rider.
- Keep your hands on the handlebars.
- Observe pedestrians' right-of-way on walks, paths, and streets.
- Be alert for off-road areas with tire-puncturing cacti and sandspurs.
- Look out for soft sand that can cause a wipeout.
- Use a front-lighted white lamp and a rear red reflector when riding at night.
- Corolla—Ocean Atlantic Rentals, NC 12, Corolla Light Town Center (252) 453-2440
- Duck—Ocean Atlantic Rentals, NC 12 (252) 261-4346
- Kitty Hawk—Kitty Hawk Cycle Co. Off NC 12, MP 2.5 (252) 261-2060
- Kill Devil Hills—Bike Barn, Wrightsville Ave., (252) 441-3786
- KDH Cycle, NC 12, MP 8½, (252) 480-3399
- Ocean Atlantic Rentals, US 158, MP 9.75, (252) 441-7823
- Avon—Ocean Atlantic Rentals, NC 12, (252) 995-5868

- Hatteras Village—Lee Robinson General Store (252) 986-2381
- Ocracoke—Slushie Stand, NC 12 (252) 928-1878
- Beach Outfitters, NC 12, (252) 928-6261

i Unsure what to do? Something fun is always happening in Manteo. Check the website www.townofmanteo.com for details of current festivities. Events are being added frequently.

BEACH OUTFITTERS
NC 12, Ocracoke
(252) 928-6261, (252) 928-7411
Beach Outfitters, in the Ocracoke Island Realty office, is open all year and accepts reservations. You can rent bikes for $15 a day or $40 a week. See the Weekly and Long-Term Cottage Rentals chapter for more information.

BOWLING

Even the most dedicated sun-worshippers need an occasional afternoon or evening in air-conditioned comfort.

NAGS HEAD BOWLING CENTER
US 158, MP 10, Nags Head
(252) 441-7077
Open for year-round league and recreational play, this is the Outer Banks' only bowling center. Twenty-four lanes are available for unlimited members of a party as well as a billiards room, pro shop, video arcade, and a cafe serving light meals, sandwiches, wine, beer, and hamburgers. Laser light and glow-in-the-dark bowling is offered at 10 p.m. on Friday and Saturday nights. Nags Head Bowling is open from 10 a.m. to midnight

Mon through Thurs and 10 a.m. to 1 a.m. Fri through Sun. Call for league information.

CLIMBING

Rock-climbing walls are available for all ages at the following locations.

KITTY HAWK KITES/CAROLINA OUTDOORS
Monteray Plaza, NC 12, Corolla
(252) 453-3685, (800) FLY-THIS
www.kittyhawk.com

If you're itching to climb, try one of Kitty Hawk Kites/Carolina Outdoors's climbing walls. Two climbs and basic instruction cost $7 per person. Rappelling equipment, climbing shoes, and ropes are all part of the package. In the Nags Head store, scale the 22-foot-high wall with four main routes and an overhang for extra challenges. At Monteray Plaza, there's a 25-foot climbing wall with four main routes and an overhang. The Nags Head location is open year-round, but only on weekends in winter. The climbing wall in the Nags Head location is indoors, while the walls at Corolla and Hatteras are outside. Consider the weather when choosing the wall to climb. Call for hours at other locations, which are at: across from Jockey's Ridge, US 158, MP 13, Nags Head, (252) 441-4124; and Hatteras Landing, NC 12, Hatteras Village, (252) 986-1446.

DOLPHIN TOURS, BOAT RIDES & PIRATE TRIPS

Most Outer Banks boat cruises are included in the Water Sports and Fishing chapters. However, a few unusual ventures are mentioned here. These trips, of course, are weather dependent and available only during warmer spring and summer months. Reservations are recommended for each of these tours. Unlike

sailing and more participatory water adventures, you don't have to be able to swim to enjoy these activities, and you probably won't even get wet on board these boats as they ply through the shallow sounds.

Nags Head

GROG'S WATERSPORTS
Nags Head-Manteo Causeway,
Nags Head
(252) 441-8875
www.grogswatersports.com

For an up-close glimpse of bottlenose dolphins playing in Roanoke Sound, this company has daily trips throughout the summer. Dolphin trips are led on a 40-foot pontoon boat that can accommodate up to 44 passengers. Along the way you'll see the Bodie Island marshes, the Bodie Island Lighthouse, Pelican Island, osprey nests, and a variety of other wildlife, including dolphins. This company also offers thrill-a-minute WaveRunners, parasailing, and boat and kayak rentals along the same area south of Nags Head. Look for Grogs under the 30-foot wooden observation tower.

NAGS HEAD DOLPHIN WATCH
Willett's Wetsports
Nags Head–Manteo Causeway,
Nags Head
(252) 449-8999
www.nagsheaddolphinwatch.com

If you're interested in bottlenose dolphins, this is the best way to get to know more about them. Nags Head Dolphin Watch is run by a team of independent dolphin researchers who conduct the trips to pay for their ongoing research. The team of expert naturalists leads dolphin watches through Roanoke Sound three times a day, six days a week, beginning the week before Memorial

Day through the end of September. Two-hour tours are given on a speedy pontoon boat holding 36 people. Along the way you'll see bottlenose dolphins and learn about their fascinating feeding and social behavior and also about local ecology, history, and wildlife. The researchers take photos of the dolphins' dorsal fins on every trip, and they call dolphins they see by name.

i Insect repellent intensifies the sun's effect on skin. If you are going to be out in the direct sun and need insect repellent, try putting repellent on your clothes and sunscreen on your body. Bad burns can be caused by the combination of sunscreen and insect repellent.

Roanoke Island

CRYSTAL DAWN
Pirate's Cove Marina, Manteo
(252) 473-5577
http://crystaldawnheadboat.com
Sunset cruises around Roanoke Island take place every evening except Sunday throughout the summer on this sturdy, 2-story 65-foot vessel that accommodates 100 passengers. Trips include commentary about the Outer Banks, while the boat cruises past Andy Griffith's house, Roanoke Island Festival Park, and Jockey's Ridge. The boat departs at 6:30 p.m., returning about 90 minutes later. This is also a fishing headboat; for additional information see the Fishing chapter.

OUTER BANKS CRUISES
Queen Elizabeth Avenue, Manteo
(252) 473-1475
www.outerbankscruises.com
Outer Banks Cruises offers dolphin tours, sightseeing tours, and evening cruises aboard the 53-foot covered pontoon boat *Capt. Johnny,* which can accommodate 49 passengers. The dolphin-watch tours are offered in Roanoke Sound from June through October, and ninth-generation native Capt. Stuart Wescott has a knack for finding the playful mammals. He even recognizes many of them by their fins and knows the names given them by local researchers. Dolphin sightings are guaranteed: If you don't see any on your trip, you are given a rain check for a free ride another time. The shrimp and crab cruise is educational, fun, and very popular. Evening cruises are available by charter; call for schedules and rates. The *Capt. Johnny* is docked on the Manteo waterfront next to the little bridge that heads to Roanoke Island Festival Park.

DOWNEAST ROVER
Manteo Waterfront Marina, Manteo
(252) 473-4866, (866) 724-5629
www.downeastrover.com
A 55-foot topsail schooner, the *Downeast Rover* tall ship is a modern reproduction of a 19th-century sailing vessel. Two-hour cruises onto the placid waters of Roanoke Sound delight passengers with views of dolphin, osprey, heron, and seabirds. A hands-on adventure is also possible on this lovely boat: Passengers may help trim the sails and take a turn at the wheel. Tickets can be purchased on the *Downeast Rover,* which also has a ship's store and restroom on board. Deck seating and a belowdecks lounge are available. Reservations are recommended but not required. Private charters for weddings, parties, and other special occasions are available. The *Downeast Rover* sails from early spring to late fall.

Hatteras Island

CAPTAIN CLAM

Oden's Dock, NC 12, Hatteras Village
(252) 986-2365

The Captain Clam is a fishing headboat (see the Fishing chapter) that also offers family-style pirate cruises that are a hit with the kids. The pirate cruise is Wed, Thurs, and Fri in summer from 6 to 7 p.m. The crew dresses as pirates and tells tales about Blackbeard and the area's pirate history as you cruise around Pamlico Sound. Complimentary swords and eye patches are given to every passenger. Cruises are available June through September. The boat can hold 40 people.

MISS HATTERAS

Oden's Dock, NC 12, Hatteras Village
(252) 986-2365
www.breakwaterhatteras.com/dockmain.html

The headboat *Miss Hatteras,* which ties up at Oden's Dock, offers dolphin tours on Wed, Thurs, and Fri from 6:30 to 8 p.m. in summer. Bird-watching cruises are available.

Ocracoke

THE WINDFALL II

The Community Store Docks
NC 12, Ocracoke
(252) 928-7245
www.schoonerwindfall.com

Sail around Blackbeard's former haunts aboard this gaff-rigged schooner that seats up to 30 passengers. One-hour cruises depart from the Community Store docks several times daily during summer months and cost $40 per person. Call for the schedule.

GO-KARTS

If you're looking for a way to race around without getting a speeding ticket, several go-kart rental outlets offer riders a thrill a minute on exciting, curving tracks. Drivers have to be at least 12 years old to take the wheel at most of these places, but younger children are often allowed to strap themselves in beside adults to experience the fast-paced action.

Corolla

COROLLA RACEWAY

TimBuck II Shopping Village
NC 12, Corolla
(252) 453-9100

Corolla Raceway is the sister track of Nags Head Raceway. In TimBuck II Shopping Village, it features one large track with 16 cars. The go-kart raceway is open Easter through Nov. Corolla Raceway also has freestanding, gas-powered bumper cars. For more entertainment a family arcade is on-site. Summer hours are 10 a.m. until 11 p.m. daily.

Kill Devil Hills

COLINGTON SPEEDWAY

1064 Colington Rd., Kill Devil Hills
(252) 480-9144

Colington Speedway features three tracks and about 40 Indy-style two-seaters or NASCAR-style 5.5 horsepower cars. Riders choose a kiddie track, a family road course, or a slick track. The facility's gift shop features NASCAR items, Outer Banks souvenirs, and children's toys. Colington Speedway is open daily from Memorial Day through Labor Day until 10 p.m. The track is also open on weekends until 10 p.m. in the spring. Call for opening hours and more information.

Hatteras Island

WATERFALL ACTION PARK
NC 12, Rodanthe
(252) 987-2213
http://waterfallactionpark.com
This sound-to-sea amusement area offers the biggest selection of go-kart tracks on the Outer Banks—and more recreational opportunities in a single spot than anywhere else on Hatteras Island. Here kids of all ages enjoy seven separate race car tracks where drivers test their skills on a different style of vehicle at each pit stop. Wet racers are great for hot afternoon sprints against the wind—and other boaters. Bumper boats, two minigolf courses, waterslides, and a snack bar also are open from 11 a.m. to 10 p.m. daily May through Oct.

HANG GLIDING

The closest any human being will ever get to feeling like a bird is by flying beneath the brightly colored wings of a hang glider, with arms outstretched and only the wind all around. Lessons are available for fliers of all ages. Just watching these winged creatures soaring atop Jockey's Ridge or catching air lifts above breakers along the Atlantic is enough to make bystanders want to test their wings.

KITTY HAWK KITES/CAROLINA
**   OUTDOORS**
US 158, MP 13, Nags Head
(252) 441-4124, (800) FLY-THIS
www.kittyhawk.com
Kitty Hawk Kites, the country's most popular hang-gliding school, offers various ways to learn how to fly. The company's headquarters, in Nags Head across from Jockey's Ridge

State Park, faces the main training site on the largest sand dune in the East. Here learn to fly solo 5 to 15 feet over the soft, forgiving sand, or soar through the clouds at altitudes up to 2,000 feet with an instructor. Either method, offered at various locations along the Outer Banks, is an exhilarating experience you'll never forget and undoubtedly will return home to brag about.

If hang gliding has kindled your desire to fly, Kitty Hawk Kites can also help you train to become a certified pilot. A number of packages are designed to help you achieve your goal.

This school, the world's largest, has taught more than 250,000 students to fly since 1974. No experience is necessary, and there are no age limitations. As long as you weigh within the parameters, you can fly!

Tandem hang-gliding instruction is offered at the Currituck Airport. There are no age restrictions and no minimum weight requirement for tandem instruction, which is also accessible to the disabled. Kitty Hawk Kites offers two methods of instruction—by plane or boat. Reservations are required for most recreation, so be sure to call ahead. Discount packages are available. Ask about fun and exciting events for adventure enthusiasts of all ages throughout the season!

i The oldest continuous hang-gliding competition in the country is held at Jockey's Ridge State Park. Kitty Hawk Kites sponsors the Annual Hang Gliding Spectacular and Air Games, which began in 1973. Visit www.hangglidingspectacular.com for more information.

KITE FLYING

Kite flying is not what it used to be. Thanks to modern technology, today it's an adventurous, interactive activity, even a competitive sport. And the Outer Banks is the perfect place to try your hand at it, since one of the top kite stores in the world, Kitty Hawk Kites, is here. There are plenty of open spaces to fly kites on the Outer Banks, though Jockey's Ridge State Park in Nags Head is the absolute best because it offers acres unobstructed by power lines and trees.

KITTY HAWK KITES/CAROLINA OUTDOORS
US 158, MP 13, Nags Head
(252) 441-4124
www.kittyhawk.com

This is the only dedicated kite store in the area, and it offers an enormous range of kites, from the backyard variety to competition style, which come with an instructional video. The staff is knowledgeable about what they sell, and they can help you pick out just the right kite for your skill level. In addition to lessons and repairs, they offer kite-making workshops in summer. There are several locations of Kitty Hawk Kites on the Outer Banks, but the Nags Head location across from Jockey's Ridge has the largest selection. This company hosts several kite-flying events throughout the year, including the annual Outer Banks Stunt Kite Competition and Festival at Jockey's Ridge in October. See the Annual Events chapter for more kite events.

MINIATURE GOLF COURSES

No beach vacation is complete without the timeless activity of miniature golf. More than a dozen minigolf courses adorn the Outer Banks from Corolla through Hatteras Island. Themed fairways featuring African animals, circus clowns, and strange obstacles await even the most amateur club-swinging families. Small children enjoy the ease of some of these holes, and even skilled golfers can get into the par 3 grass courses that have been growing in numbers over recent years.

You can tee off at most places by 10 a.m. Many courses stay open past midnight for night owls to enjoy. Several of these attractions offer play-all-day packages for a single price. Almost all minigolf courses operate seasonally, and since they are all outside, their openings are weather dependent.

Corolla

THE GRASS COURSE
NC 12, Corolla
(252) 453-4198

Offering the Outer Banks' first natural-grass course, these soundside greens are open seven days a week throughout the summer season from 10 a.m. to 11 p.m. The 18-hole course includes par 3s, 4s, and 5s. The undulating hills winding around natural dunes provide intriguing challenges for beginning and better golfers. The course is open from Apr to Oct and at Thanksgiving and Christmas. The Grass Course sells hot dogs and barbecue.

Kitty Hawk

THE PROMENADE
US 158, MP ¼, Kitty Hawk
(252) 261-4900

This family fun park includes Victorian-style buildings, turn-of-the-20th-century streetlights, waterside recreation, a children's playground, and an 18-hole themed minigolf course called Waterfall Greens.

There's also a 9-hole, par 3, natural-grass putting course, complete with separate putting greens; a target driving range; a par 3 chip-and-putt 9-hole course; and an 18-hole course. A restaurant, snack bar, and picnic tables are on-site. The Promenade is open Easter weekend through early Oct. Summer hours are from 8:30 a.m. to midnight, seven days a week.

PARADISE GOLF
US 158, MP 5½, Kitty Hawk
(252) 441-7626
More challenging than the usual minigolf fairways, this natural-grass site includes two 18-hole, par 56 courses. Most holes are 110 feet from the tees. The courses are open from 10 a.m. until midnight daily during summer. For one price ($7 for adults, $5 for children), you can play all day.

Kill Devil Hills

LOST TREASURE GOLF
US 158, MP 7½, Kill Devil Hills
(252) 480-0142
Lost Treasure Golf features two 18-hole courses situated among five waterfalls illuminated with different colors at night. Kids love the little train that carts them up to the first hole and through a series of caves and mines. Professor Hacker, a fictional adventurer, tells his story about gold and diamond expeditions that kids read about as they play. Lost Treasure Golf is open Apr through Nov. Hours are 9 a.m. to 11 p.m. daily in the summer and are decreased accordingly in the off-season.

Nags Head

GALAXY GOLF
NC 12, MP 11, Nags Head
(252) 441-5875
Aliens, flying saucers, and outer space objects surround 36 lighted holes of minigolf at this popular Outer Banks course on the Beach Road. Galaxy Golf is open on weekends in Apr, early May, Sept, and Oct and daily throughout the summer. In-season hours are 9 a.m. to midnight. Children younger than four with a paying adult play free. The price doesn't change after dark as it does on many minigolf courses.

BLACKBEARD'S GOLF AND ARCADE
US 158, MP 16, Nags Head
(252) 441-4541
The Outer Banks' most infamous pirate wields his 6-foot sword above these greens. Open daily, summers only, until at least 10 p.m., Blackbeard's includes a video arcade for alternate entertainment after putting around.

JURASSIC PUTT
US 158, MP 16, Nags Head
(252) 441-6841
Life-size models of dinosaurs from the Jurassic period hover over and among Jurassic Putt's greens, delighting kids and adults alike. Two 18-hole courses wind through caves and streams and around the dinosaur models. Jurassic Putt is open daily from mid-March until Nov. Hours are 9 a.m. until midnight. Call or stop by for rates.

Hatteras Island

AVON GOLF
NC 12, Avon
(252) 995-5480
Adjacent to the Avon Pier, this 18-hole, natural-grass course is open from 11 a.m. to 11 p.m., seven days a week all summer. You can play as many games as you can squeeze in from noon until 6 p.m. for $8.

In the offseason you can play all day for $8. Avon Golf is open from Easter through the week after Thanksgiving, depending on business.

FRISCO MINI GOLF AND GO-KARTS
NC 12, Frisco
(252) 995-6325

This 18-hole championship miniature golf course is a little more challenging than the average minigolf game, though all levels of players will enjoy the experience. Waterfalls splash amid the well-manicured course, and children feed goldfish. There are also two go-kart tracks, a concession stand, and an arcade on the premises.

MOVIE THEATERS

On some steamy summer afternoons or those rainy Saturday nights, there's no better place to be than inside a dark, air-conditioned movie theater, catching the latest flick with a companion. First-run movies are offered at most Outer Banks theaters. Popcorn, candy, and sodas are, of course, sold at all movie houses.

Corolla

RC THEATRES COROLLA MOVIES
4 Monteray Plaza, NC 12, Corolla
(252) 453-2999
http://rctheatres.com

This seasonal establishment in Monteray Plaza includes four wide screens and is open from May through Labor Day. The theater reopens for shows again from Thanksgiving through New Year's Day. Movies are shown seven days a week from 2 p.m. to midnight.

Kill Devil Hills

RC THEATRES MOVIES
10 US 158, MP 6½, Kill Devil Hills
(252) 441-5630
http://rctheatres.com

This multiplex cinema houses 10 screens. Films are shown seven days a week in season from 2 p.m. until midnight. On summer days when the weather is bad, the theater adds a rainy-day showing at 11 a.m.

Roanoke Island

PIONEER THEATRE
113 Budleigh St., Manteo
(252) 473-2216

The nation's oldest theater operated continuously by one family, the Pioneer is filled with nostalgia and smells of just-buttered popcorn. And it's been showing flicks since 1934. For the inexpensive admission price—and the old-fashioned feel of the place—it can't be beat. Even the popcorn, sodas, and candy are a great deal. The Pioneer is open year-round. All movies start at 8 p.m. daily, and a ticket is only $5. Listings change weekly on Friday; call for a synopsis of the current show. See the Attractions chapter for more information.

Hatteras Island

RC THEATRES HATTERAS CINEPLEX 4
Hatteras Island Plaza, NC 12, Avon
(252) 995-9060
http://rctheatres.com

With four screens and first-run movies year-round, this large movie house shows films all day on weekends and throughout the summer, and on evenings only in the off-season.

NATURE TRAIL HIKES

The Outer Banks is home to several diverse ecosystems that house a wide variety of wildlife. If you love nature, you'll love the many self-guided nature trails that allow you to see the diversity of the Outer Banks up close. You can hike in wildlife refuges, across sand dunes, and through maritime forests. The National Park Service offers some guided walks; call (252) 473-2111 or visit www.nps.gov/caha for more information.

Corolla

AUDUBON WILDLIFE SANCTUARY AT PINE ISLAND

An unmarked trail leads through this 5,000-acre wildlife sanctuary, a protected habitat for birds, deer, rabbits, and a variety of plants. Park at the Sanderling Inn to access the 2.5-mile soundside path through a portion of the sanctuary.

Nags Head

NAGS HEAD WOODS ECOLOGICAL PRESERVE

Part of the Nature Conservancy, Nags Head Woods is a preserved maritime forest with diverse flora and fauna. There are more than 5 miles of trails through forest, dunes, swamp, and pond habitats. You'll also see 19th-century cemeteries. For maps and start locations, go to the visitor center at 701 West Ocean Acres Dr. in Kill Devil Hills or call (252) 441-2525.

JOCKEY'S RIDGE STATE PARK

Climbing the tallest sand dune on the East Coast is a challenging hike, but two nature trails wind through the lower regions of the dune. The Soundside Nature Trail is an easy 45-minute walk, and the Tracks in the Sand Trail is a 1.5-mile walk. Start at the state park visitor center at MP 12 in Nags Head.

Roanoke Island

THOMAS HARIOT NATURE TRAIL AT FORT RALEIGH

This trail winds through a heavily wooded area from the Fort Raleigh National Historic Site to Roanoke Sound. Along the way are several interpretive markers with Hariot's descriptions of Roanoke Island in the 16th century. Call the Fort Raleigh National Historic Site at (252) 473-5772 for information.

FREEDMEN'S TRAIL

This 2-mile trail commemorates the history of the Freedmen's Colony, a Roanoke Island community that provided a safe haven for freed slaves during the Civil War. Access to the trail is near the Elizabethan Gardens entrance, and exhibits are at the end of the trail on Roanoke Sound. Call the National Park Service for information at (252) 473-5772.

Mainland

ALLIGATOR RIVER NATIONAL WILDLIFE REFUGE

Two trails lead through this refuge. Sandy Ridge Wildlife Trail starts at the south end of the dirt Buffalo City Road. The trail, a half mile out and a half mile back, has footpaths and a boardwalk. Creef Cut Wildlife Trail starts on US 64 at the intersection with Milltail Road. A kiosk with parking marks the trailhead. It's also a half mile out and back. Additionally, it has a fishing dock, an overlook, and a boardwalk. Both trails are wheelchair accessible. Call (252) 473-1131 for information.

RECREATION

Bodie Island

BODIE ISLAND DIKE TRAIL AND POND TRAIL

Starting at the Bodie Island Lighthouse, two trails wind through marsh and wetlands to the sound. Call the light station at (252) 441-5711 for information.

Pea Island

PEA ISLAND NATIONAL WILDLIFE REFUGE

North Pond Trail starts behind Pea Island Visitor Center and leads hikers on a half-mile, 30-minute walk around the refuge. The quarter-mile Salt Flats Trail starts at the north end of North Pond Trail. These are favorite walks for birders year-round, but especially in late fall and winter when migrating swans, ducks, and geese winter here. Call (252) 987-2394 for information.

Buxton

BUXTON WOODS NATURE TRAIL

Starting at Cape Point Campground, this 0.75-mile trail leads through maritime forest, across dunes, and into freshwater marshes. Small plaques along the way explain the fragile maritime forest eco system.

Ocracoke

HAMMOCK HILLS NATURE TRAIL

This 0.75-mile trail, about a 30-minute walk, leads through the salt marsh and forest. The trailhead is north of the village on NC 12; signs direct you to it. Call the Ocracoke Island Visitor Center at (252) 928-4531 for information.

PORTSMOUTH ISLAND

This ghost-town island is accessible only by boat, but once you get there you'll find numerous trails that lead you on a fascinating exploration of this island, past abandoned but restored buildings. A 2-milelong trail leads from the village to the beach through the heart of the island. Call Cape Lookout National Seashore for information at (252) 728-2250.

PARASAILING

If you've always wanted to float high above the water beneath a colorful parachute, adventures await at various locations along the Outer Banks. Although a boat pulls from below, allowing the wind to lift you toward the clouds, you don't get wet on these outdoor trips over the sounds unless you want to. You take off and land on the back of the boat. Riders soar with the seagulls above whitecaps and beach cottages. People of any age, without any athletic ability at all, enjoy parasailing and find it one of their most memorable experiences. And it's safe, too; unbreakable ropes are standard.

Corolla

NORTH COROLLA WATERSPORTS
NC 12, Corolla
(252) 453-6900
www.corollawatersports.com
Parasailing trips are offered at heights from 400 to 1,400 feet above the Currituck Sound. Call ahead for reservations and rates. Parasailing is offered in the spring, summer, and fall.

Duck

NOR'BANKS SAILING CENTER
NC 12, Duck
(252) 261-7100
http://norbanks.com
Specializing in single, tandem, and triple flights, this was one of the original parasailing locations on the Outer Banks. All vessels that give you your ride are Coast Guard–inspected and are able to take passengers up 400 to 1,400 feet. Parasailing is available from May through Oct.

Kitty Hawk

THE PROMENADE WATERSPORTS
US 158, MP¼, Kitty Hawk
(252) 261-4400
The Promenade offers parasailing with an experienced captain in Currituck Sound. Persons of any age can take off for a single, tandem, or triple ride up to 1,400 feet.

Nags Head

WILD BILL'S WATERWORKS
US 158, MP 17, Nags Head
(252) 441-9453
http://obxwaterworks.com
Parasailing captains from the Waterworks can take you high. Uplifting experiences are offered daily from Apr through Nov. These 8- to 15-minute flights allow you to float at 400 to 1,400 feet; cost depends on how high you want to fly.

RACES

NAGS HEAD WOODS ANNUAL 5K RUN
Nags Head Woods Preserve
Kill Devil Hills
(252) 441-2431

The Nags Head Woods Run is a well-loved spring tradition on the Outer Banks. Close to 400 runners, from ages 6 to 60 and beyond, gather to run (or walk) the soft dirt road that winds through this rare maritime forest. Afterward, an awards ceremony then a big party are held at a local restaurant. There is no race-day registration so you must register early.

OBX MARATHON AND GATEWAY BANKHALF MARATHON
Kitty Hawk and Jockey's Ridge to Roanoke Island
www.obxmarathon.com
The second Sunday in November is the day 4,000 athletes pound the pavement and sand of the beautiful Outer Banks. The full marathon takes off in Kitty Hawk, and the half marathoners join in at Jockey's Ridge. Both groups cross the Washington Baum Bridge to Roanoke Island, where the race finishes. The total purse is $25,000. Music, food, T-shirts, and more await the finishers. Registration is online only.

ADVICE 5K ANNUAL TURKEY TROT
Duck
(252) 255-1050
www.advice5.com
The annual Turkey Trot is a Thanksgiving Day tradition in Duck. The race starts on Scarborough Lane and ends at the Red Sky Cafe for a post-race party. There is no race-day registration. You must register in advance at the Red Sky Cafe at 1197 Duck Rd. (NC 12) or by mail: Advice 5K, c/o Advice 5¢, PO Box 8278, Duck, NC 27949. The race is limited to 350 people.

TENNIS

Many cottage rental developments through-out the Outer Banks have private tennis courts for their guests. If you don't own a racquet or left yours back on the mainland, you can rent one by the day or week from Ocean Atlantic Rentals (see the Weekly and Long-Term Cottage Rentals chapter). Out-door public tennis courts include the follow-ing free courts:

- **Kill Devil Hills**—two hard-surface courts are located near the Kill Devil Hills Fire Department at MP 6 on US 158, and four hard-surface courts are beside the Kill Devil Hills Water Plant on Mustian Street.
- **Nags Head**—a public court is behind Kelly's Restaurant, off US 158 at MP 10½.
- **Roanoke Island**—courts are available at Manteo High School on Wingina Avenue and at Manteo Middle School on US 64/264 after school hours.
- **Hatteras Island**—courts are available at Cape Hatteras School on NC 12 in Buxton after school hours.

Corolla

PINE ISLAND RACQUET CLUB
NC 12, between Corolla and Duck
(252) 453-8525
Home to the Outer Banks' only indoor ten-nis courts, Pine Island is 2.5 miles north of the Sanderling Inn. It is open to the public year-round for recreational play, and several tournaments are held each season.

Three hard-surface courts are under a vaulted roof for air-conditioned or heated comfort, while two clay courts and two platform tennis courts are outdoors. Rest-room, locker, and shower facilities are included.

Pine Island also has two ball machines, a radar gun for timing serves, and a video-tape analysis machine to help improve your game. Tennis pro Rick Ostlund and his assis-tant Betty Wright teach clinics for adults and children and offer individualized instruction at any skill level. The pro shop sells racquets, clothes, and tennis accessories and provides stringing services.

Reservations are suggested for indoor and outdoor courts. Indoor courts rent for $32 an hour, and the outdoor court is $28 per hour. Pine Island is open every day except Christmas from at least 9 a.m. in the offseason and from 8 a.m. in season.

WATERSLIDES, ARCADES & OTHER AMUSEMENTS

On hot afternoons when you're ready for a break from sand and salt water, slip on down to a water park and splash into one of its big pools. Most of these parks are open daily during the summer—some well into the evening. Waterslides generally close on rainy days.

Among the recreational outposts, many include video arcades in their offerings, but the Outer Banks' amusement centers also offer brightly lit computerized games and other unusual activities. We can't list every-thing the owners of these establishments include, so you'll have to experience these places for yourself to discover all the sur-prises in store.

HATTERAS ISLAND WATERFALL ACTION PARK
NC 12, Rodanthe
(252) 987-2213
www.waterfallactionpark.com

You can't miss this palm-tree-lined playground, geared for hours of fun for both adults and kids. An Outer Banks fixture for more than 20 years, this amusement park has more than 20 rides and the area's only bungee-jumping outlet for daredevils. Two waterslides, the Corkscrew and the Cyclone, give heart-thumping, thrill-filled rides. But this wonderland has a multitude of other offerings: two minigolf courses, model Grand Prix race cars, Winston Cup stock cars, Outlaw sprint cars, NASCAR super trucks, and free-fall go-karts—not to mention speedboats and bumper cars. Children have to be at least 12 years old to ride the adult rides. Kiddie Land features rides for the under-12 set. There's no admission charge to get into the park; call for prices to ride. Your best deal can be had with one of the 40 combination tickets, which save you more money the more you ride. Waterfall Action Park is open daily 10 a.m. to 9 p.m. from Memorial Day through Labor Day.

FRISCO MINI GOLF AND GO-KARTS
NC 12, Frisco
(252) 995-6325

This miniature golf and go-kart establishment also has an 1,800-square-foot arcade that keeps kids entertained on a rainy day with pool tables, air hockey, video games, and other games. A concession booth sells ice cream, snow cones, cotton candy, hot dogs, and drinks.

WATER SPORTS

Water is the Outer Banks' biggest draw. Everywhere you look on the Outer Banks there's wet, wonderful H20—the deep, blue Atlantic Ocean; the wide, shallow Currituck, Croatan, Roanoke, and Pamlico Sounds; brackish bays and estuaries teeming with wildlife; thick, sopping marshes; and dark, man-made canals sluicing through the islands. And everywhere you look there are people on or in the water. Whether it's on a surfboard, a kiteboard, a sailboard, a Jet Ski, a kayak, or just in a bathing suit, everyone eventually finds his or her way to the water. Numerous water-sports establishments happily accommodate anyone's wish to get wet.

In this chapter we give you a rundown of water sports and a list of places to rent or buy equipment and take lessons. We list prices to give you a general idea of how much things cost, but be aware that prices are subject to change.

SURFING

Warmer than New England waters and wielding more consistent waves than most Florida beaches, the Outer Banks' surf is reputed to have the best breaks on the East Coast. Local surfing experts explain that since we are set out farther into the ocean in deeper waters than most other coastal regions, our beaches pick up more swells and wind patterns than any place around. Piers, shipwrecks, and offshore sandbars also create unusual wave patterns. Along with those swells, the Outer Banks has the added bonus of sharp drop-offs and troughs right offshore, which make the waves break with more power and force.

The beaches from Corolla through Ocracoke are some of the only spots left that don't have strict surfing regulations: As long as you keep yourself leashed to your board and stay at least 300 feet away from public piers, you won't get a surfing citation.

The best surfing is from late August through November in hurricane season, when swells from storms are likely to roll toward shore. Midsummer is traditionally the worst time for surfing. On small summer waves it's more fun to surf a longboard.

Since the beaches are getting increasingly crowded with summer surfers, some folks understandably don't want to reveal their favorite wave-catching locales. And breaks, which are affected by shifting sandbars, change every year. After fall hurricane season and winter nor'easters, no one really knows which breaks subsided or where they reappear. It takes some looking around in the spring to find new breaks and relinquish old ones.

Piers always make for good breaks because of the sandbars that form around them. In Corolla there is a good break on the beach in front of the Corolla Light swimming pool. You can't park there unless you're staying in the resort, so park at the south ramp road next to the lighthouse and walk up the beach. Swan Beach in the four-wheel-drive area is also good. Kitty Hawk Pier in Kitty Hawk and Avalon Pier in Kill Devil Hills each boast ample parking and pretty good waves. Also check out the area around First and Second Streets in Kill Devil Hills. Nags Head Pier is a good spot, but also check out the beaches north and south of there, especially around milepost 13.

i Though good surf breaks tend to form around fishing piers, it's illegal to surf within 300 feet of a pier—for the surfers' own protection, of course.

When swells come from the south, Hatteras Island beaches have the best waves. If you don't mind hiking across the dunes with a board under your arm, Pea Island and Coquina Beach both have waves worth the walk. Rodanthe has always been a popular destination, and its name sparks fond recognition with surfers all over the world. If there are waves you'll have no trouble spotting the area because you'll see hundreds of surfers squeezing into wet suits along the roadside. The surf is just a short hop over the dunes from the road. The ramps north and south of Salvo are also worth a try. Ramp 34, just north of Avon, is another location, as are the turnout north of Buxton, ramp 49 in Frisco, Frisco Pier, and the public beach access area between Frisco and Hatteras Village.

The best and biggest waves by far roll in around the original site of Cape Hatteras Lighthouse. Here at Cape Point, the beaches jut closest to the Gulf Stream and face in two directions, doubling the chances for good conditions. Concrete and steel groins jut out into the Atlantic, though, so beware of being tossed into these head-bashing barriers.

Surf Reports

Local radio station WVOD 99.1 offers a daily surf report at 8:45 a.m. For an online surf report, visit www.surfchex.com or http://surfreport.corollasurfshop.com, or check out surf-cams for the following location websites: Hatteras Lighthouse (www.surfline.com) or Avalon Pier (www.avalonpier.com).

Most surf shops have an even more up-to-the-minute pulse on the surf, but not all provide a formal "surf line" service. Following is a list of numbers to call for the daily wave report. Most shops give the scoop only on the portion of the beach in their geographical area.

COROLLA SURF SHOP & COROLLA SURF MUSEUM
Corolla
(252) 453-WAVE

WAVE RIDING VEHICLES
Kitty Hawk
(252) 261-3332

THE PIT
Kill Devil Hills
(252) 480-3128

WHALEBONE SURF SHOP
Nags Head
(252) 441-6747

RODANTHE SURF SHOP
Rodanthe
(252) 987-2435

NATURAL ART SURF SHOP
Buxton
(252) 995-4646

ℹ️ Is your teenager looking for a happening beach hangout? The Pit in Kill Devil Hills is popular Mon, Wed, and Fri evenings when a drug-free, alcohol-free dance party is held from 9:30 p.m. to 1 a.m. during the season. Here teens can find out which beach accesses everyone will head to in the daylight hours. As the surf breaks change, so do the gathering spots.

Surf Shops

Ranging from sublime to specialized to hip, the Outer Banks is inundated with surf shops—hot spots for wave riders of all ages and skill levels. Each summer surf-shop managers post competition schedules for beginners through surfing-circuit riders near the storefronts. Most shops stock gear, and many offer instruction during the season. The following list highlights some favorites of Outer Banks surfers.

COROLLA SURF SHOP & COROLLA SURF MUSEUM
Monteray Plaza
NC 12, Corolla
(252) 453-9283
www.corollasurfshop.com
Corolla Surf Shop is a full-service shop with boards, lessons, sales, repairs, and rentals. The store also has a full line of new surfboards for sale (more than 100 boards are in stock). A good stock of used boards is available for purchase, along with new skateboards, skimboards, and body boards. The store carries a full skateboard department, clothing, shoes, shades, and jewelry. Check out the surfer's museum too!

Surf lessons, including all equipment, start at $65 per student for a 2-hour lesson. Up to five people take lessons together. Special needs surf lessons are available for ages 9 and up. Rentals are available on a daily and weekly basis. Rentals start at $20 a day and $50 per week. The shop is the home of the Nalu Kai Surf Museum, a free exhibit of 15 collectible surfboards and other surfer memorabilia. Corolla Surf Shop is open year-round. Winter hours vary.

DUCK VILLAGE OUTFITTERS
1207 Duck Rd., Duck
(252) 261-7222
www.duckvillageoutfitters.net
With surfboards and body boards, Duck Village Outfitters is surf-shop central for Duck. Surfing lessons are offered daily during the summer season. The shop conducts kayak tours every day in the summer and has a large assortment of rentals and retail items, including bikes, wet suits, fishing equipment, kayaks, and ocean toys.

WAVE RIDING VEHICLES (WRV)
US 158, MP 2, Kitty Hawk
(252) 261-7952
www.waveridingvehicles.com
Carrying top-of-the-line surfboards, apparel, and accessories since 1967, WRV focuses on what the owner calls "the godfather of water sports"—surfing. This year-round shop also sells skateboards and snowboards. It's one of the largest full-service surf shops on the barrier islands. WRV is also the biggest surfboard manufacturing company under one label on the East Coast. The company produces private-label surfwear, which is sold from Maine to Florida and overseas. Surfboards rent daily and weekly.

THE PIT SURF SHOP, BAR AND GRILL
US 158, MP 9, Kill Devil Hills
(252) 480-3128
www.pitsurf.com

The Pit bills itself as a "surf hangout." The setup includes a 3,000-square-foot surf shop that covers all board sports—surfing, body boarding, skimming, and skateboarding. Owners Steve Pauls and Ben Sproul, both devout surfers, sell a large selection of new, used, and custom boards, including the locally made Gale Force boards, plus a selection of wet suits and related accessories. All boards are available for sale or rent. Surf lessons and camps are offered in the summer months for groups or individuals. Lessons run about 2 hours and include board rental and a T-shirt.

i Waves look good for body surfing? Be sure that the waves are not breaking right on shore. There is a steep rise at the edge of the water and body surfers risk broken bones if the water breaks at the edge of the beach. Try surfing farther out in the open water.

WHALEBONE SURF SHOP
US 158, MP 10, Nags Head
(252) 441-6747
www.whalebonesurfshop.com
Surfer-owned and -operated, Whalebone boasts that it has been in business since the 1960s. Major brands of surfboards, and the best of the smaller brands, are available at this well-stocked store. Surfboard rentals are available for trials. The store is open year-round, but hours vary so call ahead.

SECRET SPOT SURF SHOP
US 158, MP 11, Nags Head
(252) 441-4030
www.secretspotsurfshop.com
No secret to surf enthusiasts, Secret Spot is one of the old-timers of the barrier islands'

surf scene and claims to have the most boards available. Packed with the best of contemporary and classic boards and favorite surfwear, the store prides itself in catering to both younger and older surfers. The business has manufactured its own surfboards since 1977; the shop opened five years later. A full line of shortboards, longboards, and custom and used boards is available, along with a selection of wet suits.

Surfboards can be rented and lessons are available. Call the shop or visit the website for surf reports. Secret Spot also sells items for women and girls, including sundresses, T-shirts, bathing suits, shorts, shoes, and accessories. The skate store has a full selection of skateboard paraphernalia, including decks, trucks, wheels, and accessories.

CAVALIER SURF SHOP
NC 12, MP 13½, Nags Head
(252) 441-7349
This classic shop, the only one on the Beach Road, has been in business since the 1960s. The family-run operation is dedicated to the surfing lifestyle. Cavalier rents a variety of surfboards, boogie boards, and skimboards, plus gloves, booties, and wet suits. They also rent umbrellas, chairs, and rafts for long beach days. Surfboard rental is available. When you're not in the surf, rent a surf video for excitement. New and used boards are for sale, and Cavalier also sells boards by consignment. You'll also find a huge collection of stickers and sunglasses, watches, and clothing for men and women.

RODANTHE SURF SHOP
NC 12, Rodanthe
(252) 987-2412
Rodanthe Surf Shop owners Randy Hall and Debbie Bell moved to the southern Outer

Banks to surf, and the shop evolved naturally from their lifestyle. A hands-on, no-frills operation, the shop sells only the boards it makes, Hatteras Glass Surfboards, along with surfing equipment and surfer lifestyle clothing. Get a true surfing experience by renting a real fiberglass board here. The shop is closed Thanksgiving through Mar.

i When you're surfing or kayaking in the ocean waves, look out for your fellow surfers and for swimmers. Do not cut across the path of someone actively riding a wave. Courteously ask swimmers to move down the beach a bit if they're swimming in the best breaks.

HATTERAS ISLAND SURF SHOP
NC 12, Waves
(252) 987-2296
www.hiss-waves.com
Veteran surfers Barton and Chris Decker have operated Hatteras Island Surf Shop since 1971. They expanded their ventures to include windsurfing. The surf shop offers new and used equipment, rentals, and lessons. It sells surfboards, balsa boards, longboards, body boards, ocean toys, kayaks, and in-line skates. Wet suits, surfwear, beach clothing, and bathing suits are also for sale in this no-nonsense surf shop. The shop closes in Jan and Feb.

HATTERAS ISLAND BOARDSPORTS
NC 12, Avon
(252) 995-6160, (866) HIB-WAVE
www.hiboardsports.com
Just like the name suggests, this surf shop has boards—pick from all styles of surfboards (including custom designs), skimboards, and body boards. Wet suits and surf clothing are sold as well.

NATURAL ART SURF SHOP
NC 12, Buxton
(252) 995-5682
Natural Art specializes in both custommade surfboards and a full line of handmade surf wear for men, women, and kids. The shop also carries shoes, wet suits, skatewear, and videos. The surfboards are shaped by owner Scott Busbey in a separate shop in the backyard. Busbey has gained a national reputation for his beautiful craftsmanship and reasonably priced boards. Rent surfboards, boogie boards, and wet suits here.

RIDE THE WIND SURF SHOP
NC 12, Ocracoke
(252) 928-6311
www.surfocracoke.com
In business since 1985, Ride the Wind features two floors of merchandise, ranging from the latest contemporary surf gear to casual, comfortable clothing and footwear for men and women. Ride the Wind rents surfboards, body boards, wet suits, and practically all Outer Banks water-sports equipment, except windsurfing items. Surfboards can be rented here. The shop is open seven days a week from Mar through Dec and is closed for the winter. Ride the Wind also offers outfitting trips to Portsmouth Island and a surf and kayak day camp for kids. Beginner surf lessons are available for adults and kids.

i Don't know how to surf, and not sure you want to learn? Try purchasing a boogie board and you'll still have big fun on the waves. No instruction is necessary; only good swimming skills and a board are required.

WINDSURFING

Springtime on the Outer Banks brings a specific annual migration, mostly from Canada and the northern United States. From a distance we know where these migrating flocks are from and why they're here, for their vehicles give them away. Their luggage racks are laden with windsurfing equipment, and some tow trailers stacked with boards and sails for every wind condition. Tourism officials estimate that as many as 500 windsurfing enthusiasts a week arrive at the Outer Banks in spring and fall. Dozens of other visitors try the sport for the first time while vacationing in Dare County.

Owing to our position in the Atlantic, plus the area's prevailing winds, shallow sounds, and temperate weather, Hatteras Island is a sail-boarding mecca on the East Coast. When the wind whips just right, hundreds of sails soar along the sound and ocean shores, skimming over the salty water like bright butterflies flitting near the beach.

Windsurfing is not an easy sport, although once you get the hang of it, it is one of the most intoxicating experiences imaginable. It's clean and quiet and just as easily lends itself to solitary excursions as it does to group outings. With the proper equipment, sailboarders glide into a sunset or cruise more than 40 mph across choppy breaks. On the Outer Banks sailboarders can usually find some wind to ride year-round. Windsurfing is permitted any place you can set your sails, except lifeguarded beaches. This sport truly allows the rider to feel a part of the natural surroundings—and it's an incredible rush to fly with the wind.

Canadian Hole & Other Places to Windsurf

Hatteras Island's Canadian Hole, so named for all of our visitors from the far north, has often been touted in international windsurfing circles as one of the continent's best sailboarding spots. Formed in the early 1960s, Canadian Hole was created after a storm cut an inlet across Hatteras Island, just north of Buxton, and workers dredged sand from the sound to rebuild the roadway. Dredging activities carved troughs just offshore in the Pamlico Sound. The deep depressions, which extend well beyond 5 feet, help create ideal conditions for sailboarders. Additionally, Canadian Hole flanks one of the barrier islands' narrowest landmasses. The walk from ocean to sound is less than five minutes, enabling sailboarders to easily switch between the two bodies of water.

Besides the sound and the Atlantic, Canadian Hole's amenities include a 100-space paved lot in which to park big vans and trailers, toilets and showers, a phone booth, and trash cans. The beach at Canadian Hole is much wider than other soundside stretches of sand—it's about 50 yards wide and accommodates sunbathers, coolers, and plenty of spectators.

Nags Head's soundside beaches also provide areas that are great for sailboarding. The sounds are shallower than at Canadian Hole, and thus safer for beginners. The town of Nags Head has a soundside access at milepost 16 with plenty of parking. Jockey's Ridge State Park's soundside access area also provides parking and a small beach for launching sailboards. In Duck most people launch on the sound. There are dozens of launch areas on the soundside all along the Outer Banks.

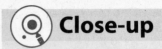

Close-up

Canadian Hole

Wide-open sky, unobstructed by trees and skyscrapers, hovers over a ridge of sand. The wind blows from every direction, sweeping sometimes gently, sometimes with excited fury, across the island from sea to sound or sound to sea. Welcome to Canadian Hole.

Long before sailboarders and kiteboarders arrived in droves at Canadian Hole, Hatteras Island's local fishermen toiled night into day, day into night, plying fish from the salt- and freshwater sound. Arriving upon the shore, they toted their boats and fishing equipment, crossing the island at one of its narrowest locations to the Atlantic's beach.

Some days their journey took them from the ocean to the sound at this place, dubbed "the Haulover." The crossing was frequently made here between Avon and Buxton, where the ocean has met the sound in past storm rages and will do so again one day.

For now Canadian Hole is available for wind and water lovers to use. It is a privilege granted by the National Park Service, which holds jurisdiction over the land as part of Cape Hatteras National Seashore. Americans, Canadians, and indeed people of the world come here to sail across the shining seas known as the prime windsurfing and kitesailing spot on the United States' East Coast.

The place has a smell of its own, dusted by wind, sun, and island brush, wetted with rain and salt spray. At times windriders wait in a quiet hush, lazily aware, keen to every movement of the wind. When the wind picks up, the scurry begins. Dashing across the parking lot, board over head, squeezing between cars, trucks, and vans, sailboarders in wet suits head to the shallow sound while new arrivals find a parking space, scope the scene, assess the wind speed, and follow suit.

The spot attracts visitors from Canada seeking warm water and air often accompanied by steady wind. The drive is accomplished in a day or two, consuming 16 to 20 hours from eastern locales, with eager anticipation pushing the wind lovers south.

A few resident sailboarders remember when the sport was new and first brought to the island in the early 1970s. One or two wet-behind-the-ear windsurfing pioneers ventured into the shores meeting the Graveyard of the Atlantic, where shoals and unpredictable shifting conditions wrecked more than 1,000 ships.

Enthusiasts soon determined that windsurfing in the safer sound is fun, not only for beginners but for intermediate and advanced wind sailors as well. At times, hundreds of sails flit about, dancing upon the sparkles.

Some brave and skilled sailors carry their boards and sails across the highway, over the dune, and ride the waves into the Atlantic. The experience, if successful, is surreal, intoxicatingly beautiful. But many a daredevil has been smashed by the surf and "denied" entry or has been swept along in a wicked current or lost equipment and pride, which is renewed in the next great session. More and more dedicated enthusiasts become wave sailors, enticed by the never-ending challenges and thrills.

Now kiteboarding has found its perfect spot. Those with kites rather than sails park along the sound in the sand and sail where the water is definitely shallow, away from the crowd of windsurfers, at Kite Point. Kite Point is just south of the Hole but part of the same park.

Despite the rise of windsurfing, followed by the rise of kiteboarding, the water is the same, and so is the wind. It's beautiful and free. Whether holding a sail or a kite, sailors smile, tasting freedom, keeping the feeling forever and ever.

KITESURFING

Kitesurfing, or kiteboarding, is a relatively new sport, and it's the latest rage among sail-boarders, wake boarders, and surfers alike. The Outer Banks is widely recognized as one of the top places in the world to kitesurf because of the ever-present wind and shallow sounds. Kitesurfers favor the Pamlico Sound off Hatteras Island because it is so wide and has few obstructions to the kite lines. Some daredevil types also kitesurf in the ocean.

Kitesurfing does offer significant advantages over windsurfing: The gear is much more portable, you can do it in a wider range of winds (even low winds), and most people say it's much easier to learn. However, windsurfing is safer. Kite-surfing is a dangerous sport, though it's hard to perceive that danger when you're watching from the shore. The amount of wind power behind the kite is enormous.

For this reason you cannot simply rent a kite and board at the local outfitters and go on your merry way. You must attain a basic level of certification before you are allowed to rent or buy kitesurfing equipment, and some outfitters don't rent the gear at all, saying the risks are just too great.

Two types of kites are used in kitesurfing: an inflatable kite and a foil kite. The inflatable kite is crescent shaped, with an inflatable leading edge that allows it to float. This kite is easier to use, is more stable and predictable, and can be used in a broader wind range. The foil kite is flatter and it fills with wind for a more powerful, high-performance ride. The foil kites are a little more unpredictable and are subject to unexpected gusts.

Kitty Hawk Kites Kite Surfing School does rent equipment, but only to people who have completed their Professional Air Sports Association–certified training courses at Carolina Outdoors at MP 16 in Nags Head. It takes about 4 hours of training to become certified, and then you are able to rent gear. The amount of training time depends on your previous kiting skills. If you're not familiar with kite physics, trainers suggest that you practice with a trainer kite until kite-steering techniques become ingrained.

If you want to buy kitesurfing gear, the whole setup will cost you $1,500 or more. If you want to watch or compete in kitesurfing, check out Kitty Hawk Kites Kiteboarding Center at milepost 15½ in Nags Head.

Shops & Lessons

Whether you're looking for a lesson, need a sail or a fin of a different size, or want advice, more than a dozen shops stock windsurfing and kitesurfing supplies, and many provide instructors in season.

KITTY HAWK WATERSPORTS
US 158, MP 16, Nags Head
(252) 441-2756
www.kittyhawkwatersports.com
Dealing in windsurfing on the Outer Banks for more than 20 years, Kitty Hawk Watersports was one of the first windsurfing operations on the barrier islands. At its site on Roanoke Sound, the center is open almost all year-round and offers windsurfing instruction in spring, summer, and fall. With a $65, 2-hour lesson, instructors guarantee you'll be skimming the Roanoke Sound on your own. Call the number listed for rates. Kitesurfing lessons are available, but rentals are not. Wind- and kitesurfing equipment is also for sale.

KITTY HAWK KITES KITE SURFING SCHOOL
US 158, MP 15½, Nags Head
(252) 449-2210
www.kittyhawk.com

Kitty Hawk Kites Kite Surfing School at Carolina Outdoors offers kitesurfing lessons with highly qualified instructors at this location on the Roanoke Sound in Nags Head, right next to Windmill Point restaurant. Lessons cost $200. This school offers Level I, II, and III certification that is recognized by the Professional Air Sports Association. Once you have achieved a certain level of certification, you can rent kitesurfing gear at this location. Call for rental prices.

OCEANAIR
NC 12, Avon
(252) 995-5000, (866) 995-6644
www.oceanairsports.com

With private access to Pamlico Sound, this widely respected store was opened in 1988 as Windsurfing Hatteras by a group of dedicated local sailboarders. Now known as OceanAir, the operation offers windsurfing and kitesurfing lessons and clinics every year for both beginners and advanced students. The clinics are staffed by some of the best kite- and windsurfing talent around.

Lessons come with guaranteed success for beginners. Windsurfing lessons include all equipment and on-water instruction. Windsurfing boards and rigs can be rented at the site. Kiteboarding lessons are offered by highly qualified instructors. Kitesurfing gear is not available for rent. Call for rates on renting surfboards, body boards, kayaks, Hobie Cats, and other fun-inspired items. OceanAir stocks everything you could possibly need for wind- or kiteboarding.

HATTERAS ISLAND SAIL SHOP
NC 12, Waves
(252) 987-2292
www.hatterasislandsurfshop.com

On the soundfront, this windsurfing shop was opened in 1996 by the owners of Hatteras Island Surf Shop, which is 250 yards south. They offer sales, rentals, and lessons. Owner Barton Decker says the sailing site is the largest grassy rigging area on the Outer Banks with a sandy beach launch. With about 150 new and used boards in stock, the store also has necessary accessories in its complete inventory. Windsurfing lessons are available as well as rentals. Kiteboarding lessons are offered; no rentals are available. Standup paddleboards and kayaks can be rented or purchased here. The store closes in Jan and Feb.

REAL KITEBOARDING
Cape Hatteras
(252) 995-4740, (866) REAL-KITE
www.realkiteboarding.com

REAL Kiteboarding is a full-service kiteboarding center that offers gear and instruction. With home bases on Hatteras Island and Puerto Rico, they offer instruction in many areas of the East Coast. Three-day Kite Camps are offered on Hatteras Island in spring, summer, and fall, and after one of these intense camps, you'll certainly be ripping. Less-expensive lessons require less time but still cover basic skills. Kid's camps are also offered.

HATTERAS ISLAND BOARDSPORTS
NC 12, Avon
(252) 995-6160, (866) HIB-WAVE
www.hiboardsports.com

For windsurfing and kiteboarding equipment, new or used, for sale or to rent, visit Hatteras Island Boardsports. Instructors teach all levels, catering to your specific needs, particularly with private lessons. The shop stocks casual clothing for the beach and to wear at home. Kayaks, kayak tours, and other water-sport needs are served here. The shop is open all year; call for hours.

KAYAKING & CANOEING

The easiest, most adaptable, and most accessible water sports available on the Outer Banks—kayaking and canoeing—are activities people of any age can enjoy. The lightweight paddlecraft are maneuverable, glide almost anywhere along the seas or sounds, and afford adventurous activity as well as silent solitude. They're also relatively inexpensive ways to tour uncharted waterways and see sights not observable from shore.

In recent years more than a dozen eco-tour outlets have opened on the barrier islands. Stores offer everything from rent-your-own kayaks for less than $40 a day to guided, daylong, and even overnight tours around uninhabited islands. With no fuel to foul the estuaries, no noise to frighten wildlife, and no need for a demanding skill level, kayaks and canoes offer a sport as strenuous or as relaxing as you want it to be.

Unlike the closed-cockpit kayaks used in whitewater river runs, most kayaks on the Outer Banks are a sit-on-top style from 7 to 10 feet long. They're molded in brightly colored plastic, are light to carry to a launch site, and are manufactured in one- and two-seat models. A double-blade paddle and a life jacket are the only other pieces of equipment needed, and these are included with rentals and lessons.

Canoes are heavier and harder to get into the water but slightly more stable than kayaks. They seat two or three people and include a more sheltered hull to haul gear or picnic lunches. Single-blade paddles, usually two per boat, are needed to maneuver this traditional watercraft.

These sports lend themselves to solitary enjoyment just as easily as group fun. Thrill seekers can splash kayaks through frothy surf in the Atlantic or paddle past the breakers and float alongside schools of dolphin. For more tranquility kayakers and canoeists can slip slowly through mysterious, marshy creeks at the isolated Alligator River National Wildlife Refuge, explore narrow canals that bigger boats can't access, or slip alongside an uninhabited island in the middle of the shallow sound. There are historical tours around Roanoke Island, nature tours through maritime forests, and self-guided trails with markers winding through a former logging town called Buffalo City on the Dare County mainland.

Learning to Paddle

Unlike other water sports, little to no instruction is needed to paddle a kayak or canoe. It is best to know how to swim, in case you capsize, but since most of the sounds are only a few feet deep, you can walk your way back to shore if you stay in the estuaries—or, at least, jump back in your boat from a standing position. If you fall out of your boat and cannot touch bottom to stand, try to grab onto the canoe or kayak and float to where you can stand.

Different strokes are required for each type of craft. For single kayaks, double-blade paddles are designed to be used by one person. The blades are positioned at opposing angles so you can work across your body with a sweeping motion and minimal rotation and paddle on both sides of the boat. The trick is to get into a rhythm and not dig too deeply beneath the water's surface. Double kayaks are paddled by two people alternating rhythmic strokes on opposing sides of the kayak. Canoeing is done with one person paddling on each side of the boat, if there are two passengers, or a single operator alternating sides with paddle strokes.

Most kayak- and canoe-rental outfits offer lessons. Even if you prefer to be on your own rather than with a guided group trip, people renting these watercraft are happy to share advice and expertise. If you have any questions or need directions around the intricate waterways, ask.

The sounds around the Outer Banks are ideal for kayaking and canoeing because they are shallow, warm, and filled with flora and fauna. There are marked pathways at Alligator River National Wildlife Refuge; tours through Nags Head Woods; buoys around Wanchese, Manteo, and Colington; and plenty of uncharted areas to explore around Pine Island, Pea Island, Kitty Hawk, Corolla, the Cape Hatteras National Seashore, and Portsmouth Island. Unlike other types of boats, canoes and kayaks don't require a special launching site.

Rentals

KITTY HAWK KITES
Monteray Shores Plaza, NC 12, Corolla
(252) 453-3685
www.kittyhawk.com
Carolina Outdoors, a division of Kitty Hawk Kites, offers kayak rentals for paddlers who want to explore the sound.

KITTY HAWK SURF COMPANY
NC 12, Corolla
(252) 453-6900
www.khsurf.com
Kitty Hawk Sports, behind TimBuck II Shopping Village, offers kayak rentals and kayak ecotours in Currituck Sound. Call for details. The Corolla store is open Memorial Day to Labor Day.

NOR'BANKS SAILING CENTER
NC 12, Duck
(252) 261-7100
www.norbanks.com
Single as well as tandem kayaks are available for sale or rent here. Prices range from around $15 an hour for a single kayak to $100 a week for a tandem kayak when used on-site. Open May through Oct.

DUCK VILLAGE OUTFITTERS
1207 Duck Rd., Duck
(252) 261-7222
www.duckvillageoutfitters.net
These folks will take you wherever you want to go in a kayak. Their preplanned tours are ocean kayak dolphin tours and scenic tours through the estuaries of Kitty Hawk Nature Preserve, Kitty Hawk Bay, and Ginguite Creek. The 2-hour soundside tours cost $33 for a single kayak or $59 for a tandem. Kayak rentals cost around $15 an hour or $20 for tandem models. Tours are conducted daily in the warm seasons, but call in the off-season and one of the enthusiastic guides will take you out. The shop is open all year.

KITTY HAWK KITES
US 158, Nags Head
(252) 441-4124, (800) 334-4777
www.kittyhawk.com

Kitty Hawk Kites' water-sports operation offers a selection of sound tours from Corolla to Hatteras, in addition to sea and surf kayak lessons. No experience is necessary, and tours include all necessary equipment, including single and tandem kayaks, paddles, and life jackets. Tours are offered around Kitty Hawk Woods, Manteo and Roanoke Island, Alligator River, and Pea Island. Sunset tours, dolphin tours, lighthouse tours, and tours with historical narration are offered. Tours range from 1 hour to more than 2 hours. Long, specialty tours are available; see the website for more information. Sea, surf, and touring kayaks as well as a selection of personal sailboats are available for sale, including Escape boats and the Wind Rider trimarans. Special programs for kids are available in summer months. Equipment can be rented by the hour, day, or week.

KITTY HAWK WATERSPORTS
US 158, MP 13, Nags Head
(252) 441-6800
www.kittyhawkwatersports.com
A division of Kitty Hawk Sports, the kayak service offers tours ranging from 2 hours to extended expeditions and covers the soundside areas from Corolla to Portsmouth Island, including Pea Island and Alligator River. Launch sites are in Corolla, Kitty Hawk, Nags Head, and Avon. Sales and rentals are available. Lessons for any experience level, from beginner to advanced, are available. Two-hour tours start at $39 for adults, $25 for children. Alligator River tours cost $49 for adults and $25 per child. Kayak rentals start at $30 per day, depending on the craft.

WILD BILL'S WATERWORKS
US 158, MP 17, Nags Head
(252) 441-8875

Right on the sound in Nags Head, the Waterworks offers kayak and canoe rentals for those who want to be alone. Rent a variety of kayaks for adventures in the sound behind the shop.

KITTY HAWK KITES
Queen Elizabeth Street, Manteo
(252) 473-2357, (800) 334-4777
www.kittyhawk.com
Carolina Outdoors rents kayaks from its location, which is right on Shallowbag Bay in downtown Manteo. Ecotours through Shallowbag Bay and surrounding canals are given throughout the day. The tours last about 1.5 hours. Sunset and moonlight tours are also available.

HATTERAS ISLAND BOARDSPORTS
NC 12, Avon
(252) 995-6160, (866) HIB-WAVE
www.hiboardsports.com
Rent a kayak (single or double) for the sound or ocean. Choose from a variety of styles and makes. Rent for a half day, a whole day, three days, or a week. HIB delivers, or you can pick up the gear yourself. Single surf kayaks rent for $15 for 4 hours, regular single kayaks rent for $20 for 4 hours.

CAROLINA OUTDOORS ISLAND SHOPS
NC 12, Avon
(252) 995-6060, (800) 334-4777
www.kittyhawk.com
These locations of Kitty Hawk Kites/Carolina Outdoors offer kayak rentals for the sound as well as the ocean. They also perform kayak ecotours on the sound. Another location is at Hatteras Landing NC 12, Hatteras Village, (252) 986-1446, (800) 334-4777.

KITTY HAWK KITES KITEBOARDING CENTER
Waves Village Resort
NC 12, Rodanthe
(252) 987-2528
www.wavesvillage.com

This huge retail store offers everything you need for kiteboarding. There is ample space to set up, and pros are on hand to help you with your skills. Enthusiasts can rent before buying gear. Warm showers and a restaurant are also on the premises.

RIDE THE WIND SURF SHOP
NC 12, Ocracoke
(252) 928-6311
www.surfocracoke.com

Ride the Wind offers four two-and-a-half-hour kayak tours (the Sunrise, the Midday, the Sunset, the Full Moon) of Pamlico Sound and the surrounding estuarine waters every day in spring, summer, and fall, weather permitting.

Any size group can be accommodated with advance notice. The fee includes kayak, life jackets, and a four-page plastic field guide to area fish, shellfish, and fauna. Call for prices. Reservations are strongly suggested during summer.

SCUBA DIVING

Although cloudier and cooler than waters off the Florida Keys and the Caribbean Islands, offshore areas along the Outer Banks offer unique scuba-diving experiences in the Graveyard of the Atlantic. The area owes its moniker to the more than 1,000 shipwrecks (at least 200 named and identified) whose remains rest on the ocean floor from Corolla to Ocracoke. Experienced divers enjoy the challenge of unpredictable currents while exploring beneath the ocean's surface. From 17th-century schooners to World War II submarines, wreckage lies at a variety of depths in almost every imaginable condition.

Some underwater archaeological shipwreck sites are federally protected and can be visited but not touched. Others offer incredible souvenirs for deepwater divers: bits of china plates and teacups, old medicine and liquor bottles, brass-rimmed porthole covers, and thick, handblown glass that's been buried beneath the ocean for more than a century. If you prefer to leave history as you find it, waterproof cameras bring back memorable treasures from the mostly unexplored underwater world.

Sharks, whales, dolphins, and hundreds of varieties of colorful fish also frequent deep waters around these barrier islands. The northernmost coral reef in the world is off Avon. Submerged Civil War forts are scattered along the banks of Roanoke Island in much more shallow sound waters.

Dive-boat captains carry charter parties to places of their choosing. Some shipwrecks have become popular with scuba divers and are among the most frequently selected sites. The freighter *Metropolis,* also called the "Horsehead Wreck," lies about 3 miles south of the Currituck Beach Lighthouse off Whalehead Beach in Corolla, 100 yards offshore and in about 15 feet of water. This ship was carrying 500 tons of iron rails and 200 tons of stones when it sank in 1878, taking 85 crewmen to a watery grave. Formerly the federal gunboat *Stars and Stripes* that worked in the Civil War, this is a good wreck to explore in the off-season. If you have a four-wheel-drive vehicle, you can drive up the beach and swim out to this shipwreck site.

Off the shores of Kill Devil Hills, an unidentified tugboat rests about 300 yards south of Avalon Pier, approximately 75 yards off the beach, in 20 feet of water. Two miles south, the Triangle Wrecks—*Josephine, Kyzickes,* and *Carl Gerhard*—sit about 100 yards offshore, about 200 yards south of the Sea Ranch Motel, in about 20 feet of water. These vessels sank in 1915, 1927, and 1929, respectively. You can access these wrecks by boat or swim from the beach.

Nags Head's most famous dive site is the USS *Huron,* a federal gunship that sank in 1877, taking 95 crewmen to the bottom. This wreck is about 200 yards off the beach at MP 11, resting in an estimated 26 feet of water with many salvageable artifacts. The tugboat *Explorer* is nearby.

Long known as the East Coast's most treacherous inlet, Oregon Inlet rages between Bodie Island and Hatteras Island. It's infamous for the hundreds of ships—and scores of lives—that it has claimed through the ages. The liberty ship *Zane Grey* lies about a mile south of this inlet in 80 feet of water. A German sub sank northeast of the inlet in 100 feet of water in 1942. The *Oriental* has been sitting about 4 miles south of Oregon Inlet since sinking in 1862; its boiler is visible above the surf. Most of these dive sites can be accessed only from boats.

About a mile north of Rodanthe Fishing Pier, 100 yards offshore, the *LST 471* lies in only 15 feet of water. This ship sank in 1949 and is accessible by swimming from shore. Nearby off Rodanthe, about 22 miles southeast of Oregon Inlet, the tanker *Marore* is approximately 12 miles offshore. It sank when torpedoed in 1942 and lies in about 100 feet of water.

Experienced deepwater divers enjoy the *Empire Gem,* a British carrier that sank in January 1942, torpedoed by a German U-boat. This shipwreck sits about 17 miles

off Cape Hatteras in 140 feet of water and was one of the first vessels to go down in these waters in World War II. It, too, must be reached by boat.

Before You Dive

If you're going scuba diving, you might want to jot down these important numbers.

Emergency Numbers

US Coast Guard
24-hour Search and Rescue and all boating/diving emergencies
(252) 995-6411

US Coast Guard Aids to Navigation Team
(252) 986-2177

Divers Alert Network (DAN)
(919) 684-2948, 8:30 a.m. to 5 p.m. daily,
(919) 684-8111 after hours

Ocean Rescue Squad
(helicopter available)
911

US Coast Guard Stations
Oregon Inlet
(252) 441-1685

Hatteras Inlet
(252) 986-2175

Ocracoke Inlet
(252) 928-3711

Learning to Dive

Unlike most other water sports, scuba diving isn't something you can learn on your own. You have to be certified to do deep dives. This takes special training by certified instructors—and practice in a pool. Average recreational dives are 80 to 100 feet deep, while extreme divers reach depths of more than 300 feet. There are dangers associated with such deep dives, however. Every seasoned diver knows the perils associated with the sport: the potential for death in underwater caves, shark attacks, and the hazards of surfacing too fast and being afflicted with "the bends." Divers universally agree, however, that the thrill and tranquility of deep-wreck diving justify the risks.

Several Outer Banks dive shops offer lessons, advanced instruction, and the equipment you'll need to get started. This is a relatively expensive sport. Divers say it takes at least $1,500 just to get the necessary tanks, hoses, wet suits, and other paraphernalia to take the first plunge. Dive boat charters, which all dive-shop workers help arrange, begin at about $600 per day, depending on how far offshore you want to go.

Some dive shops can also recommend shallow dive spots that you don't need a boat to get to, as well as nearby-shore or sound areas that you can explore with a face mask and snorkel. All Ocean Atlantic Rentals locations rent fins, masks, and snorkels (call 252-261-4346). The National Park Service has sporadic snorkeling adventures along the Cape Hatteras National Seashore in the summer. Call (252) 473-2111 for tour times and information.

Dive Shops

OUTER BANKS DIVE CENTER
US 158, MP 12½, Nags Head
(252) 449-8349
www.obxdive.com
This center in Nags Head meets the needs of all divers onboard its 46-foot crew boat named the *Pelican*. Guided beach dives are offered at the wreck of the *Huron* in Nags Head. Dive trips are offered to the offshore wrecks of the *Advance,* the *Jackson, U-85,* and others. The shop supplies all levels of diving instruction, rentals, equipment, repairs, and tank fills. It's open all year. Visit the website for information about trips, dives, and equipment.

OUTER BANKS DIVING AND CHARTERS
57540 NC 12, Hatteras Village
(252) 986-1056
www.outerbanksdiving.com
Offering daily dives on Gulf Stream wrecks for individuals and groups, Outer Banks Diving and Charters specializes in family and group outings. Dive trips are made on *Bayou Runner*, a 42-foot US Coast Guard–certified vessel, which is docked at Teach's Lair Marina, 1 mile from the dive shop. This full-service facility is open year-round and has equipment sales, full rental gear, tank fills, and Nitrox.

SAILING

Sir Walter Raleigh's explorers first sailed along these shores more than four centuries ago. Private sailboat owners have long enjoyed the barrier islands as a stopover while en route along the Intracoastal Waterway. Many sailors have also dropped anchor beside Roanoke or Hatteras Islands—only to tie up at the docks permanently and make Dare County their home.

Until recently you had to have your own sailboat to cruise the area waterways. Now shops from Corolla through Ocracoke rent sailboats, Hobie Cats, and catamarans to weekend water enthusiasts. Others offer introductory and advanced sailing lessons. Some take people who have no desire to learn to sail on excursions across the sounds aboard multipassenger sailing ships. Eco-tours, luncheon swim-and-sails, and sunset cruises have become increasingly popular with vacationers. From 40-passenger cata-marans sailed by experienced captains to piratelike schooners carrying up to six pas-sengers to single-person Sunfish sailboats, you can find almost any type of sailing vessel you desire on these barrier islands.

Unlike loud motorized craft, which pol-lute the water with gasoline, sailing is a clean, environmentally friendly sport that people of all ages enjoy. You can sail slowly by marshlands without disturbing the water-fowl or cruise at 15 mph clips in stiff breezes. It all depends on your whim—and the wind.

If you've never sailed before, don't rent a boat and try to wing it. Winds in this area are trickier than elsewhere and either increase in intensity or shift direction with-out a moment's notice. If you get caught in a gale, you could end up miles from land if you don't know how to maneuver the vessel. A 2-hour introductory lesson is worth the mini-mal investment to learn basic sailing skills such as knot tying, sail rigging, and steering.

Sailors with basic on-water experience manage to navigate their way around the shallow sounds. All boat passengers should always wear a life jacket.

Sailboat Cruises, Courses & Rentals

Prices for sailboat cruises depend on the amenities, length of voyage, and time of day. Midday trips sometimes include lunches or at least drinks for passengers. Some sunset tours offer wine, beer, and appetizers. Almost all of the excursions let people bring their own food and drink aboard, and some even accept dogs on leashes. Special arrangements can also be made for disabled passengers. Prices generally range from $30 to $60 per person. If you'd like to book a boat for a private charter for you and your friends, some captains also offer their services along with the sailboats, beginning at $50 per hour per vessel.

Lesson costs, too, span a range, depend-ing on how in-depth the course is, what type of craft you're learning on, and whether you prefer group or individualized instruction. Costs start at $10 and go to $50 per person. Call ahead for group rates for more than four people in your party.

If you'd rather rent a craft and sail it your-self, Outer Banks outfitters lease sailboats by the hour, day, or week. Deposits generally are required. Costs range from $25 to $60 per hour and $50 to $110 per day. Most shops accept major credit cards.

KITTY HAWK WATERSPORTS
NC 12, Corolla
(252) 453-6900
www.kittyhawkwatersports.com
On the sound behind TimBuck II Shopping Village, Kitty Hawk Watersports rents day sail-ers and catamarans. Call for rates.

NOR'BANKS SAILING CENTER
NC 12, Duck
(252) 261-7100
www.norbanks.com
In recent years Duck has become one of the Outer Banks' busiest sailing hubs and is among the easiest places in the area to learn to sail or take a calm cruise. Nor'Banks rents day sailers and catamarans hourly, by the half day, or daily and is open May through Oct.

KITTY HAWK KITES/CAROLINA OUTDOORS
1215 Duck Rd., Duck
(252) 261-4450, (800) 334-4777
www.kittyhawk.com

A division of Kitty Hawk Kites, Carolina Outdoors rents the Wind Rider trimaran, a stable sailing vessel, for hourly and daily rates. The lightweight Escape, a less destructible and more portable version of the Sunfish, is also available for rent or sale. The Escape is equipped with a Windicator, which sets the sail by measuring wind speed and direction. Wind Rider trimarans are also available to rent in Corolla. Call (252) 453-3685.

THE PROMENADE WATERSPORTS
US 158, MP ¼, Kitty Hawk
(252) 261-4400
At the foot of the Wright Memorial Bridge, the Promenade is the only full-service watersports center in Kitty Hawk. Of its multitude of services, it offers sailboat lessons and rentals. Try out a Precision 13, an 18-foot day sailer, Hobie Cats, or a 20-foot trimaran in the sound behind the Promenade. Call for prices. Reservations are recommended.

WILD BILL'S WATERWORKS
US 158, MP 17, Nags Head
(252) 441-8875
Sailboat rentals are offered at this complete water-sports center March through November. Try out a 14- or 18-foot day sailer or a Sunfish. This area of the Roanoke Sound is safe for day sailing. Stop and explore the several small islands for a break.

KITTY HAWK WATERSPORTS
US 158, MP 16, Nags Head
(252) 441-2756
www.kittyhawkwatersports.com
Kitty Hawk Watersports rents day sailers and catamarans from its soundside Nags Head location. This is a great place to learn to sail on a not-too-windy day. The sound is wide with few hazards to look out for—except Jet

Skiers and other water-sports enthusiasts. Personal watercraft and kayaks are also available here.

HATTERAS ISLAND SAIL SHOP
NC 12, Waves
(252) 987-2292
www.ncbeaches.com/outerbanks/
waves/shopping/surfshops/
hatterasislandsailshop/
Catamarans, day sailers, and Hobie Cats are available for rent by the hour at this extension of the Hatteras Island Surf Shop. Kayaks and other ocean vessels are also available to rent. Sound access is on-site. Lessons are offered. Call for more information. The sail shop is closed in Jan and Feb.

KITTY HAWK KITES/CAROLINA OUTDOORS
Island Shops, NC 12, Avon
(252) 995-6060
www.kittyhawksports.com
The Avon location of Carolina Outdoors rents Wind Rider trimaran sailboats, probably the easiest boats to learn to sail on. Carolina Outdoors also offers kayak rentals.

BOATING

From small skiffs to luxurious pleasure boats, there is dock space for almost every type of boat on the Outer Banks. Most marinas require advance reservations. Space is extremely limited on summer weekends, so call as soon as you make plans to visit the area. Prices vary greatly, depending on the dock location, amenities, and type of vessel you're operating.

If you don't own your own boat, you can still access the sounds, inlets, and ocean around the Outer Banks by renting powerboats from area outfitters. Most store owners don't require previous boating experience. If you leave a deposit and driver's license, they'll include a brief boating lesson in the rental price. Whether you're looking to lease a craft to catch this evening's fish dinner or want to take an afternoon cruise, you can find a vessel to suit your needs at a variety of marinas. Slow-going pontoon boats are popular with vacationers because they're easy to handle and accommodate a crowd of boaters. Prices range from $15 an hour to more than $100 per day, depending on the type of boat. Some places require a 2-hour or more minimum. Most accept major credit cards. See the Fishing chapter for charter information. If you're interested in a boat tour, see the Recreation chapter.

Public Boat Launch Ramps

Find free public launch ramps at these locations:

- Whalehead Club in Corolla
- Soundside end of Wampum Drive in Duck
- Bob Perry Road on Kitty Hawk Bay in Kitty Hawk
- Avalon Beach off Bay Drive in Kill Devil Hills (small boats only)
- Washington Baum Bridge on Nags Head–Manteo Causeway, opposite Pirate's Cove
- Thicket Lump Marina near Thicket Lump Lane in Wanchese
- Foot of the bridge leading to Roanoke Island Festival Park in Manteo
- Oregon Inlet Fishing Center
- Oceanside end of Lighthouse Road in Buxton
- Frisco Cove in Frisco
- Between Cedar Island/Swan Quarter ferry docks on Ocracoke Island

Marinas & Dock Space

The following Outer Banks marinas offer services to boaters, such as fuel, bait and tackle, ice, supplies, and weighing stations. If you're interested in dockage at a marina, see the Getting Here, Getting Around chapter. If you're interested in chartering a boat at one of these marinas, see the Fishing chapter.

DOCK OF THE BAY
Bob Perry Road, Kitty Hawk
(252) 255-5578

This fuel dock and convenience shop is a welcome service to boaters on the northern beaches. Dock of the Bay is easily accessed by boat from Kitty Hawk Bay. It offers ice, gas and diesel fuel, snacks and drinks, fishing tackle, and bait. Fishing and crabbing are allowed on the docks as well. It's located at the end of Bob Perry Road, on the Loving Canal at Hog Island, past the Dare County boat landing.

PIRATE'S COVE YACHT CLUB
Nags Head–Manteo Causeway, Manteo
(252) 473-3906, (800) 367-4728
www.fishpiratescove.com

This full-service marina is known for its good service and many amenities. It offers a fuel dock with gas and diesel fuel, and diesel is now available at every slip. An on-site restaurant, Pirates Cove Dockside Restaurant, serves lunch and dinner. Professional fish-cleaning staff is on-hand at the dock, or do it yourself at the facilities. The dock master's office monitors marine radio channels 16 and 78. Pirate's Cove is open year-round. For boat-ramp access head across the street to the site just under the west side of the Washington Baum Bridge. This site has concrete ramps and plenty of parking for vehicles with trailers.

MANTEO WATERFRONT MARINA
207 Queen Elizabeth Ave., Manteo
(252) 305-4800

Located within walking distance of restaurants, a movie theater, a bookstore, and retail shops, this marina has 53 slips and accommodates boats up to 130 feet.

Air-conditioned heads and showers are available as well as laundry facilities, a picnic area with gas grills, e-mail access, and rental cars. Fuel is not available. Both 30-amp and 50-amp power is on-site. Block and cube ice are sold on-site. Ask about weekend packages and sailing and fishing charters. Manteo Waterfront Marina is open all year.

THICKET LUMP MARINA
Thicket Lump Road, Wanchese
(252) 473-4500

This family-owned and -operated, 28-slip marina rents dock space to pleasure and fishing vessels up to 45 feet by the day, week, month, or year. A ship's store and tackle shop are at the marina, and both gas and diesel fuel are available. Thicket Lump offers inshore and offshore charters; call for information. The marina is open throughout the year.

i The extralong parking spaces near boat ramps are for vehicles pulling boat trailers. These are the only spaces for them to park and unload or load their boat. Vehicles with no trailers should be parked in the normal-size spots.

MANNS HARBOR MARINA
US 64, Manns Harbor
(252) 453-5150

The Manns Harbor Marina serves boaters with a boat ramp that's the perfect put-in spot for those fishing for striped bass on the Manns Harbor and Croatan Sound bridges. Gas and diesel fuel are available. A bar/lounge and a small motel are also on-site.

OREGON INLET FISHING CENTER
NC 12, Bodie Island
(252) 441-6301
www.oregon-inlet.com

The closest marina and fuel dock to Oregon Inlet, Oregon Inlet Fishing Center is on the north side of the Herbert C. Bonner Bridge, about 10 miles from Nags Head. The fishing center accommodates anglers with gas and diesel fuel and a well-stocked bait and tackle shop that opens at 5 a.m. The tackle shop carries a complete line of surf, inshore, and deep-sea fishing equipment, plus drinks, snacks, coffee, hot dogs, T-shirts, ice, sunscreen, sunglasses, and other items. The boat ramp at Oregon Inlet Fishing Center, with five concrete ramps, is one of the nicest in the area, with plenty of parking for vehicles and trailers. Restroom and trash facilities are on-site.

HATTERAS HARBOR MARINA
NC 12 and Gulfstream Way, Hatteras
(252) 986-2166, (800) 676-4939
www.hatterasharbor.com

This marina accommodates boats up to 68 feet for a day, month, or year. Call for in-season rates and annual charges. Hatteras Harbor also has five apartments available for customers to rent. A full-service deli and ship's store are located at the marina. Diesel fuel is available. Hatteras Harbor is open year-round, and its public laundry facilities are open 24 hours a day.

WILLIS BOAT LANDING
NC 12, Hatteras Village
(252) 986-2208

This marina accepts small craft up to 25 feet for short-term stays. About 20 boats can be accommodated at a time. Boat and motor repairs can be done on-site. Bait and tackle are available. Willis Boat Landing is open year-round.

HATTERAS LANDING MARINA
NC 12, Hatteras Village
(252) 986-2205, (800) 551-8478

Hatteras Landing offers a complete ship's store with tackle, fresh and frozen baits, lures, sportswear, and a market with beer, ice, and groceries. Gas and diesel fuel are available. Hatteras Landing has fully metered slips, laundry facilities, bathrooms, and a fish-cleaning service. It's open year-round.

ODEN'S DOCK
NC 12, Hatteras Village
(252) 986-2555
www.odensdock.com

Oden's Dock has a deep draft that accommodates vessels up to 65 feet. Of the 27 slips at the marina, 20 are deep draft. Reservations are suggested during the peak season.

A seafood market and Breakwater Island Restaurant are at Oden's Dock. Diesel fuel and gasoline are sold at the ship's store, along with bait, tackle, food, and beverages. Showers are available during business hours, and fish-cleaning facilities are also available for anglers. One headboat and a charter fishing fleet dock here. Oden's is open year-round. Hours vary during the off-season. Please call ahead for details.

TEACH'S LAIR MARINA
NC 12, Hatteras Village
(252) 986-2460
www.teachslair.com

This year-round, full-service marina has 95 slips accommodating boats up to 65 feet. Two launching ramps are also located at the marina. Teach's Lair has a bathhouse, dry storage, and a ship's store. Fuel (diesel and gasoline), oil, and tackle are all available at the store. A headboat, charter fishing fleet, and two dive boats dock here. Parasailing adventures leave from the marina.

NATIONAL PARK SERVICE SILVER LAKE DOCK
Ocracoke Village
(252) 928-4531

April through November, dockage costs $1.25 per foot (except if you are over 62 years old—then the rate is half price) plus $3 a day for 110-volt electricity hookups, or $5 a day for 220-volt connections. The rest of the year, the cost is 40 cents per foot, while the electric hookups stay the same price. There's a two-week limit on summer stays, and dock space is assigned on a first-come, first-served basis. No water is available in the winter season. If no ranger is on-site when you arrive, pay at the visitor center across the street.

ANCHORAGE MARINA/OCRACOKE FISHING CENTER
NC 12, Ocracoke
(252) 928-6661
www.theanchorageinn.com

Right in the heart of Ocracoke on Silver Lake, Anchorage Marina has 35 slips accommodating boats up to 120 feet long. Diesel fuel and gas are available. The marina is open year-round with no limit on the length of stays. The dock-side sMacNally's Raw Bar is next door, and Anchorage offers bike rentals and small-boat rentals. Boaters have swimming pool and shower privileges.

Boat Rentals

If you don't own a powerboat but want to explore the vast waters of this region, rent one. Lots of places, even marinas or rent-all services, rent boats. Following are some reliable sources for motorboats.

NORTH DUCK WATERSPORTS
NC 12, Duck
(252) 261-4200

North Duck Watersports is on the west side of Duck Road, directly on Currituck Sound. Sport boats, pontoon boats, kayaks, and bicycles are all available. North Duck is open spring through fall. Call for rates.

THE PROMENADE WATERSPORTS
US 158, MP ¼, Kitty Hawk
(252) 261-4400
www.promenadewatersports.com

Right across from the Wright Memorial Bridge on the Currituck Sound, the Promenade bills itself as the only full-service water-sports center in the Southern Shores, Kitty Hawk, and Kill Devil Hills area. If you want to rent a boat, you are quite likely to find what you want at this complete fun spot. Sailboats, kayaks, pontoon boats, and 16-foot fishing and crabbing skiffs are all available for rent. The Promenade is open spring through fall.

WILD BILL'S WATERWORKS
US 158, MP 17, Nags Head
(252) 441-8875

Not only can you rent 19-foot powerboats, pontoons, and jet boats at the Waterworks, you can also get any kind of watercraft supplies, plus a complete line of bike, kayak, and beach equipment rentals. This water-sports center is the only one in the area that sells

and repairs Yamaha watercraft, boats, and Yamaha outboard motors.

ANCHORAGE MARINA
NC 12, Ocracoke
(252) 928-6661
www.theanchorageinn.com

Anchorage Marina rents 16- to 24-foot skiffs for half days, whole days, and weekly. Call for rates. The marina is on Silver Lake and is open year-round.

PERSONAL WATERCRAFT

If you feel a need for speed and enjoy the idea of riding a motor-powered vehicle across the water, Outer Banks businesses rent personal watercraft by the hour. Personal watercraft (PWC) are most known and referred to by their brand names—Sea-Doo, Jet Ski, and WaveRunner. No experience is necessary to ride these powerful boatlike devices, although a training session is a must if you've never before piloted a PWC. Unlike landlocked go-karts and other speedy road rides, there are no lanes on the open sound or ocean. But that doesn't mean you should ride with reckless abandon. With more and more people riding PWCs, it is imperative that each person practice responsible and safe riding.

Several styles of PWCs have developed over the past decade. WaveRunners allow drivers to maneuver these crafts sitting down with a second passenger holding on, also sitting, from behind. Most Jet Skis don't have seats and accommodate only one person at a time in a standing or kneeling position. Newer Runabouts, also known as blasters, give riders the choice of standing or sitting. WaveRunners are the easiest style craft to balance and control. Jet Skis are, however, more suitable for tricks—and prone to spills. Almost all of these motorized vessels cruise for up to 2 hours on five gallons of fuel.

PWCs are akin to motorboats with inboard motors that power a water pump. Like other motorized boats, however, PWCs are loud and are dangerous if you are not extremely cautious and aware. Most rental places include brief instructions and sometimes even a video on how to handle Wave-Runners, Jet Skis, and Runabouts.

i Know the rules of the water before you operate a boat! Observe No Wake signs, and slow down for smaller craft so that your wake doesn't swash them. Sail craft always have the right-of-way. When you pass through a channel, the red markers should be on your left as you're moving out to sea and on your right as you're coming in. Use this mnemonic device—Red on Right Returning—to remember which side of the channel to stay on.

Most rental shops are on the sound side of the Outer Banks, where the water's surface is generally slicker and depths are much more shallow. A few PWC outlets let you take the vessels into the ocean. There shore break and offshore waves challenge experienced Jet Ski drivers. Watch out for surfers, swimmers, dolphins, turtles, sharks, and birds—and other Jet Ski drivers who might not see you coming.

Those who own their own PWCs can launch their craft at public boat ramps. Be aware, however, that PWCs are banned in certain areas of the Outer Banks. The National Park Service does not allow the launching of PWCs anywhere in Cape Hatteras National Seashore. The town of Southern Shores requires PWC launchers to get a permit from the police department. To get this permit you must show proof of insurance and that you have taken a boating-safety course. You must stay at least 400 yards offshore in Southern Shores. In Nags Head PWCs must stay at least 600 yards offshore and away from piers. Ocracoke Island forbids the use of PWCs.

Renting Personal Watercraft

New PWCs sell for $5,000 to $13,000. Several Outer Banks rental shops sell used PWCs for cheaper prices at the end of the summer. You'll probably need a trailer to haul these vessels behind your vehicle.

Shops from Corolla to Hatteras Island rent PWCs by the half hour. Price wars occasionally result in very low prices. More powerful models are generally more expensive. Additional charges sometimes apply for extra riders. PWCs also can be rented by the hour, day, or even week at some places.

When you're out riding through the waves, keep in mind these personal watercraft rules:

- Stay in designated buoyed areas at all times.
- Stay at least 50 yards away from other personal watercraft, swimmers, and boaters.
- Give sail craft, such as sailboarders and sailboats, the right-of-way.
- Do not excessively flip your vehicle.
- Wear a life jacket.
- Keep the lanyard attached to your wrist at all times.
- Be aware that PWCs are low profile and often difficult for others to see. Stay a safe distance away.

- Return to shore immediately if the gas gauge has turned to "reserve" or if any mechanical problems are apparent.
- Do not wake jump, splash, race, or interact in any way with other watercraft.
- Check local regulations before using a PWC in a new area. Some municipalities, such as Ocracoke Island, strictly forbid their use.

COROLLA WATERSPORTS
TimBuck II, Corolla
(252) 453-6900

At this store you can rent WaveRunners and kayaks. Also go parasailing, play miniature golf, and shop in the retail store. Call for rates and more information. Corolla Watersports is open May through Oct.

KITTY HAWK WATERSPORTS
NC 12, Corolla
(252) 453-6900
www.kittyhawkwatersports.com

Kitty Hawk Watersports, behind TimBuck II Shopping Village, rents WaveRunners by the half hour and hour. Call for prices and more information. Water bikes, paddleboats, kayaks, and parasailing are also offered through this store. Kitty Hawk Watersports is open in Corolla from early spring through fall. The Nags Head location at milepost 16 on US 158 stays open longer.

NOR'BANKS SAILING CENTER
NC 12, Duck
(252) 261-7100
www.norbanks.com

Nor'Banks Sailing Center rents WaveRunners and Sea-Doo jet boats. It is open spring through fall.

THE PROMENADE WATERSPORTS
US 158, Kitty Hawk
(252) 261-4400

Before you arrive at the Outer Banks from the Wright Memorial Bridge, the Promenade is on the right. A water-sports and kiddie recreational park, Promenade includes enough to keep everybody delighted on land as well as on Currituck Sound on a PWC. WaveRunners and Runabouts rent by the half hour, hour, half day, or full day. Early-bird specials are offered on WaveRunners. Call for price information. The Promenade says it has the largest riding area of any other PWC rental business because its share of Currituck Sound is not restricted by municipal regulations. Promenade closes in winter.

WILD BILL'S WATERWORKS
US 158, MP 17, Nags Head
(252) 441-8875

One of the many activities and services Waterworks offers is PWC rental. Jet Skis, Sea-Doos, and WaveRunners are available at half-hour and hourly rates. Call for prices. Waterworks also sells PWCs, including Yamaha and Sea-Doo. Rentals are available Mar through Nov.

KITTY HAWK WATERSPORTS
US 158, MP 16, Nags Head
(252) 441-2756
www.kittyhawkwatersports.com

This complete store rents WaveRunners by the half hour and hour. The store is on the sound in Nags Head, so launching is easy. Water bikes, paddleboats, and kayaks are available for purists. Call for prices.

RODANTHE WATERSPORTS AND SHORELINE CAMPGROUND
NC 12, Rodanthe
(252) 987-1431
www.watersportscampground.com

This soundfront campground and watersports operation rents WaveRunners as well as surfboards, bikes, kayaks, and sailboats.

HATTERAS WATERSPORTS
NC 12, Salvo
(252) 987-2306
www.hatteraswatersports.com

Hatteras Watersports rents WaveRunner personal watercraft. The store is on the sound side, across from the Salvo Volunteer Fire Department.

FISHING

If fishing is your passion, these barrier islands should be enough to send you reeling. Situated as we are in the Atlantic, not only do we have fabulous close-range ocean and inlet fishing but we're so close to the Gulf Stream and its bounty that offshore trips are just as popular. Half-day and full-day charters are available year-round, or if you're a seasoned boater with an ocean-worthy vessel, you can make the trip yourself. If you're looking to spend only a couple of hours' worth of angling, you can surf fish along nearly 100 miles of wide sandy beaches, or you can wet a line at any one of a number of fishing piers. And that's just covering the ocean. Our sound waters are home to numerous finned species, and interior freshwater ponds are stocked with fish. Outer Banks angling is the stuff of which dreams are made. The following fish stories are for real.

OVERVIEW

The International Game Fish Association lists 92 world records for fish caught in Outer Banks waters, though some of those are now retired. These record holders include a 405-pound lemon shark caught off of Buxton, a 67-pound amberjack caught in Oregon Inlet, a 41-pound bluefish, and a 72-pound red drum landed off Hatteras. A 348-pound bluefin tuna was caught in Hatteras waters as well, along with record-size black sea bass, Spanish mackerel, oyster toadfish, bigeye tuna, kingfish, and sheepshead landed in waters from Kill Devil Hills to Ocracoke. Even if you don't tip the scales with a record-breaking catch, you're bound to fill your coolers with anything from albacore to wahoo. Depending upon the season, where you fish, and your choice of bait, you'll also find speckled trout, gray trout, flounder, striped bass (or rockfish), black drum, largemouth bass, tautog, cobia, a variety of pan fish, and the big attraction, billfish.

You might think that the variety here draws expert anglers, hence the great catches. Chances of a good catch are enhanced by physical conditions existing here that don't exist anywhere else. And that's no fish story! We outline these characteristics in the offshore section that follows.

Another factor that hugely influences the catch is our charter fleets. Many consider the local sportfishing boats, called Carolina boats, the most beautiful in the world, and these vessels house the complete package of brains, talent, and beauty. Our experienced captains are without peer, and their charter mates will awe you with their knowledge, their skill, and the manner in which they work. Some mates move as if their actions are choreographed: simultaneously working lines, assisting members of the fishing party, keeping the captain apprised of catches in progress, arranging poles, gaffing fish, and encouraging you to keep reeling when it feels as if your arm just won't manage another revolution. A good mate is worth his or her weight in gold.

While anyone who's ever gone fishing knows you can't predict catches, the local charter boat captains know what species may be in the area, and they will guide you. Charters leave the docks for inshore and offshore fishing every day that the weather permits. When you call to book a boat (see the Marinas listing in this chapter), you may find it hard to decide what kind of trip to choose unless you've fished before. Booking agents at each marina will help you.

In the following sections we describe offshore and inshore angling, backwater, surf, fly, and pier fishing. Offshore trips generally leave the docks at 5:30 a.m. and return no later than 6 p.m. Inshore trips are half-day excursions that leave twice daily, generally at 7 a.m. and again around noon. Intermediate trips can last all day but generally don't travel as far as the Gulf Stream.

If you decide to fish without a guide or charter captain, the North Carolina Division of Marine Fisheries (800-682-2632) is a wealth of information. It's your resource for all available licenses, including recreational, commercial gear, and standard commercial licenses. A license to land flounder is available only through this Morehead City office. The division publishes an annual recreational-fishing handbook, the *North Carolina Coastal Waters Guide for Sports Fishermen*, a comprehensive guide to licenses, limits, and sizes. The helpful staff will also direct you to the appropriate contacts for obtaining federal permits for tuna and other controlled species.

For information on freshwater fishing permits and regulations, you'll need to contact the North Carolina Wildlife Resources Commission in Raleigh. The number for hunting and fishing licenses is (919) 662-4370. A regulations digest is available at sporting goods stores and tackle shops. Call either Wildlife Resources or the North Carolina Division of Marine Fisheries for information on motorboat registration. Official weigh stations are listed toward the end of this chapter.

OFFSHORE FISHING

The Outer Banks is famed as the Billfish Capital of the World. Though other fishing destinations debate that point, the Outer Banks waters are home to an incredible number of billfish—white and blue marlin and sailfish. These fighting fish are caught from spring through early fall, with peak catches for blue marlin in June and peak catches for white marlin and sailfish in August and September. To protect the species, billfish are almost always caught and released. You still get bragging rights for your released fish, though; the mate flies one flag per released billfish on the outriggers of the boat so everyone at the dock sees how many your party reeled in that day.

Next to billfish, some of the most pursued Gulf Stream fish are the yellowfin tuna and bluefin tuna. Other fish you're likely to catch are bigeye tuna, blackfin tuna, dolphinfish (mahimahi), king mackerel, wahoo, and mako shark.

The majority of Outer Banks captains who lead the way to offshore fishing grounds have been working these waters for years. Many are second- and third-generation watermen. They generally choose the daily fishing spot depending on recent trends, seasons, and weather. Occasionally, when there's a slow spell, a captain moves away from the rest of the fleet to play out a hunch. If the maverick meets with success, it's common for him or her to share this find with the rest of the fleet. In other words, the area fleets have a brother- or sisterhood that visiting anglers say they've experienced nowhere else. This camaraderie enhances the fishing experience—plus fishing together is safer.

Anglers fishing offshore for big game fish generally troll (drag bait behind the moving boat). If you run into a school of fish, such as mahimahi, the captain stops the boat so the party can cast into the water that's been primed with chum, or fish bits. Chumming also is used on bluefin tuna trips. All these techniques are explained the day of the trip. Expect to pay $900 to $1,500 for six people to charter a fishing excursion. Bluefin tuna trips cost a bit more. Gulf Stream charters leaving from Hatteras marinas tend to be less expensive than those near Oregon Inlet.

One offshore area frequented with great regularity is called the Point (not to be confused with Cape Hatteras Point). Approximately 37 miles off the Outer Banks, this primary fishing ground for local boats is rich in game fish such as tuna, dolphin, wahoo, billfish, and shark. Blue marlin, wahoo, and mahimahi show up at the Point in April and May. Yellowfin, bigeye, and blackfin tuna are the anglers' mainstay year-round. A significant population of yellowfin inhabits this area in the winter, providing a tremendous seasonal fishery. You have to be patient to fish in the winter because plenty of bad-weather days make traveling offshore a waiting game.

The Point has unique characteristics that give it a reputation for attracting and harboring a great variety and quantity of fish, from tiny baitfish to massive billfish. Deep-swimming reef fish, such as grouper, snapper, and tilefish, also inhabit the Point. Because of the strong current, however, you must travel a little bit south of the Point to fish effectively.

i A fishing license is required to fish anywhere on the Outer Banks, including up to 3 miles offshore. If you are younger than age 16, you are exempt. July Fourth is a free fishing day in North Carolina. No license is required, but recreational size and possession limits are still enforced.

What also helps set this spot apart is its proximity to the edge of the continental shelf. Where there's a drop-off, baitfish concentrate because of the nutrient-rich waters and the currents playing off the edge, stirring things up. Anglers don't have to travel far to get to the Point since the continental shelf is particularly narrow off Cape Hatteras. The Point is the last spot where the Gulf Stream appears near the shelf before it veers off in an east-north-easterly direction. Weather permitting, some days the Gulf Stream entirely covers the Point. Other days prevailing winds push it farther offshore.

At about 50 miles wide and a half mile deep, the Gulf Stream's temperatures rarely drop below 65 to 70 degrees, providing a comfortable habitat for a variety of sea life. The Gulf Steam flows at an average rate of 2.5 mph, at times quickening to 5 mph.

This steady flow carries millions of tons of water per second, continually pushing along sea life in its path, including fish, microscopic plants and animals, and gulfweed. Gulfweed lines the edge of the Gulf Stream when winds are favorable, creating a habitat for baitfish. You can pull up a handful of vegetation and find it teeming with miniature shrimp and fish. Anglers fish these "grass lines" as well as the warm-water eddies that spin off from the Gulf Stream. These warm pockets, which vary in size from 20 to 100 miles long by a half mile to a mile wide, are sometimes filled with schools of dolphin, tuna, and mako shark. The Gulf Stream is about 30 miles off the Outer Banks. It takes about 2 hours to get there from Oregon Inlet, and about an hour and a half from Hatteras Inlet, depending on the prevailing winds and the speed of your boat.

Catch-and-release fishing for bluefin tuna has anglers from across the globe traveling to Hatteras Island to partake in a bonanza that revived winter offshore charter fishing along the Outer Banks. In 1994 captains began noticing a massive congregation of bluefin tuna inhabiting the wrecks about 20 miles from Hatteras Inlet. The quantity of bluefin available and the frequency with which they bite are phenomenal. Bluefin fishing takes place on the southern Outer Banks, with trips leaving from Hatteras and Ocracoke marinas. Charter boats that ordinarily dock on the northern Outer Banks make their home base on Hatteras during the bluefin months. Many motels on Hatteras Island gladly stay open year-round to accommodate bluefin anglers.

Bluefin tuna weighing 200 to more than 800 pounds have been caught in these waters. These giants are a federally protected species, so anglers almost always must release them. Restrictions state that during bluefin tuna season anglers may keep one fish from 27 to 73 inches per boat per day. The length of the tuna season is determined annually by the National Marine Fisheries and is contingent on overall poundage caught.

i Always dress in layers for an Outer Banks fishing trip. Cold mornings have been known to transform into a warm afternoon on many fall and winter days. Of course, the opposite is also true, and gales and thunderstorms notoriously appear out of nowhere.

Reeling in a bluefin of any magnitude makes the blood of an avid angler run hot! The bluefin seem to strike with less provocation on the choppy days—plus there are fewer boats present during rougher weather. On days when the fish are spooked by excessive boat traffic or simply aren't biting for whatever reason, mates chum the water to increase the chance of a strike. These giants often jump 4 feet out of the ocean to bite bloody bait.

Local anglers troll, chum, and use live or dead bait. Many anglers even catch bluefin tuna and other game fish on a fly. We've seen great success with 130-pound test line. Some folks like to use lighter tackle for the sport of it, but the heavier the line, the better the condition of the fish when it's released. Circle hooks are also recommended, for they tend to lodge in the mouth cartilage rather than in the fleshy gullet or gills.

Even though most of the fish are caught on heavy tackle, carefully handled, and subsequently released, recreational charter boat captains are contemplating a self-imposed quota for catch and release to protect the fish even further. When there are large groups of boats present day after day, it's likely the same fish will have to do battle over and over.

You can enjoy offshore fishing year-round, but for bluefin fishing off Hatteras, book a trip from January through Mar. Some fish may show up earlier, and there are bluefin available in early April, but by then captains begin concentrating on yellowfin again. Bluefin boats leave the dock between 5:30 and 7 a.m.

Offshore fishing charters accommodate six people. If your party is shy of six, many times the booking agents or captain can hook you up with another small party. Anglers are expected to bring their own food and drinks on the trips. Coolers for any fish you want to take home can be left in your car at the dock to save room on the boat. Fish-cleaning facilities are available at all docks, and fish-cleaning services (for a fee) are available at most. Bring sunscreen and seasickness remedies (see the sidebar on preventing seasickness). All bait, tackle, instruction, and advice are included in the price of your charter. Mates work for tips, so be sure to tip them at least 15 percent and up to 20 percent of the cost of your trip.

If you really love offshore fishing, consider entering one of the fishing tournaments listed in the Annual Events chapter. If you're not up for Gulf Stream fishing but want to see the fish, show up at these docks at about 4 p.m. to watch the boats unload their catches. You'll see mahimahi, tuna, wahoo, cobia, and others, but no billfish since those are catch-and-release species.

INSHORE & SMALL-BOAT FISHING

Inshore opportunities strike the fancy of the novice or expert angler. Inshore generally refers to inlet, sound, lake, river, and some close-range ocean fishing on a boat.

Inshore captains generally book half-day trips but also offer intermediate all-day trips to take you farther out. If you're interested in bluefish, Spanish mackerel, cobia, king mackerel, bonito, trout, flounder, croaker, or red drum, book trips from virtually any marina. Half-day trips are a little easier on the pocketbook.

Spanish mackerel are a mainstay of the area. Ocracoke Island captains begin looking for them in late April and typically enjoy catches through late October. Farther north on the Outer Banks, Spanish mackerel usually arrive the first or second week in May, depending on the water temperature. Casting is the most sporting way of catching them. We suggest that you use 8-pound test on a medium to medium-light spinning rod with a pink and white Sting Silver. Other colors work well also; if the people next to you are catching fish and you aren't, see what lures they are using.

If it's flounder you're after, you can find these flat fish in both Hatteras and Oregon Inlets, in clear water. Anglers drift bottom rigs on medium-light spinning tackle. Croakers are found in the sounds around deep holes, oyster rocks, and sloughs.

You can dine on almost all inshore species. Tarpon, a bony fish with little food value, cannot be overlooked. A release-category fish, the tarpon is probably one of the strongest fighting fish inshore. While the Outer Banks is not a destination spot for tarpon, a handful of locals fish for them around

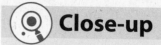 **Close-up**

Battling and Preventing Seasickness

Almost everyone who has ever been on the water has gotten seasick or at least battled that unmistakable queasy feeling. We've spent plenty of time on the water and know what it's like to want to throw yourself overboard. Here are some suggestions to help you avoid that feeling. Experiment to find what works best for you.

1. Take an over-the-counter remedy for motion sickness the night before your trip and again an hour before departure. This allows time for the medicine to get into your system. Ask your pharmacist about the specifics on these medications. Some will make you more sleepy than others. If you're bringing children along, find out whether the medication is safe for them, too.

2. Topical patches are also available over the counter. The patch fits behind your ear or on your wrist and administers medication through your skin.

3. Eat nongreasy food the night before the trip (and go easy on alcohol), and always eat a nongreasy breakfast. Pancakes and toast are good choices. Despite what you may think, a full stomach is much better than an empty one.

4. Pack a lunch that is neither spicy nor greasy. It also helps to nibble on saltines or ginger snap cookies through the day. Ginger is an Asian remedy for motion sickness. Some people take ginger capsules, but we like the cookies.

5. Some swear that you should drink a lot of fluids while offshore. This makes sense when it comes to dehydration, but we've seen plenty of people get even sicker by downing a soda hoping to ward off the oncoming surge. Always bring water. While some people refrain from drinking anything until the latter part of the trip, others replenish fluids all day. Again, this is a highly personal choice.

6. If you do get sick, the worst may be over if you follow this simple rule: Eat immediately after getting sick (so says Hatteras native Capt. Spurgeon Stowe of the *Miss Hatteras*).

7. If you're feeling queasy, stay out on deck in the fresh air. Don't hole up in the salon, and do not go into the head (bathroom). If you're going to throw up, do it overboard. This is common and acceptable. Concentrate on the horizon if possible. Orient yourself with a stable point, and you should feel better. Above all, don't be embarrassed.

Ocracoke in Pamlico Sound and south to the mouth of the Neuse River. We recommend fresh-cut bait, such as spot or trout, and very sharp hooks to penetrate the tarpon's hard mouth. Remember, it's one thing to hook up and a whole other to bring a tarpon to the boat. Good luck!

Outer Banks anglers enjoy fishing for rockfish (also called striped bass or stripers) year-round. They are fun to catch and make a great-tasting dinner. Though stripers are a regulated species, they've steadily been making a comeback during the last decade or so. Each year stripers spawn inland,

and the young live in estuaries for several years before joining the Atlantic migratory population.

The ocean season for stripers is open year-round, but limits vary according to season. Though stripers are present in our waters year-round, the sound inhabitants are protected by restrictions. Since the sound fishing season fluctuates, call a tackle shop for up-to-date regulations. If you want to catch and release, go at it anytime.

When a cold snap hits the Chesapeake Bay area, stripers migrate down past Corolla into Oregon Inlet. November is one of the best months to fish for them around the Manns Harbor Bridge that connects Roanoke Island to the East Lake community. Anglers also fish in the winter for stripers behind Roanoke Island in East and South Lakes.

Stripers tend to congregate around bridge pilings. They cluster near these nutrient-covered supports that entice smaller baitfish. You can troll, use spinning tackle with lures, fly cast, or surf fish. Stripers are bottom feeders, so a planer can be used to catch them. Insiders suggest using a butter bean with a white buck-tail on the end or Rat-L-Traps. You can catch these fish on slick calm days and in rougher weather, but a little current seems to help.

Summertime finds Outer Bankers fishing the sounds from Manteo to Ocracoke for speckled trout. Insiders suggest you move to the surf or a pier to catch them in fall. The speckled trout fishing is excellent in early fall around Oregon and Hatteras Inlets. They are best caught on light tackle with artificial lures or on a fly rod. Light spinning tackle is another good choice. Artificial lures are the norm. Insiders suggest using a lead head jig with a soft plastic twister tail for sound,

bridge, and inlet fishing. For the beach, try Mirrolures. Currently a keeper must be a 12-inch total length minimum. Call your local tackle shop for more information.

OFFSHORE & INSHORE CHARTERS

To book offshore and inshore charters, contact one of the marinas listed here. You can request a certain boat and captain or let them offer you one. All of these marinas represent reputable, licensed captains. Call at least a month ahead, but earlier if you know your schedule. Fishing trips continue year-round. If everything is booked, ask to be put on a waiting list; somebody might cancel. You should know that it is the captain's call on whether to go out in inclement weather. Always defer to the captain's judgment. Prices are for full-day trips, unless specified otherwise.

PIRATE'S COVE YACHT CLUB
Nags Head–Manteo Causeway, Manteo
(252) 473-3906, (800) 367-4728
www.fishpiratescove.com

Pirate's Cove is a world-class fishing center known for its boats, captains, and large-purse tournaments. By far the most modern marina on the Outer Banks, its prices reflect its high quality. Seventeen sportfishing boats operate out of this marina, each at a price of $1,650 cash, plus mate's tip, for a full day of Gulf Stream fishing. Booking is centralized through the marina. Pirate's Cove Yacht Club is about a 15- to 20-minute boat ride from Oregon Inlet, the northernmost ocean-sound inlet on the Outer Banks. The Gulf Stream is about a 2-hour ride from the inlet. Pirate's Cove is the central booking agent for four inshore boats. Trips run year-round.

Pirate's Cove sponsors several fishing tournaments each year; see the Annual Events chapter.

CUSTOM SOUND CHARTERS
152 Dogwood Trail, Manteo
(252) 216-6765, (252) 986-2201
www.customsoundcharters.com

Capt. Rick Caton has long been fishing the Outer Banks waters, both inshore and offshore, and offers a wide variety of trips. Year-round you can charter sound-fishing trips with Caton, who specializes in catching striped bass. He'll take you fly fishing or light-tackle fishing for trout, puppy drum, flounder, striped bass, and bluefish. Everything you need is furnished. Caton's inshore trips are offered on the 42-foot *Free Agent*. Caton also conducts shrimping and crabbing trips, inshore Spanish mackerel trolling trips, and light-tackle bottom fishing over wrecks for triggerfish and black sea bass. Or you can choose to anchor and chum for sharks, cobia, and king mackerel. Call for more information.

TIDELINE CHARTERS
Thicket Lump Marina, Wanchese
(252) 261-1458

The 34-foot custom Carolina boat called the *Tideline* takes full- and half-day inshore and intermediate trips. Half-day inshore trips and full-day intermediate trips are offered.

NAGS HEAD GUIDE SERVICE
(252) 475-1555

Capt. David Dudley offers light-tackle inshore trips for stripers, flounder, trout, bluefish, mackerel, cobia, drum, and largemouth bass.

OREGON INLET FISHING CENTER
NC 12, Bodie Island
(252) 441-6301, (800) 272-5199
www.oregon-inlet.com

The Oregon Inlet charter fishing fleet is a historic landmark on the Outer Banks. Most of the 31 sportfishing boats in this marina were locally made and have the famous Carolina flared bow. Some of the Outer Banks' most seasoned captains fish from this marina and have done so since it opened in the 1960s. Five boats offer near-shore and intermediate trips from Oregon Inlet Fishing Center. Inlet intermediate trips of 5 to 10 miles are available.

HATTERAS HARBOR MARINA
NC 12, Hatteras Village
(252) 986-2166, (800) 676-4939
www.hatterasharbor.com

This marina represents about 20 vessels that take anglers to the Gulf Stream via Hatteras Inlet. The Gulf Stream is about a 90-minute boat ride from Hatteras Inlet. Inshore fishing trips are chartered year-round from this marina on one of two 24-foot boats. Half-day trips are available.

HATTERAS LANDING MARINA
NC 12, Hatteras Village
(252) 986-2077, (800) 551-8478
www.hatteraslanding.com

Hatteras Landing Marina represents 12 offshore fishing boats. Call for current pricing. If you don't have a full party, Hatteras Landing can put one together for you if you're willing to wait on standby for a couple of days.

ODEN'S DOCK MARINA
NC 12, Hatteras Village
(252) 986-2555, (888) 544-8115
www.odensdock.com

The chaser sport fishing charter boat operates out of Oden's Dock and takes anglers offshore for a day of fishing. Oden's books inshore charters on a 22-foot boat and a 24-foot that each handle four people. These boats fish in the sound only. A larger 42-foot boat operates in the sound or ocean and accommodates six people.

TEACH'S LAIR MARINA
NC 12, Hatteras Village
(252) 986-2460
www.teachslair.com

Fourteen boats operate out of Teach's Lair. Bluefin trips are popular. Teach's Lair books inshore charters on morning or afternoon half-day trips. Morning trips run from 7 to noon, and afternoon trips run from 12:30 to 5:30.

ALBATROSS FLEET
Foster's Quay, Hatteras Village
(252) 986-2515
www.albatrossfleet.com

The Albatross Fleet of Hatteras, established by Capt. Ernal Foster in 1937, was the first charter fishing operation on the North Carolina coast. The original boat, the *Albatross,* still takes anglers to the Gulf Stream. The *Albatross* was designed by Foster to perfectly accommodate offshore fishing parties, and it was built across the sound in Harkers Island. The fleet now consists of three boats, all named *Albatross,* and is now operated by Foster's son, Ernal Foster Jr., who began working as a mate on his father's boat in 1958. The *Albatross I, II,* and *III,* all 44 feet, dock at Foster's Quay.

OCRACOKE FISHING CENTER AND
ANCHORAGE MARINA
NC 12, Ocracoke Village
(252) 928-6661

Four boats offer full-day offshore charters out of this marina. Full-day trips cost around $900 to $1,200. These boats use Ocracoke Inlet when heading to the Gulf Stream.

OFFSHORE & INSHORE HEADBOAT FISHING

Headboat fishing can give you a great fishing experience without the expense of chartering a private boat. Several large boats take parties into the intermediate waters (in the ocean, though not as far as the Gulf Stream) all day, while others ply the inshore waters for half days. Ocean trips typically track bottom species, such as black sea bass, triggerfish, tilefish, amberjack, snapper, tautog, grouper, and occasionally small sharks. The species vary slightly from north to south. Generally on these trips you're dropping a line down over artificial and natural reefs and wrecks, not trolling. Inshore trips ply the sounds and inlets and sometimes go several miles offshore to the wrecks on calm days. The trips usually yield croaker, trout, spot, flounder, sea mullet, blow toads, and pigfish. There is one headboat, the *Country Girl* out of Pirate's Cove, that takes trips to the Gulf Stream.

Headboats are built to accommodate a multitude of passengers, each person paying "by the head," hence the name. Open deck space from bow to stern holds anglers comfortably, and sometimes there is an enclosed cabin area. The boats are generally between 60 and 75 feet long and can hold up to 50 anglers. All gear and bait are supplied. All you have to bring is food, drinks, and sunscreen. Some boats provide snacks and drinks, so you should check when making reservations. You don't even need a fishing license. If you're new to fishing, the mates will help you with everything from baiting your hook to identifying your catch. Be sure to dress in layers if you're fishing any time other than summer. Mornings and evenings can be cool, even when days are warm.

Inshore headboat trips are the most suitable choice for families with young children, mainly because they're shorter. Deep-sea trips are full-day trips that can be as long as 8 to 10 hours, and the captain will not turn around except in a real emergency. Seasickness is not an emergency. Inshore trips are typically a half day. Watch the kids carefully on the boats. The decks are often slippery, so you should enforce a no-running policy. Plus these boats carry large crowds of people and fishing gear. Getting hooked can ruin a trip. That said, headboats are great places to teach children how to fish for a very small amount of money. Remain positive when fishing with kids. Everywhere in the world, there are days when the fishing is slow. If you're having one of those days, let the trip be a positive lesson in nature, patience, and people. A positive attitude will go far in hooking your kids on fishing for life. Besides, you often see dolphins, birds, turtles, and sometimes whales on these trips, so the day won't be a total loss.

CRYSTAL DAWN AND COUNTRY GIRL
Pirate's Cove Yacht Club
Nags Head–Manteo Causeway, Manteo
(252) 473-5577
www.crystaldawnheadboat.com
This 65-foot, 2-story vessel offers inshore (inlet and sound) bottom-fishing trips from May through October. The boat holds up to 55 passengers. All bait and tackle are provided, but you have to bring your own snacks and drinks. In peak season (Memorial Day to Labor Day), trips run from 7 a.m. to noon or 12:30 to 5 p.m. The rest of the time, the boat heads out from 8 a.m. to 1 p.m. *Crystal Dawn* also takes sightseeing trips in the evenings (see the Recreation chapter).

Country Girl heads offshore from 5 to 35 miles, depending on the weather and the fishing. This is a full-day trip, lasting from 7 a.m. to 4:30 p.m. Older children and teenagers are welcome, but younger children are not. *Country Girl* offers trips from May through October.

MISS OREGON INLET
Oregon Inlet Fishing Center
NC 12, Bodie Island
(252) 441-6301
www.oregon-inlet.com
Miss Oregon Inlet is a 65-foot headboat that offers half-day inshore fishing trips for around $36 per person or $26 for kids age 6 and younger. In early spring and fall, the boat makes one trip per day (except Sun), leaving at 8 a.m. and returning at 12:30 p.m. From Memorial Day through Labor Day, there are two trips: 7 to 11:30 a.m. and noon to 4:30 p.m. Buy tickets one day in advance, if possible, because the boat often fills up.

MISS HATTERAS AND CAPTAIN CLAM
Oden's Dock, NC 12, Hatteras Village
(252) 986-2365
www.odensdock.com
The *Miss Hatteras* headboat ties up at Oden's Dock in Hatteras Village and operates from Feb through Nov. She offers half-day fishing trips on Mon, Tues, and Thurs from 8 a.m. to noon and Tues and Thurs from 1 to 5 p.m. On Wed, Fri, Sat, and Sun, she offers full-day bottom-fishing trips from 6:30 a.m. to 4:30 p.m. The boat accommodates 45 people. In late Oct and early Nov, she offers full-day king mackerel

fishing trips. All gear is included in the cost of the trip, and a snack bar is on board. In the summer, when the *Miss Hatteras* is booked, Oden's Dock also offers the *Captain Clam,* a 40-person-capacity headboat that conducts half-day, inshore sound, and inlet fishing trips. These trips run Mon through Sat from 8 a.m. to noon and 1 to 5 p.m. Call for current rates.

MARINAS

The Outer Banks is dotted with many marinas with slips, boat ramps, gas and diesel fuel, tackle, and supplies. Almost all offer fishing charters as well. We've listed the fishing opportunities available at marinas in the Offshore and Inshore Headboat Fishing category in this chapter. For information pertaining to slip rental, see the Getting Here, Getting Around chapter; and for information on amenities offered to boaters, such as boat ramps, gas, and supplies, see the Water Sports chapter.

BACKWATER FISHING

Fishing the backwaters means fishing the more-protected inland sounds, rivers, and lakes, either brackish or freshwater. The Croatan Sound, between Roanoke Island and the mainland, is a popular fishing spot for striped bass, also known as stripers or rockfish in these parts. Striper fishing is a year-round sport on the Outer Banks, though you can keep those caught in the sound only at certain times of the year. The Manns Harbor Bridge is renowned for its striper activity. Stripers congregate at the bridge, feeding around the pilings. They also feed over oyster bars located near the bridge. Be on the lookout for diving gulls and terns, which is a good identifying marker of the location

of stripers. Both sides of the bridge have public parking and access for waders, but the western side has a marina with a boat-launch ramp. The Croatan Sound Bridge, just beyond the Manns Harbor Bridge, has proven itself as a striper-attracting structure, so you should try both bridges. Many anglers fly fish for stripers. Others swear by live eel, jigging with a bucktail or grub, or casting a Rat-L-Trap.

Backwater fishing also includes the Alligator River and South and East Lakes. You can troll, spin cast, bait cast, or fly fish year-round in the backwaters. You'll find an interesting mix of freshwater and saltwater species, including crappie, striped bass, largemouth bass, flounder, bream, sheepshead, drum, perch, croaker, spot, catfish, and trout. It all depends on the season.

If you'd like a guide, there are a few that offer backwater services. The fishing is so laid-back that you might find the guide throwing in a line with you. Since these waters are more protected and less prone to harsh offshore winds, you can often fish here when you can't elsewhere. This is a nice alternative to ocean fishing, and it's a good choice for families. Bring your camera. You might spot birds, deer, and bears on land and alligators in the water.

You don't have to hire a guide, though. You can launch your own boat from any number of local ramps (see the Water Sports chapter) or contact a tackle shop or marina for information.

i When booking a fishing trip, ask about cash discounts. Occasionally charter captains will save you some money if you pay without swiping a credit card or debit card.

PHIDEAUX TOO
PO Box 343, Manns Harbor, NC 27953
(252) 473-3059
Capt. V. P. Brinson uses a 150-hp Pathfinder to get you to the fish. Brinson offers spin-casting, fly rod, bait-casting, and trolling charters in lakes, sounds, and rivers. Fish for rockfish, trout, red drum, flounder, bass, bream, crappie, and perch. Call for prices.

CUSTOM SOUND CHARTERS
152 Dogwood Trail, Manteo
(252) 986-2201, (252) 216-6765
www.customsoundcharters.com
Light-tackle backwater trips are taken on the *Iron Will*, an 18-foot center-console. Capt. Rick Caton books trips on this boat in the spring and fall. Call for prices.

i If you're going fishing without a local captain or guide, check on current fishing regulations before embarking on your trip. Size and bag limits change frequently, and fines for illegal fish can be substantial.

FLY FISHING

The fly-fishing bug on the Outer Banks started in the 1960s and 1970s, when a few well-known fly anglers and locals cast flies into the surf for bluefish and were quite successful. In 1979 Chico Fernandez fly fished the Outer Banks, catching a white marlin. In 1981 he set an International Game Fish Association Fly Rod record with a 42-pound, 5-ounce red drum on a 12-pound tippet. Since then anglers have slowly discovered the Outer Banks' varied fly-fishing opportunities. Fly-fishing magazines and television shows now regularly feature the Outer Banks and its fly-fishing guides.

Fly anglers fish in the same places conventional anglers do. Fly anglers catch dolphin, tuna, and marlin in the Gulf Stream. They catch amberjack, mackerel, albacore, and cobia on inshore wrecks. They reap pompano and bluefish in the surf and stripers in the sounds. The most successful and accessible fly fishing is in the sounds, where you'll find speckled trout, stripers, red drum, bluefish, and Spanish mackerel.

It can be difficult to learn to fly fish the Outer Banks, especially the vast Pamlico and Roanoke Sounds. Hiring a guide is the quickest way to learn the area. If you prefer to go on your own, ask for advice at local tackle shops.

FLAT OUT FLY-FISHING & LIGHT-
**   TACKLE CHARTERS**
(252) 449-0562
www.outerbanksflyfishing.com
Capt. Brian Horsley and Capt. Sarah Gardner are true insiders when it comes to Outer Banks fly fishing. Both halves of this fly-fishing duo are guides and well-known fishing writers.

Horsley's *Flat Out* and Gardner's *Fly Girl* dock at Oregon Inlet Fishing Center. They run near-shore fly-fishing/light-tackle charters from Apr through Nov, though they move both boats to Harkers Island on the southernmost Outer Banks during October and November for false albacore fishing. They fish the Pamlico, Roanoke, and Croatan Sounds for speckled trout, bluefish, puppy drum, little tunny, flounder, and cobia.

RIOMAR FLY-FISHING AND LIGHT
**   TACKLE**
(252) 202-7962
www.fish-riomar.com

Capt. David Rohde offers inshore, near-shore, and soundside charters onboard his 18-foot Parker boat, the *Riomar*. He offers fly and light-tackle trips for speckled trout, bluefish, stripers, and drum. Rohde operates the *Riomar* in Harkers Island in the fall for albacore fishing. Call to arrange a meeting place.

CAPTAIN BRYAN DE HART'S COASTAL ADVENTURES GUIDE SERVICE
507 Barlowe St., Manteo
(252) 473-8632

Captain De Hart books light-tackle fly-fishing charters inshore, in brackish and saltwater, and in coastal rivers and sounds. On the backwaters De Hart uses an 18-foot War Eagle, and in the open sound, he fishes from a 22-foot Javelin. De Hart has been featured on ESPN's *Fly-Fishing America* program and is a regular on *The Carolina Outdoor Journal*.

OUTER BANKS WATERFOWL
67 East Dogwood Trail, Kitty Hawk
(252) 441-3732
www.outerbankswaterfowl.com

Capt. Vic Berg runs sound and inlet fly- or spinning-tackle fishing trips. Everything you need is included, or if you like, you can bring your favorite tackle. Berg also offers instruction on fly or surf fishing. Family and group rates are available for lessons. Berg is US Coast Guard licensed.

Berg is also an experienced hunting guide who leads hunting trips that can yield many species of waterfowl. A typical bag of 10 ducks can contain seven different species. Berg's blinds are located between Oregon Inlet and Pea Island and have proven their success for more than 25 years. He also offers swan-hunting trips.

SURF FISHING

Surf fishing is a popular Outer Banks pastime for the competitor or amateur alike. While there are miles of beach from which to cast a line, experienced local anglers say a surf caster's success will vary depending on sloughs, temperature, currents, and season. One of the hottest surf-casting spots on the Outer Banks is Cape Point, a sand spit at the tip of Cape Hatteras. Anglers often stand waist deep in the churning waters, dutifully waiting for red drum to strike.

About nine months out of the year, anglers can fish for red drum on the Outer Banks. The best time to catch big drum is mid-October through mid-November. During this period large schools of drum are feeding on baitfish called menhaden that migrate down the coastline. Cape Point is the hot spot for drum, but it tends to be a very crowded place to fish. A good second choice is the beach between Salvo and Buxton. But in the fall you can catch them from Rodanthe down to Hatteras Inlet. From mid-April through about the third week in May, red drum show up around Ocracoke Inlet, both in the ocean and shallow shoal waters at the inlet's mouth and also in the Pamlico Sound.

Serious drum anglers fish after dark for the nocturnal feeders. Insiders prefer a southwesterly wind with an incoming tide and water temperatures in the low 60s. Big drum are known to come close to the surf during rough weather. Puppy drum (or juvenile drum) are easier to catch than the adult fish. They show up in the surf after a northeast blow in late summer or early fall. Anglers use finger mullet with success as well as fresh shrimp (and we do mean fresh). Red drum are a regulated fish, both in size and limit. Call your local tackle shop for more information. If you're interested in learning more about red drum tag-and-release programs, call the Division of Marine Fisheries at (252) 473-5734 or (252) 264-3911.

There's a lengthy list of fish regularly caught at Cape Point. Common species include dogfish, bluefish, pompano, striped bass, and Spanish mackerel as well as bottom feeders such as croaker, flounder, spot, sea mullet, and both gray and speckled trout. More uncommon are tarpon, cobia, amberjack, jack crevalles, and shark weighing several hundred pounds.

Shoaling that takes place off Cape Hatteras makes Cape Point a haven for baitfish, and the influence of the nearby Gulf Stream and its warm-water jetties also contribute to excellent fishing. The beach accommodates many four-wheel-drive vehicles, and during peak season (spring and fall) it's packed with anglers. If you want to try fishing Cape Point, take NC 12 to Buxton and look for signs to vehicle access ramp 43. (For more information about driving on the beach, please see the Getting Here, Getting Around chapter.)

A section on surf fishing would not be complete without discussing bluefish. For years anglers enjoyed the arrival and subsequent blitzes of big bluefish during the Easter season and again around Thanksgiving. During a blitz, big blues chase baitfish up onto the beach in a feeding frenzy. This puts the blues in striking distance of ready surf casters. It's a phenomenal sight to watch anglers reel in these fat and ferocious fish one after the other. Anglers line up along the shore like soldiers, and many a rod is bent in that telltale C-shape, fighting a bluefish. Some days you can see a sky full of birds hovering, waiting to feast on the baitfish that the bluefish run toward the shore for.

The last few years the blues have not blitzed like they used to. As with most species, population figures (or at least landings) tend to rise and fall in cycles; perhaps they're tending toward a low point in the pattern. Maybe the big bluefin tuna, which feed on bluefish, are taking over these days, but blitz or not, you can usually catch some bluefish in the surf or in greater numbers offshore.

JOE MALAT'S OUTER BANKS SURF FISHING SCHOOL
415 Bridge Ln., Nags Head
(252) 441-4767
www.joemalat.com

For some pointers from an angler who has certainly put his time into the sport, pick up a copy of Joe Malat's *Surf Fishing*. This easy-to-read, illustrated book outlines methods of catching species common to our area. Malat shares tips on the lures, rigs, baits, and knots favored by local surf anglers. You can also read about catch-and-release techniques and how to locate and land fish. This comprehensive book includes useful information about tides, currents, wind, and other factors that affect surf fishing. Malat's *Pier Fishing* (Wellspring, 1999) includes all you should want to know about pier fishing plus information on 15 species of fish. For even more information, read Joe Malat's Fishing Notebook, which appears weekly in the *Outer Banks Sentinel*.

Malat's Outer Banks Surf Fishing School offers a two-and-a-half-day course that includes one day of classroom instruction, one-and-a-half days of on-the-beach instruction (bait included), classroom materials, and a copy of Malat's book. Malat and instructor Mac Currin offer personal instruction in an enjoyable, relaxed atmosphere, teaching students about such things as "reading the beach," fish identification, tackle, bait and lures, knot tying, casting, and beach driving.

PIER FISHING

Pier fishing is a true Outer Banks institution and has delighted anglers young and old for decades. The appeal is obvious: low cost and a chance to fish deeper waters without a boat. The variety of fish available also lures anglers. Depending on the time of year, you can catch croakers, spot, sea mullet, red drum, cobia, and occasionally a tarpon, king mackerel, sheepshead, or amberjack.

Bait and tackle are sold at each pier, or you can rent whatever gear you need. Avid anglers usually come prepared, but newcomers to the sport are always welcome on the pier, and staff are more than willing to outfit you and offer some fishing tips. Pier fishing is a good way to introduce kids to the sport. Many Outer Banks locals spent their youth on the pier soaking in know-how and area fishing lore. For instance, Garry Oliver, who owns the Outer Banks Pier in South Nags Head, spent many a summer day at the Nags Head Fishing Pier when he was a lad. Today Garry is a member of an award-winning surf-casters team.

The Outer Banks has no oceanfront boardwalks, but the piers more than make up for it. The smells of salt air and creosote-treated lumber greet you as you walk the wide planks over the ocean water. Looking down between the cracks, you see the waves crashing beneath you. You don't have to fish to appreciate the piers. For a small fee you can just walk out on the piers to enjoy the vantage points.

AVALON FISHING PIER
NC 12, MP 6, Kill Devil Hills
(252) 441-7494
www.avalonpier.com

Avalon Pier, in the heart of Kill Devil Hills, was built in the mid-1950s and is 705 feet long. The pier has lights for night fishing, a snack bar, a bait and tackle shop, ice, video games, and rental fishing gear. A busy place in season, the pier is open 24 hours a day. The pier house is open from 6 a.m. until midnight. The pier is closed Dec through mid-March. People with disabilities are admitted free.

NAGS HEAD FISHING PIER
NC 12, MP 12, Nags Head
(252) 441-5141
www.nagsheadpier.com

This is one of the most popular fishing piers on the Outer Banks. It is 750 feet long and has its own bait and tackle shop. Enjoy night fishing, game tables for the kids, and a restaurant. The Pier House Restaurant features fresh seafood and wonderful views of the ocean. The restaurant serves breakfast, lunch, and dinner. (See the Restaurants chapter for more information.) The pier closes in Dec and reopens in Mar or Apr, depending upon whether the fish are biting. It is open 24 hours during the season.

OUTER BANKS PIER AND FISHING CENTER
NC 12, MP 18½, South Nags Head
(252) 441-5740
www.fishingunlimited.net

This 650-foot ocean pier was originally built in 1959 and rebuilt in 1962 after the Ash Wednesday storm. Owner Garry Oliver has all you need in the bait and tackle shop for a day of fishing along this stretch of beach. A 300-foot sound fishing and crabbing pier is also available on the Nags Head–Manteo Causeway. The piers are open 24 hours a day from Memorial Day until mid-October and close from Thanksgiving through Easter. Call for rates. Snack at the pier's on-site oceanside deli.

HATTERAS ISLAND FISHING PIER
NC 12, Rodanthe
(252) 987-2323, (800) 331-6541
www.obxfishingpier.com
After massive poundings by Hurricanes Dennis and Floyd, this pier collapsed in 1999. Even the land on which the pier house stood disappeared due to storm erosion. The land was refilled and in 2000 the pier reopened, a little farther back from its original location. The pier house sells drinks, snacks, sandwiches, tackle, and bait. The pier and pier house are open every day in the summer, 7 a.m. to 11 p.m. from Memorial Day to Labor Day and 7 a.m. to 10 p.m. the rest of the season. The Rodanthe pier is closed Jan 1 through Apr 1.

AVON GOLF & FISHING PIER
NC 12, Avon
(252) 995-5480
www.avonpier.com
Avon Golf & Fishing Pier has a reputation for being a hot spot for red drum. The all-tackle world-record red drum, weighing in at 94 pounds, 2 ounces, was caught about 200 yards from the pier in 1984, and the record holds to this day. The pier opens at the beginning of Apr and remains open through Thanksgiving. Purchase or rent your fishing supplies here, buy sandwiches and drinks, and pick up nautical gifts, including T-shirts and sand mirrors. They also offer an 18-hole natural-grass putting green on the premises.

Play is unlimited, and you can come and go as you please.

i When buying waders or boots, always buy them one-and-a-half sizes larger than your shoe size. The larger size will enable you to slip them off in the event that you step in a slough or fall overboard.

CITATION FISH

Citation fish are caught in the waters off the Outer Banks every year. The North Carolina Division of Marine Fisheries manages the North Carolina Saltwater Fishing Tournament, which recognizes outstanding angling achievement. The tournament runs yearlong. Other than charter boat captains and crews for hire, everyone is eligible for a citation fish award. Eligible waters include North Carolina sounds, surf, estuaries, and the ocean. This tournament is for the hook-and-line angler; use of electric or hydraulic equipment is not allowed. There is one award per species, and all fish must be weighed in at an official weigh station. Anglers receive a certificate after the close of the tournament. There is no registration fee. Following is a list of the area's weigh stations, where you can pick up a species list and receive rules for the tournament. Citations are also awarded for the catch and release of some species.

OFFICIAL WEIGH STATIONS
Corolla

TW'S BAIT AND TACKLE
NC 12, (252) 453-3339

Duck

BOB'S BAIT & TACKLE
NC 12, (252) 261-8589

Kitty Hawk

KITTY HAWK BAIT & TACKLE
US 158, MP 4½
(252) 261-2955

TW'S BAIT AND TACKLE
US 158, MP 4
(252) 261-7848

WHITNEY'S BAIT & TACKLE
US 158, MP 4½
(252) 261-5551

Kill Devil Hills

AVALON FISHING PIER
NC 12, MP 6, (252) 441-7494

STOP 'N' SHOP CONVENIENCE AND DELI
NC 12, MP 8½, (252) 441-6105

Nags Head

NAGS HEAD FISHING PIER
NC 12, MP 12, (252) 441-5141

OUTER BANKS PIER AND FISHING CENTER
NC 12, MP 18½, (252) 441-5740

OUTER BANKS FISHING UNLIMITED
Nags Head–Manteo Causeway
(252) 441-5028

TW'S BAIT AND TACKLE
US 158, MP 10½, (252) 441-4807

WHALEBONE TACKLE
Nags Head–Manteo Causeway,
(252) 441-7413

Manteo

PIRATE'S COVE
Nags Head–Manteo Causeway,
(252) 473-3906

Oregon Inlet

OREGON INLET FISHING CENTER
NC 12, 8 miles south of Whalebone
Junction, (252) 441-6301

Rodanthe

HATTERAS JACK
NC 12, (252) 987-2428

MAC'S TACKLE & ISLAND CONVENIENCE
NC 12, (252) 987-2239

Salvo

FISHIN' HOLE
NC 12, (252) 987-2351

Avon

FRANK AND FRAN'S FISHERMAN'S FRIEND
NC 12, (252) 995-4171

Buxton

DILLON'S CORNER
NC 12, (252) 995-5083

RED DRUM TACKLE SHOP
NC 12, (252) 995-5414

Frisco

FRISCO ROD & GUN
NC 12, (252) 995-5366

FRISCO TACKLE
NC 12, (252) 995-4361

Hatteras Village

HATTERAS HARBOR MARINA
NC 12, (252) 986-2166

ODEN'S DOCK
NC 12, (252) 986-2555

PELICAN'S ROOST
NC 12, (252) 986-2213

TEACH'S LAIR MARINA
NC 12, (252) 986-2460

WILLIS BOAT LANDING
57209 Willis Ln., (252) 986-2208

Ocracoke

OCRACOKE FISHING CENTER
NC 12, (252) 928-6661

O'NEAL'S DOCKSIDE TACKLE SHOP
NC 12, (252) 928-1111

TRADEWINDS
NC 12, (252) 928-5491

BAIT & TACKLE SHOPS

Full-service tackle shops are scattered from Corolla to Ocracoke. They are good sources for not only rods, reels, bait, and other fishing equipment and accessories, but also for tips on what's biting and where. You'll find bait and tackle at all Outer Banks fishing piers and most marinas, too. Just about every department store and general store on the barrier islands carries some sort of fishing gear, and many shops also offer tackle rental. You can ask for guide information at any one of the following shops.

Duck

BOB'S BAIT & TACKLE
NC 12, Duck
(252) 261-8589
Stop in Bob's if you're looking for advice on where to catch the really big one. The old building is left over from Duck's early days, when a soundside dock out back was the distribution point for shiploads of fresh ocean fish. The shop carries a good supply of rods, reels, bait, and tackle. Bob's also books offshore charters and provides a hunting and fishing guide service.

Kitty Hawk

TW'S BAIT AND TACKLE
US 158, MP 4, Kitty Hawk
(252) 261-7848
TW's Bait & Tackle, next to the 7-Eleven in Kitty Hawk, is a great place to find the right stuff for your fishing adventure. Owner Terry "T. W." Stewart has been in business since 1981 and can sell you what you need, including ice and live bait. TW's also books inshore and offshore charter fishing trips. There is another location in Corolla (252-453-3339) at the Food Lion Shopping Center, but it's closed during Jan and Feb. The Kitty Hawk location stays open year-round. TW's has a Nags Head store at milepost 10½; call (252) 4414807. The Nags Head location is open all year also. You can reach the second location in Corolla at (252) 453-3339.

WHITNEY'S BAIT & TACKLE
US 158, MP 4½, Kitty Hawk
(252) 261-5551
Whitney's specializes in custom rods made by Whitney Jones, plus offshore and inshore bait and tackle. The shop also offers rod and reel repairs. The walls at Whitney's are lined

with Jones's impressive freshwater and salt-water citations and trophies. Call for Whitney's fishing report.

Kill Devil Hills

STOP 'N' SHOP CONVENIENCE AND DELI
NC 12, MP 8½, Kill Devil Hills
(252) 441-6105
Located on the Beach Road across from the Kill Devil Hills beach access, Stop 'N' Shop has about anything you might need for a day of fishing or a day at the beach. This is a full-service tackle shop, with fishing and beach items that include bait, tackle, local information, beer, ice, gas, and rental equipment. Owners Tom and Vickie Byers stock a surprising amount of goods for anglers. Stop 'N' Shop is open seven days a week year-round.

T.I.'S BAIT & TACKLE
US 158, MP 9, Kill Devil Hills
(252) 441-3166
T.I.'s is a member of the North Carolina Beach Buggy Association. The shop offers quality tackle and fresh bait and is an authorized Penn parts distributor and repair station. T.I.'s is also a factory-authorized Daiwa service warranty center. The shop is open year-round. Check out their other location across from Cahoon's grocery on NC 12, milepost 16½, in Nags Head; call (252) 441-5242.

Nags Head

WHALEBONE TACKLE
Nags Head–Manteo Causeway,
Nags Head
(252) 441-7413
Whalebone is a full-service tackle shop offering ice, fresh bait, tackle, and rod and Penn reel repairs. As they say at the store, "All roads lead to Whalebone Tackle, the center of the universe." The store is open year-round.

FISHING UNLIMITED
Nags Head–Manteo Causeway,
Nags Head
(252) 441-5028
www.fishingunlimited.net
Fishing Unlimited specializes in fresh bait and is a full-service tackle shop. You can purchase live bait, custom rigs, and lures here as well as crabbing supplies, snacks, and drinks. Services include 16-foot outboard and 20-foot pontoon boat rentals. Fish or crab from the 300-foot sound pier. You can rent rods and reels. The shop is open from Easter until early Dec.

Salvo

FISHIN' HOLE
NC 12, Salvo
(252) 987-2351
Operating on the Outer Banks since 1976, The Fishin' Hole is a full-service tackle shop that sells live bait, tackle, beach supplies, groceries, and T-shirts. Rod and reel repairs for Daiwa, Penn, and other brands are available here. It's an official weigh station for the North Carolina Beach Buggy Association. The shop is open from the end of Mar through mid-December.

Avon

FRANK AND FRAN'S FISHERMAN'S FRIEND
NC 12, Avon
(252) 995-4171
A full-service tackle shop and headquarters for the local Red Drum Tournament held every October, Frank and Fran's is an emporium of fishing gear. This is another official

weigh station for the state and the North Carolina Beach Buggy Association.

Buxton

DILLON'S CORNER
NC 12, Buxton
(252) 995-5083
Stop here for an assortment of tackle, including custom rods and bait. The shop also carries a wide selection of gifts, T-shirts, and lighthouse replicas (see the Shopping chapter). The shop offers rod repairs and has gas pumps. Dillon's Corner is open all year but has shorter hours in winter.

RED DRUM TACKLE SHOP
NC 12, Buxton
(252) 995-5414
Get the latest in fishing information and select gear at Red Drum Tackle Shop. It offers everything you need in the way of custom rods, bait, and tackle, plus reel repairs. They're a Penn warranty center and official weigh station for the state, the North Carolina Beach Buggy Association, and the Cape Hatteras Anglers Club.

Frisco

FRISCO ROD & GUN
NC 12, Frisco
(252) 995-5366
www.friscorodgun.com
Frisco Rod & Gun is a one-stop shop for everything you need for a hunting or fishing trip. The owner calls it his "hobby gone wild." You'll find inshore and offshore fishing equipment, fly-fishing gear, custom rods, guns, ice, bait, tackle, and one of the biggest and best selections of knives you'll ever see. They also offer rod and reel repairs and can help you find a hunting or fishing guide.

Taxidermy services can be arranged. Camping supplies, name-brand outdoor apparel, Sperry footwear, T-shirts, groceries, gas, and convenience items round out the offerings.

Ocracoke

TRADEWINDS
NC 12, Ocracoke
(252) 928-5491
www.fishtradewinds.com
Tradewinds is a one-stop tackle shop that can supply all your fishing needs, including fresh and frozen bait, tackle, clothing items, and plenty of good advice about fishing. The shop also offers tackle rentals and rod and reel repair. Tradewinds is an official North Carolina weigh station and is open seven days a week from Mar through Dec.

O'NEAL'S DOCKSIDE TACKLE SHOP
NC 12, Ocracoke
(252) 928-1111
O'Neal's offers fresh and frozen bait as well as fishing, marine, and hunting supplies and can furnish you with any license you need. They are a full-service tackle shop and offer tackle rentals. These folks have been in business for more than 20 years and are official North Carolina Wildlife and Marine Fisheries agents. If you have any questions on official regulations, stop here.

FISHING REPORTS

For the latest word on what's biting, check with the following sources. Also read the *Virginian-Pilot* daily North Carolina section and the *Carolina Coast* for Damon Tatem's report. Check out Joe Malat's informative weekly column in the *Outer Banks Sentinel*. The *ReelFisher News* is a free quarterly tabloid available at retail outlets throughout the

FISHING

Outer Banks; it has folksy fishing editorials
plus a directory to area piers, ramps, marinas,
and weigh stations.

NAGS HEAD FISHING PIER
(252) 441-5141

PIRATE'S COVE YACHT CLUB
(252) 473-3906

OREGON INLET FISHING CENTER
(252) 441-6301

RED DRUM TACKLE SHOP
(252) 995-5414

FRISCO PIER
(252) 986-2533

O'NEAL'S DOCKSIDE TACKLE SHOP
(252) 928-1111

GOLF

Whether you're a scratch golfer or a duffer, you'll find play to suit your game and style on or near the Outer Banks. Part of the pleasure of golf almost everywhere is in the lushness of the environment, but few locations outside of this area offer the astounding ocean-to-sound views you'll find at many courses along these barrier islands. Such distraction might not be good for your game, but it'll do wonders for the soul!

In this section you'll find golf courses from Corolla to Hatteras Island, plus courses on the Currituck mainland just north of the Wright Memorial Bridge. We've also included an excellent course in Hertford that's only an hour's drive from the heart of the Outer Banks.

Golfers have it made during the off-season and shoulder seasons. Accommodations are a bargain from the fall through the spring, and many hotels, motels, and cottage rental companies package special golf vacations. Depending on the season you can usually plan a visit on the spur of the moment if you want to play at off-peak times. The temperatures on the Outer Banks remain fairly moderate throughout the year. A day in January might bring temperatures of 60 degrees or higher, so keep an eye on the weather and your clubs close at hand. To avoid disappointment, call for tee times at your course of choice before your visit; more and more golfers are discovering the Outer Banks in the off-season.

All the regulation courses in the following section are semiprivate, meaning the public can pay to play, and all welcome beginners and newcomers. Yardage and par figures are based on men's/white tees.

REGULATION & EXECUTIVE COURSES

THE CAROLINA CLUB
US 158, Grandy
(252) 453-3588
www.thecarolinaclub.com
More and more Outer Banks golfers are discovering the courses on the Currituck mainland, and the Carolina Club, designed by Russell Breeden, is one of the nicest of the bunch. Located in Grandy, the course is just 13.5 miles past the Wright Memorial Bridge, about a 20-minute drive from Kitty Hawk. The 7,000-yard, par 72 course has, according to the southeastern director of the US Golf Association (USGA), "among the finest putting surfaces in the eastern US." Indeed, the Carolina Club management prides itself

on its high level of course conditioning, slick bent-grass greens, and plush Tifway Bermuda fairways. Five sets of tees allow you to match your game to an appropriate level of challenge. On this course you will encounter wetlands, woodlands, water, and bunkers galore. Hole 7, a par 3, has an island green that will challenge your club-selection skills. The par 5 hole 18 offers the ultimate in risk versus reward. Water and wind direction factor in on this hole, where the tee shot must be right on the mark.

There's a snack bar on the premises, plus a pro shop. Rental clubs and carts are available. Individual and group lessons are offered. Greens fees, including cart, are a good value, ranging from $99 in June to $35 in January, but they change monthly so call for accurate prices. Youth rates are available. Tee times are booked up to three months in advance. The course is open all year.

THE CURRITUCK CLUB
NC 12, Corolla
(252) 453-9400, (888) 453-9400
www.thecurrituckclub.com
When the Currituck Club opened in 1997, *Golf* magazine named it one of the "Top 10 You Can Play." In 1999 *Golf Digest* ranked it as one of the top 25 courses in North Carolina, a great compliment for a young course in a renowned golfing state. The Currituck Club was rated in 2004 *Golf Digest's* best places to play. This 6,885-yard, par 72 course is situated on 600 acres of pristine wetlands along Currituck Sound, surrounded by luxurious homes in the Currituck Club resort community. The natural beauty of this course makes it one of the most peaceful golfing spots around. Prominent golf architect Rees Jones designed the stunningly scenic links-style course with respect for the wildlife

and waterfowl that populate the area. While protecting their habitats, he offers golfers a course set amid dunes, wetlands, and marsh fringes. From the rolling dunes golfers enjoy views of the Atlantic Ocean and Currituck Sound. Within the property lie 15 acres set aside for the historic and private Currituck Shooting Club, whose lineage dates from 1857. The back nine has several holes with some of the most beautiful views you'll ever see. The view from the elevated 13th tee offers a panorama of the ocean, sound, and the Currituck Beach Lighthouse.

The course features a full driving range. Lessons are offered year-round, along with weekly clinics by PGA professionals. Golf schools take place from June through Aug on Tues, Wed, and Thurs from 9 to 11 a.m. Junior golf school is offered on Thurs from 5 to 7 p.m. Rates include golf cart rental and vary according to the season. The clubhouse includes a restaurant, a bar and lounge with full ABC permits, a pro shop, locker rooms, bag storage, and a private members' lounge.

DUCK WOODS COUNTRY CLUB
50 Dogwood Trail, Kitty Hawk
(252) 261-2609
www.duckwoodscc.com
Duck Woods is the club to play on windy days, since it provides more shelter than the soundside clubs. This 18-hole, 6,161-yard, par 72 course was built in 1968. Designed by Ellis Maples, Duck Woods features a traditional layout with tree-lined fairways. Shots must be placed with care, especially on the par 5 14th hole, where water dissects the fairway. Water comes into play on 14 holes. You might want to warm up before your round; the course begins with a 481-yard par 5 and ends with a 506-yard par 5.

While the club accommodates 900 members, it accepts public play year-round. Nonmembers can take advantage of the driving range and putting green on the day of play only. Target greens and a practice bunker are available. Duck Woods' pro shop is complemented by the presence of golf pro Brian Liebler. Club rentals are available. Members enjoy clubhouse and locker room privileges and the bar and restaurant. Beer and wine are sold to nonmembers, but no other alcoholic beverages are available, as the club does not hold a liquor license.

Riding is mandatory for nonmembers. Booking is accepted a week in advance for members and two days in advance for nonmembers. Call for more information. Greens fees vary.

GOOSE CREEK GOLF AND COUNTRY CLUB
US 158, Grandy
(252) 453-4008, (800) 443-4008

Goose Creek, a 5,943-yard par 72 public course on the mainland, offers an easygoing track complete with a hospitable atmosphere and some of the most affordable greens fees in the area. The greens and fairways on this flat course are blanketed with Bermuda grass. Greens are relatively small. Trees line the course, with tighter fairways on the first nine but more undulating and open terrain on the back.

Designed by Jerry Turner and built by Jernigan Enterprises, Goose Creek is a player-friendly golf course. Goose Creek has a Class A PGA golf professional on staff. Water comes into play on five holes. Hole 13 is considered the signature. The hole plays differently according to the wind (it's generally to your back during the summer and in your face in fall and winter).

The clubhouse is a former hunting lodge that the owners converted into private locker rooms. Take some time to relax in the pine-paneled lounge for a cool drink. The clubhouse menu includes all sorts of sandwiches, plus everything from buffalo wings to crab cakes.

A driving range and practice green are available. Walking is allowed for members only. This is a great course for the entire family, and children are both welcome and encouraged; however, it's recommended that young golfers check in after noon.

HOLLY RIDGE GOLF COURSE
US 158, Harbinger
(252) 491-2893
www.cathyjohnstonforbes.com

Holly Ridge Golf Course is 1.5 miles north of the Wright Memorial Bridge in Harbinger. Holly Ridge is under the management of Wright Flight Golf. The front nine wind through a peaceful forest of native trees and picturesque ponds, while the more open back nine are affected by winds. Holly Ridge has a full-length, fully lighted grass practice area and putting green. LPGA major champion Cathy Johnston Forbes teaches golfers of all levels. Private lessons and group clinics are available, as are private lessons with video analysis. The pro shop carries apparel, accessories, and equipment, and the staff helps with selecting the right clubs. Walking is allowed on this course. Pull carts, golf clubs, and, of course, golf carts are available to rent. Greens fees are a good value here, and they vary throughout the year, so call ahead. Juniors may play for half price but must have a valid driver's license to operate a cart.

MILL RUN GOLF AND COUNTRY CLUB
US 168, Currituck
(252) 435-6455
www.millrungolfclub.us

If you're willing to drive a ways, Mill Run Golf and Country Club offers a great bargain for Outer Banks golfers. The course, opened in 1999, is just south of Moyock on US 168, about 50 miles from the Outer Banks on the mainland and about 5 miles south of the Virginia state line. The course is fun and enjoyable, not overly difficult; so if you're looking for a good-time game, come here.

Mill Run is a great course for beginners. Course architect James Overton Sr. designed the 6,651-yard course to take advantage of the natural terrain and to provide challenging play for golfers of all levels. Mill Run is relatively flat and plays somewhat like a links-style course, though it's nowhere near the ocean or sound. It does offer some challenges with wind, ponds, and woods. Bunkers are still being added to the course. The signature hole is number 17, a par 3 with the carry over water. Greens are in tip-top shape. A driving range, practice putting green, and chipping green are available, and golf professional Buddy Lawrence offers lessons. Walking is allowed here. The pro shop is well equipped, and the on-site Hackers Grill serves breakfast and lunch.

i Snakes! Tiny slivers of snakes and much bigger ones slither through the tall grasses and marsh. Look out for them and proceed carefully, especially when retrieving a ball from the brush or near rocks, where they often hide. Snakes want to avoid you, but if trapped or surprised, they may strike in defense.

NAGS HEAD GOLF LINKS
5615 South Seachase Dr., Nags Head
(252) 389-9079
www.nagsheadgolflinks.com

This soundside 18-hole Scottish links–style course is in the Village at Nags Head off US 158 at milepost 15½. Architect Bob Moore left most of the natural setting intact, and the 6,100-yard, par 71 course is a real beach beauty. Golfers enjoy idyllic views of Roanoke Sound from nearly every hole. With the sound to the west and the ocean to the east, wind plays a significant role here.

It doesn't take but one quick gust of wind to blow your ball off course on the 221-yard 15th hole, a lengthy par 3. The green is fronted by a pond. All but four holes are affected by water here.

Nags Head Golf Links pros are on hand and invite you to try this mercurial course. The environment is so refreshing that we think it's worth a round regardless of what's controlling the shots. Golf school is held mornings three days a week during summer.

Golf Digest called the holes along the sound "among the most beautiful in the eastern US," and went on to say that "Nags Head Golf Links is the longest 6,100 yards you'll ever play." The same journal awarded the course 4½ stars.

Cart and greens fees vary, and starting times may be reserved up to one year in advance. Seniors pay special off-season rates. A nine-hole scramble is played June through August late Sunday afternoons; call to sign up.

Enjoy good food and excellent views of Roanoke Sound from the Links Grill, which is open for lunch only. Nags Head Golf Links also has a bar, golf shop, driving range, putting green, and rental clubs. The course is open every day, except Christmas, from sunrise to sunset. Call for more information.

THE POINTE GOLF CLUB
US 158 East, Powells Point
(252) 491-8388
www.thepointegolfclub.com

"Golfer's heaven" well describes this 5,911-yard, par 71, 18-hole championship golf course on the mainland. Both the recreational golfer and the professional will find a challenge on this verdant course created by Russell Breeden. Breeden's unique design features soundfront views from wooded and links-style holes with gentle mounds and slopes. This was the first course in the country to feature A1 bentgrass greens, a new disease-resistant dense grass. It's no surprise because the folks at Pointe are grass experts. Pointe owner Keith Hall is the president of United Turf.

The course sports a traditional design, with water hazards coming into play laterally on 15 holes. The signature hole is number 6, a 457-yard par 4 with a carry over wetlands, a blind shot to the fairway, water, bunkers, and slopes to the right.

You can fine-tune your game on the driving range, in the practice bunker, or on the full-size putting green. The Pointe offers a full-service pro shop headed by resident golf pro Doug Kinser. Other amenities include a clubhouse, carts, lessons, sales, and rentals. The Pointe Restaurant, which serves breakfast and lunch, has views of the 9th green and the 10th tee.

Walking is allowed after noon for greens-fee pass holders, Oct 1 through May 24. Greens fees vary, so it's a good idea to call for information. Annual golf packages are offered through Outer Banks Golf Getaways (800-635-1559) and Outer Banks Golf Packages (800-916-6244); accommodations packages are available through area rental companies. The golf course is located 3.5 miles north of the Wright Memorial Bridge. Call for tee times up to a month in advance.

SEA SCAPE GOLF LINKS
300 Eckner St., Kitty Hawk
(252) 261-2158
www.seascapegolf.com

Keep your eye on the ball and not the view on this 18-hole, links-style championship course. You get a real taste of Outer Banks beauty with water vistas from almost every hole, especially from the elevated ninth tee. Sea Scape is cut into Kitty Hawk's maritime forest, just off US 158 East at milepost 2½. Designed by Art Wall, the 6,052-yard, par 72 course features bent-grass greens and fairways, which are fairly wide. Sea Scape was host of the 2000 North Carolina Open.

Opened in 1965, the links-style course has been modernized, and now you can expect cart paths on all holes. Wind is a factor here, and you may find yourself puttering around in the sand and brush looking for your ball. Expect a challenge on number 11: Look to play against the wind on this 410-yard, par 4 hole. Sea Scape will test your ability as well as your patience, with five par 3s and five par 5s.

A scheduled golf clinic is offered for all ages from June through August. Sea Scape offers club fitting, rental clubs, and a driving range, bar, restaurant, and fully stocked pro shop. Sea Scape pro Danny Miller is available to discuss your game or the course. Sea Scape's clubhouse features a fully stocked pro shop and Sully's Restaurant, serving breakfast and lunch.

Walking is not allowed. Greens fees range from $50 to $100, including the cart.

Call ahead for tee times, especially if you plan to play during the summer (there's no established rule, but we were informed that eight months in advance isn't too soon). The course is open every day except Christmas from 7:30 a.m. until dark.

THE SOUND GOLF LINKS
101 Clubhouse Dr., Hertford
(252) 426-5555, (800) 535-0704
www.soundgolflinks.com
Tucked within Albemarle Plantation, the Sound is a 6,504-yard, par 72, 18-hole course. It's also a world-class golfing and boating community at the tip of the Albemarle Sound near Hertford. The beautiful 12,000-square-foot clubhouse overlooks the water. Owner and designer Dan Maples stamped his signature here. As with all Maples-designed courses, you get a break on the par 4s and 5s, but the par 3s are extremely difficult. It's a target golf course with a few similarities to a links course.

Fairways are narrow, and marsh must be carried frequently. It's a fair course overall but a tough one from the back tees. On the 7th and 13th holes, the landing areas are extremely small. Both are par 4s.

A golf pro is available here. The clubhouse includes a golf shop and restaurant, the Soundside Grille, which serves lunch and dinner. A driving range and putting green are also available. The marina, available to the public, is the largest in the area.

Walking is restricted, so call for details. Tee times may be booked up to nine months in advance. The course is a little over an hour's drive from Kitty Hawk. Call for greens fees.

PRACTICE RANGES

THE PROMENADE
US 158 East, MP ½, Kitty Hawk
(252) 261-4900
www.promenadewatersports.com
Along Currituck Sound at the eastern terminus of the Wright Memorial Bridge, this 30-acre adventure spot features a nine-hole chip-and-putt course on natural grass. Separate putting green and target driving range facilities are available.

LIVING HERE

In this section we feature specific information for residents or those planning to relocate here. Topics include real estate, education, and retirement.

REAL ESTATE

There's a certain feeling that many of us get when we cross a bridge to the Outer Banks. It's excitement mixed with awe, blended with the spirit that something wonderful might happen at any moment. It's also a feeling of coming home. Any visitor to these shores who has that feeling should know one thing: It only gets stronger, and it makes leaving increasingly difficult. When you get that feeling, you know that it's time to look at Outer Banks real estate.

It's the desire to belong here, as much as the desire to own here, that puts the ink on all those real estate contracts. Before you take up a pen, however, realize that no matter how much experience you have buying and selling real estate in other areas, you need a deep understanding of the Outer Banks and its unique real estate market in order to make a sound decision. There's a lot to learn about seasonal versus residential neighborhoods, coastal and wetlands regulations, investing in an income-producing property versus buying a second home, buying an existing home versus building—you get the picture. It's not unusual for real estate agents to work with prospective buyers for two or three years before it all comes together. Then again, you may find exactly what you want your first day out looking.

So if you're serious about buying on the Outer Banks, begin by reading this chapter, and when you're done, consider that you've learned just enough to be dangerous. Do two things: (1) Start interviewing real estate professionals, and (2) begin collecting and reading everything you can get your hands on that will help you decipher the real estate market. Subscribe to the local newspapers and get to know the areas, the issues, and the prices. Search the Internet and pick up the free real estate magazines. Smart buyers begin performing this due diligence well before they're ready to make a purchase.

UNDERSTANDING THE LOCAL MARKET

As you learn about the Outer Banks, you'll come to understand that the market varies quite a bit by township and by proximity to water. Nowhere is the old adage about location, location, location more important than here on the Outer Banks. The rules of supply and demand apply, period. The closer to the ocean, the greater the demand—and nothing is more precious than an oceanfront lot. Bear in mind that all oceanfront lots aren't created equal. The shoreline along the entire East Coast is in a constant state of flux. With such a dynamic scenario, some areas of the beach will experience erosion, some will experience accretion, and it's all subject to change. There's always an element of risk in owning property in a coastal environment.

The priciest real estate on the Outer Banks is in Corolla, where the newer ocean-front homes sell for up to $7 million. Still, there are many excellent, established neighborhoods in other areas of the Outer Banks where you can buy a cottage for around $220,000 and still walk to the ocean. This chapter touches upon the flavor of the various sections of the beach; for more information on townships, see the Area Overview chapter.

WORKING WITH A REAL ESTATE AGENT

Whether you decide to buy an existing home or build your own, a good real estate agent can supply you with the information you need to make a smart decision and can save you a great deal of time and, very often, money. You are wise to enlist the services of a knowledgeable agent when you buy real estate on the Outer Banks given the uniqueness of the market economics and the local environment.

Interview a few agents before you decide with whom you'd like to work. Ask around for referrals. It's important for you to know that any real estate agent or broker can represent your interests, but be careful to select an agent with expertise in the communities in which you're most interested. Generally you're better off to work with an agent whose office is located near your preferred areas. An agent who understands the market in Corolla probably won't be quite as knowledgeable of markets in Hatteras or Manteo.

Real estate agents and brokers are licensed by the State of North Carolina and are subject to its laws and regulations. A Realtor is an agent or broker who also belongs to the Board of Realtors, represented in our area by the Outer Banks Association of Realtors. What sets a Realtor apart from any licensee is the Realtor Code of Ethics, a set of stricter rules of conduct to which members subscribe, and access to the Multiple Listing Service, the most comprehensive database of properties for sale. For a listing of local Realtors, contact the Outer Banks Association of Realtors, PO Box 1070, Kill Devil Hills, NC 27948; (252) 441-4036; www.outerbanks realtors.com. This organization represents more than 900 Realtors on the Outer Banks.

When you choose an agent or broker, technically you're entering into an agreement not only with that agent but also with the agent's firm. You'll need to decide whether you want exclusive representation from a buyer's agent, whether you're content to work with the seller's agent, or whether under certain circumstances you'll allow your buyer's agent to represent both you and the other party to the transaction, which makes your agent a "dual" agent. There are specific rules governing these relationships, and all agents and brokers are required to explain these rules at the first substantive contact with a prospective client or customer. You will be asked to sign an agency agreement; make sure you understand your options and your obligations to your agent as well as her or his obligations to you. Most agents collect their fees from the proceeds of the sale, but this is not always the case. Make sure you understand the compensation arrangement before you commit to an agent. According to North Carolina statute, even if an agent does not represent you, the agent must still be fair and honest and disclose to you all material facts that the agent knows or reasonably should know.

A conscientious, hardworking agent or broker will supply you with extensive information on the market—including comps (comparable properties currently listed and recently sold), neighborhood amenities and covenants, and financing options—and will be conversant in the pros and cons of building your own versus buying an existing home. She or he can also help you estimate the costs of ownership and what you might expect to realize in terms of income if you decide, as many owners do, to rent your home to others.

At the end of this chapter are listings of real estate companies and the areas they specialize in. Along with some community listings, we've supplied contact information for the developer, but do be aware that you don't have to work with the developer or the developer's agent directly; you should feel free to use your own buyer's agent if that's your preference.

BUILDING YOUR OWN

If you decide to build, your agent can help you choose a building contractor, or you can ask for a list of members from the Outer Banks Homebuilders Association, 105 West Airstrip Rd., Kill Devil Hills, NC 27948; (252) 449-8232, http://obhomebuilders.org.

If you decide to build your own home, first be clear about its intended use: Do you want a second home, rental property, or year-round residence? Your answer will determine where you build and the style

of home. If you're designing for the rental market, you'll have to keep in mind not only your preferences but those of others as well. Talk with your builder and property managers to learn the features that will make your home a popular rental. You'll be wise to listen to their advice.

Ask your builder to not only show you floor plans but also take you through other houses he or she has built. (If you do this in the off-season, you'll have a better chance of viewing homes, for they will probably be vacant. Understandably, property managers try not to interrupt their guests' summer vacations.) If your goal is to achieve the maximum income, ask a property manager whose firm represents a lot of homes in your area to show you the most popular rentals in their inventory, but be careful to focus on homes similarly located to the lot you've selected. You can't compare income on an oceanfront to income on a house four rows back from the ocean.

You'll want to familiarize yourself with the building codes and regulations unique to our area, including regulations relating to environmental protection set by the North Carolina Coastal Management Authority (CAMA).

Throughout the process, keep in mind that your intended use of the property will dictate its design and construction. A home intended for weekly rental is usually substantially different in design than a home intended for year-round residential use. Wandering through open houses and model homes is a fun and informative way to refine your ideas before you begin to set them down on paper.

TUNE IN TO REALITY

Many prospective buyers wander into real estate offices insisting they be shown properties that will "pay for themselves." Trust this insider: If that many properties paid for themselves, there would be precious few for sale. Even if you're planning to rent out your new home at the beach, know that in 99 percent of cases you'll have to shell out more money than you'll take in for the privilege of owning it. Just how much you'll have to pay is highly variable. It depends on how much you paid for the property, the financing terms you've arranged, and how much rental income it generates.

When you buy a beach cottage with the intention of realizing rental income, what you're really doing is operating a business, so learn about it. As an owner you have a great deal of influence over how much income your property generates. Participate in setting your rates. Keep your home in good repair, and be realistic about the funds you'll need to designate for annual maintenance and periodic replacement of housewares and furnishings. Discuss your goals with your agent and speak with property managers at a few carefully selected real estate firms (see the chapter on Weekly and Long-Term Cottage Rentals). You'll also want to consult your tax adviser, since the IRS has specific rules you must follow depending on how you use your property.

Once you place your property in service, review its performance at least annually with your property manager and pay close attention to any complaints or comments from renters. Keep a guest book in the cottage for renters' comments and think of it as a quality-control device.

Nearly all owners realize that by renting out their cottages, they are letting others subsidize their dream of owning a home by the sea. Over time, as property values and rental rates creep up and other costs stabilize, many cottages will operate at break-even or better. Your best bet is to be conservative in your expectations and be pleasantly surprised when they're exceeded.

What follows is a brief overview listing the main residential resort communities, as well as information on time-share properties and a listing of real estate companies. Please also refer to the Area Overview chapter for more information.

RESIDENTIAL RESORT COMMUNITIES

We've listed a combination of newer and more established oceanside and sound-side residential communities to give you an idea of what's here on the Outer Banks. We start our journey in the four-wheel-drive beaches north of Corolla and then move south through the Outer Banks, ending on Ocracoke Island. These communities include resorts and developments that offer recreational amenities and easy access to the ocean and sound, those that provide a mixture of both seasonal and year-round living, and neighborhoods with more of a year-round lifestyle.

Most developments have strict architectural guidelines, or covenants, to ensure quality development. It should also be noted that there are many one-road (cul-de-sac) subdivisions scattered throughout the Outer Banks. Some of these subdivisions offer private roads and private ocean or sound accesses. These neighborhoods offer great rental opportunities but fewer amenities. Call your local real estate professional for more information about sales or rentals (see the Real Estate Sales Firms section at the end of this chapter).

The Four-Wheel-Drive Beaches

CAROVA, NORTH SWAN BEACH, SWAN BEACH, SEAGULL, AND PENNY'S HILL SUBDIVISIONS
Off the paved road north of NC 12

Access to these subdivisions is by four-wheel-drive vehicle only. Depending upon how far north you're heading, you'll drive 5 to 20 minutes once you cross the beach access ramp just north of the Villages at Ocean Hill. (Read the rules of the road.) Although there's no paved road linking these communities to the asphalt in Corolla, once you drive up the beach, you'll discover a network of dirt roads throughout the four-wheel-drive area. Many of these have standing water after heavy rains, so watch for puddles and deep holes. Even though these are some of the widest beaches anywhere, we recommend that you drive at low tide. Some parts of the beach are home to the remains of a petrified forest—an indication of how much this barrier island has migrated throughout the centuries. The black stumps are mysteriously beautiful but can easily puncture a tire. Use extra caution in these areas, especially at night. At one time the beaches were open to vehicular travel clear past the northernmost town of Carova up to Virginia. Driving into Virginia is no longer permitted from here, and a fence and a gate prevent crossing the border. Watch for the wild horses!

Virginia's False Cape State Park borders Carova on the north, and North Swan Beach borders Carova on the south. As you continue southward you come to Swan Beach, Seagull, and Penny's Hill subdivisions. Development began in Carova Beach in 1967, followed by development in North Swan Beach and Swan Beach. Carova Beach is the largest subdivision off the paved road.

Carova consists of approximately 2,000 lots. Resales are available in most areas. There are approximately 400 improved lots from Ocean Hill to the Virginia line and 2,500 property owners, of which a small number are year-round residents. The Seagull and Penny's Hill subdivisions are much smaller than Carova, which offers lots fronting canals, sandy trails, and open water between Currituck Sound and the Atlantic Ocean. Swan Beach and North Swan Beach are ocean-to-sound developments. Ocean Beach and Penny's Hill do not include sound frontage. Basic amenities are offered, including electricity, cable TV, Wi-Fi, telephone service and water/sewer by individual well and septic system. Some mail delivery is available to a bank of locked boxes.

Real estate agents working in Corolla tend to be the most knowledgeable about this area. Find one that specializes. The quality of lots varies widely, and some areas are more prone to erosion than others.

Corolla

OCEAN HILL AND THE VILLAGES AT OCEAN HILL
NC 12, Corolla

Ocean Hill and the Villages at Ocean Hill lie at the northernmost end of the paved road in Corolla. The Villages at Ocean Hill is a unique resort community covering 153 acres, including lakefront, oceanfront, and soundside lots. This development of primarily rental homes is still very much available to the buying public. Amenities include oceanfront and lakefront pools, tennis courts, and a freshwater lake. Wide, white, sandy beaches are also part of the package.

Strict architectural guidelines ensure quality development. The adjacent Ocean Hill has no amenities to speak of, although lot sizes are larger.

COROLLA LIGHT RESORT VILLAGE
NC 12, Corolla

More than 200 acres compose this northern Outer Banks resort. Construction began in 1985, and some very large luxury homes were built here as well as elegant three-bedroom condos and four-bedroom villas. Home sizes range from 1,300 square feet to 3,600 square feet. This beautiful ocean-to-sound resort boasts an oceanfront pool complex, tennis courts scattered throughout the resort, a soundside pool, and an indoor sports center that houses a competition-size indoor pool, tennis courts, racquetball courts, and exercise rooms.

WHALEHEAD BEACH
NC 12, Corolla

Whalehead Beach is the most established beach neighborhood in Corolla. Its wide beaches stretch for more than 3 miles along the ocean and have a dozen public beach-front walkways. Public parking lots are scattered throughout. Though Whalehead doesn't have a central water system (properties have individual wells) and there are few other amenities, its 20,000-square-foot lots are a remarkable draw.

MONTERAY SHORES
NC 12, Corolla

While Whalehead Beach occupies only the east side of NC 12, Monteray Shores is situated on the sound side (or west side) of this northern Outer Banks area. Its Caribbean-style homes have red tile roofs, arched verandas, spacious decks, and an abundance of windows, contrasting with the wooden structures found in most Outer Banks residential communities. But if you prefer Outer Banks–style homes, they also are available here. The community features single-family residences and offers sound or ocean views from every homesite. While there are no oceanfront lots, the full gymnasium, sound-side clubhouse, junior Olympic swimming pool, hot tub, four tennis courts, jogging trails, stocked fishing ponds, boat ramps, and other recreational amenities provide a dash of sophistication.

BUCK ISLAND
NC 12, Corolla

In a small section of the northern Outer Banks lies the exclusive community of Buck Island. This oceanfront and oceanside development is across from the TimBuck II Shopping Village on Ocean Trail. Buck Island is reminiscent of the nautical seaside villages of Kiawah and Nantucket and boasts timeless Charlestonian architecture along a promenade of hardwood trees and turn-of-the-20th-century streetlights. Amenities include a guarded entrance, pristine ocean beach, beach cabana, spa, pool, and tennis courts.

CROWN POINT
NC 12, Corolla

Crown Point is 1 mile north of Ocean Sands and 10 miles north of Duck. This is a single-family subdivision with oceanfront and oceanside properties. It is completely separate from the Ocean Sands subdivision. There are approximately 90 homes here. Amenities include a swimming pool, tennis courts, and private beach-access walkways.

OCEAN SANDS
NC 12, Corolla

Ocean Sands is an oceanside and ocean-front planned unit development, or PUD, considered to be a model of coastal development by land-use planners, government officials, and environmentalists alike. The Ocean Sands concept is centered around clusters of homes that form small colonies buffered by open space. This design eliminates drive-through traffic while increasing privacy and open vistas. Clusters are devoted to single-family dwellings, multifamily dwellings, and appropriate commercial usage. Many of the approximately 600 residences at Ocean Sands are placed in rental programs. Amenities include tennis courts, nature trails, and a fishing lake stocked with bass. The development has guarded private roads. Tucked within Ocean Sands is Ocean Lake, a little neighborhood with a 3-acre lake, tennis courts, and a large swimming pool. Ocean Sands is a family-oriented community buffered on the east by the Atlantic Ocean and on the west by the exclusive Currituck Club community. Lots are 6,000 square feet.

SPINDRIFT OCEAN TRAIL
Near the Currituck Club Corolla

Spindrift is a small gated community with about 30 40,000-square-foot lots—large in comparison to neighboring developments. The single-family residential development offers few amenities, but the privacy here can't be beat. You can build a dream home and be assured you will not be within an arm's length of your neighbor.

THE CURRITUCK CLUB
NC 12, Corolla
(252) 453-9445
www.thecurrituckclub.com

This 600-acre world-class golfing community is bordered by the Currituck Sound and sports an 18-hole championship golf course (see the Golf chapter). Single-family homes, villas, and patio homes are available. The upscale, gated community features tennis, basketball, and volleyball courts; swimming pools; lighted bike and jogging paths; and a full fitness center. Private ocean access is available with a trolley system, and there's even a beach valet service. Overall density is just more than one family per acre. Located in a maritime forest environment, on the grounds of the historic Currituck Shooting Club, the scenery can't be beat. Don't miss touring the development's Mainstreet Corolla model homes.

PINE ISLAND
NC 12, Corolla

Pine Island resort is on 385 acres, with 300 single-family homesites and 3 miles of oceanfront. This planned oceanfront and oceanside community is bordered on the west by 1,500 acres of perpetually preserved marsh, islands, and uplands that compose the National Audubon Society Pine Island Sanctuary. Homesites are generous and have strict architectural guidelines. Central water and sewer and underground utilities are available. Residents have access to a tennis court, two community swimming pools, beach club, jogging paths, and more. Property owners also have access to a private landing strip.

Duck

PALMER'S ISLAND
NC 12, Duck

Located between Pine Island and Sanderling, the exclusive Palmer's Island is an ocean-to-sound community with fewer than 15 homesites. Beach frontage ranges from 120 feet to 225 feet per lot, and the enormous homes are magnificent. This is the narrowest stretch of land on the Outer Banks, so residents have breathtaking views of both the ocean and Currituck Sound. Although no property is available in Palmer's Island, home values begin at several million dollars.

SANDERLING
Duck Road (NC 12), Duck

This ocean-to-sound community several miles north of Duck consists of nearly 300 homes and lots and is one of the most desirable residential communities on the Outer Banks. The heavy vegetation, winding lanes, and abundant wildlife offer the most seclusion of any resort community on the beach. Developers have taken care to leave as much natural growth as possible, and strict building covenants ensure privacy and value. The Sanderling Inn Resort is just north of the residential area.

Home owners have their own recreational amenities, including miles of nature trails, the Soundside Racquet and Swimming Club, and sailing and canoeing opportunities.

PORT TRINITIE
Duck Road (NC 12), Duck

Port Trinitie, situated on 23 acres of ocean-to-sound property, stretches across Duck Road and offers gorgeous soundfront views. Located 2 miles north of Duck, amenities include two swimming pools, two tennis courts, a soundside pier and gazebo, and an oceanfront sitting area. This development began with condominiums, which are co-ownership properties, but Port Trinitie now offers an even mixture of whole ownership single-family dwellings (cottages and townhomes) and co-owned condos.

i A number of real estate developers have on-site model homes open to the public. For an up-close and personal glimpse of some stunning design and architecture, look for the Open House signs. The Outer Banks Home Builders Association also has an annual Parade of Homes. For more information call (252) 449-8232 or check the website at www.obhome builders.org.

SEA RIDGE AND OSPREY
Duck Road (NC 12), Duck

This area, 1.5 miles north of the village of Duck, claims to have the best views on the Outer Banks and has lots and three- and four-bedroom single-family homes available. Natural beauty is this development's calling card.

NORTHPOINT
Duck Road (NC 12), Duck

Fractional ownership is popular at North-Point, though some lots remain for individual ownership and development. Residents enjoy an enclosed swimming pool, tennis and basketball courts, and a long soundfront pier for fishing, crabbing, and small boat dockage. One of the first fractional ownership developments on the northern Outer Banks, North-Point has enjoyed good values on resales.

SHIPS WATCH
1251 Duck Rd. (NC 12), Duck
(252) 261-2231, (800) 261-7924
www.shipswatch.com

Mid-Atlantic Country magazine portrayed this community as "the Palm Beach of the Outer Banks." Ships Watch is a community of luxurious seaside homes on the northernmost

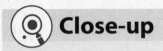

Close-up

Beach House Names

Houses have been given names almost since there have been houses. Literature is full of them, from Emily Brontë's Wuthering Heights to Margaret Mitchell's Tara. Presidential homes are famously named, from Washington's Mount Vernon and Jefferson's Monticello to James Madison's Montpelier.

Beach house names have evolved to have a character all their own, though the first structures weren't named at all. By all accounts, the first Outer Banks beach vacation homes were built in the 1830s by wealthy plantation owners who went to "take the summer waters" on the Outer Banks and thus escape the malarial swamps of their plantations. The popularity of the beach at Nags Head grew, and before the Civil War, there were many summer houses and even a hotel that could accommodate 200 people. Interestingly enough, the hotel didn't seem to have a name, nor did any of the vacation homes, though it is noted that families generally stayed in the cottages in season while the hotel was filled to capacity with unmarried men.

When the modern cottage rental market was in its infancy, it competed with a robust motel market. A 1967 accommodations directory for the Outer Banks lists more than 60 motels and motor lodges, with names like "the Journey's End Motel," "the Sea Oatel," "the Beacon," and "the Sea Ranch." While several hundred individual cottages were available for rent, most were simply referred to by the surname of their owner. Very few motels were named for their owners (the John Yancey Motor Hotel was a notable exception), but cottage courts (groups of two to 10 cottages) seemed to bridge the gap between motels and cottages and often carried both a beachy name as well as the family name, like "Evan's Sun-Fun Cottages" and "Eggleston's Sea Haven."

Beach house owners eventually caught on, and gave their houses names of their own. A Southern Shores rental directory from 1970 listed 95 houses for rent, with only 12 of them named for something other than the owner. The names were fairly straightforward, like "Juniper" and "Surfview," with no fewer than six named "Seashore." By 1977 the same Southern Shores directory listed 180 cottages for rent, and 29 had creative names, including "Southern Comfort," "Rebel Hill," and "Hi Life."

Naming vacation homes today has become the norm (indeed, some rental companies highly recommend a proper name), and these names reflect a wide range of wit, style, and taste. While there are still many called names like "Sea Haven" and "Sun-Fun," others have branched far afield, with names like "Duck Work" and "Life's a Beach." At least three are named for Jimmy Buffet songs, while many use word play and puns, like "Dare-E-Aire," "Duck Down," "Fish Upon a Star," "Katmandunes," "Breaking Winds," and "Seagullable."

Some house names are of dubious etymology, like "Conch Potato," seemingly named for the mispronunciation of the conch shell, a name often erroneously given to the locally found whelk. One house is called "We Ge," and is said to have once been called "Wet Age," but was renamed after it lost a couple of letters.

Other names only shine when you know their story. One family owns a beach house and a sound house and calls them "Sunrise" and "Sunset," respectively. One house in Southern Shores is named "Checkmate." The owners were a retired Air Force family who had moved many times in their career. The matriarch of the family swore the move to the Outer Banks would be her last, and she named the house "Checkmate," representative of their final and best move.

end of the village of Duck. Complete service, home maintenance, and attention to details are characteristics of this resort. Carefully placed on high rolling dunes, the homes offer spectacular views of the ocean, Currituck Sound, or both. An Olympic-size pool, tennis courts, jogging trail, soundside pier and boat ramp, and weekly socials offer entertainment options for the whole family. Full concierge service includes arranging tee times, dinner reservations, and babysitting. The resort provides rentals, along with fractional and whole ownership. Fractional, one-tenth deeded ownerships are available. Developer Buck Thornton and his associates have experienced great success with this high-end resort. Contact Ships Watch for sales and rental information.

SEA PINES
Duck Road (NC 12), Duck
Sea Pines is a 61-lot development tucked away in the heart of Duck. Lot sizes for this oceanside village range from 15,000 to 20,000 square feet. There still are lots to choose, including some with ocean views from upper-level living areas. Amenities include a swimming pool and tennis court.

SCHOONER RIDGE BEACH CLUB
Duck Road (NC 12), Duck
Schooner Ridge is in the heart of Duck, but its oceanfront/oceanside homes are well hidden from the hustle and bustle. The high, sandy hills fronting the Atlantic Ocean are perfect for these large single-family homes with ample windows and decks. All lots are sold, but resales are available. The community offers indoor and outdoor recreational amenities. Bike paths wind through the area, and the shops in the village are within walking distance.

NANTUCKET VILLAGE
Duck Road (NC 12), Duck
Nantucket is an upscale private resort consisting of 35 large condominiums with garages and spacious decking. Situated on a high hill overlooking Currituck Sound, these units have panoramic views and magnificent sunsets. The year-round development offers an indoor pool and tennis court as well as sandy soundfront beaches, a pier with gazebo, and boat launch facilities. The sound beach is ideal for wading, children's activities, crabbing, fishing, windsurfing, and other watercraft sports. Units in two luxury duplex condominium buildings have about 1,750 square feet of living space, two-car garages, three bedrooms, two-and-a-half baths, gas fireplaces, and panoramic water views.

OCEAN CREST
Duck Road (NC 12), Duck
Near Nantucket Village, Ocean Crest is an ocean-to-sound resort consisting of 54 lots of 15,000 square feet or larger zoned for single-family dwellings. This is an upscale neighborhood with strict architectural guidelines. Homes must be 2,000 square feet or larger. Amenities include a swimming pool, tennis courts, private ocean access, and good water views.

Kitty Hawk

MARTIN'S POINT
US 158, MP 0, Kitty Hawk
Martin's Point is an exclusive waterfront community of custom homes and homesites with stringent building requirements, a guarded entry, and some of the most beautiful maritime forests found anywhere. Homes range from 1,200 square feet to 13,000 square feet. This primarily year-round neighborhood features a marina, dock, and

pier on the Currituck Sound. Owners have easy access to the local elementary school, shopping, and golf.

When you arrive on the Outer Banks at the eastern terminus of the Wright Memorial Bridge, the entrance to Martin's Point is on your immediate left. The community is closed to drive-through inspections, but if you're considering a permanent move to the Outer Banks, it's an upscale area you should look at.

SOUTHERN SHORES
US 158 and NC 12, Kitty Hawk

Southern Shores is a unique 2,600-acre incorporated town with its own government and police force. Although there are two shopping centers on its western boundary, commercial zoning/development is not allowed elsewhere. The town has dense maritime forests along the soundside fringe, wide-open sand hills in the middle, and beachfront property. The substantial year-round population attests to the popularity of Southern Shores. Kitty Hawk Land Company has carefully paced development through the years, and there are still many vacant lots. Southern Shores is considered one of the most desirable places to live on the Outer Banks.

KITTY HAWK LANDING
West Kitty Hawk Road, Kitty Hawk

This is a residential community with mostly year-round home owners. It's on the far western edges of Kitty Hawk. To get there, turn west off US 158 at milepost 4 onto West Kitty Hawk Road and just keep driving until you see the signs. The community borders Currituck Sound. It has deep canals, tall pines, and gorgeous sunsets.

SANDPIPER CAY CONDOMINIUMS
Sand Dune Drive, Kitty Hawk
(252) 261-2188

This resort community consists of 280 condominium units and is near Sea Scape Golf Course. About 155 of the units are second homes; some 40 percent of the units are either long-term rentals or primary residences, making this a year-round resort. Some units are available for short-term or weekly leases. All the original inventory has been sold, though some resales are available. Amenities include a large outdoor pool, clubhouse, and tennis court. Homeowner fees apply. Contact Sandpiper Cay for more information.

Kill Devil Hills

FIRST FLIGHT VILLAGE
First Street, Kill Devil Hills

This is one of the Outer Banks' most popular year-round neighborhoods in the central area of the beach. The entrance to First Flight Village is on the west side of US 158 at milepost 7½. This is a family-oriented neighborhood, so if you're considering a permanent move to the Outer Banks with kids in tow, you should investigate this community. First Flight Village real estate is considered moderately priced.

Colington Island

COLINGTON HARBOUR
Colington Road, Colington Island

Colington Island is a popular spot for families and boaters. To get there turn off US 158 at the stoplight just south of the Wright Brothers National Memorial onto Colington Road. Colington Harbour is about 4 miles down the winding road.

The community has some 12 miles of bulk-headed deepwater canals and soundfront lots, all easily accessing Albemarle Sound. Oregon Inlet, the closest ocean inlet, is approximately 25 miles by boat south of Colington Island. Choices range from extremely affordable starter homes to upscale soundfront or canal-front homes with private boat docks. This community combines a year-round population of more than 2,000, with seasonal and weekly renters. The picnic area, playground, sandy beach on Kitty Hawk Bay, boat ramp, boat slips for rent, and fuel dock are available to all residents, including year-round renters. Clubhouse activities, an Olympic-size swimming pool, a children's pool, and a tennis court are available to club members. What makes Colington Harbour popular is its private entry and the many canals that offer waterfront living to many residents. Colington Harbour is one of the best places to keep a deep-draft boat.

COLINGTON HEIGHTS
Colington Island

This subdivision is within Colington Harbour. There are 23 lots on approximately 35 acres. The inventory includes wooded interior lots, waterview lots, and waterfront properties. Essentially this is a maritime forest development. Large 3-acre lot sizes contribute to the area's privacy. Roads are private, and there is private beach access on Albemarle Sound. Architectural controls are in effect, and the developer has paid all of the water-impact fees, making the real estate even more attractive.

WATER'S EDGE
Off Colington Road, Colington Island
(252) 261-2131, (800) 488-0738
www.outerbankshome.com/
waters-edge.asp

Water's Edge is a gated, year-round residential neighborhood on Colington Island. The community has a swimming pool, marina, and boat ramp with access to Roanoke Sound and its own owners' association. Sales are handled exclusively by Kitty Hawk Land Company.

Nags Head

SOUTH RIDGE
Off US 158, MP 13, Nags Head
(252) 441-2800

This 42-acre parcel is a no-frills community with 140 homesites on the hill behind the Nags Head Post Office. The development features quarter-acre ocean- and soundview lots but no soundfront property.

THE VILLAGE AT NAGS HEAD
US 158, MP 15, Nags Head
(252) 441-8533, sales
www.villagerealtyobx.com

The Ammons Corporation began developed this ocean-to-sound community, which has become one of the best sellers on the Outer Banks. The golf course (with a beautiful clubhouse and popular restaurant) and the oceanfront recreational complex with tennis courts and an outdoor pool make this attractive residential community most desirable. Single-family homes and townhomes provide something for everyone. The oceanfront homes are some of the largest and most luxurious anywhere. There's plenty to do here. It's an excellent choice for beach living, or vacation rentals.

Roanoke Island

PIRATE'S COVE
Nags Head–Manteo Causeway, Manteo
(252) 473-1451, (800) 762-0245
Pirate's Cove is a distinctive residential marina resort community. Hundreds of acres of protected wildlife marshlands border Pirate's Cove on one side, while the peaceful waters of Roanoke Sound are on the other. Deepwater canals provide each owner with a dock at the door, and the centrally located marina is home to many large yachts and fishing boats. They offer homesites, homes, condominiums, and "dockominiums" fronting deepwater canals. Activities abound. Fishing tournaments seem as important as sleeping to many of the residents, with locals and visitors getting in on the fun. Other recreational amenities include a hot tub, sauna, fitness center, restaurant, and beautifully appointed clubhouse, plus swimming pools and lighted tennis courts. Scheduled recreational activities for all ages are available. One of the prettiest Outer Banks settings enhances the Victorian nautical design of these homes.

SHALLOWBAG BAY CLUB
US 64/264, Manteo
(252) 261-5500, (800) 395-2525
www.pirates-cove.com/shallowbag.htm
Manteo's newest development, this luxury condominium complex and marina has breathtaking views. There are 60 luxury three-bedroom condos in the Harbor and 17 condo suites in the Point. Amenities include 91 private boat slips, a full-service marina, a waterfront restaurant, fitness center, pool and hot tub, meeting room, water taxi to downtown Manteo, and clubhouse.

Association fees are charged to owners. The entrance to Shallow-bag Bay Club is on US 64/264, right behind McDonald's.

ROANOAK VILLAGE
Manteo
Roanoak Village offers options for building a variety of homes ranging in size from 860 to 2,100 square feet. The development is being built in three phases and encompasses nearly 8 acres with a potential of 57 homesites. Interiors range from two-bedroom, one-bath styles to four-bedroom, two-and-a-half-bath homes. Some models feature hardwood floors. For the new neighborhood, local architect John Wilson IV designed approximately 10 house plans in keeping with the older building styles still evident in downtown Manteo, giving the project a homey feel with a historic thrust. The neighborhood is within walking distance of Roanoke Island's bike trails, the public library, local churches, town, and the Manteo waterfront.

HERITAGE POINT
Pearce Road, Northern Roanoke Island
(252) 473-1450
This year-round resort community is subdivided into 111 lots off US 64/264 next to Fort Raleigh National Historic Site. Restrictive covenants are in place. Interior, soundview, and soundfront lots overlooking the Croatan and Albemarle Sounds are available. Lot sizes range from a half acre to more than three-and-a-half acres. Each lot has a boat slip, and there is a fishing pier for home owners. The community sports two tennis courts, and a parking area and common beach are provided. Homeowner association fees apply.

THE PENINSULA
Russell Twiford Road, Manteo
(252) 453-3600
This exclusive boating community includes 34 private waterfront homesites with a lighted dock in excess of 2,000 feet, a boat ramp, a pump-out station, deepwater canals, and three gazebos over the water. These homes on the Manteo sewage system feature looped water lines to prevent sediment buildup. Homes have direct access to the sound. Some covenant restrictions apply.

Hatteras Island

RESORT RODANTHE
Rodanthe Drive, off NC 12, Rodanthe
This resort consists of one building with 12 two-bed and 8 one-bed condominium units. Views of the ocean and sound vary by unit. Lower floor units have sound views. The condos are for sale, but owners also rent them. Amenities include a swimming pool and private ocean access.

HATTERAS HIGH CONDOMINIUMS
Resort Rodanthe Drive, off NC 12, Rodanthe
Hatteras High features four oceanfront condominium buildings with 12 units in each. These two-bed, two-bath condos connect to the beach by boarded walkway. A swimming pool is behind the buildings.

MIRLO BEACH
NC 12, Rodanthe
This sound-to-oceanfront resort community is 12 miles south of the Oregon Inlet Bridge, adjacent to Pea Island National Wildlife Refuge. There are approximately 10 large oceanfront cottages in Mirlo Beach, each of which comfortably sleeps an average of 12.

Amenities include tennis courts and private beach and sound accesses. This resort has a solid rental history.

ST. WAVES
NC 12, Waves
This subdivision was developed during the 1980s. Properties offer ocean, sound, and lake views. The homes are upscale, and architectural controls are in effect. Amenities include a swimming pool, a tennis court, and a centrally located lake. St. Waves maintains an excellent rental history.

KINNAKEET SHORES
NC 12, Avon
Once a desolate stretch of narrow land between the Atlantic Ocean and Pamlico Sound, Kinnakeet Shores is a residential community being quickly developed. It consists of 500 acres next to beautiful marshlands and one of the best windsurfing areas in the world. Recreational amenities include swimming pools and tennis courts. This is the largest development on Hatteras Island, and the homes tend to be big, reminding us of the ones on the northern beaches. This is primarily a second-home development, offering one of the most popular rental programs on the island.

HATTERAS PINES
NC 12, Buxton
This 150-acre subdivision nestles in a maritime forest in the heart of Buxton. It consists of 114 wooded lots rolling along the dunes and ridges. The roads for this development are intact, along with protective covenants. A pool and tennis court are part of the package.

REAL ESTATE

SUNSET VILLAGE
Sunset Strip, Frisco
(252) 995-3313
www.landsendinc.com

Only a few homesites are currently available in this new soundside community, but the area is beginning to develop. Lots come with a deeded boat slip.

HATTERAS LANDING
NC 12, Hatteras Village

This development features 41 homesites, a restaurant, gift shop, bookstore, deli, convenience store, coffee shop, clothing stores, and other retail opportunities. Home owners have access to the on-site Holiday Inn Express pool. Oceanfront and soundfront lots are available. Home owners build the homes of their choice.

HATTERAS BY THE SEA
NC 12, Hatteras Village

This rather small community of 36 lots on 25 acres is one of the last oceanfront areas available for residential living. The southern end of the Outer Banks has little land, and a good portion is preserved by the national seashore designation. A large pool and some carefully designed nature paths are included. Sunrise and sunset views are unobstructed here.

Ocracoke Island

OCRACOKE HORIZON CONDOMINIUMS
Silver Lake Road, Ocracoke
(252) 928-5711

These five soundfront condominiums were developed by Midgett Realty in Hatteras but are handled by Sandy Shores Realty on Ocracoke Island. Features include 2 two-bedroom and 3 three-bedroom units with either two or two-and-a-half baths and

whirlpool tubs. The units overlook Pamlico Sound and Portsmouth Island. Sales and rentals are available.

TIME-SHARING

Time-sharing is a deeded transaction under the jurisdiction of the North Carolina Real Estate Commission. A deeded share is $\frac{1}{52}$ of the unit property being purchased (one week of a year). This deed grants the right to use the property in perpetuity. Always ask if the property you're inspecting is a deeded time-share because there is such a thing as undeeded time-shares—these give the right to use a property, but the property reverts to the developer in the end.

What you buy in a time-share is the right to use a specific piece of real estate for a week per year. The weeks are either fixed at the time of sale or rotate yearly. Members trade their weeks for different time slots at a variety of locations around the world. Qualifying for the purchase of a time-share unit can be no more difficult than qualifying for a credit card, but be aware of financing charges that are higher than regular mortgages.

Most time-share resorts on the Outer Banks are multifamily constructions with recreational amenities varying from minimal to luxurious and sometimes include the services of a recreational director. Time-share units usually come furnished and carry a monthly maintenance fee. Tax advantages for ownership and financing are not available to the purchaser of a time-share.

Many time-share ventures offer "free week-ends"—you agree to a sales pitch and tour of the facilities in exchange for accommodations. Listen, ask questions, and stay in control of your money and your particular situation. If you get swept away, you'll only have five days to change your mind, according to the North Carolina Time Share Act that governs the sale of time-shares.

It is best to keep the purchase of time-shares in proper perspective; your deeded share only enables you to vacation in that property during a designated time period each year for as long as you own that share. This makes time-share very different from other potential investments.

All real estate investment decisions require thorough research and planning, and time-share is no exception. Time-share salespeople are licensed (to everyone's advantage) and earn commissions. Some great arrangements are out there, while others are not so good. Check thoroughly before buying. Several Outer Banks companies specialize in time-sharing. The following list includes some of these.

BARRIER ISLAND OCEAN PINES
NC 12, Duck
(252) 261-3525
Ocean Pines offers time-sharing opportunities featuring oceanfront one- and two-bedroom condominiums. Amenities include an indoor pool, tennis courts, whirlpool tubs, and, of course, the beach.

BARRIER ISLAND STATION
NC 12, Duck
(252) 261-3525
Barrier Island, one of the largest time-share resorts on the Outer Banks, is on a high dune area of ocean-to-sound property. These are multifamily units of wood construction.

There is an attractive, full-service restaurant and bar with a soundside sailing center, in addition to the beach. A full-time recreation director is on board for a variety of planned activities and events. Indoor swimming, tennis courts, and other recreational facilities round out a full amenities package. This is a popular resort in a just-as-popular seaside village.

BARRIER ISLAND STATION AT KITTY HAWK
1 Cypress Knee Trail, Kitty Hawk
(252) 261-4610
www.bistation.com
Barrier Island Station at Kitty Hawk is a multifamily vacation ownership resort set in a maritime forest. The 100 acres of private land sport a million-dollar sports complex featuring an indoor pool, free weights, circuit training, and aerobic and massage facilities. Shoot pool or play table tennis in the game room. Condominiums have one, two, or three bedrooms. The community is near two shopping centers.

SEA SCAPE BEACH AND GOLF VILLAS
US 158, MP 2½, Kitty Hawk
(252) 261-3837
There are plenty of recreational opportunities here: tennis courts, three swimming pools, an indoor recreation facility, an exercise room, and a game room. The villas are next to the Sea Scape golf course. The two-bed, two-bath units are of wood construction, and they are on the west side of US 158. Sea Scape offers a unique opportunity for time-share ownership and an active rental program.

OUTER BANKS BEACH CLUB
NC 12, MP 9, Kill Devil Hills
(252) 441-6321
The round, wooden buildings of the Outer Banks Beach Club were the first time-sharing opportunities built and sold on the Outer

Banks. The 160 units include oceanfront and oceanside units, plus clubhouse units across the Beach Road, near the clubhouse and its indoor pool. There are two outdoor pools in great oceanfront locations. One-, two-, and three-bedroom units have access to whirlpools, tennis courts, and a playground. There is a full-time recreation director offering a variety of activities and games.

OUTER BANKS RESORT RENTALS
Croatan Centre, MP 13½, Nags Head
(252) 441-2134
This company deals exclusively with timeshares, handling rentals and resales at all the time-share complexes on the Outer Banks. All the units this company represents are furnished and self-contained, and all have swimming pools.

DUNES SOUTH BEACH AND
RACQUET CLUB
NC 12, MP 18, Nags Head
(252) 441-4090
Townhome time-sharing at this resort features two- and three-bedroom units with fireplaces, washers and dryers, and whirlpool tubs. The 20 units are mostly oceanfront; the remainder of the units are oceanside. A pool, tennis court, putting green, and playground make up the recreational amenities.

REAL ESTATE SALES FIRMS

Following are some Outer Banks real estate sales companies, their locations, and contact information. While this list is not all-inclusive, it is representative of reputable real estate sales companies on the Outer Banks. Most, if not all, of these companies are members of the Outer Banks Association of Realtors.

RIGGS REALTY
Austin Building, 1152 Ocean Trail,
NC 12, Corolla
(252) 453-3111
www.riggsrealtycorp.com
Riggs specializes in northern beach land and home properties, especially in the fourwheel-drive areas like Swan, North Swan, and Carova Beach. Riggs Realty has 30-something years of real estate experience.

TWIDDY & COMPANY REALTORS
NC 12, Duck
(252) 261-8311, (800) 342-1609
www.twiddy.com
Twiddy represents properties from Carova through Kitty Hawk. Another location is at NC 12 and Second Street, Corolla, (252) 453-3325, (800) 579-6130.

STAN WHITE REALTY &
CONSTRUCTION
812 Ocean Trail, Corolla
(252) 453-3161, (800) 753-6200
www.builderouterbanks.com
Stan White represents properties from Corolla to Hatteras Village. Another location is at US 158, MP 10½, Nags Head, (252) 441-1515, (800) 753-9699.

BEACH REALTY & CONSTRUCTION/
KITTY HAWK RENTALS
790-B NC 12, Corolla
(252) 453-3131
www.beachrealtync.com
Steve Blaisdell is one of the expert consultants at Beach Realty, which handles real estate sales, rentals, and construction. The firm represents property from Carova to South Nags Head. Other locations are at: 1450 NC 12, Duck, (252) 261-6600; US 158, MP 2, Kitty Hawk, (252) 261-3815, (800)

849-9888; and US 158, Kill Devil Hills, (252) 441-1106.

KARICHELE REALTY
66 Sunset Blvd., TimBuck II, NC 12, Corolla
(252) 453-4400, (800) 453-2377
www.karichele.com
Karichele covers properties from the Virginia line to Nags Head.

STAN WHITE REALTY
NC 12, Duck
(252) 261-2224, (800) 992-2976
www.outerbanksrentals.com
Stan White Realty represents property from Corolla to Nags Head.

SOUTHERN SHORES REALTY
NC 12, Southern Shores
(252) 261-2000, (800) 334-1000
www.southernshores.com
Southern Shores Realty represents properties from Corolla to Nags Head.

JOE LAMB JR. & ASSOCIATES, REALTORS
US 158, MP 2, Kitty Hawk
(252) 261-4444, (800) 552-6257
www.joelambjr.com
Joe Lamb represents properties from northern Duck to South Nags Head.

KITTY HAWK LAND COMPANY
US 158, Kitty Hawk
(252) 261-2131, (800) 488-0738
www.kittyhawklandcompany.com
Kitty Hawk Land Company has been in the real estate business for more than 50 years. KHL is credited with developing Southern Shores, Spindrift on the Currituck Outer Banks, WatersEdge on Colington Island, Sea Pines and Oceancrest in Duck, and the Currituck Club in Corolla. They offer properties within these developments as well as select listings of outside properties on the Outer Banks.

OUTER BANKS VACATION REALTY
US 158, MP 2½, Kitty Hawk
(252) 261-5500, (866) 884-0267
www.outerbanksvacations.com
Properties from Kitty Hawk to South Nags Head are offered through Outer Banks Vacation Realty.

KITTY DUNES REALTY
US 158, MP 5, Kitty Hawk
(252) 261-2173

COROLLA LIGHT TOWN CENTER
Unit 1110, Corolla
(252) 453-DUNE
www.kittydunes.com
Kitty Dunes represents Corolla to South Nags Head. This company also owns Colington Realty. Residents of Canada can contact the Canadian representative at (514) 252-9566.

JIM PERRY & COMPANY
Executive Center, US 158, MP 5½, Kill Devil Hills
(252) 441-3051, (800) 222-6135
www.jimperry.com
Jim Perry represents properties in all areas of the Outer Banks.

RE/MAX OCEAN REALTY
US 158, MP 6, Kill Devil Hills
(252) 441-2450
www.obxrealtor.com
RE/MAX represents properties from Corolla to Hatteras Village.

HARRELL AND ASSOCIATES
US 158, MP 7, Kill Devil Hills
(252) 441-7887
www.harrellandassociates.com
This company specializes in property throughout Dare County, including commercial and residential listings, plus many condominiums.

COLINGTON REALTY
2141 Colington Rd., Colington Island
(252) 441-3863
www.colingtonrealty.com
Colington Realty specializes in Colington Harbour properties.

SUN REALTY
US 158, MP 9, Kill Devil Hills
(252) 441-8011
www.sunrealty.com
This realty represents properties throughout the Outer Banks. Other locations are at: NC 12, Corolla, (252) 453-8811; NC 12, Duck, (252) 261-4183; US 158, Kitty Hawk, (252) 261-3892; NC 12, Salvo, (252) 987-2755; and NC 12, Avon, (252) 995-5821.

GATEWAY REALTY
2808 North Croatan Hwy., Nags Head
(252) 480-0093, (800) 633-4491
www.gatewayobx.com
Gateway specializes in sales, long-term rentals, and property management from North Currituck beaches to South Nags Head.

NAGS HEAD REALTY
US 158, MP 10½, Nags Head
(252) 441-4311, (800) 222-1531
www.nagsheadrealty.com
Nags Head Realty represents property from Corolla to Oregon Inlet.

COVE REALTY
Between NC 12 and US 158 MP 14,
Nags Head
(252) 441-6391, (800) 635-7007
www.coverealty.com
Cove represents Nags Head and South Nags Head and specializes in Old Nags Head Cove.

VILLAGE REALTY
US 158, MP 14½, Nags Head
(252) 480-2224, (800) 548-9688
www.villagerealtyobx.com
Village Realty represents properties from Corolla through South Nags Head.

PIRATE'S COVE
Nags Head–Manteo Causeway, Manteo
(252) 473-1451, (800) 762-0245
www.pirates-cove.com
The realty arm of Pirate's Cove Yacht Club represents properties in this boating paradise.

MIDGETT REALTY
NC 12, Rodanthe
(252) 987-2350
www.midgettrealty.com
Midgett Realty represents properties on the southern end of the Outer Banks. Other locations are at: NC 12, Avon, (252) 995-5333; and NC 12, Hatteras Village, (252) 986-2841, (800) 527-2903.

SURF OR SOUND REALTY
NC 12, Rodanthe
(252) 987-1444, (800) 237-1138
www.surforsound.com
Surf or Sound represents properties from Rodanthe to Hatteras Village. Another location is at NC 12, Avon, (252) 995-6052.

CAPE ESCAPE
NC 12, Salvo
(252) 987-2336, (800) 996-2336
www.capeescaperealty.com
Cape Escape, across from the local post office, handles sales in Rodanthe, Waves, and Salvo.

OUTER BEACHES REALTY
NC 12, Waves
(252) 987-1102, (800) 627-3750
www.outerbeaches.com
Outer Beaches Realty specializes in properties throughout Hatteras Island. Other locations are at: NC 12, Avon, (252) 995-6041, (800) 627-3150; and NC 12, Hatteras, (252) 986-1105, (888) 627-3650.

HATTERAS REALTY
NC 12, Avon
(252) 995-5466, (800) HATTERA
www.hatterasrealty.com
Hatteras Realty covers residential and commercial lots and homes on Hatteras Island.

DOLPHIN REALTY
NC 12, Hatteras Village
(252) 986-2562, (800) 338-4775
www.dolphin-realty.com
This company provides real estate properties in the villages of Avon, Buxton, Frisco, and Hatteras for buyers and sellers on Hatteras Island.

OCRACOKE ISLAND REALTY
NC 12, Ocracoke
(252) 928-6261, (252) 928-7411
www.ocracokeislandrealty.com
Ocracoke Island Realty represents Ocracoke Island properties.

RETIREMENT

When some people dream of retirement, they might picture themselves strolling along stretches of deserted beaches on a mild winter afternoon. Perhaps later they would enjoy a round of golf with friends on an award-winning course to be followed by a good meal at one of many area restaurants. Sound too good to be true? It's possible right here on the Outer Banks. But beware, this isn't your normal retirement community! The retirees here eagerly pursue an active lifestyle, participating in the many activities the beach has to offer. Many seniors also enjoy working with the public, filling a spot in the workplace through retail sales or other tourist-oriented jobs. As for fun activities, the senior centers offer all kinds of group trips and classes.

If you're thinking of retiring to the Outer Banks, you're in good company. Each year it seems that more retirees are lured to these barrier islands by some sort of siren call. Moderate winters (remarkably quiet due to the small year-round population) provide for a tranquil environment, and 90-plus miles of broad, soft-sand beaches might figure into the equation as well. North Carolina is now the third most attractive state to retirees, after Florida and Arizona.

These are retirement locations that tend to attract early-retiring baby boomers who are seeking out relatively remote areas on the water where outdoor recreation is an integral part of life. Options for any type of dwelling abound all along the Outer Banks. If you're looking for a seaside mansion in a gated community, you'll find it. And if your tastes lean more toward a bungalow in the woods or to a traditional three-bedroom home with a yard, you'll find those, too.

OVERVIEW

If you're looking for property, check out the Real Estate and Area Overview chapters before you start shopping. For information on our community's senior services, read on.

Seniors are encouraged to participate in the Outer Banks Senior Games sponsored by Dare County Older Adult Services. But be warned, these senior athletes are a dedicated and talented bunch, capable of putting much younger athletes to shame. This is a year-round program to promote health and fitness for Dare County residents age 55 and older. Competition events include track and field, bicycle racing, swimming, tennis, bowling, golf, softball and football throwing, basketball shooting, archery, shuffleboard, billiards, horseshoes, and croquet. Medal winners automatically qualify to compete at the North Carolina Senior Games in September. Besides athletics, there is a Silver

Competition for the visual and performing arts. See the listings in the Annual Events chapter under April, or call the Thomas A. Baum Center, (252) 441-1811, for more information.

i **You don't have to limit yourself to the senior centers to socialize. Cultural arts nonprofit groups such as the Theatre of Dare, Dare County Arts Council, and Outer Banks Forum offer plenty of opportunities for you to volunteer your time and offer your expertise. See the Arts & Culture chapter for more information.**

SENIOR CENTERS

THOMAS A. BAUM CENTER
300 Mustian St., Kill Devil Hills
(252) 441-1181
The Thomas A. Baum Center is named after a Dare County native who was a pioneer in ferry transportation. His daughter, Diane Baum St. Clair, arranged for the town of Kill Devil Hills to purchase the land, known locally as the Baum Tract, on very generous terms. Dare County bought a section of the land, which today is home to the senior center, water plant, library, two public schools, the local chamber of commerce, and the town's administration and water departments.

The senior center was dedicated in 1987. The 10,000-square-foot-plus building houses the senior center and the county's older adult services. A handful of paid staff and countless senior volunteers operate the center, which is the hub for senior activity north of Hatteras Island. Dare County residents or property owners who are age 55 or older may use the center for free; if you are younger than age 55 but your spouse meets the age requirement, you also may use the center.

The facility includes a multipurpose room with a stage where the center's drama group, Center Front, performs various productions annually. The Outer Banks Senior Chorus, which performs two concerts per year, also uses this room for practice sessions. The Baum Center is home to the Wright Tappers, a seniors tap-dancing group, and the Dare Devils, the official cheerleaders for the Outer Banks Senior Games. Line- and square-dance groups round out the foot-tapping activities. And going hand in hand with its name, the multipurpose room does double-duty for aerobic classes three days a week.

A full-service kitchen is used for social functions and fund-raisers such as the popular annual eat-in or take-out spaghetti supper. The center does not offer daily lunches on the premises.

Head to the lounge to chat, relax, or read a paperback book borrowed from the center's honor-system library. Adjacent to the lounge is the game room, where you can play bridge weekly, work puzzles, play cribbage or canasta, or sit in on seminars in history, tax aid, or health education, to name a few. The center also hosts support-group meetings for such organizations as the Outer Banks Cancer Support Group and the Amputee Coalition of Coastal Carolina. Twice a month seniors gather at the center for an afternoon movie with popcorn.

If you're an outdoor lover, eat lunch on the deck or watch for resident deer and foxes. Five picnic tables and various chairs encourage relaxation or conversation. The nearby yard is host to a football target that tests throwing accuracy, horseshoe pits, and spin-casting targets. Outer Banks Senior

Games contenders practice discus and shot put as well as archery using bales of hay for targets.

The recreation room comes alive as competitors play a leisurely game of billiards, table tennis, or shuffleboard. There's plenty of elbow room in this spacious area, complete with three pool tables, two Ping-Pong tables, and several huge, floor-painted shuffleboard games. Coffee is available in the kitchenette just off the recreation room, and cups are in the cabinet. Donations are welcome. Bring your lunch and store it in the refrigerator or heat it in the microwave.

Off the rec room is a craft room complete with two sinks, a projector, storage space, seven tables with four chairs each, and a sewing machine. Check the center's newsletter, *Senior Soundings,* for craft courses and special activities that take place in this room. The newsletter comes out by the 15th of the month and is available at both county senior centers and the three public libraries.

The center has an information and referral room where you can sign up for programs on preparing healthful food, bird watching, growing perennials, and acrylic painting. Some activities have a small supplies fee; scholarships are available. A wall of pamphlets cover topics such as taxes, health, and fire safety. Countywide information is available via the computerized Senior Connection information and referral system. Questions on Alzheimer's disease, in-home services, marriage licenses, and the like can be answered by using this program staffed by trained volunteers.

A small computer room is set up with Internet connections. An exercise suite features a treadmill, a rowing machine, and four stationary bicycles, and a staff exercise specialist offers regular exercise programs.

Seniors can take advantage of the center's 20-seat conference room complete with a telephone and white marker board. Community groups also use this space from time to time.

The senior center plays a vital role in providing transportation for elderly and disabled Dare County residents. A paid staff member is on hand at the center to schedule free rides to doctor appointments and hospitals in Chesapeake and Norfolk, Virginia, as well as Greenville, North Carolina. The transportation volunteer needs 24 hours' notice.

Rides also are available for shopping trips and getting to and from the center and to the nutrition site at Mount Olivet United Methodist Church in Manteo, where lunch is served Monday through Friday. Seniors are asked to make a $1 donation, but it's not mandatory. Menu selections may include herb-baked chicken with mixed vegetables and rice pilaf or spaghetti with a tossed salad. Two-percent milk and dessert top off the meal. The meals are prepared off the premises by the Columbia 4-H center. A day's notice is all they need to make sure the food count is correct. If you can't make it to the luncheon, home delivery is available.

The Baum Center is open Mon through Fri from 8:30 a.m. until 5 p.m. and for special functions.

FESSENDEN CENTER
NC 12, Buxton
(252) 995-3888

The Fessenden Center offers services and programs for county residents and property owners of all ages, although you must be age 55 or older to participate in the older adult activities for free. However, the center schedules activities, such as aerobic classes, for adults of all ages for various fees.

The building has a gym with a basketball court. The center operates as a senior center and a site for youth athletic activities. The gym is open from 3 to 5 p.m. Mon through Fri. You can enjoy basketball and volleyball as well as fishing, believe it or not. Throw a line in the creek off the back deck—chances are you'll snag a puppy drum (juvenile channel bass).

The full-service kitchen/conference room is available for preparing meals. Every second and fourth Thursday of the month, seniors attend a luncheon. The second Thursday lunch is prepared at the center by seniors; the fourth Thursday lunch is a covered-dish affair. Funds for the lunches are provided by Festivities, a volunteer senior group that raises money by running the center's concession stand at athletic functions. Seniors contribute a $1 donation if they are able. The kitchen/ conference room does double duty as a county meeting facility.

The center also sports an activity room, a sitting room, and a library. Seniors are invited to hone their skills at the outdoor tennis courts or play with grandchildren at the on-site playground. The soccer and baseball fields give them plenty of room to stretch or jog.

Adults can participate in organized step aerobics, toning and stretching, abdominal exercise, tae kwon do, tai chi, walking, basketball, and dance. Take Spanish or sign language classes; attend seminars, workshops, and classes on fire safety, cardiac rehabilitation, credit fraud, nutrition, home decorating, quilting, and painting; or take cultural arts trips to shows and parks outside the area. Minimal fees are attached for supplies ($5 to $10).

Transportation is available through the center's coordinator by calling the center's main number. Shopping trips are scheduled for seniors and disabled adults with transportation problems. Rides are available to medical appointments and out-of-town hospitals and doctors' offices in Norfolk and Chesapeake, Virginia, as well as Elizabeth City, Nags Head, and Greenville, North Carolina.

The Fessenden Center is open Mon through Fri from 8:30 a.m. to 5 p.m. and weekends for youth and special activities.

i The local chapter of SCORE (Service Corps Of Retired Executives) provides free counseling on business matters such as putting together a marketing plan, starting a business, compiling financial statements, computerizing an office, obtaining small business loans, and expanding business plans. Weekly sessions are held on Tuesday at the Outer Banks Chamber of Commerce in Kill Devil Hills. For more information call the chamber of commerce: (252) 441-8144.

SENIOR SERVICES

HELPING HAND
Manteo Police Department
410 Ananias Dare St., Manteo
(252) 473-2069
Working from a list of voluntary participants, Manteo officers check on more than 70 elderly or disabled citizens twice a week in person or by phone to make sure they are healthy and their needs are being met. The town list is divided among the officers, who prefer to go in person but telephone from time to time. Participants include seniors, disabled individuals, and persons who live alone. This program is particularly useful in a community like the Outer Banks, where

storms occasionally threaten the coast and require residents to evacuate. Officers are in such close contact with the community that they are able to alert homebound individuals in the event of a weather emergency. If you're interested in being on the Helping Hands list, call the police department. Anyone there will give you more information on this free service.

LITTLE GROVE UNITED METHODIST CHURCH MONTHLY LUNCHEON
NC 12, Frisco
(252) 986-2149
Little Grove usually has a luncheon the third Thursday of the month for anyone interested in food and fellowship. The luncheon includes singing and storytelling that begins at 11:30 a.m. Call the above number on the Monday before the third Thursday of the month to reserve your space. Donations are appreciated.

EDUCATION & CHILD CARE

Education has evolved since the days when some Outer Banks kids paddled their skiffs to the one-room schoolhouse. Today there are more than 4,700 students attending 11 schools on the Outer Banks, 10 in Dare County and 1 on Ocracoke Island.

Higher education opportunities on the Outer Banks include a community college campus, College of the Albemarle, in Manteo. COA provides associate degrees, certificates, and diplomas, and many of the hours are transferable to other colleges. Some students make a 45-minute commute to Elizabeth City to attend that city's College of the Albemarle campus or Elizabeth City State University. Other students commute over an hour and a half to attend Old Dominion University in Norfolk, Virginia, or over two-and-a-half hours to attend East Carolina University in Greenville, North Carolina.

For children who are not school age or who need care after school, Outer Banks parents depend on a patchwork of day-care providers: grandparents, teenagers, and the neighborhood retiree who cares for one or several children in the home; licensed home providers who care for a number of children in their homes; after-school care services at local schools; or day-care centers that watch dozens of children in a more controlled and regulated setting. We cannot provide listings for grandparents, teenagers, and neighborhood retirees here, but we have provided information about area preschools, day-care facilities, and babysitting services.

EDUCATION

Public Schools

DARE COUNTY SCHOOLS
(252) 473-1151
www.dare.k12.nc.us

More than 4,700 elementary and secondary students from Corolla to Hatteras Island attend one of the 11 Dare County schools—5 elementary schools, 2 middle schools, 1 combination middle and high school, 2 high schools, and 1 alternative high school.

As the population of year-round residents grows, the Dare County Board of Education searches for new ways to meet

the demands of more students. With almost every one of the current schools at, near, or over capacity, the biggest goal is more space.

But for all the concerns over raising enough funds and providing better classrooms, Dare County offers children a quality education. It is one of the top-scoring districts statewide. Despite the area's remoteness and distance from cultural and educational hubs, schools here have measured up exceedingly well. Dare County schools have consistently ranked in the top five on student achievement among school systems statewide. The district, one of the first to connect to the state's web system in 1994, provides computers in every classroom, Internet access for students, and a commitment to technological advancement. Each school has an interactive room with audio and visual equipment.

Dare County schools open before Labor Day and close early in June. All elementary schools have after-school day care available until 6 p.m. (See the Child Care section of this chapter for information.)

For more information about the Dare County schools, contact the Dare County Board of Education at (252) 473-1151.

KITTY HAWK ELEMENTARY (K–5)
US 158, MP ½, Kitty Hawk
(252) 261-2313

FIRST FLIGHT ELEMENTARY SCHOOL (K–5)
Run Hill Road, off Colington Road, Kill Devil Hills
(252) 441-1111

FIRST FLIGHT MIDDLE SCHOOL (6–8)
Run Hill Road, off Colington Road, Kill Devil Hills
(252) 441-8888

FIRST FLIGHT HIGH SCHOOL (9–12)
Veteran Drive, off Colington Road, Kill Devil Hills
(252) 449-7000

NAGS HEAD ELEMENTARY SCHOOL
3100 Wrightsville Ave., Nags Head
(252) 480-8880

MANTEO ELEMENTARY SCHOOL (K–5)
US 64/264, Manteo
(252) 473-2742

MANTEO MIDDLE SCHOOL (6–8)
US 64/264, Roanoke Island
(252) 473-5549

MANTEO HIGH SCHOOL (9–12)
Wingina Avenue, Manteo
(252) 473-5841

DARE COUNTY ALTERNATIVE SCHOOL (9–12)
US 64/264, Manteo
(252) 473-3141

CAPE HATTERAS ELEMENTARY SCHOOL (K–5)
NC 12, Buxton
(252) 995-5730

CAPE HATTERAS SECONDARY SCHOOL (6–12)
NC 12, Buxton
(252) 995-5730

THE OCRACOKE SCHOOL
1 Schoolhouse Rd., Ocracoke Island
(252) 928-3251

Part of the Hyde County school system, the Ocracoke School is one of the smallest public schools in the United States, serving an island where the entire year-round population is only 750. It is a K–12 school and in 2005 had about 100 students, with only seven graduating seniors. The Ocracoke School was built in 1931. For the last several years it has been designated a School of Excellence, a state honor awarded to schools where more than 90 percent of students are performing at or above their grade level. The Ocracoke School is also repeatedly honored as an Exemplary School, which means that academic growth has exceeded expectations by more than 10 percent. Though small, the Ocracoke School is sophisticated. Every classroom is equipped with computers that are linked to the rest of the state via the

Internet. Student clubs, a student newspaper, and a basketball team provide extracurricular activities. The basketball team is not in a league but plays numerous independent games throughout the season.

Private Schools

THE WANCHESE CHRISTIAN ACADEMY
39 The Lane, Wanchese
(252) 473-5797
www.wanchesechristianacademy.com
The oldest private school on the Outer Banks, this K–12 facility was founded in 1978 by members of the Wanchese Assembly of God Church, who wanted to teach their children moral values and Bible studies. This Christian school is open to members of any religion. About 110 students from Currituck to Avon attend. (Transportation is not provided.) The Wanchese Christian Academy meets North Carolina private-school requirements.

i The North Carolina Sea Grant Extension Program, the aquatic equivalent of Cooperative Extension, offers classes on a broad range of water-related skills, especially for anglers. Most seminars are free and include instruction on crab shedding, shrimping, and net making. The Nags Head office at Caribbean Corners is also a resource for environmental information about water. Call (252) 441-3663 for more information.

Higher Education

COLLEGE OF THE ALBEMARLE DARE CAMPUS
132 Russell Twiford Rd., Manteo
(252) 473-2264
www.albemarle.edu/dare_sitemap.php

The Manteo campus of the College of the Albemarle (COA) was established in 1984 as a second branch of the main campus in Elizabeth City. A third branch is in Edenton. The College of the Albemarle is part of the state's 59-member North Carolina System of Community Colleges. This is the only institution of higher learning on the Outer Banks and is a great asset to the citizens of these remote islands. The campus includes classrooms, laboratories, offices, a library, a student lounge, a technology building, an auditorium and conference facility.

Certificate, diploma, and associate degrees are offered in numerous areas. For example, associate degrees are offered in arts, fine arts, and general education; associate of applied science degrees are offered in business administration, office systems technology, information systems, early childhood education, criminal justice, electronics, and computer engineering; diplomas are offered in heating and air-conditioning; and certificates are offered in nursing assistance, real estate, and medical transcription. This, of course, does not cover all areas of study. A Cisco Systems Academy prepares students to work with Cisco Systems network. The campus is connected to the North Carolina web system so that students may take classes or seminars from remote locations. The school has an active student government association. Students at the Dare branch can apply credits earned at COA toward degrees at other state colleges and universities. Day, evening, and weekend classes are scheduled during the school year and summer. Federal financial aid and other student assistance is available.

Continuing-education programs are wide ranging at COA. Certifications, trainings, and just-for-fun classes are offered in nursing assistance, notary, effective teacher training, computers, Spanish, science, English as a second language, yoga, cooking, photography, art, and more. The college's Small Business Center, based in Elizabeth City, loans videos, books, audio tapes, and CD-ROMs. A list of publications is available by calling (252) 335-0821, ext. 223.

CHILD CARE

North Carolina law mandates child/staff ratios at licensed day-care centers and home providers that are different for each age group and type of facility. The state also requires that all teachers meet certain criteria for health and continuing education. Anyone who watches more than two children (who are not relations) for more than 4 hours a day must be licensed. Home-care providers can care for a maximum of eight children with no more than five preschoolers in the group, including the provider's own kids (if the provider has school-age children, they are not counted toward the eight children). Regulators inspect facilities and teacher records on an annual basis. For information on ratios and license requirements, call the state Division of Child Development at (800) 859-0829.

Recently some centers have stretched their hours to accommodate parents who work nights in one of the restaurants across the barrier islands. Others have put out the welcome mat for tourists who need child-free time during vacations. A list of registered and licensed providers is available from the Dare County Department of Social Services. Contact the office at (252) 473-5857.

Dare County schools offer the After School Enrichment Program to serve working parents of K–5 students. Children are cared for in the same building where they attend school, but their after-hours time is spent in free play inside or on the playground. Crafts and games are available for kids to play with one another and the staff. Help with homework is also available, and an optional homework period is set aside every day. Call the Dare County Board of Education, (252) 473-1151, for scheduling and information.

The North Carolina Cooperative Extension 4-H provides summer camp programs for elementary and middle school youth, rolling child care and supervised fun activities into one service. And 4-H also offers day care at the schools during spring and winter breaks. Contact the Cooperative Extension office in Manteo at (252) 473-1101, ext. 243. Also see the Kidstuff chapter for a list of summer camps.

Additional day-care options are available through a Head Start program run by the Economic Improvement Council, (252) 473-5246.

Preschool/Day-Care Facilities

FIRST ASSEMBLY OF GOD PRESCHOOL AND DAYCARE
812 Wingina Ave., Manteo
(252) 473-2664

At this Christ-centered facility, children are given Bible lessons daily. Attendees do not have to be Christian. Children age 3 through kindergarten age are taught preschool three times a week, including phonics and numbers. The kids are also taken on regular field trips to educational attractions, such as the aquarium or the Norfolk Zoo. The school invites members of the community, such as firefighters or police officers, to give on-site presentations.

The school is conducted Tues, Wed, and Thurs from 8:30 a.m. to noon. Full-time day care, which includes preschool, is available. Sessions include lunch and two snacks daily. A transitional class for children not quite ready for kindergarten is also offered. The day care is state certified. Hours are 7:30 a.m. to 6 p.m. Mon through Fri. Drop-off service is not available.

HERON POND MONTESSORI SCHOOL
3910 Poor Ridge Rd., Kitty Hawk
(252) 261-6077
Based on the philosophies of Italian physician/educator Maria Montessori, Heron Pond offers half-day and full-day licensed daycare programs, kindergarten programs, and junior elementary programs through the sixth grade. Both locations of the school are in historic Kitty Hawk Village, one of them in the Unitarian Universalist Church building. The staff of nine well-trained teachers has extensive child-care and educational experience and is trained in the Montessori method.

The Montessori spirit of education is rooted in the belief that children are naturally eager to learn, and all the teaching tools at Heron Pond are centered on encouragement of the child's ability to teach him- or herself. The school has a summer program. Another location is at 831 Herbert Perry Rd., Kitty Hawk, (252) 261-5358.

MUNCHKIN ACADEMY
NC 12, across from Cape Hatteras School, Buxton
(252) 995-6118
This state-certified facility offers preschool, prekindergarten, after-school care, and full-time and drop-in child-care service. The only A-licensed child-care facility on Hatteras

Island, Munchkin Academy also offers 4-H summer camp programs for school-age youth. A homey center with an unusually large playground, the academy provides care for children ages birth through 12 years. All teachers are certified in first aid and CPR and have state child-care credentials. According to director Kyle Williams, the facility far exceeds state standards for teacher/child ratio. A registered nurse is also on-site. Preschool and pre-K are held Mon through Fri from 7:45 a.m. to 5:15 p.m. Two-, three-, and four-day schedules are available. Call ahead to reserve a drop-in space. Munchkin Academy is open Mon through Fri year-round from 7:45 a.m. to 5:15 p.m.

Child-Care Centers & Services

AT YOUR SERVICE
(252) 261-5286
www.atyourserviceobx.com
The oldest babysitting service on the Outer Banks, At Your Service offers bonded adult babysitters who drive themselves to your home. Sitters are screened thoroughly, and all references are checked. At Your Service is the only business of its kind recommended by the Outer Banks Chamber of Commerce. Rates are based on the number of children and number of hours (there is a 4-hour minimum). Parents must pay the travel expenses of the sitter. The service also provides linen, maid, housekeeping, delivery, personal chef, and grocery services. At Your Service is available year-round. Call for rates and off-season information. (See the listing in the Weekly and Long-Term Cottage Rentals chapter.)

OCRACOKE CHILD CARE, INC.
45 Old Beach Rd., Ocracoke
(252) 928-4131

EDUCATION & CHILD CARE

What's unique about Ocracoke Child Care, the only licensed center on Ocracoke Island, is that it is owned by its members. For an annual fee participants are entitled to attend membership meetings and receive the quarterly newsletter. The center, which has a capacity of 40 children, is overseen by a six-member board of directors, which sets rules and policies. Fully trained staff who prefer to think of themselves as teachers rather than babysitters care for children ages 6 weeks to 12 years. The facility has a special infant-toddler room and an age-3-and-older preschool room. Based on the motto "Peace begins in the playground," Ocracoke Child Care has structured playtime as well as indoor and outdoor play areas and revolves activities around a different theme each week. Visitors to the area are asked to come in a day in advance to fill out forms. Immunization records are not necessary for out-of-towners. Ocracoke Child Care is open 7:45 a.m. to 5:15 p.m. Mon through Fri all year.

INDEX

INSIDERS' GUIDE®

The acclaimed travel series that has sold more than 2 million copies!

Discover: Your Travel Destination.
Your Home. Your Home-to-Be.

Albuquerque

Anchorage & Southcentral Alaska

Atlanta

Austin

Baltimore

Baton Rouge

Boulder & Rocky Mountain National Park

Branson & the Ozark Mountains

California's Wine Country

Cape Cod & the Islands

Charleston

Charlotte

Chicago

Cincinnati

Civil War Sites in the Eastern Theater

Civil War Sites in the South

Colorado's Mountains

Dallas & Fort Worth

Denver

El Paso

Florida Keys & Key West

Gettysburg

Glacier National Park

Great Smoky Mountains

Greater Fort Lauderdale

Greater Tampa Bay Area

Hampton Roads

Houston

Hudson River Valley

Indianapolis

Jacksonville

Kansas City

Long Island

Louisville

Madison

Maine Coast

Memphis

Myrtle Beach & the Grand Strand

Nashville

New Orleans

New York City

North Carolina's Mountains

North Carolina's Outer Banks

North Carolina's Piedmont Triad

Oklahoma City

Orange County, CA

Oregon Coast

Palm Beach County

Palm Springs

Philadelphia & Pennsylvania Dutch Country

Phoenix

Portland, Maine

Portland, Oregon

Raleigh, Durham & Chapel Hill

Richmond, VA

Reno and Lake Tahoe

St. Louis

San Antonio

Santa Fe

Savannah & Hilton Head

Seattle

Shreveport

South Dakota's Black Hills Badlands

Southwest Florida

Tucson

Tulsa

Twin Cities

Washington, D.C.

Williamsburg & Virginia's Historic Triangle

Yellowstone & Grand Teton

Yosemite

RECEIVED JUN 2 7 2012

**To order call 800-243-0495
or visit www.Insiders.com**